PERSPECTIVES ON
ACADEMIC WRITING

PERSPECTIVES ON ACADEMIC WRITING

Alice Calderonello
Bowling Green State University

Donna Nelson-Beene
Bowling Green State University

Sue Carter Simmons
Bowling Green State University

Allyn and Bacon
Boston ■ London ■ Toronto ■ Sydney ■ Tokyo ■ Singapore

Executive Editor: Eben Ludlow
Editorial Assistant: Liz Egan
Marketing Manager: Lisa Kimball
Editorial Production Service: Chestnut Hill Enterprises, Inc.
Manufacturing Buyer: Suzanne Lareau
Cover Administrator: Linda Knowles

Copyright © 1997 by Allyn & Bacon
A Viacom Company
Needham Heights, MA 02194

Internet: www.abacon.com
America Online: keyword: College Online

Library of Congress Cataloging-in-Publication Data

Calderonello, Alice Heim.
    Perspectives on academic writing / Alice Calderonello, Donna
Nelson-Beene, Sue Carter Simmons.
        p.   cm
    Includes bibliographical references (p.) and index.
    ISBN 0-02-318295-4 (paper)
    1. English language–Rhetoric.   2. Interdisciplinary approach in
education.   3. Academic writing.   4. College readers.   I. Nelson
-Beene, Donna.   II. Simmons, Sue Carter.   III. Title.
PE1408.C273 1996   96–32113
                                                    CIP

Printed in the United States of America
10 9 8 7 6 5 4 3 2   01 00 99 98 97

❦ Contents

PART III: Group Research Projects

✳ PREFACE

Educators have long realized that writing is important, not just for conveying information but also for clarifying thought and exploring ideas. For these reasons, writing has become an integral part of every discipline within the academy, from the humanities to the social sciences to the sciences. We believe that one important role of the first-year writing course is to show beginning college students how various disciplines produce and use writing. Accordingly, our central aim in *Perspectives on Academic Writing* is to reflect our commitment to writing across the disciplines in all aspects of our discussion. For instance, when we discuss report writing, we give examples of various kinds of assignments students might receive—whether in chemistry, journalism, or marketing. In describing how to write reports, we provide explanations and examples relevant to a number of different disciplines. In this way, we hope to sensitize our student-readers to the many contexts in which they will write during and after their college careers and to equip them with the skills necessary to assess each rhetorical situation and to select appropriate strategies to produce effective writing.

In order to inform ourselves and our readers about the different kinds of writing actually being required within different disciplines, we collected over a hundred different assignments from disciplines as diverse as sociology, psychology, environmental studies, marketing, elementary education, sports management, chemistry, computer science, and ethnic studies, to name a few. These assignments, coupled with conversations with our colleagues in other academic departments, have strongly influenced the instruction, the writing assignments, and the readings in the text.

Perspectives on Academic Writing has been designed for use by first-year students in courses focused on academic and research writing. It is divided into three parts. Part I discusses the writing process and the nature of collaboration. Part II, the core of the text, consists of eight chapters on the skills and kinds of writing students will be required to use throughout their college careers. Chapters 3 through 8 focus on writing personal histories, observing, reporting, critiquing, evaluating, and synthesizing. Chapters 9 and 10 guide students through the research process with library and nonlibrary sources. Part III consists of three collaborative research projects equally suitable for a small group or for an entire class. The projects are designed to give groups great latitude in devising and producing their work and to afford students the opportunity to write in a variety of academic formats.

One distinctive feature of *Perspectives on Academic Writing* is that many of the readings within the chapters are taken from scholarly journals of the sort students will work with as they progress through their studies. In selecting these readings, we chose pieces that demonstrate disciplinary perspectives and approaches but are, at the same time, accessible and interesting. The pages of *Perspectives on Academic*

Writing include discussions of how McDonald's won the hamburger wars, reviews of controversial films, and a report of a search for the identity of an unknown growth discovered in a pickle jar.

Because a central component of writing across the disciplines over the past several decades has been attention not just to writing but to language experiences across the curriculum, we have incorporated the pedagogy of collaboration—which we know permeates many disciplines and professions—throughout the text. *Perspectives on Academic Writing* provides not only carefully sequenced writing assignments that reflect the kinds of writing commonly assigned across the disciplines, but also special guidance on how to collaborate and how to organize and reorganize the social relations in which learning will occur.

We believe that *Perspectives on Academic Writing* is unique in accomplishing the following:

- Providing practice with a variety of academic writing assignments sequenced from easy to complex. These activities will help first-year students master the academic writing skills that they will need throughout college and beyond.

- Empowering students to become analytical, perceptive readers. Each of the disciplinary readings in *Perspectives on Academic Writing* is accompanied by questions requiring the kind of critical thinking that leads to sustained critical responses.

- Motivating students by providing them with a peer audience for their writing and ideas. According to current theory in composition and rhetoric, students learn more quickly and write more effectively when they are given audiences other than their teachers. This theory is fundamental to the approach of *Perspectives on Academic Writing*, which provides students with an audience of their peers each time they are asked to write.

- Helping students work together to become active researchers. *Perspectives on Academic Writing* does not merely instruct students to do research but provides a research process and teaches them how to investigate primary as well as secondary sources.

- Including activities of interest to nontraditional learners as well as to traditional learners. These activities have proved accessible to a wide range of first-year college writers.

- Providing students with reading and writing activities that introduce current rhetorical theory at a level of understanding appropriate for first-year students.

- Teaching students to become successful collaborators. *Perspectives on Academic Writing* shows students how to collaborate in each assigned discussion and planning activity. In addition, the text teaches students to reach collective judgments in all phases of the writing process—invention/prewriting; drafting/revision; final editing/publishing. This, in turn, encourages students to take their ideas seriously and to modify them or revise them in the light of others' ideas. Students also learn to recognize and tolerate differences and, ideally, to see the value systems or sets of beliefs that underlie these differences.

ACKNOWLEDGMENTS

In producing this text, we were greatly influenced by the ideas of many people within our own discipline, whose discussions of writing theory and practice have proved invaluable to us. Our work has been informed by the contributions of contemporary teacher/theorists such as Kenneth Burke, James Kinneavy, Peter Elbow, Pat Belanoff, Lisa Ede, and Andrea Lunsford, as well as by the work of classical rhetoricians such as Aristotle. And, of course, we are indebted to our students from whom we have learned and continue to learn.

We would also like to thank the reviewers of our manuscript: Janet P. Bean, University of North Carolina—Greensboro; Jeffrey Carroll, University of Hawaii at Manoa; Dan Dieterich, University of Wisconsin—Stevens Point; Michael C. Flanagan, University of Oklahoma; Cheryl Glenn, Oregon State University; Susan H. McLeod, Washington State University; Harvey Wiener, City University of New York. We also thank the following faculty, whose writing assignments helped us to craft the samples provided in Chapters 2 through 10: Pamela C. Allison, Roger Anderson, Elliott Blinn, Nancy Brendlinger, Ed Danziger, Bonnie Fink, Paul Fischer, Sue Gavron, Paul E. Haas, Vikki Krane, Ron Lancaster, Laura Leventhal, Barbara Moses, Janet Parks, Gary Silverman, Marc Simon, Ofir Sisco, Joe Spinelli, Roger Thibault, and Jim West.

Finally, we would like to thank the following able members of the General Studies writing staff, Connie Allison, John Clark, and Barbara Little; English Department secretaries Joanne Lohr, Mary Jo Smith, Mary Ann Sweeney, and Jessica Wade; English Department Chair, Rick Gebhardt; our patient spouses, John Calderonello and Gregory Nelson-Beene; and Laura Simmons, who anticipated the publication of this book almost as much as her mom.

CHAPTER 1

HOW WRITERS WRITE

WHAT WRITERS DO WHEN THEY WRITE

It is no exaggeration to say that there are as many different writing habits as there are writers. Each writer possesses a unique collection of rituals and practices. Some writers spend days or weeks thinking about and discussing a topic and, then, in response to a feeling of readiness, write a first draft alone in one sitting; others set aside a regular block of time each day for writing and hold conversations on a regular basis to develop and refine their ideas. Some writers do most of the thinking about what they're going to write in their heads; others reveal these thoughts and strategies on paper. While some writers compose a first draft on paper, others write everything on a computer.

Knowing what you do when you write is important in order to improve your efficiency and make writing more productive and satisfying. After giving a general discussion of the important processes in which all writers engage, this chapter will provide a series of descriptions and exercises that should help you discover your writing behavior.

Invention

Much has been written about how people discover what to write about and what to write. *Invention,* or the processes by which writers generate information and ideas, is a crucial component of any journey toward a completed text, whether that text be single-authored or cowritten.

Many writers have no idea about what they do when they invent, particularly if whatever they do produces the desired effect. These writers use unconscious strategies, alone or in concert with others, to come up with ideas and information, to plumb their memories, jog their minds, and make connections, and to create relationships. Other writers have an array of invention techniques and procedures that they self-consciously employ by themselves or with others, sometimes in a particular order, depending on the circumstances. Many of these techniques have been simplified and taught to apprentice writers. For the most part, beginning writers are encouraged to devote plenty of conscious time to the inventing process because research studies show that fluent, competent writers seem to spend more time inventing than inexperienced ones do. Also, experienced writers are sufficiently flexible to engage in invention activities whenever necessary throughout the writing process—not just at the beginning before they start drafting.

In general, *invention* techniques fall into one of two categories. Some primarily generate information and ideas; others generate and arrange them. Here is a common invention technique that *generates* information:

> *On a separate sheet of paper or sitting at your computer, write for <u>two</u> minutes anything that comes to your mind in response to this sentence, "When I begin writing, I _____." Begin immediately and do not stop writing for two minutes. If you can't think of anything to write, then write (and keep on writing) "I can't think of anything to write."*

This easy-to-use and effective technique is known as timed *freewriting*. Usually timed freewriting sessions last from five to ten minutes. Writers who frequently employ freewriting may alternate timed sessions with untimed ones, which last for as long as a writer wants, and they can produce many pages of text. Try freewriting whenever you want to generate ideas quickly or to explore or probe a topic—especially if you don't have others with whom you can converse.

To give you an example of an invention technique that *generates* and *arranges* ideas and information, here is a simple version of an invention strategy that you will learn more about in a subsequent chapter:

> *"When I begin writing, I _____."*
>
> *Answer the following questions (1–3) in response to the previous sentence. You may freewrite your answers if you wish, but try to spend a couple of minutes on each question:*
>
> 1. Where *do you usually begin writing? Describe one place where you often begin writing. If you don't have such a place, then imagine an ideal place to begin writing, and describe it.*
>
> 2. When *do you begin writing? What time of day (in the morning? late at night?) do you prefer to begin writing? Why is that time preferable?*
>
> 3. Whom *do you think of when you begin writing? The teacher who gave you the assignment? Your audience? Yourself? Your ninth grade history teacher? Your mother? Do you always think of the same person—yourself, for example—or does it depend on the assignment, the state of your mind, and so forth? Explain.*

As you can see from your brief experience with these invention procedures, some are simple and require little effort; others are more complex and invite the user to create relationships among and categories within the ideas and information that they generate. In contrast to freewriting, the second exercise you performed didn't just assist you in bringing forth information about writing; it divided that information into three categories related to *where* you write, *when* you write, and *whom* you think of when you write. Many writers prefer to begin with a simple invention technique, such as freewriting, to discover ideas and to jog their memories. Then they follow this initial invention with a more elaborate procedure that sorts or "clusters" information.

One invention tool that lends itself readily to either simple or complex inventing strategies is the computer. Even with the most simple word processor, writers can easily freewrite or generate lists. Computers also enable writers to manipulate the writing that they produce. Chunks of text can easily be moved or reproduced and inserted in more than one part of a freewriting. Likewise, lists can be moved, combined and recombined, keyed in different fonts, and so on. Any of these strategies can enable writers to reconceptualize, expand on, or discover connections among their ideas. Besides the functions that a word processor provides, software designed to assist with various stages of the writing process is increasingly becoming available. Such software can help writers invent by offering them specific questions to answer about their topic.

Now that colleges and universities are making the Internet more accessible to their students, this powerful resource can also be a valuable stimulus to invention. Many writers find that a powerful way to stimulate their thought process is to read or converse with others on matters related to their topic. The Internet is a vast network that reaches every corner of the globe. It offers users a relatively simple way to access a variety of documents on a multitude of topics or to converse with people who share particular interests or possess specific expertise.

Planning

It is difficult to separate components of the writing process from one another because they often occur simultaneously or recur throughout the act of writing. However, some useful distinctions can be made. *Planning* is the name given to those activities that shape the material (generated by invention) into an organizing principle or thesis. This principle or thesis then determines an appropriate structure. Unlike invention, planning cannot be easily accomplished through the use of one or more standard methods or procedures, so it is a challenge for writers, especially inexperienced ones.

Fortunately, even though there are no absolutely dependable methods for helping a writer discover a thesis, writing texts and teachers do offer some helpful techniques to accomplish this task. Some recommend the use of powerful invention procedures that arrange the generated information into complex groupings or patterns that reveal hidden or subtle relationships; such relationships can suggest interesting and provocative organizing principles. Other people maintain that a rigorous process of generating data, focusing on a small portion of that data, and then repeating the process by generating and then focusing again—especially if this process is informed by feedback from teachers or peers—can help a writer determine a thesis.

Once a writer has come up with a provisional thesis, the most commonly offered method of planning is a simplified variation of the outline. Although most writers do not produce a formal outline (with roman numerals and capital and small letters and so forth), many sketch a tentative structure to guide their drafting of an essay after they've decided on an organizing principle or thesis. Such an organizational plan might consist of several blocks of notes, each block describing a part of the essay; a series of summaries of what should go in the introduction, the first paragraph, the second, the third, and so forth; or a set of objectives that direct the writer to "talk about" certain items in a particular order.

In arriving at a workable outline or organizational plan, a writer can use the computer to good effect. A word processor enables writers to reorder sections of their plans, to easily add and delete details and ideas, or to save several alternate plans that can be compared, modified, or combined. Currently, there is also hypertext software designed to help writers create various organizational plans by allowing them to create links between topics and subtopics. And of course, many widely available software packages for word processing enable writers to craft formal outlines.

Although some writers can visualize the structure of a text before they begin to draft it, others must discover the form that their writing will take by writing. These writers usually do not benefit from an initial outline or organizational plan. This is not to say that writers who must discover their forms by writing can never benefit from an outline, however. Writers who discover form after they have begun drafting often outline a first or an early draft; such outlines are useful because they frequently suggest theses or organizational plans that can be helpful in crafting subsequent revisions.

For writers who discover form while drafting, the computer can also be extremely helpful. It can enable such writers to rearrange their drafts and highlight and draw out key lines from which they can create topic outlines. A computer can even allow a writer to rearrange portions of text, produce several alternate drafts, and create outlines comprising the first (or first several) lines of each paragraph. These outlines can then be compared, modified, and combined. Regardless of their planning strategies for shorter papers, however, most writers prepare detailed outlines before they begin drafting when they produce long papers that synthesize information from a variety of sources.

Drafting

Drafting is the designation commonly given to the act of writing a text; it can—but doesn't always—follow inventing and planning activities such as freewriting or outlining. That is, some writers do a lot of inventing and sketch out detailed plans before they actually begin drafting. For these writers *drafting* means the writing they do when they make a first attempt to construct a text after they have completed any initial inventing or planning. Other writers, however, produce their best work when they begin writing a paper immediately—without any preliminaries. Such writers do not do any conscious inventing or planning, Later in their writing process, as they work on subsequent drafts, these writers may use freewriting or other inventing strategies, as needed. They discover an organizational structure as their texts become more finished.

When a person begins writing immediately, it is hard to characterize that process as either drafting or inventing—since it is probably both. Moreover, although it is widely believed that drafting usually takes place after some invention and planning has occurred, invention paragraphs that resemble drafts are common enough to have been given a name: *discovery* (or *zero*) *drafts*. Because *discovery drafts* are special, experienced writers treat them differently from more conventional drafts that are composed following substantial inventing or planning sessions.

Once again, no matter how a writer drafts, the word processor is an important tool. Even those writers who absolutely must compose a first draft on paper often transfer that draft to the word processor so that they can more easily make revisions and edit their texts. However, many writers do their initial drafting with a word processor. Such a means of drafting offers several advantages. Drafting on a computer enables writers to write fast enough to keep pace with their thoughts—no matter how quickly these occur. It simplifies the processes of deleting, adding, or reordering words, sentences, or larger pieces of text, so these operations don't interfere with drafting. Moreover, for those who have done freewriting or other inventing on a computer, moving from inventing to drafting is easier.

Revising and Rewriting

As we said earlier, it is not unheard of for writers to produce an almost-finished draft the first time they sit down to write. This does not mean, however, that such writers have done no revising; it simply means that the revising occurred in their minds and could not be observed. *Revising*, therefore, refers to any and all of the activities, performed alone or in concert with other people, that a writer does to transform successive versions of text into a finished product. Some writing teachers like to point out that the word *revision* consists of the prefix *re-* and the root *vision*, meaning to "see again." This is a helpful way to think of the term because the most productive revisions often may transform whole concepts and structures within an emerging text. Also, if you think of revision as "re-vision," you won't confuse it with editing, the practice of removing blemishes (such as awkward sentences or misspelled words) from a text.

In contrast to revising, which can be mental or physical, *rewriting* is strictly a physical, observable process. That is, it is possible to see just what a writer does while rewriting. Also, if a writer uses a pen, pencil, or typewriter to draft, the physical traces of textual changes—such as crossed-out and added words or arrows indicating changes in ordering—can be examined. However, for those who use a computer to write, the line between drafting and revising and rewriting is often blurred. Word processing makes the act of changing even large portions of text so simple that writers routinely make significant alterations while producing initial drafts. Word processors can also make it more difficult to observe rewriting because each alteration, no matter its scope, creates a "new" text. When a paragraph (or word) is omitted, for example, all traces of it are erased; the deleted paragraph (or word) doesn't remain on the screen with an X drawn through it. On the other hand, if a writer uses a word processor to write and revise, it is easy to print out, and thus save, progressive drafts of a text.

You probably throw away all of your early drafts after you hand in a finished copy to your teacher, but the next few times you compose a paper, you might save drafts so that you can look over your rewriting and determine the kinds of changes you make, especially if these changes are in response to comments or criticisms you have received from others. In the interim, to get an idea of what you do when you rewrite, you might think of the last time you had to compose an essay, and try to recall the kinds of revisions you made on your paper (or on the screen of your word processor). Did you omit unnecessary words or phrases; move things around to make the ordering of the sentences in a passage less confusing; or add some necessary detail or information that you had omitted? There are four kinds of changes you and other writers make when rewriting: adding, subtracting, substituting, and rearranging. Usually rewriting means making one or more of these kinds of changes right on the paper or screen. However, if a draft is a discovery (or zero) draft, which as you recall is similar to inventing, rewriting could involve starting all over with a blank page or an empty screen.

Editing

Editing is the act of polishing a piece of writing so that it is error-free. Most often, writers correct errors based on their own knowledge of grammar. They also may turn to reference aids such as grammar handbooks or on-line handbooks to help them identify and correct errors. Although editing is usually performed at the end of the process of producing a text, many writers correct misspelled words, fix grammatical and punctuation problems, or rewrite awkward sentences while they are drafting. We even know writers who try to correct spelling errors while they are freewriting! However, no matter how little or how much editing they might have done while constructing a text, meticulous writers do a careful editing of a final draft by reading it several times to ensure that they have eradicated every word- and sentence-level mistake.

Because editing is usually less intellectually demanding than inventing, planning, drafting, and revising, beginning writers sometimes don't give it the attention it deserves. This is a serious mistake. The quality of editing often determines the overall look and feel of a piece of writing. A sloppily edited paper can give the impression that the writer is lazy or careless. Copious editing errors can also annoy or irritate readers. Fortunately, however, writers tend to commit their own inventory of "bloopers," which they can learn to anticipate—and eliminate. An important step in becoming an effective editor, therefore, is to become sufficiently familiar with your writing so that you are aware of the types of errors you make. Skillful editing requires careful attention to your own special inventory of problems and to transcription errors that inevitably occur during the act of writing.

These days a variety of word processing aids such as spellchecks and grammar checks have become increasingly available. On occasion, we have been asked whether these have eliminated the need for careful editing. The answer is a resounding no.

Spellchecks often help writers detect misspelled words, but because they don't respond to the context in which words are used they can easily "overlook" errors. The same is true for grammar checks, which also cannot evaluate the context in which words and sentences appear. A spellcheck would find nothing odd about this sentence despite its peculiarity: "In the sprung, birds sing noisy because their building nests for there babes." Because all of the words within the sentence exist and can be spelled as they are, a spellcheck would find nothing amiss. Grammar and spellchecks, then, can be useful tools for the writer, but they are meant to enhance, *not* to replace, a careful job of editing.

DISCOVERING YOUR OWN BEHAVIOR

Do you play a musical instrument? Are you—or were you ever—a serious basketball player? Or perhaps you design and sew clothes. If you've already practiced one or more skills seriously, then you know that *how* you perform cannot be separated from *what* you perform. You have probably had to learn to observe and dissect your own behavior to rid yourself of ineffective habits and to build a repertoire of strategies that lead to success. Like any other skill, your writing will improve if you make an effort to examine and modify what you do. Here's a true story to illustrate how this might work:

> *Kathy often put off working on a writing assignment, sometimes until the night before it was due because she "wrote best under pressure," yet she found that these last-minute sessions were extremely unpleasant. However, when keeping a log of what she did when writing an essay, Kathy discovered something curious: She could not write any part of her essay until the introduction was letter-perfect. After she finally got through the introduction, the rest of the paper "flowed." Kathy timed the process and found that it took her as long to do the introduction (typing and retyping it) as it did to do the rest of the essay.*

> *When she shared the results of this discovery in class discussion, several of her classmates as well as her teacher suggested that next time she wrote an essay she should try to keep on writing beyond her initial introduction—no matter how flawed she thought it was. Then she could go back and fix her introduction after her draft was finished.*

> *Kathy was determined to try this suggestion, so the next time she wrote she forced herself to continue drafting even though her introduction wasn't exactly the way she wanted it. To her delight, the rest of the essay flowed just as easily as it had when she had spent twice as long on the introduction, and it was easier to go back and revise the beginning of the essay after she had a completed draft. As the semester progressed, Kathy found that diminishing the stress of producing a perfect introduction at the beginning of her writing process lessened her fear of writing. Her diminished fear, in turn, helped her to stop procrastinating. By the end of the semester, Kathy concluded that giving herself more time to write produced better results than putting herself in a pressure cooker.*

If you haven't examined your own behavior as a writer, this part of the chapter will help you begin to understand it better. As you read through each section, you may also discover strategies to help you improve your writing.

Your Writing Environment

Have you ever thought about the conditions you need to do your best writing the most comfortably? Do you require three-hour blocks of time, or do you perform better when you write in short, regular intervals? When do you write more easily: in the early morning or late at night? Must your environment be absolutely quiet or does background music help you? Do you require food, drink, "tools" (extra pens, pencils, or paper; a dictionary or thesaurus; a pair of scissors, a stapler, or tape), notes, books, or friends nearby, or do you want nothing near you *except* a pen and paper or your word processor? Most successful writers have a pretty good idea about their own habits; whenever they write, they arrange everything to suit their needs. To give you an idea of the range of these needs, here are some of the more unusual requirements of some of the successful writers we've interviewed:

> *John: I write in a closet (no kidding), which is painted dark blue. My desk, which holds my typewriter, fits in there rather snugly. When I go into my closet to write, I need a thermos of black coffee.*

> *Amy: I must begin every paper by lying on the floor, on my stomach, with a legal-size pad and several black fine-point pens. To support my head, I have a special small pillow, which I place under my chin. I work best if at least one of my roommates is there to bounce ideas off of.*

> *LaRuth: When I write, I need absolute quiet. So I go to a carrel at the back of the eighth floor of the library; nobody ever comes up there. I need to have all my notes with me, and I also bring about three or four packs of gum because I chew one stick after another.*

Now that you have an idea of what some other writers need when they write, here are a few questions to answer about your own writing environment:

Please circle the appropriate responses.

I write in the same place.

Always   Usually   Sometimes   Never

When I write, noise bothers me.

Always   Usually   Sometimes   Never

When I write, I need a friend nearby to help me.

Always   Usually   Sometimes   Never

I can't be too relaxed when I write.

    Strongly Agree   Agree   Disagree   Strongly Disagree

When I write, food or drink is a distraction.

    Strongly Agree   Agree   Disagree   Strongly Disagree

For each of the following questions, please check *all* of the responses that apply.

I usually write

_____ in the morning   _____ in the afternoon

_____ in the early evening   _____ late at night (9 to 12 P.M.)

_____ really late at night (after midnight)   _____ whenever I feel like it

_____ when I have time

_____ other (describe) _____

I need to write in

_____ large blocks of time (3 to 5 hours)

_____ small, regular intervals (1 to 2 hours)

_____ other (describe) _____

I need to write

_____ in my own room   _____ in a classroom

_____ in a study carrel at the library   _____ at a table in the library

_____ in a classroom   _____ in a study lounge

_____ in my friend's room   _____ at my friend's apartment

_____ other (describe) _____

When I write, I must

_____ sit at a desk

_____ sit at a table (specify size and kind) _____

_____ recline in a comfortable chair, with a pad on my lap

_____ lie on my back on a bed, propped up with a pillow

_____ lie on my stomach, on a bed

_____ lie on my back on the floor, propped up with a pillow

_____ lie on the floor, on my stomach

_____ other (describe) _____

When I write, I use

_____ an erasable ink pen   _____ a pencil

_____ a fine-tip pen   _____ a mechanical pencil

_____ a typewriter   _____ a word processor

_____ a ballpoint pen (specify color) _____

_____ a felt-tip pen (specify color) _____

_____ other (describe) _____

When I write, I use

_____ lined white paper   _____ unlined white paper

_____ lined yellow paper   _____ lined, legal-size yellow paper

_____ a spiral notebook   _____ a word processor

_____ a word processor plus scratch paper (specify) _____

_____ the blank side of used paper (specify) _____

_____ other (describe) _____

When I write, I must be able to reach

_____ a dictionary   _____ a thesaurus

_____ a stapler   _____ tape

_____ scissors   _____ a scribble pad

_____ the telephone   _____ an eraser

_____ notes   _____ other papers I've written

_____ books and readings   _____ paper clips

_____ colored felt-tip pens (specify) _____

_____ other (describe) _____

While I write, I need

_____ absolute quiet

_____ some background noise (specify) _____

_____ the sound of people talking

_____ soft music (specify) _____

_____ loud music (specify) _____

_____ other (describe) _____

While I write, I must have

_____ gum   _____ water

_____ coffee   _____ sugarless gum

_____ hot food (specify) _____

_____ cold food (specify) _____

_____ snacks (specify) _____

_____ candy (specify) _____

_____ a carbonated beverage (specify) _____

_____ other (describe) _____

 **Activity 1**

If your teacher has assigned you to a group, then this activity can be done together with other group members. If your teacher has not yet assigned you to a group, then this activity can be done in pairs; you can work with a person sitting near you. Groups should have at least one person jot down notes of your discussion and designate someone else to get the discussion started and keep it going if it lags. If you work in pairs, one person should report his or her answers while the other takes notes and records responses and questions; then reverse roles.

For about five minutes, share the results of your answers to the previous questions with your partner or group members. Note similarities and differences. What requirements and habits seem to be productive; are there any that are not so helpful? How might these be modified? Did your partner or group fill in any of the "other" slots with unusual answers?

After discussing your writing environments, prepare a brief (two- or three-minute) summary to present to the class. Try to highlight the most interesting and useful information you found.

Avoiding Writing

Penny: I just got a writing assignment.

Milagros: Oh really?

Penny: Yeah, time to do my laundry.

Because writing can sometimes be an emotionally trying experience, many writers try to avoid it—even successful, experienced ones. For this reason, Penny (in the previous conversation) could just as easily be a published author as a first-year college student. Sometimes the ways in which individuals successfully avoid writing can be interesting and imaginative; most often, though, writers choose surprisingly similar avoidance strategies. Listen to Kathleen, Mark, and Lila describe their own habits. Do you sometimes do what they do?

> *Kathleen: When the time comes for me to write, I convince myself that my apartment must be spotless. I wash the dishes, sweep, mop the floors—I even clean the bathroom.*

> *Mark: I do all of my other homework before I start writing. Sometimes I even do assignments that aren't due yet.*

> *Lila: The only time I ever write letters is when I have to do a paper. For some reason, I can't start writing until I've written letters to my friends back home.*

Lila's, Mark's, and Kathleen's methods of avoiding writing are fairly common, but they didn't realize this until they discussed their avoidance behavior in class. Although they suspected that others occasionally felt anxious about writing from time to time, they had assumed that they were the only ones who put off writing and felt guilty about procrastinating. However, it is probably not coincidental that writers show similar avoidance behavior. Notice that by cleaning her apartment strenuously, Kathleen elevates her pulse rate and probably makes herself more alert and ready to perform at her best. Cleaning may also clear her mind, allowing ideas for writing to pass through her head while she mops and scrubs. Similarly, the activities that Mark and Lila select to postpone writing require reading (an activity that is cognitively related to writing) or actual writing, although of a different sort.

Think about your typical reaction when you receive a writing assignment. Do you begin working on it in good time, or do you put it off? If you're not sure (or can't remember) how you feel or what you do when it's time to start writing, the following questions may be helpful:

For each of the following questions, please check all of the responses that describe how you feel.

Before I begin writing, I feel

_____ anxious to begin

_____ excited about what I'm going to say

_____ worried that my mind will go blank

_____ worried that I won't be able to decide what to write

_____ confident that I'll finish

_____ worried that I won't be able to finish

_____ happy that I'll be able to express myself

_____ depressed because my writing won't be good

_____ confident that I will like what I've written

_____ worried about my teacher's reaction

_____ worried about my grade

_____ confident in my ability as a writer

_____ depends on the circumstances (explain) _____

_____ other (specify) _____

Once I've begun writing,

_____ I feel relieved

_____ I always worry that I'll get stuck

_____ I feel elated

_____ every word is torture

_____ time seems to disappear

_____ the excitement builds until I'm finished

_____ I keep wishing I were finished

_____ I'm never satisfied with what I write

_____ I am often surprised—and pleased—by my brilliance

_____ I think I'd rather be doing *anything* else

_____ the experience isn't as unpleasant as I thought it would be

_____ my writing comes out better that I expected

_____ I can't stop thinking about my grade

_____ I constantly worry about what my teacher will think

_____ depends on the circumstances (explain) _____

_____ other (specify) _____

I put off writing a paper by

_____ cleaning my room   _____ cleaning my apartment

_____ paying bills   _____ doing laundry

_____ doing other homework   _____ jogging

_____ exercising (specify) _____   _____ eating

_____ writing another paper   _____ writing letters

_____ watching TV   _____ writing in a journal

_____ talking to friends   _____ going to a movie

_____ taking a nap   _____ worrying that I'm not writing

_____ This is a silly question; I *never* put off writing.

_____ depends (explain) _____

_____ other (describe) _____

 **Activity 2**

Work with the same partner with whom you completed Activity 1. If you have been assigned to a group, work with your group partners. Share your responses to the preceding questions with one another. Do particular avoidance behaviors seem to correlate with particular emotional responses? Does any member of your group (or your partner) *not* engage in avoidance behavior; if so, has this always been true or has the person's writing behavior changed?

Once you have discussed your answers, make a tentative list of "avoidance" strategies that, in fact, enable a reluctant writer to begin writing. Do all of these strategies usually help a writer start writing, or does the effectiveness of some or all of them depend on the individual or the circumstances? Compile a list of strategies that you recommend to get a writer started. Note, if relevant, any reservations you have about particular strategies. Present your list, including your reservations, to the class.

Your Writing Process

Earlier in this chapter you read that every writer must invent, plan, draft, revise, and edit to produce a polished, complete piece of writing. You also read that writers differ from one another, sometimes quite dramatically, with regard to how they perform these operations and that a writer's behavior isn't necessarily consistent. If you haven't had the opportunity to scrutinize your own writing process, we hope that the remainder of this chapter will pique your interest and suggest aspects of your behavior that deserve your attention.

Invention and Planning. When you have to write a paper, how do you get started? Do you follow a standard set of steps in a particular order, or do you just try to get going any way you can? Do you do some planning before you start to draft an essay, or do you usually jump right in, figuring the sooner you start writing, the sooner you'll be done? Here are some questions to help you understand your own behavior:

Please circle the appropriate responses.

I begin drafting right away to save time.

> Always   Usually   Sometimes   Never

Only writing teachers do inventing.

> Strongly Agree   Agree   Disagree   Strongly Disagree

I never invent on paper, just in my head.

> Strongly Agree   Agree   Disagree   Strongly Disagree

I spend lots of time thinking before I write.

> Always   Usually   Sometimes   Never

An outline is essential to my writing.

> Always   Usually   Sometimes   Never

I don't know what I do to invent, but it works.

> Strongly Agree   Agree   Disagree   Strongly Disagree

I would feel better if I knew some invention procedures.

> Strongly Agree   Agree   Disagree   Strongly Disagree

I would feel better if I knew some planning strategies.

> Strongly Agree   Agree   Disagree   Strongly Disagree

I never invent once I've begun drafting.

> Strongly Agree   Agree   Disagree   Strongly Disagree

I do my best planning *after* I've completed a draft.

> Always   Often   Sometimes   Never

For each of the following questions, please check *all* of the responses that are appropriate.

When I invent, I

_____ freewrite

_____ jot down as many ideas as I can

_____ write answers to a series of questions about the topic

_____ carry paper around with me in case I get an idea

_____ come up with too many ideas

_____ think of my readers to get ideas

_____ don't come up with enough ideas

_____ think about ideas while I'm doing something else (specify) _____

_____ sometimes use definite procedures and sometimes don't

_____ never know what I'm doing

_____ feel worried because I have no set of steps

_____ I really don't think that I invent

_____ other (specify) _____

After I invent, I

_____ don't know how to use what I generate

_____ immediately begin planning

_____ don't know how to proceed to the next step

_____ have trouble deciding what to use

_____ invent again, using a different method

_____ invent again, using the same method

_____ begin drafting immediately

_____ talk to my teacher for ideas about what to do next

_____ talk to friends for ideas about what to do next

_____ get stuck

_____ plan and then do more inventing

_____ plan, draft, and then do more inventing

_____ am not sure what I do

_____ other (specify) _____

 ## Activity 3

Again, work with your partner (from Activities 1 and 2) or with your group members. Discuss your responses to the questions about how you invent and plan. Do some invention and planning strategies seem more effective than others? Did you discover some strategies that you don't currently use that you'd like to try? After your discussion, work together to construct two lists of strategies that you'd suggest for apprentice writers, one list for invention strategies and one for planning strategies. Share your lists with the class. Perhaps the class can compile two master lists from those that the various groups or partners suggested.

Drafting. From your experience, you already know that drafting is a significant and time-consuming part of the writing process. Because writers may encounter difficulties while drafting, experienced ones usually develop strategies to help them move forward when they get stuck or keep them going when they want to quit. Some of the stories about what famous writers have done to keep themselves "on task" are pretty remarkable. It is said, for example, that Victor Hugo asked to be locked in a room, naked, with nothing but pen and paper, a drastic measure, indeed! While we're not suggesting that you use such a strategy, this example is meant to illustrate that staying put and writing is not always easy, even for the experienced, successful author.

When all is said and done, perhaps the most distinctive feature about successful writers is that they have a variety of methods to cope with problems. However, before you build your own set of tried-and-true strategies to help you become the best drafter you can be, it's probably a good idea to examine what you do currently so that you can modify or add strategies to your usual practices. The following questions will help you begin:

Please circle the appropriate responses.

Once I begin drafting, the hardest part of writing is over.

    Strongly Agree   Agree   Disagree   Strongly Disagree

Once I begin drafting, the real work begins.

    Strongly Agree   Agree   Disagree   Strongly Disagree

When I draft, my attention is on "where I'm going," not on each sentence.

    Always   Usually   Sometimes   Never

I can keep on drafting even if I want to quit.

    Always   Usually   Sometimes   Never

Drafting is easier if I've done lots of inventing first.

    Always   Usually   Sometimes   Never

Drafting is easier if I write out a plan first.

    Always   Usually   Sometimes   Never

For each of the following questions, please check *all* of the responses that apply.

When I draft, I

_____ always have a pad or notebook handy to jot down ideas

_____ usually finish in one sitting

_____ lose track of time

_____ try to avoid thinking of my audience

_____ seem to get stuck every minute

_____ have a hard time keeping my mind on my writing

_____ want to get up too soon

_____ set goals for myself (describe) _____

_____ write quite a lot very quickly

_____ don't worry about "little" things like words and sentences

_____ don't write quickly, but sentences come out at a regular pace

_____ produce chunks of writing in spurts

_____ constantly think of my readers

_____ worry about getting stuck

_____ leave "spaces" if I can't think of what to write

_____ other (specify) _____

To continue drafting when I want to quit, I

_____ promise myself food if I keep on writing

_____ promise myself a treat (specify) _____

_____ promise to reward myself (specify) _____

_____ promise myself that I can stop after I've written for (specify length of time)
_____

_____ promise myself I can stop after I've written (specify amount) _____ pages,
paragraphs, words

_____ imagine how good my finished paper will be

_____ imagine the mess I'll be in if I don't finish

_____ allow myself a short break (specify length) _____

_____ I always quit when I feel like it

_____ other (specify) _____

When I get stuck while drafting, I

_____ panic

_____ quit

_____ take a short break (specify length)

_____ stop and begin writing again the next day

_____ try freewriting

_____ use an invention method other than freewriting (specify) _____

_____ review my plan for writing

_____ modify my plan for writing

_____ reread what I have written

_____ read through my notes

_____ read what I have already written out loud

_____ read through the papers that I have successfully completed

_____ do vigorous exercise (specify what and for how long) _____

_____ other (specify) _____

 Activity 4

Discuss your drafting behavior with the other members of your group (or with your partner). Decide which habits seem to be the most productive, which are the least helpful, and which should be modified or eliminated. Then, together, prepare a one-page report that describes strategies that lead to the most productive drafting; address your report to novice writers. Be sure to cover strategies that can help a writer overcome drafting problems, such as getting stuck.

Revising and Rewriting. Drafting and revising are intimately tied to one another because the extent to which a draft is or isn't "finished" determines the amount and nature of revising a writer must do. Writers who don't begin drafting until they've engaged in extensive inventing and planning often produce texts that require very little rewriting, especially if they've modified their plans extensively in response to others' reactions. On the other hand, writers who begin drafting almost immediately, without much inventing and planning, may use drafting as a kind of inventing and planning activity and can produce first drafts that resemble freewriting. These kinds of drafts rarely exhibit much structure or unity; as a consequence, many writers prefer to read them over for the ideas they suggest about possible theses or ways of structuring. Then they begin an entirely new draft. Because writers can use a variety of strategies when they compose a text, it is important for them to have some expectations about the nature of the first draft that they are likely to produce. These expectations can then guide them in selecting appropriate revision strategies.

Think about your own drafting behavior. Do you use the strategy of writing initial discovery drafts? As you consider your answer, review your revising behavior. Do you rewrite drafts significantly, or do you make minimal changes in them? If you aren't sure of what you do, the following questions will help you think about the nature and amount of revising you do while you draft, or the types of changes you make when you rewrite.

Please circle the appropriate responses.

I must do all of my revising before I begin drafting, because my first draft always comes out almost finished.

    Strongly Agree   Agree   Disagree   Strongly Disagree

I do most of my revising while I'm inventing and planning.

    Always   Usually   Sometimes   Never

Almost all of the revision I do is unconscious.

    Strongly Agree   Agree   Disagree   Strongly Disagree

I do major revising after I've begun drafting.

    Always   Usually   Sometimes   Never

I only do revisions required by my teachers.

    Strongly Agree   Agree   Disagree   Strongly Disagree

My first draft is usually a "discovery" draft.

    Strongly Agree   Agree   Disagree   Strongly Disagree

I only do minor revisions, like fixing words or sentences.

    Strongly Agree   Agree   Disagree   Strongly Disagree

I fix problems if they're pointed out, but I have trouble seeing them myself.

    Strongly Agree   Agree   Disagree   Strongly Disagree

Revising is not an important part of my writing process.

    Strongly Agree   Agree   Disagree   Strongly Disagree

For each of the following questions, please check off of the responses that apply.

When I revise, I

_____ make the major changes in my head

_____ make many major changes on paper

_____ make most of the changes during inventing and planning

_____ am not aware of the major changes that I make

_____ change my written plan several times

_____ rearrange whole portions of a draft

_____ cut out major portions of a draft

_____ replace major portions of a draft with new material

_____ add a lot (more than a few sentences) to a draft

_____ am willing to start an entirely new draft if necessary

_____ sometimes have to replace my introduction

_____ sometimes have to replace my conclusion

_____ sometimes have to add entire paragraphs

_____ almost always have to omit digressions

_____ often have to rework the structure of my essay

_____ usually need to add more explanations or illustrations

_____ rarely do more than fix words or sentences

_____ only correct errors in spelling and grammar

_____ wait until a draft is finished before I make changes

_____ make small changes while I'm drafting

_____ make major changes while I'm drafting

_____ other (specify) _____

Editing. Recent writing studies suggest that novice writers often think of revising and editing as being the same operation, perhaps because they are unaware of the global changes they make in the design of a text while they are in the process of producing it. Studies have also suggested that writers who lack confidence often become preoccupied with errors in spelling, grammar, and sentence structure—a preoccupation that can minimize their attention to other, more important aspects of the writing process.

Perhaps for these reasons, many contemporary writing texts and teachers say to "put error in its place"—that is to make attention to error an important part of the writing process, but not a central concern. However, even though attention to error has been minimized within the context of many textbooks or writing classes, this does not mean that the majority of readers notice errors any less frequently. The effectiveness of even a well-written paper can be diminished by a preponderance of error.

Through our conversations with students, we know that most want to eliminate errors when they edit. However, for a variety of reasons, many don't have helpful or efficient strategies. Here are comments from several of our students that describe how they feel about and what they do when editing:

> *Janella: When I'm done with a paper, I'm worn out. It's all I can do to add a conclusion. I try to edit, but I'm sick of writing; I just want to be finished.*

> *Bob: I just read over my mistakes. I don't see them until someone else points them out.*

> *Eddy: I edit while I type my final draft. When I'm done typing, the paper is ready to hand in.*

> *Barb: Sometimes when I'm writing I see something wrong, but I don't want to stop and break my train of thought. Then I don't catch the problem later, but my teacher always does.*

Are you exhausted like Janella when it's time for you to edit your paper? How long do you wait after you've finished your final draft before you begin editing? Do you do other things, like copy over your paper, while you're editing? Here are some exercises to help you answer these and other questions:

Please circle the appropriate responses.

I edit while I'm writing, so I don't need to do it again when my paper is done.

> True   False

I can edit carefully at the same time as I'm copying over or typing my paper.

> True   False

I have friends who help me edit my work.

> Always   Usually   Sometimes   Never

I go to the writing center to get help with editing.

> Always   Usually   Sometimes   Never

I do several readings to locate and correct my errors.

> Always   Usually   Sometimes   Never

Are you familiar with the kinds of errors you write? Check *all* of the responses that seem appropriate.

_____ I don't have any idea about the kinds of errors I write.

_____ My errors don't fit any pattern.

_____ I really don't make very many errors.

When I write, I sometimes have problems with

_____ spelling	_____ verb forms and endings
_____ subject-verb agreement	_____ possessives
_____ pronouns	_____ comma splices
_____ fragments	_____ run-on or fused sentences
_____ faulty parallelism	_____ dangling or misplaced modifiers

_____ similar-sounding words like *they're*, *their*, and *there*

_____ punctuation (specify) _____

_____ sentences that are too long and complicated

_____ other (specify) _____

For each of the following questions, please check all of the responses that describe your habits.

I edit

_____ whenever I'm writing, even during freewriting

_____ only when I'm just about finished with my paper

_____ several times, at different stages (specify) _____

_____ with a ruler to help me focus on each word

_____ after I've waited at least (specify amount of time) _____ after finishing a paper

_____ by reading a paper backwards

_____ for errors in sentence structure by reading out loud

_____ when I'm alert and rested

_____ very minimally

_____ by marking errors to come back to later

_____ once, immediately after I've finished writing

_____ for particular errors that I know I make

WRITING ASSIGNMENTS

As you have discovered from examining your own behavior as a writer and from comparing your habits with those of others, each individual has a unique way of performing the act of writing. Some writers have very elaborate requirements. Others seem to be quite flexible about their needs.

The assignments that follow are meant to focus your attention on what you do when you write. Following the writing topics and procedures are three short pieces about writing by three composition instructors who teach in our program. These selections will give you some more ideas about what others do or how they feel when they write. Do you see some similarities between their behaviors or attitudes and yours?

Writing Topic

Select **one aspect** of your writing behavior (the environment you require; your avoidance behavior; what you do to "keep on task"; your revising behavior, etc.) and write a three-page description of it. Use your answers to the questions in this chapter and your discussions with your group members or partner to help you generate ideas. Be sure to include as many concrete, vivid details as you can. Conclude your paper with a discussion—at least one-half a page long—in which you react to your description. Your reaction might be an explanation of why you think the aspect of your behavior that you described is unusual, an assessment of its effectiveness, and so forth.

In selecting which aspect of your behavior to write about, consider choosing something that you think is unusual or distinctive, or if the questions within this chapter led you to discover an aspect of your behavior about which you were previously unaware, you might describe the practices that make up this behavior. In any case, avoid writing about an aspect of your behavior that is largely unconscious. That is, if you aren't the least bit aware of what you do when you revise, you shouldn't choose your revising behavior as a topic for this paper.

Writing Procedures

By now, you may have been assigned to a writing group. The following procedures will help you and your group (or partner) assist one another in preparing this assignment.

1. Review your answers to the questions in this chapter and your discussions with your partner or group members. Tentatively select an aspect of your writing behavior for this assignment.

2. Freewrite for at least ten to twenty minutes on your topic. If you run out of things to say in *less than* ten minutes, select another topic and freewrite about it.

3. Share your freewriting and any ideas for your paper with your group/partner. Jot down suggestions, questions, and ideas.

4. Use your freewriting, discussion notes, answers to chapter questions, and so on to write an informal statement of purpose (thesis) for your paper. An example of such an informal thesis might be the following: *I used to think that I was the only person who put off writing. But now I know that my behavior is quite typical. To avoid writing, I do other homework, clean my room, or write bills.*

5. Keeping your informal thesis in mind, look over your freewriting and see if you can arrange the ideas and information within it into several areas or subtopics. For example, if you are writing about the writing environment that you require,

see if you can arrange the aspects of your environment into several broad categories (perhaps, how it is typical in some respects and unique in others). Also, jot down notes for the reaction portion of your paper. In reacting to your environment, for example, you might explain that you wish to modify particular practices and requirements and give the reasons why.

6. Write out a detailed plan for your essay. Jot down where you might include specific details and examples (from your freewriting, from answers to questions within the chapter, etc.). Share your detailed plan with your group/partner, and revise it based on the suggestions you receive.

7. Use your revised plan to write a first draft of your paper.

8. Wait at least one full day (preferably two) before you examine the draft that you wrote. Read it over and make any revisions you consider necessary.

9. Edit the final draft of your essay, and turn it in to your instructor.

READINGS

The Pleasures and Frustrations of Writing

Billie Jones Waisanen

Writing is both a pleasurable and frustrating experience for me. In fact, some of the pleasure is a by-product of the frustration. Upon returning to college, I took a first-year composition class, in which I experienced early success and much positive reinforcement. At this point, writing was a pleasure because it provided me with the satisfaction of a job well done. Later, a history professor with a very narrow writing style in mind frustrated me to the point that I developed a writing phobia. Writing was no longer a pleasure, but an arduous chore. Although I have overcome some of this feeling, there is still a lingering sense of dread over some writing projects.

Probably the biggest change in my writing process itself has been my switch from composing in longhand on legal pads to keyboard composition. Since part of me still regards computers as early humans might have reacted to fire, I still experience the delight of a small child on Christmas whenever I cut and paste to find just the right progression of words, thereby converting frustration to pleasure in a key stroke or two.

Despite my affinity for the magical cut-and-paste, however, my analytical mind loves the permanence of writing. I can study each subtle nuance of every word. Furthermore, I can look back at previous writings and see where I've been, which helps me to see where I'm going. The pleasure of writing is in the conquering of the frustration. Finding that elusive word, completing that lengthy assignment, discovering new meaning through the process—that is the pleasure of writing.

A Beauty Dimly Seen

Yewon Kim

Writing for me has always been a mystery and a strange phenomenon. I've tried to figure out how the writing process happens—to split it apart and look for the inside. After reading great pieces of work by famous authors, still dizzy from their effects, I ask myself, "How is it done?" I analyze the work or a passage to figure out meanings—is it the words? the phrasing? the sentence structure? I still don't know the answer. But I've discovered some things from my own writing process.

Good writing certainly doesn't happen by magic or by chance; good writing is, for the most part, difficult. But it is also too easy to say it's difficult. Writing happens sometimes by thinking and sometimes by doing the opposite. Take freewriting, for example. I have surprised myself by how many good ideas flow from some unconscious source in my mind. I have written many journal entries this way, which have given me ideas to start other writing projects with clear focus and force. The generative power of writing is amazing, but obviously there is no such thing as a formula for good writing. One constantly has to create new tracks and discover new ways of seeing.

The writing process is justifiably ambiguous. It should not be plain and familiar. Mary Wollstonecraft wrote in her *Vindication,* "[t]he fancy has hovered around a form of beauty dimly seen—but familiarity might have turned admiration into disgust; or, at least, into indifference, and allowed the imagination leisure to start fresh game." I love this sentence. It represents writing for me.

Writing and Speaking

Kawita Kandpal

In the beginning of my undergraduate study, I settled on the task of writing because my professors told me this was a prerequisite for graduation. Writing was also a method of showing them how much "knowledge" I had digested during my classes. Sometimes when I read a book, I wrote a paper. Sometimes when I read a book, I contributed to class discussions. It was only during these classroom debates, though, that the correlation between speaking and writing became meaningful to me. In order to discuss and debate with my peers, speaking clearly and coherently was necessary. I reasoned that if I could learn to speak in a particular manner during class discussions, then paper writing couldn't be that much different.

Writing and Speaking *(cont'd.)*

In class discussions as well as well as on paper, I had to learn to introduce my topic, make points to support that topic, show further support through examples, and—most of all—be prepared to offer counterarguments in response to attacks from my peers. Speaking and writing were not separate entities that were independent of one another. They were, instead, like right and left hands. They could and often would work together if and when I allowed them to. I also realized that writing was a form of artistic expression that could evoke emotions from readers—the words in my papers had to approximate my voice in class discussions.

It was only when I recognized the connection between speaking and writing that I began to understand the importance of writing. I also realized that writing was not simply an assigned chore; writing could be a passionate form of self-expression, if and when I allowed it to be. During classroom discussions, I was learning to develop my speaking voice. After classroom discussions, I was learning to develop my written voice through writing papers. As this process continued, I found that I was *choosing* writing instead of *settling for* writing.

Writing and speaking. One is the right hand; the other is the left. Both work together with one another. Both lend voice to and allow passion in expression.

CHAPTER 2

WORKING TOGETHER

BEGINNING TO COLLABORATE

Most likely, you have had the experience of working together with other people on some project. Perhaps you worked with a group of friends to plan a party or special celebration. In high school, you may have played a team sport, worked to produce a play, or collaborated with others to publish a newspaper or a yearbook. In previous classes, you may have worked in groups as well. For example, you may have worked in groups in your high school English class to respond to one another's ideas or papers. You may have worked in groups in a science class to perform an experiment or develop projects for a science fair. In any of these situations, you were working in a collaborative group, that is, in a group of people working together to achieve a common goal.

By now you have undoubtedly realized that group work can be an important part of a writing class; however, a writing or English course is not the only class where collaboration may be involved. Many careers and professions routinely entail collaborative work, and an important aspect of college training is learning to work in groups. As a consequence, students in a marketing class may be required to work in teams to research and promote a new product. Likewise, students in a chemistry class may be put into permanent groups for weekly lab work.

You can see, then, that learning to work in groups is an important part of your education. The ability to collaborate successfully with others may also be a requirement in your future career. In addition, group work is a *central* means by which you will learn to be a better writer. For these reasons, we are devoting this chapter to helping you learn more about what collaborative groups are, how they may be used in writing classes, and what responsibilities group work entails.

Reasons for Working in Groups

From this brief overview, you can see that in college you may be working in groups, but perhaps you do not understand why. One reason teachers require students to work in small groups is to provide them with greater opportunities to express or clarify their opinions on a wide variety of subjects. In a traditional classroom setting, when a discussion takes place among the members of a whole class, only one person at a time can speak; thus perhaps only 20 percent of the students are able to contribute to a "class discussion." However, when a large class is divided into small collaborative groups, numerous people may express opinions at the same time—and, in doing so, learn to address one another, rather than their instructor. Small groups thus offer some students better opportunities to express their opinions, ask questions of others, and talk through their ideas. Talking about ideas and opinions—rather than just thinking about them—is important, because vocalization helps to clarify thinking and provides speakers with a chance to hear how other people respond to their ideas. It also encourages students to develop and defend their own points of view, instead of always looking to the teacher for the "right answer."

Small groups are also ideal for ensuring that each student in a class receives individual attention and response. In traditional classrooms, teachers attempt to provide individual attention to each student but are often unable to do so. In classrooms composed of small groups, each group member can be assisted by his or her peers during the class period.

Another reason why small groups are used in many classes is that they are an ideal way to provide students with assistance through all of the phases of writing a paper, from invention to final editing. Within collaborative writing groups, ideas for papers can be discussed and developed. Writing groups can also help group members determine various methods for selecting and structuring their ideas and for revising and editing their papers. Group collaborators help one another with all stages of writing.

As mentioned earlier, however, besides the benefits provided to writers, working with a small group can be excellent practice for careers after college. Many professions—including medicine, law, business, science, and technology—rely heavily on consultation and collaboration as the most effective way to operate. Industries, for example, often depend on the effective collaboration of people with a variety of specializations. To produce a product such as a backpack may require the combined efforts of designers, textiles experts, metalworkers, patent attorneys, marketing experts, and publicists.

Types of Collaboration

There are a variety of collaborative activities in which a group can engage. Within a university or college setting, of course, the way in which groups are constituted and how they function can vary across disciplines. Still, people who have studied collaborative groups have identified some common group activities. These are knowledge making, investigating/researching, workshopping, and coauthoring.

- **Knowledge Making.** *Knowledge making* is any activity in which the group's primary purpose is to share knowledge about the subject at hand or to create a new and more complete pool of knowledge. Knowledge making may involve generating ideas, searching memories, or enlarging and expanding points of view. Knowledge making is especially productive in small groups, as the different members are put in dialogue with one another, which leads to broader perspectives or a fuller synthesis of the subjects under discussion. If you watched a group of people involved in knowledge making, they would be talking to one another, with some moments of silence for thinking. You might observe some writing if, for example, group members were charged with preparing a report for their class or with brainstorming a list to be used in a later activity. Under these and other circumstances, then, group members might occasionally jot down notes; however, in the act of knowledge making, for the most part, group members would be engaged in discussion. Knowledge-making activities may end when the group reaches an agreement or consensus about the subject under discussion or produces a synthesis of or conclusion about the members' points of view. Alternatively, knowledge making may result in different conclusions being reached by different group members.

- **Investigating/Researching.** Collaborative groups can enlarge their knowledge by sharing what they know with one another, yet they can also expand their collective pool of knowledge by investigating a subject together. The processes of *investigating* and *researching* involve identifying useful information sources, both those located in libraries (which we discuss in Chapter 9) as well as those located elsewhere (which we discuss in Chapter 10). While library or nonlibrary research can be performed by individuals, it is not uncommon for people in a group to pool their individual research. In addition, people conducting nonlibrary research—for example, conducting an opinion survey—may codesign materials and collect data together. Within the sciences and social sciences, research is routinely performed by teams, which may (or may not) be lead by a "primary" investigator.

- **Workshopping.** *Workshopping* is the term used to describe the kind of help that group members can provide for one another throughout the writing of individual projects. It can occur in professional contexts but most often takes place in a classroom setting. Workshopping allows writers to test their ideas and plans with actual readers, to get immediate feedback on drafts, and to get help with editing. Thus workshopping usually involves examining thesis statements and plans, drafts, or revisions. The procedures groups use for workshopping vary. People may report orally on their plans or read papers out loud, with listeners offering comments, questions, and suggestions orally. Sometimes copies of papers are distributed so that group members can read them silently, write comments on them, and then discuss them together with other group members. In addition, teachers often give groups a written set of directions to follow in responding to drafts, perhaps the criteria by which papers will be graded or an editing checklist.

- **Coauthoring.** When we use the word *coauthoring*, we are referring to a process in which two or more people produce a single piece of writing by working together at every stage, from generating ideas to drafting to revising and editing. Coauthoring takes many forms. One common variation is for a group to decide together what the overall design of a text will be, to draft sections separately, and then to revise and edit together. Another (less common) variation is for coauthors to draft an entire text together, sitting beside one another at a word processor. Depending on the number of writers working on a project, coauthoring can be a highly structured activity coordinated by a particular individual or it can be loose and unstructured with participants adopting a variety of roles.

Although knowledge making, investigating/researching, workshopping, and coauthoring are common group activities, the form these activities take as well as the extent to which they are acceptable practices may vary. Most instructors do not object when students engage in knowledge making; in fact, many colleges and universities provide students with a variety of opportunities to join discussion groups related to their classes, current topics, courses of study, and the like. However, the appropriateness of other collaborative activities is not so clear-cut.

If, for example, students in a particular class are assigned to write individual term papers, the instructor may or may not find it appropriate for them to engage in group investigating/researching. Likewise, students who decide to coauthor a paper without clearing it with their instructor may encounter difficulty. Even workshopping, in which students gain feedback about their papers from others, may be considered inappropriate by some instructors, who may consider it a form of cheating. It is always prudent, then, to be aware of disciplinary or professional conventions regarding group work, as well as the attitude and expectations of your instructor, if you wish to employ collaborative practices in producing your class assignments.

Being an Effective Group Member

Now that you have been acquainted with several kinds of group activities, it is time to learn more about how to make groups work well together. There are two major areas to consider: the different roles people play in groups and effective guidelines for group work.

Different Group Roles. When people work together in small groups, there are many functions they can serve. As you practice these functions, you will get better at performing each one and at becoming more adaptable. That is, if you learn to play the role of a leader at times and of a questioner or a timekeeper at others, you will contribute to the success of any groups you work in. Within a group, members can assume a variety of roles such as researcher, organizer, note taker, leader, and so forth. However, despite this diversity, several roles are crucial in making groups work effectively. As we have suggested, these roles should be assumed by each member of the group on differing occasions. In this way, the group itself will not become overly dependent on the skills of particular individuals who may be absent from time to time, and each group member will become more adaptable. Because people vary in their ability to play particular roles, if you and your peers are given the opportunity to form your own group, you should try to balance your membership.

Consider such matters as gender, ethnicity, course of study, and interpersonal skills as you form your collective.

- **Initiator/Facilitator.** A key group role is that of initiator/facilitator. Whoever assumes this role manages group work, initiates discussion, and raises questions that encourage group members to respond to issues in detail. Within a linguistics class discussion, for example, the initiator/facilitator might ask, "What are some specific ways that this conversation illustrates the maxim of relevance?" Frequently, a group initiator/facilitator may draw connections among points raised by individual group members. Doing so is important because it allows group members to enlarge their own perspectives in order to see an issue more globally. Finally, the person who assumes this role should work to draw all members into each discussion. If one or more members aren't speaking, the initiator/facilitator might direct questions to specific individuals: "Bob, can you give us another example that illustrates the maxim of relevance?"

- **"The Boss."** As we were trying to come up with a name for this function, we discarded some of these possibilities: the Taskmaster, the Enforcer, the Disciplinarian, and the Wagon Master. As these rather whimsical titles suggest, the person who assumes the role of "the Boss" must work to keep the group on task. That is, as you know from experience, when people get together, even if they are charged with accomplishing a particular goal, it is human nature to digress or to chat with one another. Most people, including students, have tight schedules and need to make effective use of their time. Some of the specific duties of "the Boss" are clarifying directions, setting and keeping time limits, and cutting off or redirecting digressions and unnecessary socializing. A characteristic remark from the individual who assumes this role might be a direct statement that informs group members of time constraints and sets forth a task: "We only have ten minutes left, so we need to think of a couple of examples that illustrate intangible power."

- **Questioner.** Because people who share similar characteristics such as age, background, and so forth may reach a consensus or adopt a particular point of view without much deliberation, an important group role is that of the questioner. The individual who serves this function must play devil's advocate. It is his or her job, then, to ask questions like "Why are you making that assumption about the results of our survey?" or "What kind of evidence do you have to support the idea that educational level is an important variable related to quality of life in this community?" While we don't want to suggest that the questioner should be combative, we do want to emphasize that this person should invite and sometimes even challenge a group to examine different perspectives and question interpretations and conclusions that have been arrived at too easily.

- **Note Taker/Summarizer.** The person who assumes the role of note taker/summarizer ordinarily does not do as much talking as other group members. This is because he or she is busy taking detailed notes of the group's discussion. Such notes are valuable resources because they provide continuity and a record of all of the ideas, perspectives, and information that the group discovers. In addition, the notes are often a record to help determine the agenda of future group work and may become the substance of a paper that the group will write. Although we have suggested that the note taker/summarizer does not do a great deal of talking, periodically this individual may wish to summarize the group's accomplishments or decisions that have been reached or that need to be made.

Guidelines for Effective Collaboration. For some students, and perhaps for you, working in groups in a classroom setting may be a new way of learning. Reliance on the teacher rather than on peers—and working alone rather than in groups—have been far more often the norms within classrooms. Therefore, you may feel some initial anxiety or uneasiness about group work. For many students, though, uneasy feelings disappear after the first session or two of group work, when they begin to learn more about working effectively together.

Learning to work effectively within a community of writers is not automatic, so it is not reasonable to expect your collaborative group to work easily together at first. Groups need time to gel, to find their own comfort zone—and doing so takes effort from all members of the group. Group members need to determine what responsibilities are entailed in order for the group to work well together. The following guidelines will help your group learn to collaborate effectively; if you and the other members of your group adhere to them, you will start to work together effectively in almost no time at all.

- **Think of yourself as an important member of a team.** Just as members of all sorts of teams (athletic teams, for example) have responsibilities to their teammates, you, too, should feel a sense of responsibility to your writing class team. This means that you should attend all group meetings, be on time, and come fully prepared for the task at hand. At your initial meeting, you and your group members should exchange class and work schedules and phone numbers with one another and agree on a means for each member to get materials to the group in the event of an unforeseen illness or conflict. You and your partners should also decide together what the group should do if individuals need to miss meetings or can't come prepared. Agreeing together in advance on such strategies will help ensure that all members are treated consistently and fairly.

- **Socialize briefly, then get to work.** When your group sits down together, it is only natural to greet one another and start talking about something unrelated to your class—the weather, the upcoming football game, or a recent news story. Not only is such dialogue at the beginning of a group session a normal part of group behavior, it also is essential in helping the group establish its comfort zone and sense of identity. However, the members of your group should share the responsibility for *ending* the opening dialogue fairly quickly in order to move on to the assigned task by saying something like "Okay, folks, let's get on to this project." Once your group has become engaged in working, members should not bring up unrelated topics of conversation, such as "Hey, did you get your hair cut?" Should such comments occur, group members need to draw the group's attention back to work, perhaps with comments like "Yes, I did. Now what do you think about my conclusion? Do I need to add more details there?"

- **Practice good communication skills.** During each session it will be important for all members of your group to practice good communication skills such as making eye contact with one another and using group members' names when you are referring directly to them. When you are responding to Marina's paper, for example, you should look at her and say, "Marina, I liked the way you started with a question. That got my interest right away." Your group should also make sure that everyone receives an equal amount of time to speak and that anyone who tends not to speak be encouraged to do so. If, for example, you notice that a group member has not contributed to the discussion, you might ask, "Al, you haven't said anything about this paper yet. What do you think about it?" Your aim should be a conversation among all the members; hence you should avoid conversations with only one person in the group, since this will divide his or her attention (and yours) from what the larger group is discussing.

- **When you disagree, be respectful.** Undoubtedly, there will be times when you will disagree with what a fellow group member is saying. When disagreement occurs, it is important not to interrupt another person, but to listen patiently until it is your turn to speak. When you do speak, you should explain your own point of view or your reaction to what is being said in a paper—without directly attacking or "putting down" the group member. For example, if you disagree with the stand someone has taken in a paper criticizing affirmative action programs, that person would probably feel you were launching a personal attack if you said, "That's the most stupid argument I've ever heard—affirmative action discriminates against white people! How can you believe that?" Instead of an emotional response that may put the writer on the defensive, a message that describes what has been said or written and how you feel about it is preferable: "Alisha, I know that you think that affirmative action is discriminatory against white people, but I feel that it's necessary to correct a long history of discrimination in employment that you aren't acknowledging in your paper."

  On some occasions, you and your group members may feel that it is desirable to achieve a consensus or agreement on potentially divisive issues, especially if you want to keep working together on a project or to share one another's writing. Realize, however, that there are differences among people that simply cannot be erased. Consequently, at times it may be more respectful to "agree to disagree" with one another than to push toward compromise or agreement.

- **Offer constructive criticism of the writings.** Many times your group will meet for the purpose of discussing one another's writing. During these sessions, you should note particular strengths in each person's paper and offer praise where praise is due. When you note weaknesses, you should be honest yet tactful in describing the problems and in offering explanations or suggestions. Most especially, it is important to offer specific advice or criticism. Global comments such as "I liked it" or "It doesn't flow" are not clear or helpful. Consider how much more helpful the following comments are:

> *Daniel, I think your main point, about how the essay we read changed your view of hunting, is really clear. I also liked the story you opened with because it helped me see why you feel the way you do now. But I had some trouble following parts of your paper. When you moved from the story at the beginning to the rest of the paper, it felt pretty choppy. And later, on page 3, I didn't understand why you included the last paragraph. How does it connect to your main point?*

In addition to being specific about a paper's specific strengths and weaknesses, to be a helpful group member, you should offer suggestions to your partners and ask questions that will help them clarify thinking, generate ideas, and focus their texts. If, for example, you are unsatisfied with the conclusion of a group member's paper, you might ask questions that would help the writer to see additional reasons why he or she chose to write on this topic or why other people might be interested in the paper.

- **Be open to suggestions.** When your own writing is being discussed by your group members, you should be open to their responses and not be offended by their constructive criticism. Some writers are uncomfortable about sharing their writing with others because they are afraid that someone else—a teacher or a peer group member—will "rewrite" their paper. If you feel this way, realize that you are the author of your own work and are therefore responsible for deciding whether and how to incorporate the suggestions of your readers. Sometimes writers are reluctant to hear feedback from readers for an additional reason: They do not want to hear that the paper isn't finished yet.

  If you are uncomfortable about sharing your writing with group members for whatever reasons, a good way to handle your feelings may be to take more control of the situation. That is, instead of waiting for group members to identify problems in your paper, you may feel more comfortable sharing your own evaluation of the paper first and then soliciting their opinions as in this example: "When I was writing this paper, I wasn't sure if I was being detailed and specific enough. Do you think I need more examples?" An additional strategy that may help you gain more control over the feedback process is to ask questions of your group members. If, for instance, someone suggests using more examples, ask what kinds, and where they should be added.

- **Plan time carefully.** Because time passes quickly when groups are busily working together, it's important to budget time wisely. In order to do this, at the beginning of each session, your group should decide what you need to accomplish and how you will spend the time allotted. If, for example, your task is to discuss drafts of essays written by the three people in your group and you have an hour to work, you should devote no more than twenty minutes to discussing each text. An appointed timekeeper should keep an eye on the clock and make sure that everyone's work receives an equal amount of time and attention by keeping the group moving forward with comments such as this: "We could probably say a lot more about Ralph's essay, but now we need to move on to Max's paper."

- **Make plans for your next meeting.** Shortly before the close of each session, your group should make plans for the following session and decide what each group member's responsibilities will be to prepare for it. If your group is researching a topic together for a research paper, you might decide to do the following: "At the next class meeting, we will brainstorm what we know already about our group topic. We will each locate three sources in the library and bring our research notes with us." It may be wise for group members to take notes at this point, in order to remember exactly what the group has decided and what individual members are responsible for next time. That is, everyone should write notes about exactly what reading to complete, what writing to complete, and what notes or books to bring to the next meeting.

Although the guidelines we have outlined can help your group function effectively, sometimes collaborative groups can encounter difficulties. One common problem is unequal participation of group members. To resolve problems related to participation, it is always best to try to discover what is affecting a particular group member's behavior. Underlying causes for unequal participation can be diverse. Sometimes an inordinately heavy work or class schedule can make it difficult for a person to attend meetings; group efforts to accommodate such individuals by changing the times or places for meetings or allowing them to do other work in lieu of attending can be effective in these situations. Other times, group members may not respond during discussions or produce much work for a project because they feel that their ideas are not being valued—either by the group as a whole or by an individual who seems to dominate group activities. In these cases, periodic evaluations—in which group members assess the effectiveness of the group as a whole as well as their own contributions—can be helpful.

Ordinarily, when members evaluate the effectiveness of their group as whole they consider factors such as the extent to which all members have contributed, whether one or more persons have been dominant, whether members have assumed a variety of roles, and so forth. When members evaluate their own contributions, they try to determine in what way they have made contributions (by providing leadership, asking questions, etc.) and in what ways they can improve their participation (by listening more and talking less, by building on what others have said rather than disagreeing, by initiating group action rather than waiting for someone else to act, etc.) Sometimes instructors give their students forms to fill out or a series of questions to answer to assess group performance. Even if your instructor does not provide you with such aids, your group should discuss its performance from time to time. The writing assignment at the end of this chapter will help you with that endeavor.

Another common problem that groups experience is in reaching a consensus. As we have said, making an effort to disagree respectfully as well as listening carefully to others' points of views can help groups reach a consensus or decide on a course of action. However, this may not always be possible. If your group cannot decide how to proceed with a project because of strong, irreconcilable differences, it is probably wise to ask your instructor for assistance. In fact, any serious problems that you and your group members cannot deal with on your own—for example, repeated absences by a member—should be discussed with your instructor.

WORKING IN GROUPS

From reading the first part of this chapter, you should have a general understanding that working in groups can be beneficial for both students and professional writers. However, "working in groups" is a broad phrase that encompasses many possible procedures. In this section, we offer guidelines for some of the more commonly used methods of collaboration; of course, there can be numerous variations on these. As you become more comfortable with the process of collaboration, you and your group members probably will want to devise procedures of your own.

Procedures for Collaborating

Because collaborative activities include knowledge making, researching/investigating, workshopping, and coauthoring, a useful way to discuss procedures is within these contexts. The following sections describe procedures for these four kinds of activities, which you and your group members can try out to see how well they work for you. It is important to remember, though, that the first time your group works with a particular procedure, you may not make as much progress as you would like; collaborating effectively takes *practice.*

Knowledge Making.   As the phrase suggests, *knowledge making* means combining or synthesizing ideas or information in an original way, thereby creating knowledge that is new. Knowledge can be "made" by one person working alone, of course, but for our purposes we will discuss only the kind of knowledge making that occurs when group members talk or write with one another. Obviously, it would be impossible to exhaust all of the procedures for knowledge making; therefore, we will offer two examples that are intended to help you think of other possibilities.

To help you fully realize the usefulness of the procedures we are recommending for knowledge making, we want you to think of them in the context of the following assignment: Let's say that each student in your class has been assigned to select an article and to write a critique of it (which includes a summary and an evaluation). Although this assignment conceivably could be completed independently, your instructor has asked you to work in small collaborative groups throughout the process. To prepare for your upcoming collaborative session, your instructor has asked everyone to select two possible articles and prepare brief rationale statements about why they might make good choices for the assignment.

The purpose of your first collaborative session, then, would be to help one another decide which of the two articles would work best for the assignment. As you might imagine, in order to have an effective session, the members of the group would not be able to talk whenever they felt like it; instead, they would need to follow a systematic procedure that allowed time for each person to summarize his or her articles and rationale statements and for the other group members to respond. The following are two alternative procedures that could be used:

Procedure 1 for Knowledge Making

Each person is allotted an equal amount of time (say, five minutes) to summarize one of his or her articles and the accompanying rationale statement. Immediately following each person's summary, the group takes five minutes to discuss the benefits and limitations of using the article for the assignment. Each group member contributes to this discussion. After each person's first article has been dealt with in this manner, the procedure is repeated for the second article. This time around, however, the group makes a recommendation regarding the preferred article—or perhaps, a recommendation that neither article should be used for the assignment.

Procedure 2 for Knowledge Making

Each person is allotted an equal amount of time (say, ten minutes) to summarize both of his or her articles and rationale statements. Immediately following each person's summaries, the group takes ten minutes to discuss the benefits and limitations of using the articles for the assignment and makes a recommendation about the preferred choice. Each group member contributes to this discussion.

Investigating/Researching. If you look ahead to Chapters 9 and 10 in this textbook, you will see that we have provided detailed information about gathering and utilizing information from both library and nonlibrary sources. The point we want to make in this chapter is that working in collaborative groups can greatly increase the effectiveness of researching and investigating. As you would assume, there are numerous workable procedures for collaborating as a "research team"; the following discussion should help you start thinking of various possibilities.

To provide a concrete basis for understanding the options we discuss, we want you to assume that you are a member of a collaborative group that has decided to investigate the topic "gender and interruption" for an introductory linguistics class; that is, you want to learn who interrupts other people's speech more frequently—

men or women? Through your research, your group hopes to learn whether there is a significant difference between the genders regarding interruption, whether men interrupt other men to the same degree as they interrupt women, whether women interrupt other women to the same degree as they interrupt men, and so on. This topic could be researched by a group using a variety of procedures, including the following:

Procedure 1 for Working as a Research Team

Following a group discussion of how to divide up tasks, each member of the group is assigned (or volunteers to do) a specific kind of research. That is, one person investigates library sources; one person observes conversations between men and women and keeps track of the interruptions on a self-designed tally sheet; one person interviews a linguistics professor who has done research on the topic of interruption; and one person designs and distributes a survey to find out people's overall perceptions regarding the topic. Each group member is responsible for designing whatever research tool he or she will use (survey, tally sheet, list of interview questions, etc.). The research tools are critiqued by the group so that individual members can make adjustments, if necessary. When all of the information has been accumulated, the group members meet to share and interpret their findings.

Procedure 2 for Working as a Research Team

Before any research is conducted, the group works together to design the tools they will use. They collaborate to design a survey; to prepare a list of interview questions; to decide how and when information from observations will be gathered; and to decide on the kinds of library sources that will be used to investigate the topic. After the tools are established, the responsibilities for conducting the research are divided among the group members. When all information has been accumulated, the group members meet to share and interpret their findings.

Workshopping. Perhaps the most frequently used collaborative activity in college classrooms is workshopping. A broad term, *workshopping* refers to the help that group members can give one another during any part of the writing process. It is likely that you already have engaged in workshopping with classmates in college classes or even in high school. Workshopping is used by students and professionals throughout all disciplines.

Because workshopping is used to assist writers at various stages of the writing process, it is necessary to think about workshopping procedures in terms of writing stages. It is not possible to establish procedures that are appropriate for working with all stages of writing, so we offer the following workshop procedures, which are designed to help groups invent, prewrite, and plan; draft and revise; and edit. As with the other procedures we have discussed, these can be varied as a group gains more experience working together.

The first stage in the writing process is the invention of ideas. Ideas are invented in writers' heads, of course, but the physical act of writing them down (prewriting) in the form of notes, diagrams, or lists enables writers to generate even more information and to see connections among ideas. Through prewriting, writers are able to discover and narrow topics, arrive at potential thesis statements, and determine possible strategies for developing ideas within a paper; although these procedures also occur when the writer actually begins drafting, they are begun to a large degree during prewriting. Prewriting often occurs as a solitary act; however, the quality of the prewriting can be greatly enhanced through the help of group members working together. And in general, the more thorough the prewriting, the more effective the paper will be. The procedures that follow illustrate two ways in which group members can assist with prewriting:

Procedure 1 for Workshopping—Prewriting

The group members meet to discuss the prewriting they have done separately in response to a writing assignment. Each person comes prepared with a substantial amount of prewriting. The first person reads his or her prewriting aloud, with the other group members listening carefully. Then the group members respond with questions and comments about the prewriting to help the writer see where ideas are especially convincing, where there are gaps, where additional support is needed, where thinking is unclear, and so on. During this discussion, the writer takes notes on what the others say. Finally, the group works together to help the writer devise a tentative plan for structuring the paper. In the course of the session, every group member's prewriting is dealt with in the manner just described, with an equal amount of time devoted to each.

Please note that in the procedure just described, group members can come prepared with any kind of prewriting they wish, such as freewriting, brainstorming, listing, and so forth. We realize that at this point you and your classmates may not yet be familiar with various kinds of prewriting; however, you can expect to be introduced to them as you proceed through this book. Later in this chapter, in fact, you will be introduced to "brainstorming" and to ways of using this technique as you work in groups. Other prewriting techniques that you will be introduced to include clustering, note taking, heuristics, and the Pentad.

Procedure 2 for Workshopping—Prewriting

Group members convene in a manner that gives them all visual access to a chalkboard, an easel with a large sheet of paper attached, or another such tool for note taking. One person serves as the note taker while the group works together to help one member at a time prewrite on his or her topic, using any prewriting technique the member chooses. For each writer, the group together comes up with ideas that are especially convincing and well developed. After a writer has been assisted in prewriting, the group works together to help him or her devise a tentative plan for structuring the paper. Each writer copies the notes that the group generates or keeps the notes that were taken by the designated note taker during the discussion of his or her paper. In the course of the session, every group member's prewriting is dealt with in the manner just described, with an equal amount of time devoted to each.

Now, we will offer sample procedures for assisting one another with revising drafts. Such workshopping activities are probably the most common kind that you will encounter throughout your college courses. In providing assistance with revising, group members not only may help one another construct initial drafts, but they may also actively help one another read drafts with a critical eye and make necessary—and often substantial—changes. During this stage of the writing process, instructors often provide students with questions to use as they consider one another's drafts or students devise their own. Here are some typical examples: "What is the thesis or main point?" "How does the writer support or illustrate the main point (list arguments and examples)?" "In what way can the structure be improved?" "Where can additional examples or explanation be added?" "What is the most effective part of the essay?"

Procedure 3 for Workshopping—Revising

After individual group members each have completed a draft of a paper, they bring enough copies to class so that each person in their group can have one—but they do not distribute them right away. During the actual workshopping, the group works through the following directions:

- One at a time, each member reads his or her paper aloud to the group. Other members listen carefully to each reader, with paper and pens ready to jot down notes. While listening to each paper, members take notes on strengths and weaknesses and note any questions they have, any areas where they have difficulty picturing what the writer is trying to convey, and any places where connections are abrupt.

- Immediately after a paper is read, copies are distributed to each group member. Using their notes, the group members mark their copy of the paper with suggestions for revision, focusing their comments on substantive issues: whether the paper has a clear controlling idea, whether the paper has vivid details, and whether the paper presents a distinctive, critical voice, and so on.

- Afterwards, comments are discussed by all group members—including the writer of the paper. In particular, group members focus on problem areas. During this stage of workshopping, problem areas are explained to each writer as precisely as possible so that the writer can understand *why* particular passages need to be revised. In addition, group members try to offer at least one or two suggestions for revising for each problem area they have identified. Comments that explain problems and offer suggestions for revision are written on copies of each paper and returned to the writer.

As you will see, the following workshopping activity for revision is similar to the preceding activity. In this activity, however, the members of the group bring enough copies of their drafts to class so that each group member can have one—and they *do* distribute them right away.

Procedure 4 for Workshopping—Revising

After the members of the group each have completed a draft of a paper, they bring enough copies to class so that each group member can have one. They distribute them right away and begin to work through the following procedures:

- One at a time, each person in the group reads his or her paper aloud, with the others following along on their copies. As group members listen to one another's papers, they observe strengths and weaknesses, as well as note any questions they have, any areas where they have difficulty picturing what the writer is trying to convey, and any places where connections are abrupt.

- Immediately after a paper is read, the writer spends a few minutes discussing his or her intentions in the paper and explaining where he or she believes the writing is strong—and where it needs work. The writer identifies any difficulties the paper is presenting.

- Next, the group discusses the paper in terms of the writer's comments and makes suggestions for revision. Comments focus on substantive issues: whether the paper has a clear controlling idea, whether the paper has vivid details, whether the paper presents a distinctive, critical voice, and so forth.

- As the group members discuss their comments with one another and with the writer, they again keep in mind that the writer will benefit most if the group offers precise explanations about why problems exist. In addition, at least one or two suggestions for revising each problem area are offered. Comments are written on copies of each paper and then returned to the writer.

- The previous procedures are repeated for each writer in the group, ensuring that everyone's paper receives equal time.

The final stage in the writing process—editing—sometimes is overlooked by students who are eager to be finished with writing a paper. However, a paper should never be viewed as a finished product until it has been edited, that is, proofread and polished. Editing includes such concerns as spelling, punctuation, usage, verb tense, sentence construction, and word choice.

Although we recommend that students strive to learn to be effective editors of their own writing, we also know that workshopping with a group can be a useful way of ensuring that all errors are corrected—as well as a way of helping one another master editing techniques. The following procedures represent two examples of the numerous possibilities for editing with a group:

Procedure 5 for Workshopping—Editing

Each student comes prepared with enough copies of his or her paper for each member of the group. Copies should be typed or "hard copies" (computer printouts) in order to ensure that group members will have no questions about any writer's intentions because of illegible handwriting. Group members read the first writer's paper carefully, marking the paper whenever they see (or suspect) an editing error. When everyone has completed this, the group discusses the paper, paragraph by paragraph, helping the writer to correct his or her errors. If a group is unsure about whether something in the paper is correct, a handbook or the instructor is consulted. This procedure is repeated for each writer in the group so that everyone's paper receives equal time.

Procedure 6 for Workshopping—Editing

Each student comes prepared with enough copies of his or her paper for each member of the group. Again, copies should be typed or "hard copies" (computer printouts) in order to ensure that messy handwriting will not cause misinterpretations. Instead of trying to work on all concerns of editing at once, the group examines a paper for one concern at a time. That is, the group members read each paper several times. On the first reading of a group member's paper, the group may pay attention only to punctuation concerns. On the second reading, the members may review and discuss the paper for spelling. Subsequent readings may focus on usage, word choice, and so on. After one paper has been edited in this fashion, the procedure is repeated for each writer in the group, ensuring that everyone's paper receives equal time.

As we have said, workshopping is an effective activity during all stages of writing a paper. We hope that your group not only will utilize the procedures we have recommended but that together you will design and use some of your own procedures. In particular, editing procedures can be tailored to address the specific editing needs of members in your group.

Coauthoring. The final collaborative activity that we will discuss is coauthoring, the activity that takes place when one or more writers work together to produce one final product. As we said earlier in this chapter, coauthoring is gaining in popularity, both in classrooms and in professional arenas. As you might expect, coauthoring can be accomplished in many workable ways; the suggestions we provide are intended to help you start thinking of various possibilities.

To provide you with a basis for understanding Procedure 1, which follows, we want you to assume that your sociology instructor has given your class a semester to construct group projects on a social issue of your choice. To fulfill this assignment, your group has decided to coauthor a booklet on the topic "alcoholism." Procedure 1 illustrates one method that would help your group coauthor this project.

Procedure 1 for Coauthoring

In coauthoring your booklet, your group works through the following procedures:

- The members of your group meet to decide on the aspects of alcoholism that you wish to address in your booklet (examples might include causes of alcoholism, co-dependency, family problems and alcoholism, alcoholism and college students, alcoholism and the law, and treatments for alcoholism.) As a group, you plan the overall structure for your booklet and discuss points that should be made in each section. When a tentative plan has been made, responsibilities for writing and researching the various sections are divided among group members. In addition to deciding who will draft the various sections, the group selects individuals who are responsible for writing an introduction, a table of contents, and a conclusion.

- Throughout the term, group members meet periodically to assist one another with the drafting process. Group members provide honest feedback and are serious in their efforts to provide useful assistance.

- When the parts of the project have been drafted, they are compiled into one work. Group members then read through the work as a whole and determine where connections need to be made among the sections. Group members work together to write the necessary connections, to revise any parts that need revision, and to produce a final draft of the booklet that reads smoothly and whose parts are logically connected.

In the coauthoring procedure just described, the parts of the booklet are planned by the entire group but most of the drafting is done by members working independently. However, if your group is asked to coauthor a shorter piece, such as an essay, you may want to use a quite different procedure. In the following procedure for coauthoring an essay, notice that all group members are engaged in every stage of writing the piece.

Procedure 2 for Coauthoring

In coauthoring your essay, the group works through the following procedures:

- Group members meet to decide on a topic and tentative thesis for the essay. Together they do substantial note taking on their topic and determine a possible structure.

- The second time the group meets, they work together to actually begin drafting the essay. The group members may choose to sit before a computer screen with one person entering words or they may choose to sit in a small circle with one person writing by hand. (As you might imagine, this activity works best for groups that are composed of only two or three members.) During this stage of writing, group members cooperate to construct the draft but are sure to voice individual opinion about the best strategies.

- When the group has a completed the first draft of the essay, some time is allowed to pass before plans for revision are discussed. Then the group works together to determine whether the thesis is adequately supported, whether the argument ever gets off track, whether all parts of the paper are adequately developed with details and examples, and so on. The group works together to make the necessary revisions.

- As a last step, the group works together to eliminate all editing errors.

To summarize this section, knowledge making, researching/investigating, workshopping, and coauthoring are collaborative activities with which we hope that you will gain practice as you proceed through this textbook—and through college and your career beyond. There are multiple procedures that can be effective for each activity, and the more practiced you become with collaborating, the more readily you will design your own procedures.

BRAINSTORMING

We hope that by this point you are not only beginning to see the value of collaboration for a writer but also to understand that collaboration can play a significant role in every phase of the writing process. As we have said earlier in this chapter, prewriting is one phase of the writing process that often is handled independently, but it can be enhanced through collaboration. As we also explained, prewriting can take many forms.

In this chapter, we will introduce you to one widely used method of prewriting: *brainstorming*. Brainstorming is the process of choosing a general topic and then quickly jotting down, usually in the form of a list, ideas you have that are related to the topic. Your prewriting list should include all ideas that occur to you, regardless of how insignificant or unworkable they might seem; oftentimes, the seemingly insignificant or unworkable ideas will trigger some of the best ideas on your list.

The process of writing down your ideas in this fashion helps you to probe your memory, generate ideas, and fully develop your topic.

A brainstorming list might look like the one by Yolanda that follows. Yolanda's assignment is to write an essay that explains the significance a particular person has had in her life.

MY NEIGHBOR LIZZIE

eccentric woman
seemed old—about seventy?
never smiled at anyone, seemed unfriendly, made me sort of afraid of her
lived in my apartment complex so I saw her coming and going a lot—drove old
    Chevy
chased cats out of the apartment dumpsters so she could browse
tall person, walked proudly, reminded me of a statue
bathrobe
washed her car every day
        even in winter
        used bucket of water and a mop
I imagined scary things about her (will need to explain)
I was afraid
wore curlers in her hair a lot
wouldn't say hello
picked things out of dumpster and put them in her car—lamps, boxes
what happened that made me decide that she wasn't so weird after all—early
        April morning, 5:00 A.M., I had to be up to work on a project
        —sun was coming up, beautiful sky
        —saw Lizzie in middle of field behind complex, sitting there watching the
        sunrise, seemed to be meditating
        —seemed to be praying or meditating or something
        —wearing straw hat and billowy red pj's
        —Lizzie stayed in field till sun was high, then came in carrying cardboard
        "prayer rug"
Need a good ending about Lizzie's ability to be peaceful or to use her time wisely,
        how she didn't seem so scary to me anymore, what I learned from Lizzie

As with all brainstorming lists, Yolanda's is made up of phrases and words that appear in no particular order. However, from creating this list, she came to realize that she wanted to focus her paper on the incident that made her aware that her neighbor had more dimensions than Yolanda had earlier perceived. In addition, the list enabled Yolanda to group related items on her list, exclude items that did not really seem to fit, and decide on a tentative organizational plan for her paper.

As you can see, a writer can easily complete a brainstorming activity alone. However, the following activities should help you to see the benefits of working together during the process of brainstorming and will give you practice with both individual and collaborative brainstorming. Activity 1, which follows, will give your group practice with brainstorming together; Activities 2 and 3 will give your group practice in using your brainstorming to draft a paragraph.

 ## Activity 1

The members of your group should spend five minutes or so independently brainstorming a list of details that could be used to construct a paragraph on the topic "Why Writing Is Important." You should write quickly, without worrying about forming complete sentences or using correct spelling or punctuation. The idea is to get your ideas on paper.

Next, the members of the group should meet to compile a collaborative list of details on the topic "Why Writing Is Important." One person in the group should serve as note taker for the day. In collaborating on such a list, it is helpful if everyone in the group can see what the note taker is writing down. A chalkboard or easel works particularly well for group brainstorming, but if one is not available, a large piece of paper, located where everyone can see it, will suffice.

Everyone in the group should contribute ideas to the list. Many of the ideas, of course, will come from the lists that each of you brainstormed independently. However, the process of creating this new, collaborative list will help group members think of ideas that they had not previously thought of; these new ideas, too, should be included in the list. Remember that no idea is too insignificant to be included in the brainstorming.

 ## Activity 2

When your group has developed a fairly substantial list of details (from completing Activity 1), you should discuss possibilities for writing a collaborative paragraph on the topic "Why Writing Is Important." Your group should examine your brainstorming list to determine categories of information and decide which to include or exclude. You should think about ways that you might introduce the topic and ways that you might conclude the paragraph. Your group should work together to decide on the most effective organizational plan. As the members reach agreement, the note taker should be writing down the tentative plan for the paragraph.

 ## Activity 3

After completing Activities 1 and 2, your group is ready to work together to write a draft of the paragraph. During this process, group members should offer ideas, agree and disagree, and reach a consensus regarding the words that will be used. The note taker should write down the paragraph as the group makes decisions. When the paragraph has been written, the group should discuss any changes members wish to make in content, organization, syntax, style, or mechanics, and then, perhaps, construct a revised version.

WRITING ASSIGNMENT

The following assignment builds on the work you completed in Activities 1, 2, and 3. It will also help you assess the effectiveness of your group's collaboration and of your own individual contribution to your group. In working through this assignment, first complete Part A and then do Part B. You may wish to hand these in together or to hand them in one at a time, whichever your instructor requires.

Part A

In order to complete Activities 1, 2, and 3, your group worked together as you brainstormed collaboratively and coauthored a draft of a paragraph. For this part of the assignment, you will write two to three pages that *evaluate* how well your group worked together as you completed the activities.

As you write your evaluation, you should be honest and open, yet tactful. You might explain procedural matters, such as how the note taker was chosen, how the group managed (or failed to manage) to stay on task, or how disagreements were resolved. Be sure that your evaluation includes the strengths you saw emerging as your group worked together, as well as suggestions you can offer for the group to try.

After everyone has completed writing an evaluation, your group should meet to discuss them and to collaborate on setting several "group goals" for your upcoming collaborative sessions.

As a reminder, if your group did encounter some problems in working as a team, you should not feel dismayed or as though you somehow failed. As we stated earlier, it ordinarily takes some time for groups to gel. With practice and commitment, your group will develop stronger collaborative skills.

Part B

Again, reflecting upon Activities 1, 2, and 3, think about yourself as a part of your group. For this part of the assignment, you should write two pages evaluating your own role. You might consider some of the following questions: How comfortable did you feel within the group? How did your comfort level make you react? How much and what kind of support did you provide? Based on your experience, do you have personal goals for upcoming collaborative sessions?

After everyone has completed writing his or her two-page self-evaluation, your group should meet to share members' feelings on this topic.

✣ CHAPTER 3

WRITING THE PERSONAL HISTORY

INTRODUCTION

Although you may not be aware of it, you and many of your peers already have experience with some of the skills and subject matter that you will be studying more formally in college. You probably don't have to be told that tickets will be scarce and therefore costly if there is limited seating at a concert given by a popular rock group. This example illustrates the principle of supply and demand, which you will study in more depth and detail if you enroll in an economics class. College instructors sometimes assign personal histories because they realize that students may learn basic terms, operations, or disciplinary ways of conceptualizing if they can make connections with their own experience. The personal history is a kind of writing that tells about a significant event or series of events in the life of the writer, and how these events relate to a central idea or focus.

In addition to making abstract concepts and ideas such as supply and demand more concrete and immediate, writing personal histories also provides students with a comfortable way of learning about a discipline with which they may be unfamiliar or about which they have anxiety. Examining your feelings about past experiences with a particular subject matter can allow you to understand that past difficulties may have been due to a variety of factors, not just to personal inadequacy. The result of writing a personal history may be a more positive attitude toward and improved performance in an academic discipline.

In writing a personal history, you will necessarily engage in reflective thinking. Many experts in learning theory feel that the learning process is assisted by reflective thinking, that is, thinking that engages a person in an assessment of past behaviors and attitudes. They believe that reflective thinking helps students reach a higher stage of learning than can be achieved solely through memorization and conventional testing.

SAMPLE ASSIGNMENTS

Although interesting and useful, personal history assignments are not as common as many of the other types of writing tasks that you will encounter in your college career. The writing you may be required to do in conjunction with this type of assignment may also run the gamut from formal essays to more informal pieces, such as journal entries. To give you an idea about the different kinds of personal history assignments, we have selected a few examples that illustrate some of the variations you may encounter.

- **Mathematics Assignment.** In one or two pages, discuss your early memories of learning math, either at home or in school. Describe your present attitudes toward math and explain how your early experiences may have shaped these attitudes. As you review your memories, does a particular friend or teacher come to mind? Is this person partly responsible for your present success or failure at math? Hand in this "paper" on a computer disk. Use 12-point type, double-spacing, and end justification. Underline your title. Be sure to use correct grammar and punctuation.
- **American Literature Survey Assignment.** You undoubtedly were assigned to read many works of fiction by American authors when you were in junior high or high school. You may have read such authors as Mark Twain, Nathaniel Hawthorne, Herman Melville, Kate Chopin, Alice Walker, or works such as *The Scarlet Letter, Huckleberry Finn, Sister Carrie,* and *Invisible Man.* Recall an early encounter with one such work. Was your reading experience mostly positive or negative? Did you want to read more fiction, especially by this author? In what ways, if any, did the reading make you think about what it means to be an American? To what extent, if any, were you able to relate events in the fiction to your own life? Craft an essay of approximately three to four typewritten pages in which you explore your early experience with American literature.
- **Computer Literacy Journal Assignment.** Select a friend (or create an imaginary one) whom you consider to be intimidated or even victimized by computer technology. Write a letter to that person in which you describe one or more of your experiences with computers that enabled you to develop a positive attitude toward them. What capabilities of computers attracted you? If you experienced difficulties (access, use, attitude, etc.), how did you overcome them?

As is evident from the preceding assignments, writing a personal history usually requires you to narrate events or experiences from your life, which, in turn, involves self-disclosure. We have found that some students are comfortable writing about their experiences—even painful ones—while others find this difficult. Regardless of the level of disclosure you elect, however, a personal history must contain concrete, specific details; otherwise, such writing is liable to have a generic, cookie-cutter quality and seem as if anyone could have written it.

Because personal history writing is often assigned to help students discover their attitudes or past experiences with a particular subject, such writing is usually addressed to two audiences, the teacher and the student. Both of these audiences are important. As a consequence of thinking and writing about experiences with a particular subject matter, students often gain useful insights that help them acquire new knowledge and skills.

Of course, your instructor is also a significant reader, since he or she undoubtedly had a purpose in assigning the writing task and will, very likely, be responsible for evaluating it. When you write a personal history, your teacher will be particularly interested in your selection of experiences and details as well as how these relate to your organizing principle and to the subject matter of your class.

In the event that you receive an assignment to write a formal personal history (as opposed to an informal, ungraded writing task), your essay should contain the following:

1. A clear controlling idea that establishes your purpose for writing

2. Specific details and incidents that illustrate or support your controlling idea

3. A distinctive, unique voice that examines the significance of the narrated events from a critical perspective.

CREATING A DISTINCTIVE VOICE

Perhaps the most challenging aspect of writing a personal history is the ability to project a distinctive, unique voice. Although no other human being is exactly like you, it is not easy to convey your uniqueness within a short paper that focuses on merely one or a few events. How do you manage, in such a limited space, to sound like yourself and no one else at the same time that you present your readers with a clear, focused piece of writing? There are no pat formulas to accomplish this; however, the way in which you select and portray details is of paramount importance, as is your selection and sequencing of events.

Description: Selecting and Crafting Details

The Importance of Detail. The essence of describing an object, person, or event is detail. Without sufficient detail, descriptions are vague, overly general, and uninteresting. Lack of detail can also cause ambiguity, which can confuse or mislead readers. "Large and mostly round" isn't nearly as precise as "egg-shaped and approximately fifteen feet in diameter." "Cold" doesn't convey the same information as "frigid, with a windchill factor of minus twelve degrees Fahrenheit"—especially because a person living in Hawaii might have a very different notion of "cold" than a person living in northern Minnesota. Of course, the amount and type of detail you select must always be dictated by your audience and, where appropriate, the expectations of a profession or discipline.

There are many different types of details, each of which can lend specificity, precision, and vividness to writing. Details that appeal to the senses are powerful because they evoke sights, sounds, tastes, smells, and textures. Skillfully presented visual details can paint pictures in readers' minds of objects, places, and people; details related to other senses such as taste ("bitter, tin-like") or touch ("nubby and rough, like the peel of an avocado") can increase the vividness of a description as well as contribute to the mood or tone a writer wishes to convey. Factual details ("first-year student, majoring in fashion design"), details about emotional states ("horrifying"; "intoxicating"), as well as quotes and dialogue ("You still don't understand," he snarled) all lend sharpness and focus to a piece of writing.

Notice how the italicized details within the following passage from *The God Particle* illustrate exactly what Leon Lederman means when he says that "Columbia was a hotbed of physics in the 1950's":

> Columbia was a hotbed of physics in the 1950's. *Charles Townes would soon discover the laser and win the Nobel Prize. James Rainwater would win the Prize for his nuclear model, and Willis Lamb for measuring the tiny shift in hydrogen's spectral lines. Nobel laureate Isadore Rabi, who inspired all of us, headed up a team that included Norman Ramsey and Polykarp Kusch, both to become Nobel winners in due course. T. D. Lee shared the Nobel for his theory of parity violation.* The density of professors who had been anointed with Swedish holy water was both *exhilarating* and *depressing. As young faculty, some of us wore lapel buttons that read "Not Yet."* (italics added)

Without details that include the names and discoveries of past and future Nobel prizewinners, readers wouldn't have any idea of the density of superstars in Columbia's physics department at the time or the importance of their work. It's no mean feat to "discover" the laser or to measure infinitesimal shifts in the spectral lines of hydrogen. Given the numbers and accomplishments of Leon Lederman's colleagues, it's no wonder that he and other junior faculty felt both exhilarated and depressed. Notice also how nicely the detail that some faculty "wore lapel buttons that read 'Not Yet' " helps readers experience this feeling.

 Activity 1

Although writers sometimes have difficulty recalling details as they construct personal histories, lived experience is, quite literally, composed of details. You may not realize it, but if you try, you will be able to remember many details about even a brief period of time during which you performed the most routine activity.

To show you how this works, think about the trip you took a few moments earlier to get to your composition class. Mentally retrace your steps, jotting down as many details related to your short trip as you can. Here are some questions and suggestions to help you:

- What was the weather like? (temperature, sun, clouds, wind, rain, humidity, etc.)
- What were you thinking about? (this class, a meal, your roommate, a song, a member of your family, another class, etc.)

- What physical entities did you pass? (buildings, people, bushes, cars, benches, trash cans, bulletin boards, piles of dirty snow, etc.) You might find it helpful to draw a map of the portion of campus through which you traveled. Then you can trace your route on your map and add major objects such as trees, barriers, or buildings as well as particular objects, people, and animals that attracted your attention (an overflowing dumpster, two students playing Frisbee with a dog, etc.).

- What encounters did you have with other people? (how many interactions did you have and with whom; how long did they last; what was the nature of each encounter; what did people say to you; what did you say to them; etc.)

- What particularly attracted your attention? (an argument you witnessed; food you smelled; a hat—or other piece of clothing—you liked; buds on a tree; the sound of laughter; etc.)

- What, if anything, happened that was out of the ordinary? (you almost were run over by a person on a bicycle; your homework blew away and you had to chase it; a stranger complimented you on your coat; etc.)

Selecting Detail. Although a personal history should contain details to be effective, a history that does not have a discernible focus or organizing principle can be confusing or distracting. No reader wants to muddle through a barrage of seemingly unrelated particulars. Details within a well-written personal history must, therefore, convey a perspective that is unique to the writer, contribute to the central focus or organizing principle of the essay, and meet the needs of a particular audience or discipline.

A unique perspective is important because it helps readers to understand why an event or a series of events—even commonplace ones—were special or significant for the writer. As a consequence of adopting a perspective, writers don't just passively record what happened to them; they actively and consciously reexamine, recreate, and interpret past events. To convey a unique perspective within a personal history, writers often contrast a former self (naive, defeatist, overconfident, overly passive, know-it-all; etc.) with a more knowledgeable present self (sadder-but-wiser, confident, cautious; etc.) As you might imagine, a writer's perspective is very much bound up with what he or she will eventually select as a thesis or organizing principle. This is because perspective determines which events are significant, why they are important, ways in which past and present emotional responses, behaviors, or attitudes are linked, and so forth.

A writer's perspective is an important means by which details for a personal history can be generated and selected. In addition, a useful technique you can try to accomplish this end is to think about the dominant impression you'd like your essay to convey. Ordinarily, the events we experience are accompanied by emotional responses, most of which we don't recall because they may seem mild, or "neutral." When you consider which event to write about, we suggest that you select an incident about which you *can* recall the dominant emotional state (or states) you experienced at the time, because this dominant impression is a good way to begin to move toward a unique perspective and controlling principle. As you scan your memory, you can, very likely, remember many experiences and their attendant emotional states: terror, embarrassment, exhilaration, frustration leading to a sense of triumph, disappointment, pride, anger, inadequacy, contentment, the feeling of being special, and so forth. One or more of these may be a good starting point from which to begin your personal history.

Suppose, for example, you are assigned a personal history in your introductory college algebra class that requires you to write about one or several significant experiences with math that you feel have determined your present attitude, level of confidence, and work habits. You may begin to recall the time when you were assigned homework that included a particularly difficult problem that you didn't understand and that you knew would be on the next exam. As you think about that experience, you may recall how you felt: furious at your teacher; worried about the upcoming exam; frustrated as you tried again and again to understand and work through the problem. Then, well into the night, you finally got it. How did you feel? Exhilarated? Triumphant? And what did you learn from this experience? That you could persevere and learn on your own; that if you persisted you would succeed—even at math?

Some details would be relevant in creating a dominant impression about your math "incident": throwing your book across the room or the way your stomach turned when you thought about the upcoming exam. Similarly, too many details about what other people were doing in math class (what the weather was like that day or the exact way in which the teacher tried and failed to explain the problem) would be distracting. Such details might also shift the focus to external events rather than your perspective on an important experience, which is the purpose of a personal history.

 ## Activity 2

Together with your group, choose the list of details that *one* member generated about his or her walk to class (see Activity 1).

1. Select two of the following scenarios and discuss which details from the list you chose would be relevant in creating a dominant impression of each scenario, and which would not.

   Scenario 1: You found out that you failed a major test in your previous class.

   Scenario 2: Just before your walk to class, a friend who works at the Bursar's Office told you that your long-awaited and desperately needed check from financial aid had finally arrived.

   Scenario 3: You overslept or got out of your previous class late and are rushing to get to class on time. Your instructor has already said something to you about being late too often.

2. Write two paragraphs, one for each of the scenarios you selected, that convey a dominant impression through detail. In both of your paragraphs include a sentence that explains what happened to cause the dominant impression you are trying to convey.

Narrating Events

Not only are details important in writing a personal history, you also need to tell your audience about particular events. You have undoubtedly been telling stories to other people throughout your life, whenever you have told family or friends about what happened in a movie you saw, in a class they missed, or on a weekend trip. You should be able to draw on such experiences in writing a personal history because you will be telling a relevant story, or a series of related stories, to your audience.

Telling stories isn't as straightforward as you might think at first. If you reflect on what you do when you tell someone a story, you'll probably find that you necessarily make decisions—consciously or unconsciously—about what to tell and what to leave out. That is, if you set out to tell a friend about what you did over the weekend, you wouldn't tell the person about every single thing that you did over the course of two or three days. Yet you would need to talk about some particular event or events in detail if you wanted your friend to understand what a great (or disastrous) weekend you had. Likewise, when you write a personal history for a college course, your instructor isn't likely to want to read a five-thousand-word history of your life. Even if you tried to write down everything that you did over just the past month, day by day and hour by hour, you would write far more than five thousand words. More importantly, your instructor is likely to expect you to focus on particular events from your own experience that are relevant to the purpose of the writing assignment.

A key to writing personal histories, then, is to choose an event or series of events that are relevant for your audience, your purpose, and the class for which you are writing. The event or events you write about should be representative of your history with the particular subject or field of study that is the focus of your assignment. That is, you should choose one event or a few events that generally represent your experiences or attitudes. For example, suppose that your predominant attitude toward writing is that you prefer to do it quickly and get it over with so that you can move on to do something else that you enjoy more. To convey this attitude in a personal history, you wouldn't need to recount every writing experience you have had. More likely, you would make a stronger impression on your audiences if you focus on one or two experiences that are typical of your experience generally or that represent your dominant attitude toward writing. With a focus on one or a series of events, you will be able to develop sufficient detail to convey the controlling idea of your paper.

In ordinary situations, people don't pay much attention to the tension between telling too much and telling too little. Your friends may well alternate between the two extremes. Suppose a friend of yours, John Dull, rented several Arnold Schwarzenegger movies and spent his weekend watching them. If you ask him to recommend which Schwarzenegger movie you should see, he might say to you, "Well, my favorite one was *The Terminator*. It's about this cyborg who came from the future and got killed." On the other hand, John might respond by telling you far more than you wanted to know, enough even that you might have no desire left ever to see the movie yourself: "First when the opening credits are rolling . . . there's this scene in the future where scientists have created a killing machine in the shape of a human being. . . . The Terminator comes to Los Angeles and . . . Then Linda Hamilton, who's the boy's mother in the sequel. . . . The Terminator says 'Hasta la vista, baby!' Then the guy . . . ." Neither response tells you what you want to know to decide whether to see the movie yourself.

It's important, then, to be aware of what your audience is interested in—and what they are not. In other words, when writing a personal history, you ought to tell the events and provide details that are relevant to your audience and to your purpose in writing—and you should omit those that digress from your main points. When people tell stories orally, they frequently digress from their main points by including details or events that aren't relevant to their audience or to their purpose. Perhaps you've had a friend who witnessed an unusual event like a car accident. When you meet her for the first time afterward, you want to hear what happened; she digresses: "I was on my way to the laundromat on Main and Third. I always use that one because the seats are more comfortable, and there's a tanning salon next door. Did I tell you that I'm going to Fort Lauderdale for spring break? My roommate got a terrific deal on a condominium, and after the way I spent my last spring break, I really wanted. . . ." You may well be thinking, "Come on, tell me about the accident!" John Dull, from the earlier example, might recount his problems as he was watching *The Terminator*, for example, the damaged video-tape he had to exchange at the video store or the way he made microwave popcorn that didn't burn. These trials and tribulations are undoubtedly interesting events to John, but they are not likely to influence your decision about whether to watch the movie.

When you are writing personal histories, you will always face the tension between telling too much and telling too little. You need to select particular events that will help to create and develop the controlling idea of your paper.

 **Activity 3**

First, each member of your group should write down *exactly* what you each did during the first half hour after you got out of bed this morning. Try not to leave out any activities. Be as specific as possible. Don't simply say "I got up, got dressed, and went to school." Instead tell *exactly* what actions you performed and in what order. Fill at least one page. Try to write as much as you can.

Next, compare your narration of events with those of your group members. Approximately how many words did you each write? Who wrote the most? Compare specific activities that you all performed, such as brushing your teeth, taking a shower, or getting dressed. Who described those activities in the most exact sequence and detail? Were there particular activities that some of you forgot about or omitted? In what ways, if any, did knowing you would share your list with class members influence what you wrote on your list? Why?

WRITING THE PERSONAL HISTORY

When Self-Disclosure Is Required

From reading the preceding section, you probably have determined that creating a distinctive voice requires you to present events and details that are unique to you and, therefore, personal. For this reason, writing a personal history inevitably requires self-disclosure, which can present writers with several challenges. Writing about events that recreate highly charged emotions may deprive a person of the critical distance needed to craft a coherent, focused personal history essay. Disclosing personal information also requires writers to examine their notions of privacy and to assess their attitudes toward past emotions and events.

Revealing or disclosing personal information is easy for some people but difficult for others. Some individuals are used to, and therefore comfortable with, talking about themselves, their experiences, and their feelings. Other people often feel uncomfortable or embarrassed when talking about themselves. Then, too, we all have different attitudes about what we do or don't consider to be "personal." For example, one woman might be willing to share intimate details about her experience in childbirth with relative strangers, but feel uncomfortable talking about the arguments she had with her parents when she was an adolescent; another woman might feel more comfortable talking about her arguments with her parents and wish to keep her experiences during childbirth to herself. Because of our personalities, life experiences, cultural backgrounds, and many other factors, each of us is different with respect to what we do or don't consider private.

Although writing a personal history requires disclosure, writers can always control what they reveal by adapting a topic or assignment. Suppose, for instance, that you get an assignment that requires you to narrate a story from your childhood about an important incident in a physical education class. If you have no wish to reveal one of your own experiences because you can only remember ones that are too personal, you can still respond to the assignment. You can describe an event that you witnessed happening to someone else, focusing on how this event affected and influenced you. In this way, you would be interpreting the assignment in a manner that enables you to complete it while respecting your own privacy.

In rare circumstances, adapting an assignment may not be sufficient to protect your privacy satisfactorily. In this case, you should speak with your instructor, who may suggest ways of modifying the assignment or your approach to it. After talking with your instructor, you may be able to complete the assignment if you are assured that your privacy will be respected and that no one else will read your final draft. Your instructor may also suggest that you need not share intermediate drafts with personal details during group revision sessions. However, if you are still uncomfortable with the self-disclosure necessary, you will need to find a way to reinterpret the assignment.

Mining Your Memory: Loop Writing

Regardless of when in your writing process you determine what you wish to disclose, you will need to search your memory for an event or events about which to write as well as generate details that you can use to recreate your experiences for your reader. Either freewriting or brainstorming may be helpful in this process, but another inventing technique you may find useful is loop writing.

Loop writing consists of a series of activities that can enable writers to think more productively and creatively by encouraging them to narrow their focus and vary their perspective.

Step 1: Freewrite for about five to ten minutes on your topic. If you are assigned a personal history, your topic will be one or more of the experiences about which you may write.

Step 2: Read over your freewriting and select a portion or chunk that captures your attention and about which you can write some more. Elaborate as much as you can on that small portion of your text. You can do additional freewriting or jot down ideas, details, commentary, dialogue, whatever.

If you cannot immediately think of how to expand the portion of freewriting you selected, here are some exercises that can help. These activities, often suggested with loop writing, will help you generate details, make connections between your ideas, and provide you with different perspectives about your topic.

- Convert the chunk you have selected into an event (unless it already is one). If, for example, the part of your freewriting that you chose describes an emotion you were feeling, recall the surrounding circumstances that caused you to feel that emotion; if you cannot remember the matters that caused you to feel the emotion very well, recreate or imagine the circumstances that might have caused it. (If your personal history is about a difficult writing experience, think of where you wrote, how long the process took, how you felt, who was near you while you were writing, and so forth.)
- Recreate a conversation between yourself and someone else that took place during the event; or imagine and describe a conversation that you wish had occurred. (If your personal history is about an event that occurred in a physical education class, try to recall the conversation you had with one or more of your classmates, or imagine a conversation you wish you had with your classmates or with your teacher.)
- Describe everything that happened during the event to at least two different audiences. One should be sympathetic, such as your very best friend; one should be skeptical, such as your parent or your teacher.
- Describe the event from the point of view of one of the principal characters besides yourself.
- Imagine and then recreate the incident in another time or place. (If you are writing a personal history about an experience you had with a math teacher when you were in elementary school, imagine and describe how that experience would have been if you were an adult when it occurred. You might also imagine what would have happened if the incident had taken place where you live and your parents, family members, and friends had all been present.)

- Write a letter to one of the principal characters in the event.
- Imagine that you were casting the event as a play or movie. Whom would you select to play yourself and the other major characters?

Step 3: Write out, in several sentences, a tentative focus for your essay. If you are unable to do so, repeat the activities listed in Step 2, as necessary.

 ## Activity 4

Assume that you will be composing a personal history about your writing experiences for this class. Jot down ten memorable writing experiences that occurred before taking this class. Write them down as quickly as possible. Choose two that you remember the most vividly, and freewrite for five to ten minutes about each of them. Then select a portion from one of your freewritings for loop writing. Use one or more of the activities described in Step 2. After you complete these activities, write out a tentative focus in two or three sentences (see Step 3). Share your loop writing and your tentative focus with your group partners.

Planning and Structuring Your Personal History

Mining your memory and remembering relevant events will help you to get started in writing a personal history. However, once you have completed these activities, you will need to think consciously about how to shape your loop writing into a coherent paper.

Articulating Your Controlling Idea. One of the most important parts of a personal history is the controlling idea. This is a direct statement, in one or a few sentences, of the central importance or significance of the event(s) discussed in your paper. It's important to directly state your controlling idea in a personal history so that your instructor and other readers will clearly understand the purpose of your paper. Establishing your controlling idea as you begin an assignment will also help you draft and revise because the idea will keep you on track. However, you should be aware that your controlling idea may change as you write and revise a draft. Thus as you revise your paper, you will probably also need to revise your controlling idea or make it more specific.

In articulating your controlling idea, you will need to think about your course and the assignment. If you took notes as your professor discussed his or her expectations for the assignment, reread those notes. If your professor gave you a written assignment sheet, reread it. Think also about the purpose of the course and your reasons for taking it.

In formulating a controlling idea, you not only will need to consider what the assignment is asking you to do. You will also need to consider the expectations of your professor, the discipline, and even the course itself. When you are able to find a controlling idea for your paper that is consonant with those expectations, you will greatly increase your likelihood of writing a successful paper and of doing well in the course. You should also realize that your instructor will expect to see evidence of reflective thinking in your paper, namely, some critical insight about your past experiences. Your personal history will necessarily reveal some particular perspective toward the subject matter or discipline you are writing about, or perhaps toward the course in which the personal history is assigned. You should think carefully about what kind of perspective your professor would like you to assume—that of an interested learner, perhaps, or someone ready to meet a challenge. While you want to sound intelligent and authoritative, you should avoid writing in a language that is inflated on the one hand or too colloquial on the other.

 Activity 5

The following controlling ideas were composed by students who had been asked to write a personal history of their experiences with reading literature for a required Introduction to Literature course. With your group members, evaluate each controlling idea, deciding the degree to which each is appropriate or inappropriate for this course and for college courses in general.

Reading literature gives me a broader perspective on my own life. I understand through literature that all problems, even those I face, are universal.

Reading is a waste of time; TV is better.

Although reading literature takes a lot of time and has been difficult for me, the more I am exposed to it, the more appreciation I develop.

Engineers shouldn't have to take literature; we'll never use it after college.

 Activity 6

1. Working individually, read through the material you wrote as you completed Activity 4, including the tentative focus you wrote. Again, assume you are writing a personal history for the writing course you are currently taking. Write a controlling idea that you feel would be reflective of your experiences yet consonant with the values of this course and instructor.

2. Compare your controlling idea with those of your group members. Which controlling ideas do you feel are most consonant with the values of the course or discipline and with your teacher's expectations? Are any of the controlling ideas problematic? Do any contain language that is either too inflated or too colloquial? Are any likely to create an unfavorable impression of the writer because of the tone or the ideas expressed?

Structuring a Personal History. In writing a personal history, you will need to determine whether to focus on one event or a series of events. To do this, you should first consider your assignment. Does it clearly ask you to focus on how one event influenced you? Does it specifically ask you to consider your personal development through several events or across a long period of time? If the assignment does not specify whether to focus on one or a series of events, think about your own personal experiences and the controlling idea you are articulating. Is there one experience that best typifies your past experiences or attitudes regarding the assigned topic? Is your current attitude toward the topic the result of your development through several related events over a period of time?

As we have said earlier, in telling about any personal experience, you cannot possibly narrate every single action that occurred. You will, therefore, have to leave out actions or details that are irrelevant or that your audience might perceive as digressions. Such omissions will necessarily result in gaps that your readers may find difficult to bridge. Thus, a central challenge you will face in writing a personal history is how to create connections among details and actions.

You can create connections—or coherence—in narrating an event by paying attention to two areas: the sequence of actions and the passage of time. Because you will probably be using chronological order in retelling an event or series of events, you need to make sure that your readers properly follow the sequence of actions you describe. Words or phrases such as *initially, then, next, at the same time,* and *finally* make the relationship between actions explicit. In addition, you can use time markers to let readers know how much time has lapsed in your narration: *after two minutes, a little bit later, meanwhile, at 10:00 A.M.,* and *the next day.*

In addition to establishing coherence using sequence or time markers, you can create coherence using metadiscourse. Metadiscourse is language, ordinarily a sentence or group of sentences, that helps a reader move though a text more easily. A major function of metadiscourse is to establish links among the parts of a piece of writing. Thus, the more complicated a text is, the more likely readers will need metadiscourse to help them understand it. In a personal history essay, rather than furthering the action of or providing more details about a particular event, metadiscourse may summarize or make explicit its significance or relate it to the controlling idea. Also, if an essay relates a series of events, metadiscourse can help readers move more easily from one event to the next. The following are some examples of metadiscourse from personal histories:

As this story illustrates, my confidence in my writing ability has been formed through the encouragement my teachers have given me.

At this young age, I already had developed a liking for computers.

Thus, I was embarrassed at being singled out in front of my classmates. My third grade physical education teacher had made me feel like a klutz. This was nothing, however, compared to the thorough humiliation I would experience in the sixth grade.

Notice how these examples might help readers make connections between the parts of the essay they are reading or see the relationship between these parts and the controlling idea.

 **Activity 7**

For this activity, you will first need to read the personal history essays that appear at the end of this chapter. Then you will work in class with your group members to answer the following questions.

1. Examine two of the essays to see how the writers use sequence or time markers in telling about an event.

2. Examine the excerpt from "The God Particle" and "Birth of an Entomologist" to see how the writers use metadiscourse to help their readers follow their texts.

3. Examine the opening few paragraphs of "The Covered Wagon Geologist" and "Birth of an Entomologist." What actions trigger the beginnings of the narrative passages? What kind of background information do the authors provide? Where does it appear?

4. Examine endings of narrative passages from at least two of the essays. What is the final action in each passage? How do the writers establish closure?

Placing Your Controlling Idea within Your Paper. Most often, in academic writing, you will need to make your main idea clear to your readers. Academic readers such as your college instructors usually expect a student writer's meaning to be self-evident in the written text, and they highly value writing that clearly states its purpose or main idea. In writing your personal history, it is especially important for you to clearly state your controlling idea in one or several prominently placed sentences in your paper. Doing so will help ensure that your readers understand that the personal experiences you are relating are relevant to their interests or to the assignment they have given you.

Where should you place your controlling idea? There are two main places, at the beginning or at the end of your paper, as well as a few variations on these. You can begin your paper with a direct statement of your controlling idea in your opening paragraph. Doing so will cue readers in immediately to your purpose in writing about your personal experiences. Notice how Edward O. Wilson initially states his controlling idea in the opening paragraph of "Birth of an Entomologist":

> I am often asked how I came to be an entomologist, a scientist who specializes in insects. The main part of the answer is simple. Most children have a bug period; I never grew out of mine. But as in the lives of scientists generally, there is more to the story. Every child wants to visit a magic

kingdom. Mine was given to me at the age of ten, when my father, a government accountant, moved his little family to Washington, D.C. We took up residence in an apartment on Fairmont Street within walking distance of the National Zoological Park—commonly called the National Zoo—and a cheap streetcar ride from the National Museum of Natural History. For me the location was an extraordinary stroke of good luck.

In the preceding paragraph, Wilson begins by explaining that his childhood experiences growing up in Washington, D.C., will illustrate how he came to be interested in studying insects.

Placing your controlling idea in the opening paragraph is what you generally should plan to do in academic writing. However, you may find that in particular cases you can gain a better effect by placing your controlling idea at the end of your paper, at the beginning *and* the end, or by revealing it gradually throughout the paper.

Placing the controlling idea at the end of your personal history can be an effective strategy if you want to highlight a particularly gripping event or to capture your reader's imagination early in your paper, as you can see in this excerpt by Charles N. Gould from *Covered Wagon Geologist*. Gould begins by setting the stage for the primary event he focuses on, the first lecture he heard about geology:

> It was a hot August night in 1889. Some fifty country boys and girls, prospective school teachers, were seated in a stuffy schoolroom in Kingman, Kansas, listening to a lecture on the geology of Kansas.

Gould goes on to recount the lecture, including the moment when the speaker held up two pieces of sandstone from the local river. He ends by describing the effect that the lecture has had on his life and professional career. The drama of that event would undoubtedly be lessened if Gould began with a direct statement about why he decided to become a geologist. Such a statement comes, instead, at the end of the excerpt, when he reveals the influence of the lecture on his life:

> This lecture changed the entire current of my life. At that time I did not know what a geologist did, but I then and there resolved that whatever things a geologist did, those things must I do.

Occasionally you may want to state your controlling idea at both the beginning and the end of your paper, especially if your paper is long or if you are relating a series of events. Doing so may help ensure that your readers understand your main point, because they will be reading it at two prominent places in your paper.

In addition, if you are writing about a series of events, you may find that your paper coheres better if you provide some statement of your controlling idea as you introduce each event. Suppose, for example, that you are trying to show that the process of becoming a competent volleyball player was long and arduous, and that a series of events helped you learn the necessary skills, gain confidence in your ability, and practice in a supportive atmosphere. You may well need to provide a restatement of your controlling idea as you move from the first event to the second and so forth, probably in topic or transition sentences such as these:

> [at the beginning of one paragraph] While learning to spike was important, I still lacked confidence in my ability to perform in a real game in which my teammates were counting on me. That confidence came during the third varsity game I played as a sophomore in high school.

> [at the beginning of the next paragraph] Yet I could not perform at my best in the competitive atmosphere that Coach Wilson established. It was only when Coach Perkins came to our school that I found the supportive atmosphere that helped me to enjoy playing volleyball.

Notice here how these transition sentences remind readers of the sequence of the events being written about as well as of the way that each event is connected to the ones preceding and following it.

 ## Activity 8

1. Using the controlling idea you wrote and evaluated in Activity 6, write an informal outline or a tentative plan for a personal history that identifies what the major parts of your paper would be. If the paper would cover a series of events, which specific ones would you write about? If it would focus on one event, what actions occurred in what sequence?

2. Next, decide where you would state your controlling idea—at the beginning, at the end, in both places, or throughout the paper as you move from one event to the next? If you plan to restate your controlling idea as you move from one event to the next, tentatively write out the topic and transition sentences that you will need.

3. Finally, share your ideas with your group. Together, look over the writings you have each produced in the preceding activities related to your writing experiences. Could you use these materials for your major writing assignment in this chapter? Are there particular strengths in your writings? Are there events or ideas that you would like to explore more thoroughly? Are there events and ideas that your group would like to learn more about? Alternatively, would you find writing (and reading) about another topic more challenging or interesting?

Drafting and Revising

In writing any personal history, keep in mind that you probably have three audiences. Your teacher is certainly an important one, because he or she has assigned this type of writing and will use it in evaluating your overall performance in the course. In addition, as we have said before, when teachers assign personal histories, they usually expect students to learn something about themselves through self-reflection. So *you* are an important audience for this paper as well. As you are writing a personal history, then, you should think about what your teacher's purpose was in assigning it, what you believe your teacher expects you to learn, and to what extent your writing should be guided by a disciplinary or professional perspective. You also want to remember that your classmates may well be reading or hearing your personal histories, particularly if your teacher reads papers aloud in class or has students workshop one another's papers.

Once you are writing, you may need to refer to notes and plans. Therefore, in preparation for drafting, you should gather all relevant materials. Review what you have received and written so far: your assignment, the notes from mining your memory, any brainstorming or any other inventing, your controlling idea, and your plan or outline. With these materials, you should have a good sense of how to get started. If you don't, just start writing anyway; you can always go back over your draft later to revise it.

If you are especially reluctant to begin or find that you are blocking, set aside a short period of time to spend on drafting, approximately thirty to sixty minutes. Sit down during that time and do nothing but write. It may also be helpful to refer to the strategies in Chapter 1 for getting unstuck. Some writers find it helpful to envision a supportive audience. For example, you might imagine that your best friend is sitting across from you and write your first draft as though you were talking to that person.

Although many writers begin a text by first crafting an introduction, if you find it particularly hard to write the first paragraph, move to another section of your paper. Alternatively, you may find it easier to begin by drafting the middle of your paper and adding an introduction later. Make notes to yourself as you write about additional ideas or concerns that arise. Ordinarily, as you draft, you should have a sense of how to connect one idea or event to the next. If you lose this sense, write a note to yourself to flesh out the connection later—but keep on drafting. It is usually wise to continue writing as long as you have momentum, even if you recognize that there are areas that need reworking. You can always solicit advice about revising those areas later from your teacher or your peers. The important thing to remember about drafting is this: Don't put it off; just start! Don't stop just because you have problems from time to time.

Once you have written a draft, put it aside at least overnight before you begin to rework it. When you revise, you also should have specific goals in mind. In this way, you will be able to focus your attention on the most important criteria for the kind of writing you are doing or the assignment you are completing. As you revise your personal history, make sure that your controlling idea is clear, that you describe specific details and events, and that you write with a distinctive, critical voice.

A Clear Controlling Idea. As you recall, your controlling idea should be clearly stated in the paper at a point where your readers will be likely to pay attention to it. Therefore, when you read your draft, locate and mark those places where you have stated your controlling idea. Are there additional places where you might state it?

Can you think of a more effective placement? Next, if you state your controlling idea more than once, make sure those statements are consistent with one another and with the rest of your paper. If you discover any inconsistencies, you will need to determine whether to modify the controlling idea or portions of your narratives, or both.

Specific Details and Events. In writing a personal history, your stories will not be effective nor will they illustrate your controlling idea unless they are developed with specific, concrete detail. Only a detailed account of an experience can help a reader to understand how it may still be influential, perhaps ten or fifteen years after it occurred. Imagine, for example, if Edward O. Wilson, in his essay "Birth of an Entomologist," had described the National Zoo this way:

> Here I spent happy days looking at big animals like tigers and crocodiles, as well as small ones like birds and lizards.

Most readers would not understand from that account how Wilson's boyhood fascination with animals forged an interest that led him to become a scientist who specializes in insects. When you are reading your draft, then, look for places that seem to be vague, poorly described, or overly spare. Add details to make your descriptions as evocative as possible.

A Distinctive, Critical Voice. Perhaps your greatest challenge in writing a personal history will be to create a distinctive, critical voice. As you draft, you may feel that simply writing about events that happened to you will be enough to make your writing distinctive, but this may not be the case. Often people have very similar experiences. Just think about it: Many of your peers have been embarrassed in class, yelled at by a teacher, or praised highly for a particular piece of writing. What will make your recounting of these experiences distinctive is how you express them. The best way to construct a distinctive voice is to avoid clichés. For example, if you are trying to convey that you were nervous, avoid saying that you "sweated bullets" or were "freaked out." Remember also that everyone experiences similar emotions such as anger, sadness, or happiness, but the ways in which these emotions are expressed differs dramatically. To say that your algebra teacher "became furious" doesn't convey much. For some people, fury could mean pursed lips and a red face; for others, fury could mean physical violence. Compare, for example, these two passages of how one might describe an excited co-worker:

I

> Suddenly Gilberto went crazy. He became so excited that he jumped up and down with glee. He ran around the laboratory like a chicken with its head cut off.

II

> Suddenly Gilberto went stark, raving wild. "Mamma mia! Regardo incredibilio! Primo secourso!" (Or something like that.) He shouted, pointed,

lifted me up in the air—even though I was six inches taller and fifty pounds heavier than he was—and danced me around the room.

"What happened?" I stammered.

"Mufiletto!" he replied. "Izza counting. Izza counting!"

As you may realize, the second version is a passage from Leon Lederman's *The God Particle*. Note how Lederman has avoided clichés like "jumped up and down with glee" or "ran around like a chicken with its head cut off." Instead, Lederman's description of his response to his co-worker's behavior is unique and distinctive.

WRITING ASSIGNMENTS

Writing Topics

Select one of the following topics and write a personal history. Besides yourself, your audience should be your teacher and your classmates, who will be listening to your ideas and reading your paper as you compose it.

1. Explain why you chose the major or profession that you plan to enter by writing a personal history. Narrate a particular event or series of events to explain the reasons for choosing your major or future profession, as well as your attitudes toward it.

2. Select one of the personal history assignments from the Sample Assignments section of this chapter. You may, for example, want to write a math history because you are taking a required math course but have never consciously reflected on how your past experiences with the subject have influenced your present attitudes and performance in the course.

3. Write a personal history about your experiences with and attitudes toward writing. Select a particular aspect of your writing behavior to focus on, or select the dominant attitude you have about writing. Narrate an event or series of events that have led to your present attitude or behavior. Alternatively, you could write about your best or worst experience with writing and explore how that experience has influenced your attitudes or writing behavior.

Writing Procedures

1. Meet with your group and discuss all the preceding topics. Consider these factors in your discussion:

   - Different approaches to each assignment
   - The relative ease/difficulty of each assignment
   - The number of your relevant memories
   - The richness and specificity of the details in your memories
   - Your own comfort level with the kinds of self-disclosure required for each assignment.

2. Tentatively select a topic and, individually, brainstorm about it for ten minutes, focusing on your memories, relevant details, your ideas, and various approaches to the topic. Then meet with your group to share your selections and brainstorming. As you listen to each group member's selection and brainstorming, offer suggestions, and where relevant, suggest alternatives or other topics that might be more interesting or appropriate.

3. Once you've selected a topic, do loop writing to mine your memory for relevant experiences and concrete details and to explore your attitudes toward the topic. Do loop writing for at least thirty minutes; several short sittings will probably be easier than doing the writing all at once.

4. When you feel that you have mined your memory and explored your topic sufficiently, write out a controlling idea in two or three sentences. If you can't write at least that much about your controlling idea, you should continue loop writing or consider writing on a different topic. Once you have articulated a controlling idea, write out a tentative structure for your paper, identifying what particular experience or experiences you will write about.

5. Steps 1–4 should help you choose a good topic, explore it well, and devise an appropriate structure and focus for your personal history. Once you have done these, you should be ready to begin drafting. As you draft, pay attention to the continuity of your writing, noting where there are changes you may need to make later or transitions you may need to add.

6. After you have completed a draft, bring copies of it to class to workshop with your group members. In workshopping with your group, follow one of the procedures described in Chapter 2.

7. Based on the feedback you get from your group workshop session or from your instructor, revise and then edit your final copy. In revising, you should pay particular attention to the following:

   - The clarity of your controlling idea
   - The concreteness and specificity of your supporting details
   - The distinctiveness of your writing voice.

   In addition, you should consider your own confidence about the degree and type of personal information you disclose in the paper. You will want to take into account the purpose of the assignment, your controlling idea, and the audiences with whom you will share your paper.

READINGS

Wilson, Edward O. "Birth of an Entomologist." *Discover* (November 1993), pp. 86+.

from Gould, Charles N. *Covered Wagon Geologist.* Norman: University of Oklahoma Press, 1959.

from Lederman, Leon. *The God Particle.* Boston: Houghton Mifflin, 1993. William Morrow & Company, 1972.

Moon, Alison. "Living to Read," class assignment.
Clark, Emily. "Sharing 1000 Lives," class assignment.

The six pieces of writing at the end of this chapter resemble the personal histories you may be required to write. Three of them are excerpts from longer works; one is an essay from a science magazine; and two are essays that were written by college students for a class. "Birth of an Entomologist" describes how Edward O. Wilson, unlike most children, "never grew out of" his bug period and became a scientist who specializes in insects. The excerpt from *Covered Wagon Geologist* explains how hearing a single lecture on a hot August night before the turn of the century opened the world of geology to Charles N. Gould. *The God Particle* is a book for lay readers about modern particle physics. The selection that appears here describes, in Lederman's own words, his "entrapment" into this exciting discipline. The last two essays, written by college students, both detail the writers' personal histories with reading.

Questions

As you read these selections, answer the following questions. You may want to discuss them with your group members.

1. What is the controlling idea of each piece? How, in what way, and where is that controlling idea expressed?
2. In each selection, locate details that you think are particularly effective in recreating events, objects, or people. Explain why they are effective.
3. How are the details used overall to support the controlling idea in each reading?
4. Leon Lederman, Edward O. Wilson, and Charles N. Gould all explain how they became scientists, and yet they sound very different from one another. How does each portray a unique, critical voice? How would you characterize what is distinctive about each voice?

Birth of an Entomologist*

By Edward O. Wilson

I am often asked how I came to be an entomologist, a scientist who specializes in insects. The main part of the answer is simple. Most children have a bug period; I never grew out of mine. But as in the lives of scientists generally, there is more to the story. Every child wants to visit a magic kingdom. Mine was given to me at the age of ten, when my father, a government accountant, moved his little family to Washington, D.C. We took up residence in an apartment on Fairmont Street within walking distance of the National Zoological Park—commonly called the

*Edward O. Wilson © 1993 The Walt Disney Co. Reprinted with permission of *Discover* Magazine.

Birth of an Entomologist *(cont'd.)*

National Zoo—and a cheap streetcar ride from the National Museum of Natural History. For me the location was an extraordinary stroke of good luck.

Here I was in 1939, a little kid, an only child open to any new experience, with a world-class zoo on one side and a world-class museum on the other, both free of charge and open seven days a week. Unaffected by the drab surroundings of our working-class neighborhood, I entered a fantasy world made weirdly palpable. I spent hours at a time wandering through the halls of the national museum, absorbed by the unending variety of plants and animals on display there, pulling out trays of butterflies and other insects, lost in dreams of distant jungles and savannas. There was romance in human terms. I knew that behind closed doors along the circling balcony, their privacy protected by uniformed guards, labored the curators, shamans of my new world. I never met one of these important personages; perhaps a few passed me unrecognized in the exhibition halls. But just the awareness of their existence—experts of such high order going about the business of the federal government in splendid surroundings—fixed in me the image of science as a desirable profession. I could not imagine any activity more elevating than to acquire their kind of knowledge, to be stewards of animals and plants and to put the expertise to public service.

The National Zoo, the second focus of my life, was a living museum of equal potency with the National Museum of Natural History. It was and is in fact administered as part of the same organization, the Smithsonian Institution. Here I spent happy days following every trail, exploring every cage and glass-walled enclosure, staring at the charismatic big animals: Siberian tigers, rhinoceroses, cassowaries, king cobras, reticulated pythons, and crocodiles big enough to eat a boy in two bites. There were also smaller animals that eventually became equally fascinating. I developed a liking for lizards, marmosets, parrots, and tree-dwelling Philippine rats.

Close by the zoo was Rock Creek Park, a wooded urban confine within earshot of passing automobiles and the conversations of strollers. I found neither elephant herds to photograph nor tigers to drop-net, but insects were everywhere present in great abundance. So Rock Creek Park became Sumatra writ small. The collection of insects I began to accumulate at home was a simulacrum of the national museum. During excursions with a new best friend, Ellis MacLeod (who was later to become a professor of entomology at the University of Illinois), I acquired a passion for butterflies. Using homemade nets fashioned of broomsticks, coat hangers, and cloth bags, we captured our first Red Admirals and Great Spangled Fritillaries and sought the elusive Mourning Cloak along the shaded trails of Rock Creek. We were inspired by Frank Lutz's *Field Guide to the Insects* and W. J. Holland's *Butterfly Book*. Poring over R. E. Snodgrass's *Principles of Insect Morphology*, which we could barely begin to understand but which we knew was real science, we decided we would devote our lives to entomology.

About that time I also became fascinated with ants. One day as Ellis and I clambered over a steep wooded slope in the park, I pulled away the bark of a rotting

Birth of an Entomologist *(cont'd.)*

tree stump and discovered a seething mass of citronella ants underneath. These insects, members of the genus *Acanthomyops*, are exclusively subterranean and can only be found by digging in the soil or in fallen pieces of decaying wood. The worker ants I found were short, fat, brilliant yellow in color, and emitted a strong lemony odor. The smell was the chemical citronellal, which 30 years later (in my laboratory at Harvard) I discovered is secreted by glands attached to the mandibles of the ants and is used by them to attack enemies and spread alarm through the colony. That day the little army quickly thinned and vanished into the dark interior of the stump heartwood. But it left a vivid and lasting impression on me. What netherworld had I briefly glimpsed? What strange events were happening deep in the soil?

I devoured an article entitled "Stalking Ants, Savage and Civilized," by William M. Mann, in the August 1934 issue of *National Geographic.* In what was to be one of the more remarkable coincidences of my life, Mann was at that time director of the National Zoo. Like the still anonymous keepers of the museum, he became my hero from afar. To run a great zoo while writing about his adventures around the world with ants—what a role model! In 1957, when I was a beginning assistant professor at Harvard, Mann gave me his large library on ants (an important source for my later research). He also escorted my wife and me on a special tour of the zoo, a truly fulfilling event. In 1987 I was awarded the silver medal of the National Zoological Park for my work on ants and other animals: now I had come home in a deeply satisfying way.

Completing the circle, I have often returned to the National Museum of Natural History. The dwellers of that Olympus, all a new generation since 1940, have acquired names and faces and become friends and colleagues. The great collections they attend behind the closed doors are familiar ground.

There is today a quickening of purpose, a sense of rising importance and responsibility, at both the institutions that influenced me 50 years ago. Michael Robinson, the current director of the zoo, prefers to speak of his domain as a biopark, where animals will be released from the isolation of cages and placed in natural settings of plants and animals from their place of origin. The public can then view them not as caged curiosities but as parts of ecosystems, on which biological diversity—and the health of the planet—ultimately depend.

A short distance away, on the Mall, the curators of the National Museum of Natural History continue their role in building one of the world's largest collections of plants and animals. They too must feel the future in their bones. Recent studies indicate that between 10 and 100 million species of plants, animals, and microorganisms exist on Earth, but only about 1.4 million have been studied well enough to have received scientific names. Many of these species are vanishing or being placed in imminent danger of extinction by the reduction of habitat and other human activities. The loss in tropical rain forests, thought to contain a majority of the species on Earth, may exceed half a percent a year.

Birth of an Entomologist *(cont'd.)*

So there is a lot for those who study the diversity of life to do, as well as a new respectability. But I have a confession to make. The boy who experienced the magic of the zoo and the museum is still strong inside me. I would have followed the same path regardless of what happened in the rest of the world.

The Old Home In Ohio*

Charles N. Gould

It was a hot August night in 1889. Some fifty country boys and girls, prospective school teachers, were seated in a stuffy schoolroom in Kingman, Kansas, listening to a lecture on the geology of Kansas. The girls all wore bustles and most of the boys had sandburs in their trousers.

This was during the summer Normal Institute, which in those days was held in each Kansas county for the training of teachers.

The speaker was L. C. Wooster, the conductor of the institute. He had gone down to the banks of the Ninnescah River, which flows through Kingman, and had picked up two slabs of red sandstone, each about an inch thick. These he held up before us so that we might see that on one slab there were ripple marks, and on the other mud cracks.

Professor Wooster explained to us simply but clearly that these slabs were once part of a sea beach. He told us that the ripple marks were formed by the action of waves on the sand, just as ripple marks were being produced along the banks of the Ninnescah today, and that if we would go down to the river we might see mud cracks very similar to those on the slab he was holding up before us.

He explained that at the time when these sandstones were being deposited the greater part of Kansas, as well as much of North America, was an open sea, and that at that time neither the Rocky Mountains nor the Appalachian Mountains were in existence. He said that the same forces of nature—wind, rain, running water, heat, cold, and chemical agencies which we could see today—have been active throughout all geologic time, and that by these agencies our world is still being shaped. He gave us the foundation stone of the science of geology, viz., "All rocks have been laid down under water," and explained that by great convulsions of nature mountains were raised, and then by the processes of erosion these mountains were again worn down.

I hung entranced on every word. As Professor Wooster continued his lecture unfolding nature's handiwork, I felt the spinal shiver which betokens the last word in emotional appeal. This was my conversion.

The Old Home In Ohio *(cont'd.)*

Up to that time, I do not believe that I had heard the word geology spoken. I may have run across the word in my reading, but it certainly had no place either in my vocabulary or in my thinking.

This lecture changed the entire current of my life. At that time I did not know what a geologist did, but I then and there resolved that whatever things a geologist did, those things must I do. I then and there resolved that, in as much as in me lay, I would devote my life to learning how the rocks had been laid down and how they had been all mussed up.

And now for nearly a decade more than half a century I have constantly kept before my eyes the resolution made that hot August night.

The Entrapment of Leon*

Leon Lederman

I started out as a molecules kid. In high school and early college I loved chemistry, but I gradually shifted toward physics, which seemed cleaner—odorless, in fact. I was strongly influenced, too, by the kids in physics, who were funnier and played better basketball. The giant of our group was Isaac Halpern, now a professor of physics at the University of Washington. He claimed that the only reason he went to see his posted grades was to determine whether the A had a "flat top or a pointy top." Naturally, we all loved him. He could also broad-jump farther than any of us.

I became intrigued with the issues in physics because of their crisp logic and clear experimental consequences. In my senior year in college, my best friend from high school, Martin Klein, the now eminent Einstein scholar at Yale, harangued me on the splendors of physics during a long evening over many beers. That did it. I entered the U.S. Army, with a B. S. in chemistry and a determination to be a physicist if I could only survive basic training and World War II.

I was born at last into the world of physics in 1948, when I began my Ph.D. research working with the world's most powerful particle accelerator of its time, the synchrocyclotron at Columbia University. Dwight Eisenhower, president of Columbia, cut the ribbon dedicating the machine in June of 1950. Having helped Ike win the war, I was obviously much appreciated by the Columbia authorities, who paid me almost $4,000 for just one year of ninety-hour weeks. These were heady times. In the 1950s, the synchrocyclotron and other powerful new devices created the new discipline of particle physics. . . .

*Excerpts from *The God Particle* by Leon Lederman with Dick Teresi. Copyright © 1993 by Leon Lederman and Dick Teresi. Reprinted by permission of Houghton Mifflin Co. All rights reserved.

The Entrapment of Leon *(cont'd.)*

In those days the scientific problems seemed very clear and very important. They had to do with the properties of what's called the strong nuclear force and some theoretically predicted particles called pi mesons, or pions. Columbia's accelerator was designed to produce lots of pions by bombarding innocent targets with protons. The instrumentation was rather simple at the time, simple enough for a graduate student to understand.

Columbia was a hotbed of physics in the 1950s. Charles Townes would soon discover the laser and win the Nobel Prize. James Rainwater would win the Prize for his nuclear model, and Willis Lamb for measuring the tiny shift in hydrogen's spectral lines. Nobel laureate Isadore Rabi, who inspired all of us, headed up a team that included Norman Ramsey and Polykarp Kusch, both to become Nobel winners in due course. T. D. Lee shared the Nobel for his theory of parity violation. The density of professors who had been anointed with Swedish holy water was both exhilarating and depressing. As young faculty, some of us wore lapel buttons that read "Not Yet."

For me the Big Bang of professional recognition took place in the period 1959–1962 when two of my Columbia colleagues and I carried out the first-ever measurement of high-energy neutrino collisions. Neutrinos are my favorite particles. A neutrino has almost no properties: no mass (or very little), no electric charge, and no radius—and, adding insult to injury, no strong force acts on it. The euphemism used to describe a neutrino is "elusive." It is barely a fact, and it can pass through millions of miles of solid lead with only a tiny chance of being involved in a measurable collision.

Our 1961 experiment provided the cornerstone for what came to be known in the 1970s as the "standard model" of particle physics. In 1988 the experiment was recognized by the Royal Swedish Academy of Science with the Nobel Prize. (Everybody asks, why did they wait twenty-seven years? I don't really know. I used to give my family the facetious excuse that the Academy was dragging its feet because they couldn't decide which of my great achievements to honor.) Winning the Prize was of course a great thrill. But that thrill does not really compare with the incredible excitement that gripped us at the moment when we realized our experiment was a success.

Physicists today feel the same emotions that scientists have felt for centuries. The life of a physicist is filled with anxiety, pain, hardship, tension, attacks of hopelessness, depression, and discouragement. But these are punctuated by flashes of exhilaration, laughter, joy, and exultation. These epiphanies come at unpredictable times. Often they are generated simply by the sudden understanding of something new and important, something beautiful, that someone else has revealed. However, if you are mortal, like most of the scientists I know, the far sweeter moments come when you yourself discover some new fact about the universe. It's astonishing how often this happens at 3 A.M., when you are alone in the lab and you have learned something profound, and realize that not one of the other five billion people on earth knows what you now know. Or so you hope. You will, of course, hasten to tell them as soon as possible. This is known as "publishing" . . . .

The Entrapment of Leon *(cont'd.)*

The scientist, however, cannot depend on Eureka moments to make his life fulfilling. There must be some joy in day-to-day activities. For me, this joy is in designing and building apparatus that will teach us about this extraordinarily abstract subject. When I was an impressionable graduate student at Columbia, I helped a world-famous professor visiting from Rome build a particle counter. I was the virgin in this and he a past master. Together we turned the brass tube on the lathe (it was after 5 P.M. and the machinists had all gone home). We soldered on the glass-tipped end caps and strung a gold wire through the short, insulated metal straw penetrating the glass. Then we soldered some more. We flushed the special gas through the counter for a few hours while hooking an oscilloscope to the wire, protected from a 1,000-volt power supply by a special capacitor. My professor friend—let's call him Gilberto, because that was his name—kept peering at the green trace of the oscilloscope while lecturing me in faultlessly broken English on the history and evolution of particle counters. Suddenly Gilberto went stark, raving wild. "Mamma mia! Regardo incredibilo! Primo secourso!" (Or something like that.) He shouted, pointed, lifted me up in the air—even though I was six inches taller and fifty pounds heavier than he—and danced me around the room.

"What happened?" I stammered.

"Mufiletto!" he replied. "Izza counting. Izza counting!"

He was probably putting some of this on for my benefit, but he was genuinely excited that we had, with our hands, eyes, and brains, fashioned a device that detected the passage of cosmic ray particles, registered them by small blips in the sweep of the oscilloscope. Although he must have seen this phenomenon thousands of times, he never got over the thrill. That one of these particles may just possibly have started its voyage to 120th Street and Broadway, tenth floor, light-years ago in a distant galaxy was only part of the excitement. Gilberto's seemingly never-ending enthusiasm was contagious.

 **Living to Read**

Alison Moon

I cannot remember a time when I couldn't read. I cannot remember a time when I didn't want to read. For me, reading is nourishment, as necessary as the food I eat and the air I breathe. Sure, there are times when I have been reading for so long that my eyes get googly and my head starts to ache; but even then, I promise myself that I will pick up the book again as soon as my vision clears and the headache dissipates. Like the girl's mother in the essay we read in a class, my mother was always trying to tear me away from my books and encouraging me to call a friend or play

Living to Read *(cont'd.)*

outside. Ironic, when all my friends' mothers were *paying* their kids 50 cents an hour to read, anything just to make them read.

I am always relieved to hear similar stories from other people . . . it seems that those of us who would rather read than eat are a rare breed, and I am always faintly embarrassed to admit on those interest surveys that my primary hobby is reading. "What about hiking or mountain biking?" they ask. "Do you like to go jogging to relieve stress?" And their faces are always slightly incredulous (just for an instant) before they retrieve their glossy smiles and say brightly, "No? Well, that's *wonderful* (gushgush) that you are educating yourself," and walk away slightly bewildered that someone would *want* to do something as nerdy as reading.

My love for reading obviously began in the home rather than school because I was reading long before I started school. My parents are both readers, but reading doesn't seem to be as driving, as necessary to them as it is to me. That makes me wonder: Is a love for reading inborn? Is it instilled in the home environment? Nature / Nurture / Nature / Nurture / Freak of Nature? I must have caused my parents to wonder. But they were proud, proud because the reading made me smart ("My, what a large vocabulary for such a little person!"), proud because the reading would take me places ("Congratulations, you have been selected to receive a full-tuition scholarship . . ."), and they encouraged me.

I had an "only-childhood" for four years before the first of my five sisters and brother came along, so Mom and Dad had plenty of time to feed my insatiable appetite for printed material. They showed me books, games, magazines, words on TV, street signs, even cereal boxes, and plenty more that I'm sure I can't remember. Trips to the library were a weekly event. As my sisters and brother came along, reading was often my escape from a chaotic household. I didn't actually have to leave the room in which my younger sibs were playing: I simply had to open a book for instant peace. Somehow, once the book was open, my ears were closed. To this day, opening a book is the trick I use to soothe myself in the midst of confusion . . . sort of like offering a pacifier to a baby.

Some people say the same thing about their writing . . . that has never been the case for me. People often assume that, because I read, I must also love to write. This is not the case. I don't mind writing for my classes, and I've been told I'm proficient at it (a result, I'm convinced, of having read for long enough to know what feels right and what doesn't). The thing is, people often write to make their voices heard when it seems that no one else will listen (here I think of the nineteenth-century housewives who kept all those diaries). Yet, I have never had any trouble making my own voice (my physical, actual vocal voice) heard, despite the size of my family and the chaos that sometimes ruled in my house. Adding my voice to the chaos was never a problem: Escaping from it was, and reading provided this escape.

I think that if I could name any books I remember above all others, it would be the "Little House" books by Laura Ingalls Wilder. My father first introduced them to me by reading the first in the series, *Little House in the Big Woods,* chapter by chapter as a bedtime story every night. I was hooked. To read and own all the books in the series became my quest; and once I achieved this goal, I simply started over

Living to Read *(cont'd.)*

by reading all the books again. And again. I think now, fourteen years later, I could still quote sections from the Little House books. I loved them first because they were a series: My primary dissatisfaction with books until this point was that they had to end. I would become so involved with a book that its ending was actually like a death to me: However, with the Little House books, I could put off this sadness because when one ended, there was another waiting to take its place and continue the story of the Ingalls family. I also loved them because they lent themselves to play so well: I would coerce my friends and babysitters into playing the parts of Laura, Mary, Ma, and Pa. The creek behind my house became "Plum Creek," and all our efforts were spent trying to create the dugout in which Laura and her family lived in *On the Banks of Plum Creek.*

People who know me ask me to name the point at which I started reading. I might as well try to remember the point at which I started breathing . . . I can't. I just know that I always have read, and I imagine I always will. When I look at my parents and how little they read (apart from the newspaper and magazines and children's books for my little sisters), I wonder if there will come a time when I will become like them, not having the time to read the way I need to. What will happen when I have children? Reading is a selfish habit, I've found, and I can't expect to be selfish and care for others at the same time. I don't want to become like my parents; but at the same time, I want more than anything to be exactly like them. I would hate to read the way they read and the things they read, but they are the ones who made me read the way I read and the things I read. What a dichotomy.

That's why I have chosen to become a teacher . . . to share my love for reading with my students (I don't think a teacher will be successful unless she loves what she is teaching) and to encourage them to develop their own love (or at least, appreciation) of reading. Yet, I know that all I can do is to encourage it and nurture it: I can't force it. Why are there people who love to run twenty-six-mile marathons? The very thought makes me shudder, just as the thought of reading makes others sick to their stomachs. I just don't think the need to read can be instilled by someone else all the time. Maybe it is circumstantial, maybe it is inborn . . . to me, it remains a mystery.

 ## Sharing 1000 Lives

Emily Clark

Reading seems to have always had a big impact on my life. I feel as if I was born reading, and have since gone from character to character and adventure to adventure. In my life, I have read for school, for pleasure, for information, and for necessity.

Sharing 1000 Lives *(cont'd.)*

I feel as though I have shared a thousand lives with a thousand people and now carry a small piece of each of them with me through my life. My reading has served the purpose of educating me, amusing me, bonding me to friends, and giving me a true feeling of self-worth.

My earliest remembrances of reading are of my parents reading to me. I can still picture my father carrying me up the stairs at night to my bedroom to take me into the world that my favorite characters could make come alive for me. My father and I have always been close; this was a special bonding time for us. Although my older brother was always there to hear the stories too, they were always read in my room. I probably always had my own pick of what was read, as well. My mother also read to me during the days, which I enjoyed, but nothing was as special as falling asleep to the words of my favorite stories rolling off of my father's tongue.

In elementary school, I loved to read at home, but hated the boring books and workbooks of school. *Stuart Little* was, by far, my favorite book to read. I must have cried, laughed and gasped with him at least a hundred times. No matter how many times I read about his adventures, I would still cringe at the crucial moments, not sure if everything would turn out alright, again.

This was also a time of great competition for me against my older brother. When he learned to write cursive, I would spend excruciating hours with pen in hand trying to recreate the curves, loops, and spirals that he was so lucky to be learning about in school. My mother was constantly bombarded by offerings of my "writing" while I begged her to find something among the scribbles that remotely resembled some human writing. As could be expected, I was just as competitive with our reading. I always wanted to read the work that he was expected to read and show everybody how amazingly smart I was. I never surpassed him, but that was not because of a lack of effort on my part.

My reading in junior high really seemed to have an important role in my social life. I was always a person who had many friends, but was somewhere "in the middle," socially. However, in eighth grade, I found a way to climb that social ladder. V. C. Andrews was the author of choice among anybody who was anybody. I, being the lucky person that I was, just happened to have all four books in her series. Of course the books were really my grandmother's, but nobody had to know that. I was finally on top; people had to come to me and ask to be put next in line for my books. I also was among the first people to read each edition, so I was *the* source of knowledge on the topic of these books. Life was good (in this aspect).

The only problem was, junior high English left much to be desired. My days were filled with grammar, composition, tree diagrams, and any other aspect of English that could possibly bore me to tears. Nobody seemed to enjoy this, and I can't say that I ever got any real knowledge out of it that truly helped my writing or reading abilities.

The only English class that I ever truly enjoyed was Advanced Placement English, which I took my junior year of high school. During this class, our assignments consisted of reading novels (picked out by the teacher, of course), and then coming

Sharing 1000 Lives *(cont'd.)*

to class and discussing them, as well as writing papers about them. I loved this class because it was the first time that a teacher actually made us feel as though what we had to say was worthwhile. I was also exposed to books that I never would have thought to read. Had I gone to the library on my own, I never would have even considered picking *Lord of the Flies* or *Alas, Babylon* off of the shelf. But, because they were required I actually read them and enjoyed them. Imagine that. I actually started to feel fear that my own flesh could be preyed upon by the barbaric young beasts of the first story. I finally realized that exploring new types of literature could be enjoyable.

I still love to read, but my opportunities for it are few and far between because of my hectic college schedule. Any time that I begin a book and really find myself enjoying it, I remember my stacks of homework. I finally put the book of my choice back on a shelf and draw out my required texts, read through them (remembering nothing of importance), and then fall asleep out of boredom. I have had a few classes that allow some freedom of choice in what I read, but the pace is so hectic that I am not able to savor each word as I so enjoy doing.

I have managed to squeeze a few of my own reading into my time in the last few years. Of these, my favorites would have to be *The Firm* and *The Bridges of Madison County.* These books were totally different, but both equally stimulating to fill some of my void of true literary treasures. *The Firm* really took me on an adventure like I hadn't experienced in a very long time. The scandalous plot kept me excited (and away from my school work) and reminded me how such I missed living through the life of my favorite characters. In a totally different way, *The Bridges of Madison County* also kept me spellbound. But, this book was not long enough for me. I locked away certain passages in my mind, keeping them safe so that I could pull them out and savor them from time to time like a small child might do with a precious stone or favorite trinket. The story in this book was great, but I fell in love with the words in a way I never before knew was possible. I have purchased Walker's next book, but I am saving it for a time when I know I can become totally engulfed. I hope to feel the same rush of emotion as I did before.

My friends still seem to be in the same mode as they were all through school. They still read the same types of books (yes, two of them even still follow V. C. Andrews's latest novels), and still even seem to have plenty of time to read. I envy them for the latter, but pity them for never seeming to explore beyond the limits that reading from only one or two authors can set. They have offered me the latest editions of Andrews's novels, but I have left them to collect dust for the time being. I have a hard time accepting the fact that her novels live on without her, even though I am told they all have the same mood as when she composed the words herself. I imagine that some day I will enjoy slipping back into the dark, sadistic world that these offer, but for now I want to keep exploring and discover how many new worlds I can uncover to stimulate my imagination.

As an elementary education major, I hope to instill my love of reading into my students. I want them to understand that they can explore any world they wish to

Sharing 1000 Lives *(cont'd.)*

through stories, and that anything they want to read can be acceptable. I feel that their reading and writing abilities can be best strengthened by using literature that is enjoyable for them. They might find that a good book could give them the escape that they need from whatever they are feeling dragged down by in life. I will share my stories with them, and show them (by example) that reading can be enjoyable and does not have to be a chore.

❧ CHAPTER 4

OBSERVING

INTRODUCTION

The Importance of Careful Observation

If you consider the way you have acquired information and skills throughout your life, you will soon discover that much of what you have gained has come as a result of observation. You didn't learn how to tie your shoes or climb trees, for example, by reading a book or by hearing someone describe what to do. Additional opportunities to sharpen your observation skills will undoubtedly come as you progress through your college courses, because an important part of your education is to acquire a habit of mind that doesn't automatically accept information without testing it to see if it is accurate.

Many of us are familiar with assertions that seem true because most people don't question them. "Women talk more than men" is a good example of a belief so commonly held that it hardly seems worth the bother to confirm it. Yet when trained observers (linguists and social scientists) have watched men and women talking with one another, they have found that men talked more often than women in many circumstances. As this and similar examples illustrate, the habit of careful observation is vital; it allows you to see whether a particular claim or conclusion accurately reflects the data on which it is based.

The ability to observe carefully is not only an important consequence of a general education, it is also the foundation of many disciplines—especially the sciences and social sciences. Part of the training you will receive within your academic major and as a professional will be to learn how to observe from the perspective of that discipline. For this reason, this chapter does not offer a particular research methodology to guide your observations. If you become a sociology major, you will learn to observe like a sociologist. If you major in biology, you will learn to observe like a biologist. Whatever your major course of study—nursing, chemistry, interior design, computer science, or accounting—you will learn to conduct observations in ways that are deemed important within your discipline. Some experience in observing now will better prepare you for the particular methodology you will work with later.

The Relationship between Observing and Reporting

Although observing and reporting are closely related, our coverage of each is separate. This chapter focuses on observing while the next chapter is devoted to reporting, but in practice, it is virtually impossible to totally divorce one activity from the other. You can't report without having observed first; and continued observation is based, in part, on sensory feedback—a kind of self-reporting. Then, too, you will often perform follow-up observations that are modified to reflect information reported in earlier ones.

We would have preferred to discuss observing and reporting in one unit. However, covering the necessary information for both would have resulted in an enormous chapter. In the interest of accessibility, we have separated the two, beginning with observation. We chose this order because in most cases (if not always) observing initiates a process that may culminate in a report. Reporting also seems secondary because it cannot occur unless it has been preceded by some kind of information gathering, such as observation. On the other hand, observations do not necessarily have to be reported to others. If you perform an observation, you may keep the information to yourself.

SAMPLE ASSIGNMENTS

In college you may be asked to complete assignments that require you to observe an activity, person, or object in one way or another. Sometimes an observation may be the focus of the task; sometimes it may culminate in a written report. On occasion, your professor may instruct you to use the research methodology of a particular discipline to guide your observation or to develop procedures of your own. To show you the range of assignments you might encounter, we have selected examples that are fairly common.

Physical Education Assignment. (1) Select a physical education or recreation activity involving either adults or children. (2) With your selection in mind, review the materials from your textbook and class notes. Then develop a mental plan for how to conduct your observation and a checklist on which to record information. (3) Perform the observation. (4) Articulate and summarize your observations in an organized manner in four typewritten pages.

Sociology Assignment. Select a group of which you are a member (family, peer, recreational, work, etc.). The next time you are with this group, perform an observation. As you observe, try to adopt the role of a sociologist; you should attempt to be unbiased and to avoid influencing the behavior you are observing. Describe the group features: type, size, membership characteristics (age, gender, race/ethnicity, etc.). Provide an analysis of the group's structure: division of labor, status, leadership, and roles played by group members. Write up a report of your findings in which you include the advantages and disadvantages of observing a group of which you are a part.

Linguistics Assignment. Review the readings about interruption within same-sex and opposite-sex interactions. Plan to observe three groups of speakers for the same length of time. As much as possible, match groups in terms of size and member characteristics. One group should consist of men; one group should consist of women; and one group should consist of a relatively equal number of men and women. During your observation of each group, record the number of interruptions, noting the gender of both interrupters and those who are interrupted. Write a report of your findings in which you compare group behavior with respect to this feature. Offer a possible analysis or interpretation of your data.

Biology Field Notebook Assignment. Turn in a portion of your field notebook that contains the following information:

1. Date, time, and other relevant information (air temperature, water temperature, weather conditions, etc.)
2. Goal of investigation. This should include a description of your goal plus notes about your expectations.
3. Observations. Include detailed information about objects, their relationship to one another, setting, etc.
4. Questions that arise as a result of your observation. These can include queries about unexpected findings, tentative hypotheses ("same species?"), and so on. You can also include tentative answers and any plans for additional investigation in this section.

Although the previous assignments seem different from one another, they actually share a number of features. First, they all contain assumptions about the intended audience. For most college assignments, the principal reader is, of course, your instructor. However, depending on the assignment, an additional audience may be implied. The field notebook assignment, for example, is devised, in part, to acclimate students to writing for an audience of scientists. Such writing must be systematic and detailed so that recorded work can be understood and, if necessary, carried on by others.

Next, observation assignments always imply or explicitly state expectations about the observer. It is impossible to observe without a perspective or point of view; therefore, assignments may provide precise directives ("adopt the role of sociologist") or assume that students will adopt a perspective suggested by the course or discipline. Even when an assignment instructs you to be "objective" or "unbiased," remember that you are a unique individual with your own history, interests, and abilities. The resources you bring to an assignment will, necessarily, differ from those of your classmates.

Finally, observation assignments usually suggest procedures about how to conduct the observation and write up a report. However, as the preceding examples illustrate, the amount of detail and direction required by a particular assignment can range from minimal to substantial.

If you are given an observation assignment, you must consider to what extent it provides you with assistance. Whether an assignment is lengthy or brief, you always need to determine:

1. The role or perspective from which your observation should be conducted
2. The procedure to be used for your observation
3. The format or organization your written findings should take.

YOUR POINT OF VIEW AS AN OBSERVER

Observations are often presented as if they are neutral or totally objective. That is to say, written or oral reports of observations often appear as if they have no point of view or orientation. Common examples of this kind of writing are news stories that describe an event or reports that focus on "the facts and only the facts."

Despite conventional wisdom, there is no automatic, predetermined "neutral zone" from which to observe anything "objectively." Whether you want to or not, every time you observe, you do so through your own experience, which is shaped by matters such as your family, friends, religious background, social and economic status, racial and ethnic background, and gender. Therefore, it is important to be conscious, as much as you are able, of your role as an observer, that is, of your own point of view during a particular observation as well as of the role an assignment is creating for you.

Different Points of View

Although it may seem an easy matter to assess your point of view as you prepare to do an observation, accomplishing this may not be simple. Think of some of the roles you may occupy currently—student, son or daughter, athlete, youth counselor, employee—and how these affect the way people think of you and you think of yourself. Others' expectations as well as your own sense of "who" you are at a particular time influence your point of view and may cause it to shift subtly or even quite dramatically.

You may, of course, think that when you receive an assignment you act in your role as "student." Still, a college or university might enroll two thousand or forty thousand students. Are you the same as every first-year student or every undergraduate? Of course not. You bring a unique personal history and your own set of resources to each assignment you receive.

As you assess the resources you bring to an assignment, your role as an observer should become more clear. If, for example, you are assigned to observe people's behavior for an introductory psychology class, you should anticipate that those who come from similar backgrounds as your own may seem to behave "normally" with respect to voice level, gesture, large body movements, and so on. This may cause you to observe them less carefully or not to consider their behavior as noteworthy. By the same token, if you consider the behavior you have experienced and take for granted as "normal" or "regular," you may overemphasize unfamiliar behavior or characterize it as "strange," "unusual," or "inappropriate." In assessing the resources you bring to an assignment, it is also important to take stock of and compensate for your relative strengths and weaknesses. Here is an example of one way you might prepare for the previous observation assignment:

> *Because I come from a small town with a homogeneous population, I don't have much experience observing lots of different people. I may overlook or overemphasize aspects of my subjects' behavior because of this lack of experience. But I have done sketching for many years; I can use my attention to detail to focus my eyes on smaller matters like hand movements, which might force me to observe everyone more carefully and more uniformly.*

 **Activity 1**

With your group members select one of the assignments from the Sample Assignments section of this chapter. First, brainstorm together some of the "typical" ways that students might perform the observation. On what aspects of the objects or persons to be observed would you expect most students to focus? What aspects would you expect most students to overlook or misinterpret? Next, determine how your own experience and background might influence the nature or results of your observation. Compare the influence upon your observation with the influences other members of your group report.

The Observer That the Assignment Creates

Although course assignments often require students to acquire and synthesize information or practice a skill, many—particularly those that involve observation— are designed to offer practice in playing a particular role (scientific observer, sociologist, historian, teacher, physical trainer, etc.). In designing an assignment, for example, instructors may wish to help apprentices-in-training to see through the eyes of a professional, and thus catch a glimpse of what their future work might be like. They might also want to give students who haven't had much exposure to a particular academic discipline the experience of observing from the perspective of that discipline. In addition to fostering a professional or disciplinary perspective, assignments may encourage students to play a more practical role, such as careful consumer or concerned citizen, or to observe with a particular attitude such as "objective," "meticulous," "dispassionate," or "empathetic."

Because observation assignments often imply information about the perspective from which the instructor expects you to observe, it is wise to consider this in your preparation. In addition to taking stock of your own personal experiences and qualities and how they might affect your observation, it is also important to ask yourself, Who does this particular assignment want me to be? An assignment may want to you be something particular like an art lover or an ecologist; or it may want you to adopt the more general stance of a person who is receptive to a new way of looking at or thinking about the world.

 **Activity 2**

> With your group partners select another assignment from those listed in the Sample Assignments section of this chapter and assess the observer roles it implies. Then determine the different approaches that might be adopted by two different students, one with interest or experience in the subject of the assignment and one without either of these.

Anticipating Questions and Details

Once you have decided on an observer's role, you are ready to make final preparations for your task. We suggest that this preparation involve at least two steps:

1. Anticipating the questions that would be asked from the perspective of the role you have assumed

2. Using these questions to generate a list of the particular details to which you should attend.

Following these two steps will help you to be selective and to focus your attention, which is important because it is impossible to carefully attend to everything during even the most careful observation.

Anticipating Questions. If you have a good sense of your perspective, it shouldn't be too difficult to imagine in advance the kind of information that would be of particular interest. Suppose, for example, that you are assigned to watch an intramural game. You may have adopted an observer role from a number of possibilities: team member, coach, physical education teacher, activities director, or playground supervisor. The particular role you select should help you generate questions. If you observe from the perspective of coach, you might be interested in some of the following questions: How do the players on my team interact with one another, given the current configuration? What are the weak spots in each team's defense? Which players are the weakest? Which are the strongest? On the other hand, if you observe from the perspective of an activities director, some of these questions might interest you: Are all of the participants having a good time? How much interaction between players is occurring? Does interest in the game seem to diminish after a while or is it sustained throughout?

Generating Details. With the role or perspective from which you are observing in mind, you can generate a list of questions to help you determine, in advance, what details you need to watch for. Details are by nature small and easily over-looked, which is why you should be alert to them before you begin. Notice how the questions in the previous example might lead an observer to pay attention to some details and to ignore others. The person observing in the role of a coach wouldn't be much interested in the amount or nature of verbal interaction between players; likewise, the activities director wouldn't be focusing attention on particular moves or plays within the game.

We suggest that you observe at least twice, if possible. Unfortunately, regardless of how carefully you construct your role as an observer and how thoroughly you antic-ipate questions and details, actual observations often suggest issues you didn't antici-pate, thus causing you to overlook crucial details. Two observations afford you the opportunity to compile an additional list of questions and details based on your first experience, which you can use to guide you in a second, more focused examination.

 **Activity 3**

> Together with your group partners, select an assignment from the Sample Assignment section of this chapter and articulate a particular role from which one or more of you could conduct the observation. Then brainstorm a set of questions a person observing from that perspective would want to answer. Finally, using your set of questions, generate a list of details that these questions suggest. Given your selections, what details might you *disregard* during your observation? Why wouldn't these details be significant?

THE OBSERVATION

Preparing for Your Observation

In order to do an observation that will provide you with useful, sufficient data, you will need to devote a substantial amount of time to preparing for the observation. What you must do to prepare depends, of course, on the nature of the observation that you are planning to do as well as the disciplinary perspective from which it must be conducted. These suggestions should help you think of the kind of prepa-ration that you will need to do before you head off to make an observation.

Making Contacts. If you are planning to observe methodologies or strategies of a teacher in his classroom, a supervisor in her office, a scientist at work in her lab, or any other person doing his or her job, it will be necessary to contact the person beforehand in order to obtain permission to do the observation, to arrange a time for the observation, and to discuss any information that the person may want you to know. Of course, you will need to be clear about who you are and about your rea-sons for wanting to do the observation. You also will need to explain what you will do with the information once you have obtained it. Generally, people are more than willing to accommodate a college student working on an assignment.

Getting Your Tools Ready. If you are planning to use a tape recorder during the observation, you will need to obtain permission from the people whom you wish to record. If you will need an electrical outlet in order to do the taping, you will need to find out whether your intended site has an outlet, where it is located, and whether its location will be convenient for your needs.

If you are planning to perform a scientific experiment and observe the results, as in a chemistry lab, you will need to carefully prepare by reading directions for the experiment, making sure that you know how to handle the chemicals properly and that you have the right equipment (including goggles and safety clothing, if required) and the proper amounts of chemicals, and so on. You should gather all necessary materials and carefully lay them out before you begin the experiment. You also will need to decide beforehand how, exactly, you will record the results of your experiment. If you plan to take notes during the experiment, be sure to have a notepad ready.

If you are planning to observe people's behaviors in a public setting, such as in an elevator, in a shopping mall, or in a dentist's waiting room, you will need to think beforehand about where you will position yourself during the observation in order to be inconspicuous. For such observations, it would be wise to prepare a list of behaviors that you expect to see and to leave room on the list to add the behaviors that you do not expect to see. You may want to prepare your list as a chart, of sorts, so you will be able to tally how many times each behavior takes place during your observation. Figure 4–1, for example, a chart designed to assist in the observation of elevator behaviors, allows the observer to quickly tally the various behaviors of up to twelve different subjects.

Researching a Topic. If the purpose of your observation is to help you gather information in an area in which you have little expertise, it may be wise to visit the college library to do some background reading in preparation for the observation. If you are observing the way that a group of small children share their toys, you may want to do some reading on stages in child development; if you are observing the behaviors of an autistic child, you may want to do some reading on autism; if you are observing a display of impressionistic artwork in order to focus on common features, you may want to do some reading on impressionism; and so on. Often you will be able to find sufficient background information in standard reference books such as specialized dictionaries or encyclopedias. You also might examine your textbook for background information or ask your teacher for suggestions about where you might find additional background information.

Conducting Your Observation

Learning to Recognize Important Information. Undoubtedly, the most important step towards making a useful observation is training your senses to recognize and focus on details that are important to your observation. Learning to recognize such details, however, is not as easy as it may at first sound: During your observation,

Elevator Behavior in a University Library												
Behaviors						**Subjects Being Observed**						
	1	2	3	4	5	6	7	8	9	10	11	12
Standing away from others												
Invading others' "personal space"												
Leaning against side of elevator												
Eating												
Reading												
Initiating conversation (list examples)												
1.												
2.												
3.												
4.												
5.												
6.												
Making eye contact												
Avoiding eye contact												
Standing near the door												
Standing in the back												
Fidgeting												
Looking at ceiling												
Looking at other people												

Figure 4–1.

your senses will be bombarded by everything you see, hear, smell, feel, and even taste.

One way to focus on the details that are important to your observation (so that you can record them) and to ignore the details that are not important is to keep your "role" as an observer in mind throughout the observation. If, for example, you are observing a second-grade classroom in the role of principal, you probably will focus on the teacher: whether he or she adheres to the lesson plan, whether he or she is able to deal effectively with questions and problems, and so on. If you are observing the classroom as a parent who is thinking of enrolling a child in the school, you may have some of the same concerns as the principal might have. But it is also likely that you will focus more on the children: whether they seem to be receiving an adequate amount of praise and attention, whether they demonstrate respect for the teacher and for one another, and whether they seem to be excited by the learning environment. If you are visiting the class in the role of a social worker, you probably will focus on the way a particular child interacts with other students and with the teacher. If your role is that of a government investigator who has been sent to observe a classroom because racial discrimination charges have been filed against the school, you probably will focus on the way the members of the various racial groups interact with one another and on the way the teacher treats each group.

These examples show that understanding your role as an observer is a key element in recognizing important information. As we have said, when you are asked to make an observation for one of your classes, your professor may assign you a specific role to assume or will explain a specific context for doing the observation. However, if your professor does not assign such a role or context, you would be wise to select an appropriate role for yourself and to make this role clear as you write up a report of the observation.

 **Activity 4**

To prepare for this activity, your collaborative group must meet briefly a day or so beforehand to decide on an object that one of the group members will bring to class for the group to observe. The object could be anything that the group finds interesting and would like to observe: a seashell, a sculpture, a pine cone, a piece of fruit, a toy, even a kitchen gadget. When your group meets to perform the observation, each person should select a different "role" to guide him or her in selecting details. If the object to be observed is a persimmon, for example, group members could assume the roles of chef, botanist, artist, customs agent, and shopper; the notes group members take will vary according to their assigned roles. Allow about ten minutes for everyone to examine the object and to take notes, each of you keeping in mind your respective role.

When everyone in your group has finished, compare your notes and observations and discuss the various details that are important for each assigned observer role.

Recording Information During the Observation. Because information can be recorded in a variety of ways, you will need to decide the most useful way of recording data for your particular observation. What you *should never* plan to do, though, is leave the details solely to your memory; you undoubtedly will lose important information this way. If you adopt the following recommendations for your note-taking process, the result, in all likelihood, will be specific notes that will help you write a strong report.

Be specific. Gathering specific details is perhaps the most important aspect of good note taking; however, most people need practice to learn to take specific notes while they are performing an observation. You might think of the key to specificity in note taking as "show, don't tell," a phrase that is often recommended for good writing. Suppose that you were observing the behaviors of a child playing with a friend on a playground. Here are examples that illustrate how to write notes that "show" rather than "tell."

Weak details that "tell"	*Improved details that "show"*
looks happy	shouts, "I like this swing!"
looks mean	clenches fist and grimaces
takes turns/shares	asks, "Do you want to use the slide now?" "Let's both play in the sandbox."
gets angry/fights	throw a pebble in anger spits at other child
acts mischievous	hides from parent pokes other child in back

Write as much as you can, as quickly as you can. Writing quickly in order to get down as many useful details as you can is somewhat difficult, considering that you are also observing; still, you will need to generate as many useful details as you can in order to truly capture and remember your observation. One strategy for helping you to write quickly is to use some system of shorthand that you develop, which works well for you. For example, if you are observing a classroom, you might shorten the word *teacher* to *teach*, the word *chalkboard* to *chalkbd*, the word *discipline* to *discip*, and so on. You also might use abbreviations such as *w/o* for *without* and *b/c* for *because*. As you take notes, you should not worry about writing complete sentences or correct punctuation and spelling. Your goal should be to write down as much relevant information as possible.

Include metacommentary. As you make an observation for a particular class, you occasionally may see connections to the materials you have been studying for the class. Including in your notes commentary that explains such connections certainly will be to your advantage when you write a report. Here is an example that shows why this type of commentary, more precisely defined as "metacommentary," is helpful. Suppose that you have been asked to observe a children's birthday party as an assignment for your Child Development class. Watching the children as they interact with one another, you become aware that some of the children seem more mature than others and that their behaviors match the stages of development described by the theorist Piaget. Your metacommentary, then, might include information about Aletha, a five-year-old whose speech is so egocentric that nearly all of her sentences begin with "I" or "My." Because you recognize that Aletha's stage of development, as defined by Piaget, is the "Concrete Stage," you should include that information in your notes. Your notes also might include information about Sonia, an eight-year-old who sees others' points of view and is working to ensure that all children are included in the games. When you recognize that Sonia's stage of development, as defined by Piaget, is the "Pre-Operational Stage," you should include that information in your notes.

Sketch out information that is harder to explain in words. Suppose, for example, that an assignment for your secondary education techniques class requires you to observe the use of peer groups in a high-school classroom. Rather than try to explain in your notes the arrangement of the various groups in the classroom and the movement of the teacher from group to group, you probably will have a more accurate record if you note the information visually (see Figure 4–2). Furthermore, using such a sketch will save you time.

Take advantage of every perspective available to you. If it is feasible for you to move from place to place during an observation, do so in order to get more than one perspective. If, for example, you are observing shoppers in a mall, you will acquire a more complete understanding of their activity if you do not stand in one spot throughout the entire observation. Of course, if moving around would hinder the activity of those you are observing or would be somehow inappropriate, you will need to find a location from which to observe and then remain there.

Pretend that you've never seen this activity before. Although an assignment may ask you to observe something that is entirely new to you, observation assignments often require students to observe something with which they are familiar. In many ways, observing something with which you have familiarity is more difficult than observing something new. If the object or situation to be observed is familiar (shoppers at a mall or a teacher in a classroom, for example), many students tend to take fewer and less detailed notes. The trick is to observe as though you're seeing the situation for the first time.

Decide whether to use a tape recorder. Tape recorders are wonderful tools that can greatly assist a person who is trying to record important details. However, using a tape recorder can have drawbacks: A tape recorder is a machine, and machines can break down or fail to function properly; a tape recorder is sometimes intimidating to people who are being observed, so they alter their normal behavior; a tape recorder, especially one that requires a cord and an outlet or a change of tapes during the observation, can be a physical nuisance.

If, after considering the possible drawbacks of using a tape recorder, you still decide to use one to assist you with an observation, you will need to keep several things in mind. First, even if you use a well-functioning tape recorder during an observation, *you will still need to take notes* according to the guidelines discussed throughout this chapter. Writing your own notes is mandatory for helping you acquire a "dominant impression" of the activity or object you observe; for helping you focus on what is important to you in your particular observer's "role"; and for helping you to remember more details when you organize information and write a report.

Again, anytime you use a tape recorder during an observation, you will need to obtain permission from those being taped, practice using the taping equipment before the actual observation, and keep the recorder in as unobtrusive a place as possible during the observation.

Rewriting Your Notes. After you have done an observation, as soon as you can, you will need to take ample time to rewrite your notes, filling in gaps with any additional, relevant information that you can remember and clarifying any information that was sketchy when you first recorded it. Your revised notes should become far more extensive, more complete, and more organized and systematic than your original notes. As you write your revised notes, you not only should elaborate on and clarify

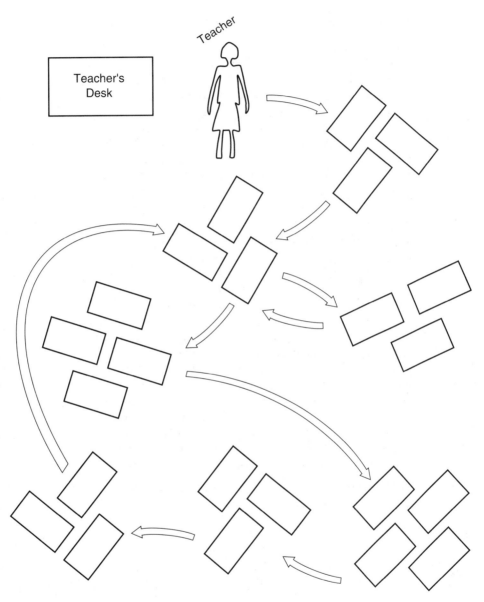

Figure 4–2.

information in your original notes, but also think carefully about the observation and decide on a "dominant impression" of the observation, if you haven't already done so. In other words, you will need to decide on a primary focus around which to construct a report.

In some instances, it is possible that one observation will not provide you with a sufficient amount of information for writing a strong report. If this is the case, and if doing a second observation is feasible, you probably will want to arrange for a second observation.

USING CLUSTERING TO ORGANIZE YOUR NOTES

Once you have taken notes from an observation, it can be challenging to discern possible organizational patterns that convey the most important information in a manner that will be accessible to others. This is because inexperienced writers often try to use a format suggested by the notes themselves rather than by the information within them. Two common patterns suggested by notes are chronological and spatial. During an observation, you must, of necessity, observe and record in a chronological time sequence; therefore, observational notes often reflect this structure. While chronological structure may be evident within a set of notes, it is not ordinarily the best way to convey information from those notes to a reader. On occasion, observation notes may be structured spatially. This happens particularly when you are observing a large object or area. For example, if you observe a room full of people, you may find it useful to divide your notes into quadrants that reflect activities within those particular areas of the room. Although convenient, organizing a report according to the way notes were taken may not reveal important trends or relationships.

Clustering is a strategy that may be of use in helping you discover useful alternatives for organizing your notes. It can help you use spatial configurations to develop your thoughts and make connections between them by providing a visual map of your ideas.

The guidelines for clustering are simple. The only materials you'll need are a few sheets of paper and, if you like to highlight differences visually, several colored pens or markers. If you decide to use clustering to discover ways of organizing the information you gathered while observing, it is best to do it *without* looking at your notes. Remember, the goal is to invent new organizational patterns so that you do not rely on the chronological or spatial order that may be reflected in your notes.

Here are several simple steps that explain how to do clustering. Accompanying each step is an illustrative example performed by Sue, an early childhood education major who has been asked to observe the play of preschool children.

1. Write the subject of your observation in the center of a sheet of paper and circle it.

   As noted, Sue was assigned to observe the play of preschool children from the perspective of an early childhood education major. Therefore, *Play* is the subject of her observation.

2. Write down topics related to your main subject as they occur to you, circling them and drawing lines that connect them to the main subject or to one another. If you first think of topics related to your main subject, your lines will resemble spokes on a wheel. On the other hand, if you keep developing one smaller topic, your lines and circles will resemble a chain.

   In most cases, though, your clustering will contain examples of both, as illustrated in the following clusters.

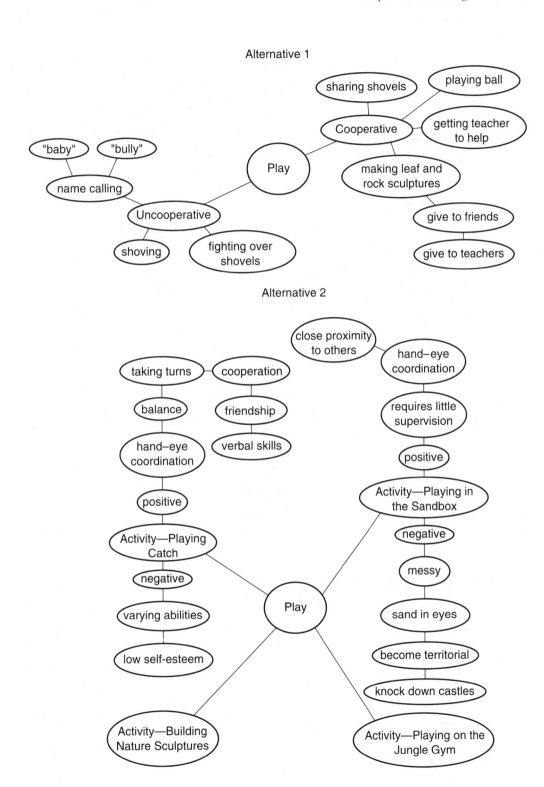

Clustering has enabled Sue to think of two possible ways of structuring her information. In the first cluster, Alternative 1, she has organized by types of behavior, *cooperative* and *uncooperative*. In the second cluster, Alternative 2, she has organized by types of activity: *Playing in the Sandbox, Playing on the Jungle Gym, Playing Catch,* and *Building Nature Sculptures.* Notice that Alternative 2, Sue's second attempt at clustering, also has suggested a number of interesting subtopics for her to explore.

3. Continue to search your memory, to develop your cluster diagram. If a new idea or train of thought strikes you, begin at the subject or from any of the subtopics and write down words radiating outward.

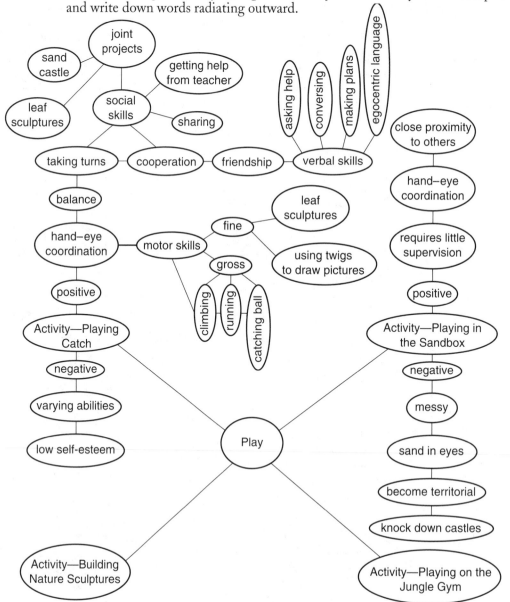

Notice that while Sue was clustering according to activity, she started to pursue several new trains of thought that led her to expand on the topics "motor skills" and "verbal skills." This in turn led her to discover a new topic, "social skills," and as a consequence, a new organizational scheme, "three important skills developed by play activities." Sue's new organizational pattern will be particularly relevant because her assigned observational role is that of a prospective early childhood educator.

Once clustering has enabled you to explore several alternate methods of structuring the information from your observation, you can select the structure that reveals important (or interesting) patterns and is most relevant to your role as observer. At this time, a review of your notes is helpful to fill in gaps and add details. On occasion, an idea from clustering may motivate you to perform an additional observation to confirm or pursue an emerging pattern, trend, or relationship.

 **Activity 5**

Earlier in this chapter (in Activity 4), you and your group practiced observing an object to recognize important details and information from different perspectives. Use the notes you generated in Activity 4 to practice clustering now. First, review your notes and your group's discussion. Then draw at least two different clusters to organize the information you have gathered. You may wish to have your group's object available for additional observation. Finally, share your clustering and organizational plans with your group members, focusing on (1) how clustering enabled each of you to see alternative ways of structuring ideas and (2) how different observer roles influenced the nature and arrangement of details.

Like brainstorming and freewriting, clustering can help you generate ideas and mine your memory. Clustering also can help you see the different patterns of meaning that can be drawn from your ideas. If you have a writing assignment that specifically tells you how to organize your paper, clustering can help you arrange ideas and information within the relevant parts. When you begin to cluster, simply write down the major topics you must discuss as a group of circles around your central subject, and write related ideas and details radiating outward. On the other hand, if your writing assignment doesn't provide you with a structure—as was the case for Sue—clustering can help you not only generate ideas but also discover ways to structure your paper. In any event, try clustering several times. Like most writing techniques, it is most useful when you practice it several times.

OBSERVING ASSIGNMENTS

Select one of the following activities and perform the suggested observation. To prepare for each, be sure to articulate a perspective from which you will conduct your observation. You may approach an assignment from the point of view of a prospective major who is interested in learning about a possible future career, or you may adopt the perspective of someone who's interested in observing a person or process relevant to summer employment. For example, you may be able to observe the food operation within a restaurant where you'd like to work. If you haven't decided on a major or don't wish to investigate employment opportunities, use this assignment to pursue an interest or to explore something about which you are curious.

After you have conducted your observation, write up detailed notes and cluster these notes. Then compose a brief paragraph outlining a possible organizing principle and come up with subtopics you might use to structure a report if you were required to submit one. Alternatively, you can make a list of questions and attendant details that you would ask or look for if you were to conduct a second observation.

1. Observe a teacher instruct a class in which you are *not* enrolled. You may perform this individually or with your group partners. If you and your group choose this option, each of you should observe from a different perspective or for a different purpose (e.g., from the perspective of a parent of a student in class who is having difficulty, a future teacher preparing for student teaching, or a principal observing a new teacher). Afterwards, compare the results of your observations.

2. Observe an aspect of group behavior. Here are some possibilities: children on a playground taking turns, sharing, or name calling; players in an intramural game exhibiting competitive or cooperative behavior; or people standing in line talking to one another, cutting in front of one another, or ignoring one another. If you and your group partners select this option, observe the same behavior from different perspectives or for different purposes and compare the results.

3. A location or place often influences behavior because of stated (or unstated) rules of conduct or because it projects a certain atmosphere. Select a place and observe an aspect of people's behavior within it, focusing your attention on the ways in which the place modifies that behavior. Here are some suggestions: people arriving, leaving, or conversing within a place of worship; students talking, taking notes, or exhibiting behavior that indicates attention (or lack of it) within a large lecture hall (again, use a class in which you are *not* enrolled); or shoppers strolling, conversing, and examining goods within a mall. If you and your group choose this option, be sure to select the same place to observe and compare your findings.

4. Observe a professional doing his or her work "live" in a real setting (in other words, no films or TV recordings). Here are some examples: a science professor in her laboratory; a psychology professor conducting an experiment with human subjects; a lawyer arguing a case; a director conducting a rehearsal; an actor or musician performing; a city council person during a meeting; or a cook or baker in a restaurant, kitchen, or bakery.

5. Observe an intricate object, a large structure, or a collection of objects. You may observe the thing with regard to a particular feature. Some ideas: the ornamentation on one or several buildings; the arrangements of a particular product (or

products) in a place of business; a bridge; a portion of a highway, such as an overpass; the glass collection (or a portion of it) in an art gallery; or a photographic exhibit.

READINGS

Pirsig, Robert. "Nothing to Say," from *Zen and the Art of Motorcycle Maintenance.* New York: William Morrow & Co., 1974, pp. 170–172.

1. Initially, the student Pirsig describes can't think of five hundred words to write about the United States. Describe a similar experience when you felt unable to say or write anything about a topic that was familiar to you.

2. Why did Pirsig switch the student's topic from the "United States" to "Bozeman" to "the main street of Bozeman"?

3. Why did writing about the first brick and then the second and then the third help this student find something to say?

4. What does Pirsig mean by "seeing directly" for yourself? Why is seeing directly so important for writers?

Scudder, Samuel H. "Take This Fish and Look at It."

1. What role do you suppose Scudder's teacher, Professor Agassiz, was expecting Scudder to assume when he asked him to observe the fish? How significant is knowing this role as you note the kind of details that Scudder reports to his professor?

2. What strategies does Scudder use during the process of observation? In what ways are these various strategies effective?

3. In the last sentence of the essay, Scudder states that his observation of the fish was "of greater value than years of later investigations in [his] favorite groups." Why does he value this particular observation activity so highly?

Tio, Adrian. "On Observation."

1. In his essay, Adrian Tio, a professor and practicing artist, says that graphic artists must represent "a three-dimensional image . . . on a two-dimensional surface." How do the observation techniques he describes facilitate this process?

2. In crafting a drawing, an artist must select a portion of what he or she sees to represent. How do the observation techniques Tio offers assist with the process of selection and focus?

Geertz, Clifford. "The Fight," from "Deep Play: Notes on the Balinese Cockfight."

1. Elsewhere in the essay from which this excerpt is taken, Geertz reports that the colonial government had made cockfighting illegal, perhaps because of the

gambling associated with it and because of concern for treatment of the fighting cocks. In "The Fight," what kind of tone does Geertz adopt toward the practice of cockfighting? Does he write about it negatively, as a barbaric activity, for example? Or more positively, as an honored ancient tradition? Or more neutrally, as a phenomenon that he objectively records? Is his tone consistent throughout this excerpt, or does it change? Find specific passages to support your findings. How does Geertz's tone help shape your attitude toward the practice of cockfighting?

2. Throughout his chronological description of typical cockfights, Geertz presents readers with background information necessary to understand the meaning various aspects of cockfights have for the Balinese people. In addition, Geertz uses and defines a variety of Balinese terms (*sehet, pengangkeb*). How do these two strategies strengthen Geertz's authoritativeness?

3. Despite the short length of "The Fight," Geertz manages to include a great many details. Comment upon the nature and type of these details. What kinds of sensory details are included? Do they provide measurements? To what extent do the details allow readers to imagine a typical fight?

 ## Nothing to Say*

Robert Pirsig

He'd been innovating extensively. He'd been having trouble with students who had nothing to say. At first he thought it was laziness but later it became apparent that it wasn't. They just couldn't think of anything to say.

One of them, a girl with strong-lensed glasses, wanted to write a five-hundred-word essay about the United States. He was used to the sinking feeling that comes from statements like this, and suggested without disparagement that she narrow it down to just Bozeman.

When the paper came due she didn't have it and was quite upset. She had tried and tried but she just couldn't think of anything to say.

He had already discussed her with her previous instructors and they'd confirmed his impressions of her. She was very serious, disciplined and hardworking, but extremely dull. Not a spark of creativity in her anywhere. Her eyes, behind the thick-lensed glasses, were the eyes of a drudge. She wasn't bluffing him, she really couldn't think of anything to say, and was upset by her inability to do as she was told.

It just stumped him. Now *he* couldn't think of anything to say. A silence occurred, and then a peculiar answer: "Narrow it down to the *main street* of Bozeman." It was a stroke of insight.

*Text from pp. 170–172 of *Zen and the Art of Motorcycle Maintenance* by Robert Pirsig. Copyright © 1974 by Robert Pirsig. By permission of William Morrow & Company, Inc.

Nothing to Say *(cont'd.)*

She nodded dutifully and went out. But just before her next class she came back in *real* distress, tears this time, distress that had obviously been there for a long time. She still couldn't think of anything to say, and couldn't understand why, if she couldn't think of anything about *all* of Bozeman, she should be able to think of something about just one street.

He was furious. "You're not *looking*!" he said. A memory came back of his own dismissal from the University for having *too much* to say. For every fact there is an *infinity* of hypotheses. The more you *look* the more you *see*. She really wasn't looking and yet somehow didn't understand this.

He told her angrily, "Narrow it down to the *front* of *one* building on the main street of Bozeman. The Opera House. Start with the upper left-hand brick."

Her eyes, behind the thick-lensed glasses, opened wide.

She came in the next class with a puzzled look and handed him a five-thousand-word essay on the front of the Opera House on the main street of Bozeman, Montana. "I sat in the hamburger stand across the street," she said, "and started writing about the first brick, and the second brick, and then by the third brick it all started to come and I couldn't stop. They thought I was crazy, and they kept kidding me, but here it all is. I don't understand it."

Neither did he, but on long walks through the streets of town he thought about it and concluded she was evidently stopped with the same kind of blockage that had paralyzed him on his first day of teaching. She was blocked because she was trying to repeat, in her writing, things she had already heard, just as on the first day he had tried to repeat things he had already decided to say. She couldn't think of anything to write about Bozeman because she couldn't recall anything she had heard worth repeating. She was strangely unaware that she could look and see freshly for herself, as she wrote, without primary regard for what had been said before. The narrowing down to one brick destroyed the blockage because it was so obvious she *had* to do some original and direct seeing.

He experimented further. In one class he had everyone write all hour about the back of his thumb. Everyone gave him funny looks at the beginning of the hour, but everyone did it, and there wasn't a single complaint about "nothing to say."

 ## Take This Fish and Look At It

Samuel H. Scudder

It was more than fifteen years ago that I entered the laboratory of Professor Agassiz, and told him I had enrolled my name in the Scientific School as a student of natural

Take This Fish and Look At It *(cont'd.)*

history. He asked me a few questions about my object in coming, my antecedents generally, the mode in which I afterwards proposed to use the knowledge I might acquire, and, finally, whether I wished to study any special branch. To the latter I replied that, while I wished to be well grounded in all departments of zoology, I purposed to devote myself specially to insects.

"When do you wish to begin?" he asked.

"Now," I replied.

This seemed to please him, and with an energetic "Very well!" he reached from a shelf a huge jar of specimens in yellow alcohol. "Take this fish," he said, "and look at it; we call it a haemulon; by and by I will ask what you have seen."

With that he left me, but in a moment returned with explicit instructions as to the care of the object entrusted to me.

"No man is fit to be a naturalist," said he, "who does not know how to take care of specimens."

I was to keep the fish before me in a tin tray, and occasionally moisten the surface with alcohol from the jar, always taking care to replace the stopper tightly. Those were not the days of ground-glass stoppers and elegantly shaped exhibition jars; all the old students will recall the huge neckless glass bottles with their leaky, wax-besmeared corks, half eaten by insects, and begrimed with cellar dust. Entomology was a cleaner science than ichthyology, but the example of the Professor, who had unhesitatingly plunged to the bottom of the jar to produce the fish, was infectious; and though this alcohol had a "very ancient and fishlike smell," I really dared not show any aversion within these sacred precincts, and treated the alcohol as though it were pure water. Still I was conscious of a passing feeling of disappointment, for gazing at a fish did not commend itself to an ardent entomologist. My friends at home, too, were annoyed when they discovered that no amount of eau-de-Cologne would drown the perfume which haunted me like a shadow.

In ten minutes I had seen all that could be seen in that fish, and started in search of the Professor—who had, however, left the Musem; and when I returned, after lingering over some of the odd animals stored in the upper apartment, my specimen was dry all over. I dashed the fluid over the fish as if to resuscitate the beast from a fainting fit, and looked with anxiety for a return of the normal sloppy appearance. This little excitement over, nothing was to be done but to return to a steadfast gaze at my mute companion. Half an hour passed—an hour—another hour; the fish began to look loathsome. I turned it over and around; looked it in the face—ghastly; from behind, beneath, above, sideways, at three-quarters' view—just as ghastly. I was in despair; at an early hour I concluded that lunch was necessary; so, with infinite relief, the fish was carefully replaced in the jar, and for an hour I was free.

On my return, I learned that Professor Agassiz had been at the Museum, but had gone, and would not return for several hours. My fellow-students were too busy to be disturbed by continued conversation. Slowly I drew forth that hideous fish, and with a feeling of desperation again looked at it. I might not use a magnifying-

---

Take This Fish and Look At It *(cont'd.)*

glass; instruments of all kinds were interdicted. My two hands, my two eyes, and the fish: it seemed a most limited field. I pushed my finger down its throat to feel how sharp the teeth were. I began to count the scales in the different rows, until I was convinced that was nonsense. At last a happy thought struck me—I would draw the fish; and now with surprise I began to discover new features in the creature. Just then the Professor returned.

"That is right," said he; "a pencil is one of the best of eyes. I am glad to notice, too, that you keep your specimen wet, and your bottle corked."

With these encouraging words, he added: "Well, what is it like?"

He listened attentively to my brief rehearsal of the structure of parts whose names were still unknown to me: the fringed gill-arches and movable operculum; the pores of the head, fleshy lips and lidless eyes; the lateral line, the spinous fins and forked tail; the compressed and arched body. When I finished, he waited as if expecting more, and then, with an air of disappointment:

"You have not looked very carefully; why," he continued more earnestly, "you haven't even seen one of the most conspicuous features of the animal, which is plainly before your eyes as the fish itself; look again, look again!" and he left me to my misery.

I was piqued; I was mortified. Still more of that wretched fish! But now I set myself to my task with a will, and discovered one new thing after another, until I saw how just the Professor's criticism had been. The afternoon passed quickly; and when, towards its close, the Professor inquired:

"Do you see it yet?"

"No," I replied, "I am certain I do not, but I see how little I saw before."

"That is next best," said he, earnestly, "but I won't hear you now; put away your fish and go home; perhaps you will be ready with a better answer in the morning. I will examine you before you look at the fish."

This was disconcerting. Not only must I think of my fish all night, studying, without the object before me, what this unknown but most visible feature might be; but also, without reviewing my discoveries, I must give an exact account of them the next day. I had a bad memory; so I walked home by Charles River in a distracted state, with my two perplexities.

The cordial greeting from the Professor the next morning was reassuring; here was a man who seemed to be quite as anxious as I that I should see for myself what he saw.

"Do you perhaps mean," I asked, "that the fish has symmetrical sides with paired organs?"

His thoroughly pleased "Of course! of course!" repaid the wakeful hours of the previous night. After he had discoursed most happily and enthusiastically—as he always did—upon the importance of this point, I ventured to ask what I should do next.

"Oh, look at your fish!" he said, and left me again to my own devices. In a little more than an hour he returned, and heard my new catalogue.

Take This Fish and Look At It *(cont'd.)*

"That is good, that is good!" he repeated; "but that is not all; go on"; and so for three long days he placed that fish before my eyes, forbidding me to look at anything else, or to use any artificial aid. "Look, look, look," was his repeated injunction.

This was the best entomological lesson I ever had—a lesson whose influence has extended to the details of every subsequent study; a legacy the Professor had left to me, as he has left it to so many others, of inestimable value, which we could not buy, with which we cannot part.

A year afterward, some of us were amusing ourselves with chalking outlandish beasts on the Museum blackboard. We drew prancing starfishes; frogs in mortal combat; hydra-headed worms; stately crawfishes, standing on their tails, bearing aloft umbrellas; and grotesque fishes with gaping mouths and staring eyes. The Professor came in shortly after, and was as amused as any at our experiments. He looked at the fishes.

"Haemulons, every one of them," he said; "Mr. ―――― drew them."

True; and to this day, if I attempt a fish, I can draw nothing but haemulons.

The fourth day, a second fish of the same group was placed beside the first, and I was bidden to point out the resemblances and differences between the two; another and another followed, until the entire family lay before me, and a whole legion of jars covered the table and surrounding shelves; the odor had become a pleasant perfume; and even now, the sight of an old, six-inch worm-eaten cork brings fragrant memories.

The whole group of haemulons was thus brought in review; and, whether engaged upon the dissection of the internal organs, the preparation and examination of the bony framework, or the description of the various parts, Agassiz's training in the method of observing facts and their orderly arrangement was ever accompanied by the urgent exhortation not to be content with them.

"Facts are stupid things," he would say, "until brought into connection with some general law."

At the end of eight months, it was almost with reluctance that I left these friends and turned to insects; but what I had gained by this outside experience has been of greater value than years of later investigation in my favorite groups.

 ## On Observation

Adrian Tio

Artists make full use of all their senses during the creative process. To a visual artist such as a painter or graphic designer, no sense is more critical than sight.

On Observation *(cont'd.)*

Through extensive training and constant practice, a visual artist learns to observe his or her environment with greater clarity, observing the visual relationships of not only objects, but colors, shapes, forms and textures. These elements of art are the basic building blocks that the artist utilizes to visually represent to the viewer a three-dimensional image observed by the artist, and recreated with marking tools on a two-dimensional surface. Observation is the key to solving this creative task.

When most people are asked to hold a hand in front of them and describe what they see, the usual response is, ". . . my hand." Ask artists what they see, and they will mention the hand and then begin to describe the spaces between the fingers. Similarly, most individuals think a landscape is painted or drawn the way it is seen, with priority given to people, buildings, animals, and trees. The sky and ground are usually mentioned as an afterthought if at all. But to an artist, the order is reversed. Let's imagine drawing a typical northwestern Ohio landscape together to discover how an artist observes our world.

For our visual journey we'll be using a modest sketchpad of white paper, say 18″ × 24″, and charcoal in stick and pencil form. We'll also use plastic and kneaded erasers to create textures and change values as needed. Let us assume that we are in Grand Rapids, Ohio, sitting on the bank of the mighty Maumee River. Behind us lies a picturesque nineteenth-century river town situated on the rapids just below a WPA-era dam. Before us lies the river, over half a mile wide at this point. Behind the river stands the Ludwig Mill, operational since the early 1800s. Surrounded by tall trees with broad leaves, the mill is perched between the river and a section of the old Erie Canal still in use today. On our left, an old rail bridge straddles the river, another remnant of the town's shipping and trading past. On the right, our view is blocked by a more contemporary concrete auto bridge, often clogged with tourists on the weekend. Our task is to draw this scene in a manner that will encourage others to come visit and see Grand Rapids for themselves.

Our first step is to visualize the rectangular format of the drawing pad as the viewfinder of a camera and to sight our composition. To do this, we might find it helpful to cup our hands together in the shape of an oval and look through the opening at the surrounding landscape. This will enable us to find an interesting composition without being overwhelmed by the sheer scale of our subject. At this point, we also consider whether we want a vertical or horizontal composition, and hold the sketchpad accordingly.

Now, holding the charcoal pencil lightly, we quickly draw a horizontal line that extends off the sides of the page. This line represents the horizon line, where we think the sky and land meet behind the buildings and trees. Next, we add quick vertical and diagonal lines that indicate where the mill and trees are located, adding the bridges, as well, if we are including them. At this point, we stop and break off half an inch of the narrow vine charcoal stick and—without worrying about objects or details—we gray in those areas of the page that do not need the white of the paper to show through. Since we are looking at a complex arrangement of

On Observation *(cont'd.)*

structures that are in color and are being affected by the position of the sun, we can be messy. We aren't afraid to use the palm of our hand and our fingers to rub the charcoal over the surface of the paper. As a rule, the more expressive artists are at this stage, the more likely they will be able to recreate a scene.

The next stage is to begin darkening in larger areas of the page in relation to the scene before us. Again, it's important to be suggestive rather than analytical. We're still discovering the shape arrangements on the page that will represent the various natural and manmade forms without worrying about detail. We treat these values of gray as if we were seeing the landscape on a black-and-white television set, saving the details for last, along with the darkest values. At this point, we are not afraid to make mistakes because vine charcoal has a weak binder in it that makes erasing easy. If we wish to erase, we use the plastic rather than the kneaded eraser; it will do less damage to the surface of the paper.

Our composition now looks as if the scene before us were drawn in a fog. Objects can be located, but without much clarity. So we switch, now, to the harder compressed charcoal stick and begin to further darken in those areas that are in shade. In contrast, areas lit by the sun are left as light as possible. Again we use one of our erasers to lighten specific areas. The plastic eraser cleans best, but the kneaded eraser can be used to gently lighten values without erasing the surface entirely.

As our drawing emerges from those early marks and smears, we continue to compare our page with the scene we are depicting. Since we do not see details in the distance, areas such as the sky and distant trees and land shapes can be left in a more sketchy state, usually in vine charcoal alone. The greatest contrasts in value (light to dark) are in those areas nearest us. This is where we'll now add those details necessary to create the clarity of texture needed to convince the viewer of what he or she is seeing. We notice, with pleasure, how effective some of those early vine charcoal smears now appear in comparison to the whole composition.

Once we have a somewhat completed sketch, we are ready to critically examine our work in comparison to the actual scene before us. As we view the entire drawing, we make those changes necessary to create a better representation of the subject, being careful to compare the whole composition with the entire landscape. Rather than worrying about accuracy, we compare our initial impression of the landscape with our drawing and with our scene. Although there is a great deal to be seen in nature, we can only focus our attention on one small area at a time—and so will the viewer when observing our completed artwork.

As we contemplate our finished product, we need to remind ourselves of an important fact. We really haven't drawn a landscape; we've actually arranged values and textures of charcoal on a paper surface in such a way that viewers are reminded of a similar scene that they've seen at another time.

The Fight*

Clifford Geertz

Cockfights (*tetadjen; sabungan*) are held in a ring about fifty feet square. Usually they begin toward late afternoon and run three or four hours until sunset. About nine or ten separate matches (*sehet*) comprise a program. Each match is precisely like the others in general pattern: there is no main match, no connection between individual matches, no variation in their format, and each is arranged on a completely ad hoc basis. After a fight has ended and the emotional debris is cleaned away—the bets have been paid, the curses cursed, the carcasses possessed—seven, eight, perhaps even a dozen men slip negligently into the ring with a cock and seek to find there a logical opponent for it. This process, which rarely takes less than ten minutes, and often a good deal longer, is conducted in a very subdued, oblique, even dissembling manner. Those not immediately involved give it at best but disguised, sidelong attention; those who, embarrassedly, are, attempt to pretend somehow that the whole thing is not really happening.

A match made, the other hopefuls retire with the same deliberate indifference, and the selected cocks have their spurs (*tadji*) affixed—razor-sharp, pointed steel swords, four or five inches long. This is a delicate job which only a small proportion of men, a half-dozen or so in most villages, know how to do properly. The man who attaches the spurs also provides them, and if the rooster he assists wins, its owner awards him the spur-leg of the victim. The spurs are affixed by winding a long length of string around the foot of the spur and the leg of the cock. For reasons I shall come to presently, it is done somewhat differently from case to case, and is an obsessively deliberate affair. The lore about spurs is extensive—they are sharpened only at eclipses and the dark of the moon, should be kept out of the sight of women, and so forth. And they are handled, both in use and out, with the same curious combination of fussiness and sensuality the Balinese direct toward ritual objects generally.

The spurs affixed, the two cocks are placed by their handlers (who may or may not be their owners) facing one another in the center of the ring.[9] A coconut

---

*From "Notes on the Balinese Cockfight," reprinted by permission of *Daedalus*, Journal of the American Academy of Arts and Sciences, from the issue entitled, "Myth, Symbol, and Culture," Winter 1972, Volume 101, Number 1.

[9]Except for unimportant, small-bet fights (on the question of fight "importance," see below) spur affixing is usually done by someone other than the owner. Whether the owner handles his own cock or not more or less depends on how skilled he is at it, a consideration whose importance is again relative to the importance of the fight. When spur affixers and cock handlers are someone other than the owner, they are almost always a quite close relative—a brother or cousin—or a very intimate friend of his. They are thus almost extensions of his personality, as the fact that all three will refer to the cock as "mine," say "I" fought So-and-So, and so on, demonstrates. Also, owner-handler-affixer triads tend to be fairly fixed, though individuals may participate in several and often exchange roles within a given one.

The Fight *(cont'd.)*

pierced with a small hole is placed in a pail of water, in which it takes about twenty-one seconds to sink, a period known as a *tjeng* and marked at beginning and end by the beating of a slit gong. During these twenty-one seconds the handlers (*pengangkeb*) are not permitted to touch their roosters. If, as sometimes happens, the animals have not fought during this time, they are picked up, fluffed, pulled, prodded, and otherwise insulted, and put back in the center of the ring and the process begins again. Sometimes they refuse to fight at all, or one keeps running away, in which case they are imprisoned together under a wicker cage, which usually gets them engaged.

Most of the time, in any case, the cocks fly almost immediately at one another in a wing-beating, head-thrusting, leg-kicking explosion of animal fury so pure, so absolute, and in its own way so beautiful, as to be almost abstract, a Platonic concept of hate. Within moments one or the other drives home a solid blow with his spur. The handler whose cock has delivered the blow immediately picks it up so that it will not get a return blow, for if he does not the match is likely to end in a mutually mortal tie as the two birds wildly hack each other to pieces. This is particularly true if, as often happens, the spur sticks in its victim's body, for then the aggressor is at the mercy of his wounded foe.

With the birds again in the hands of their handlers, the coconut is now sunk three times after which the cock which has landed the blow must be set down to show that he is firm, a fact he demonstrates by wandering idly around the ring for a coconut sink. The coconut is then sunk twice more and the fight must recommence.

During this interval, slightly over two minutes, the handler of the wounded cock has been working frantically over it, like a trainer patching a mauled boxer between rounds, to get it in shape for a last, desperate try for victory. He blows in its mouth, putting the whole chicken head in his own mouth and sucking and blowing, fluffs it, stuffs its wounds with various sorts of medicines, and generally tries anything he can think of to arouse the last ounce of spirit which may be hidden somewhere within it. By the time he is forced to put it back down he is usually drenched in chicken blood, but, as in prize fighting, a good handler is worth his weight in gold. Some of them can virtually make the dead walk, at least long enough for the second and final round.

In the climactic battle (if there is one; sometimes the wounded cock simply expires in the handler's hands or immediately as it is placed down again), the cock who landed the first blow usually proceeds to finish off his weakened opponent. But this is far from an inevitable outcome, for if a cock can walk, he can fight, and if he can fight, he can kill, and what counts is which cock expires first. If the wounded one can get a stab in and stagger on until the other drops, he is the official winner, even if he himself topples over an instant later.

Surrounding all this melodrama—which the crowd packed tight around the ring follows in near silence, moving their bodies in kinesthetic sympathy with the movement of the animals, cheering their champions on with wordless hand motions, shiftings of the shoulders, turnings of the head, failing back en masse as the cock with

The Fight *(cont'd.)*

the murderous spurs careens toward one side of the ring (it is said that spectators sometimes lose eyes and fingers from being too attentive), surging forward again as they glance off toward another—is a vast body of extraordinarily elaborate and precisely detailed rules.

These rules, together with the developed lore of cocks and cockfighting which accompanies them, are written down in palm-leaf manuscripts (*lontar; rontal*) passed on from generation to generation as part of the general legal and cultural tradition of the villages. At a fight, the umpire (*saja komong; djuru kembar*)—the man who manages the coconut—is in charge of their application and his authority is absolute. I have never seen an umpire's judgment questioned on any subject, even by the more despondent losers, nor have I ever heard, even in private, a charge of unfairness directed against one, or, for that matter, complaints about umpires in general. Only exceptionally well trusted, solid, and, given the complexity of the code, knowledgeable citizens perform this job, and in fact men will bring their cocks only to fights presided over by such men. It is also the umpire to whom accusations of cheating, which, though rare in the extreme, occasionally arise, are referred; and it is he who in the not infrequent cases where the cocks expire virtually together decides which (if either, for, though the Balinese do not care for such an outcome, there can be ties) went first. Likened to a judge, a king, a priest, and a policeman, he is all of these, and under his assured direction the animal passion of the fight proceeds within the civic certainty of the law. In the dozens of cockfights I saw in Bali, I never once saw an altercation about rules. Indeed, I never saw an open altercation, other than those between cocks, at all.

This crosswise doubleness of an event which, taken as a fact of nature, is rage untrammeled and, taken as a fact of culture, is form perfected, defines the cockfight as a sociological entity. A cockfight is what, searching for a name for something not vertebrate enough to be called a group and not structureless enough to be called a crowd, Erving Goffman has called a "focused gathering"—a set of persons engrossed in a common flow of activity and relating to one another in terms of that flow.[10] Such gatherings meet and disperse; the participants in them fluctuate; the activity that focuses them is discrete—a particulate process that reoccurs rather than a continuous one that endures. They take their form from the situation that evokes them, the floor on which they are placed, as Goffman puts it; but it is a form, and an articulate one, nonetheless. For the situation, the floor is itself created, in jury deliberations, surgical operations, block meetings, sit-ins, cockfights, by the cultural preoccupations—here, as we shall see, the celebration of status rivalry—which not only specify the focus but, assembling actors and arranging scenery, bring it actually into being.

In classical times (that is to say, prior to the Dutch invasion of 1908), when there were no bureaucrats around to improve popular morality, the staging of a cockfight was an explicitly societal matter. Bringing a cock to an important fight

[10]E. Goffman, *Encounters: Two Studies in the Sociology of Interaction* (Indianapolis, 1961), pp. 9–10.

The Fight *(cont'd.)*

was, for an adult male, a compulsory duty of citizenship; taxation of fights, which were usually held on market day, was a major source of public revenue; patronage of the art was a stated responsibility of princes; and the cock ring, or *wantilan,* stood in the center of the village near those other monuments of Balinese civility—the council house, the origin temple, the marketplace, the signal tower, and the banyan tree. Today, a few special occasions aside, the newer rectitude makes so open a statement of the connection between the excitements of collective life and those of blood sport impossible, but, less directly expressed, the connection itself remains intimate and intact. . . .

CHAPTER 5

REPORTING

INTRODUCTION

In this chapter, we continue the sequence started in Chapter 4 by discussing reporting, a type of writing based on an observation. You may have heard library research papers, essays about books, or short papers referred to as "reports." We are using the word *report* in a particular sense, defining it more narrowly as "a written paper that is based primarily on a writer's observations." Undoubtedly, you have been making reports based on observations for most of your life. You probably made verbal reports as a child to your parent or to your teacher that were based on your observation of your sibling's or a classmate's misbehavior (and perhaps you were called a tattletale, too). Your friends may have asked you for a report—"What happened?"—after you were sent to the principal's office. In any of these circumstances, you were making a report based on your observations.

Reports may be written for a variety of reasons. Primarily, they are written to share the results of one or more observations with an audience, in order to inform or educate them or to bring about a change in attitude or policy. For example, specialized books and magazines are readily available at libraries and bookstores with advice—based on observations—about buying computer hardware and software, stereo systems, and new or used cars. Reports may also be written to persuade a group of readers to hold a particular point of view on an important or controversial issue. If there is a proposal to build a nuclear waste incinerator in your community, a watchdog group might write a report based on observations of the environmental impact of similar incinerators in other communities. In some fields, such as journalism, reporting serves the additional aim of creating an historical or legal record.

Whatever their purpose, reports are often written as part of a professional's duties. Social workers, doctors and nurses, engineers, and other professionals are called on to observe a particular person, object, or situation; report their findings; and make a recommendation. In the sciences, reporting has a special function, as well. When scientists write lab reports, they record the methods and materials they used and the results they observed so that others can replicate their findings.

What subjects are reports written about? The subject of a writer's observations largely depends on the purpose of the observation and how the written report will be used by readers. News reports are written about events to describe actions that have occurred or are predicted to occur. Many lab reports describe phenomena that have been observed in an experiment, or compare what actually happened with what a theory predicted. Reports may be written about a group's or an individual's performance, as when a principal visits a teacher's classroom. Reports can also be written about an object or set of objects, as with consumer magazine reports that compare several brands of a similar product and make recommendations about their performance. Similarly, reports can be written about a process or series of related events, such as registration at your university or the procedure by which a city council enacts a new ordinance.

Given the variety of professionals who write reports, there are also many types of reports: journalists' news accounts, medical reports, chemistry lab reports, manufacturing process reports, and so on. Despite their variety, however, observation reports share several features. They are informative and are usually developed with detailed descriptions. They can draw on a variety of sources for their information, although the major source is observation. As a result, effective reports appear authoritative, in part because of the self-presentation, or *ethos*, of the author. Finally, reports usually reveal how the information they present was collected. That is, a routine section of a lab report is a discussion of the materials and methods used in the experiment.

When you are assigned to write observation reports, your teachers will have a particular purpose in mind. They may be using a report to assess how careful an observer you are and determine whether you are learning to observe in the conventional ways of a particular discipline. They may also want to familiarize you with a report format common in your field.

SAMPLE ASSIGNMENTS

Because of the diverse instructional functions that reports serve, many of your college instructors will require you to produce written reports based, at least in part, on observation. However, features will vary depending on factors such as the purpose of your report, your teacher's expectations, and disciplinary or professional conventions. Some reports may require rigid formats including, for example, sections that contain detailed, precise descriptions of the method by which the observations were conducted. Others may require technical information or specialized terminology (jargon).

The following assignments are examples of commonly assigned reports. Before you examine them, you may wish to review the observation assignments in the Sample Assignments section of Chapter 4, because many of these also require written reports.

Journalism Assignment. Using the information you have acquired in this class about observing, note taking, and interviewing, you will write three 1-page reports that focus on a single session of our journalism class. You may report on any class session that is held within the next three weeks. For one of the reports, you should take the stance of an objective observer, writing from your own perspective only; for another report, you should interview either instructor (Mr. Rosen or me), thereby allowing you to base the report on an instructor's perspective; for the final report, you should interview several students in the class, thereby allowing you to base the report on their perspectives. The paper you submit should conclude with a two- or three-page discussion of what you have learned about the nature of reporting as a result of completing this exercise.

Environmental Studies Assignment. The two ponds located on campus (one between the Student Recreation Center and the Music Building and the other just south of Darrow Hall) will be examined throughout the semester. Chemical, biological, and microbiological measurements will be made to determine the quality of each pond, possible pollution sources, possible uses of the water, and differences between the systems. A key objective of the laboratory component of this course is to develop an understanding of the dynamics of these two ponds during the fall season.

Six procedures have been set up. Student groups will have two weeks to conduct each procedure on both ponds. In addition to making the designated measurements, groups must pay careful attention to quality assurance, preparation of standards, and proper disposal of waste chemicals. It is the responsibility of each student to read and understand the laboratory instructions before the laboratory period. All work is to be recorded in a laboratory notebook. Before a procedure is complete, data must be entered in the laboratory computer. Every two weeks a laboratory report will be due (on the Tuesday following completion of the laboratory procedure), detailing the techniques and results of a particular measurement in the laboratory notebook. Each report should include summaries of results, final concentrations, and a discussion of the significance and applications of the findings.

Assignments for Biology. All laboratory reports written for this class are to be presented in the following sequence and format. (No deviations from this strict, standard format will be allowed.)

I. *Abstract.* An abstract is a brief summary of the report that relates purpose, methods, results, and implications. An example of an abstract appears on page 5 in the lab manual that accompanies this course.

II. *Introduction.* The introduction should provide an overview of the whole report, including the purpose of the study, hypotheses (if any), a review of any historical information, and a justification for the study.

III. *Materials and methods.* This section should include an explanation (in paragraph form rather than a list) of procedures; instrumentation and equipment; and places, dates, and times (when relevant).

IV. *Results.* This section should present the information learned and the facts discovered in the study. Data should be presented in tabular or graphical format with an accompanying description in the text. Often statistical comparisons and illustrations may be called for.

V. *Discussion.* This section consists of an interpretation of the results in relation to the experimental objectives or hypothesis. In a report encompassing experimental design, the results section should be brief and the discussion longer to explain the results. In labs observing habitats or behavior, results should be descriptive and generally more elaborate.

VI. *References.* Books, articles, or other sources referred to in the report should be documented using the CBE format, which is thoroughly covered in the textbook for this course.

As the assignments in this and the preceding chapter show, reports based on observation vary considerably. Nevertheless, observation reports share several features. Thus, when you are assigned to write a report based on an observation, your paper should show the following:

1. Specific, carefully selected details

2. An appropriate, authoritative self-presentation (or *ethos*)

3. An organization or structure that presents information from the observation, as well as the method by which it was gathered, in a clear, accessible manner

4. Format, documentation, and conventions appropriate to the profession or discipline.

REPORTING INFORMATION

While you undoubtedly have been making informal oral reports based on observations for most of your life, there are differences involved in writing more formal ones. Most especially, written reports should provide clear, explicit information for readers and follow formats or styles with which readers are familiar. In short, written reports need to be informative. Thus, reports are a type of writing that emphasizes the *subject* being written about or the *information* being reported, not the writer's feelings, the audience being addressed, or the language itself.

Because the primary purpose of reports is to inform readers, there are certain areas that writers need to think about as they plan and write. Reports will not be informative unless they present information in an easily accessible manner for readers. Therefore, reports should be readable and clear. Likewise, reports should emphasize "facts," and the information reported in them should appear credible. Finally, part of making a report appear believable rests on the way in which readers perceive the writer. People may not trust information from unreliable sources. When you write a report, you must present yourself as a credible source of information. There are, then, three primary areas for you to consider in writing observation reports: making information appear authoritative, making information accessible to readers, and presenting yourself effectively in your report.

Making Information Appear Authoritative

Two particular writing strategies are especially relevant for writing authoritative observation reports: using specific details and using supplemental materials.

Using Details. The use of detail is important in enhancing the authoritativeness of a report because details can lend a factual, immediate quality to a text. Although many types of details are useful to the report writer, sensory details, especially visual ones, are most effective because they enable readers to imaginatively experience aspects of an observation. In the following excerpt, notice how the details writers Barry J. Drucker and Dan W. Knox use offer readers a coherent sense of the physical characteristics of "The Blob":

> The tissue, which the ME had earlier removed from the glass jug, was now in four pieces, and it reeked of vinegar. The veterinarian observed that it was composed of two main parts: the largest appeared to be a seven-pound muscle-like mass which fit in the palms of two cupped hands, and which contained internal cavities. The other piece was longer, with small ridges, and it resembled a tongue or a tentacle.

Using images that are familiar and evocative, the descriptive details inform readers of how the blob smelled ("it reeked of vinegar"), its size ("the largest . . . fit in the palms of two cupped hands"), its shape ("resembled a tongue or a tentacle"), and its composition ("muscle-like mass"; "with small ridges").

Along with sensory details, factual information (such as specific times and dates or proper names) enhances the authoritative nature of observation reports. A passage claiming that you observed "several groups of children at a local day-care center for about one week" does not create the same impression as one reporting that you observed "five different play groups of three to five youngsters at Laffore's Day Care from March 1 through March 10." Precise measurements ("1.5 kilohertz" or "ten feet") and other factual information such as price ("$234.95 retail"), number counts ("twelve different brands of high-fiber cereal") also give the impression that an observation was conducted carefully. It is, of course, important when providing measurements and factual information to inform readers whether such data is exact ("the distance was six feet three inches") or approximate ("I stood about eight or nine feet from the group I observed").

Another means of including detail that can be appropriate for some reports is a narrative passage. Narrative passages enable a writer to recreate important events with precision, in the way that a zoom lens enables a photographer to give film viewers a vivid, close encounter. In the following passage from Elisabeth Rosenthal's "Burning Down the House," notice that the narrative involves readers with the text and creates the impression that the speaker is directly observing events in the emergency room:

> "It's in," I said, withdrawing the syringe.

> "Good," she answered in a voice that was raspy and barely audible. Uh-oh.

"Is that how you normally speak?" I asked.

"No," she answered with difficulty. "I started to get hoarse in the waiting room." It was obvious that the swelling that had started on her skin had now moved down to her vocal cords.

Notice also that the direct quotes provide readers with details about an allergic reaction, which can progress rapidly and become life threatening.

Although details are always important in report writing, which to select and how to present them depends on factors such as the purpose of the report, disciplinary writing conventions, and readers' expectations. Some conventions discourage the use of dialogue in reports, because doing so gives too much prominence to individual human actors rather than to the events or objects being observed. Whether precise or approximate measurements are appropriate, how persons should be designated ("Mary Jones"; "the female subject"; or "the woman who witnessed the accident"), and the nature of description ("shaped like a loaf of bread" or "rectangular with rounded corners") are also determined by conventions, audience, and purpose.

Using Supplemental Materials. Another way to make information authoritative in an observational report is to use supplemental materials. In many reports, supplemental materials—tables, line graphs, bar graphs, charts, illustrations, photographs, artwork, audiotapes, videotapes—complement written texts by visually highlighting the data discussed.

Supplemental materials usually take time to design. Therefore, as a general guideline, you should create supplemental material that will help illustrate your information effectively. If, for example, you wrote a report based on the various behaviors you observed in an elevator in your university library, you might record those behaviors on a chart and include a copy of it, with your tally marks neatly filled in (see Figure 5–1). If you preferred, you could illustrate the same information in the form of a bar graph or a line graph (see Figures 5–2 and 5–3). Depending on the focus of your report, another possibility might be a sketch of the elevator floor, showing where people tended to stand, which direction they tended to look, and so on. Keep in mind that supplemental materials present a great deal of important information for the reader. Therefore, you should never simply include supplemental material in a report; you should also discuss it in the body of the report.

Often, you can prepare supplemental materials easily by yourself, as in the case of sketches or simple tally sheets. On the other hand, if you want a more formal or precise look, use a computer spreadsheet program, which can create graphs and charts. (Your college Computer Services Office is a good place to ask for help.) Finally, the discipline in which you are writing the report may have special requirements regarding supplemental materials, which may be discussed in your textbook or within the assignment itself.

After you have created supplemental material, you will need to decide where to include it in your report: *after* the section of text that discusses it; *before;* or in a separate *appendix* at the end of the report. Different disciplines or instructors will have

Elevator Behavior in a University Library												
Behaviors — Subjects Being Observed												
	1	2	3	4	5	6	7	8	9	10	11	12
Standing away from others	X		X	X	X	X						
Invading others' "personal space"		X										
Leaning against side of elevator	X	X				X						
Eating (Banana)	X											
Reading						X						
Initiating conversation (list examples)												
1. To man with banana		X										
2. About weather				X	X							
3.												
4.												
5.												
6.												
Making eye contact			X		X	X						
Avoiding eye contact	X					X						
Standing near the door				X	X							
Standing in the back			X									
Fidgeting	X											
Looking at ceiling												
Looking at other people			X	X								

Figure 5–1. A chart for recording elevator behavior.

their own preferences regarding the placement of supplemental material. If you include more than one type of supplemental material in your appendix, you should label each separately as *Appendix A, Appendix B, Appendix C,* and so on.

Making Information Accessible to Readers

In addition to appearing authoritative, effective informative discourse should be "reader-friendly"; it should not be unnecessarily complex or difficult to follow for its intended audience. One of the best means of making reports accessible is to use disciplinary or professional conventions, which help writers decide such matters as how to structure a text, how much background information to provide, and when to use specialized terminology.

Conventions. Think of the last time you asked someone for directions. You probably heard something like this: "Go two traffic lights and turn left at the Sunoco

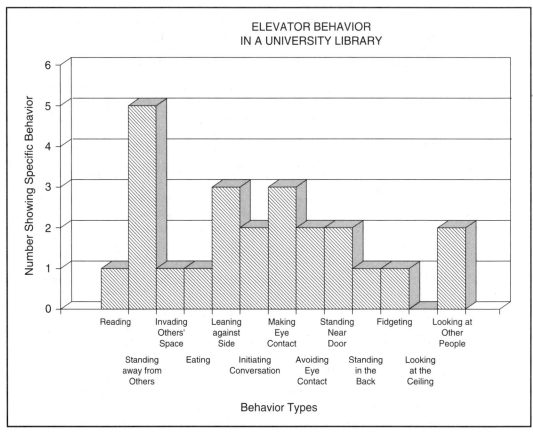

Figure 5–2. A bar graph reporting elevator behavior.

Station. You'll be on Kramer Road. Stay on Kramer for about three miles or about five minutes, then. . . ." To relate directions, most people use landmarks ("traffic lights" "Sunoco Station"), estimate time or distance ("two traffic lights," "about three miles," and "about five minutes"), describe actions chronologically, and use the imperative ("turn left"; "Stay on Kramer"). Yet the "usual" way of imparting directions isn't the only way to do so. Direction givers could, for example, start with a question: "How much time or gas have you got?" They could also relate events in a more "expository" format: "Basically, there are three main parts to your trip. The first involves getting to a neighborhood called Bakerstown; the second involves getting to Main Street; the third. . . ." Although the conventional format for direction giving isn't the best or only way to give directions, the fact that so many direction givers use it suggests that it helps listeners retrieve information from their memories.

When particular ways of presenting ideas and information are used repeatedly—for whatever reason—people come to expect them, and eventually these practices become codified, or *conventionalized*. As you might imagine, there are

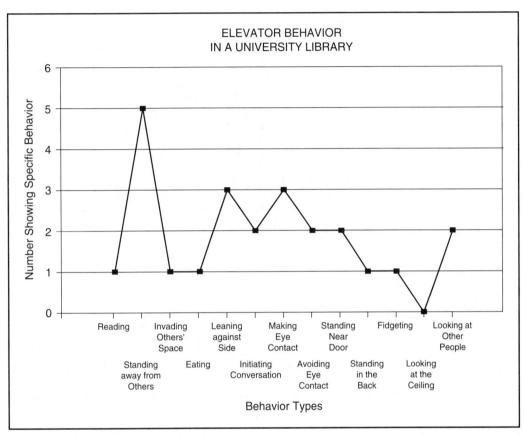

Figure 5–3. A line graph reporting elevator behavior.

numerous conventions about writing, including report writing, which can influence a range of features such as organization, sentence structure, and word selection.

Although conventions play an important part in informative writing, they are not easy to learn because all disciplines and professions use a variety of different ones. In addition, although professional organizations and publications produce style sheets or offer guidelines that specify particular conventions regarding documentation (e.g., use of footnotes or endnotes) or format, many conventions are not stated explicitly. The passive voice, for example, is expected in some disciplines and discouraged in others. Thus whether "Two play groups were observed on four separate occasions" (passive voice) is or is not preferable to "We observed two play groups on four separate occasions" (active voice) must be determined by the writer, based on his or her knowledge of what is appropriate.

In general, when crafting reports, writers must consider what they can expect readers to know, what sort of content is or is not appropriate, and what tone and level of formality is suitable. In addition, the sentence length and complexity; point of view; amount and nature of background information; use of tables, charts, and graphs; appropriateness of humor; and a variety of issues related to usage, such as whether contractions are permissible, are examples of aspects of writing that are, at least in part, determined by conventions.

Because part of becoming proficient within a discipline or profession is learning to communicate appropriately, many of your instructors will, undoubtedly, familiarize you with writing conventions. When assigning observation reports, for example, they may provide detailed instructions about format, point of view, word use, and so forth. However, teachers and textbooks are limited in their ability to acquaint you with *all* of the appropriate conventions within a particular profession or discipline, particularly those that aren't stated explicitly. Therefore, once you have determined your particular interests, you should begin to read as much professional writing within your major as possible. Reading will help you learn many conventions that are not obvious or easy to define and will assist you in becoming a confident, fluent writer in your field.

 **Activity 1**

---

1. With your group, select and photocopy five different articles from professional or scholarly journals. Your articles should reflect a variety of disciplines; at least one article should represent a social science, one a science, and one an art or humanity. Also select and photocopy one article from a popular magazine devoted to a particular discipline, such as *Discover, Omni, Psychology Today, Scientific American,* or *Smithsonian.*

2. Read all six articles. (You may wish to make copies for each group member.) As you read, pay attention to matters governed by convention: point of view, format, sentence length and complexity, supplemental materials, and so forth.

3. Together with your group members, discuss the features you discovered in the articles. Do any articles follow a fixed format? Which use specialized terminology? Is any terminology defined? Do any use dialogue or direct quotes?

4. As a group, prepare a brief report of your findings (a table comparing the articles, a written report, or both). What different textual features did you find? For the disciplines represented by your articles, can you generalize about conventions that govern formality, the presence of the writer in the text, and other features you examined?

Although conventions about how to prepare a report vary from discipline to discipline, we can generalize about several important aspects of report writing. These are structure, background information, and specialized terminology.

Structure. A carefully wrought structure can help make information accessible to a reader, particularly if the information is complex and multifaceted. However, the best way to structure a report isn't always obvious. Hence, inexperienced writers often organize reports chronologically, reflecting the order in which events occurred during an observation. Here is one such example:

> *On October 23, I observed Ms. Croft's English 9 class from 10:00–10:55 AM. The lesson for that morning was on improving stylistic fluency.*
>
> *Ms. Croft began class by taking attendance and making announcements. Next, she distributed an information sheet while students took out paper. To begin the discussion of style, Ms. Croft told the class to read and compare two paragraphs that she projected onto a screen with the overhead projector. "What differences do you see between these two passages?" she asked. When no one volunteered the answer, she asked everyone to jot down differences and provided a specific example of several.*
>
> *After several minutes, she asked the class the same question. This time seven people raised their hands. First, Ms. Croft called on a young woman who . . . . Next, a young man explained that . . . .*

Although organizing a report chronologically to reflect the structure of an observation ("First this happened"; "then this happened," etc.) may be convenient for the writer, it is not necessarily the best way to fully disclose information or make it accessible to a reader. Often, during an observation, many significant events occur simultaneously. Chronological ordering makes it difficult—if not impossible—to report these simultaneous occurrences with any sort of coherence. In addition, organizing a report chronologically may obscure significant patterns or trends.

Unless a particular format is specified by disciplinary or professional conventions, the structure of a report based on an observation should reflect significant aspects or features of that observation. Let us suppose, for instance, that Ms. Croft, the teacher in the previous example, employed writing in her class in several different ways. A prospective teacher observing her class, might consider this use of writing to be the most innovative aspect of the class and structure the report to reflect that finding:

> *On Friday, October 23, I observed Ms. Croft's English 9 class from 10:00–10:55 A.M. The lesson for that morning was on improving stylistic fluency. In general, Ms. Croft maintained a high level of interest in the class. Students contributed to class frequently, responding to one another and to Ms. Croft. Although Ms. Croft moved around the room, used the chalkboard and overhead projector, and maintained good eye contact, I believe that her innovative use of writing was what motivated students to participate. During class, Ms. Croft used writing in three different ways to stimulate discussion.*
>
> *First, in several instances, Ms. Croft used writing to stimulate discussion when students were unable (or unwilling) to respond to questions. Soon after class began, to initiate a discussion of style, Ms. Croft told her students to read and compare two paragraphs that she projected onto a screen with an overhead projector. "What differences do you see . . . ."*
>
> *Second, Ms. Croft also used writing to . . . .*

Notice how the structure in this example permits the presentation of detail and accurate chronology, while at the same time enabling the reader to understand an important pattern that the writer observed. Well-crafted observation reports, then, present information in a way that reveals important trends and patterns.

Although we have suggested that structuring a report requires a writer to carefully examine the results of an observation for trends or patterns, some disciplines, particularly the sciences and social sciences, prescribe very specific methods of investigation as well as the overall structure, or format, of a research report. If you have written laboratory reports in science classes, you have had experience with a conventional report format, probably with headings or separate sections for explaining the **purpose** of the experiment, describing the **method** or procedures used, reporting the **results** attained (including measurements, observations, calculations or data analysis), and ending with a **discussion** of the results. Regardless of whether a discipline or profession requires a conventionalized format, however, organizing a text to facilitate readers' comprehension of information is always the writer's responsibility.

Two conventional aspects of structuring reports can help writers make reports accessible to readers: headings and metadiscourse. Headings, whether a prescribed part of a conventional format or a formatting decision made by a writer, help make information accessible by allowing readers to anticipate the function and contents of various portions of a text. Notice how the following headings, taken from different reports, suggest both function and content as well as the order or placement of the sections of text they might introduce:

A Brief Overview of Elevator Behavior

A Close-Up of One Play Group

Phase One

Suggestions for Future Study

As with overall structure, the appropriateness of headings is determined by convention.

In addition to headings, metadiscourse can also enhance the impact of an effective structure by providing readers with a kind of road map to assist them as they move through a text. Passages that make sequencing and content explicit enable readers to anticipate overall structure as well as to place the portion of text that they are reading into a larger context: "This report is organized into four parts. Part One will offer a description of the physical conditions of the playground at Rogers Day Care . . . . Part Two will . . . ." In conjunction with such passages, coherence can be strengthened with phrases that reiterate "where" the reader is and phrases that summarize content ("Once the observation was completed, the tape recording was transcribed and the notes were analyzed to reveal significant trends. The analysis revealed three patterns of behavior, which will be referred to as . . . .").

❧ Activity 2

Reexamine the six articles you and your group gathered for Activity 1. This time compare how each was structured. Which articles seemed to use conventional formats? What overall or global means of structuring can you discover? Underline metadiscourse and circle headings.

Next, discuss your findings with your group. What overall conclusions can you draw, if any? For example, which articles employ headings or metadiscourse most often? How do the articles begin or end? What patterns do you see according to discipline, if any? Prepare a brief report (1 to 2 pages) of your findings. As before, you may present your results in writing, in a table, or both.

Background Information. Another important way to make reports accessible to readers is by providing background information. You can consider background information to be any information provided in a report that is not part of the observations being reported. Generally, background information is found in observation reports for two reasons. It may be provided to educate or inform general readers so that they can appreciate the significance of the observations being reported. Second, background information may be given to enable expert or professional readers to place the particular observations within a larger field of related ongoing research. While it is somewhat unusual, observation reports may contain both kinds of background information if they are addressed to general *and* specialized readerships.

Frequently, reports directed toward a general readership contain background information to explain why readers should attend to a particular observation. In this excerpt from *Failing at Fairness*, Myra and David Sadker provide background information to explain the significance of the gender bias they have observed in school:

> In elementary school, receiving attention from the teacher is enormously important for a student's achievement and self-esteem. Later in life, in the working world, the salary received is important, and the salary levels parallel the classroom: white males at the top and minority females at the bottom.

Such information is important, given that their book is directed to the general public, who might dismiss a school teacher's gender bias as unimportant.

When reports are directed toward experts or professionals in a particular field or discipline, background information serves to frame the observations for that readership. You may have seen scientific research studies that include a section called **Review of the Literature**. The information provided there is background information about other published studies similar to the one being reported. This section helps establish the credibility of the writer, by showing that he or she is knowledgeable about current work on the same topic. This section also shows other researchers how the present study is related to research in the field.

In "The Blob: Investigating the Abnormal," authors Barry J. Drucker and Dan W. Knox provide a lengthy section of background information that explains what happens when wine sours:

> In nature, wine is spoiled, or converted to sugar, generally by mixed cultures of acetic acid bacteria, which can oxidize ethanol to acetic acid. Members of the family *Acetobacteraceae*, these consist of two genera, *Gluconobacter* and *Acetobacter*. . . .

This section, from which the above excerpt was taken, explains the biological process by which "The Blob" was produced, scientific information of interest to readers of this article, published in the *Journal of Environmental Health*. In addition, this section uses references—the numbers listed in parentheses—to relate the growth of "The Blob" to current scientific knowledge in previous research studies.

One of the decisions you will face in writing observation reports, then, is when to use background information, and how much to use. In making such decisions, you should consider who your readers will be, what knowledge you can assume them to have about the subject, and what they need to know in order to understand the significance of your observations.

 **Activity 3**

Reread the articles your group selected in Activity 1, looking for examples of background information. In which articles is background information provided to make the subject understandable to general readers? Locate specific instances. In which articles is background information also provided to relate the subject to ongoing research or work by other professionals? Find examples. How much background information is there? A small part of an article, or a significant part of it? Estimate percentages for each article. Where is the background information located? Throughout the article in several snippets? Or primarily in one part of the article, under a heading like **Review of the Literature**? Be prepared to make a brief report to your class of your findings

---

Specialized Terminology. In writing observation reports, you also need to consider your selection of vocabulary, because an important part of making information accessible to readers is the words you use. In reporting observations, precision is necessary, both to communicate effectively to your readers and to create an authoritative impression of yourself as an observer. In reporting an eyewitness account of a car accident, for example, the phrase "a blue car" is much less informative than the phrase "a powder-blue '67 Mustang."

A more important area for you to consider, however, is how to use specialized terminology. Whenever people live or work together, they develop a shared vocabulary to refer to situations, objects, or processes they face again and again. You may have observed particular slang expressions used on your campus to refer to the student health center or to special campus events or traditions. In the same way, people who work together in the same discipline or profession develop a specialized vocabulary called *jargon*.

Jargon serves particular purposes for professionals. A verbal shorthand, it enables writers and readers to work efficiently by using a word like *carburetor* rather than a lengthy descriptive phrase such as "the long-ish black thing somewhere under the hood." Jargon also gives professionals the vocabulary they need to talk about the specialized kinds of work they do. While most people know words such as *noun*, *verb*, and *sentence*, linguists have a more detailed jargon, such as *phonology*, *syntax*, and *morphology*, which enables them to study specialized aspects of language. Professional jargon enables its users to refer precisely to aspects of their work with the assurance that other professionals will understand their exact meaning.

This does not mean that you should always use jargon when writing an observation report or any other writing in your college courses. Part of learning jargon is, in fact, learning *how* to use it—that is, when to use it, when to define it, and when to avoid using it. In making such decisions, you should consider the needs of the people who will be reading your writing. For example, if you are addressing a group of writing teachers, you probably can use a term like *thesis statement* without needing to define it. However, if you were helping a young child with his or her English paper, you would need either to explain the term or avoid using it. When some or all of your readers will be unfamiliar with specialized terms that you must use, you need to define them. Generally, terms that are central to the subject of the report should be defined in detail. On the other hand, terms that are more peripheral can be defined more briefly.

There are several ways of defining terms. You can often provide a brief definition within a sentence, using commas, dashes, italics, quotes, or parentheses to set off the definition or the term. Elisabeth Rosenthal provides such a definition of the term *histamine* in her article "Burning Down the House":

> Cells called mast cells release powerful chemical messengers—histamines—that pour into the bloodstream and cause smooth muscle to contract and blood vessels to open wide and become leaky.

On the same page, she uses a brief phrase to define *Hydrocortisone:* ". . . I began to order medicines: Hydrocortisone, a steroid to reduce further inflammation . . ." In both examples, brief definitions suffice to inform general readers of *Discover* magazine about what these two terms are, since neither is central to understanding what happens during an allergic reaction.

In contrast to how these peripheral terms might be defined, however, more important terms need longer or more formal definitions that provide more detailed explanations. Longer definitions are most important when readers must understand a particular concept in order to understand or appreciate the observations being reported. In "Burning Down the House," Rosenthal provides a somewhat detailed definition of the most common and most important drug used to treat anaphylaxis (a technical term for an allergic reaction):

> But the most crucial drug was to be injected under the skin: .3 cc's of epinephrine. Epinephrine is another name for adrenaline, the "fight or flight" hormone that can also counteract many of the dangerous effects histamine has throughout the body; it raises blood pressure, relaxes spasms in the airways, and quiets the stomach and bowel. It also puts great stress on the heart. . . .

Note that Rosenthal provides such a detailed definition of epinephrine because it is "the most crucial" drug used to treat Meg's allergic reaction, and is thus important to understanding what anaphylaxis is and how it is treated.

 **Activity 4**

Use the articles your group selected in Activity 1. As a group, reread the articles for examples of specialized terminology. Make a list for each article of specialized terms that are used but *not* defined and specialized terms that *are* defined. Based on your findings, what inferences can you draw about the intended readers? Would the definitions provide help to any other readers? Why or why not?

Presenting Yourself Effectively in Your Report

In addition to making a report authoritative and accessible, the image of yourself that you construct within your writing, or *ethos*, is also important. When you recount the results of an observation, readers should be confident of your accuracy and trust your ability as an observer. Readers should believe you capable of noting significant details and patterns.

Constructing an Effective Ethos. More than two thousand years ago Aristotle, a Greek philosopher and educator, wrote a treatise called *Rhetoric*, in which he explained how to address the public. Aristotle said that it was important for a speaker "to construct a view of himself as a certain kind of person" if he was to be persuasive to his audience. Specifically, he argued that audiences trusted three qualities in an orator's presented self: practical wisdom, virtue, and good will.

Since Aristotle's time, subsequent books about how to speak and write have discussed ethos in terms of the qualities he identified, often referring to them as *good sense*, *good will*, and *good character*. Good sense has to do with a self-presentation that emphasizes the speaker's or writer's ability to make sensible, reasonable judgments. Good character suggests that the speaker or writer is an ethical person, someone who can be trusted. Finally, good will implies that the writer or speaker has the audience's best interests at heart and is offering beneficial advice or information.

An ethos that projects good sense is very important in an observation report. For such a report to be credible, readers must believe that the author used good judgment in conducting the observation as well as in writing about it. Because readers of reports rarely know authors personally, the writer's good sense must be established within the text. An important way of doing so is to provide background information, such as clear explanations of the procedures used to conduct the observation, and detailed descriptions of decisions made.

Knowing how much and what kind of background information to provide, though, is not a clear-cut matter. In reporting an observation of a chef preparing a complex meal, for example, you would appear foolish if you described in detail how the burners and oven were ignited. Of course, as a novice writing a report for a disciplinary or professional context, you may not have sufficient expertise to distinguish the significant from the superfluous. In addition, your instructor may be more knowledgeable about both your observation and related professional literature than you are. Under such circumstances, you should realize that although you cannot demonstrate the same level of expertise as your teacher, you can still create the impression that you worked diligently to make careful, intelligent decisions when you conducted your observation by fully explaining the basis of those decisions.

Also important in creating an effective ethos is good character, which has to do with the projection of honesty or trustworthiness. In observation reports, this quality is essential, because most readers assume that writers who possess good character observe what they record accurately and don't fabricate data. People of good character strive to overcome personal bias and, thus, do not exaggerate findings or ignore data—even data that is unanticipated or conflicts with their personal beliefs.

As with good judgment, you cannot assume that readers will ascribe to you such qualities as honesty and trustworthiness; these traits must be projected as a part of your ethos. When you write observational reports, avoid biased, judgmental language (such as "her disgusting behavior" or "his bizarre practices") in order to show that you are attempting to be fair and impartial. Also, provide justifications for assumptions that govern your observation and your reporting ("I chose to elaborate on the interaction within this play group because it is representative of the other four that I observed in several ways . . . ."). This implies that you have operated in a manner that is thoughtful and governed by principle rather than by unexamined biases.

To create an effective ethos in an observation report, you need to know about conventions related to four factors: (1) the extent to which the writer should be present in the text; (2) the extent to which observations should be mediated by the observer's opinion; (3) the proper distance between reader and writer; and (4) a suitable tone. These factors are important and vary with respect to a particular discipline or profession.

Because the focus of informative writing is on information, a writer's presence within such a text is usually minimized. In fact, within some disciplines the *overt* presence of the author, expressed by the use of the first person (*I/we*), suggests bias and lack of objectivity. For this reason, the conventions associated with report writing often discourage the use of the first person and promote, instead, the use of the third person (e.g., *he, she, they, the observer,* or *the researcher*).

Along with the third-person point of view, the passive voice can also remove the writer from a text, as can turning a subject-verb combination (*I examined*) into a noun that denotes the action expressed by the verb (*examination* revealed that). In each of the examples below, notice how point of view, active versus passive voice, and the manner in which action is expressed controls the extent to which the writer is overtly present:

First-Person Point of View

I inoculated three solutions with the virus.

Third-Person Point of View

The experimenter inoculated three solutions with the virus.

Active

I observed the children for three days.

Passive

The children were observed for three days.

Subject–Verb

I examined the paintings carefully and noted this pattern.

Verb into Noun

A careful examination of the paintings yielded this pattern.

Stylistic options such as these allow writers to control the extent to which they are present in a text. However, as the Readings section of this chapter demonstrates, conventions regarding authorial presence vary across disciplines. Therefore, when assigned to write an observation report, you should consult your instructor or appropriate models of similar writings before drafting.

The extent to which a writer should describe an observation as factual and unmediated by his or her perceptions, biases, or life experiences is also an important factor in report writing. While the difference between "Their behavior *was* aggressive" and "Their behavior *appeared* aggressive" may seem minimal, one statement presents the writer's perception as fact and the other suggests interpretation by means of the word *appeared*. Verbs such as *appeared* or *seemed* lessen the certainty of what is being reported as do words such as *perhaps*.

Depending on the disciplinary or professional context, explicit interpretations ("I felt that they exhibited aggressive behavior" or "My interpretation was that their behavior was, in fact, aggressive") or expressions of uncertainty ("I was unable to determine whether their behavior was aggressive or merely hyperactive" or "I began to wonder if my position as an observer would enable me to accurately assess what I was seeing") may be discouraged or highly desirable.

Finally, tone and distance between writer and audience are important considerations in report writing. Tone has to do with the feel or mood that a piece of writing projects. Ordinarily, readers don't notice the tone of reports because these are written to present information, not to entertain or to create aesthetically pleasing effects. For this reason, reports of unpleasant events and circumstances (earthquakes, homelessness) are often presented in a dry, dispassionate manner, and expressions of judgment or condemnation are avoided. In "Missing in Interaction," for example, note how the authors of *Failing at Fairness* report observations of teachers silencing their female students; they do so without expressing indignation or making judgments about the character or competence of these instructors. As with other conventions associated with report writing, however, what is considered an appropriate tone can vary. Although humor is ordinarily not associated with report writing, you will notice that "The Blob," a report published in *The Journal of Environmental Health*, is both informative and entertaining.

The neutral, impersonal tone characteristic of many reports is both enhanced by and helps maintain distance between the writer and reader. Unlike expressive or even persuasive writing, which often creates an intimacy between writers and their audiences, informative writing ordinarily separates these parties. This distancing is accomplished in several ways. Observation reports are usually written in a semiformal style; they are rarely informal or colloquial. Readers are not appealed to or directly addressed with the pronoun *you*. Inflammatory language is avoided. Regardless of the emotions an observation may inspire in the writer (elation, disgust, or indignation), results are presented in a dispassionate—distancing—manner. Of course, some reports are crafted not only to inform readers but also to move them to some action. Under these circumstances, conventions that govern distance may vary. An environmentalist reporting her observation of a rapidly deteriorating wetland may well try to move her readers to identify with her and her values more closely in an effort to inspire them to act.

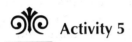 **Activity 5**

Together with your group, select three of the journal articles that you examined for Activities 1–4; one should be from the popular magazine (*Discover, Psychology Today,* etc.). Compare the articles in terms of (1) the tone, (2) the distance between the audience and writer, (3) the presence or absence of the writer, and (4) the extent to which information is presented as fact or is mediated by the writer's opinion. What generalizations, if any, can you offer about disciplinary or professional conventions? How do conventions associated with these four areas differ for the article that is addressed to a more general readership? Be prepared for one or several members of your group to deliver a brief oral report of your findings to the class.

 **Activity 6**

Using the same journal articles that you chose for Activity 5, your group must select several short (200-word) passages that enhance the writer's credibility through a skillful self-presentation or ethos. Together, analyze each passage, examining word choice, tone, point of view, and so forth, to show how the ethos was created. Then select one passage and rewrite it (as a group) to diminish the writer's credibility. You might, for example, replace specific detail and precise terminology with vague, general words or content, or you might add inappropriate judgments about information in the passage.

Responsibilities toward Your Readers and Your Subject. If you construct an effective ethos or self-presentation, your readers will perceive you as a trustworthy source and thus feel that your observations are factual. That is, when you use conventions to construct a credible, authoritative ethos as a reporter, readers are likely to believe what you tell them. In writing observation reports, you are engaging in a kind of writing in which you have a particular responsibility to be fair toward the subject you are writing about and to be a credible source for the information you are providing.

As you might expect, writing observation reports can cause conflicts between your sense of responsibility to your observation subject and the constraints of existing conventions. Both students and professionals face such conflicts, and may face pressure to ignore them. In the sciences, for example, researchers can be pressured to falsify data or draw unreliable conclusions in order to maintain economic support for their research. Because reports are perceived as factual, research findings from them are used to influence decisions about people's lives and about the environment. Thus, in many fields professionals recognize their responsibilities toward their subjects. It is customary for research universities, for example, to have a faculty committee review and approve research proposed by faculty that involves human beings.

Such measures work in a variety of settings to ensure some minimal standards for the ethical treatment of people who participate in research studies. However, they do not ensure that people seriously consider how their *writing* influences their readers' impressions of the people, events, or objects that are written about. That is, while research methods themselves are regulated in some form or another, the language in which research reports are written is not. Yet the language used in research reports does help form readers' impressions of the research subjects.

In writing observation reports, writers ordinarily must use the specialized terminology of a particular field. As a consequence, they may refer to the people they observed—whom they know as Johnny or Mrs. B.—as "the participants" or "the subject." They may use a phrase like "sensori-motor skills" to refer to the abilities young children displayed as they built a sand sculpture, or the word *decentering* to refer to the pain Billy seemed to feel when his best friend was stung by a bee. Such specialized terminology frequently does not convey the richness or fullness of observed experience, nor does it adequately reflect the feelings or point of view of the people observed. Worse yet, such specialized terminology can seem to turn a real human being into an object—"Caucasian female, aged twenty-five...."

Because language usage within an observation report can shape the perceptions of readers, it is important to choose descriptive words carefully, and to ensure that they have connotations appropriate for the behavior actually observed. For example, in a playground observation, you may report that one child "shoved" another. This word choice implies that one child was deliberately pushing another. Yet if one child was losing her balance and pushed against someone else nearby to keep herself from falling, using the word *shoved* would misrepresent the situation and the child's action.

As well, when you are writing a draft, you should be exact and explicit about the observations you report. Your readers will form impressions about the people, objects, or events you report based not on their own observations, but on your writing. Thus you should carefully distinguish what you actually observed from assessments or inferences that you are making. There is a big difference between reporting that "Kevin touched Jacob on the cheek" and reporting that "Kevin was pretending to shave Jacob's face" or "Kevin was aggressive toward other children." The latter statements are inferences or conclusions, which should be clearly indicated as such with qualifying statements like "It appeared that Kevin was pretending to shave Jacob's face" or "I felt Kevin was aggressive toward other children." Usually, inferences like these should also be supported with additional explanations or details.

Whatever care you take to present your observations precisely and to state them in a responsible manner, you may face conflicts. It may not always be possible, for example, to add a phrase like "I felt" to qualify a statement, particularly if the conventions of your field or discipline obligate you to write an "objective" report and to omit first-person pronouns or value judgments. You may sense conflicts between the conventional expectations of your field or of your teacher and your own obligations to be truthful, honest, or fair to your readers or to the people, places, or events you are reporting about. If such conflicts arise, you will need to determine the best means to resolve them. You can consult with your teacher about the assignment, explaining your reservations and soliciting advice for ways to resolve them. Or, perhaps you could supplement your report with photographs, audiotapes, or videotapes, which could give readers a closer look for themselves at the phenomena you observed. You may also be able to enlarge your own observation by interviewing the people you observed; doing so may enable you to include their own views or their own words in your report. You should realize that an important part of learning to work as a professional in any field is learning how to negotiate such issues as these.

 **Activity 7**

> With your group members, choose one of the writing assignments from the Sample Assignments section of this chapter and select a real or imaginary person, event, or object as your observation subject. What responsibilities would you have toward your subject? Would conflicts be likely to arise between your responsibilities and the expectations of the teacher or field involved? What, if any, jargon would you be expected to use? How might jargon affect readers' perceptions of your subject?

WRITING AN OBSERVATION REPORT

Using the Pentad to Determine a Focus

Like any other type of college writing, observation reports require a specific focus or purpose, which may or may not be explicitly stated within an assignment. Assignments may be quite vague, asking you to "observe" a particular object, person, or event and then "write up the results." Some—for example a laboratory report for an introductory biology class—may provide you with the purpose of the experiment and a rigid format for your writing to follow. In contrast, most report assignments will reflect a middle ground, offering guidance about focusing and organizing your report, but not providing a ready-made purpose and structure. Despite such specifics, we believe that it is best to use clustering or some other prewriting along with your observation notes to plan a draft. Even if provided with a focus for a report, you can use clustering to determine how details are related to one another and to assist you in distinguishing significant details from unimportant or superfluous ones.

In writing observation reports, you may need to manipulate and integrate a great deal of information during the course of report writing. Another useful inventing and organizing tool is the Pentad, which was developed by Kenneth Burke. It is a set of questions similar to those that journalists use:

What happened?

Where/When did it happen?

Who caused it to happen?

Why did it happen?

How did it happen?

The Pentad, or set of journalistic questions, is a powerful means of generating information because taken together, the questions cover all matters related to an event, a series of actions, or the results of these. To see how the Pentad might help you integrate information and discover patterns, let us suppose that you and one other person in your group decide to do a report assignment that involves observing a teacher. Let us also suppose that you choose to observe from the perspective of a future teacher preparing for student teaching. After recording observations of an hour-long class, you would undoubtedly have several pages of notes, with details about what the teacher said, questions she asked, student responses, and so forth.

To pull together different aspects of your notes, you could, for example, focus on a particular question, such as *What* happened? Under this question, you could list all of the responses students gave in class; you might even begin to subcategorize these in different ways: verbal responses, facial expressions, gestures and other body language, and positive responses versus negative responses. Once you had gathered together information by asking, *What* happened? you might further examine that data by asking the question? *Who* caused it to happen? Asking *why* in conjunction with *what* might help you to suggest a tentative explanation for various responses:

> *The class engaged only a few students because of the types of questions asked and the lack of eye contact on the part of the teacher.*

These explanations could be used to craft a thesis or focus for your report.

The Pentad might also help you to see other patterns if you emphasize different questions. Focusing on the question, *Where* did it happen? would require you to list the characteristics of the classroom (size, seating, arrangement of seats, etc.). Pairing *where* with *who* could reveal a relationship you might not have noticed—for example, how the physical setting of the classroom (whether seats are movable or fixed or arranged in tiers) can cause teachers to behave in a particular way (to lecture, to be open to questions, or to listen to student responses). Finally, to help generate background information for your readers, the Pentad can't be surpassed. For example, responding to *Where/When* did it happen? can help you recall details about the location and duration of the observation.

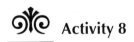 **Activity 8**

Use the Pentad with the notes from the observation you conducted at the end of Chapter 4. First, use all five questions to organize your notes and to generate additional information. Next, pair questions to generate new focuses. For example, if you feel the time or place influenced your observation, you might focus on the question, *What* happened? and pair that with the question, *Where/When* did it happen? Finally, use all or several of the questions to generate background information that will be useful to your readers.

Structuring Your Report

As you work to determine a focus or controlling idea for your report, simultaneously you will make decisions about content. Observation reports ordinarily contain four main types of content: details from the observation, background information, explanation of the procedures used, and discussion or interpretation of the results of the observation. Structuring these types of content requires careful planning, even for a report in a discipline that prescribes a rigid structure.

Because the main purpose of a report is to inform or to educate readers, your task as a writer is to structure details from the observation to best accommodate your readers. In general, readers have difficulty accessing information that is presented in the same order as that of the original notes, as the first example of an observation report of Ms. Croft's class (page 123) reveals. A different kind of structure will be best for your readers, a structure that will allow you to make points and offer interpretations about the information you are presenting. Again notice how the revised version of the observation (page 123)—organized around the three ways Ms. Croft used writing in her class—arranges the information in an accessible way for readers.

In coming up with a controlling idea and overall structure for your report, then, examine your notes and consider other ways that the material could be organized. As you decide how to structure your information, you also will find ideas for topic sentences to provide readers with a "map" to move them easily from one category to another as they read your report.

Even if your report contains sufficient details about the observation, it will probably also need background information; the exact amount will depend on the familiarity you believe your intended audience has with the topic. In addition to deciding how much background information to include, you will need to carefully consider where to place it. One method is to place all or most background information in the introductory section, in order to provide readers with information that will prove useful as they read subsequent sections of the report. On the other hand, background information can be placed near the end of a report, after the observation has been discussed, to help explain the results.

You should know, though, that placing most of your background information at either the beginning or at the end of your report may not be the best way to hold your readers' interest. Very often, report writers provide background information at regular intervals throughout the entire piece of writing, accompanying their discussions with appropriate background information as they address specific issues. If you examine "Burning Down the House" by Elisabeth Rosenthal, you will see that large chunks of background information about anaphylaxis appear in several places throughout the report. As you work on structuring your own report, you might experiment by placing background information in various places; doing so will help you determine the most effective location for this data in your report.

Another important component of observation reports is a discussion of the procedures used in the observation. Depending on the discipline, this section may be a minimal, moderate, or significant part of the report. As discussed previously in this chapter, report assignments, particularly those in the sciences, may require a prescribed set of procedures and a detailed explanation of them. If you are writing such reports, you won't have to worry about where to place certain pieces of information because their appropriate placement already has been determined for you. However, it is important to include *all* information relevant to your procedures. As you plan your structure for scientific reports or other reports with prescribed formats, it is wise to write extensive notes on each step in the prescribed procedure and then check off portions of your notes as you include them in your draft.

Many observation report assignments will not prescribe a format, however, and you will have to decide how much explanation to provide about procedures used and where to place this explanation. For reports of observations that used methodical or scientific procedures, a separate **Procedures or Methods** section may be necessary. On the other hand, some other kind of structure may be more appropriate for other types of procedures. When you read "The Blob" by Barry J. Drucker and Dan W. Knox, you will see that while the topic is scientific, the writers chose to include explanations of the procedures they used throughout the entire piece of writing, placed at appropriate points in the narrative.

Finally, all observation reports should include discussion or interpretation of the results. The writer of a successful report never leaves it up to the reader to interpret the results, but structures the report in such a way that the reader is shown how to interpret them and is at least reasonably compelled to agree with the results. Once again, in scientific writing a discussion of results ordinarily is expected to be in a separate section at the end of the report. This placement may be effective in other kinds of reports as well. However, writers of observational reports also can present and discuss results throughout. Just as you must consider the most effective placement for details about the observation, background information, and an explanation of the procedures used, you also must consider various options for including your discussion or interpretation of the results.

As you work to structure these four components of your report, you will, of course, need to make them work effectively together to create a unified piece of writing. In order to do this, you should remember to use metadiscourse and to create effective transitions throughout the report.

Revising a Report

Whenever possible, you should plan to draft your report and then allow yourself some time—at least overnight—before you begin to revise it. Putting the draft aside for a day or two will allow you to reread it with a more critical eye and to set particular goals to achieve as you revise. When you revise, you should remember that your teacher undoubtedly assigned an observation report to gauge both your ability to observe carefully and your ability to write an informative report. You should, then, pay careful attention as you revise your report to any particular directions or criteria your teacher has given for the assignment. Whatever specific expectations your teacher may have, there are also three general areas to consider in revising observation reports: improving the accessibility, strengthening the authoritativeness, and polishing your ethos, or self-presentation.

An accessible report has a clear structure that readers can predict because they are informed about it. If you have employed a conventional form, make sure, during revision, that you have adhered to the prescribed structure. If you have not followed a conventional form, carefully examine the organization of your report to ensure that it makes information accessible for readers unfamiliar with your subject. You may wish to check, for example, to be sure that your report has an introduction and explains the purpose of the observation. Beyond examining the structure and contents of your paper, you should also determine whether you have used sufficient metadiscourse to make your organization clear. If not, insert metadiscourse to keep readers informed about the order of parts within your report, as shown in this example:

> *Following a description of Happy Time Day Care and its playground, I will present my observation and then . . . . First, background will be provided on the observation site, the coffee shop Grounds for Thought. Then detailed findings will be presented, and discussion will follow about . . . .*

In addition, you can improve the accessibility of your report by eliminating extraneous or digressive information and by adding necessary information that has been omitted. Once you have finished a draft and your primary focus is more definite, you may realize that details you had included are peripheral to the central points you actually make or that your slightly modified focus requires additional details or explanation.

Another important step in revising for accessibility is to make sure you have used specialized terminology effectively. Generally, your intended audience and your purpose in writing should help you determine whether you need to add or omit jargon. When revising, check to ensure that you have defined necessary jargon adequately. When writing to a highly trained audience, you may need to determine whether you have used relevant specialized terms correctly because it is easy to misuse terms that are not part of your daily vocabulary. As a student writing to a teacher more knowledgeable than you are, you should generally define most of the jargon that you employ in a report.

Once you've completed a draft, you may discover that additional details from your observation notes are needed to support your conclusions. You may also decide to include supplemental materials to present detailed information in a short space, as, for example, Myra and David Sadker do in the classroom transcript they provide and in the close descriptions they give of a fifth-grade boy and girl. Supplemental materials lend an air of authoritativeness to a report that cannot be gained through a summary of your notes.

In addition to revising for accessibility and authoritativeness, you should also revise to improve your ethos, or self-presentation, primarily to make your report present you as a careful and reliable observer. Read your draft closely, paying attention to your word choice. If you have used imprecise words, they should be replaced with more precise ones. Likewise, any words or phrases that have unwanted or distracting connotations—for example, in an observation of a five-year-old on the playground, the phrase "bawled like a baby"—should be replaced or rewritten.

In revising to strengthen your self-presentation, you should also consider the tone of your report. As you review your draft, first check to see if your tone is consistent throughout your report. Changes in the tone that come about accidentally should be revised for consistency. In addition, the tone of your report should be somewhat serious. Writing with too casual or flip a tone may convey the impression that you don't care about the assignment or the subject you are studying. Certainly the humor in "The Blob" does add to its readability. Yet the authors' tone is balanced by their professional ethos, as well as by the gravity of their recommendations. As a student, you will be safest if you strive for a tone that is serious, considered, and consistent.

WRITING ASSIGNMENTS

Writing Topics

Select an assignment from the Assignments section of Chapter 4, and write a report based upon the observations you conducted. Use your notes, inventing (clustering, the Pentad, etc.) and other writings to help you begin. In addition, if your instructor permits groups to coauthor a report, consult Chapter 2 for ideas about collaborative procedures.

Writing Procedures

1. Meet with your group to discuss and evaluate one another's notes, inventing (clustering, Pentad, etc.), organizational plans, or questions for a subsequent observation. Advise one another about whether individuals need to conduct follow-up observations, change to a different topic, or conduct a new observation.

2. If you select another topic, once you have completed your observation or follow-up observations, use clustering or the Pentad (or both), to help you determine a focus, select details, and generate background information. Whether you continue to work with your original topic or select a new one, be sure to consider your role as an observer, the purpose of your report, and your audience as you refine the focus of your report. Present a detailed description of your organizing principle or focus orally or in writing to your group members for their feedback.

3. In one to two pages, use the information you've gathered to write out a tentative structure for your report. Your structure should reflect the major sections of your report, the ordering of these sections, and approximate contents for each. Share your structuring plans with your group and discuss your summaries of each section, determining whether the proposed content is sufficient, whether there is irrelevant information, and so on. Based on your group's response, revise your plan to reflect any changes you think are necessary.

4. Write a first draft of your report, using your revised plan, notes from your observation(s), and your prewriting. Use your observation notes and prewriting for concrete details. Insert headings and metadiscourse to create continuity as you move from one section to another.

5. After you have completed a draft, bring copies of it to class to workshop in your group. Use one of the draft workshop procedures described in Chapter 2.

6. Based on the feedback you get from your group workshop and/or your instructor, revise and then edit your final copy. In revising you should pay particular attention to specific, concrete details that reflect what you observed; an authoritative, unbiased ethos; and an organization or structure that presents your observations and your discussion of them in a clear, accessible manner. Be sure also to consider your responsibilities toward your readers and toward the subjects you observed. Finally, if your instructor has prescribed particular conventions about structure, word choice, and the like, be sure to follow them.

READINGS

Sadker, Myra and David. "Missing in Interaction," from *Failing at Fairness: How America's Schools Cheat Girls*. New York: Scribner's, 1994.

1. The authors make several generalizations based on their observations. How does the detail they provide, particularly transcripts and detailed narratives, support and lend authority to their claims?

2. Find at least two instances in which the authors refer directly to the reader as "you." How do such direct references lessen the distance between the readers and the writers? How do they strengthen the reasonableness of the writers' self-presentation?

3. The Sadkers use a variety of devices to increase their authoritativeness, such as statistics, citing the number of observations they have made, and so on. Locate several instances in which these and other devices make the report appear more authoritative. Explain how they do so.

Drucker, Barry J., and Knox, Dan W. "The Blob: Investigating the Abnormal." *Journal of Environmental Health* 56 (September 1993), 19–23.

1. Although "The Blob" has a rather humorous tone that makes it enjoyable to read, the article concludes with a serious and lengthy list of recommendations for environmental health professionals. How does the humor contribute to the accessibility of the material? How do both the humorous and serious tones enhance the writers' ethos?

2. Drucker and Knox enhance the authoritativeness of their report in a variety of ways. They provide details about their observations, use technical terminology, refer to published studies, and so forth. Locate specific instances in which they employ these and other devices to strengthen the authoritativeness of their report; explain how each instance does so.

Rosenthal, Elisabeth. "Burning Down the House." *Discover* (May 1993), pp. 30–32.

1. "Burning down the House," employs a great deal of jargon as well as the names of specialized drugs. Find specific instances in which jargon and drug names are used and explain how they are made accessible to general readers.

2. Saying, as did Meg Swift, "It's just allergies," can get you killed. That is, anaphylaxis is a common yet potentially life-threatening condition. How did Rosenthal structure her report of her observation of Meg to make the information accessible? Describe the nature of the details. Why are these details effective enough to motivate readers to take anaphylaxis seriously?

Thomas, Elizabeth Marshall. "Misha's Traffic Management Skills," from *The Hidden Life of Dogs.* Boston: Houghton Mifflin, 1993, pp. 11–20.

1. How might "Misha's Traffic Management Skills" have read if Thomas had structured it to reflect the late-night meanderings of Misha? Examine this report and describe how it is structured.

2. Many readers may not consider the behavior of dogs to be an interesting subject. How does Thomas enhance the authoritativeness of her report on Misha's behavior? In particular, look at her descriptions of mundane activities such as Misha's urinating or greeting another dog.

3. Thomas repeatedly refers to herself as "I" throughout this piece and also describes the reasoning process she used to reach conclusions. How does Thomas's use of the first-person pronoun as well as her descriptions of her reasoning processes affect readers' perceptions of her ethos and judgment?

 Missing in Interaction*

Myra and David Sadker

"Candid Camera" would have a field day in elementary school. There would be no need to create embarrassing situations. Just set the camera to take a photograph every sixty seconds. Since classroom action moves so swiftly, snapshots slow down the pace and reveal subliminal gender lessons.

Snapshot #1	Tim answers a question.
Snapshot #2	The teacher reprimands Alex.
Snapshot #3	Judy and Alice sit with hands raised while Brad answers a question.
Snapshot #4	Sally answers a question,
Snapshot #5	The teacher praises Marcus for skill in spelling.
Snapshot #6	The teacher helps Sam with a spelling mistake.
Snapshot #7	The teacher compliments Alice on her neat paper.
Snapshot #8	Students are in lines for a spelling bee. Boys are on one side of the room and girls are on the other.

Missing in Interaction *(cont'd.)*

As the snapshots continue, the underlying gender messages become clear. The classroom consists of two worlds: one of boys in action, the other of girls' inaction. Male students control classroom conversation. They ask and answer more questions. They receive more praise for the intellectual quality of their ideas. They get criticized. They get help when they are confused. They are the heart and center of interaction. Watch how boys dominate the discussion in this upper elementary class about presidents.

The fifth-grade class is almost out of control. "Just a minute," the teacher admonishes. "There are too many of us here to all shout out at once. I want you to raise your hands, and then I'll call on you. If you shout out, I'll pick somebody else."

Order is restored. Then Stephen, enthusiastic to make his point, calls out.

STEPHEN: I think Lincoln was the best president. He held the country together during the war.

TEACHER: A lot of historians would agree with you.

MIKE (seeing that nothing happened to Stephen, calls out): I don't. Lincoln was okay, but my Dad liked Reagan. He always said Reagan was a great president.

DAVID (calling out): Reagan? Are you kidding?

TEACHER: Who do you think our best president was, Dave?

DAVID: FDR. He saved us from the depression.

MAX (calling out): I don't think it's right to pick one best president. There were a lot of good ones.

TEACHER: That's interesting.

KIMBERLY (calling out): I don't think the presidents today are as good as the ones we used to have.

TEACHER: Okay, Kimberly. But you forgot the rule. You're supposed to raise your hand.

The classroom is the only place in society where so many different, young, and restless individuals are crowded into close quarters for an extended period of time day after day. Teachers sense the undertow of raw energy and restlessness that threatens to engulf the classroom. To preserve order, most teachers use established classroom conventions such as raising your hand if you want to talk.

Intellectually, teachers know they should apply this rule consistently, but when the discussion becomes fast-paced and furious, the rule is often swept aside. When this happens and shouting out begins, it is an open invitation for male dominance. Our research shows that boys call out eight times more often than girls. Sometimes what they say has little or nothing to do with the teacher's questions. Whether male comments are insightful or irrelevant, teachers respond to them. However, when girls call out, there is a fascinating occurrence: Suddenly the teacher remembers the rule about raising your hand before you talk. And then the girl, who is usually not as assertive as the male students, is deftly and swiftly put back in her place.

Missing in Interaction *(cont'd.)*

Not being allowed to call out like her male classmates during the brief conversation about presidents will not psychologically scar Kimberly; however, the system of silencing operates covertly and repeatedly. It occurs several times a day during each school week for twelve years, and even longer if Kimberly goes to college, and, most insidious of all, it happens subliminally. This micro-inequity eventually has a powerful cumulative impact.

On the surface, girls appear to be doing well. They get better grades and receive fewer punishments than boys. Quieter and more conforming, they are the elementary school's ideal students. "If it ain't broke, don't fix it" is the school's operating principle as girls' good behavior frees the teacher to work with the more difficult-to-manage boys. The result is that girls receive less time, less help, and fewer challenges. Reinforced for passivity, their independence and self-esteem suffer. As victims of benign neglect, girls are penalized for doing what they should and lose ground as they go through school. In contrast, boys get reinforced for breaking the rules; they are rewarded for grabbing more than their fair share of the teacher's time and attention.

Even when teachers remember to apply the rules consistently, boys are still the ones who get noticed. When girls raise their hands, it is often at a right angle, arm bent at the elbow, a cautious, tentative, almost insecure gesture. At other times they raise their arms straight and high, but they signal silently. In contrast, when boys raise their hands, they fling them wildly in the air, up and down, up and down, again and again, Sometimes these hand signals are accompanied by strange noises, "Ooh! Ooh! Me! Me! Ooooh!" Occasionally they even stand beside or on top of their seats and wave one or both arms to get attention. "Ooh! Me! Mrs. Smith, call on me." In the social studies class about presidents, we saw boys as a group grabbing attention while girls as a group were left out of the action.

Another way to observe in a classroom is to focus on individual children and record and describe their behavior for an extended period of time. Here is what we found when we watched two children for a forty-five-minute class. Perhaps you will see yourself in their behavior. Maybe you will see your son or daughter.

The fifth-grade boy sits in the fourth seat, second row. Since there are more than thirty other children in the class, getting the teacher's attention is a very competitive game. Watch how he plays.

First the boy waves his hand straight in the air so that the teacher will select him from the surrounding forest of mainly male arms. He waves and pumps for almost three minutes without success. Evidently tiring, he puts his right arm down only to replace it with the left. Wave and pump. Wave and pump. Another two minutes go by. Still no recognition. Down with the left hand, up with the right. He moves to strategy two—sounds: "Ooh, me. C'mon. C'mon. Pleeze. Ooooh!" Another minute without being noticed. Strategy three: He gets out of his seat, stands in front of his desk, and waves with sound effects for another thirty seconds. He slumps back

Missing in Interaction *(cont'd.)*

into his seat, momentarily discouraged. Five seconds later there's the strategy-four effort: He holds his right arm up in the air by resting it on his left as he leans on his elbow. Three more minutes go by.

"Tom." His name. Recognition. For a brief moment he has the floor. The eyes of the teacher and his classmates are on him, the center of attention. He has spent more than nine minutes in his effort to get a half-minute in the sun. Post response: He sits for four quiet minutes. Then up shoots the arm again.

There is another student in the same class on the other side of the room, a little more toward the front. She begins the class with her arm held high, her face animated, her body leaning forward. Clearly she has something she wants to say. She keeps her right hand raised for more than a minute, switches to the left for forty-five seconds. She is not called on. She doesn't make noises or jump out of her seat, but it looks as though her arm is getting tired. She reverts to propping the right arm up with the left, a signal she maintains for two more minutes. Still no recognition. The hand comes down.

She sits quietly, stares out the window, plays with the hair of the girl in front of her. Her face is no longer animated. She crosses her arms on the desk and rests her head on them, which is how she spends the final twelve minutes of class time. Her eyes are open, but it is impossible to tell if she is listening. The period ends. The girl has not said a word.

When we videotape classrooms and play back the tapes, most teachers are stunned to see themselves teaching subtle gender lessons along with math and spelling. The teacher in the social studies class about presidents was completely unaware that she gave male students more attention. Only after several viewings of the videotape did she notice how she let boys call out answers but reprimanded girls for similar behavior. The teacher who taught Tom and the silent girl did not realize what effort it took to get attention. Surprised and saddened, he watched on videotape how his initially eager female student wilted and then faded from the activities of the classroom.

In our workshops for educators we call boys like Tom "star students" or "green-arms." Teachers smile with weary recognition as we describe students whose hands are up in the air so high and so long that the blood could have drained out. Our research shows that in a typical class of twenty-five students, two or three green-arm students may capture 25 percent of the teacher's attention.

Most students are not so salient. Rather, nominally involved, they are asked one or two questions by the teacher each class period. Even though nominal students don't wave arms and make birdlike noises, they do exhibit their own distinct patterns. If you were a nominal student, you can probably remember the following from your own school days: As the teacher approaches, you tense. The question is asked. Your shoulders rise, your adrenaline pumps, and your heart pounds so loudly that the teacher's voice is barely audible. You answer. Correct!

Missing in Interaction *(cont'd.)*

You exhale with relief. The teacher's shadow and cologne move on. You've paid your dues. If the teacher asks you another question, you're likely to think, "He's picking on me."

When teachers ask students to read aloud one after the other down the row, one paragraph after another, nominal students count ahead and practice their paragraph silently. Can you remember industriously working on an impending passage only to have the student in front of you flub his, leaving you to stumble over unknown literary ground? If you can picture yourself in this scene for at least part of your school career, you were probably a nominal student.

In the typical classroom we found that approximately 10 percent of students are green-arms and 70 percent are nominal. Who's left? The remaining 20 percent, about four or five students in most classrooms, do not say anything at all. Of course some boys are shy and some girls are assertive, but we found that male students are more often stars and female students are more often stifled.[1] One researcher found that for every eight star-boys there is only one star-girl.[2]

Boys cast in starring classroom roles are often high achievers. Bright boys answer the questions, and their opinions are respected by the teacher. Low-achieving boys also get plenty of attention, but more often it's negative. No surprise there. In general, girls receive less attention, but there's another surprise: Unlike the smart boy who flourishes in the classroom, the smart girl is the student who is least likely to be recognized.[3]

When we analyzed the computer printouts for information about gender and race, an intriguing trend emerged. The students most likely to receive teacher attention were white males; the second most likely were minority males; the third, white females; and the least likely, minority females. In elementary school, receiving attention from the teacher is enormously important for a student's achievement and self-esteem. Later in life, in the working world, the salary received is important, and the salary levels parallel the classroom: white males at the top and minority females at the bottom. In her classroom interaction studies, Jacqueline Jordan Irvine found that black girls were active, assertive, and salient in the primary grades, but as they moved up through elementary school, they became the most invisible members of classrooms.[4]

References

1.   Sadker, Myra, and David Sadker. *Year 3: Final Report: Promoting Effectiveness in Classromm Instruction.* Washington, DC: National Institute of Education, 1984.
Sadker, Myra, and David Sadker. "Sexism in the Classroom: From Grade School to Graduate School," *Phi Delta Kappan* 67:7 (March 1986), pp. 512–15.
Leinhardt, Gaea, Andrea Seewald, and Mary Engel. "Learning What's Taught: Sex Differences in Instruction," *Journal of Educational Psychology* 71:4 (1979), pp. 432–39.
Jones, M. Gail "Gender Issues in Teacher Education," *Journal of Teacher Education* (January-February 1989), pp. 33–38.

Missing in Interaction *(cont'd.)*

Wellesley College Center for Research on Women. *How Schools Shortchange Girls: The AAUW Report.* Washington, DC: American Association of University Women Educational Foundation, 1992.

Sadker, Myra, David Sadker, and Lisa Stulberg. "Fair and Square? Creating a Nonsexist Classroom," *Instructor* 102:7 (March 1993), pp. 45–46, 67.

2. Gore, Dolores. *Sex-Related Differences in Relation to Teacher Behavior as Wait-Time During Fourth-Grade Mathematics Instruction.* Unpublished doctoral dissertation, University of Arkansas, 1981.

3. Wilkinson, Louise Cherry, and Cora Marrett (eds.). *Gender Influences in Classroom Interaction.* Orlando, FL: Academic Press, 1985.

4. Irvine, Jaqueline Jordan. "Teacher-Student Interactions: Effects of Student Race, Sex, and Grade Level," *Journal of Educational Psychology* 78:1 (1986), pp 14–21.

 ## The Blob: Investigating the abnormal*

Barry J. Drucker and Dan W. Knox

Abstract

A strange mass of tissue was discovered in St. Louis County, Missouri—and for some time it defied identification by numerous authorities. Finally, it was identified as a massive "pellicle," composed of a colony of Acetobacter xylinum bacteria and its fibrils of extracellular cellulose. The investigation is recounted, retrospectively analyzed, and recommendations are offered to others who may find aberrant objects. These recommendations focus on the following: 1) deciding on responsibility; 2) obtaining support of management; 3) considering security; 4) working with the news media; 5) trusting intuition, and; 6) avoiding paradigms.

"The field sanitarian," wrote Dr. Ben Freedman (2), "goes about his duty from day to day, performing routine services and keeping alert for signs . . . of the abnormal in the environment." Sometimes, signs of environmental abnormalities just land on the sanitarian's doorstep. This paper recounts one such incident.

While attending a routine staff meeting, St. Louis County Department of Health (DOH) managers were apprised of a mysterious mass of tissue being held at the Office of the Medical Examiner (ME). A month had passed since the police had submitted the "five gallon glass jug containing unknown matter," which they

*Barry J. Drucker and Dan W. Knox. "The Blob: Investigating the abnormal." *Journal of Environmental Health* (September 1993), pp. 19–23. Reprinted with the permission of the publisher.

The Blob: Investigating the abnormal *(cont'd.)*

had found along a remote highway. During that time, the ME had ascertained that the contents were not human remains, yet the exact identity of the strange material remained unknown. Since the tissue was no longer evidence of possible foul play, the ME permitted other staff members to try to identify it.

It came from outer space . . . not!

Although many DOH employees possessed backgrounds in life sciences, none had seen anything as bizarre as this object, and it was quickly nicknamed "The Alien." It appeared to have been a living animal, or at least part of one—thus, some of the managers thought it was an organ or some kind of a tumor. To others, it resembled a marine creature. All agreed, however, that it was highly exotic, so it was necropsied by the county animal control manager, a veterinarian experienced with exotic animals.

The tissue, which the ME had earlier removed from the glass jug, was now in four pieces, and it reeked of vinegar. The veterinarian observed that it was composed of two main parts: the largest appeared to be a seven-pound muscle-like mass which fit in the palms of two cupped hands, and which contained internal cavities. The other piece was longer, with small ridges, and it resembled a tongue or a tentacle. Although the mass was palpated, teased, dissected, x-rayed, stained and examined microscopically, it continued to defy description.

Eventually, the examination focused on the tentacle-like object. Since it resembled part of a squid or an octopus, we contacted marine biologists and, as they requested, shipped the organism across country for their examination. They guessed that the specimen was not of marine origin, and it was possibly some sort of land creature, but their examination was inconclusive.

The news media to the rescue?

Having made little progress in identifying the object, our puzzlement and frustration grew. Surely, there had to be *someone* who knew about the thing. Therefore, in order to elicit information from the public, we considered informing the news media. Actually, no attempt had been made to conceal the aberrant find, but word of its existence was spreading rapidly, so we knew that media involvement was just a matter of time. We hoped that if their information came from *us*, the chance for a sensational story might be minimized. None of us wanted to see a headline that read: "Health Officials Hiding Alien Being in County Morgue."

Accordingly the Director of DOH took a proactive stance, and released our message in a news release. It seemed like a good idea at the time, but soon we were to learn that Stephen C. Stuyck (3) was correct when he wrote that "Public health agencies often have unrealistic expectations about message control."

The fact that the object was discovered around Halloween was not lost to the media, and they had great fun exploiting that association. In addition, although the county veterinarian had referred to the oddity in consistently objective terms, labeling it "the thing" or the "mass of tissue," immediately reporters renamed it "The

---

The Blob: Investigating the abnormal *(cont'd.)*

Blob." Soon, the national wire services joined in the "feeding frenzy" and DOH was deluged with requests for interviews.

In the face of mounting media pressure, we found that humor was helpful. For example, when interviewers sought to sensationalize the issue by asking if "The Blob" could have come from outer space, our veterinarian deadpanned "I'm not doubting the existence of extraterrestrial life, but I'd assume it wouldn't come to Earth in a glass bottle." Humor relieved tension, a fact which everyone seemed to appreciate.

Against the backdrop of the media circus, research continued, and eventually The Blob was examined by a wide array of life scientists. Among them were forensic and animal pathologists, zoo officials, meat scientists, bacteriologists, mycologists and other assorted botanists.

The plot sickens

Interestingly, the meat scientists found bovine hairs among the tissue and what they *thought* were erythrocytes. Although these findings seemed to confirm the earlier judgment of the marine biologists that The Blob was a land creature, the hairs probably came from cattle that grazed near the creek where the jug was first found. Subsequent heavy rains, which we knew had occurred, may have washed them into the flooded creek, whereupon they floated into the jar. The "erythrocytes" were probably crystals produced by the inappropriate use of an *animal* stain on what we finally learned was *botanical* matter.

Incredibly, everyone had placed The Blob in the wrong kingdom. It was not an animal; it was a plant. In particular, as we were soon to discover, the curious mass had been produced by a species of acetic acid bacteria, which convert alcohol to vinegar (4, 5) and which can synthesize abundant amounts of cellulose (6, 7, 9, 10, 11, 12, 13, 14, 15, 16).

As expected, the first key to the puzzle came from someone who had seen the story in the news. A worker reported that while cutting weeds along a creek bank in a small Missouri town, he saw the narrow mouth of a glass water jug sticking out of the gravel. Although it was filthy and filled with muddy water from a recent flood, immediately he saw its potential as a terrarium, so he hid it from his coworkers, planning to retrieve it after work. When he returned for it, however, it was gone.

The lead seemed to be promising, since the creek bank he specified was less than 10 miles from where the police had recovered the bottle. Consequently, the authors visited the town, and engaged in face-to-face interviews with many of the residents. Unfortunately, we could not locate the owners of the town's French restaurant, who had, as we would learn, played pivotal roles in the intrigue. The following week, however, the restaurateurs saw The Blob on television, and suspecting their part in the bizarre riddle, they called the station. Soon the story began to unfold.

The investigation sours

A hobby of one of the restaurateurs was making flavored wine vinegars, having learned the process as a youth in her native France. Since her departure from

The Blob: Investigating the abnormal *(cont'd.)*

Europe, however, she had been unable to find the familiar bacterial culture, "mother of vinegar," or "mère de vinaigre" (4). Then, one day, as she decanted some commercial Spanish vinegar, she recognized the speck of protoplasm in the bottom of the bottle. It was "La Mère!" Carefully, she filtered it and assembled the other recipe ingredients for her vinegar.

Filling two glass, five-gallon water jugs with "good wine," she added the culture and, for flavor, fresh berries. She then stored the jugs in a dark corner of the restaurant's cellar. Normally, this "slow generator process" takes three to six months (5). During that time, the bacteria form a light veil which increasingly penetrates the liquid, forming a thick, folded, sticky skin (4). Under static (not agitated) conditions, this film of cellulose will rapidly cover the surface and produce a remarkably thick mat (6, 7). These batches were static for a very long time; incredibly, they had been forgotten for eight years. During that time, the once tiny specks of La Mère had proliferated wildly, and eventually filled the jugs with grotesque progeny.

Evidently, this is what happened: In nature, wine is spoiled, or converted to sugar, generally by mixed cultures of acetic acid bacteria, which can oxidize ethanol to acetic acid. Members of the family *Acetobacteraceae*, these consist of two genera, *Gluconobacter* and *Acetobacter* (7, 8).

Some species of *Acetobacter* synthesize cellulose (6, 7, 9, 10, 11, 12, 13, 14, 15, 16, 17, 18, 19), one of the most abundant organic macromolecules on earth, being found in cell walls throughout the plant kingdom (7, 10, 13, 15). Among these cellulose synthesizing species, the gramnegative *Acetobacter xylinum*, produces an abundance (13,15,16) of high purity (7,16, 20, 2 1) material, which is extruded (6, 12, 13, 23) from the cell in ribbons of loosely intertwined microfibrils (6, 10, 12, 13, 15, 18, 19, 20, 21, 22, 23, 24, 25). A giant colony of *A. xylinum* made "The Blob."

As the mass grew larger, the microfibrils of extracellular cellulose entrapped bacterial cells and formed a "pellicle" (6, 7, 12, 13, 15, 16, 18, 23, 24, 25), a structure thought to aid the growth and survival of the microorganism (12). Natural pellicles are eaten in some societies (15, 25, 26), and, when carefully grown, they provide unique products for medicine and industry (11, 15, 16, 25). Pellicles may range in thickness from a thin skin (6, 27) to a thick surface mat (6, 10, 18) as in this case.

The fact that this pellicle was enormous and well-organized, however, may have been attributable to the extended period of stasis. Ross *et al.* (7) state that when the culture is shaken or stirred, round balls of cellulose are typically observed, and Couso *et al.* (14) found that shaking favors the production of different, xanthan-gum-like substance.

Furthermore, we speculate that the berries were responsible for the pellicle's grotesque shapes and gruesome colors, both characteristics of which were more evident in the second jug, which had not been subjected to the harsh effects of the elements. When this tissue was dissected, we observed a gray-brown substance that resembled loose, cooked ground beef, and which we presumed to be the seed-laden, berry residue. This coarse material originally may have served as nuclei upon which subcolonies of bacteria produced numerous individual pellicles.

The Blob: Investigating the abnormal *(cont'd.)*

As these grew, absorbing the red pigment from their substrate, the propulsive force of the fibril extrusion (24) increasingly pressed them against their neighbors and against the confining walls of the glass jug, resulting in folded and coiled structures. Similarly, a softer, more amorphous material also observed may have been produced by this stress of compression. Brown (18) notes that when cells come in contact with immobile objects they may synthesize a different physical form of cellulose which has no microfibrillar structure. Accordingly, much material from the second jug grossly resembled coiled pink intestines and lobes of dark red liver.

Seeing these bizarre structures, the restaurateur realized that something had gone wrong, so she put one of the jugs on the loading dock, to be cleaned later by the kitchen staff. However, before the staff arrived, the jug was stolen and hidden in the gravel bed of the nearby creek, where it later was discovered by the worker.

The events that followed the theft of the jug from the worker are conjecture. Possibly, some of the opaque liquid spilled from the jug in transit, revealing its disgusting contents to the thief, to whom it may have looked like toxic material or the remnants of a grisly murder. We know the robber eventually discarded his loot by the roadside, where it was later discovered by a horseback rider, who reported it to the police.

Recommendations

Hopefully environmental health professionals finding abnormal objects will benefit from our experience, and in this spirit, we make the following recommendations.

- *Decide on responsibility*—Initially, a decision should be made whether an investigation is to take place and who is best qualified to coordinate the study. In doing so, one must bear in mind that there are risks in deciding *not* to investigate.

  For example, if one is apathetic about the discovery of an aberrant object, and later it proves to be toxic or stolen, one may be liable for damages. Apart from legal, ethical and public health considerations, indifference could damage your credibility with the public.

- *Obtain support of management*—Top managers within St. Louis county government, including the county executive and the director of DOH were informed, involved and supportive throughout the investigation. Accordingly, there were at least three benefits from their participation: 1) they were able to provide guidance and make critical decisions throughout the investigative process; 2) their support facilitated cooperation between departments, such as health and police, and between divisions, such as the ME office and environmental protection; and 3) they permitted the investigators to work outside their normal fields of work for extended periods.

- *Consider security*—An abnormal object may have priceless scientific value, so it should be protected until more is known. Hailed as "the world's most intact ancient human," the 5,300 year old "Iceman" found recently in the

The Blob: Investigating the abnormal *(cont'd.)*

Alps is one such example. Because of the extraordinary circumstances surrounding its interment, it appeared initially to be a fresh corpse, and careless workers nearly destroyed the discovery (28, 29, 30, 31).

Similarly, Mastodons and wooly mammoths, extinct since the last ice age, are routinely uncovered with the flesh intact (32, 33). Occasionally, these priceless, neolithic specimens are so "fresh" they appear to have died only recently. They are at risk, therefore, of being skinned by careless humans, or eaten by present day canines, such as wolves and camp dogs (33).

Furthermore, science lost the first live Coelocanth discovered in recent times. This unusual fish, which provides a "missing link" to air breathing animals, was once thought to be extinct for 60 million years, but the modern fishermen who caught it were concerned principally with the animal's edibility. Thus, observing it was bony and scaly, they let it rot (34). Fourteen years would pass before another was caught (32).

- *Work with the media*—Contact with the news media, which first we had approached with apprehension, ultimately proved invaluable to the investigation. Generally, reporters are like the rest of us: they are simply trying to do a good job. However, keen competition sometimes will produce undesirable effects. According to journalism professor Phillip Meyer (35), "The intensity of this competition creates the incentive to distort (and emphasize) the most outlandish or most alarming aspect of a situation." It is necessary, therefore, when dealing with an aberrant discovery, that the person chosen to interact with the media be helpful, honest, credible and report the facts concisely.

   Reporters will appreciate your help in securing their story. Thus, they may tend to be more helpful to you when reporting it. However, in your attempt to help the reporter, you should not allow yourself to be induced to conclusions which are not warranted by facts.

   The spokesperson must be highly credible. Usually this will mean that a scientist should be chosen to speak on technical matters arising from your discovery. Not only will a professional scientist be perceived as qualified to speak on the phenomenon, but that person's training will impart the necessary objectivity to the interview.

   Stories in the electronic news media frequently take the form of "sound bites," and even the print media employ short paragraphs, sometimes written at the fifth-grade level. Therefore, the spokesperson should avoid jargon and drawn out discourses. Construct your message in advance of the interview, stick to it, and relate it concisely. By doing so you will minimize the risk that someone else will edit your message and quote you out of context.

- *Trust your intuition*—If we had succeeded in locating the restaurateurs, we might have resolved the mystery one week earlier. From the time we learned that the jug originally was found in the creek on the grounds of the French restaurant, our *intuition* told us that the restaurant somehow was

The Blob: Investigating the abnormal *(cont'd.)*

involved. We interviewed some restaurant employees, but stopped short of questioning the owners. In retrospect, we should have been more persistent.

- *Avoid paradigms*—Paradigms serve as filters to incoming data, screening out that which does not fit our expectations or assumptions. Often they are useful, providing order and structure for our lives, but they may also be limiting. When too much data are removed we may fail to see, distort or reject experience and information that does not fit our paradigm (36).

Although cellulose is generally associated with plants, it is also found in varying amounts in animals (15, 20, 37). More surprisingly, there are even a few reports that cellulose may be a normal but small component of mammalian cells and that under certain disease conditions in humans, notably scleroderma, cellulose is produced in abundance (20). "But what medical doctor would think to look for cellulose in human tissues," asks botany professor R. Malcolm Brown, Jr., "and what botanist would think to ask a physician about this?" Their paradigms are mutually exclusive.

Our veterinarian thought he saw skin, tendons, coelomic cavities and other animal-like structures. Similarly, the meat scientists, finding bovine hairs and red artifacts, incorrectly assumed that the object was meat. Everyone seemed to interpret The Blob in terms of his or her own specialty. Why did each see only that which was familiar?

According to Thomas Kuhn (38), who has written extensively on the subject of paradigms in science, it is because those phenomena "that will not fit in the box are often not seen at all." Perhaps the strange appearance of this anomalous object may have so violated the expectations of the scientists that it could not be seen for what it was. Therefore, while often it may be advantageous to follow one's hunches, one should remain inquisitive, flexible and open to new possibilities.

Conclusion

Every day in the U.S. alone, many thousands of sanitarians and other environmental health personnel practice their profession. Given the variety of their specialties and diversity of environments in which these are practiced, inevitably abnormal objects will be discovered. Determining their identity will satisfy an obligation to the public and will enrich the sanitarian's everyday work.

References

1. Scott, H.G. (1981), New Developments: The sanitarian's need to stay informed, *J. Environ. Health* 44(3):131–133.
2. Freedman, B.(1977), *Sanitarian's Handbook: Theory and Administrative Practice*, 4th ed., Peerless Publishing Co., New Orleans, LA, pp. 16–17.
3. Stuyck, S.C. (1990). Public Health and the Media: Unequal Partners?, In: Atkins, C. and W. Lawrence (eds.), *Mass Communication and Public Health: Complexities and Conflicts*, Sage Publications, Inc., Newbury Park, CA, p. 73.
4. Turgeon,C. and N. Fround (eds.) (1961), *Larousse Gastronomique: The Encyclopedia of Food, Wine and Cookery*, Crown Publishers, Inc., New York, NY, p. 1000.

The Blob: Investigating the abnormal *(cont'd.)*

5. Manchester, R. B. (1987), *Amazing Facts: The Indispensable Collection of True Life Facts and Feats,* Galahad Books, New York, NY. pp. 325–326.
6. Kreig. N.R. and J.G. Holt (eds.) (1984), *Bergey's Manual of Systematic Bacteriology, Vol. 1,* The Williams & Wilkins Co., Baltimore, MD. pp. 268–271.
7. Ross, P., R. Mayer and M. Benziman (1991), Cellulose biosynthesis and function in bacteria, *Microbiol. Rev.* 55(l):35–58.
8. Matsushita, K., H. Ebisuya, M. Ameyama and O. Adachi (1992), Change of the terminal oxidase from cytochrome a1 in shaking cultures to cytochrome o in static cultures of *Acetobacter aceti, J. Bacteriol.* 174(1):122–129.
9. Kösebalaban, F. and M. Özilgen (1992), Kinetics of wine spoilage by acetic acid bacteria, *J. Chem. Tech. Biotechnol.* 55:59–63.
10. Ross, P., H. Weinhouse, Y. Aloni, D. Michaeli, P. Weinberger-Ohana, R. Mayer, S. Braun, E. de Vroom, G.A. van der Marel, J.H. van Boom and M. Benziman (1987), Regulation of cellulose synthesis in *Acetobacter xylinum* by cyclic diguanylic acid, *Nature* 325:279–281.
11. Aldersey-Williams, H. (1989), Bacteria weave luxury headphones, *New Scientist* 121:31.
12. Williams, S.W. and R.E. Cannon (1989), Alternative environmental roles for cellulose produced by *Acetobacter xylinum, Applied and Env. Microbiol.* 55(10):2448–2452.
13. Lin, F.C., M.R. Brown, Jr., J.B. Cooper and D.P. Dellmer (1985), Synthesis of fibrils *in vitro* by a solubilized cellulose synthase from *Acetobacter xylinum, Science* 230:822–825.
14. Couso, R.O., L. Ielpi and M.A. Dankert (1987), A xanthan-gum-like polysaccharide from *Acetobacter xylinum, J. Gen. Microbiol.* 133:2123–3135.
15. University of Texas (1992), *Cellulose Research at the University of Texas,* Dept. of Botany, The University, Austin, TX, pp. 1–13.
16. Brown, Jr., R.M. (1992), Emerging technologies and future prospects for industrialization of microbially derived cellulose, In: Ladisch, M.R. and A. Bose (eds.), *Harnessing Biotechnology for the 21st Century,* American Chemical Society, Washington, DC pp. 76–79.
17. Brown, A.J. (1886), On an acetic acid ferment which forms cellulose, *Trans. J. Chem. Soc.* (London) 49:432–439.
18. Brown, Jr., M.R. (1989), Cellulose Biogenesis and a Decade of Progress: A personal perspective, In: Schuerch, C.S. (ed.), *Cellulose and Wood—Chemistry and Technology,* John Wiley & Son, New York, NY, p. 649.
19. Brown, Jr., M.R. (1989). Biosynthesis of cellulose II in *Acetobacter xylinum,* In: Schuerch, C.S. (ed.), *Cellulose and Wood—Chemistry and Technology,* John Wiley & Son, New York, NY, p. 689–704.
20. Brown, Jr., R.M., C.H. Haigler, J. Suttie, A.R. White, E. Roberts. C. Smith, T. Itoh and K. Cooper (1983), The biosynthesis and degradation of cellulose, *J. Appl. Polymer Res.:* Applied Polymer Symposium 37:33–78.
21. Brown, Jr., M.R., K. Kudlicka, S.K.Cousins and R.Nagy (1992), Gravity effects on cellulose assembly. *Am. J. Bot.* 79(11):1247–1258.
22. Kuga, S. and R.M. Brown, Jr. (1988), Silver labeling of the reducing ends of bacterial cellulose, *Carbohydrate Res.* 180:345–350.
23. Haigler, C.H., R.M. Brown, Jr. and M. Benziman (1980), Calcofluor white ST alters the *in vivo* assembly of cellulose micorfibrils, *Science* 210(4472):903–906.
24. Brown, Jr., R.M., J.H.M. Willison and C.L. Richardson (1976), Cellulose biosynthesis in *Acetobacter xylinum:* Visualization of the site of synthesis and direct measurement of the *in vivo* process, *Proc. Nat'l. Acad. Sci. U.S.A.* 73(12):4565–4569.
25. Brown, Jr., R.M. (1989), Bacterial cellulose. In: Kennedy, Phillips & Williams (eds.), *Cellulose: Structural and Functional Aspects,* Ellis Horwood Limited, West Sussex, England, pp. 145–151.
26. Lapus, M.M., E.G. Gallardo and M.A. Palo (1967), The nata organism—cultural requirements, characteristics and identity, *Philippine J. Sci.* 96(2):91–111.
27. Hensyl, W.R. and J.O. Oldham (eds.) (1982), *Stedman's Medical Dictionary,* 24th ed., The Williams and Wilkins Co., Baltimore, MD, p. 1045.
28. Jaroff, L. (1992), Iceman, *Time,* 26:62–66.

The Blob: Investigating the abnormal *(cont'd.)*

29. Fritz, S. (1993), Who was the Iceman?, *Popular Science* 242(2):46–88.
30. Seidler, H., W. Bernhard, M. Teschler-Nicola, W. Platzer, D. zur Nedden, R. Henn, A. Oberhauser and T. Sjøvold (1992). Some anthropological aspects of the prehistoric Tyrolean ice man, *Science* 258(5081):455–457.
31. Harrigan, S. (1992), The long-lost hunter, *Audubon* 94:92–97.
32. Laycock, G. (1973), *Strange Monsters and Great Searches,* Doubleday & Company, Inc., Garden City, NY, pp. 16–23.
33. Sanderson, I.T. (1972), *Investigating the Unexplained: A Compendium of Disquieting Mysteries of the Natural World,* Prentice-Hall, Inc., Englewood Cliffs, NJ, pp. 93–98.
34. Burton, M. (1956), *Living Fossils,* Jarrold & Sons, Ltd., London, England, p. 17.
35. Meyer, P. (1990), News Media Responsiveness to Public Health, In: Atkins, C. and W. Lawrence (eds.). *Mass Communication and Public Health: Complexities and Conflicts,* Sage Publications, Inc., Newbury Park, CA, p. 57.
36. . . . (1993), What's your paradigm?, In: *Training Tribune,* Vol. 7, Division of Personnel, St. Louis County Government, Clayton, MO, pp. 1–2.
37. Hall, D.A., F. Happey, P.F. Lloyd and H. Saxl (1960), Oriented cellulose as a component of mammalian tissue, *Proc. Roy. Soc. Lond.* Series B 151:497–517.
38. Kuhn, T.S. (1970), *The Structure of Scientific Revolutions,* 2nd ed., University of Chicago Press, Chicago, IL, p. 24.

 ## Burning Down the House*

Elisabeth Rosenthal

When Meg Swift first noticed the itchy red blotches erupting on her skin with the regularity of fireworks on the Fourth of July, she didn't even consider the idea that anything could be terribly wrong. After all, she'd never been seriously ill before. She guessed she must be having an allergic reaction, but she had no idea what she was reacting to—she'd never had allergies before, either. In any case, she figured, it didn't matter, since allergies are no big deal. She decided to just finish reading the newspaper and wait to see if the itchy hives would go away by themselves.

As the minutes passed, however, the itching didn't go away; instead it spread to her stomach and legs. It was getting so bad she couldn't concentrate. Worse still— was it her imagination?— her eyes and lips were beginning to feel puffy. She looked in the mirror. They did look a little swollen, but then again, she hadn't slept well the night before. After staring intensely at herself for another minute, she turned away, worried that she was becoming a hypochondriac.

An allergy pill should do the trick, she thought. So she rummaged through the medicine chest in the hope of finding the pills her sister had once given her as part

Burning Down the House *(cont'd.)*

of a first-aid kit to take on a camping trip. But when she stepped back from the medicine chest, she caught another glimpse of herself in the mirror. Already her lips and eyelids were growing bigger. They were beginning to resemble water balloons. She called out to Matthew, her husband, to come and see—and noticed that her throat felt clumsy when she tried to swallow or speak.

Since they were new to town and didn't yet have a doctor, Matthew insisted they take a taxi to the nearest hospital outpatient clinic, just to get her checked out. Meg protested that she felt silly going to a hospital for an allergy attack, after all, her mother and sister had taken pills for hay fever and asthma for as long as she could remember. If only she had found some in the medicine chest—then she could forget about the emergency room.

But by the time they arrived at the hospital, she was feeling a bit woozy and had to lean on her husband's arm. And her eyes were so itchy and swollen that all she could see was a narrow slit of light. Still, when the guard at the hospital's front desk asked if she wanted a wheelchair, she waved him off. "I'm 25; its just allergies," she said. He had her write her name on a registration list and and take a seat in the waiting room until the triage nurse got a chance to check her out. It all seemed fairly routine.

So she was startled when the nurse in charge, who had come to the waiting room to speak to the family of another patient, made a big fuss upon seeing her. The nurse asked her a few quick questions and then rushed Meg into the emergency room itself, straight into a treatment bed.

Until this point, I'd been unaware of Meg Swift's plight; I'd been sitting at the doctor's desk in the ER, filling in some patients' charts. But as the nurse passed by with Meg, she said one word to me—"anaphylaxis." My heart started pounding, and I immediately fell in behind her.

Anaphylaxis, the malevolent kingpin of allergic reactions, makes a mockery of a patient's assertion that "it's just allergies." Anaphylaxis is a misguided attack by the body's immune system against a generally benign foreign substance—usually a food, drug, or insect venom. In this type of relentless allergic reaction, an overzealous immune system seeks to expel a harmless intruder by burning down the house. It is so overwhelming that it can leave virtually every body system in a state of collapse, and so ferocious that a patient can be dead in minutes despite the best medical treatment.

Anaphylaxis occurs when the body recognizes the presence of a foreign intruder, or antigen, that it has seen before and for some unknown reason has deemed henceforth unwelcome. During the first encounter there is no outward reaction to the antigen. But the body takes an irrational dislike to the substance, creating immune molecules called antibodies that remember its chemical structure. If and when it intrudes again, these scouts detect its presence and sound a chemical alarm. Cells called mast cells release powerful chemical messengers—histamines—that pour into the bloodstream and cause smooth muscle to contract and blood vessels to open wide and become leaky. Tissues become swollen as fluid leaks

Burning Down the House *(cont'd.)*

from the vessels. And this inflammation occurs not only externally—causing hives—but internally as well.

When I first saw Meg Swift, it was clear she was having a severe attack: her pale, puffy face seemed to be all lips and eyelids. In fact, her eyes were now sealed shut. But that was not what worried me. An allergic reaction that confines itself to the skin can make patients look like monsters and go wild with itching, but it is rarely dangerous. The other symptoms Meg had mentioned to the nurse (with a touch of embarrassment, confessing she was sure they were "all in my head") were what caused me concern: terrible cramping in her stomach, a funny tightness in her throat, wooziness, and a weird whistling sound when she breathed.

She was definitely not imagining things. Even from the foot of her stretcher I could hear the wheezes and see the saliva running from the corner of her mouth. I knew she needed treatment right away and that niceties like taking a history and performing an exam would have to wait.

As the nurse and I each hooked up an IV line to give her fluids, I began to order medicines: Hydrocortisone, a steroid to reduce further inflammation, 100 mg, through the IV. Diphenhydramine, an antihistamine, 50 mg, also through the IV. Zantac, a drug that would help calm her crampy intestine, 50 mg, again through the IV

But the most crucial drug was to be injected under the skin: .3 cc's of epinephrine. Epinephrine is another name for adrenaline, the "fight or flight" hormone that can also counteract many of the dangerous effects histamine has throughout the body; it raises blood pressure, relaxes spasms in the airways and quiets the stomach and bowel. It also puts great stress on the heart, and in an older person or someone with hypertension or a heart condition, it can do more harm than good. So as the nurse prepared the epinephrine injection I asked Meg if she had any heart problems. She shook her head no.

"Okay, then," I told her. "I'm going to give you a shot of adrenaline, which will make your heart pound and make you feel really jumpy, but you need it to break the attack." I stuck the needle into her arm. I remembered, from my childhood bouts with asthma, the blessed relief such shots could bring, but also the hours of jitters and sleeplessness that followed them. "It's in," I said, withdrawing the syringe.

"Good," she answered in a voice that was raspy and barely audible. Uh-oh.

"Is that how you normally speak?" I asked.

"No," she answered with difficulty. "I started to get hoarse in the waiting room." It was obvious that the swelling that had started on her skin had now moved down to her vocal cords.

The quick exam that followed confirmed my initial impression that her reaction was widespread and serious. Her blood pressure was extremely low—only 78/50, compared with a normal pressure of 120/80—because of the fluid leaking out of her blood vessels and the widening of those vessels. This meant that she was in danger of going into shock—or even dying—because less oxygen was reaching her brain and other vital organs. Her lungs were in trouble, too: with my stethoscope

Burning Down the House *(cont'd.)*

I could hear the wheezes even more precisely. Her belly was tender. And as she was being helped into a gown she started vomiting.

It was obvious that quite a few of Meg's organs were involved in the reaction, and that worried me. I was relieved to note, however, that no single system in her body had reached the point of total collapse.

So after giving her the first dose of epinephrine, the nurse and I held vigil at her bedside, peppering her with questions. It was no easy task, since the antihistamine she had received—used to block the further release of histamine from mast cells—can make even the heartiest of souls profoundly sleepy.

"I'm going to be a pest," I told her, trying to keep her awake. "How's your breathing feel?"

"Better," she said, her eyelids dropping. But her voice seemed even raspier than before.

Suddenly she sat bolt upright and grabbed her neck. "I feel like I'm choking. Like it's closing off."

"Another epinephrine, right now," I said to the nurse at my side.

A battle was being waged between her body's own aberrant immune chemicals and the ones we had given her to block their way. All I could do was watch the nurse give the second round of epinephrine and pray our side would win.

After a few minutes I looked at Meg's arms and noticed that her hives were fading. Through her boggy eyelids I could see slivers of green. Her blood pressure was up to 110/70. When she spoke, I heard a more resonant voice.

The immediate crisis had been averted but now came the hard work: we had to figure out what had provoked this life-threatening episode. Anaphylactic reactions tend to get worse each time they occur, so it's crucial to know what caused the first one and to prevent any subsequent exposure to that antigen.

People who develop an allergy—to a specific drug, for instance—frequently react with disbelief. "Allergic to Bactrim? Couldn't be. I took that last year." But that's just the point: in allergies, the immune system only reacts to vanquish foes it has already met.

The meeting may be brief, however, so brief that the patient is not even aware of it. A person may become sensitized to penicillin, for instance, from trace quantities of the drug in cow's milk. At other times, the encounter is not with the allergenic substance itself but with a different, though chemically related, substance. For instance, a person may become allergic to insect venom after being pricked by a sea urchin spine.

In Meg's case, I probed and probed to find a culprit, any culprit, but with each line of questioning I ran into a dead end. She and her husband, who joined us once the crisis had passed, insisted that she was taking no medicines. I asked about new shampoos, new soaps, new powders—anything that could be absorbed through the skin. Nothing. She had no history of allergies and had had no insect bites.

It's not always this difficult to track down the reason for a severe allergic reaction. I took care of one man who knew he was allergic to peanuts but thought he

Burning Down the House *(cont'd.)*

might be able to get away with eating a few on his birthday. He survived, but 24 hours on a breathing machine in the intensive care unit was the price of his little snack.

Although the severity of a reaction is loosely related to the amount of a substance that enters the bloodstream (the man who ate the peanuts had gotten away with eating a few on special occasions before), in people who are sensitized, even a minuscule portion can be perilous. And the reaction each time is unpredictable.

The medical journals contain reports of a man allergic to fish who died after eating french fries that had been cooked in oil used to fry cod earlier in the day. Likewise, they tell of a woman with a peanut allergy who succumbed to anaphylaxis after eating a turkey sandwich cut with a knife that had previously been used to slice a peanut butter and jelly sandwich. A friend of mine, who is allergic to celery, has had several severe reactions after eating dishes that she was assured by waiters were celery-free; she now carries epinephrine with her everywhere. For people allergic to foods that restaurants commonly use as minor ingredients for texture or flavor, eating out can be like walking through a minefield.

Having tried everything else I could think of, I had to assume that Meg's attack was caused by a food allergy as well. So we started to go through the foods she'd eaten for breakfast, since anaphylactic reactions tend to start within several hours of exposure to the offending substance.

I was hoping Meg would tell me that she'd had an unusual meal that morning, one that included a type of food commonly associated with severe allergic reactions—nuts (an apple walnut muffin?), chocolate (a chocolate croissant?), berries (strawberries on her cereal?). But no luck. She told me she was a creature of extreme habit. Every morning she had coffee, orange juice, and a bagel with cream cheese or grape jam.

Still, I pushed her to go over every last spoonful of food. And it was worth it, because we sparked something in Matthew Swift's memory.

"Wait!" he suddenly exclaimed. "We did have grape jam, but it wasn't the one we usually eat. It was from that gift basket we got for Christmas." It was not a very satisfying lead, but I clung to it nonetheless. Who knew what substance had been dumped into the vat to make the jam sweeter or purpler or stickier?

But I was still left with a problem. Meg would soon be ready to leave the emergency room—her voice was already back to normal and the hives had disappeared—and I had to give her instructions about what foods to avoid. I would have loved to be able to tell her right there and then that she had developed an allergy to grapes or to grape jam. But the only way to tell for sure would be to do some kind of allergy testing, and the devastating internal aftermath of an anaphylactic attack made that an impossibility. The body's exhausted immune system needs time to rebuild and replenish itself so that it can react normally when challenged with a suspect antigen. The drugs that we used to suppress the near-fatal reaction would skew any test results as well.

Burning Down the House *(cont'd.)*

The best I could do was to warn Meg to avoid anything and everything she had eaten that morning—including coffee and bagels. And since allergy attacks sometimes rebound, even after successful treatment, I explained that she would have to continue taking the antihistamines and the steroids to break the cycle of inflammation. After all, some of the substance that had precipitated this near disaster might still be in her blood, so it was wise not to drop our defenses.

I arranged for Meg to see an allergist two weeks later—by which time her system would have recovered. The allergist would use one of two methods to find her nemesis: he might mix small samples of her blood with a wide variety of potential antigens to see which caused the cells in her blood to release histamine, or he might simply perform a prick test, dropping a minute amount of each chemical onto the skin, making a tiny pinprick beneath it, and looking for a local reaction.

In the end, the allergist—using the first of the two methods—found that Meg had indeed reacted to something from that gift basket. But the culprit wasn't the grape jam she'd told me about. She'd forgotten that she had also taken a tiny taste of papaya jelly that morning. Her body, however, had remembered.

The day she left the ER, though, I still could not name her enemy. So instead I gave her a prescription and a piece of advice. The prescription was for an EpiPen—a syringe of epinephrine that injects automatically when pressed into the flesh of the thigh. I told her to use it if she felt an attack coming on and felt that she couldn't breathe—and then to return to the hospital immediately. And my piece of advice was this: "Remember," though I knew she would, "anaphylaxis is not 'just allergies.'"

 ## The Hidden Life of Dogs*

Elizabeth Marshall Thomas

Another very important skill of Misha's was his management of traffic. Cambridge suffers from some of the worst drivers in the nation, but no car as much as touched Misha, who, like a civil engineer, had divided the streets and their traffic into four categories and had developed different strategies to deal with each. The worst and most dangerous areas were congestions of multidirectional traffic, such as are found in Central, Porter, or Harvard Square. These areas Misha completely avoided. If he needed to be on the far side of one of them, he simply went around it. The second

The Hidden Life of Dogs *(cont'd.)*

category was composed of a few limited-access highways, such as Alewife Parkway and Memorial Drive, where the heavy traffic of speeding cars was especially dangerous to dogs, not only because no legal or moral responsibility is attached to killing a dog, but also because dogs are down low, where motorists can't see them. Misha couldn't avoid the highways and still go where he wanted, so, adopting a humble attitude, he approached the cars with diplomacy and tact in an attempt to appease them.

Perhaps not surprisingly, many dogs treat cars as if they were animate. Dogs who chase cars evidently see them as large, unruly ungulates badly in need of discipline and shepherding, and can't help trying to control them. But Misha didn't chase cars. Being a husky and wearing very lightly the long domestication of his species, he felt no compulsion to assist mankind. However, he well understood that cars could be tremendously dangerous, especially when they seemed to be acting angrily and willfully, as they did on the limited-access highways. So he offered them respect. At the edge of the highway Misha would stand humbly, his head and tail low, his eyes half shut, his ears politely folded. If the cars could have seen him, they would have realized that he didn't challenge their authority.

But the moment the cars became few, Misha's humility would vanish. His ears would rise, his tale too, and he would bound fearlessly among them, the very picture of confidence. Over the highway he would skip, and go happily on his way. Never while I was observing him did I hear a scream of tires. Sometimes, though, he would lose me beside a limited-access highway. I lacked his courage, also his speed and skill, and I usually had to wait much longer than he did before the traffic conditions met my requirements for crossing. If traffic separated us, Misha would wait for a while on the far side, but sooner or later he would assume that I had lost interest and would travel on. Calling him back was out of the question for me—I couldn't have asked him to risk the traffic again on my behalf. Rather, if we became separated, I would simply go home. There he would find me waiting whenever his voyaging abated for a time.

Misha's third category of traffic included the main city streets. Cambridge's famous Brattle Street offers a perfect example, especially because Misha often used this street as a thoroughfare. Or rather, he used the sidewalk of Brattle Street as he traveled from one neighborhood to another, just as a human pedestrian would do. When crossing an intersecting street, however, Misha used a better and more intelligent method than his human counterparts. Unlike us, he didn't cross at the corner. Instead, he would turn up the intersecting street and go about twenty feet from the corner, cross there, and return on the sidewalk to Brattle Street's sidewalk, where he would continue his journey. At first I couldn't understand this maneuver, although Misha invariably used it. Then I saw its merits, and copied him thereafter. Why is Misha's method safer? Because at any point along the block, traffic comes from only two directions instead of from four directions, as it does at the intersection. By crossing at midblock, one reduces one's chances of being hit by a turning car. Since learning the midblock technique from Misha, I have noticed that almost

The Hidden Life of Dogs *(cont'd.)*

all free-ranging dogs do likewise, as do people who need extra time to cross or who depend on their hearing for safety. Certain blind people, for instance, use the same technique.

Safety, however, was not Misha's only consideration. Usually, a tree or lamppost or mailbox or fire hydrant stands just behind the building line at the place where a traveling dog likes to cross the street. For dogs, the object serves the same function as a wayside inn at the ford of a river, a place that most travelers would visit of necessity, and therefore a good place to leave a message or a sign. Misha would visit these fixed objects, and after careful investigation would turn around and lift his leg. This is a very familiar sight to most dog owners. Virtually all male dogs mark permanent items (or what they believe to be permanent items) as they progress along a street. Sometimes Misha would mark repeatedly, passing a little urine, investigating his stain, and passing urine again, sometimes repeating the procedure as many as five or six times before he seemed satisfied and ready to carry on. Sometimes he rotated his body until his belly tilted upward, meanwhile standing on tiptoe to place his mark almost three feet above the ground. But even these very high stains did not always please him. If they weren't to his satisfaction, he would turn around and stretch even more, so that when he investigated, he would find his mark at his own eye level or higher.

What did it mean? Surely more than emptying the bladder. If Misha wanted merely to empty his bladder, he wouldn't bother to lift his leg at all but would bend his knees slightly, so as not to wet his hind feet, and release his urine, puppy-style, on the ground. Was Misha's leg-lifting an attempt to mark territory? That certainly was the popular explanation, an explanation that I had accepted as fact before my observation began. So I kept track of all the places Misha stained in order to learn what he felt he owned. Soon, though, I had an unwieldy sprawl of data that showed his alleged territory to be virtually everywhere he went. Was this possible? Wouldn't a dog as savvy as Misha want to discriminate to some degree between his home ground and distant places? Wouldn't he act one way in the place where he lived and another way in a distant area which he might visit only once? In fact, Misha's leglifting was about the same however far from home he happened to be.

In the residential streets, Misha's demeanor changed. Here he took no precaution about cars and never used a sidewalk, but instead moved daringly and purposefully up the middle of the street, eyes front, head and ears forward, tail up, the very picture of intent confidence. Even when he crossed an intersection, he did not alter his demeanor but kept scanning the street ahead. The trouble was that he couldn't see the cars speeding toward him on the cross street. Yet, amazingly, he always escaped them. How did he manage that?

I might never have learned if both his ears had been like the ears of most other huskies, stiff and upright. But they weren't. His left car was soft at the tip, and when Misha was trotting along in a relaxed manner, the soft left tip bounced. When he was alert and tense, however, or when he noticed or thought of something important, the tip of his left ear would shoot up and stand stiff like the tip of his right ear.

The Hidden Life of Dogs *(cont'd.)*

One day, while following Misha down a side street on the bike I had taken to using for my dogological studies, I saw his left ear stiffen as he approached an intersection. As was his custom, his eyes never left the street ahead, but the nearer he got to the intersection, the more his two ears stiffened and rotated outward, pointing sideways, so that by the time he was ready to cross, which he always did without changing his speed or shifting his gaze, the cups of his ears were pointing up and down the cross street. If a car was coming, he heard it. What was more, his hearing gave the speed of the car as well as its location, so that all Misha needed to do to avoid being hit was to pick up his pace or slow down, either to beat the car to the intersection or else to let it go across ahead of him. Scanning the street along which he was proceeding, never shifting his gaze to confirm what he heard coming from the sides, Misha would trot across the intersection smoothly, radiating coolness and self-confidence.

Why didn't he look at the cars? Because he was using his eyes to monitor the scene on the far side of the intersection. There, sensing Misha's approach, all the loose dogs of the neighborhood would leave their yards and porches and run out into the street. And Misha wanted to be ready for them. He wanted to see them before they saw him, so he could prepare himself mentally for the meeting. Inevitably, the nearest dog would approach Misha with its tail and ears raised. When the approaching dog was about thirty feet away, Misha would slow his pace and advance more stiffly, his attention closely focused on the other dog, and gradually the two would come together.

Then Misha's neck would arch and his tail would rise. The other dog would stand still to meet him. Misha would approach stiffly and rapidly, and the two would stand slightly past each other, their heads by each other's necks. Misha usually averted his head to look sideways into the eye of the other dog, who usually looked directly but inquiringly at Misha and then averted his head slightly. Holding his tail high during these meetings, Misha kept his ears forward and the hair of his mantle slightly raised. If the other dog tried to investigate his groin or anus, Misha would leap sideways with his rear legs to avoid the investigation. Finally he would make his conclusive gesture: he would face the other dog's side with his neck highly arched and his nose pointing down almost into the other dog's hackles. Only after this would he sometimes switch his stance again and let the other dog investigate him.

Everyone has watched such a meeting. Sometimes just as the tension seems to be relaxing, one dog knocks the other with his hips. Sometimes the second dog does not react visibly and the circling goes on, but sometimes the second dog staggers slightly, then folds his ears and lowers his tail a bit. No person knows exactly what the hip test tells the participants, but probably the dogs have felt each other's mass. At any rate, the test seems to help them reach an agreement. They usually separate soon afterward, each going his own way. Very inconspicuously, Misha would administer the hip test to every dog who cared to encounter him, and invariably emerged from the encounter with his tail high, a sign of his transcendence over

The Hidden Life of Dogs *(cont'd.)*

the other dog, who emerged with his tail low. Then Misha might invite or be invited by the other dog to play, and the two might frisk briefly. Misha might invite the other dog to follow him, which he did by trotting onward, looking back at the other dog meanwhile.

Always pragmatic, Misha never bothered to circle tiny dogs, but just swept by them or stepped over them, and he never tried to circle huge dogs, whom he pretended to ignore. Anyone would know that he was superior to the tiny dogs, and evidently he didn't want anyone to notice that the huge dogs could have been physically superior to him. Instead, he concentrated on dogs within ten or fifteen pounds of his own size (a size range that probably included more than 90 percent of the dogs he encountered) and circled to establish his superiority to them. He spent more time circling the male dogs than the female dogs, who tended to be less forthcoming, often circling Misha only long enough to learn his sex and attitude before backing off. Whatever the sex of his challenger, though, the moment the encounter ended, Misha, with his supremacy intact, would continue up the street to repeat exactly the same behavior with every dog who didn't retreat from him. On and on he traveled, in long straight lines about the city, concluding his business in one residential neighborhood only to penetrate another, where once again, radiating coolness, he would circle all comers.

✤ CHAPTER 6

CRITIQUING

INTRODUCTION—WHAT IS A CRITIQUE, AND WHY WRITE ONE?

A critique is a piece of academic writing that provides a summary of the content of something—such as a book, article, play, film, art exhibit, lecture, or concert—and offers an evaluation of it. As a college student, you commonly will be assigned to write critiques for classes, and as a reader of magazines, newspapers, and scholarly journals, you frequently will come across critiques in your reading. In critiques, writers explain the criteria they used to make their evaluations and illustrate their points according to those criteria. Simply saying that something was "interesting," "not very good," or "so-so" without explaining *why* does not suffice for a critique.

Although, as we have said, critiques evaluate various kinds of written texts, performances, events, exhibits, and so on, this chapter will focus solely on critiques of written texts; other kinds of critiques (which we will refer to as "evaluations") will be dealt with in Chapter 7. We devote an entire chapter to the critique of written texts because the skills required to write them are of crucial importance in the academic and professional development of college students. In this chapter, you will gain practice in reading, note taking, and summarizing, skills that are important not only in writing critiques but in several other kinds of academic writing.

College teachers frequently assign critiques because they are one means by which teachers can measure their students' ability to apply the skills and knowledge being taught. In order to write an effective critique, you must fully understand the content of the piece you are critiquing, including any key terms. It is necessary to understand the other course material well enough to apply it to the piece you are critiquing. Critiques make for interesting assignments because students often reach very different conclusions about a source.

In assigning critiques of written texts, teachers are helping you to acquire educated opinions about issues in your discipline and to become conversant about these issues. As you write critiques, you will gain valuable experience in working with the kinds of material that you will be using throughout college, and you will develop a much fuller understanding of the materials than you would by merely reading them. Because you are forced to evaluate the materials, you will internalize their content, think about how they relate to other materials within your discipline, and remember them more readily.

SAMPLE ASSIGNMENTS

Critiques are a very common type of writing in college. While you may think of analyzing written texts as the business of people in the humanities, you should realize that people in all professions or disciplines read and analyze professional writings as a routine part of their work. Critiques, then, provide practice in this type of critical reading and writing. To show you some of the types of critiques you may be required to write, we have selected a few representative assignments from several fields. As you read these assignments, look for similarities among them.

Computer Literacy Assignment. To complete this assignment you will first need to read one of the novels listed on the class syllabus. All of these are available in paperback from the Campus Bookstore. The purpose of this assignment is to give you an opportunity to assess the accuracy with which computers are portrayed within a work of popular fiction and to practice your word-processing skills.

The essay. Craft an essay of at least three pages in which you explain how well you think the author understands computers. Justify your thesis with specific references to the novel. For example, what current capabilities of computers are depicted, and how accurately are they described? If the author extrapolates about computer technology, how plausible are these speculations?

Format. Please use a 12-point Palatino font with headings and interline spacing as described on page 2 of the course syllabus. Page numbers should be printed on each page.

Political Science Assignment. Several times this term you will be required to submit a reading journal, which should include *one- to two-page* (typed or word-processed) summaries of articles from *The Christian Science Monitor* dealing with comparative politics (two per week). For your summaries, use the following format:

Citation:

Last Name, First Name. "Title of article," *The Christian Science Monitor,* date, page numbers.

Summary of article:

Your comments and analysis:

(Be sure that you write more than one or two sentences here.)

Biology Assignment. This is an assignment designed to familiarize you with the Science Library and to give you an opportunity to become acquainted with the format and contents of literature published in the life sciences. It requires you to critically examine a journal article, using the questions that follow.

To complete this assignment, you must select one of the journals listed on the attached sheet. Use issues of journals *published within the last ten years.* Do not select review articles or short reports. If you are unsure about whether the article you have selected is suitable, consult with your lab instructor.

After you have read your article, answer *all* of the following questions. You may number and answer each question separately or you may group questions together; however, you will need to write out the complete citation for the article you selected (using the format we have discussed in class) at the top of your paper.

1. Identify the journal you selected, and briefly (in one paragraph) describe its contents.

2. Identify the publisher of the journal (a society? a university press?), and briefly describe what you consider to be its intended readership.

3. Discuss the contents of the abstract: How fully does it describe the contents of the article? If you read the abstract first, did it help you read the article? Explain.

4. Select one of the figures (or a table of data) in the article, and describe what it illustrates. Are such figures or tables important? Explain.

5. List the subheadings of the article. Do they identify all of the major sections? Explain the importance of such subheadings.

6. Describe the way in which other research studies are cited within the article. Why is citing other studies important?

7. From your examination of the article you selected, what do you consider to be the most important function of this type of writing? (To answer this question, you might ask yourself, "Who reads this, and why?")

8. Attach a photocopy of the first page of your article to this assignment when you hand it in.

Journalism Assignment. Select a nonfiction book, other than an autobiography, written by someone trained as a journalist, and write a two- or three-page paper in which you answer the question "What can aspiring journalists learn about reporting, researching, or writing from this book that they could apply to their own work?" Summarize your book as necessary within your paper; as part of the background information, you will need to provide the author's credentials and experience as a journalist. Be sure to include specific examples (negative or positive) to support your opinion.

Economics Assignment. To earn extra credit in this class, you may write and turn in a critique of any of the articles distributed in class. A critique must consist of the following:

- An identification/explanation of two positions regarding the controversy (1 point)
- A discussion of the position you find more credible, including a rationale for your selection (2–4 points)

Your discussion of the position you have selected will be more convincing if you show a full, detailed understanding of *both* sides of the controversy. In addition, citing other sources (material from your textbook, other distributed articles, etc.) will strengthen your argument.

As you can see from these assignments, critiques involve reading, summarizing, and/or analyzing a written text. Usually such assignments require students not just to summarize but to support their opinions about the written texts they critique. However, there are some assignments, such as the Political Science Assignment, that ask students to summarize a written text without providing any analysis of it. While such assignments are occasionally used in college, it is our experience that most often critique assignments expect both summary and opinion. In fact, if you receive an assignment that asks you to "write a summary" of a book or article, it's a good idea to check with your instructor to see whether he or she actually expects you to write a critique—a combination of summary and analysis or opinion.

Whatever field they are written for, critiques like those described in the sample assignments share a number of features:

1. Appropriate summary of or background information about the text being critiqued is provided as and where needed.
2. Criteria are used to evaluate a written text.
3. The criteria used are relevant to the type of writing being critiqued.
4. The criteria are consistent; they relate to the purpose of the critique and support a controlling idea or judgment.
5. The controlling idea or judgment is supported with specific references to or supporting details from the text being critiqued.

READING, SUMMARIZING, AND CRITIQUING

To write a critique, you will need to pay attention to three particular areas: critical reading, summarizing, and determining the criteria with which you will evaluate a text. Critical reading enables you to *understand* and *assess* the text that you will be critiquing. Summarizing provides readers of critiques with information about the content of the text that is being evaluated. Finally, every critique should use criteria that are appropriate to the subject matter or topic and that are clearly related to the controlling idea.

Critical Reading

As we have already implied, critical reading consists of at least two important components: **comprehension** of the content of whatever is read and **assessment** or evaluation of that content. That is, to merely *understand* what a writer says is not sufficient when you are reading critically; you need also to evaluate the content for qualities such as accuracy, comprehensiveness, and fairness. It has been our experience that students are often unfamiliar with the subject matter or inexperienced with the level of difficulty of the reading they are assigned in college. A good strategy for you to practice, therefore, is to perform two separate readings, one to fully understand the content of what you have read and the other to evaluate that content.

Reading for Comprehension. Obviously, a reader's first task in confronting a text is to be able to fully understand what is says. If a piece of writing deals with a simple or familiar topic and is well organized and clearly written, this does not ordinarily present a challenge. However, writing that deals with highly complex content, particularly if the subject matter is unfamiliar, is often hard to understand. Because comprehending a piece of writing can be hard, seasoned readers ordinarily develop strategies that assist them in constructing meaning.

Readers often exploit some of the same concepts as writers when they read for comprehension. As you know, skilled writers consider their audience and purpose when crafting a text; they also consider the rules or conventions related to the particular type of writing, or *genre,* in which they are engaged. In reading for comprehension, therefore, it is wise to begin by getting a sense of the genre (research report? textbook? editorial?) with which you are dealing. Determining this may help you locate important information more easily. A research report, for example, may be preceded by an abstract that highlights the purpose, methods, and results of the study. Book reviews often begin or end with an overall assessment.

Because a variety of informative writing genres require that purpose be stated explicitly, many of the readings you examine will contain statements of purpose or intent: "This essay is a report of. . . ." Such statements are often accompanied by brief previews of the contents or organization of the text to follow: "We will first examine the three basic approaches that we observed. Following this examination, we will. . . ." An explicitly stated thesis accompanied by a "road map" that tells the reader what to expect is a powerful aid to comprehension. This is especially true if the text also highlights important sections with headings—**The First Approach, The Second Approach, The Third Approach,** and **Our Assessment of Their Effectiveness.**

Of course, not all texts explicitly state a thesis or contain headings that identify major portions. However, metadiscourse can—and often does—appear throughout a text. It is always a good reading strategy, therefore, to look for and underline or highlight each occurrence because metadiscourse can alert you to important parts of content and structure, as the following examples illustrate:

> *A third reason we did not agree with their judgment is because. . . .*
>
> *Contradictory to our expectations, we began to observe that. . . .*
>
> *To conclude, Whery's approach was inconsistent with. . . .*
>
> *Although Keen's explanation seemed reasonable when I first encountered it, I began to question. . . .*

Looking for explicit thesis statements and headings, as well as examining instances of metadiscourse, then, can assist you in understanding the contents of a written text.

It can sometimes be difficult to find indications of large or macro-structures (explicit thesis statements, metadiscourse, headings, etc.) within a text, especially if the text is lengthy and complex. Therefore, as you read, you should also try to determine the meaning of smaller, more local chunks. The easiest way to identify such smaller portions is to work paragraph by paragraph. Look for topic sentences, which are usually located at the beginning or end of a paragraph. If a paragraph doesn't seem to contain a topic sentence, repeated words or phrases—particularly those that function as the subjects of sentences—often point to the main idea. Also, paragraphs often consist of claims or generalizations, accompanied by examples that illustrate or support them, so it can be instructive to differentiate these. Sometimes you can work backwards from illustrative examples or evidence and use them to identify the claims or generalizations that they support.

Because critical reading that focuses on comprehension can be quite involved, many readers underline key words and phrases, make marginal comments, or jot down important notes as they move through a text. If you follow our suggestion and do two critical readings, one for comprehension and one to evaluate contents, you may wish to use two different-colored markers or two different-colored ink pens; in this way, you can differentiate your marks and notes for each reading. Another easy way to differentiate underlining, commentary, and so forth from two separate readings is to make two photocopies of your text; one copy can be used during a reading for comprehension, the other during an evaluative reading.

The following brief article illustrates the kinds of notations a person might make during a reading for comprehension. The article was originally published in *Ms.* magazine in April 1980.

The Great Person-Hole Cover Debate

A Modest Proposal for Anyone Who thinks the Word "He" Is Just Plain Easier . . .*

Lindsy Van Gelder

I wasn't looking for trouble. What I was looking for, actually, was a little tourist information to help me plan a camping trip to New England.

But there it was, on the first page of the 1979 edition of the State of Vermont *Digest of Fish and Game Laws and Regulations:* a special message of welcome from one Edward F. Kehoe, commissioner of the Vermont Fish and Game Department, to the reader and would-be camper, *i.e.,* me.

Gelder was offended by reading literature addressed to sports<u>men</u>

This person (*i.e.,* me) is called "the sportsman."

("We have no 'sportswomen, sportspersons, sportsboys, or sportsgirls,'") Commissioner Kehoe hastened to explain, obviously

message from book

The Great Person-Hole Cover Debate *(cont'd.)*

anticipating that some of us sportsfeminists might feel a bit over-looked. "But," he added, "we are pleased to report that we do have many great sportsmen who are women, as well as young people of both sexes."

It's just that the Fish and Game Department is trying to keep things "simple and forthright" and to respect "long-standing tradition." And anyway, we really ought to be flattered, "sportsman" being "a meaningful title being earned by a special kind of dedicated man, woman, or young person, as opposed to just any hunter, fisherman, or trapper."

Commissioner explains how term includes everyone not just men (reason for his message)

I have heard this particular line of reasoning before. In fact, I've heard it so often that I've come to think of it as The Great Person-Hole Cover Debate, since gender-neutral manholes are invariably brought into the argument as evidence of the lengths to which humorless, Newspeak-spouting feminists will go to destroy their mother tongue.

She heard this reasoning before and is going to try to prove it's illogical

Consternation about woman-handling the language comes from all sides. Sexual conservatives who see the feminist movement as a unisex plot and who long for the good olde days of *vive la différence,* when men were men and women were women, nonetheless do not rally behind the notion that the term "mankind" excludes women.

(1)

some believe "man" includes everyone

But most of the people who choke on expressions like "spokesperson" aren't right-wing misogynists, and this is what troubles me. Like the undoubtedly well-meaning folks at the Vermont Fish and Game Department, they tend to reassure you right up front that they're only trying to keep things "simple" and to follow "tradition," and that some of their best men are women, anyway.

(2)

some people say keep language simple

Usually they wind up warning you, with great sincerity, that you're jeopardizing the worthy cause of women's rights by focusing on "trivial" side issues. I would like to know how anything that gets people so defensive and resistant can possibly be called "trivial," whatever else it might be.

(3)

some people say this issue is trivial

The English language is alive and constantly changing. Progress—both scientific and social—is reflected in our language, or should be.

* thesis ?

Not too long ago, there was a product called "flesh-colored" Band-Aids. The flesh in question was colored Caucasian. Once the civil rights movement pointed out the racism inherent in the name, it was dropped. I cannot imagine reading a thoughtful, well-intentioned company policy statement explaining that while the Band-Aids would continue to be called "flesh-colored" for old time's sake, black and brown people would now be

first example to back up her point — language can exclude

The Great Person-Hole Cover Debate *(cont'd.)*

considered honorary whites and were perfectly welcome to use them.

Most sensitive people manage to describe our national religious traditions as "Judeo-Christian," even though it takes a few seconds longer to say than "Christian." So why is it such a hardship to say "he or she" instead of "he"?

Second example to back-up her point — it's worth the effort to use longer terms

I have a modest proposal for anyone who maintains that "he" is just plain easier: since "he" has been the style for several centuries now—and since it really includes everybody anyway, right?—it seems only fair to give "she" a turn. Instead of having to ponder over the intricacies of, say, "Congressman" versus "Congressperson" versus "Representative," we can simplify things by calling them all "Congresswoman."

Is she being serious here? I don't think so. Her solution would suggest not. She's being sarcastic

Other clarifications will follow: "a woman's home is her castle". . . "a giant step for all womankind" . . . "all women are created equal" . . . "Fisherwoman's Wharf." . . .

And don't be upset by the business letter that begins "Dear Madam," fellas. It means you, too.

If this issue is so trivial, how do you feel about these terms?

In this example, a variety of simple graphic devices—underlining, circles, arrows, asterisks, brackets, numbers—accompany the marginal commentary. These devices, especially the numbering of arguments in paragraphs 7, 8, and 9 and the use of arrows and lines that connect circled and underlined words and phrases with each other or with marginal commentary (paragraphs 2 and 4; 5 and 6; 7; 14 and 15) draw the eye to key points. They also provide visual links that connect parts of the article with one another or with the reader's commentary. Some marks are used sparingly to call attention to significant parts of the text; the asterisk (*) is used just once—to call attention to a possible thesis in paragraph 10. Marginal commentary is spare and tends to paraphrase important points.

 **Activity 1**

Carefully reread "Burning Down the House" and "Missing in Interaction" in Chapter 5. Use graphics (underlining, circles, asterisks, etc.) and marginal notation to identify and comment on what each text reveals about its main idea or thesis, its important parts or aspects, and how these parts/aspects fit together and support one another.

Compare your marking and notations with those of your group partners. Did you all identify the same central purpose and main ideas for each essay? Compare your commentary, underlining, and so on with respect to the two essays. Was it easier to identify a thesis, metadiscourse, main points, and the like for one essay rather than the other? If so, why? For both essays, if you and your group partners disagreed about the main point or points, discuss why and see whether you can reach a consensus.

Assessing What You Read. To understand a piece of writing is only a portion of what is necessary in a thorough critical reading. A careful evaluation or assessment is also a requirement.

Because an author of a novel might review his or her own work quite favorably or a person who has been a victim of crime might argue for stiffer penalties for felons, it is important to consider a writer's relationship to his or her subject matter when assessing a piece of writing. People's life experiences, as well as factors such as age, social class, race, and religious background, influence their perception and judgment, even when they make serious attempts to be "fair" or "impartial." Careful readers, then, have an obligation to consider what they know or can infer about these factors, because taking these into consideration can help them conduct an informed reading.

The familiarity of writers with their subject matter—either through formal training, prior experience, or information gathering—is crucial. How confident, for example, would you be about following advice on the purchase of a used car if the person who offered it had no experience buying such automobiles, was not an experienced mechanic, and had not done any related research? Similarly, when you read critically, you should take into account what you know or can infer about the writer's qualifications to speak authoritatively on a particular topic. What are the writer's credentials, such as degrees or evidence of specialized training? Writers often provide information about their training, experience, and other qualifications for the reader. In addition, these can be listed with an author's name or provided in a section at the beginning or end of a journal, magazine, or book.

In addition to an author's qualifications, the source in which a piece of writing appears is important. Information about dieting, for example, might appear as a small filler in a local newspaper, within a magazine written for teenage girls, or within the pages of the *New England Journal of Medicine*. These and other publications vary dramatically in the extent to which they do or don't identify their authors and in what they expect of their authors in terms of qualifications, objectivity, and so forth. Some sources are very particular about the writing they publish. Editors or experts with specialized training "referee" what can be published, selecting only a very few pieces written by highly qualified individuals from the many that are submitted. Reputable publishers of books, magazines, or newspapers also ordinarily require that "facts" be verified and that sources be corroborated so that false information isn't circulated. They also publish the identity of writers of important pieces so that readers can assess their qualifications or biases.

You can evaluate a source of publication for a piece of writing by examining any information the source provides about the editorial (selection) policy, publisher, and intended readership. Many sources also publish statements about their purposes or goals, often revealing their biases in a forthright manner ("a liberal magazine dedicated to . . . "). If a source does not provide much information about itself, examining the audience to whom it is addressed can be helpful. What type of advertisement is included? How technical and detailed is the information? What type of subject matter is covered? These and other features of a publication offer clues about the attributes its audience is expected to possess, such as level of education, familiarity with specialized information, political or religious affiliations, and so on.

Another factor important to critical reading is the historical context in which the writing occurred. Significant events, public opinion, the state of knowledge about a particular subject all influence what writers say, or don't say. Because, for example, the issue of how language might affect women was not a widely discussed topic in the United States before the 1970s, it would have been unusual—and noteworthy—if "The Great Person-Hole Cover Debate" had been published in the 1930s. It can also be argued that Americans' attitudes about when and how they should become involved in armed conflict was very much affected by the war in Vietnam. Therefore, it would be important to note the date of an essay that assesses the circumstances under which Americans should (or should not) engage in military action.

Finally, a careful assessment of the contents of a reading should involve some attention to the writing itself, especially the type of examples provided, the quality and extent of the argument or explanation used to support claims, and indications of the writer's attitudes toward the topic. An essay that makes claims about the value of a college education, for example, should provide ample reasoning that supports these claims as well as specific examples that illustrate the benefits of a college education or data with respect to relevant criteria such as job satisfaction, level of responsibility, salary, and so forth. In addition, the tone (humorous, serious, ironic) is an important factor to consider; an ironic or sarcastic tone suggests that the writer means the opposite of what is said. An essay entitled "Ten Reasons Not to Attend College" written in an ironic tone would be arguing that persons should pursue their education beyond high school.

Reproduced a second time is the article "The Great Person-Hole Cover Debate," this time with markings that assess or evaluate the content. Notice how the comments reflect attention to the source (*Ms.* magazine), the writer, the time the article was written, the nature of the argument and examples provided, and the tone.

The Great Person-Hole Cover Debate

Is this a reference to Swift's essay "A modest propsal"?

A Modest Proposal for Anyone Who thinks the Word "He" Is Just Plain Easier . . .*

never heard of her; no b'ground info given on her

Lindsy Van Gelder

I wasn't looking for trouble. What I was looking for, actually, was a little tourist information to help me plan a camping trip to New England.

article published 1980 — so this happened to her recently

catchy beginning— Interesting

But there it was, on the first page of the 1979 edition of the State of Vermont *Digest of Fish and Game Laws and Regulations:* a special message of welcome from one Edward F. Kehoe, commissioner of the Vermont Fish and Game Department, to the reader and would-be camper, *i.e.,* me.

This person (*i.e.,* me) is called "the sportsman."

"We have no 'sportswomen, sportspersons, sportsboys, or sportsgirls,' " Commissioner Kehoe hastened to explain, obviously anticipating that some of us (sportsfeminists) might feel a bit overlooked. "But," he added, "we are pleased to report that we do have many great sportsmen who are women, as well as young people of both sexes."

She calls herself a feminist

It's just that the Fish and Game Department is trying to keep things "simple and forthright" and to respect "long-standing tradition." And anyway, we really ought to be flattered, "sportsman" being "a meaningful title being earned by a special kind of dedicated man, woman, or young person, as opposed to just any hunter, fisherman, or trapper."

Is this how others see her?

I have heard this particular line of reasoning before. In fact, I've heard it so often that I've come to think of it as The Great Person-Hole Cover Debate, since gender-neutral manholes are invariably brought into the argument as evidence of the lengths to which (humorless, Newspeak-spouting feminists will go to destroy their mother tongue.)

Consternation about woman-handling the language comes from all sides. Sexual conservatives who see the feminist movement as a unisex plot and who long for the good olde days of *vive la différence,* when men were men and women were women, nonetheless do not rally behind the notion that the term "mankind" excludes women.

she's biased — has a strong opinion

a feminist magazine

But most of the people who choke on expressions like "spokesperson" aren't right-wing misogynists, and this is what

The Great Person-Hole Cover Debate *(cont'd.)*

troubles me. Like the undoubtedly well-meaning folks at the Vermont Fish and Game Department, they tend to reassure you right up front that they're only trying to keep things "simple" and to follow "tradition," and that some of their best men are women, anyway.

Usually they wind up warning you, with great sincerity, that you're jeopardizing the worthy cause of women's rights by focusing on "trivial" side issues. I would like to know how anything that gets people so defensive and resistant can possibly be called "trivial," whatever else it might be.

Do people really get defensive? Is she right

thesis

The English language is alive and constantly changing. Progress—both scientific and social—is reflected in our language, or should be. *her opinion — do I agree?*

Not too long ago, there was a product called "flesh-colored" Band-Aids. The flesh in question was colored Caucasian. Once the civil rights movement pointed out the racism inherent in the name, it was dropped. I cannot imagine reading a thoughtful, well-intentioned company policy statement explaining that while the Band-Aids would continue to be called "flesh-colored" for old time's sake, black and brown people would now be considered honorary whites and were perfectly welcome to use them.

Are the examples sufficient to support her point?

Most sensitive people manage to describe our national religious traditions as "Judeo-Christian," even though it takes a few seconds longer to say than "Christian." So why is it such a hardship to say "he or she" instead of "he"?

What about atheists & other religions? Are they being excluded?

Is she being ironic like Swift?

I have a modest proposal for anyone who maintains that "he" is just plain easier: since "he" has been the style for several centuries now—and since it really includes everybody anyway, right?—it seems only fair to give "she" a turn. Instead of having to ponder over the intricacies of, say, "Congressman" versus "Congressperson" versus "Representative," we can simplify things by calling them all "Congresswoman."

Other clarifications will follow: "a woman's home is her castle" . . . "a giant step for all womankind" . . . "all women are created equal" . . . "Fisherwoman's Wharf." . . .

Catchy ending

And don't be upset by the business letter that begins "Dear Madam," fellas. It means you, too.

I think she has persuaded more with her writing style & sense of humor than with well-developed arguments or evidence

 **Activity 2**

As a group, select one of the readings from this chapter, and individually assess the writer's attributes, such as formal education and training, other specialized credentials, clinical or personal experience, research on the subject or related areas, and political views. Use information provided by the source or your inference skills to make this assessment. How do you think the writer's attributes affected his or her overall purpose and the points he or she made? Did the writer seem to be biased? Was the writer expert enough to write on the topic? Did you accept his or her claims as valid? Compare your assessment with that of your group partners. Try to account for differences of opinion.

 **Activity 3**

Together with your group partners, collect an example of each of these types of sources: a tabloid such as *National Enquirer;* a magazine about celebrities or entertainment such as *People;* a popular news magazine such as *Time* or *Newsweek;* a more specialized popular magazine such as *Discover* or *Psychology Today;* and a scholarly or professional journal. (Your teacher may need to help you find a copy of the scholarly journal.) Bring the copies of your sources to class. Then together as a group, compare them in terms of reliability, editorial policy, criteria for inclusion of writings, readership, and so forth. You might like to make a chart or table on which to record this information. As a group, prepare a brief oral report of your findings for your classmates and decide who will present it to class.

 **Activity 4**

With your group partners, select a reading from one of the sources you worked with in Activity 3. Read it carefully and, together, determine the author's controlling idea and main points. Then, locate instances in which data or examples are used to support the writer's claims. Find at least one passage in which the author used reasoning to defend the main ideas. (Hint: Look for words like *because, therefore,* and *thus*).

Assess the quality and extent of the examples or data you found. Also evaluate the reasoning the writer employed. Do you consider it convincing? Why or why not? Finally, comment on the tone of your selection. Is it serious or ironic? How does the tone affect the way in which the content is presented?

Summarizing

Summarizing—or providing a brief restatement of the main points of a text—is a skill that is often used in academic writing. In your college courses, you will see that summarizing is done for a variety of purposes. Sometimes teachers will ask you to summarize in order to determine whether you have read and understood a text they assigned you to read. As you study for various courses, you may also choose to summarize the materials to keep track of the main points you encounter or to review for an exam.

When writers summarize, their goal is to provide a condensed restatement of the original piece of writing. The exact length of a summary, though, depends on the summary's purpose. Standing alone, a summary of a three-hundred-page novel could be four or more pages; however, as part of a five-page critique of that same novel, the summary sections might make up less than two pages. In either case, a good summary represents the original as accurately and as fairly as possible. It is true to the original in content, emphasis, structure, and tone.

Although a summary is written in the words of the summarizer rather than in lines or passages borrowed from the original piece, it does not ordinarily include the summarizer's opinions, recommendations, or conclusions. In general, summaries cover *only* the main points of the original piece, eliminating any examples, illustrations, minor points, or statistics, although any details that are especially relevant to the thesis may be mentioned. Summaries that stand alone should be well-written, coherent texts with clear thesis statements, not a series of unconnected points that were taken from the original piece. Summaries that serve a function within a larger text also require careful construction and should be placed logically and coherently within a larger text.

To write an effective summary, you must first conduct a careful, critical reading. If the piece you are summarizing is fairly complex, you may need to define terms using a dictionary or discuss the piece with your instructor or with a classmate in order to completely understand the contents.

After you feel comfortable that you have a solid grasp of the piece you are summarizing, you should write out detailed notes. If the piece you are summarizing is a narrative, notes listing main events in chronological order probably will suffice; however, if you are summarizing an argument of some kind, you probably will find your notes most useful if they consist of a more formal outline of the original piece.

Before you construct a rough draft of a summary, you should consider its ultimate purpose. If your goal is to write a summary that will stand alone, you will need to decide on the main points or events from the original text and then plan a summary that will make connections between these points or events. If you are drafting a summary that ultimately will be placed within a larger text, you may decide that you cannot completely draft the summary in advance of writing the rest of the text; to ensure that the summary directly relates to the argument or discussion in the larger text, you may decide to write both parts together.

ᐁᑫ Activity 5

Read "Burning Down the House" by Elisabeth Rosenthal, which appears in Chapter 5. As a group, compose a one- to two-page summary of the piece. In order to do this, you will need to decide what the focus of the essay is (about Meg or anaphylaxis?) and, therefore, how much information should be included about Meg. When each group has finished, the groups should read their summaries aloud in class.

The Function of Summarizing within a Critique. The critique is one kind of academic writing that always contains summarizing. By providing a summary of the main points of the piece of writing you are critiquing, you are giving the reader information that is essential to understanding the points of your critique; such summarizing is essential for the reader who is unfamiliar with the text you are critiquing or who has not recently read it.

As with most kinds of academic writing, there is no one standard form for writing a critique and, therefore, no standard way of incorporating a summary. The amount of summarizing that should be included, the location of the summary, and the structure of the summary itself may vary greatly, depending on the audience, the purpose, and even upon the genre of the writing that is being critiqued.

As you prepare to write a critique, an important consideration is where, exactly, to place your summarizing. Conceivably, some—or even all—of it could be placed within a lengthy introductory section, or it could appear as one large chunk following the introduction. Another means of organization, however, is to include only a very brief amount of summarizing at the beginning and to intersperse the major portions of the summarizing throughout the critique, in the appropriate sections.

"Repugnant Is to Aversion . . . *A Look at ETS and the New SAT I,*" which appears at the end of this chapter, is a good example of this second way to include summarizing. In this article, a critique of the new SAT exam, Smith does not give a summary of the contents of the exam in the opening section. Instead, he summarizes—and then immediately critiques—the contents of the exam, one component at a time, throughout the body of the article.

When critiquing a novel or any other descriptive writing, you will find that summarizing interspersed throughout the critique is often the most helpful way to guide your reader's understanding. On the other hand, if you are asked to critique an argumentative essay—for example, a treatise that advocates the raising of taxes for people in the middle class—you probably will need to summarize the main points of the argument before proceeding to critique its various parts. Without a clear understanding of the overall logic and of the points within an argument, readers will have difficulty understanding your critique.

♋ Activity 6

With your group, read and examine the sample critiques that appear at the end of this chapter. Note where any summarizing is placed. Is the summarizing presented all in one chunk, in several large chunks, or in numerous sections interspersed throughout the critique? In each case, what specific purpose does the summarizing serve? Who are the intended readers of the critiques? How does the summarizing accommodate these readers? For example, in which (if any) of these samples does the author assume that readers have read the work being critiqued?

Determining Criteria

Perhaps the most crucial step you will face in writing a critique is determining what criteria to use to evaluate the written text you are critiquing. In fact, the most important aspect of a paper that states a writer's opinion is the set of criteria used to support or defend that opinion. Criteria are any standards of judgment that can be applied to a piece of writing (or anything else you are evaluating) in order to help assess its effectiveness. As you saw in the Sample Assignments section of this chapter, some critique assignments explicitly state the criteria writers should use. Other assignments, however, may not specify the criteria to be used. To respond to such assignments, you need to determine what criteria to use in assessing the text you are to critique. College instructors often want students to develop their own criteria for a critique; this way teachers can gauge students' reading and writing abilities and their growing knowledge of writing conventions within a particular field.

It's always a good idea to keep in mind the course for which you are writing a critique. In introductory or lower-level courses, you will not yet be able to write a critique as a practicing sociologist, journalist, chemist, or art therapist would, and your instructors will not expect you to. What they will expect is to see that you can read critically and assess the value of what you read. Thus, when critique assignments ask for your opinion about a text, instructors are asking you to develop a considered opinion based on your close reading and to explain and support your opinion with appropriate criteria. Your instructors most likely want you to appear to be a critical, observant, and intelligent adult reader who can maintain distance from what he or she observes and who does not believe everything he or she reads. You will, of course, augment that general ability with more specific knowledge as you enter particular disciplines—knowledge about, for example, what constitutes good research or writing in sociology or in other fields.

In addition to considering what kind of course you are writing a critique for, you should consider what kind of text you are evaluating because there are no universal criteria for critiquing any and all written texts. Instead, some criteria are more relevant to particular types or genres of writing. Informative writing, for example, should be *clear* to the people who will read it. A textbook should use language that can be understood by most of the students likely to read it. Likewise, people who buy a new coffee maker should be able to follow the written directions that come with it. However, for literary writings—poetry, short stories, novels, and plays—clarity may be a sign of the author's limitations, rather than his or her skill. Many people enjoy reading literature precisely because doing so requires them to work hard, as readers, to interpret what they think the author is saying. A criterion more appropriate for reading literary writing, therefore, might be the beauty of its style. We expect literature to be written in a style that is carefully crafted and that calls attention to itself, perhaps through the use of rhyme, rhythm, imagery, assonance, and alliteration.

Rather than depending on seemingly universal criteria for evaluating all writing, then, you should consider what general kind of writing you are critiquing. You should consider the functions this kind of writing serves for its readers, as well as what the author's primary purpose for writing is. A text that tries to entertain readers, for example, should use humor effectively. One that tries to inform should anticipate the background knowledge of its intended readers and provide definitions of specialized terms.

Choose Relevant Criteria. When determining criteria for critiquing a piece of writing, you should carefully consider the writer's intentions. It's probably not relevant to dismiss a research article from a scholarly journal as "boring," and it would be equally inappropriate to lambaste a humorous column from the Lifestyle section of a newspaper for being about a trivial subject. Certainly if a writer's intention is to entertain, then a relevant criterion for critiquing a short story or humorous essay is the aesthetic style of the language. However, that criterion would not be relevant for many informative writings, in which the writer's intention is probably to provide instructions, not entertainment. You would appear foolish if you faulted an instruction manual for using repetitive vocabulary and sentence structure, yet you would be justified in criticizing a short story on that basis.

The credibility of the author may also be an appropriate criterion for evaluating a piece of writing. In critiquing writing, it is important to examine the credentials, training, expertise, or experience a person has and to decide whether these qualifications are relevant for the subject of the piece. Just because people write about a subject does not mean that they are qualified to do so. Suppose a medical journal has published a research study that concludes that listening to rock music leads to health problems such as suicide and pregnancy among teenagers. If the study was conducted by a medical doctor, you well might wonder whether a sociologist or psychologist would be a more credible source.

To reiterate, then, there are no universal criteria for evaluating writing, a point that is illustrated in the Sample Assignments section of this chapter. Instead of looking for universal criteria to determine what makes writing good, you should consider the writer's purpose and the course in which the critique is assigned to help you determine what criteria may be relevant.

Choose Criteria That Support a Thesis.   Because there are no universally applicable criteria, if you think about it you will realize that a single piece of writing could be critiqued from a variety of perspectives, using different criteria. Several different criteria may be relevant given the writer's purpose, the type or genre of the writing, and the course for which you are writing the critique. In fact, the more familiar you become with your major or discipline, the easier it will be for you to see various criteria to use in critiquing writing in your field. To write an effective critique, however, you must select from the many *only* those criteria that will actually work together to support your thesis or overall judgment about the writing. Obviously you should use whatever criteria, if any, are directly stated in an assignment. Beyond that, however, you should choose those criteria that best support your overall judgment about the text.

For example, in "Outlaws in Cyberspace," a critique of the book *Secrets of a Super Hacker,* the major criterion reviewer Ed Krol uses is the author's ethics in writing the book. That is, Krol questions the author's purpose in divulging ways of breaking the law. Consider how different this critique might be if the reviewer had used different criteria. The book could have been evaluated with respect to its entertainment value, an approach that might be relevant for the course Computers in Contemporary Popular Culture or simply for determining whether the book would appeal to a wide audience. Similarly, the book might have been critiqued for its informativeness and accessibility; that is, when examined as a how-to guide, a criterion might have included the extent to which the book provides adequate information in a manner that would be understandable to its readers.

 **Activity 7**

Assume you were asked to read the essay "The Great Person-Hole Cover Debate" in one of the following classes and to write a critique of it:

- Introduction to Journalism

- Women's Studies 101

- Critical Thinking and Argument

- Political Science 301: Contemporary Issues

- Creative Writing 343: Humor and Satire.

With your group, pick two of the classes. For each of the classes, decide what criteria might be relevant for critiquing this article. Justify your answers for each class.

 **Activity 8**

Using the periodicals you and your group collected in Activity 3, select one article for your group to use now. Imagine that you and your group members are taking one of the classes previously listed, or another of your choice, and that you have been assigned to write a critique of the article you selected. What criteria might you use to critique the article? As a group, prepare a brief oral report for your class.

WRITING A CRITIQUE

Although some assignments present students with a particular text to critique, many provide a choice of readings. Therefore, the first challenge in producing a successful critique can be selecting an appropriate piece.

Selecting and Critically Reading the Text You Will Critique

Choosing a text to write about is not a trivial task, because a hastily selected piece may cause problems in the long run. To select an appropriate text, you should skim a few possibilities, while considering several factors as you make your choice. First, it is wise to keep the purpose of both the course and the assignment in mind. If, for example, you are taking a course that emphasizes the reading and evaluation of research reports, you should make sure that you select a research report that you can understand and about which you can make evaluative statements.

As you examine possibilities, don't select a reading just because it is short. Short pieces are often brief because they are densely packed with information—and, therefore, difficult to comprehend. Short, "simple" pieces, on the other hand, may not contain sufficient material for you to evaluate. Similarly, it is not advisable to make a selection based on a title alone. Catchy, attention-grabbing titles can precede readings with highly complicated or technical content.

Once you have identified several (three or four) promising readings by glancing through them and getting a sense of their scope and topic, you can narrow your choice by skimming each of your selections. Such quick readings enable you to jot down possible ideas for a critique. Skimming several possibilities will also give you a clearer idea of each text's level of difficulty.

After you have selected your text—or if you are given one to critique—you will need to do several careful readings to ensure that you fully understand the contents and to provide a careful, thorough assessment of these. It is, of course, best to review the assignment before you begin so that as you are reading and taking notes you can keep in mind any relevant information or requirements as well as possible criteria you may use later.

ꙮ **Activity 9**

Using the strategies previously described, select the text that you will critique for this chapter. (See the Writing Assignments section on page 189 of this chapter.) As these assignments suggest, you have several possibilities from which to choose. You may, for example, decide to critique a textbook or a piece of written material circulated on your campus, such as a directory, handbook, or catalogue. You may critique readings from within this book. Alternatively, you may elect to critique the coverage (within your campus newspaper or a local publication) of a local event. Once you've made your selection, jot down your reasons for choosing it.

In a meeting with your group partners discuss your selection and the reasons for your choice. When it is your turn to report, try to give as much detail as possible so that others can offer helpful suggestions—or perhaps convince you to make another selection. When others are reporting their selections, try to ask questions and offer suggestions that will help them determine criteria for their critique, reread for clearer comprehension, or reassess their choices.

Choosing Criteria and Generating a Focus

As you were reading and taking notes, undoubtedly you were keeping in mind the particular requirements of your assignment. If you've done a good job of reading and note taking, your notes will probably include many particular details and several possible criteria. To relate these criteria to one another, you may find it helpful to organize your notes better or try to use invention techniques such as clustering or the Pentad. Both of these writing activities can help you to easily and quickly organize your existing notes, recognize relationships among the details and comments you recorded, organize your criteria, and generate a focus. For example, suppose you were critiquing the textbook used in your chemistry course, for the textbook critique assignment in this chapter. Your notes might well contain details about (1) how the chapters are organized, (2) whether special features such as an index or a glossary are included, and (3) how often visual aids such as headings, photographs, charts, graphs, and tables are used. Using clustering or another invention technique may lead you to see a connection between these three areas: All have to do with the readability of a textbook. You could focus your critique on how readable your chemistry textbook is; two criteria for your critique could be the text's format and it's use of visual aids.

On occasion you may find that you have a criterion related to your emerging focus but have few supporting details or examples in your notes to support it. For the textbook critique just discussed, you might have notes on how much trouble you had understanding the textbook explanation of the difference between reactive and nonreactive elements, which suggests an additional criterion: Textbooks should effectively explain key concepts or processes. Alone, this example isn't sufficient evidence to claim that the textbook authors do or don't provide effective explanations.

However, you could do additional reading and note taking on their explanations of other key concepts or processes to determine how effectively they are explained. If you experience similar difficulty understanding their explanations of the difference between acids and bases, how to balance an equation to describe a reaction, and what titration is and how to do it, then you would have sufficient details to support a claim that the authors should revise their explanations to make them clearer to student-readers.

As you go through your notes, you might also find one or two criteria that seem unrelated to your emerging focus or to your other criteria. To return to the textbook critique, you might have notes on how expensive the textbook was, along with how well a few of the chapters actually related to the lectures or to the labs for your class. These points may be valid, but they don't directly relate to your focus on the book's readability, in which case you might decide to omit them. On the other hand, if you feel that what you have to say on these points is important enough and is relevant to your assignment, you could broaden your focus to include them. For example, your critique could focus on revisions you recommend to make the book more useful to students, assuming that a useful textbook should be readable, affordable, and relevant to actual course content.

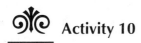 **Activity 10**

Read the text you selected to critique in Activity 9. Do several readings, taking notes as you read. Once you've completed critical reading and note taking, use clustering, the Pentad, or another invention technique to begin organizing your notes and to determine possible criteria to use. Next, with your group members, brainstorm to come up with a possible focus and a set of relevant criteria for each of your papers. Assess the focus and criteria for each group member's paper, using these questions to guide your discussion:

- Are your focus and criteria relevant for the assignment?

- Do they support a thesis or develop a main point?

- Are all the criteria relevant to the kind of writing you are critiquing? Are any of them only marginally relevant?

If you or your group members see possible problems, discuss whether to omit irrelevant criteria or devise a way to revise or recast criteria to make them better fit the focus.

Structuring Your Critique

Once you have determined your criteria and your focus, it is wise to explore how you might organize your critique. In planning a structure for your critique, it is important to make use of your criteria rather than to copy the structure of the text you are critiquing. That is, if you are critiquing a textbook that has six main parts, it is not, ordinarily, a good strategy to have six main parts in your critique—one representing each section of the textbook. In using such a structure, you would have to discuss your criteria again and again—in each section of the critique. And your readers would have to sift through repetitious information, which would make it difficult for them to gain a clear understanding of your overall evaluation.

Instead, as we have suggested, a more expedient method is to structure your critique according to the criteria you have chosen. Let's say, for example, that you are critiquing a nonfiction book for a history class. You have determined that the book is a good history text overall (it is carefully researched and up-to-date; it is written in a readable style; and it contains vivid photographs that help make the historical events become a reality for you). However, you also have determined that the book is weakened by a couple of problems (it lacks an index, which makes quick referencing virtually impossible, and its key terms are not always clearly defined). Because you have determined that there are five criteria on which you can evaluate the book (three positive and two negative), you easily can create a structure based on these criteria. Your critique would have five main parts in its body—one for each of your criteria with each part containing as many paragraphs as necessary. In ordering your criteria, you might choose to explain your two negative ones first and end with a discussion of the three stronger, positive criteria. Alternatively, you might decide to begin with a discussion with your positive criteria and end with a discussion of the two negative criteria. In either case, you would probably introduce your critique by explaining that, in general, you find the book to be an effective text for your history class but that you are troubled by two inadequacies.

After you have formulated a tentative overall structure for your critique, you will need to make some decisions about the critique's summary sections. You need to consider how much summarizing your critique will contain, how you will integrate the summary into your text, and where you will place it. Ordinarily, the amount of summarizing in a critique does not constitute more than 25 to 30 percent of your entire text. The primary purpose of a critique, after all, is to *evaluate* a text for the readers—not to *retell* it to them. Still, without a sufficient amount of well-placed summarizing, your readers will become lost. If you are writing a critique as an assignment for a course, you would be wise to ask your instructor whether there are any specifications for the amount of summarizing you should include. Finally, as you consider how and where to place summarizing within your critique it might be helpful to consider the two basic models that we described earlier.

As with any other kind of writing, an important final consideration is the kind of information you will include in the introduction and conclusion of your critique. Part of your introduction, of course, will be a brief summary of the text you are critiquing—or perhaps an extensive summary, depending on where you have decided to place the majority of your summarizing. In addition to the summary, you might want to begin with an explanation of why your critique will be useful or interesting to its readers. You might want to explain why you have chosen to critique this particular text or to provide any background regarding your special expertise for writing a critique. Depending on the kind of work you are critiquing, you might even want to begin with a powerful direct quotation taken from that work. In any case, you will want to make your introduction clear and interesting so that it prepares your readers for the critique that is to come.

As you decide what kind of information to include in the conclusion of your critique, there are also a number of possibilities that you might consider. Especially if your critique is lengthy or if it contains both positive and negative assessments, you may want to reiterate each of the criteria and explain how the text holds up for each of them. Another possibility is to explain how your perspective has been altered by the experience of writing about and thinking about the text you are critiquing. Finally, you could choose to recommend—or not to recommend—the text to other readers; a recommendation serves as a relevant conclusion for many critiques.

 **Activity 11**

With your group members, read and examine the samples of critiques provided in the Readings section of this chapter to see where criteria are listed, what basic models of overall structure are used, and where summarizing is placed within these structures. Also examine the introductions and conclusions of the critiques, discuss the contents of each, and note how the contents of each introduction and conclusion serve to frame the critique for its readers.

Revising Your Critique

After you have drafted your critique, perhaps using the plan or outline that you have developed, you will need to assess your draft to determine whether it meets your expectations and then make any changes you find necessary. Because a major challenge in constructing an effective critique is integrating the right amount of summary into the appropriate places, a good way to begin your assessment is to get an overall sense of the "summary-to-critique ratio." That is, do a quick reading to get an idea of what *proportion* of your critique is devoted to summarizing.

Some writers find it easier to see how much summary they've written if they use a pencil to draw a vertical line whenever they encounter it. If you wish to try this method, simply read with a pencil in your hand and draw a vertical line in either the right or left margin of your paper each time you find any summarizing of the text you are critiquing. Then, when you are finished, examine the vertical lines to see how much of each page they cover. Whether or not you use this technique, you need to carefully determine whether you have included too much summarizing. Again, it is rare for an effective critique to devote much more than a quarter of its total text to summarizing. Should you discover an excess of summary in your critique, you will need to determine whether some of it should be cut or whether additional discussion to explain or support your criteria should be added.

In addition to examining your critique to see whether you have included the proper amount of summary, you will also need to check the placement of your summarizing. Therefore, as you read over your first draft, see whether portions of your summarizing can be moved to more appropriate places in your text. For example, if most of your summarizing is at the beginning of your critique, it may be more effective if you place the summarizing that includes background information about your criteria *within* your discussions of those criteria.

When you are satisfied that your summarizing is appropriate for your critique in terms of amount and placement, you will also need to read your draft again to assess whether you have explained each of your criteria adequately. If, for instance, you have drafted a critique of a textbook, using *format* as one of your criteria, you must specify fully what you mean:

> *I am using* format *to refer to those features that have to do with the overall design and layout of a textbook that do (or don't) enhance accessibility for its readers. Included in my definition of* format, *then, are graphics, print size and readability, use of color, design of table of contents and index. . . .*

Explaining all of your criteria fully is important because your readers will not be convinced by your assessment if they don't understand the criteria you used.

In addition to checking that your criteria are carefully defined, you also need to make sure that each criterion is supported or developed with sufficient details. Let us suppose that the textbook you are critiquing is difficult to comprehend and should, therefore, be replaced. Let us also suppose that one of the criteria you have used to make the judgment is the textbook's format. It would not be sufficient simply to argue that the "format is poor because this textbook is difficult to follow and information is hard to locate. The format also makes it hard to read." You would, instead, need to provide specific details that show how various aspects of the format make the textbook difficult to understand. You might discuss how the various headings are not easily distinguished from one another, which makes it hard to determine which ones refer to major as opposed to minor topics. You might also explain how the size and shape of the print causes eye strain, which makes it hard for the reader to concentrate.

Finally, as you provide details to convince your readers of your assessment, you may find that you wish to use direct quotes. These can be quite convincing but should, ordinarily, be brief. As you revise, then, replace any overly long quoted passages with shorter quotes or paraphrases. Also, make sure that all of your quotes are well integrated into your text and are preceded or followed by an explanation of their relevance as shown in this example:

> *"As you can see from this passage, the style of this textbook is confusing and inaccessible:* [Quoted Sentences.] *Notice how the sentences in the preceding passage are overly long and convoluted; in addition, several highly technical terms are used but not defined."*

Whether you explain the relevance of each quotation before or after you provide it, such explanations are crucial if you want your readers to fully understand how your examples illustrate the points you are trying to make.

WRITING ASSIGNMENTS

Writing Topics

1. Critique the textbook from this or any other course that you are taking this term for the purpose of assessing whether it should continue to be used in the future. Your audience should be the instructor (or committee) responsible for selecting the textbook. Alternatively, critique this (or another) textbook for the purpose of offering useful suggestions for revision. In this case, your audience should be the authors of the text. (If you choose a textbook from another class, you will need to hand in a photocopy of the table of contents as well as of a few representative excerpts so that your instructor can get a sense of the source you are critiquing.)

2. Critique a piece of written material that is distributed to students on your campus. You may select, for example, a handbook, course catalogue, user's guide, or brochure that describes an academic program for prospective majors. Address your critique to the office or program that produced the document (Financial Aid; Student Activities; Placement Services; Computer Services; The Department of Social Work; etc.). How easy is it to use and read? Does it contain enough or too much information? Overall, how effective a document is it? (You will need to turn in a copy of the document along with your critique of it.)

3. Critique any of the readings within this textbook *for a particular course or audience that you specify.* The course or audience that you select will determine what criteria are appropriate. You may, for example, choose to critique one of the excerpts from an autobiography within Chapter 3 and pretend that the critique was assigned in a biology class. In this case, an example of a relevant criterion might be the extent to which the autobiography offers information about the "making of a scientist." On the other hard, if you critiqued the same excerpt for a journalism class, a relevant criterion might be how accessible the writing is to a broad audience of readers.

4. Select an event—a play, concert, speech, election—that has recently occurred on your campus, and critique the coverage it has received within the campus or local newspapers. Was the coverage evenhanded? Informative? Did it serve the interests of the local community or some other group or individual? Address your critique to the readers of the newspapers in which coverage of the event appeared. (You will need to turn in copies of the articles you are critiquing.)

Writing Procedures

1. By now, you have already selected a text to critique and have determined the criteria you will use. Before you begin to plan your critique, draft a one- to two-page summary of the text you are critiquing.

2. Using this summary, your notes, any inventing (Pentad, clustering, etc.), and your partners' suggestions from Activities 9 and 10, devise a tentative plan for your critique. Share your plan with your group partners. Be sure to get feedback from them about the overall structure for your critique and the placement of the summarizing. Also solicit ideas for your introduction and conclusion. After you have discussed your plan with your group, revise it based on the suggestions of your group or instructor. Include as much detail as possible in your plan.

3. Using your revised plan, create a draft of your critique. As you are drafting, use your summary and notes to provide detail and to incorporate direct quotations, as necessary.

4. After you have completed your draft, bring it to class to workshop with your group. Use one of the draft workshop procedures described in Chapter 2.

5. Based on the feedback you get from your group workshop or your instructor, revise and edit the final copy of your critique. In revising, you should be sure that the connections between your thesis and criteria are clear; that you have provided sufficient detail to support your criteria; and that your summarizing is appropriate in terms of amount and placement. When editing, keep your reader in mind. Be sure that your final copy is readable and free of error.

READINGS

Critiques

1. Smith, Michael K. "Repugnant Is to Aversion . . . *A Look at ETS and the New SAT 1.*" *Phi Delta Kappan* (June 1994), pp. 752–757.

   A critique from a popular/general periodical

2. Krol, Ed. "Outlaws in Cyberspace." Review of *Secrets of a Super Hacker* by The Knightmare. *The Sciences*. (May/June 1994), pp. 44–48.

   A book review from a popular periodical

3. Phelps, Christopher. Review of *Nazis, Communists, Klansmen, and Others on the Fringe,* by John George and Laird Wilcox. *Critical Sociology 19* (1992), pp. 135–138.

   A book review from a learned journal

Questions

1. For each of the critiques, what is the thesis or final assessment of the text being critiqued? Is this assessment directly stated in the critique? If so, underline it; if not, mark the parts of the critique where it is implied.

2. What criteria are used to develop or support that assessment? Mark in the margins where each of the criteria is discussed. Which of the criteria are directly stated; which are implied? In what way are the criteria related to the theses they

support in each critique? Explain why the criteria are relevant with respect to the type of written text they are being used to critique.

3. What kinds of support are used to explain each of the criteria? Does the writer use specific details from the text, summary, or direct quotes?

4. Overall, how are the criteria organized? Is an organizational plan directly stated in the critique? If so, where?

Original Text with an Accompanying Critique

Original Text: Sharpe, William, and Wallock, Leonard. "Bold New City or Built-Up 'Burb? Redefining Contemporary Suburbia." *American Quarterly 46* (March 1994), pp. 1–4.

Critique: Bruegmann, Robert. "The Twenty-Three Percent Solution." *American Quarterly 46* (March 1994), pp. 31–34.

An article with a critique of it, from a learned journal

Questions

1. "The Twenty-Three Percent Solution" is Robert Bruegmann's critique of the article "Bold New City or Built-Up 'Burb?" by William Sharpe and Leonard Wallock. What part of the article does Bruegmann focus his critique on? Why does he select this focus? What other focal points might he have selected for his critique?

2. What criteria does Bruegmann use to evaluate the conclusion Sharpe and Wallock reach about the racial segregation of suburbs? How does Bruegmann develop or support his criteria?

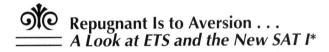

Repugnant Is to Aversion . . .
 *A Look at ETS and the New SAT I**

Michael K. Smith

For more than a decade I have been helping high school students prepare for college entrance exams. Together, we have reviewed basic formulas of high school mathematics, struggled with the word problems that appear on the exam, memorized lists of vocabulary words needed for certain parts of the verbal section, and practiced coping with the strenuous time limits of the test. As always, the Educational Testing Service (ETS) and the College Entrance Examination Board have helped me with my task by publishing collections of previously administered

Michael K. Smith. "Repugnant Is to Aversion . . . A Look at ETS and the New SAT." Phi Delta Kappan (June 1994), pp. 752–757. Reprinted with the permission of the author.

Repugnant Is to Aversion . . . *A Look at ETS and the New SAT I* *(cont'd.)*

exams.[1] It is very satisfying to see students come to "understand" this exam well enough to achieve scores that help them gain admission to the colleges they choose.

Thus it was with much anticipation that I followed the recent changes occurring with one of my favorite entrance exams. Not only did the name change (from Scholastic Aptitude Test to Scholastic Assessment Tests and, finally, to SAT I: Reasoning Test), but also, according to the College Board, the test itself was changing: "A completely redesigned SAT will be administered beginning in the spring of 1994."[2] As my students and I were preparing for the first administration of the "new SAT" on March 19, we considered with some trepidation the words of the College Board: "Developed jointly by the College Board and the Educational Testing Service, the revised SAT contains content and format changes necessary to ensure a valid measure of students' academic preparedness for college work throughout the 1990s and beyond."[3]

I know that the College Board and ETS have not ventured into this endeavor by accident; their literature informs us that "three years of extensive research and field testing" preceded the 1990 approval of the new format by the College Board trustees.[4] The College Board also adopted a recommendation of its own Commission on New Possibilities for the Admissions Testing Program that it "adapt its tests so that they assess a greater variety of skills and knowledge and thereby serve a wider range of needs."[5] The College Board was thus displaying not only its flexibility but also its prescience: "The revised SAT recognizes the increasing diversity of students in our educational system, as well as changes in how and what these students are being taught in secondary school. The new testing program will assess many of the skills important to students' success in college."[6]

Wanting to maintain my own erudition in the face of my student's demands to know how to prepare for this new exam, I scrambled for information. Once again, the College Board facilitated my task. For the past year it has been publishing a newsletter on the new SAT, which describes the changes. Furthermore, it distributed to guidance counselors, teachers, and educators a preview of the upcoming test, titled *The New SAT I: Reasoning Test.*[7] My comments below are derived from an analysis of this booklet and from statements in the College Board newsletter.

The College Board states that the new SAT gives the students more time to answer questions. According to one issue of the newsletter, "The primary benefit is that students will have more time to think about the questions in both the verbal and math sections."[8] Since time pressure has been reduced, students should feel more comfortable with the exam: "The less speeded test should also reduce student anxiety."[9] In my opinion, having more time per problem would be a tremendous advantage on this test, because students often feel that they must race through the exam in order to attempt all the problems.

So how much time are we talking about? On the old SAT verbal sections, students had 60 minutes to complete 85 problems, and average of .71 minutes per problem. On the new SAT (based on the sample test I examined), students were

Repugnant Is to Aversion . . . *A Look at ETS and the New SAT I* (cont'd.)

presented with 78 problems in 75 minutes. Thus seven problems were eliminated and 15 minutes added to the exam. This works out to an average of .96 minutes per problem on the verbal sections. Similarly, on the math sections of the old SAT, students had 60 minutes for 60 problems, an average of one minute per problem. On the new SAT math sections, students had 75 minutes for 60 problems, for an average of 1.25 minutes per problem. Thus on both sections of the SAT students now have an average of 15 more seconds per problem than test-takers had previously.

My students and I will take the extra seconds. However, I'll still have to caution them against extended reveries (unless they're restricted to the 15-second variety) and urge them to move almost as quickly through this new exam as through the old SAT. What interests me is the context in which the College Board places this revision on the time limits. The College Board notes: "The revised SAT reflects the educational reform movements of the 1980s and 1990s."[10] I believe that I have followed these reform movements pretty closely, and it seems to me that educators have called for different types of assessments: performance assessments, authentic assessments, exhibitions, portfolios, and the like. I believe that most of these new assessments would allow substantially more than a minute to solve a problem. Unless, of course, I have completely misread the literature in this area or have missed the publication of *The One-Minute Portfolio.*

Moving to more substantive changes, let's examine the verbal sections of the new SAT. As the College Board says, much remains the same on the verbal sections of the new SAT. However, some significant revisions have occurred: a separate antonym section will no longer appear, a knowledge of vocabulary in context will be required, and longer reading passages that place a greater emphasis on critical reading will appear.

To be candid, I will miss the antonym section, although my students won't. I reveled in discussing the meanings and etymologies of words and debating what would qualify as an appropriate antonym for such words as *ostentatious, mutability, querulous, pithy, propensity, daunt, burgeon, equanimity, voluble, noisome, decorum, prodigal, penchant, eclectic, abstemious, assiduous, diminution, penury, fecund, celerity, puerile, dross, salubrious, burnish, tepid, sinous, munificence, supercilious,* and *desultory.* These are just a few of the vocabulary items that have appeared on recent SATs.[11] I can no longer use my favorite motivational gambits: that *abstemious* is one of only two common words in the English language in which all five vowels appear in order or that *supercilious* derives from the Latin for "eyebrow," with the connotations of haughtiness that are associated with raised eyebrows.

Of course, the SAT has been heavily criticized for testing vocabulary out of context, and I applaud the attempt to include more context-sensitive items on the verbal test. For instance, the sentence-completion section will remain intact. My students and I will continue to discuss the strategies for determining what constitutes a

Repugnant Is to Aversion . . . *A Look at ETS and the New SAT I* (cont'd.)

grammatically, stylistically, and logically reasonable sentence. Consider the following item:

> By nature he was . . . , usually confining his remarks to . . . expression.
> (A)   acerbic . . . friendly
> (B)   laconic . . . concise
> (C)   garrulous . . . voluminous
> (D)   shrill . . . complimentary
> (E)   vague . . . emphatic[12]

From past SATs my students and I know that sentence-completion items with two blanks are often searching for answers that are complementary (words that tend to share meanings) or contrasting (words that are nearly opposite in meaning). This particular item seems to be calling for complementary responses; furthermore, the clue word "confining" indicates the type of expression. At this point, however, I have a subtle feeling that knowing the meanings of vocabulary items would help: that *acerbic* is the opposite of friendly and won't work; that *garrulous* and *voluminous* are slightly synonymous but that *voluminous* doesn't go with "confining"; and that *laconic* is synonymous with *concise*, which fits nicely with "confining." Furthermore, *laconic* derives from the Greek *Lakonia* (Sparta), who citizens were rumored to have been quite concise when they took the ancient SAT.

The analogies section also remains intact on the new SAT. I must admit that I've always found this section difficult. Not only must one discern the relationship between the given pair of words, but one must discover a similar relationship in one of five pairs that are presented as potential answers. For instance, consider the following item:

> REPUGNANT:AVERSION::
> (A)   insatiable:satisfaction
> (B)   informed:knowledge
> (C)   bigoted:judgment
> (D)   shameless:regret
> (E)   admirable:esteem[13]

The difficulty here is in the initial pair of words. Once again, without knowing the meaning of the items, a student could only guess at the relationship involved. If *repugnant* and *aversion* are recognized as somehow synonymous, then a student could conceivably narrow the choices to B and E, perhaps leaning toward the latter. After considering these sample items from the sentence-completion and analogies sections, I don't believe that I'll advise my students to discard their vocabulary lists just yet.

The readings sections on the new SAT are very similar to those on the old test. Some of the passages are longer (as promised), and the College Board notes that

Repugnant Is to Aversion . . . *A Look at ETS and the New SAT I* (cont'd.)

the passages now include "introductory information to give students a context for each passage."[14] For instance, one passage was prefaced with the following: "There has been a great deal of scientific debate about the nature of the object that exploded above Tunguska in 1908. The following passage presents one theory of what happened."[15] Furthermore, the reading material is supposed to be "more accessible and engaging."[16] In the one test that I examined, the topics of reading passages were as follows: the Tunguska object; an extract from the memoirs of poet Elizabeth Bishop; a discussion by a Japanese American about an experience during World War II; and a discussion of the architectural design of cities that contrasts English "garden cities" with modern cities.

It's been a long time since I was an adolescent, and even when I was one I couldn't claim that my interests were necessarily those of my peers. But from listening to my students talk about their interests and about what they find "engaging," I must admit that I have seldom heard discussions of English "garden cities" or unexplained explosions in Tunguska. I do not mean to advocate reading passages on "Beavis and Butt-head," but I do mean that my students must still confront reading passages that often lie totally outside their experience or areas of interest.

Instead of a separate section on antonyms, the new SAT will test knowledge of vocabulary in the context of a reading passage. After the passage on the Tunguska object, the following question appears:

> In line 4, the word "appreciation" most nearly means
> (A) increase in value
> (B) artistic interest
> (C) understanding
> (D) curiosity
> (E) gratitude[17]

The appropriate context for this item is as follows:

The thoughts came and went in a flash: there was not a chance in a billion years that an extraterrestrial object as large as Halley's comet would hit the Earth. But that was 15 years ago, when I had little appreciation of geological time. I did not consider then the adage that anything that can happen does happen—given the time.

In this context, it seems clear that the primary sense of appreciation as relating to gratitude doesn't fit. The context might incline us toward choosing "curiosity" or "understanding," with a preference for the latter. I didn't consider this item to be very hard, and the vocabulary choices were not nearly as pedantic as some I had seen in earlier SATs. I do have one small concern. I looked up *appreciation* in my unabridged *Random House Dictionary of the English Language*. The three primary

Repugnant Is to Aversion . . . *A Look at ETS and the New SAT I* (cont'd.)

meanings given are: 1) gratitude; 2) the act of estimating the qualities of things and giving them proper value; and 3) clear perception or recognition, as a course in art appreciation. In none of the primary meanings is the word *appreciation* clearly understood to mean "understanding."

I examined other examples of vocabulary items in context and found that many seemed to be testing either the third, fourth, or fifth meanings of words (as listed in the dictionaries) or perhaps a close variant, as in the case of *appreciation*. Consequently, I have been warning my students not to automatically assume the most common meanings for vocabulary items in the questions based on the reading passages. It really is an interesting paradox for me as a teacher. Some items, such as analogies, are nearly impossible to answer because the vocabulary items are much too difficult for students to recognize any of the meanings of the words, while in other items they can't use the primary meaning of more familiar words and must be wary of secondary interpretations.

The final innovation on the reading passages involves the use of a double passage that offers different points of view. The purpose here is to test students' critical reading ability by having them compare and contrast the passages. In the test that I examined, this double passage concerned the English "garden cities" as opposed to modern cities, with the passages containing more than 90 lines of text, followed by 13 questions. The time limit was 15 minutes. I must admit that I read both passages together and was overwhelmed with detail (especially since I allowed myself about two minutes to read each passage). I tried the following strategy: I skimmed the first passage and looked for test questions related to it (five questions); then I skimmed the second passage and did the test items related to it (six questions). That left two questions that genuinely tested my ability to compare and contrast the points of view in the two passages. These two questions took more time. However, they represented only 15% of the items in this section and only 5% of all the reading questions. I think my students won't be slowed down too much by this type of critical reading challenge.

Let us now turn to an examination of the mathematical reasoning sections of the new SAT. I notice that in its promotional materials the College Board suggested that the content of the new exam would remain essentially the same as that of the older version. There are two new features: 1) some questions require students to "produce" their own responses and not just choose from a set of multiple-choice alternatives, and 2) students will be encouraged to bring calculators to the exam and to use them. As the College Board notes: "The introduction of calculator use will parallel changes occurring nationally in the use of calculators in mathematics instruction."[18] The brochure then cites the advocacy for the use of calculators by the National Council of Teachers of Mathematics (NCTM) and other organizations.

I certainly applaud this long-awaited revision in testing practices. I first started using calculators in mathematics classes in the late 1970s. Most of my students tell

---

Repugnant Is to Aversion . . . *A Look at ETS and the New SAT I* *(cont'd.)*

me that they have been using calculators since they were children, and I'm glad to see that the College Board has realized that these devices are not just fads. Furthermore, 1992 field trials of the new SAT showed that 94% of college-bound seniors indicated that they owned or had access to a calculator.[19]

But here's the interesting irony. Although calculators are recommended, it seems that no test question will require the use of a calculator.[20] This presents an interesting paradox for me as I prepare my students for the exam. I will certainly encourage them to take a calculator with them, as the College Board wishes me to, but I have to ask myself to what extent will they need it. Will a calculator help at all on the test questions? Will it hinder their thinking? That is, will they be concerned with pushing buttons when they should be analyzing a problem?

Let's look for answers by considering some actual problems. Consider the following example, which is meant to be an easy mathematical reasoning problem.

> Which of the following integers is a divisor of both 36 and 90?
> (A) 12
> (B) 10
> (C) 8
> (D) 6
> (D) 4[21]

With a calculator, a student could divide all five choices into both numbers and determine that D is correct. I tried it this way, and even punching buttons quickly, it took about 30 to 40 seconds. Some students could answer the problem by a process of elimination combined with some mental arithmetic: 10 and 8 don't divide into 36; 12 won't go into 90; 6 goes into both 36 and 90; thus 4 can't be the answer, and 6 must be correct. Or perhaps a student could combine these strategies in some way. In any case, having access to a calculator wasn't all that helpful on this problem—but then, it didn't hurt either.

Consider another example:

> The sales tax on a $6.00 meal is $0.36. At that rate what would be the tax on a $14.00 meal?
> (A) $0.48
> (B) $0.72
> (C) $0.84
> (D) $0.90
> (E) $0.96[22]

If a student recognizes the correct procedure, doing this problem on a calculator is relatively straightforward: .36/6 = .06 times 14 = .84. Calculating this problem by hand, using ratios, is also not too difficult: the .36/6 ratio reduces to .06/1 which multiplied by 14 produces .84. Or, sometimes, I would encourage the student

Repugnant Is to Aversion . . . *A Look at ETS and the New SAT I* (cont'd.)

to estimate in order to eliminate some answers: $14 is more than twice the $6 meal, so the sales tax must be more than $0.72.

On some problems, however, a calculator might mean trouble. Consider the following problem.

> $P = (1-1/2)(1-1/3)(1-1/4) \ldots (1-1/16)$ The three dots in the product above represent eleven missing factors of the form $(1-1/n)$, where n represents all of the consecutive integers from 5 to 15, inclusive. Which of the following is equal to P?
> (A) 1/16
> (B) 1/2
> (C) 3/4
> (D) 7/8
> (E) 15/16[23]

If a student tries to calculate the factors $(1/2)(2/3)(3/4)$ etc., he or she is going to be quickly mired in decimal points, at least on an ordinary calculator. If a student looks at the problem, however, and recognizes that terms cancel each other regularly, then he or she should see that the answer is 1/16, although this is still a difficult problem. Another technique for solving this problem involves a process of elimination. Since the first term is 1/2 and every other factor is a fraction, then the product must be less that 1/2. And there's only one answer that is less than 1/2.

Of course, many other types of problems—those involving algebraic or geometric expressions—may not lend themselves to calculator use at all. My analysis suggests that a calculator would be unlikely to hurt a student on the new SAT, but the help it provides may be only minimal. Since most of the mathematical problems on the new SAT are nearly identical in format to those on previous exams, strategies for students still center on the ability to decode quickly what the problem is asking for and then use the appropriate mathematical knowledge.

There is one new type of mathematical reasoning problem that requires students to produce their own answers and then enter their responses on a grid in a special section on the answer sheet. I'm sure that the College Board has been influenced by recommendations from such organizations as the NCTM in designing this new type of item. In *Curriculum and Evaluation Standards for School Mathematics*, the NCTM has urged that mathematics assessments measure the ability of students to solve more open-ended problems and even to formulate problems of their own. One of the examples cited by NCTM for grades 9–12 illustrates this new trend: "You have 10 items to purchase at a grocery store. Six people are waiting in the express lane (10 items or fewer). Lane 1 has one person waiting, and lane 3 has two people waiting. The other lanes are closed. What check-out lane should you join?"[24] This problem is ambiguous and calls for the student to identify missing information and to make estimates of the missing quantities.

Repugnant Is to Aversion . . . *A Look at ETS and the New SAT I* (cont'd.)

Are these the type of student-produced responses that the College Board has in mind? A brief look at the "Directions for Student-Produced Response Questions" that appear in the sample test booklet, *The New SAT I*, suggest that these instructions are intended less to accommodate student-produced responses than to ease the scoring burden for ETS. Anyone who has ever had to blacken the ovals for each of the numbers of his or her date of birth will understand that the accuracy of entry should be among the test-takers' major concerns. Moreover, while simple numerical answers that are in the form of whole numbers, decimals, or proper fractions are merely time-consuming to enter accurately, mixed numbers appear to present a problem to the scorers. Indeed, they are outlawed. All fractional answers larger than one must be given as improper fractions or as decimals. For example, a fractions such as 2½, if entered as a mixed number, will be read as 21/2, so it must be entered as 5/2 or 2.5.

Giving the College Board the benefit of the doubt and recognizing that, with thousands of students taking the exam, an efficient means of scoring must be established, perhaps we can examine the content of these new items and determine what makes them revolutionary.

Consider the following open-ended problem.

If $3x = y$ and $y = z + 1$, what is the value of x when $z = 29$?[25]

This problem doesn't seem too difficult. Plug in 29 for z, and determine that $y = 30$. That makes $3x = 30$, which makes $x = 10$. Students can do this either by mental arithmetic, quick paper-and-pencil calculation, or by use of the calculator. The biggest problem students face is making sure that they "grid in" the number 10 correctly.

Consider another problem.

What is one possible value of x for which $1/5 < x < 1/4$?[26]

Clearly, this problem is revolutionary and could not be accommodated in a multiple-choice format, given that there are an infinite number of correct answers! What is one possible value? My students would approach this problem in terms of decimals or fractions. The numbers given should be easily recognized as decimals $1/5 = .20$ and $1/4 = .25$. Thus possible values are .21, .22, .222, etc. Once again, students must take care to "grid in" an appropriate response.

I must admit that I examined only a few sample problems of this new type. And perhaps I'm being dense, but it seems to me that this new type of problem is extremely similar to the older multiple-choice formats—except that the choices are not listed. I could see clearly why ETS would want to move this type of item, given that it takes as much time and energy to construct alternative answers as it does to write test items in the first place. However, once again, I am not privy to the details of the intensive research they conducted.

Repugnant Is to Aversion . . . *A Look at ETS and the New SAT I* (cont'd.)

I coached my students for the first administration of the new SAT, using many of the methods and strategies that have been developed over the past decade. I know that the College Board notes that coaching won't work; as Donald Powers, senior research scientist at ETS, comments, preparation courses "are of relatively limited usefulness now, and there is no reason to believe that they will become any more effective with the new test. In fact, it is more likely that these courses will be less effective."[27] Although my experience disconfirms this remark, I don't want to tangle with the exhaustive, nationwide research that ETS has conducted. I'm only thankful that the folks in charge of publications at the College Board don't totally agree with Powers' comment, because they remain the best source of study guides and test-preparation materials.[28]

I took the new SAT with my students on March 19 at Central High School in Knoxville, Tennessee. The waiting room was packed with dozens of high school juniors and seniors, together with about 20 seventh-graders who were taking the exam for a national talent search. Were the students aware of the changes to the SAT? One sleepy-eyed student responded to my query: "I didn't know I could bring a calculator until last night." After talking to several mothers of the seventh-graders, including one with whom I had attended high school two decades ago, I concluded that neither parents nor children knew much about the SAT, much less the new SAT.

After we were marched into separate classrooms for the actual testing, I discovered that the proctor for my classroom was the assistant principal of my former school, West High School. He had joined the staff one year after I graduated. He seemed nonplused that so old a person was taking the test: he asked if I was trying to get into college. I told him that I only hoped they wouldn't take away my college degrees if my performance that morning failed to measure up.

The testing session itself was utterly exhausting. After more than an hour of settling in and listening to instructions, the new SAT itself consisted of three hours of continuous testing. We were allotted only one five-minute break, during which we could go to the bathroom, and one one-minute break, during which we could stand up without conversing or leaving the room. We were allowed to use calculators on the mathematics sections, but, for some strange reason known only to ETS, the instructions demanded that all calculators be removed from our desks during the verbal sections. Perhaps ETS has conducted an unpublished study on the positive effects of calculator use on reading comprehension.

The content of the new SAT was just about what the preview test discussed above had led me to expect. The vocabulary level on this new test did not seem quite as difficult as that usually contained in the antonym sections of the old SAT. There were, however, many difficult sentence completion and analogy items, containing such words a *iconoclastic, restive,* and *reverie.* The reading passages tended to be longer than those on the old SAT; the topics covered by the passages ranged from two views of life on the prairie to a discussion of the acculturation of Chinese Americans to an analysis of the origin of Bohemian lifestyles. It's not that these passages couldn't be interesting; the Bohemian section actually contained a reference

---

Repugnant Is to Aversion . . . *A Look at ETS and the New SAT I* *(cont'd.)*

to hippies (although I was probably the only one in the room other than the proctor to whom this term wasn't strictly ancient history). It's just that the nature of the task and the intense time pressure force one to dissect the passages quickly in a quest for the right answers to some very narrowly focused questions.

I didn't use my calculator a single time on the mathematics questions. Students around me used their calculators sporadically. It was extremely difficult for me to finish the mathematics section, even though I feel I'm good at this subject. I knew that I could have done better if I'd only had 10 more minutes or even five. I wonder why ETS doesn't consider more generous time limits; the extra 15 seconds per problem allotted on the new SAT were just not quite enough. I noticed one statistics problem and one problem that related to probability; the other items tested the arithmetic, algebra, and geometry skills that have always been represented on the SAT. (My SAT scores arrived at press time: verbal 760, 99th percentile; math 720, 97th percentile.)

I talked to several students as they left the testing area. Most said they were going home to sleep, a feeling with which I heartily concurred. I know that I would not endure an experience like this again unless I were forced to (or paid big bucks for doing so). I also have much more sympathy for the students whom I tutor. It is too soon to say whether or not the new SAT is blazing a trail toward the future of assessment. But at the very least, taking the SAT will remain one experience about which both parents and children can commiserate.

1. *10 SATs*, 4th ed. (New York: College Entrance Examination Board, 1990).
2. *SAT Brochure* (New York: College Entrance Examination Board, 1991), p. 1.
3. Ibid.
4. Ibid, p. 2.
5. "The New SAT: Moving Beyond Prediction," *The New SAT Newsletter*, College Entrance Examination Board, May 1993, p. 1.
6. *SAT Brochure*, p. 2.
7. *The New SAT 1: Reasoning Test: A Preview of the Test Coming in 1994* (New York: College Entrance Examination Board, 1993).
8. "The New SAT," pp. 1, 3.
9. "Reduced 'Speededness' of Tests Allows Students to Attempt More Questions," *The New SAT Newsletter*, College Entrance Examination Board, April 1992, p. 1.
10. *SAT Brochure*, p. 3.
11. Taken from the first four editions of *10 SATs*.
12. *The New SAT 1*, p. 2.
13. Ibid., p. 17.
14. *SAT Brochure*, p. 4.
15. *The New SAT 1*, p. 6.
16. *SAT Brochure*, p. 4.
17. *The New SAT 1*, p. 6.
18. *SAT Brochure*, p. 5.
19. "SAT Field Trials Analyses Show Calculator Use Has Positive Effect for All Students," Special Report No. 3, *The New SAT Newsletter*, College Entrance Examination Board, December 1992.
20. "Calculator Use to Be Allowed on the SAT," *The New SAT Newsletter*, College Entrance Examination Board, April 1992, p. 5.
21. *The New SAT 1*, p. 8.

Repugnant Is to Aversion . . . *A Look at ETS and the New SAT I* (cont'd.)

22. Ibid., p. 9.
23. Ibid., p. 13.
24. *Curriculum and Evaluation Standards for School Mathematics* (Reston, Va: National Council of Teachers of Mathematics, 1989), p. 212.
25. *The New SAT 1*, p. 25.
26. Ibid., p. 26.
27. "Coaching Remains of Dubious Value with New SAT," *The New SAT Newsletter,* College Entrance Examination Board, March 1993, p. 2.
28. Ibid., p. 3.

 ## Outlaws in Cyberspace*

Secrets of a Super Hacker

by The Knightmare
Loompanics Unlimited, 1994
205 pages; $19.95

"What the hell is this?" was the reaction from the director of the computer center at the University of Illinois, a man I knew twenty-five years ago. He had just received in the mail an unsigned list of all valid accounts and passwords at his data center, posted from Las Vegas. The list had been sent by a hacker, who had overheard the center's security manager boasting about how impregnable it was. For the director it was a time of investigation and doubt. The most important priority should have been protecting the data center from further intrusion. Instead the director became obsessed with finding and punishing the hacker—who was never caught.

Certainly, part of the hacker's motivation for the stunt was to put a braggart in his place, but there is another reason. If you were to ask for an explanation from the Knightmare, pseudonym for Dennis Fiery (which is itself another pseudonym), author of the how-to-hack manual *Secrets of a Super Hacker,* he would offer this:

> Hacking is fun. Hell, it's exhilarating. But it's also illegal, sometimes immoral, and usually punishable. Even if what you're doing is perfectly innocent, you'll be hard pressed to find an acceptable excuse for it in court.

At the time of the Las Vegas incident, people who knew anything about computers were a small minority. Computing machines were big, expensive and slow. Translating the human-readable instructions into machine instructions took much

*Ed Krol. "Outlaws in Cyberspace." This article is reprinted by permission of *The Sciences* and is from the May/June 1994 issue. Individual subscriptions are $21.00 per year. Write to: The Sciences, 2 East 63rd Street, New York, N.Y. 10021 or call 1-800-THE-NYAS.

Outlaws in Cyberspace *(cont'd.)*

more time than it would today. Converting a program—typically hundreds of times simpler than any current word-processing program—could take hours. Writing a new program from scratch was a daunting task; days could be lost in merely trying to get the syntax of the input correct, let alone achieving the desired results. If you had a properly working program that performed one task, and you needed another program to do something slightly different, modifying the first program to create the second one was much faster than writing a new one from scratch. That shortcut led more to an ax-hewn bench than to a piece of finely crafted furniture. Taking an ax to a program to turn it into something else became the basis of the term *to hack*.

Whereas programming is like cooking in your own kitchen—a personal act of creation—hacking is like cooking in a stranger's kitchen in the dead of night. In my kitchen the spices, gadgets and appliances are laid out for my convenience and ease of cooking; as long as wonderful food is the result, the layout of the kitchen and perhaps even the precise ingredients are irrelevant. So it is with programming. The programmer places the data here and there according to his own style and makes the task of getting the computer to do his bidding easier. Hacking, however, demands more than merely following, or even inventing, a recipe. You need to locate the cumin, the zester, the mixer surreptitiously. Hacking is not for beginners.

As one might guess, *The New Hacker's Dictionary*, a collection of "in crowd" terms compiled at MIT, is chock-full of definitions of the term *hacking*. A sampling:

> 1. A person who enjoys exploring the details of programmable systems and how to stretch their capabilities, as opposed to most users, who prefer to learn only the minimum necessary. 2. One who programs enthusiastically (even obsessively) or who enjoys programming rather than just theorizing about programming. . . . 6. An expert or enthusiast of any kind. One might be an astronomy hacker, for example.

More generally, as *The New Hacker's Dictionary* notes in an appendix, hacking is "an appropriate application of ingenuity." Often, the appendix goes on to say, the ingenuity is applied in the service of "a creative practical joke." The Knightmare would certainly agree with those definitions; he offers his own similar take:

> A hacker is a person with an intense love of something, . . . who, because he or she has this love, also has a deep curiosity about the subject in question. If a hacker loves computers, then he or she is curious about every aspect of computers.

But he would probably take umbrage at the derogatory spin of the final definition in the dictionary:

> 8. (deprecated) A malicious meddler who tries to discover sensitive information by poking around. Hence *password hacker, network hacker.*

Outlaws in Cyberspace *(cont'd.)*

Therein lies the rub that has caused the honorable connotation of *hacker* to go the way of the honorable connotation of *lawyer*.

In spite of its now tainted image, however, hacking has become a requirement for living in the information age. Computer literacy has been touted as a skill all children need to acquire before they leave the school system. It implies at least that one know how to get along in a particular environment—how to work at a familiar computer without being paralyzed with fear, how to do a few simple housekeeping chores with, say, one's hard disk without losing one's disk files. Such skills are akin to the ability to sign one's name—rather than just scratch an *X*. In the past, simple computer skills were signs of sophistication; now they are rapidly becoming barely sufficient.

If you plan to tour the information superhighway or if you hope to navigate its current incarnation and presumed predecessor, the Internet, you will need to be reasonably computer literate on your own computer. From there you can reach out to other computers and gather the information you need for daily life. Indeed, learning all you can about computers and their use on the networks is a survival tactic for the year 2000. Taking part in the networks is no longer the exotic adventure it once was, but it is by no means a trip to the mall either. Frequently you may end up a reluctant traveler, without a guide, in strange places with strange names. You have to poke around—find help files, try out commands to see what they do—and become self-reliant.

Compare the foregoing activity with the Knightmare's breathless description of what confronts the hacker:

> Menus! Options! Choices to be made! Files to read and learn from, software to run, games to play. You let the directories sift past you, letting yourself be mesmerized by their framework. So much to do, and then you see connections to other sites, and more sites, and more secret files to read! You smile as you realize something: every hack, no matter its size, leads to new hacks, new computers, new horizons of exploration and gain.

Take out the cloak-and-dagger fun of breaking in and you have a description of what confronts the user of the Internet: Menus! Options! Choices! All the items in the quotation. Moving from system to system gains information for the user. That, plain and simple, is hacking. And to use the Internet to its full potential, you need to be assertive. Hacking, of course, is assertive computing in spades.

There is another reason for honest and ethical people to approach and study the methods of the hacker. When you venture outside your own computer and onto the networks, you are, by definition, not alone. With increased traffic more accidents are likely to happen. And, because the good intentions of strangers cannot be guaranteed, it makes sense to stay alert and exercise a few intelligent precautions.

Outlaws in Cyberspace *(cont'd.)*

There is always the chance—an increasing one, unfortunately, as the user population rises—that someone like the Knightmare will attempt to mug you electronically. Whether he succeeds is likely determined by your knowledge of the ways of a potential attacker. You cannot barricade yourself in your home and never leave, but you can be smart about venturing out and avoiding high-risk areas and actions. So it is with protecting information.

And yet, in spite of such high-sounding rationalizations, *Secrets of a Super Hacker* is a troubling book. Yes—to use a homespun analogy—it is useful for a store owner to have a manual of shoplifting, written by a practicing (anonymous) shoplifter, to devise measures against the crime. Yet the Knightmare has also written his book as an excuse to gloat, to show off his forbidden knowledge and to invite others to break into secure computer systems. One cannot even be sure, although it seems unlikely, that the book itself is not an elaborate hack—a feint, a misdirection for the security community or, more likely, for the naïve reader who imagines that the security measures the Knightmare recommends will make a vulnerable system safe. The Knightmare is at considerable pains—becoming almost defensive at times—about justifying what he virtually calls his "loopy code of ethics." So it is hard to say what to do with this book: encourage the free flow of the inside information, so that honest people can deal with it, or discourage its publicity to head off the encouragement it gives to bad apples. Obviously I have taken the former tack. In my view, to get around in the information age, there needs to be a little practical knowledge—a bit of the hacker—in everyone.

The techniques of hacking, in the sense relevant to the Knightmare, are typically applied to extracting information from unfamiliar computer systems—that of course is what makes them useful for travel on the Internet. Many pioneers and frontiersman of the computer culture were libertarians when it came to information, regarding it as a commodity to be shared and passed along freely, with little concern about its origin. Naturally, techniques for controlling the flow of information—passwords, user ID's, software protection schemes, computer security systems—were simply affronts to the libertarian mentality, and they themselves often became the focal points of the hackers' efforts. But in general, nothing malicious was intended, beyond perhaps demonstrating that it was uncivil—not to mention useless—to try to control the information flowing through computers. As the Knightmare puts it, a computer hacker "does not intentionally use [his] knowledge of computers to be mischievous or destructive. That sort of thing is for social-outcast junior high school kids."

Until recently, hackers were like supernumeraries in the theater, creeping through the shadows of cyberspace, doing at most a little mischief, but largely being ignored. People running computer systems had enough trouble merely keeping the systems up. If they had a night visitor who did no damage, it was hardly worth a week of effort to set traps into which the intruder might never stumble. In fact, setting the traps could well cause more damage to the system than would a hacker's visit.

Outlaws in Cyberspace *(cont'd.)*

Then, in 1988, a Cornell graduate student in computer science, Robert T. Morris Jr., built the network equivalent of a doomsday weapon, an invention that irrevocably changed the hacker community, its public image and the psyches of computer users forever. Morris wrote a program that acted like a clumsy hacker. It knew about five ways to break into a rather large class of computers, and if it broke into one computer, it would replicate itself on the new computer and use that one to break into others. The paths it took from computer to computer were along the Internet.

Morris's program invaded hundreds of computers in a day, prompting universities and defense installations to cut their Internet connections and catapulting hackers onto the six o'clock news. The FBI was called in. Police agencies raided the system operators of computer bulletin boards and confiscated their equipment—often for dubious reasons. Responding to a vague and formerly low level danger had suddenly become a witch hunt. Overnight the hacker became persona non grata.

The Morris incident reinforced the public's general fear of computing with a fear of hacking. It became taboo to play on other people's computers and to check out files and resources that were created, in fact, expressly for visiting users. Is not access to other people's computers hacking? Does the FBI not arrest hackers and confiscate their computers? Most people forgot—if they ever knew—that hacking is pretty harmless as long as the hacker avoids the temptation to cross the line and become a "malicious meddler."

In order to counteract the bad press, the hacking community tried to divide itself into good guys and bad guys. The computer junkies who adhered to the parts of the definition stressing love of systems and skill with arcane commands were the good guys. In general, those people just liked to play and learn, and they tried to retain the name *hacker* by creating the term *cracker* for the bad guys. For crackers, a major motivating force was definition number eight of *The New Hacker's Dictionary*, breaking into systems without authorization and with malicious intent. By that criterion the Knightmare has surely crossed the line, but he invents his own rules to show he too is a good guy. In any event, the distinction has failed to catch on outside the hacking community. All are still just known as hackers.

The Knightmare has something to say about the entire spectrum of hacking, good and bad. But by his own account, the book is not an encyclopedic reference on how to sneak into every imaginable system: any such volume would be out of date before it could be published. Rather, the Knightmare has produced a manual of general methods, beginning with some hacking history and some equipment recommendations for the hacking apprentice. The shopping list and the reasoning behind it could benefit any serious computer user.

The main section discusses the research the hacker must do before trying to gain access to a computer. In the past decade, thinking about computer security has matured, making it immeasurably harder for the hacker to just sit at home and break into some high-security computers—à la Matthew Broderick in the 1983

Outlaws in Cyberspace *(cont'd.)*

movie *WarGames*. It now takes legwork, undercover snooping and, in some cases, dumpster diving (raiding trash bins after hours) to gather the necessary preliminary information. The entry-level hacker can start with the easy stuff in the first few chapters—"brute force" or educated-guesses to acquire passwords—before moving on to sophisticated methods that exploit software errors, bar codes, CD-ROM data bases, telephones, bulletin board systems and human gullibility.

Only one chapter is devoted to the question, Once inside a system, what can the hacker do there? That lack of emphasis probably reflects the relatively small importance attached by hackerdom to *being* inside compared with *getting* inside. The Knightmare briefly addresses what to expect from various kinds of operating system and how to proceed with them. The techniques he mentions are probably deducible from the documentation for any of the computers one is likely to encounter, but conveniently, he has gathered some of the basic information in *Secrets of a Super Hacker*.

Finally—in perhaps the most dubious section of the book—the Knightmare addresses the budding computer criminal: How does one keep from getting caught? What does one do if one gets caught? Hackers seeking recognition for their exploits from their peers confront a catch-22: the more people who know about them, the more likely they will be caught. Just in case that happens, the wayward reader can consult the Knightmare's lengthy discussion of the applicable laws.

A question that arises throughout the book, but most sharply in the final section, is, Who is its intended reader? Is is someone like me? I help manage a computer system, and I know a lot about many kinds of computer and operating systems, but I do not become enamored with every system. I therefore consider myself a nonhacker. The book cannot be targeted at the true hacker, either, since such a person would already know the book's contents, although the tales of hacker adventure and the statements of hacker ethics would probably pique cracker curiosity. Perhaps the potential reader is a frustrated Internet user. Or maybe a computer nerd who longs for the James Bond way of life. Maybe a computer illiterate type with a voyeuristic desire to navigate cyberspace from the safety of the sofa. Most likely the reader will be the replacement for that data-center manager from twenty-five years ago, still trying to figure out what the enemy is up to.

As networking becomes the prerogative of the private citizen and perhaps the solution to many of society's problems, hacking may go the way of the Wild West. For a time, there was only frontier justice, since there was no other justice to be had. Settling differences with a gunfight at high noon was customary; but gradually the law took control, and frontier justice became a thing of the past. Remnants of the era still turn up. Western novels sell briskly, and their readers can live vicariously in the days of the frontier. Perhaps readers of *Secrets of a Super Hacker* will enjoy the book on that level.

Outlaws in Cyberspace *(cont'd.)*

Unfortunately, for the questionably hearted computer user the book is a reasonable source from which to start down the road to computer crime. It presents much information that a person—regardless of motivation—could find useful for breaking into other people's computers. Some of the information is dated, and so it will not work as a recipe. But most people who decide to try to break into a machine have no idea where to start, and for them *Secrets of a Super Hacker* is invaluable.

Does the Knightmare bear some social responsibility *not* to spread this word? He explains: "Dissemination of information is always an honorable incentive to hack." The implication that information is not bad, people are, may strike some people as simplistic and evasive, much like the motto of the National Rifle Association, Guns don't kill, people do. On the other hand, the Knightmare might look for acquittal on this point to Thomas Jefferson, who in 1810 wrote, "No one more sincerely wishes the spread of information among mankind than I do." Society, both on and off the networks, will probably never resolve all the issues of who controls information.

The discussion of how to hack does give some insight into how *not* to get hacked, but the interesting points are obscured by endless details. My father's favorite expression, *common sense,* turns out to be the worst enemy of the hacker. The Knightmare tells the story of the computer administrator who so feared hackers that he insisted passwords be ten characters long, contain nonalphabetic characters and be changed weekly. That would have solved the problem, except that no employee could remember his password, and passwords began appearing taped to the fronts of terminals. The lurking hacker peering over the user's shoulder ("shoulder surfing") had a field day.

One important insight the reader will get from this book is axiomatic among experts in security: no security measure is 100 percent effective. Any precaution that allows some people access and excludes others can be attacked. The goal is not guaranteed security, because guaranteed security leads to a system that is unusable by its legitimate users. The goal is to make things so difficult as to discourage hackers and send them looking for easier pickings. Do not use your credit card number or social security number as your password. When you dial up a computer network, take note of the date, time and place of your preceding log-in. Be wary of the charming stranger who shows up on a rainy night to fix that disk drive that has given you so much trouble. In short, become a bit of a hacker yourself; explore and stretch your capabilities. But if, on some bulletin board in a far corner of cyberspace, you encounter the Knightmare, be wary—and very polite.

Nazis, Communists, Klansmen, and Others on the Fringe, by John George and Laird Wilcox. Buffalo: Prometheus, 1992.*

Reviewed by Christopher Phelps,
University of Rochester

John George and Laird Wilcox are, respectively, professor of sociology and political science at the University of Central Oklahoma and founder of a University of Kansas archive. As its quirky title suggests, their collaborative work, *Nazis, Communists, Klansmen, and Others on the Fringe,* is a compendium of political oddities. George and Wilcox devote 37 chapters and over 500 pages to "extremist" groups ranging from the Revolutionary Communist Party to the White Aryan Resistance. The book's principal use is unintended: as a superb demonstration of how *not* to understand the far right and radical left.

If expectations are excited by this weighty volume for an informative or encyclopaedic survey of the contemporary right and left, they are soon dashed. Although the book takes the 1960s as its starting point, making its focus contemporary rather than historical, most of the groups treated are defunct, usually by several decades. These moribund subjects include, on the right, the White Citizens' Councils, the Minutemen and the *Dan Smoot Report,* and, on the left, Students for a Democratic Society, the *Guardian,* and the Communist Workers Party. Meanwhile, many groups that remain significant today—such as, on the Marxist left, the International Socialist Organization, and the journal *Crossroads*—are not treated at all. Nor are any of the currents of left-wing radicalism that do not define themselves as Marxist or Leninist.

Glaring mistakes and general confusion mar the spotty coverage. Errors that would be trivial if taken individually are, cumulatively, enough to make *Nazis, Communists, Klansmen, and Others on the Fringe* a scholarly embarrassment. To record a few representative blunders, George and Wilcox write that Communist leader Doris Healey was expelled from the C.P. in 1973, when in fact she resigned (p. 109); they date publication of Eldridge Cleaver's *Soul on Ice* as 1969, instead of 1968 (p. 132); and they make hilarious backwards reference to "Eugene Dennis (son of former CP general secretary Eugene Dennis, Jr.)" (p. 106). Such sloppiness is disastrous where authoritative treatment is claimed.

To entertain another example, George and Wilcox define Trotskyists as "those communing with the ghost of Leon Trotsky (1877–1940), who was expelled from the Soviet Union by Joseph Stalin in 1928" (p. 101). Trotsky's expulsion did not

*A book review by Christopher Phelps, which appeared in *Critical Sociology 19* (1992), pp. 135–138. Reprinted with permission from the publisher.

Nazis, Communists, Klansmen, and others on the Fringe *(cont'd.)*

occur until 1929, and it is gratuitous to impute mysticism to a rational political tradition. Such flippancy, it appears, springs from a hazy familiarity with the history of Trotskyism in the United States. George and Wilcox write, "The Socialist Workers Party was the main Trotskyist organization in America until 1985, when its leaders abandoned their commitment to Trotsky's ideas in favor of a more flexible line." The turning point was actually two years earlier, and this account is yet more misguided because it misses the point of the new SWP politics: a strict adherence to the ideas of Fidel Castro and total defense of the Cuban state, hardly a "more flexible line."

When George and Wilcox set their meager sights on more sophisticated theoretical matters, their rendering does even greater damage. Adorno's complex ideas on fascism, for example, are reduced to the crude ruminations of a dogmatist: "Theodore (sic) W. Adorno, the originator of the view that right-wingers are prone to 'authoritarianism' while left-wingers are not, was widely recognized as a Marxist and undoubtedly harbored Marxist disdain for right-wingers, whom he tended to identify with fascists and Nazis" (p. 73). Whatever one thinks of critical theory, this is an inadequate recapitulation of the ideas generated by the Frankfurt School.

Consider the similar claim by George and Wilcox, in defining Leninism, that Lenin considered the call for an eight-hour day nothing but a "tactical maneuver to improve the power position of the party" (p. 101). The reader is made to think these words are Lenin's. They belong, however, to Gabriel Almond, whose *Appeals of Communism* (1954) gives no substantiation that Lenin treated the eight-hour day so cynically. In actuality, Lenin made no such statement. In 1912, he explicitly called the demand for the eight-hour day "not reformist but revolutionary." The false imputation is doubly ironic, because George and Wilcox include an appendix of misquotations—whose fabrication, they allege, is a habit of extremists—including many attributions invented by right-wing cranks and credited to Lenin.

A poorly constructed theoretical base in part explains the book's empirical ineptness. Undistinguished apart from its manifold errors, *Nazis, Communists, Klansmen, and Others on the Fringes* is the most recent in a long tradition that equates the far right and the revolutionary left as "extremist." That tradition has as its taproot the theories of "totalitarianism" which took shape in the 1930s and 1940s among European and American intellectuals. It found far more elegant and insightful expression then. George and Wilcox see differences between right and left, but they also draw up a list of 22 common traits held universally by "extremists," including character assassination, name-calling, a Manichean worldview, inadequate proof for assertions, advocacy of repression for opponents and critics, use of intimidation, assumption of moral superiority, use of slogans, hypersensitivity, and conspiracy mongering.

Nazis, Communists, Klansmen, and others on the Fringe *(cont'd.)*

That these categories are highly subjective should be transparent. George and Wilcox lump democratic revolutionaries together with other "extremists," for example, but Marxists in the democratic revolutionary socialist tradition have repeatedly argued against conspiracy theories and defended democratic liberties, even for their opponents. Nor can such Marxists be said to habitually assume moral superiority, use intimidation, or disrespect proof. Then again, to point this out risks the charge of hypersensitivity; therein lies the trap.

George and Wilcox claim that their typology is distinct from psychological theories of extremism and that they do not seek to conflate opposing viewpoints or dismiss dissident ideas. It is difficult, however, to see how their theory does not rest upon a distinction between irrational and rational behavior. When the Spartacist League on the left is set against Lyndon Larouche on the right, that theory, with its allegation of mutual irrationality, has a certain plausibility. Mostly, however, the equation is spurious. The ability of George and Wilcox to blur distinctions between conflicting ideologies is so spectacular that they manage to group Meir Kahane's Jewish Defense League, the Nation of Islam, and assorted neo-Nazis together, all as "right-wing extremists."

Above all, the theory of "extremism" is deficient because it offers no way of explaining the dynamics of right-wing and left-wing movements. The orientation taken by George and Wilcox leads them to pay no heed to the historical, cultural, and social origins of political movements. They treat groups in isolation and in terms of their programmatic declarations alone. Only occasionally do they describe the subjective perceptions of participants in the groups they depict, and they almost never give details about internal organizational processes. Each group stands alone as a weird instance of extremism rather than as a vehicle for the organization and articulation of sentiments present in the larger society—rather, that is, than an agent of social and political conflict with wider cultural meaning.

Even the most principled characteristic of *Nazis, Communists, Klansmen, and Others on the Fringe,* its defense of civil liberties, requires some critical scrutiny. George and Wilcox are troubled by the political specimens they have put on display, but concern for the First Amendment leads them to preach toleration. Praiseworthy respect for civil liberties is thus chained to political paralysis. George and Wilcox leave the mistaken impression that moderation and inaction, apart from criminal prosecution of violence, is the only properly democratic course to take in the face of fascism. A strategy of vigilant exposure of far right activities, combined with militant mass mobilization for democratic rights and self-defense against hate crimes would in their minds have the scent of— "extremism."

Bold New City or Built-Up 'Burb? Redefining Contemporary Suburbia*

William Sharpe
Barnard College

Leonard Wallock
Hunter College, CUNY

> America has created a new form of urban settlement. It is higher, bolder, and richer than anything man has yet called city.
>   . . . Most Americans still speak of suburbs. But a city's suburbs are no longer just bedrooms. They are no longer mere orbital satellites. They are no longer *sub*.
>
> —Jack Rosenthal, "The Outer City: U.S. in Suburban Turmoil,"
>   *New York Times*, May 30, 1971

> Postsuburban regions have become the most common form of metropolitan development in this country. And this emergence has undeniably transformed our lives.
>
> —Rob Kling, Spencer Olin, and Mark Poster, eds.,
>   *Postsuburban California*, 1991

In the last few decades, the United States has become a suburban nation. Between 1950 and 1980 the number of people living in suburbia nearly tripled, soaring from 35.2 to 101.5 million. By 1990, almost half of all Americans called suburbia home.[1] But whereas the typical commuter suburbs of the 1950s were almost entirely residential, today's suburbs feature corporate headquarters, high-tech industries, and superregional malls. Consequently, about twice as many people now commute to work within suburbs as commute between them and cities.[2] Rapidly expanding suburbs contain more office space than downtowns and most of the new jobs.[3] As a result, suburbs are in the forefront of American economic development and are far less dependent upon cities than before.[4]

Such explosive growth is having a profound impact on both the landscape and people's conception of suburban life. Condominium projects, office complexes, and

Bold New City or Built-up 'Burb?
Redefining Contemporary Suburbia (cont'd.)

industrial parks abound; crowded eight-lane highways lead to commercial strips and vast shopping malls; medical facilities and research centers compete to develop land. Cultural centers, sports arenas, and multiplex cinemas have proliferated across an increasingly built-up terrain. Meanwhile, the image of the suburb as a pastoral haven from the harsh realities of the city has been shattered by the spread of homelessness, drug addiction, and crime. Relentlessly, the countryside appears to be urbanizing. The city, with its attendant problems and pleasures, seems to be coming to the suburbs.

The rapid transformation of the landscape has prompted critics to redefine the very nature of suburbia and to contend that built-up areas on the urban fringe have become cities in their own right. Some have even declared that suburbia is dead. This article reviews the current literature in order to assess the accuracy of the latest representations of suburbs and to determine the degree to which the social practices and ideals of traditional suburbia still survive.

As we will show, there has been a turnabout in the way suburbs are perceived. During the last two decades, some analysts of contemporary suburbs have begun to sound like apologists. In the 1950s, 1960s, and early 1970s, critics vigorously attacked suburbia for its racial discrimination, patriarchal familism, political separatism, and geographical sprawl and earnestly proposed solutions to overcome these ills. Such influential works as Betty Friedan's *The Feminine Mystique* (1963), Anthony Downs's *Opening Up the Suburbs* (1973), Richard Babcock and Fred Bosselman's *Exclusionary Zoning* (1973), and Michael Danielson's *The Politics of Exclusion* (1976) measured the social costs of suburban life. Many accounts stressed the disastrous consequences of suburban development for both the inner city and the nearby countryside.

By contrast, in the 1980s and 1990s, critics recognized that the problems caused by suburbanization remained unsolved, but they implicitly accepted, and in some cases enthusiastically embraced, suburbia on its own terms. Indeed, the willingness even to consider the "new city" as a utopia in the making—albeit a "bourgeois utopia"—implies that a truly searching critique of it is unnecessary.[5] Margaret Marsh has defined the best postwar studies of suburbia as those that "attempt to understand suburban communities from the point of view of the suburbanites."[6] Yet such sympathetic treatments, accepting suburban ideology at face value, may sacrifice their own critical distance. This is to a large extent what has happened with the current generation of critics; their conceptualization of the "new city" has been influenced by their own suburbanophilia.

As we will argue, the current literature reflects a skewed perception of city and suburb alike. Section one of our essay outlines the evolution, since the 1970s, of the idea that suburbs have become cities. Section two challenges that claim by pointing to the continuing social segregation within suburbs, a pattern that

Bold New City or Built-up 'Burb?
Redefining Contemporary Suburbia *(cont'd.)*

contemporary critics tend to minimize because they employ functional criteria—such as the increase in office space and retail trade—to measure suburban development. Although suburbs have assumed many of the functions of traditional cities, they are not fully comparable to cities. Nor have they become independent entities. In our view, equating suburbs with cities implies that suburbs possess a diversity, cosmopolitanism, political culture, and public life that most of them still lack and that most cities still afford.

Section three of this essay maintains that recent analysts have misrepresented the actual character of suburbia because they have too readily accepted certain mainstays of suburban ideology. They perpetuate the myths of suburbia's accessibility to all Americans, its suitability for women, and its harmony with nature, despite evidence that it excludes "undesirables," offers inadequate opportunities for women, and has a destructive impact on the environment.

Responding to the claim that "suburbia is dead," section four employs cultural rather than functional criteria to illustrate the tenacity of traditional suburban values. Just as the social exclusivity of suburbia has survived, so too have the fundamental attitudes associated with the "classic" American suburb of the 1950s. One indication of how suburban ideals persist can be found in prime-time television shows and Hollywood films; despite the increasing variety and complexity of their characters, they frequently promote the stereotyped gender roles and social hierarchies of the early postwar years. Only by considering the cultural and social context in which functional changes occur can scholars hope to assess the status of suburbia today.

Notes

1. Census figures indicate that by 1990 about 46 percent of the American population resided in suburbs. See Frank Clifford and Anne C. Roark, "Big Cities Hit by Census Data Showing Declining Role," *Los Angeles Times*, 24 Jan. 1991; and Robert Reinhold, "Chasing Votes from Big Cities to the Suburbs," *New York Times*, 1 June 1992.
2. Mark Baldassare, *Trouble in Paradise: The Suburban Transformation in America* (New York, 1986), 7.
3. William K. Stevens, "Beyond the Mall: Suburbs Evolving into 'Outer City,' " *New York Times*, 8 Nov. 1987.
4. This trend became apparent in the early 1970s: see Paul Gapp, Richard Phillips, and James Elsener, "Meet the 'New America,' " *Chicago Tribune*, 4 Feb. 1973.
5. Baldassare defines the "utopian view" as one of the three major perspectives on the future of the suburbs (*Trouble in Paradise*, 1–2, 207).
6. Margaret Marsh, *Suburban Lives* (New Brunswick, N.J., 1990), 220, n. 1.

The Twenty-Three Percent Solution*

Robert Bruegmann
University of Illinois at Chicago

In their call to arms against recent "Apologists of Suburbia," Wallock and Sharpe have given us some interesting insights, particularly in their study of the way suburban life is portrayed on television shows and in movies. In my opinion, however, these insights do not salvage their major argument.

In this essay, the authors attempt to revive the old city versus suburb debate of the 1950s and 1960s. During those years, a number of individuals, mostly academics with liberal political views teaching in urban universities in the northeastern United States, invented the concept of what Wallock and Sharpe call the "classic suburb of the 1950s." In this view, the suburbs were homogeneous, white, upper middle-class bedroom communities filled with inhabitants who had fled the city in an attempt to escape urban problems. These suburbs, we were told, replaced an urban culture of civic involvement, tolerance, and a love of the arts with a privatized, restrictive, consumption-minded, culturally impoverished existence. These antisuburban polemics were often presented as a critique of particular land-use patterns and political arrangements, but they were, at least implicitly, also attacks on the way of life of a large portion of the American population. These assertions were met with a vigorous counterattack as historians, sociologists, and others actually went out to the suburbs and reported what anyone living on the urban periphery already knew: there were rich suburbs and poor suburbs, black suburbs and white suburbs, bedroom communities and industrial satellites. In short, suburbs were as varied and as socially complex in their own ways as any central city.

"Bold New City or Built-Up 'Burb" ignores all of this latter literature and attempts to convince us that the "classic suburb" not only once existed but is with us still. The evidence presented consists primarily of census statistics, the bulwark of the earlier city-suburb cold warriors, and a new type of evidence, an analysis of the way the suburbs have been portrayed in the media. In this short review, I cannot deal with most of the argument—particularly that of the second half, which is right and suggestive but does not really carry the major burden of the authors' argument. I can only remark in passing that "Leave It to Beaver" no more accurately represents the life led by most suburbanites in the 1950s than "Escape from New York" documents the life known by most Manhattanites in the 1980s. These are

*Robert Bruegmann, "The Twenty-Three Percent Solution," copyright © 1994 by the Johns Hopkins University Press. *American Quarterly 46* (March 1994), pp. 31–34. Reprinted by permission of the Johns Hopkins University Press.

The Twenty-Three Percent Solution *(cont'd.)*

fascinating documents, but their meaning is kaleidoscopic and depends entirely on who is watching and in what circumstances.

To give, in a very limited space, some slight indication of the problems I find with the types of evidence used, the mode of argument employed, and the conclusions drawn in the Wallock-Sharpe essay, I will restrict my examination to one short passage. I have selected this passage not because it is particularly important in itself, but because it is typical of the entire argument. It reads: " . . . suburbia has remained an essentially exclusive domain. For example, in 1980, blacks constituted just 6.1 percent of suburbanites, as compared to 23.4 percent of city dwellers."

The first thing to be said about this passage is that the term "suburb," the key conceptual element in this piece, is nearly completely meaningless in the context the authors are using. As everyone who has traveled around the American city knows, demographics and political attitudes do not correspond in any kind of systematic way with municipal boundaries; this is not surprising given that, throughout most of American history, suburbs routinely became absorbed into the city and that this process still continues in many parts of the country. When the authors use the term, they are clearly thinking about it in the way a New Yorker might think about it. It simply does not apply to Indianapolis, Jacksonville, Houston, or many other American cities. So, for example, Post Oak Galleria, arguably the most conspicuous of the "suburban" centers the authors are discussing, is well within the municipal limits of Houston.

Putting aside for the moment the obvious problems with the city-suburb dichotomy, let us turn to the evidence cited: census figures on percentages of black population. The first thing to be noted is that arguments about diversity are almost always "proven" with racial statistics. No one making similar arguments ever tries to find out the ratio of fundamentalist Christians to members of more mainstream denominations, which suggests some of the political motivation involved. Like the city-suburb dichotomy, the black-white dichotomy provides an illusory simplicity that denies the actual diversity that exists as inner city neighborhoods collide with or shade imperceptibly into those outside the city. Such statistics, in any event, are never neutral "facts." The very categories used by the Census Bureau reflect the social science thinking and political views of the preceding generations.

In any case, why is 23 percent "more diverse" than 6 percent? Unless the authors believe that the higher the black populations the more "diverse" the population automatically becomes, this conclusion is hard to understand since it is actually the suburban figure that is closer to the national average than the urban one. Taking the author's ideas to their logical conclusion, can we assume that Japan or Sweden are less diverse and hence less satisfying places to live than America? Can we assume that they would advocate that the United States actively encourage increased immigration to enhance diversity? Would a uniform 23 percent of minority population in every census tract in America provide maximum diversity? What makes the authors believe that diversity is better than uniformity in the first place? If the debates about multiculturalism of the last few years have shown anything, they have

The Twenty-Three Percent Solution *(cont'd.)*

suggested the extraordinary complexity of conceptualizing, let alone accommodating, diversity.

Even setting the issue of diversity aside and accepting the figures at face value, do they at least indicate greater segregation in the suburbs than in the city? The authors write that those minorities who live in the suburbs often cluster together in relatively homogeneous neighborhoods. This is certainly true, but, to state the obvious, it is just as true in most city neighborhoods. Although it may be the case that black and white, rich and poor are thrown together more in the centers of cities than at their far edges, does it make sense to define this mere physical propinquity as "integration"? Many city neighborhoods that statistics suggest are integrated are only integrated in the sense that white people live there until they can move out or that there are poor, black families who have so far resisted gentrification. It is possible that meaningful integration is only possible when it is voluntary, when citizens have the freedom to decide not to integrate, and that, in the long run, efforts to force integration, whether school bussing or ordinances forbidding "for sale" signs to stop block busting, only delay it. It is quite possible that outlying shopping centers in the Chicago area may actually be far more "integrated" than the streets of the Loop.

Statistics do not get us very far in questions of these kinds. They can not tell us whether lot size or amount of landscaping might have an effect on the amount of racial friction in a neighborhood, for example, and they cannot inform us whether race or class is the more important determinant in the way shoppers at the mall interact. It is precisely these kinds of questions that are raised in Joel Garreau's book *Edge City*. To my mind, his chapter on Atlanta is one of the most thoughtful examinations in recent years on the race issue because it relies so little on the stereotypes created during the postwar years. This has infuriated academics of the old city-suburb cold wars, who have tried to dismiss Garreau's book as a work of right-wing, anecdotal journalism. But, to their considerable annoyance, *Edge City*, better than any previous book, described some of the forces that have shaped the urban periphery and identified the widely divergent opinions about its place in the metropolis. For this reason, Wallock and Sharpe have accused Garreau of being an "apologist" for suburbia.

If this makes Garreau an "apologist," let us have many more of them. For me, posing the question of whether the outlying areas of our cities are "good" or "bad" is about as fruitless a asking whether the city of Buenos Aires or the country of Finland are "good" or "bad." Every human community works well for some and harms others. Each is such a complex mechanism that it beggars our efforts to describe it, let alone to formulate sweeping remedies for apparent problems. In fact, such efforts, as often as not, have an uncanny knack for merely aggravating the very problems their authors are trying to eliminate. I, for one, would like to see a lot more effort to understand the issues before the call to judgment.

ᕚᕤ CHAPTER 7

EVALUATING

INTRODUCTION: WHAT IS AN EVALUATION, AND WHY WRITE ONE?

In the preceding chapter, we discussed critiques of written texts. However, as you undoubtedly realize, other kinds of subjects may be evaluated—films, plays, other kinds of performances, products, artifacts and objects, procedures, computers and computer programs, careers, services, internships, people, and complex forms of behavior (international conflicts or mate selection). Writing evaluations of such nonprint materials (which we simply will refer to as "writing evaluations" from this point on) is the focus of this chapter.

As you will see, there are similarities between writing critiques and writing evaluations, but there also are some differences. A major similarity is that in writing either a critique or an evaluation, writers must determine and assess established criteria. A major difference, though, is that critiques ordinarily discuss only one written text, but evaluations often compare and contrast a class of things. Evaluating a fast-food restaurant, for example, would involve establishing criteria that could be applied to evaluate it in comparison to other fast-food restaurants.

Why do people read and write evaluations? People read evaluations all the time in order to help them make judgments—about a product they are considering buying, about a service they are considering using, or about an action they are considering taking (such as watching a specific film). People write evaluations because they have a special perspective or expertise and wish to provide information to others. Professionals frequently write evaluations as part of their work because they possess expertise or specialized training that qualifies them to make informed judgments. An artist or designer might evaluate a store display; a theater professor might evaluate a play for the local newspaper; a business executive might evaluate the effectiveness of various departments in a large company; and a scientist might evaluate a new piece of equipment. Supervisors may be required to write evaluations about the work performance of the people they supervise. Professionals in many fields must write self-evaluations, that is, assessments of their own accomplishments at work.

Because evaluations are written so frequently in the professional world, teachers often assign them to help prepare students for their careers beyond college. Teachers also assign evaluations to assess what you know, for example your comprehension of course material or the extent to which you have assimilated a disciplinary or professional perspective.

SAMPLE ASSIGNMENTS

As we have said, there are numerous reasons for reading and writing evaluations. You can expect to receive a variety of evaluation assignments as you progress through your college courses. To show you some of the types of evaluations you may be required to write, we have selected a few representative assignments from several fields. As you read these assignments, look for similarities among them.

Journalism Assignment. For this assignment you must write a review or a critical essay about an individual piece of work or a series or collection that interests you. You may select a film, play, art exhibit, song, recording (tape, record, or CD), concert, dance performance, television series, and so forth. Your review should contain commentary about the *technical* aspects of whatever you are evaluating and discuss its significance in terms of broader issues or concerns. Minimum length: 750 words (3 pages). Recommended length: 1,200 words Publication: Please hand in with your review a brief description of the audience to whom you are writing. Although not a requirement, the title of a specific publication would be preferable.

Marketing Assignment. Prepare the product information portion of the written background study that you will use to develop a sales presentation. (You will be preparing the other portions of your background study later in the term.) The product information portion of your study should be approximately five or six typewritten pages in length and should assess your product with respect to the following criteria: *product features; general uses; benefits; extended product features; servicing;* and *competing products.*

Political Science Assignment. Select a current international dispute; it does not have to involve the United States directly. Write a brief (4- to 6-page) paper in which you use the criteria of *tangible* and *intangible power* (as found in your text) to evaluate the relative situational power of each of the parties involved as well as to assess how the parties use their power and how effective they are over time (years, months, weeks, or days). Begin your paper with a description of the dispute and the parties involved. Explain the interests of each party and the outcome each would like to achieve.

Internship Evaluation Assignment. At the conclusion of your internship, you will be required to deliver an oral presentation to your committee and other attendees in which you describe and evaluate your experience. Your presentation should be approximately thirty to forty-five minutes long, with fifteen minutes (or more) for questions/discussion. To accompany your oral presentation, you must prepare (for distribution) a ten-page (typed or word-processed) written assessment of your internship. Your assessment should include a description of your internship, a discussion of both positive and negative aspects, an explanation of how you will apply or integrate what you have learned, and recommendations about how the internship might be modified in the future for other students.

Discussion Group Assessment. This term you have been a part of a discussion group that has met regularly to assess the readings assigned for this class. Write a 1,000-word (4-page) evaluation of your group in which you address the following: member participation; distribution of leadership functions; overall focus on discussing interpretations or insights and resolving uncertainties. Also include an assessment of your contribution to your group. What positive roles did you play? In what ways might you have interfered with or hampered group effectiveness?

As you can see from these assignments, evaluations involve making an informed judgment about one or more people, objects, processes, or the like. While written critiques summarize the text being critiqued, evaluations describe the subjects being evaluated and provide readers with necessary background information to understand the overall judgment. As with critiques, that judgment must be supported and based on relevant criteria. Claiming that a person is "the best" or that a movie is "a must-see" is not sufficient for college writing (nor for professional situations). The criteria to be used may be specified by the instructor, but a significant part of some assignments may be determining what criteria are appropriate to use. Evaluations often are comparisons of two or more similar things, such as two leading candidates for a job or several pizza restaurants. Thus, evaluations are more likely to make very specific recommendations to readers.

Regardless of the particular field for which they are written, evaluations share several features, which you should keep in mind as you learn more about how to write them.

1. Evaluations contain a description of whatever is being evaluated.

2. They present an overall judgment or conclusion.

3. The judgment or conclusion is frequently accompanied by one or more recommendations.

4. The judgment is supported by relevant criteria that are used consistently, whether the subject is one or more than one persons, objects, or processes.

IMPORTANT INFORMATION ABOUT EVALUATIONS

As we have suggested, writing an evaluation is similar in many ways to writing a critique. Like critiques, evaluations must include appropriate, consistent criteria. In addition, the subject of the evaluation must be skillfully described so that it can be perceived or understood by readers. Two additional areas pertinent to writing an evaluation are selecting something to evaluate and making recommendations.

Making a Selection

In writing evaluations, sometimes people select what they will assess and sometimes they do not. An administrator, for example, may be expected to evaluate the personnel or the program she supervises. On the other hand, professionals frequently can—and do—make choices about what to evaluate. For example, a doctor may decide to assess an innovative medical technique and publish the results. Most likely, your experience will be similar to that of professionals. You may be told what to evaluate, but often you will need to make the selection yourself because your ability to make an appropriate choice may be part of what your instructor will be assessing.

If required to select your subject, you need to consider several factors. Perhaps the most important factor is accessibility. You should choose to evaluate only those subjects that you have adequate access to. If you evaluate an object, you will have to examine it often enough to become familiar with it. If you evaluate a film or a process (like registering for courses at your college), you need to be able to observe it several times. You *wouldn't,* for example, want to evaluate an exhibit at an art museum a four-hour drive away. Finally, as with observations, you may need to get permission from participants in advance and arrange convenient times for observing them.

Another important consideration in selection is the size and scope of the subject being evaluated. Objects, events, processes, and performances differ from one another in size and complexity. You can choose, for example, to evaluate *one song* or *one album* (tape or CD) with eleven or twelve selections, or *all of the recordings* produced by a particular performer or group. Likewise, you can evaluate the performance of a sport team's *defense* during *one* game or the performance of *every aspect* of that team's performance for an *entire season.* In selecting a subject to evaluate, then, consider the assignment. For a term project, it may be appropriate to assess a substantial body of work (several major works of a film director), or a complex object (campus parking) or process (the marketing of a particular product). For a more modest assignment, however, you should select something smaller in scope.

An evaluation assignment is important not only in helping you determine the scope of what you will assess; it can also help you select an *appropriate* item to evaluate, particularly if one or more criteria to be used in the evaluation are expressly stated or implied. Consider the Journalism Assignment in the Sample Assignments section of this chapter; it requires the writer to "discuss [the] . . . significance" of whatever is being evaluated "in terms of broader issues or concerns." In selecting what to evaluate for this assignment, then, you would need to consider whether and in what ways your choices were significant, and eliminate those about which you couldn't make this claim.

Finally, in selecting what to evaluate, try to choose a subject you are familiar with and interested in, when possible. It would be difficult to evaluate the parking situation at your college if you don't drive to campus. Likewise, a comparison of different ways of developing film would be inappropriate for someone who knows nothing about the subject. This is not to say that only art majors should review art exhibits, however. An interest in the visual, even in how you dress, may be sufficient to motivate someone to write an evaluation of an art exhibit, as will a desire to learn about a new area.

In addition to general factors that need to be considered in selecting something to evaluate, the process of choice can sometimes present writers with special challenges. One such challenge occurs when an evaluation must be written about an object, event, or process that will be presented as "typical" or "representative." You may, for example, be assigned to evaluate "typical" behaviors manifested by preschool children in a local play group or to assess a "typical" international dispute. As you might imagine, selecting something that is "representative" or "typical" requires a careful examination of potential choices. The word *typical* or *representative* implies similarity in all significant ways; thus to select a representative international dispute, you must be familiar with the qualities that characterize international disputes. Likewise, if you were trying to select a "typical" undergraduate recreational activity at your college or university to evaluate, you would need to investigate what most students did, for example, by contacting the Student Activities Office to secure data about attendance at and participation in campus activities.

Another problem with selection occurs when that which is being evaluated typically changes each time it occurs. Events and processes (plays, music recitals, sporting events, meetings, the passage of a bill, class registration, or manufacturing a product) never occur in exactly the same way twice. Even with the same cast, performances of a play vary, and students registering for classes using the same process may have very different experiences. For this reason, it is important when evaluating an event or process to observe and/or experience it several times, if possible. (Recall that in "The Fight" [at the end of Chapter 4] Clifford Geertz observed many cockfights before he wrote about them.)

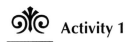 **Activity 1**

Select one assignment from the Sample Assignments section of this chapter. If you were completing this assignment for the discipline specified, what might you choose to evaluate? Would you have easy access to the object, event, or performance that you selected, or would access pose any problems? How suitable is your choice with respect to the course or discipline specified in the assignment? Is it appropriate, given the directions of the assignment? Does the scope seem reasonable? What special problems (variability, representativeness) do you anticipate for your selection?

Describing

In addition to carefully selecting what you will evaluate, you will need to describe it. In evaluations, describing serves a function similar to summarizing in critiques. Just as summarizing provides readers with an overview of the critiqued text's content and with necessary background information, in evaluations descriptions provide readers with an overall depiction of the place, object, person, or event that is being evaluated and with any necessary background information. In addition, as with summarizing, description can stand alone as a complete text. In this chapter we will not address descriptions that stand alone; we will address only descriptions that are a part of evaluations.

As you decide what description to include in an evaluation, you will need to consider whether background information should be included in addition to the description. Background information can provide facts related to the historical context, for example, about the production or formation of the object, process, or event you are evaluating. If describing the packaging of pain relievers for an evaluation, you should also explain that manufacturers made significant changes in packaging after people had tampered with boxes of pain relievers on store shelves, which resulted in several deaths.

In addition to providing background information about your subject, you may also need to provide details about its membership in a class or genre. Such information can help readers understand why you selected particular criteria. For example, if you are writing an evaluation of a movie, you probably should begin by identifying its type (romantic comedy, adventure, children's, horror, etc.). Doing so would enable you to describe the movie in terms of characteristics typical for its class. That is, as you describe a horror movie you could easily include information about its degree of suspense, amount of violence, characterization of fiendish brutes, and so on, because horror movies typically contain such features. If you are describing a children's movie, by contrast, you most likely need to include different characteristics.

Regardless of the amount and substance of background information you provide, you must, of course, describe the object, event, or process itself. Description is an important part of evaluation because readers who are unfamiliar with the subject need an overview of it in order to understand and accept your assessment of it. Moreover, even readers who are familiar with a subject are unlikely to have whatever you evaluated present with them as they read. In general, you should provide your readers with sufficient detail to give them a coherent sense of your subject as a whole and to support each of your criteria adequately.

As you are decide on the amount and kind of description to include, as always, your most important consideration is your intended audience. In the August 1994 *Consumer Reports* article, "Can Fast Food Be Good Food?" for example, the authors feel no need to describe what is meant by *fast food,* because their intended readership is people who eat fast food and know what the term means. Had their intended readership been people in a country without fast-food restaurants, a definition of the term would have been needed.

Organizing Descriptions for Placement within an Evaluation. After you have determined the kind and amount of physical description and background information needed for your evaluation, you will need to consider how to organize your descriptions most effectively. In general, you should organize them in the simplest way. That is, if you are describing an event (or something that might be perceived as an event, such as a film or television program), organize it in chronological order. Using a narrative structure, you should discuss the main parts of the event in the order in which they occurred and explain how the parts are related. Similarly, when describing a process, present each step in chronological order and explain how the steps are related to each other. By contrast, when describing an object, focus on its important parts or components. For a backpack, for example, you might describe its main storage compartment, the subcompartments, such as zippered or snapped pockets, and peripheral attachments, such as shoulder straps, pull tabs, and so on. Details can be presented as an object or component is scanned from top to bottom, from left to right, or in any other pattern that is easy to follow. Whether you are evaluating an object, process, or event, you will need to present the components or the major parts or aspects in a clear, accessible manner so that your readers can get a coherent sense of the whole and of how its parts fit together.

When you have determined how to organize the description or background information your evaluation requires, your next decision is where to place that description or background information. Our advice in this regard is similar to our advice about placing summaries within critiques. Often, especially if readers are unfamiliar with the subject being evaluated, the bulk of the description should be placed at the beginning of the piece. In this way, readers will get an overall sense of the object, process, or event being evaluated.

 **Activity 2**

> With your group, read and examine the sample evaluations at the end of this chapter. Note the kinds of description and background information that have been used and where they have been placed. Is description or background information presented all in one chunk, in several large chunks, or in numerous sections interspersed throughout the evaluation? In each case, what specific purpose does the description or background information serve? Who are the intended readers? How do the description and background information accommodate their needs? For example, do the authors assume that readers are familiar with the object, process, or event being evaluated?

Determining Which Criteria to Use

As well as carefully selecting and describing what you will evaluate, you need to consider what criteria to use in your evaluation. Evaluations use criteria, or standards of judgment, that are applied to the subject or subjects being evaluated in order to support an overall assessment or recommendation.

You can see in the Sample Assignments section of this chapter that evaluation assignments sometimes stipulate the criteria to be used. The Marketing Assignment, for example, specifies six general areas to be discussed in the product evaluation.

Likewise, the Political Science Assignment instructs students to use the criteria of *tangible* and *intangible power* to assess the power of parties involved in an international dispute. Evaluation assignments are not always this clear-cut, however. The Journalism Assignment—to review a movie, play, art exhibit, or so forth—does instruct students to comment on "the *technical* aspects." However, these are general directions, not specific criteria. In completing this assignment, you would have to determine the relevant technical aspects of your subject because these would vary depending on whether the subject was a movie, an art exhibit, or a CD. For movies, you might discuss the quality of the directing and the script; for an art exhibit, you might discuss the media used by the artists; and for a CD, you might discuss the quality of the sound engineering.

When an assignment does not specify criteria or when it gives only general directions, you will need to determine what criteria to use. In such a situation, you should choose criteria that are relevant to your subject and assignment, that support a judgment or conclusion, and that can be applied consistently to all subjects being evaluated.

Use Relevant Criteria. As with critiques, evaluations should be based on criteria that are relevant to the assignment or class and to the type of thing being evaluated. In determining which criteria could be relevant to evaluate a movie, for example, you should consider the class for which you are writing the evaluation. Suppose that you are reviewing *Schindler's List,* Steven Spielberg's 1994 movie about a German businessman who helps Jews escape Nazi death camps during World War II. For a Twentieth-Century European History class, it would be appropriate to consider how accurately the movie depicts life, and death, in the concentration camps, as well as how effectively it dramatizes an aspect of history with which many contemporary viewers may be unfamiliar. For a Contemporary Film class, however, you might focus instead on how *Schindler's List* relates to Spielberg's overall career as a director, considering such criteria as the effectiveness of his direction and his choice of subject matter.

As with critiques, there are no universal criteria for an evaluation. In selecting criteria, you should consider the nature of your subject matter and choose criteria relevant to the objects, processes, events, or so forth being evaluated. For example, cost is a relevant criteria in considering what kind of car to buy, because buying a car is usually a significant financial decision. However, in reviewing a movie, reviewers rarely mention the price of movie tickets, which is comparatively minimal. Instead of relying on universal criteria, then, you should consider the particular nature of your subject. In evaluating movies, plays, or musicals, you would generally consider the acting and directing as well as the story line. In evaluating a car, you would probably consider its cost as well as its repair record and the special features available. In evaluating a process, you would need to consider the components or the separate activities or stages of that process. For example, evaluating the process of obtaining a replacement ID at your college might involve reporting that the ID had been lost, paying for a duplicate, having a new photo taken, and picking up the completed duplicate. (At the college one of us attended, these four activities involved visiting three different buildings!)

Use Criteria That Support Your Judgment. Just as critiques support a thesis, evaluations present an overall judgment, conclusion, or set of recommendations. Obviously, if particular criteria are specified in your assignment, you should include them. When criteria are not specified, however, or when you are considering what additional criteria to use, you should choose ones that support your conclusion and that are appropriate for the focus of your evaluation. For example, in their opposing reviews, Rebecca Shugrue and Carolyn Gage ask whether *The Piano* is a feminist movie. Both writers consider the movie's presentation of the rape of Ada, the main female character, and her bargaining to buy back her piano. These are surely relevant criteria for assessing what messages the movie offers about women and thus for supporting their respective conclusions that the movie is or is not feminist. However, if you were reviewing *The Piano* for a Contemporary Film class and your assignment was to assess technical aspects of the movie, you might discuss its cinematography, sound track, and direction. In either case, you would be selecting criteria appropriate to the assignment that would work together to support your overall assessment of the movie.

Use Consistent Criteria. You may have noticed that the process of selecting criteria is similar for writing evaluations and critiques. However, in writing evaluations, keep in mind one additional aspect: The criteria you use should be consistently applied to all of the things you are evaluating. While evaluations may focus on only one object, event, or person, they are frequently written to compare more than one thing—to compare several new cars or to assess alternative methods of treating an illness, for example.

When evaluating two or more subjects, it is important to use the same criteria to evaluate them. If you were evaluating two new Italian restaurants for a newspaper, you should use the same criteria—for example, price, food quality, and convenience—to evaluate each one. Likewise, the August 1994 *Consumer Reports* article "Can Fast Food Be Good Food?" compares several menu items from several different fast-food restaurants using criteria such as serving size, calories, fat content, and taste. Think about how hard it would be to use this article if the authors had applied their criteria inconsistently—if they had reported the low-fat content but not the calories of the Hardee's roast beef sandwich, the calories but not the fat content of the Burger King basic burger, and praised the taste of one and neglected to mention the taste of the other.

Comparing more than one subject will usually result in quite a bit of information. If you are comparing several subjects and using several criteria to assess them, you might present your information in a table. *Consumer Reports* articles often use tables to summarize information; readers can find detailed information about a particular subject more easily on a chart or table than if the information were buried in a paragraph. Note the different kinds of information presented in the Ratings chart in "Can Fast Food Be Good Food?": price and serving size; total calories and fat; amounts of saturated fat, cholesterol, sodium, and protein; as well as a subjective rating of the taste and texture.

Use Criteria That You Can Justify. An important aspect of using criteria properly is being able to justify why you chose them, if it is appropriate to do so.

Generally speaking, to determine whether to state such a justification, writers consider their purpose, audience, the nature of what they are evaluating, and the general historical context. If you examine the article "Can Fast Food Be Good Food?" you will see that the authors assume that readers in the 1990s would generally accept the nutritional value and fat content as appropriate criteria for evaluating what is a "good food" and hence do not directly explain why they chose these criteria.

In deciding whether to directly state a justification for your criteria or indirectly imply one, you should take your cue from professional writers. When you can reasonably assume that your intended readers will easily accept your criteria as important and relevant, you don't need to justify them. On the other hand, however, when you are using one or more criteria that you can *not* assume readers will understand, you need to provide a rationale.

Finally, if you are concerned that readers might not understand why a criterion was *not* used, then you should explain its omission. Note that "Can Fast Food Be Good Food?" explains why the authors decided to omit a particular criterion: the presence of bacteria in the meat. As the authors explain, they consulted an expert with the U.S. Food and Drug Administration as they considered whether to include this criterion because in 1993 several children died after eating fast-food hamburgers contaminated with *E. coli* bacteria. The presence of this explanation indicates the authors' awareness of the historical context, and, thus, demonstrates that the omission of the criterion of bacterial content was not the result of their negligence or lack of expertise. In our experience, it's better for writers—especially student writers—to include such explanations about omitted criteria so that their knowledge of the subject they are evaluating won't be questioned.

 **Activity 3**

Assume that you are assigned to review a current popular movie or television series for one of these classes. With your group, select two of them:

- Journalism 342: Entertainment Writing
- Contemporary Issues in American Society
- Psychology 213: Marriage and Family
- Introduction to Women's Studies
- Creative Writing 203: Humor & Satire

What criteria might be relevant to assess the movie or series for the particular discipline of each of your choices? Would you need to directly explain why you chose some criteria and omitted others? Explain your answers.

 **Activity 4**

With your group members, select *one* of the following: a product that you all own (such as a backpack, toothbrush, or calculator), a service that you all regularly use (such as campus parking or pizza restaurants that deliver), or a local business that you all regularly frequent (such as a nearby bank). Assume that you will be writing an evaluation of your selection for potential consumers, and together with your group, answer the following questions:

1. What criteria would be relevant for evaluating the particular kind of product, service, or business that you chose?
2. Which criteria would be most important to help potential consumers make an informed choice about the subject of your evaluation?
3. In an evaluation intended for potential consumers, would you need to explain why you selected any or all of the criteria?
4. What kinds of information would you need to evaluate several different models of the product or different service providers? How would you gather information about each of the items you would be evaluating?

Take notes on your discussion and save them for a later activity.

 Activity 5

Together with your group, select two of the readings at the end of this chapter. Read each section on your own, taking notes on the following:

- Does it evaluate a single subject or more than one?
- What criteria are used?
- Does the author directly justify the criteria that was used or omitted?

After you have finished reading individually, meet with your group to compare your notes. Compare the criteria each of you identified. Discuss the appropriateness of these criteria for the subject being evaluated. What are other criteria you might select for such an evaluation? Consolidate your findings and make a brief report to your class.

Making Recommendations

Since both evaluations and critiques offer judgments, they can also provide readers with recommendations—that is, specific guidelines about what actions to take. A critique about a recipe book, for example, might contain a recommendation to "avoid buying this volume unless you live near a market that regularly stocks hard-to-prepare, unusual items." However, unlike critiques—which *may* offer suggestions to the reader—evaluations often do include one or more specific recommendations. In fact, the conventions that govern some types of evaluative writing require that recommendations accompany an assessment. Evaluations of employees contain recommendations about retention ("Based on her performance, Mary Jones should be retained for another. . . .") or compensation ("Based on her performance, Mary Jones should receive a raise of. . . ."). Evaluations of processes or procedures submitted by consultants also offer recommendations: "The current method of recruiting prospective manager trainees should be modified in the following ways. First, ..."

To determine whether—and how—to craft recommendations in an evaluation, it is wise to consider several factors. First, you should examine writing tasks or assignments carefully because these often suggest whether recommendations are necessary and specify the types that should be included. The Political Science Assignment in the Sample Assignments section of this chapter seems to have been designed to test the writer's ability to apply the concepts *tangible* and *intangible power* to a particular analysis; therefore, to include recommendations of how parties in an international dispute should modify their strategies would not be necessary. On the other hand, the Internship Evaluation Assignment requires a set of recommendations and specifies that they should address "how the internship might be modified in the future for other students."

Thinking about the task or assignment is important because it can also lead you to consider the conventions that might govern the particular type of evaluation that you are crafting. Notice, for instance, that the authors of "Choosing Among Alternative Recycling Systems: An Economic Analysis" do *not* make a specific recommendations about which recycling system should be adopted or under what circumstances. That they refrained from doing so probably had to do with the conventions governing the particular type of writing they produced. Evaluative reports, whose main purpose is to inform readers about one or more objects or processes, ordinarily do not include recommendations. On the other hand, as we have already suggested, some types of evaluative writing (such as personnel reports) may require specific recommendations. Articles within *Consumer Reports,* from which "Can Fast Food Be Good Food?" was taken, usually *do* contain recommendations because that magazine is published to help consumers make choices.

In addition to examining the writing task or assignment, considering your readers is very important in helping you decide whether to include recommendations and what to put within them. If your readers expect you to offer them guidance (about whether to see a particular film; about how the current bookkeeping system should be modified; etc.), then you probably need to include recommendations. Sometimes this can be a rather straightforward matter; you can, for example, direct your readers to take their children to see a particular film. Sometimes, however, giving advice can be more complicated because audiences rarely consist of people with the same needs and circumstances. In offering recommendations, you often have to think about how factors such as cost or accessibility may affect segments of your audience differently. If, for instance, you have evaluated several different computers that students at your school might wish to purchase, your recommendations should be directed to various segments within your audience as shown in this example:

> *For those students who will principally use the computer for word processing and to send e-mail, these four models are suitable. . . . Model XE is by far the easiest to use, the best constructed, and the most easily serviced. However, it is also quite expensive. Model CTE, while of lower quality than the XE, is still well built and fairly easy to use. For those who cannot afford the XE, it offers a reasonable alternative.*

Complex recommendations that discuss different aspects of what is being evaluated and relate these aspects to different populations are often the most helpful to the widest number of readers.

Finally, in offering recommendations, it is important to do so in a way that readers will deem responsible. Recall that in Chapter 5, we discussed the importance of an authoritative *ethos,* or self-presentation. Specifically, we talked about qualities that contribute to an effective ethos, *good sense* and *good character. Good will,* a third quality that contributes to an effective ethos, is also important in evaluative writing—especially when the evaluation offers judgments. An ethos that conveys good will implies that the writer or speaker has the readers' best interests at heart. In order to accept the judgments or advice presented in an evaluation, most readers need to feel the that the writer wishes them well. Who would trust the advice of movie critic who purposely sent people to see bad movies? Or trust (and pay for!) the advice of a consultant who deliberately suggested that an individual or group engage in destructive practices? You should take care to think about—and disclose—factors that may have affected your judgment so that your readers know you tried to be fair to the subject of your evaluation.

 ## Activity 6

> Together with your group partners, examine the readings at the end of this chapter. Which contain recommendations? How do they reflect the needs of their intended audience or disciplinary conventions? With your group, prepare a brief oral report of your findings to deliver

 ## Activity 7

> With your group members discuss the assignments in the Sample Assignments section of this chapter. Which would require recommendations? Which ones don't seem to require recommendations? Explain your answers.

❦ Activity 8

Review your notes from Activity 4 in which you developed criteria that could be used to evaluate a product or service. Together with the members of your group, use your notes to generate a list of possible recommendations that might be addressed to various segments within your audience. To which audience members would particular criteria be important? (For example, a drive-up window or ample, accessible parking wouldn't be "conveniences" for people without automobiles.) How might the relevance of particular criteria to different groups within your audience affect the recommendations you might make?

WRITING AN EVALUATION

Writing an evaluation requires a well thought out process that involves both conducting the evaluation itself and presenting the results in writing. Each part of the process deserves careful attention.

Selecting, Observing, and Note Taking

To begin an evaluation, you must select what you will evaluate, unless your assignment makes this decision for you. As we have suggested, selection is an important part of the process of writing an effective evaluation. When choosing something to assess, be sure that you have adequate access to whatever you are evaluating and that it is suitable for the assignment and appropriate in scope. Also consider the special challenges your selection may present. If what you evaluate should be representative of a class of similar objects, processes, or events, you should learn enough about the subject to select something that is, in fact, typical. On the other hand, if you evaluate an event or performance that changes each time it occurs, try to observe it several times. Also be sure to note special circumstances that may have affected an individual occurrence or performance so that you can discuss these in your evaluation.

After you have selected what you will evaluate, think about what you will need to do to conduct your evaluation and plan how to proceed. If you are going to observe an object, consider whether you can borrow or purchase it so that you can conduct your examination under ideal circumstances. If you cannot buy or borrow the object, you need to determine when and how you will observe or use it; this may include making special arrangements with store managers, for example. In addition, you may need to prepare an informal chart or table on which to record information, especially if you are evaluating more than one thing.

To evaluate a process (registering for classes, having a car wash, voting in a local election, etc.) or an event (a film, a museum exhibit, a class lecture, etc.), you need to think about when you will observe it and how you will take notes. You may want to decide in advance about the sort of information (names, dates, and hard-to-remember details) you want to jot down while you observe a process or attend an event. If you try to write down *everything,* you will distort your perception and give a false or unfair assessment; on the other hand, if you don't take any notes, you won't be able to offer specific details to support the criteria you use to make your assessment. To prepare for your evaluation, you will also need to gather materials such as pen and paper for sketching and note taking or a camera. Chapter 4 contains many good suggestions about preparing for and conducting an observation which you may wish to review to help you formulate a plan.

In addition to planning of this sort, you need to think about the type of background information your readers will need to understand your evaluation. While background information may not be part of the process of observation, it is often readily available. If evaluating a product, for example, you should examine user manuals, directions, and packaging. Plays, lectures, and exhibits often distribute programs that contain a great deal of background information.

Finally, if you evaluate several objects, events, or processes, it is important to think about and set up conditions that allow you to assess them under similar circumstances. If possible, objects should be lined up so that the features they all have in common can be compared. It would be best, for example, to place three dresses next to one another so that length, color, hemlines, bodices, sleeves, and the like can be viewed at the same time. It is not possible, of course, to experience three different events or processes simultaneously. Therefore, you need to think about how to minimize factors that might affect your judgments. If you are comparing several different brands of chicken soup, it wouldn't be fair to sample one brand when you are ravenous and the other two after you've glutted yourself on a five-course dinner.

 **Activity 9**

After reading the Writing Assignments section of this chapter, tentatively select what you will evaluate. As you make your choice, be sure to consider the subject's accessibility and suitability (in terms of size and complexity); also consider your own knowledge about and interest in your prospective selection. Does your selection change each time it occurs? Will your selection represent a particular group or class of entities; if so, how will you select something that is "typical" or representative? Discuss your choice and the factors related to your choice with your group partners. If group members raise questions or issues you didn't anticipate, will you need to change your selection?

ꙮ Activity 10

Once you have selected something to evaluate, devise a plan for conducting your observation or assessment. What information do you plan to gather? How and when will you do it? What preparations will you make before you gather information? What materials will you take? What prior arrangements, if any will you make? What kind of background or related information and materials do you need? If you are comparing more than one item or process, how can you be consistent? Share your plan with your group, and modify it on the basis of their suggestions. Using your modified plan, conduct your observation or assessment. Gather as much infor-

---

Selecting Criteria

Once you have selected the subject you will evaluate and have observed it or otherwise collected relevant information, you need to select the criteria to use in your evaluation. If your assignment specifies all the criteria you are expected to use, your instructor has done much of your work for you. If, however, your assignment gives you only general directions such as "assess the effectiveness" or specifies only one or two criteria, your next step is to begin considering which criteria to use in your evaluation.

There are several means to help you discover relevant criteria. One effective method is to explore the history and background of what you are evaluating. For example, if you are evaluating a product that you have used in the past, such as a backpack, your experience may lead you to realize what criteria (durability, comfort, or expense) are important to potential consumers. As well as being suggested by your own experience, relevant criteria can arise from the background information gathered in the course of writing your evaluation—from warranties or theater programs, for example.

In addition to generating criteria from background knowledge and information, you may be able to generate additional ones by considering your subject as part of a larger class whose members share certain similarities. Your knowledge of children's movies, for example, can lead you to assess how good a children's movie *Toy Story* is by using criteria pertinent to children's movies: the nature and amount of violence and sexual content, the language used, the quality of animation, the pace and simplicity of the plot, and the musical score. Your knowledge of how your subject *differs* from others of its class can lead you to recognize novelty, newness, or fresh approaches that are not typical for your subject. These in turn can lead you to discover appropriate criteria. In reviewing a restaurant, for example, the novelty of a chef who grows all the produce she uses is a relevant factor to consider. In such a situation, you might decide that the quality or freshness of the vegetables she serves is an appropriate criterion to employ in your evaluation.

In addition to considering how your subject is similar to or different from others of its class, you should also look at it as an isolated entity. This means carefully considering its structure and distinguishing features such as color, texture, taste, and so forth. You may need to use a product or service several times, observing and taking notes so that you can determine which criteria are most relevant for your evaluation, and perhaps comparing your experiences with those of others. If what you are evaluating is not a concrete object like a backpack, but is instead a complex process or procedure, you may find it helpful to identify the major components and assess them separately.

When you have generated a variety of criteria you might use, make sure you select and develop those that are most relevant to your subject and can best support your overall conclusion or recommendations. As we have said, evaluations, like much other academic writing, should develop a thesis, support a judgment, or make a central point. If you are comparing several banks in your community and want to conclude that one is superior because of the services it offers customers, relevant criteria might be the time it takes to complete a transaction, the range and cost of checking accounts, and special banking services like the ability to pay bills by telephone. To include a criterion such as the spaciousness of the lobby would make no sense.

Occasionally you may have an assignment that instructs you to discuss particular criteria that you initially feel are unrelated to each other. In such a situation, you should work to broaden your focus to include all the criteria specified. If your assignment directs you to evaluate both technical and aesthetic elements of a play, you might write a thesis like this: *Despite an engaging script, strong directing, and notable acting, the play fails because of its ineffective staging.* If you have difficulty finding a way to relate seemingly unrelated criteria, you might try using an invention technique such as clustering or the Pentad.

Finally, you may find that you have one or more important criteria for which you have too few supporting details. In this case, you will need to do additional observing or information gathering to ensure that you will be able to develop these criteria.

 **Activity 11**

Once you've completed one or more observations and note taking, you should begin to determine possible criteria to use. Use clustering, the Pentad, or another heuristic to help you organize your notes. Next, with your group members, brainstorm to come up with a possible focus and a set of relevant criteria for each of your papers. Assess the focus and criteria for each group member's paper, using these questions to guide your discussion:

- Are your focus and criteria relevant for the assignment?
- Are all the criteria relevant to what you are evaluating? Are any only marginally relevant?
- Do the criteria support a thesis or develop a main point?
- Do you need to justify the criteria you have selected? Do you need to explain why you have omitted any?

For each person's focus and accompanying criteria, if you or your group members see possible problems, discuss whether to omit irrelevant criteria or devise a way to revise and recast criteria to make them better fit the focus.

Structuring

After you have completed note taking on the object, process, or event that you are evaluating and have selected the criteria that you will use, you are ready to plan a tentative structure for your paper and to consider where to place descriptions and recommendations. The type of structure you choose, though, will depend on whether you are evaluating one or more than one subject.

Evaluating One Object, Process, or Event. Because inexperienced writers often organize evaluations by copying the structure of what they are evaluating, we recommend that you plan carefully to avoid this common—and problematic—practice. If reviewing a film, you should not organize your evaluation according to the plot because doing so may result in a boring paper, for example, "This happens, and then this happens." Your organization will be more effective if based on the evaluative criteria you selected—such as dialogue, camera angles, sound effects, and special effects.

Likewise, if you are writing an evaluation of a process, you should avoid structuring your paper according to the chronological events in the process. Let's say, for example, that you decide to write an evaluation of the new registration process that recently has been instituted at your university. Your first instinct might be to divide your essay into five parts, reflecting the five major parts of the registration process. However, a more useful plan would be to structure the evaluation according to the criteria you have selected: complexity of the process, fairness, clarity of guidelines, and availability of staff assistance. Using this structure, your evaluation would have four major parts, one for each of the criteria. A structure based on criteria is easier to follow, saves the writer from needlessly discussing the same criteria again and again, and more clearly supports an overall thesis or judgment.

Evaluating More Than One Object, Process, or Event. As we have said, evaluations often compare more than one object, process, or event. Evaluations of multiple subjects ordinarily require more complex structures than do evaluations of one subject. Basically, there are two types of organizational patterns to use for multiple subjects: the *block* pattern and the *alternating* pattern. The block pattern organizes according to the objects, processes, or events being compared. The alternating pattern, however, organizes according to the criteria used. Following are two simple graphic illustrations of the methods just described, for an evaluation of two Mexican restaurants. *Notice that in both organizational patterns, the same criteria are used.*

Block Pattern	*Alternating Pattern*
Introduction to Paper	**Introduction to Paper**
Margarita's Cantina	**Menu**
Menu	Margarita's Cantina
Atmosphere	La Mexicana
Price	
Service	**Atmosphere**
	Margarita's Cantina
	La Mexicana

La Mexicana
  Menu
  Atmosphere
  Price
  Service

Conclusion/Recommendations

Price
  Margarita's Cantina
  La Mexicana

Service
  Margarita's Cantina
  La Mexicana

Conclusion/Recommendations

Another challenge in evaluating more than one object, process, or event is to present your information in a way that is accessible to readers. As you structure an evaluation of multiple subjects, you might find it helpful to construct a table. Tables can simplify multiple criteria for readers by offering a quick visualization. Ordinarily, tables that are constructed to compare several objects or processes in terms of multiple criteria are organized in a particular way. To enhance readability, the subjects being evaluated are listed vertically and the criteria used to evaluate them are listed horizontally. In this way, if some readers wish to scan the criteria related to one particular product, they can do so by moving their eyes across the page, which is the way people read. The following table, designed to accompany an evaluation of backpacks, provides a simple model.

Table 7–1: An Evaluation of Backpack Design

Brand	*Durability*	*Design*	*Weight*	*Price*
Flyer	average	sleek	light	$25 to $30
StreetRunner	poor	sleek	light	$12 to $15
Carryall	excellent	bulky	medium	$35 to $40
Hefty Packer	average	bulky	heavy	$15 to $20

Notice how the previous table presents the criteria horizontally, while the products being evaluated are presented vertically.

If you include a table to simplify the presentation of your criteria, you will need to decide where to place it within your evaluation. You might want to place the table at the point in the paper where you first refer to it (introducing it with words such as "As you can see in the table below . . . "). Alternatively, you might place the table near the beginning of your paper, perhaps at the end of the introduction, where it can serve as a visual overview of the explanations that are to come in your text. In this case, you could introduce the table by saying, "The following table presents an overview of my findings." You might also place the table near the very end, where it can serve as a summation of the main points of your evaluation. If you place the table at the end, you could introduce it by saying, "Please refer to the following table for a summary of the findings discussed in this evaluation." In any case, you will need to ensure that the placement of the table is helpful rather than obtrusive for your readers and that you have adequately introduced the table and directed readers to where they can find it.

Regardless of whether you assess one or more things, in structuring your evaluation, you need to determine where to place your background information and description. As we have said, most often background information about the object, process, or event you are evaluating should be placed at the beginning of your paper to provide readers with the context necessary to understand your subject more readily. You may, however, need to provide additional description in the body of your paper as you discuss each of the criteria.

Finally, as you structure your evaluation, you need to consider where to place recommendations, if you include them. Recommendations can be put at the beginning or at the end of an evaluation. Placed at the beginning, a recommendation can serve as a thesis. If a supervisor is writing an evaluation of a worker's performance, for example, she might state in her introduction that "Priscilla has been doing an excellent job, and I recommend that we offer her a contract for the coming year." A recommendation should be placed in the beginning of an evaluation in this manner only if it can be understood without additional information. More often, however, recommendations are placed at the end of an evaluation. After reading the body of an evaluation, most readers will more readily understand and be persuaded by the recommendations. Especially if you are offering multiple evaluations, your recommendation section should appear at the end, where you can summarize your criteria and make different recommendations for different groups of people.

 **Activity 12**

With your group members, examine the sample evaluations provided in this chapter in terms of their overall structure. Where are discussions of criteria placed? Where do background information, description, and recommendations (if any) appear within the evaluation?

Revising Your Evaluation

After writing a draft of your evaluation, you will need to examine it to see if its structure has accomplished what you intended and to make any changes you think necessary. In revising the structure of an evaluation, pay particular attention to where you have placed description of and background information about what you have evaluated. Check your introduction to see if you have provided your readers with enough information so that they can get a clear sense of what is being evaluated. Description related to particular *aspects* of your object, process, or event may be more useful in the latter part of the text. Therefore, when revising, assess your introduction to see whether some of the information in it can be moved to other parts of your evaluation.

In addition to examining the placement of background information and description, you should check the location of any tables or charts that you provide. The best way to assess their effectiveness is to try to gauge your readers' response to their location as you read through a completed draft. As you read, try to determine if a table seems intrusive; if so, you need to reposition it. In addition, if you are reading information that refers to a table that you haven't yet provided, you will need to move the table earlier in your paper or refer your readers to it by using a sentence such as this one: *See the Table on page 3.*

In revising to improve the structure of an evaluation, make sure you have also included sufficient metadiscourse to help readers process your text more easily. Within evaluative writing, metadiscourse plays an important role. It can help readers recognize criteria easily ("When evaluating weight loss programs, most experts agree that three factors are crucial. . . ."). It can make justifications for particular criteria explicit ("These three factors are significant because. . .") It can also clarify the relationship between background information and what is being evaluated ("The length of time it took for staff at the Boswick clinic to design their weight loss program is significant because . . . "). When revising evaluative writing, therefore, examine the connections between the different types of information you provide (background information, descriptions of criteria, tables of information, etc.) to ensure that these connections clearly specify the relationships that you intend. If they do not, add metadiscourse where it is appropriate.

Besides examining the structure of your evaluation, when revising you also need to examine its contents carefully. To find an evaluation convincing, readers must be able to understand all of the criteria you used to make your judgment; thus, you should examine each of these to be sure that your descriptions are precise and adequately detailed.

Sometimes in evaluative writing, you may need to "operationalize" your criteria, that is, define them in a way that will clarify them or provide more precision in measurement. Suppose, for example, you have evaluated several different wallpaper pastes and one of the criteria you chose was *stickiness*. If you have described *stickiness* as "how well the paste made the wallpaper adhere to particular wall surfaces," this might not help readers compare one brand to another with any precision. You might, then, revise your description by operationalizing the term in this way:

> Stickiness *is defined as "how well each paste made the wallpaper adhere to different wall surfaces." To create a "stickiness scale," I dipped the tip of a five-inch brush into each of my samples and compared the thickness of coverage for each paste on the same size surface (12 inches square). Those brands that covered **more area** were assigned more points (1–5, with 5 being the highest); those brands that covered the area **more thickly** were assigned more points (1–5, with 5 being the highest) . . . .*

As this example demonstrates, operationalizing a criterion (where appropriate) not only gives your readers a clear sense of what it means, it also ties the criterion in concrete ways to whatever you are evaluating.

Finally, in assessing the contents of your draft, you need to determine if you have given your readers sufficient background information, especially as it relates to your criteria and to your recommendations. When you evaluate a film, it makes no sense to include the criterion "economical to make" if you don't provide background information that explains *why* this criterion should be important to viewers as well as *how much* it typically costs to make equivalent films. Therefore, when you are revising, check to see if you have provided enough background information about your criteria so that your readers will understand them fully. Likewise, recommendations often must be accompanied by background information because they frequently need to be qualified as in the following examples:

> *Quicko Cleaner ordinarily performs well under most conditions; however, it shouldn't be mixed with bleach because under these circumstances it produces a dangerous solution that* . . . .

> *The O'Keeffe exhibit is a must-see; however, it will be at the Art Institute for only two more weeks. I urge readers, therefore, to* . . . .

As you revise, then, look over the background information that you have provided to see if it is sufficient for your readers to understand—and act on—any of the recommendations you offer.

WRITING ASSIGNMENTS

Writing Topics

1. Evaluate one of the following: (a) a *process* or *procedure* (e.g., class registration or getting a replacement ID); (b) the availability/quality of a *resource* or *service* (e.g., campus student parking or the campus escort service; (c) the workings of a campus office (Financial Aid or Career Counseling). Whatever you choose to evaluate, your audience should be *either* students who (might) need to use or experience the process, service, resource, and so on *or* the administrative staff responsible for providing or managing the service, resource, office, and the like.

2. Select an object, procedure, or event that is relevant to your major field of study (or the profession for which you are preparing) and write an evaluation of it. If you are an art history major, you might evaluate an exhibit at a local gallery; if you are a marketing major, you might evaluate a major product display at (or a grand opening of) a local supermarket; if you are a science education major, you might evaluate a presentation at a nearby planetarium; if you are a history major, you might evaluate a particular collection at a nearby museum or historical society. Your audience should be other persons within your field of study. If

you are uncertain about the appropriateness or scope of your selection, check with your instructor.

3. Write an evaluation of a movie, television series, or documentary. Your audience should be people in your field of study. If, for example, you decide to review the TV series *Roseanne,* the criteria you select to conduct your evaluation will differ depending on whether you are majoring in psychology (with a specialization in marriage and family), film studies, popular culture, economics, or another subject. A film studies major might concentrate on the technical aspects of the show (timing, editing, and camera work), while a person majoring in popular culture might, instead, evaluate the show on the basis of its depiction of working-class culture in the United States.

4. Select and evaluate a product that many undergraduate students at your school are likely to buy; then write a product review directed to incoming first-year students. (If your school conducts a summer orientation for new students, you might imagine that your evaluation could be distributed at that time; or if your school sends out mass mailings to incoming students when they are accepted, you might imagine that your evaluation could be included within the mailings.) Provide a set of recommendations, taking into consideration the various subgroups within your audience. Some products you might consider evaluating are calculators, personal computers, bicycles, microwaves, popcorn makers, compact refrigerators, or coffee makers.

Writing Procedures

1. By this point, you have selected an object, process, or event to evaluate and you have determined the criteria you will use. Before you begin to plan your evaluation, draft a one- or two-page description of the objects, processes, or events that you are evaluating. Be sure to include any background information that will be relevant in your evaluation.

2. Using your description and background information (from #1), your notes, any inventing (Pentad, clustering, etc.), and your group members' suggestions (from Activity 11), devise a structural plan for your evaluation. Share your plan with your group. Be sure that your group members provide you with feedback on the overall structure for your evaluation, including the placement of description and background information. Also solicit ideas for your introduction and conclusion and for the placement of any recommendations that you will make. If you plan to construct a table in which you will present your criteria, consult with your group about the contents of the table and about its placement within your evaluation. After you have discussed your tentative plan with your group, revise it based on the suggestions of your group or instructor. Include as much detail as possible in your plan.

3. Using your revised plan, write a draft of your evaluation. To provide sufficient detail as you are drafting, consult your description, background materials, and the notes you took on what you are evaluating.

4. After completing your draft, bring it to class to discuss it with your group. Use any one of the draft workshop procedures described in Chapter 2.

5. Based on the feedback you receive from your group members or your instructor, revise and edit the final copy of your evaluation. In revising, you should make certain that the connections between your thesis and your criteria are clear; that you have provided sufficient detail to support your criteria; that your description and background information are appropriate in terms of amount and placement; that the relationship between your criteria and recommendations are clear and that your recommendations are well placed; and that any tables you may have created are easy to understand and are placed effectively within your text. As always when editing, keep your reader in mind and be sure that your final copy is readable and free of error.

READINGS

Higdon, David. "Measuring Up." *Shape.* (July 1993), pp. 46–47, 49.

1. In his evaluation, where and how does Higdon provide readers with background information about and descriptions of the methods of measuring body fat? What criteria does he use to compare the methods and where and how does he present these? Would you say that "Measuring Up" is structured chronologically, as are many narratives? Explain your answer.

2. Examine Higdon's point of view and tone. How would you characterize them? How distanced is he from his readers? What sorts of examples does he provide? Why did he decide to write about a serious health topic in the light-hearted manner that he chose?

"Can Fast Food Be Good Food?" *Consumer Reports.* (August 1994), pp. 493–496.

1. The authors of "Can Fast Food Be Good Food?" present much information that is easily measured and compared, such as the cost of food items and their fat, calorie, and sodium content. However, the article also discusses how foods look and taste, two criteria that are important yet harder to measure. How do the authors make judgments with respect to these two criteria? Look at all sections of the article that discuss taste.

2. A central part of this article is the final Ratings table. What purpose is served by the section "Notes on the table"? Compare the discussion of fat content in the main text of the article to the information about fat content in the table of Ratings. Which is more complete? Which is easier to read if you want information about a particular item? Which would you read if you want advice or conclusions?

3. Like many popular magazines, *Consumer Reports* uses sidebars, which are short boxes of self-contained information that is loosely related to the main article. How many sidebars are there in "Fast Food"? How are they related to the main article? That is, do they serve similar or different purposes?

Gutin, Jo Ann C. "End of the Rainbow." *Discover.* (November 1994), pp. 71–75.

1. What criteria does Gutin use to evaluate the Human Genome Diversity Project? Where does she state her criteria in the article? Underline or mark the appropriate passages in the margin. Do you find her criteria relevant for her subject and her audience? Note that this article was originally published in *Discover*, a science magazine directed to a general reading audience.

2. Gutin reports that different groups of people are reaching differing conclusions about the intent of the Human Genome Diversity Project. Why? What different criteria are they using to support their conclusions? What is Gutin's overall assessment of the Project?

"*The Piano*: A Feminist Film?" Shugrue, Rebecca. "Yes." Gage, Carolyn. "No." *On the Issues.* (Summer 1994), pp. 44–45.

1. Do Shugrue and Gage assume their audiences have or have not seen *The Piano*? Look for specific parts of their reviews where they either provide readers with background information about what happens in the movie or assume that their readers will not need such information.

2. Often movie reviews have a clear thesis, that people should or should not see a particular movie. In Shugrue's and Gage's reviews, however, the quality of the movie is assessed instead, and the focus is on a particular question (whether the movie is feminist). What purpose do you feel these authors intended their reviews to serve for their readers?

3. Both writers begin with the same question (Is *The Piano* feminist?), but each answers it differently. Which criteria do you find most relevant to the initial question? Do Gage and Shugrue use the same or different criteria? How do they end up with different conclusions about the movie?

Stedge, Gerald D., and Halstead, John M. "Choosing Among Alternative Recycling Systems: An Economic Analysis." *The Environmental Professional 16.* (March 1994), pp. 40–48.

1. An interesting aspect of "Choosing Among Alternative Recycling Systems" is that the authors do not discuss specific recommendations, because this is a scholarly piece directed toward a study of a process. With your group, examine what this evaluation offers readers instead of recommendations. Focus in particular on the "Study Limitations" section at the end of the article to determine its purpose within the evaluation. Although recommendations are never stated directly, does it seem to you that some might be implied? Explain your answer.

2. Because this evaluation was written for a scholarly journal, its structure follows a conventional disciplinary format. Still, the article is an evaluation, and it contains structural features that are common to all evaluations. With your group,

examine the article to see how structural features that are common to all evaluations work within the conventional format. How does the conventional format govern or influence the other structures?

 Measuring Up

How I Lost 9 Percent Of My Body Fat In 24 Hours*

David Higdon

I agreed to undergo three different body-fat composition tests for the same reason I took the SAT exam several times: I intended to count only the best score.

Ever since scientists persuaded us to chuck our bathroom scales, body-fat testing has become an important measure of fitness. It's not how much you *weigh* that matters—it's how much of this weight is made of fat.

Measuring your body's fat content would seem to be a relatively simple task in today's high-tech world. But, alas, unlike items at the checkout counter, fat and fat-free mass can't be so easily separated and weighed. Countless body-composition devices have flooded the marketplace, each offering its own interpretation of the human body. Which ones are the most accurate?

To find out, I submitted my fat for examination by the most popular methods for measuring body fat: skin-fold calipers, bioelectrical impedance and underwater weighing.

Skin-fold calipers—hand-held devices that resemble protractors from math class—are used most often, and for good reason: They're relatively cheap and simple to use. Most health clubs will test members with skin-fold calipers for free. Exercise physiologists say calipers are reasonably accurate for people who aren't obese. If done correctly, skin-fold tests offer a range of error of 3.5 percentage points.

That, however, is a big *if*, a point I fully intended to bring up if I wasn't satisfied with my tally. The tester is supposed to pinch fat at spots on your body, but accuracy gets compromised if the tester fails to pinch at the right spot or pinches too much or not enough.

My first pinch (not to be confused with my first kiss) occurred in 1979 when I was 18. David Costill, Ph.D., director of the Human Performance Laboratory at Ball State University, used skin-fold calipers to determine that my body, which was enduring two hours of intense tennis daily, was composed of 14.8 percent fat. (The recommended range for men under age 60 is 10 to 17; for women it's 18 to 25. Men with more than 25 percent body fat and women with more than 32 percent are considered to be at higher risk for heart disease, diabetes and some forms of cancer.)

In January 1993, I went back to Costill as a subject for an exercise and longevity study he was conducting. He measured me at 16.5 percent—not a bad change, considering that a two-hour tennis match now sends me crawling to the whirlpool.

Measuring Up *(cont'd.)*

As the saying goes, fat floats. That's essentially how underwater weighing works: The more your body wants to float when dunked underwater, the more fat is in your body. Underwater weighing has a relatively small margin of error, about 2.8 percentage points for young to middle-aged adults.

But the test is less accurate for children and adults over 60 and for people with lean bodies and dense bones. In fact, football star Herschel Walker was once measured by this method and found to have only 1.4 percent body fat.

Getting dunked isn't free: Very few health clubs offer this service (mine charged $10), and one fitness lab I called charges $35.

It's also an awkward procedure. You must completely rid your lungs of air, a difficult if not unnerving task, then sit motionless underwater for about 6 seconds on the platform of a giant scale. The more you "weigh" underwater, the less fat you have. (The scale is a lot more complicated than your typical bathroom variety.)

So I kneeled on the platform, exhaled vigorously, then dropped my head underwater and lay in the fetal position. I did not, as I had secretly hoped, plummet to the bottom like a cannonball. About six seconds later, I resurfaced, half expecting to see a row of grim-faced judges holding up cards scoring my body-fat dive: 20.3, 22.5, 29.7 . . .

Instead, my perky tester plugged some numbers into a computer. When I picked up the printout, she had circled the body-fat percentage figure—15.6—and written next to it. "Very good!" She must have been out of gold stars.

I then asked her, just for good measure, to test me with calipers. Several skinfold pinches and keyboard punches later, she handed me another printout. It read: 11 percent. Count it! I had dropped from 20 percent body fat one day to 11 percent the next, an astonishing fat reduction sure to shock even Richard Simmons.

Actually, my experiment demonstrated the potential for inaccuracy in body-composition analysis. Follow the experts' advice: Stick with one method and one qualified tester.

After all, as with an SAT question, there's only one right answer.

 ## Can Fast Food Be Good Food?*

Every day, America's biggest hamburger chains—McDonald's, Burger King, and Wendy's—serve more than 40 million customers from more than 25,000 restaurants around the world. KFC, the biggest chicken chain, fries or roasts another 6.6

Can Fast Food Be Good Food? *(cont'd.)*

million meals at 9000 locations. That may sound like a lot, but it's nothing compared with what's coming.

McDonald's, founded in 1955, took 13 years to open its first 1000 restaurants. Now about 14,000 outlets strong, McDonald's plans to construct approximately 1000 more golden arches this year alone. Subway, an even faster-growing sandwich chain, sets up 25 new restaurants a week (see the box an page 495). PepsiCo, which owns KFC, Taco Bell, and Pizza Hut, opens a restaurant somewhere in the world every four hours.

Although much of the expansion is overseas, the domestic industry is growing so quickly that the National Restaurant Association predicts consumers will spend $86-billion on fast food this year—more, for the first time, than they'll spend at full-service restaurants. Fast-food restaurants are also becoming an extension of the family kitchen: Nearly two-thirds of all fast food (including pizza) is takeout, and much of that goes home according to CREST, a Chicago company that tracks eating habits.

McDonald's, Burger King, and other chains are placing kiosks and mobile units where no fast-food restaurant has fit before—in mass-merchandise stores like Wal-Mart, in hospitals, in schools, and in gas stations. McDonald's now aims to serve its products "wherever customers live, work, shop, or gather."

What We Tested

With fast food such an integral part of the American diet, we decided to take a close look at what so many Americans are eating. We zeroed in on 30 items—burgers, roast-beef sandwiches, breaded- and rotisserie-chicken dishes, fish sandwiches, and french fries–from Arby's, Burger King, Hardee's, Jack in the Box, KFC, McDonald's, Popeye's, and Wendy's. (There is some overlap between Hardee's products and those at Roy Rogers, a division of Hardee's.)

We bought each item at 12 outlets and tested each for fat, saturated fat, cholesterol, protein, and sodium. We determined calorie content. And we sent a trained taster to outlets in six cities to note the firmness of the meat (or flakiness of the fish), the freshness of the vegetables and buns, the crispness of the fries, and the flavor of everything.

We rated the foods according to the percentage of calories that each gets from fat. That measurement allows for easy comparison of foods that differ in size and nutritional measures. The Ratings also include comments regarding taste and texture.

We didn't test the meat for bacteria, but we did talk to Joseph Maddern, strategic manager of microbiology in the U.S. Food and Drug Administration. He notes that since 1993, when four children died after eating Jack in the Box hamburgers contaminated with a rare strain of the bacteria *E. coli,* most fast-food chains have been paying closer attention to how burgers are cooked. At most stores, for instance, cooked burgers are checked several times an hour to make sure they're brown inside. (Bacteria are killed—and ground beef turns pink to brown—when the meat is cooked at 155° for 15 seconds.)

Can Fast Food Be Good Food? *(cont'd.)*

Such procedures follow Federal recommendations and many state laws that specify minimum guidelines for keeping food safe.

Where's the fat?

Although fast-food companies have promoted newer, low-fat offerings—such as grilled-chicken sandwiches, lean-beef sandwiches, and assorted salads—most people still order the items we tested for this report. Those staples are heavy in fat, saturated fat, and other nutrients that should be limited in a prudent diet. Five of the sandwiches we tested each provide more than half the fat that a person on a 2000-calorie diet should eat in an entire day, according to Government guidelines, and three provide half the saturated fat. The *Big Mac* and all the larger pieces of chicken have at least a third of the Government's recommended daily intake for cholesterol and sodium.

Best, nutritionally, were the basic burgers and roast-beef sandwiches. But before you celebrate with a *Whopper,* note that we're talking about the chains' *smaller* burgers: The big burgers, slathered with extras, are pretty much off limits to fat watchers. For instance, Hardee's *Frisco Burger*—topped with bacon, cheese, and sauce—had more than twice the fat, almost half the sodium, and almost all the saturated fat the Government recommends as a daily limit.

The chicken and fish sandwiches were nutritional runners-up to the basic burgers; they were fattened by their breading and mayonnaise-based sauce.

Who's the fattiest of them all? KFC's *Rotisserie Gold* chicken, in its dark-meat version. It may sound healthful because it's not fried; nevertheless, it gets 65 percent of its calories from fat. That's an even higher percentage than you'll find in a super-rich ice cream.

For the most part, an order of fries has at least as many calories and as much fat as a basic burger. And although the chains touted their change of frying oil from beef tallow to hydrogenated vegetable oil, that switch may not have helped much. The vegetable oil contains trans-fatty acids, which some studies have shown can raise blood cholesterol levels. (For a discussion of fats, see "What to Spread on Bread," in the May issue.)

It is possible to include a traditional fast-food meal in a healthy diet: just eat less-fatty food—fruit or salads, say—the rest of the day. It's even possible to make a healthy meal out of some of the foods we sampled. For a look at some strategies and how they affect nutrition, see the box at left.

Where's the taste?

No restaurant had the tastiest food overall, according to our taster, who tried the foods as they're served, complete with the usual toppings. But our taster did find at least one good dish at each chain, and a total of 10 very good items. When we compared the taste scores with our nutritional data, we found, not surprisingly, that good taste and good nutrition in fast food are often mutually exclusive.

Can Fast Food Be Good Food? *(cont'd.)*

With a few exceptions, the overall flavor and quality of the food at each chain was similar from city to city—a help to travelers who want to know that the burger they get on the road bears a passing resemblance to the one they got back home.

Still, some chains were more consistent than others. Wendy's and Arby's sandwiches were always fresh and hot; McDonald's and Burger King came closest to getting french fries right every time.

Among the problems our taster occasionally encountered were cold or overcooked meat, dry chicken that had sat around too long, and soggy french fries.

The Ratings describe each food's taste.

HOLD THE BACON, HOLD THE MAYO
HAVING IT YOUR WAY

"Healthful fast food" isn't always an oxymoron. Most chains offer salads or grilled-chicken sandwiches, some of which are good in both taste and nutrition, especially if you omit their dressing. (See "Fast Food for Fat Watchers," September 1993.) But you can make even a "regular" fast-food meal more nutritious by following a few rules:

- Hold the mayo. While you're at it, hold the tartar sauce and other mayonnaise-based dressings on sandwiches and salads. Wendy's *Breaded Chicken Sandwich* with a half-tablespoon of mayonnaise has as much fat as a *Jr. Cheeseburger Deluxe* and as many calories as a *Jr. Bacon Cheeseburger.* Order the sandwich plain, or scrape the mayonnaise off and the result is closer to a Wendy's *Plain Single* hamburger.

- No cheese, please. One piece adds about three grams of fat and 40 calories to a sandwich. Hardee's *Frisco Burger*—with two slices of Swiss cheese, plus mayonnaise and bacon—has the fat of about five regular hamburgers. Holding the additions spares you more than 240 calories and 22 grams of fat. Skip only the cheese and mayo, and you could still substitute a medium order of fries for the fat you save.

- Dip with discrimination. As if chicken nuggets didn't have enough fat, fast-food chains serve them with sauce. Worst of all: Burger King's *Ranch Dipping Sauce,* with 17 grams of fat per serving. That's more fat than there is in a small hamburger. Some other dips have little or no fat, but they do add calories. Best of the bunch is Burger King's barbecue sauce.

- Skin the chicken. When you cut straight to the meat of KFC's *Rotisserie Gold,* you lose about a third of the calories and half to three-quarters of the fat. Skinless fried chicken is much healthier, too.

- Develop a taste for baked potatoes. A serving of french fries has more fat and calories than a small hamburger does. A baked potato, available at Wendy's, has no fat at all when eaten plain—and you get twice as much potato. A pat of butter adds four grams of fat and about 30 calories.

Can Fast Food Be Good Food? *(cont'd.)*

Losing Calories and Fat

	CAL.	FAT	CAL. FROM FAT
Wendy's Breaded Chicken Filet			
As served	450	20 g.	40%
Without mayo	380	13	31
Burger King BK Big Fish			
As served	720	43	54
Without tartar sauce	540	24	40
Hardee's Frisco Burger			
As served	764	50	59
Without mayo	673	40	53
Without bacon	688	44	58
Without cheese and bacon	612	38	56
Without mayo, cheese, and bacon	521	28	48
KFC Rotisserie Gold			
White quarter, as served	335	19	51
Without skin	199	6	27
Dark quarter, as served	333	24	65
Without skin	217	12	50

FAST-FOOD 'VALUE'

IS THE PRICE STILL RIGHT?

At the first McDonald's, a hamburger cost 15 cents and a cheeseburger 19 cents. Everything else—fries, a shake, or a drink—was a dime. KFC's Colonel Harland Sanders got his start cooking chicken dinners in a dining room by his gas station in Corbin, Ky. He sold chicken, potatoes, gravy, and a roll for about a dollar.

To see how much the first hamburgers and french fries would cost today, we compared original prices with today's average prices, adjusting for inflation. The results, shown in the chart below, reveal that we're usually paying less for burgers and more for fries.

Fast-food menus have evolved to include much more than burgers and fries. During the 1980s, the big chains introduced salads, chicken nuggets, and other items.

Can Fast Food Be Good Food? *(cont'd.)*

But too much variety tended to slow service and increase costs, prompting chains to re-emphasize the original foods. That back-to-basics movement is one reason chains have adopted the "value menu," which steers customers to a limited number of combination platters or daily specials that promise more food or drink for less money.

They deliver on that promise—the package deal costs less than the individual items would—but not always as *much* less as you might think. Take McDonald's Value Meal—a medium drink, large fries, and one of three sandwiches. The chain recommends that its franchises charge $2.99, at least 20 percent off McDonald's suggested prices for those individual items. But when we recently priced a Value Meal in New York City, the savings were just 7 percent. Moreover, a value menu makes sense only if the items are what you wanted anyway. If the package tempts you to "trade up" to a bigger sandwich or soft drink or a larger serving of

	First Year	Original Price	Orig. Price, with Inflation	Today's Price	Change
Burgers					
Jack in the Box	1950	$.24	$1.46	$ .79	−46%
Burger King	1954	.18	.98	.78	−20
McDonald's	1955	.15	.82	.59	−28
Hardee's	1961	.15	.74	.75	+1
Wendy's	1969	.59	2.36	1.85	−22
Fries					
McDonald's	1955	.10	.55	1.02	+85
Hardee's	1961	.10	.49	.89	+82
Wendy's	1969	.30	1.20	.89	−26

GET 'EM WHILE THEY'RE YOUNG

As any parent knows, when it's time to pick a place to eat, the kids' choice often becomes the family's. And kids choose fast food. When children 17 and younger eat out they go to a fast-food restaurant 85 percent of the time, according to a National Restaurant Association survey.

The chains take great pains to court their youngest patrons. Burger King sends a 32-page magazine to 4 million members of its Kids Club. Since 1990, when the club began, the sale of Kids Club meals has quadrupled. Hardee's says it's going after the children's market "in a big way" in 1994. For the first time, the chain will pack its own Funmeal toys with its children's meals.

Can Fast Food Be Good Food? *(cont'd.)*

The chains compete by tying toys to movies. Burger King's toys are linked to Disney films. The ties between movies and McDonald's bind tightly indeed. The Flintstones movie features "RocDonald's," a Stone Age McDonald's replica. That prehistoric restaurant, in turn, was featured in toys for the modern restaurant's Happy Meals.

In a typical promotion, the fast-food chain pays a fee to the movie company or other licensor. The chain is in a strong position to negotiate: Its use of Fred Flintstone, say, results in widespread publicity for the movie. And landing an agreement with a fast-food chain can help a movie company reel in other cross-promotional deals—with makers of anything from clothing to lunch boxes.

Parents may wonder how much Fred adds to the price of a children's meal. Not much, say people familiar with the promotions industry. Most of the cost of licensing, developing, and making toys—and such extras as tray liners and drink cups—is absorbed by the chain. The toys act as a lure, bringing in kids who in turn bring in (or should we say drag in) parents. In the New York City area, a Happy Meal cost about a dime more than the individual items would.

9032 STORES AND COUNTING

A SUBWAY ON EVERY CORNER?

If you didn't pass a Subway shop today, the chances are good that you'll pass one tomorrow. The sandwich-maker's goal is to equal or exceed the number of outlets operated by the largest fast-food company in every market it enters. From 1989 to 1993, the number of Subway stores more than doubled, and Subway remains the fastest-growing fast-food chain around.

We analyzed Subway's top three sellers—the *BMT* (ham, genoa salami, pepperoni, and bologna), named after a New York City subway line; the *Cold Cut Combo* (turkey-based ham, salami, and bologna); and the *Subway Club* (roast beef, turkey, and ham).

We ordered six-inch sandwiches with everything, which means lettuce, tomato, cheese, onion, pickle, green pepper, olives, oil, salt, and pepper.

The *Cold Cut Combo* and the *Subway Club* were comparable in fat and calories with the other chains' roast-beef sandwiches, while the *BMT* was closer to a *Big Mac*. The sandwiches were all very high in sodium, but concerned consumers can reduce the sodium count significantly by asking that cheese, pickle, olives, and salt be left off. Eliminating the cheese and oil will lessen fat and calories.

The subs' average cost was $2.60, twice that of some other fast-food sandwiches. And we found another drawback: You get a lot of bread and fixings and not much protein for your money. None of the subs had more protein than a small McDonald's hamburger. Getting enough protein isn't a problem for most Americans, but someone with a large appetite who is expecting a meaty sandwich might finish a Subway meal unsatisfied.

Can Fast Food Be Good Food? *(cont'd.)*

Ratings: Fast Foods Excellent Very Good Good Fair Poor

Notes on the table:
Price is the estimated average, based on national and regional surveys. **Weight** and most nutrition information come from the manufacturers. **Percent calories from fat** is an index of nutritional quality. The Government recommends that people get no more than 30 percent of the calories in their overall diet from fat. If you eat a high-fat burger for lunch, you'll need to compensate by eating a lower-fat dinner. Many nutritionists say the goal should be even lower than 30 percent. The figures for **total fat, saturated fat, cholesterol,** and **protein** are rounded to the nearest gram or milligram. **Taste and texture quality** gives results of our consultant's evaluation of each item, sampled at six different

Menu item (Within type, listed in order of the percentage of calories from fat)	Price	Weight	Calories from Fat	Calories	Total Fat	Nutrition Saturated Fat	Cholesterol	Sodium
Basic Burgers								
McDonald's	$.59	4 oz.	32%	255	9 g.	3 g.	35 mg.	490 mg.
Burger King	.78	4	35	260	10	4	30	500
Hardee's	.75	3	35	260	10	4	30	510
Jack in the Box	.79	3	37	267	11	4	26	566
Wendy's Plain Single	1.85	5	39	350	15	6	70	510
Burgers with the Works								
McDonald's Big Mac	1.99	8	47	500	26	9	100	890
Jack in the Box Jumbo Jack	1.99	8	52	584	34	11	73	733
Burger King Whopper	1.99	10	56	630	39	11	90	850
Hardee's Frisco Burger	2.49	8	58	730	47	17	80	1110
Roast Beef Sandwiches								
Hardee's	1.93	4	35	280	11	4	40	870
Arby's	1.99	5	42	383	18	7	43	936
Fish Sandwiches								
McDonald's Filet-O-Fish	1.56	5	44	370	18	4	50	730
Burger King BK Big Fish	1.93	9	54	720	43	8	60	1090
Chicken Sandwiches								
Wendy's Breaded Chicken	2.68	7	40	450	20	4	60	740
Arby's Chicken Breast Fillet	2.55	7	47	445	23	3	45	958
McDonald's McChicken	2.09	7	48	470	25	5	60	830
KFC Colonel's Chicken	1.99	6	50	482	27	6	47	1060
Burger King Chicken	2.49	8	55	700	43	9	60	1400
Chicken Nuggets *(six pieces)*								
Burger King Chicken Tenders	1.99	3	43	250	12	3	35	530
McDonald's Chicken McNuggets	1.79	4	50	270	15	4	55	580
KFC Kentucky Nuggets	1.83	3	57	284	18	4	66	865
Chicken Pieces *(two pieces or 1/4 rotisserie chicken)*								
Hardee's Fried Chicken	2.49	6	49	492	27	10	184	866
KFC Original Recipe	2.30	7	50	490	27	7	185	1080
KFC Rotisserie Gold (white meat)	2.88	6	51	335	19	5	157	1104
Popeye's Chicken Dinner	3.22	5	53	390	23	10	100	900
KFC Rotisserie Gold (dark meat)	2.24	5	65	333	24	7	163	980
French Fries *(medium/regular)*								
Hardee's	.89	3	43	230	11	2	0	85
Burger King	1.03	4	45	400	20	5	0	240
Wendy's	.89	5	45	340	17	4	0	210
McDonald's	1.02	3	48	320	17	4	0	150

restaurants. Basic burgers generally come with ketchup, mustard, and pickle; Wendy's Plain Single is, as advertised, plain, and slightly larger than the others. "The works" on the bigger burgers include such additions as lettuce, cheese, dressing, and tomato. Chicken sandwiches generally come with lettuce and mayonnaise; chicken nuggets, with assorted dipping sauces; fish sandwiches, with tartar sauce.

Whopping Statistics:
Burger King sells 710 million Whoppers a year—enough, it says, to circle the Earth $2^1/_2$ times. KFC claims the chickens it cooked last year, laid head to claw, would soar 23,580 miles past the moon. No word yet on how many fries it would take to reach Neptune.

Taste and texture

Protein	Quality	COMMENTS
12 g.		Thin, very salty, slightly meaty patty that's smaller than the bun.
14		Thin, very salty, slightly meaty patty that's smaller than the bun.
10		Paper thin, very salty, slightly meaty patty that's smaller than the bun.
13		Thin, very salty, slightly meaty patty that's smaller than the bun. Sauce and onion included.
24		Square, fairly thin, tender, meaty patty that's larger than the slightly sweet egg bun.
25		Two small, thin patties between three pieces of bun. Flavors of ingredients and toppings blend well; little texture.
26		Large thin patty, crunchy lettuce, lots of mayo.
27		Large thin patty, crunchy lettuce.
28		Thick meaty patty, bacon included, on grilled sourdough bread. Firm, greasy.
18		Salty, somewhat meaty, very slight butter flavor. Gristly meat in one location.
22		Salty, somewhat meaty, slight butter flavor. Slightly springy pressed meat, but more moist and tender than Hardee's.
14		Slightly flaky fish, too much tartar sauce. Fish turns pasty when chewed.
25		Relatively large sandwich with well-balanced flavors. Somewhat flaky fish, crisp lettuce.
26		Somewhat salty, perceptible pepper. Fresh, crisp lettuce.
22		Salty, perceptible pepper, paprika and fried flavors. Firm, moist, tender chicken.
19		Very salty, somewhat meaty, slightly peppery. Dry in three locations; stale bun in one location.
21		Spicy chicken with sage, celery, nutmeg, pepper notes. Very slightly springy. Dry in two locations.
26		Moist, springy, peppery piece of oblong pressed chicken on hefty sesame bun.
16		Very salty, somewhat meaty, slightly peppery. Springy and mushy in parts.
20		Very salty, slightly meaty, some pepper and nutmeg. Moist, springy, fatty, or mushy, depending on where one bites. Gristly in some locations.
16		Salty, slightly meaty, perceptible pepper. Springy, mushy. Fat pieces, tough meat in some locations.
39		Moist, tender, meaty. Crispy brown flour coating.
46		Moist, tender, meaty. Coating partly crispy, partly soggy.
40		Plump, moist, tender, meaty, with marinated herbed coating. Very salty, greasy.
33		Moist, tender, meaty. Crispy browned flour coating.
30		Plump, moist, tender, meaty, with marinated herbed coating. Very salty, greasy. Overcooked in one location.
3		Tough, thick. Varied: some salty, some not; cold, bitter in one location, thinner; longer in another.
5		Thin, crispy. Good balance of potato, oil, salt. Would be excellent, but not consistent; soggy in one location, tough in another.
5		Tough-skinned, thick. Varied: sometimes soggy or a bit dry. Thinner in one location, slightly soapy notes in another.
4		Thin, crispy. Good balance of potato, oil, salt. Would be excellent, but not consistent; tough in two locations

Can Fast Food Be Good Food? *(cont'd.)*

Burgers.

The basic burgers may not be too bad nutritionally—but most don't taste very good. An exception is the medium-sized, unadorned Wendy's *Plain Single.*

The bigger burgers generally tasted better that the small. Hardee's *Frisco Burger* was very good; Jack in the Box's *Jumbo Jack,* Burger King's *Whopper,* and McDonald's *Big Mac* were all good. But be warned: All the big burgers are quite high in calories and fat.

Sandwiches.

The meat in Arby's roast-beef sandwich was more moist and tender than that in Hardee's. The McDonald's fish sandwich was not very flavorful; Burger King's was better. As for breaded-chicken sandwiches, Burger King's and Arby's had the moistest meat.

Chicken bits and pieces.

Although none of the chicken nuggets were very good, most of the larger pieces of chicken were. The *Rotisserie Gold* from KFC was more plump and juicy that the other chicken dishes, though it was quite greasy and salty.

Fries.

The thin-cut fries at Burger King and McDonald's were best; the thick-cut fries at Hardee's and Wendy's sometimes had unpleasant off-tastes.

Recommendations

Fast food can be good for you if you choose sensibly. Last year, for instance, we found that Arby's *Light Roast Turkey* (and *Chicken*) *Deluxe,* Wendy's *Grilled Chicken,* McDonald's *McLean Deluxe,* and several salads, eaten without high-fat dressing, were especially low in fat.

If, like most Americans, you prefer the standard foods, you'll probably sacrifice nutrition to taste. Ordering chicken or fish won't always help; sauce and breading or skin add fat and calories. In fact, the skin and dark meat of KFC's *Rotisserie Gold* chicken helps make it the fattiest food we tested. The best way to improve the nutritional value of any fast food is to avoid fried or breaded items and to leave off cheese, dressing, and other trimmings.

If you eat fast food as an occasional treat rather than a staple, enjoy it and try to eat prudently the rest of the day. Among the items that tasted best: Hardee's *Frisco Burger,* Burger King's *BK Big Fish,* Wendy's and Arby's breaded-chicken sandwiches, Popeye's and Hardee's fried-chicken pieces, KFC's rotisserie-chicken quarters, and Burger King's and McDonald's fries.

End of the Rainbow

The leaders of the Human Genome Diversity Project wanted to find a way to celebrate and preserve our genetic differences. Now they're being called racists.*

JoAnn C. Gutin

When Henry Greely is perplexed or troubled, his body English tells you as clearly as his words: the Stanford law professor and bioethicist leans back in his chair, stares into the middle distance, and slowly, absently tousles his own hair.

In his modest office this morning he's discussing the challenges of his two-year stint as one of the bioethicists on the organizing committee of the North American arm of the Human Genome Diversity Project. ("Has it only been since '92?" he wonders aloud. "It feels longer.") After two and a half hours spent grappling with variations on a single theme—"Why are some people so mad about the Human Genome Diversity Project?"—Greely's hair is decidedly the worse for wear.

That it should upset people seems curious. On paper, which is really the only place it exists so far, the project appears to be a singularly uncontroversial idea. It is merely a call for a coordinated effort by scientists on every continent to record the dwindling regional genetic diversity of *Homo sapiens* by taking DNA samples from several hundred distinct human populations and storing the samples in gene banks. Researchers could then examine the DNA for clues to the evolutionary histories of the populations and to their resistance or susceptibility to particular diseases.

Yet today the architects of the three-year-old program—a group of geneticists and anthropologists with irreproachable academic and political credentials—stand accused of being neocolonialists, gene pirates, and pawns in a conspiracy to develop race-specific biological weapons. The atmosphere surrounding the work is thick with suspicion: Greely recently heard one rumor about a medical researcher whose ongoing study in the Carribbean was abruptly shut down by charges that he would use his subjects' blood samples to clone a race of slaves. "Obviously *Jurassic Park* didn't help us," Greely says, managing a wan smile.

Clearly, though, reaction to the diversity project far exceeds mere blockbuster-induced paranoia about the perils of genetic engineering. University professors and indigenous peoples alike are voicing objections, and while the academic critique tends to be less vivid than what appears in the popular press, racism is the shared subtext. Is the Human Genome Diversity Project scientific colonialism, using the genes of Third World people to answer obscure academic questions or—worse—provide expensive medical cures for the privileged citizens of the developed world? Might it backfire and inadvertently supply more fodder for ethnic battles, as if any more fodder were needed? Or are its organizers merely victims of bad timing? Are

End of the Rainbow *(cont'd.)*

the 1990s an impossible moment in human history to launch a project touching two of the rawest nerves in the culture: genes and race?

The Human Genome Diversity Project began innocently enough in 1991 with an impassioned open letter to the readers of the journal *Genomics* by a number of prominent researchers, among them the geneticists Luigi Luca Cavalli-Sforza of Stanford and Mary-Claire King and Allan Wilson of the University of California at Berkeley. The genus *Homo,* argued the letter's authors, has reached a critical juncture: indigenous peoples are being absorbed into the larger gene pool at an escalating rate, and if the information contained in their DNA is not collected quickly, it may be lost to humankind forever. "The genetic diversity of people now living harbors the clues to the evolution of our species," they wrote, "but the gate to preserve these clues is closing rapidly." They urged members of the Human Genome Organization—an international consortium of scientists who are interested in human genetics—to "grasp a vanishing opportunity to preserve a record of our genetic heritage."

Their plea was heard not only by the nonprofit Human Genome Organization but by funding agencies that included the National Institutes of Health, The Department of Energy, and the National Science Foundation; all gave the letter's authors seed money, charging them with devising a way to collect a wider range of DNA.

Backers of the project saw it as a necessary adjunct to the much larger and better-funded Human Genome Project. The Human Genome Project often gets billed as the effort to map and sequence *the* set of human genes, but as Diversity Project organizers gently point out, that isn't quite accurate. Molecular anthropologist Ken Weiss, head of the North American Diversity Project committee, notes that the literal human genome is "the whole ball of wax," the sum of 5 billion people's DNA. What Human Genome Project researchers are actually analyzing is a sort of composite genome: 23 chromosomes pairs donated by a mere handful of U.S. and European scientists. (As one was observed, when they're finally mapped, those chromosomes will tell researchers everything there is to know "about one French farmer and a lady from Philadelphia.") And even *that* will take about 15 years and cost some $3 billion.

That's where the Human Genome Diversity Project would come in—it would supplement, particularize, and colorize the chromosome maps drawn by the Human Genome Project. As Weiss observes, "If we don't go ahead with this, then in ten years when the Human Genome Project is done, a Navajo, say, will look at those results and ask, 'Why did they bother? How well does that represent *me?*' "

From the outset, all the scientists involved called for sensitivity toward the sampled populations. These groups would include "historically vulnerable" people, warned the original *Genomics* letter, and using them merely as research subjects would inevitably lead to a "sense of exploitation and abandonment."

Yet the critiques began almost immediately. "The Human Genome Diversity ('Vampire') Project," reads as communiqué from the Central Australian Aboriginal Congress, "is legalized theft." "Your process," says a letter to the National Science

End of the Rainbow *(cont'd.)*

Foundation from Chief Leon Shenandoah of the Onondaga Council of Chiefs, "is unethical, invasive, and may even be criminal. It violates the group rights and human rights of . . . indigenous peoples around the world."

The project's friends are perplexed by the commotion, believing that aside from its giant scale, the work doesn't constitute anything fundamentally new. Researchers have been collecting biological materials from indigenous groups for years; the Diversity Project is merely a way to organize that collection. Far from being a high-tech threat, say its backers, the project will do a better job of safeguarding subjects' rights and will generate better science that the scattershot data collection that preceded it.

As the guidelines stand today, anthropologists and geneticists around the world will be asked to gather blood samples from the groups they routinely study; the groups will participate in the Human Genome Diversity Project only if they want to. In addition, all the researchers will adhere to strict and uniform standards of informed consent; the property rights of donor populations to their DNA will be protected; and the material will be stored in a gene library accessible to all qualified researchers rather than disappearing into a refrigerator in one scientist's lab. The establishment of cell lines that will survive for 20 to 25 years—an expensive process—will guarantee that scientists into the next century will be able to ask questions of the genes that no one has yet thought of.

Why is the project necessary? After all, all humans, no matter what their ancestry, share most of their DNA. As Mary-Claire King is fond of saying, "We are all different, yet we are all the same." Every human carries about 6 billion base pairs—the chemical rungs of the DNA ladder—in the nuclei of his or her cells. Our personal DNA code differs from that of a random stranger by two rungs for every thousand, or .2 percent of the whole. The differences are smaller between family members and larger between people whose ancestors are unlikely to have intermingled in recent history. Still, a random sample of people in any small group from any location in the world—from rural Sweden to the Ituri Forest to Tierra del Fuego—will turn up 85 percent of all the genetic variation our species contains.

Nevertheless, the remaining 15 percent of human genetic variation isn't distributed randomly. It has a geographic pattern, which stems from past population movements and matings. Interestingly, the larger part of that 15 percent difference is not racial: almost 9 percent is reflected in differences among ethnic and linguistic groups within any give race. Only 6 percent represents genetic differences between races.

These kinds of patterns interest anthropologists and geneticists. The interest isn't merely historical: some of the variation finds expression in physical differences that intrigue medical researchers. The Navajo, for example, have very high rates of high blood pressure, some of which may be genetic in origin. Genetic research without Navajo samples won't illuminate that problem. African Americans, as another example, experience high failure rates in organ transplants, partly because donors and recipients, even if both are of African origin, may have geographically

End of the Rainbow *(cont'd.)*

different ancestries. If geneticists understood DNA variation of the African continent, tissue matching could be done more efficiently.

But—and this is the message that Diversity Project proponents repeat like a mantra—the patterns of variation that appear at the genetic level cut across visible racial divisions. Moving from the physical traits that scientists call phenotype— things like skin color and hair type—to the genetic level is like moving closer and closer to a pointillist painting. Twenty feet from Seurat's *La Grande Jatte,* for instance, you see Parisians and their dogs, but at two feet the image dissolves into dabs of pigment that might belong to a Parisian, a dog, or a tree. It's the same way with the human phenotype and the human genotype. "The closer in you go from what you see on the surface," notes Diversity Project planner Marc Feldman of Stanford, "the more unity there is."

This genetic unity means, for instance, that white Americans, though ostensibly far removed from black Americans in phenotype, can sometimes be better tissue matches for them than are *other* black Americans. "After the Diversity Project," predicts planning-committee member Georgia Dunston of Howard University, "we won't have the luxury of drawing distinctions between one another based on skin pigmentation anymore."

That day, however, may be a long time coming, judging from the initial criticism of the project. Perhaps what's most ironic about such criticism is that the scientists most involved in the project have established track records in human rights. As Feldman observes, "All of us have worked throughout our lives in an antiracist framework. Our political credentials are in order."

Charter member and 1960s activist Mary-Claire King, for instance, was putting her genetic expertise on the political line long before the Diversity Project was proposed: in Argentina she used DNA analysis to help reunite the kidnapped children of "disappeared" political prisoners with their grandmothers. In El Salvador she's been helping UN workers identify the remains of the 794 villagers of El Mozote, who were massacred by the American-trained military in 1981.

Throughout the 1970s, three-year project veteran Feldman publicly took on Nobel Prize-winning physicist William Shockley, who argued that whites are intellectually superior to blacks, debating him at the podium and in the press; Feldman currently heads the Morrison Institute for Populations and Resource Studies at Stanford, which trains scientists and government officials from the developing world in ecology, population biology, and demographics.

And then there's Luca Cavalli-Sforza. It's Cavalli-Sforza, professor emeritus of genetics at the Stanford medical school, who remains both the project's biggest booster and the biggest target for the flak it takes. "Any sensible person can see this is important research," he says with characteristic aplomb. "But I must tell you, I was completely unprepared for the negative reactions we have encountered."

Straight-backed, silver-haired, and courtly—he registers somewhere between Marcello Mastroianni and David Niven on the charm meter—Cavalli-Sforza

End of the Rainbow *(cont'd.)*

comes by his confidence honestly. A member of the Royal Society and the National Academy of Sciences, a recipient of the Huxley Medal for Biology and the Order of Merit of the Italian Republic, the 72-year-old Cavalli-Sforza is widely regarded as one of the world's leading geneticists. Though he has worked in the United States for most of his adult life, he remains an Italian in everything from his citizenship to his accent to his style of dress, which by American scientific standards is extraordinarily debonair.

Cavalli-Sforza has spent his entire career decoding the genetic clues to our hidden past, and he recently summed up his life's work in a 1,032-page magnum opus called *The History and Geography of Human Genes.* In the preface, he and coauthors Paolo Menozzi and Alberto Piazza note that written history, linguistics, and archeology are flawed tools for reconstructing the history of human evolution: "Only genes . . . have the degree of permanence necessary," they say, for discussing *Homo sapiens'* 100,000 years of "fissions, fusions, and migrations of populations."

Yet if Cavalli-Sforza is a man entranced by genes and the evolutionary patterns they reveal, he is acutely aware of how genetic information can be willfully misused, particularly when mixed with notions of race. "I get hate mail from neo-Nazi groups all the time," he says, gesturing at the pile in his office that awaited him on his return from a six-month sabbatical in Italy.

Cavalli-Sforza considers visible racial traits mere physiological frosting, functional adaptations of an organism to its environment, but his correspondents don't agree. "To say that race doesn't exist is a lie. And only an idiot would believe it," reads one laboriously handwritten example, which attributes Cavalli-Sforza's intellectual stance to a degenerative mental disease. Others are nastier, even frightening; all are anonymous. He shrugs dismissively, immune after years of attacks. "People like this never sign their names."

The criticism that's harder to shrug off, however, comes from more respectable quarters, including some members of the scientific community, for "crimes" ranging from colonialism to outright racism. Some anthropologists suggest that Cavalli-Sforza got off on the wrong foot in 1991 by referring to African "tribes" but European "ethnic groups" before a large audience of anthropologists whose support for the project he was trying to enlist. "That's when he lost us," says one critic, who implies that the choice of words revealed a disturbing glimpse of a colonial mentality at the highest level of the project.

Ken Weiss heatedly rejects this interpretation. As for raising awareness of indigenous peoples, "I would say categorically that Luca has done more than anyone in the history of the species." He has his own explanation for the negative reaction to the project among some of his colleagues. "Many anthropologists," he contends, "are lamentably ignorant about genetics." And that ignorance breeds unwarranted suspicion, he thinks. "Laypeople sometimes have this idea that there's a black gene or a white gene or a gene for criminal behavior. And there are a lot of anthropologists who don't know much more than that. If some anthropologists are worried that the project might be used for racist purposes, then maybe that's

End of the Rainbow *(cont'd.)*

because deep down they really believe that there is a gene for race, and they are afraid to find it. But I'm not afraid of that, because I know a race gene doesn't exist. And that's what the project will show."

It seems clear that the high-profile Diversity Project has brought a long-simmering anthropological unease with genetics to a rolling boil. In particular, cultural anthropologists fear that the Human Genome Diversity Project gives intellectual legitimacy and—at a hoped-for $5 million a year for five years—a financial leg up to an approach they think shortchanges human complexity. Not surprisingly, they argue that it's more important to study and preserve the world's cultures than its genes. Greely, who has a long-standing amateur interest in anthropology, first became aware of this strain at a project-related meeting in Mount Kisco, New York, in 1993. "It was sort of like going out with somebody and being invited to Christmas dinner at her parents' house, with all of the family there," he recalls. "And suddenly they're reliving old arguments—what Uncle Joe said to so-and-so 20 years ago—and you don't have the foggiest idea what's going on. Fascinating, but I had the sense of being an outsider at a family fight."

Cavalli-Sforza attributes this family fight to a fundamental misunderstanding of how science itself works. "Some people say we should take a more *holistic* approach," he says, using quasi-audible italics to convey just how naive an idea this is. "What they don't see is that any science involves initial reductionism. You must simplify first, so you can get a handle on the problem." In an aside not calculated to win converts, he adds, "I don't think cultural anthropologists are scientists at all— more philosophers or social critics."

But cultural anthropologists are not the only ones taking serious issue with the Diversity Project. Biological anthropologist Jonathan Marks of Yale thinks its potential for answering evolutionary questions is being oversold. "You don't need molecular genetics to tell you that Danes are more closely related to Swedes than they are to Iroquois—just look at a map!" he says. "And it's not going to be able to tell you whether they're more closely related to Austrians than to Swiss, because at that level they're *all* mutts. This is 1990s genetics applied to questions anthropologists stopped asking in the 1940s."

Yet even the harshest scientific critics stop short of accusing project members of anything worse than naïveté ("a grand naïveté," Marks amends). "I think what you have here," says anthropologist Jason Clay, "is a bunch of honor roll scientists who are in way over their heads."

Clay, who founded and edited a journal focusing on the problems of indigenous peoples, supports the Diversity Project in theory. "You can't be afraid of information," he says. Yet as the head of Rights and Resources, an organization that brings together Third World agriculturists and "green" businesses like Ben & Jerry's and the Body Shop, he wonders about the details. Judging from his own experience with indigenous peoples, Clay says, well-intentioned explanations of why researchers want individuals' DNA will be useless. "Some of these groups don't know about germs, much less about genes or property rights," he explains. "What could 'informed consent' possibly mean to them?"

End of the Rainbow *(cont'd.)*

He also worries about the uses to which the samples might be put. In the past, botanicals taken from Third World countries have been used to develop new pharmaceuticals that are then sold back to their countries of origin at a profit. What if the Diversity Project were to uncover a gene that confers resistance to, say, an environmental toxin? "Indigenous peoples have been mined for their resources by big companies, and mined for their ideas by anthropologists," he says. "Now are they being mined for their molecules?"

Jon Marks concurs. "Just imagine how it seems to indigenes," he says. "'We've taken your land, we've eradicated your life-ways, we've killed your people, but—guess what—we're going to save your cells.'"

In response to these criticisms, Feldman simply sighs. "Look, if the Malaysian government is going to allow the Negrito population to be eliminated by selling their land to the Japanese timber companies," he replies wearily, "there's not much the Genome Diversity Project can do about that. We're scientists, not politicians."

Still, however acrimonious it got, the debate about the Diversity Project was confined mostly to the laboratory, the seminar room, and the faculty lounge until 1993. That's when the Rural Advancement Foundation International got into the act. RAFI, an advocacy group concerned with issues of biodiversity and intellectual property, has for a decade been sounding the alarm over what it considers to be biopiracy: the theft of intellectual property rights of indigenous peoples. And it doesn't see the Diversity Project as an exception. "I think they're very naive with regard to the commercialization of cell lines," says Hope Shand, the research director of RAFI-USA. "If the cells are in repositories that are open to everyone, what's to prevent somebody from patenting them?"

According to RAFI's point of view, First World agribusiness has made a fortune from plant strains developed by Third World agriculturists, without funneling any of the profits back to the original owners. The fledgling Diversity Project, RAFI believes, could easily become a vehicle for similar abuses—not so much by project scientists as by outside researchers who might well be less scrupulous in their use of the sampled DNA. "There is nothing in international law," notes RAFI member Jean Christie, "that assures us those abuses won't take place."

RAFI workers have told indigenous leaders of their suspicions, buttonholed delegates at conventions, and E-mailed activist groups worldwide. Partly as a result of this lobbying, the European Green party, joined by the World Council of Indigenous Peoples and the Guaymi General Congress, has called for suspension of the Human Genome Diversity Project.

All this troubles Hank Greely very deeply; he sees the intellectual property issue as a misplaced concern. "There's no reason the project and RAFI should be enemies," he says. "There's no commercial money in the project, no pharmaceutical-industry backing. This is pure science." He concedes that the patent question is a knotty one but insists "we're happy to do what's right. It's just not clear, yet, exactly what's the best way to do that."

End of the Rainbow *(cont'd.)*

While the patent question may eventually yield to time, legislation, and good intentions, it may take more heroic measures to counter the darkest charge leveled against the project: genocide. "Unscrupulous parties," warns a RAFI newsletter, could "devise cheap and targeted biological weapons," effective against specific races, by using data collected by the researchers. The Diversity Project, in RAFI's view, makes the specter of genocide a biotechnological reality.

This claim is the one that sends project scientists around the bend. "If people understood human genetics," snaps Feldman, "they'd know it can't be done."

"It's ludicrous," says University of Florida anthropologist and project committee member John Moore, "to suggest that we could be indifferent to the destruction of what most interests us."

"This is the most incredible rubbish, this DNA-poison idea," says Cavalli-Sforza. "It is part of a hate campaign waged against us."

But RAFI won't back down from its claims. "We're not scientists," says Christie, "but we've done research on biological warfare. People say our protests are naive, radical, or ill-conceived, but they're not."

Predictably, Hank Greely has a more measured response to even this dire accusation. "Governments *have* engaged in biological warfare," he says, recalling that in the nineteenth century the United States gave blankets impregnated with smallpox virus to Native Americans. "Indigenous people are right to be skeptical when people from the developed world come to them saying they want to help. It's a kind of survival trait—groups that didn't have it are probably gone now."

Greely doesn't for a moment think these fears are warranted vis-à-vis the Diversity Project, but in his view that's not the point. "If people are worried," he says, in what amounts to the ethicist's credo, "you have to deal with their fears whether or not they have any basis." It appears that his credo will guide the future progress of the Diversity Project. Feldman admits that they've made some mistakes—"You could call it arrogance," he says; "we sort of took it for granted that everyone would see this was a great project"—but he's certain they're on the right track at last. The MacArthur Foundation has awarded the North American committee a grant to develop an ethics program, and project leaders will be holding informational meetings for groups whose cooperation is being sought—meetings to explain the project as well as to answer questions about it. Feldman describes the first few such meetings, held in the spring of 1994, as "frank and good." Jon Marks applauds the trend. "Look, I think the project is a great idea; you can never have enough scientific data. The collection just has to be done right. It has to be done respectfully."

And Cavalli-Sforza, father of the Diversity Project, is heartened by the progress he's been seeing. The Chinese have established a Diversity Project committee, he reports, and collection has started in the British Isles, where the people of Cornwall have begun giving DNA samples. "We are still working on the ethics here," he says, "but that's very important. There cannot be any misunderstanding. We need to be—is the word *fireproof?* No—*bulletproof.* We need to be bulletproof."

The Piano: A Feminist Film?

Yes*

Rebecca Shugrue

bell hooks argues in *Z Magazine* that *The Piano* falls short of being a feminist film because it advances the sexist assumption that heterosexual women will give up artistic practice to find "true love." But I believe that the mute Ada makes no such sacrifice. If anything, here desire for the rough-hewn neighbor Baines, who purchases Ada's piano as a means to lure her presence, illustrates an ambition to "have it all": love, sex, and self-fulfillment through art. The fact that Ada loses interest in music when she is locked away and made a prisoner by her husband is understandably human. She is, after all, depressed and heartsick; temporarily powerless to act.

Nevertheless, Ada is far from weak. From the moment we are introduced to the Scottish widow, it is clear that she is strong-willed and self-sufficient. Her daughter and her piano fulfill her needs for companionship and expression. Unfortunately, when she arrives in New Zealand for an arranged marriage, her husband has a complete lack of understanding as to the central role of music in her life. Stewart thinks that, like a pet, Ada will somehow come to love him if he simply acts the part of a man—caring for her material, but none of her emotional needs. Leaving her piano on the beach he tells her. "I'll be back in three days, perhaps we can start fresh then." He, like Baines, wants Ada to show him some affection. But unlike Baines, he wants her not because she moves him, but because she is his wife.

In the bartering scenes, where Ada uses her sexuality in order to buy her piano back from Baines, his physical size suggests he has power and she does not. Rape is clearly his prerogative. Yet somehow Ada holds her own against him. Forget her "pale and corpse-like" body described by hooks; when Ada plays for Baines, her music is her strength, her will; her power is her passion.

Listening to Ada, Baines desires to be the object of that passion. This is what makes the bartering scene so powerful. Ada wants her piano and is willing to sacrifice her body to get it. How much her body is worth, how far she is willing to go, is up to her. Take away the fact that Baines is physically bigger for a minute, and it becomes clear that Ada really has the upper hand. She is getting what she wants. Baines is not. The more assertive she is, the more despondent Baines becomes. "I want you to care for me, but you can't. So go," he tells her, later giving her back the piano. Suddenly, without an audience to play for, Ada predictably falls for him.

These scenes raise the fundamental issue of equality in the bedroom. Campion addresses the problem of romantic love within the context of a sexist and misogynist world, where domination (by men) and submission (of women) is both eroticized

*"*The Piano:* A Feminist Film?" "Yes" by Rebecca Shugrue and "No" by Carolyn Gage. *On the Issues* (Summer 1994), pp. 44–45. Reprinted with the permission of the publisher.

The Piano: A Feminist Film? *(cont'd.)*

and considered normal. By casting tiny Holly Hunter with stocky over-built Harvey Keitel, the physical inequality inherent in this relationship is striking. The specter of rape is ever present.

In my view, *The Piano* is a feminist film because it gives us a version of female sexuality that is much more than a woman's "positive surrender" to men. It shows us the power of female passion to make music, touch souls, and defy hierarchy in the bedroom. In short, it shows the power of women to be heard, and whole, in a man's world.

No*

Carolyn Gage

The Piano is a gorgeously shot, utterly repellent film about a woman trapped between two rapists: a sleazy, blackmailing rapist and a violent, possessive rapist. The woman "chooses" the sleazy, blackmailing rapist, falls deeply in love with him (apparently because her experience of coerced sex was so hot) and ends up blissfully married to him in a cozy English cottage. And in case the misogyny of this scenario isn't enough to turn you off, there is an extra fillip of able-ism at the end: the woman, who is mute and communicates very effectively through sign language, is taught to speak by the sleazy rapist—thereby consolidating the film's claim to a happy ending.

So why am I wasting paper reviewing this silly film? Because it is by a woman, because this woman is obviously a brilliant cinematographer, and because she started to say something important.

What she started to say was something about a woman in patriarchy who decides to stop speaking and channels all of her passion and all of her love into her piano and her daughter. Jane Campion, the filmmaker and screenwriter, started to say something about male trivialization and appropriation of women's art. She started to say something very important about men as enemies, as colonizers.

The violent rapist—the woman's husband by an arranged marriage—refuses to pay for her piano to be transported to his home. The sleazy rapist then buys it from the violent rapist, transports it to his bungalow, and allows the woman to play it as long as he can masturbate to the music—or to the sight of her bare elbow, or to the feel of the hole in her stocking—or whatever it is that turns him on.

This is the first 20 minutes. Campion, a woman artist with a passion and a gift, is telling us something. And then she forgets what it is she was saying as the film deteriorates into sex, violence, and the romanticizing of rape. Or does Campion really forget?

Let's look at the scene right before the movie derails into a pro-rape piece of hetero-patriarchal propaganda. The woman has finally confronted the fact that the

---

The Piano: A Feminist Film? *(cont'd.)*

sleazy rapist is not really interested in piano lessons. He has taken the piano hostage, to force here to submit to his sexual torture. We see a few moments of her literally unspeakable agony at the horror of what men do to us around the things we love. And then she makes up her mind: she will play along. In fact, she quickly transforms herself into a hard-nose negotiator. She will "buy" back her own piano one key at a time. She learns to negotiate for more keys as he escalates his sexual demands.

Freeze frame. What is this scene saying?

It is saying that a piano is a heavy, valuable object—one that women cannot move by ourselves. One that takes man-power, man-money to move. Like, say, a feature film.

And Campion is saying we have to accept that there will be a price extorted for having access to that piano. And that price is that we will not be allowed to play for our own pleasure, but that as we play, we will have to find away to titillate and gratify the men who paid for moving it. And perhaps—melody by melody, film by film—we will one day be able to buy back our own autonomy.

And as Jane Campion plays her magnificently beautiful grand piano of a film, the men in theaters all over the world can engorge themselves on the messages of male supremacy in the film.

And the women in the audience? We will have to console ourselves with the usual last-minute lies: the lie that the victim's mute reproach will be sufficient to stop the most violent of rapists in mid-zip; the lie that the violent rapist—after it's too late—will come under the spell of the mute woman's moral integrity; the lie that a woman can exercise control over her victimization by willing herself to fall in love with the least violent victimizer. And finally, the lie that she will be abundantly rewarded for all of her passive suffering and for the sacrifice of her daughter by converting the rapist into a savior who will take her away from his world of self-created horror; who will replace her mutilated body parts with lovingly-crafted sterling silver prostheses; who will cherish her daughter; who will encourage the art he debased as an instrument of prostitution; and who will help her find her voice through his language.

And will we women be consoled? Alas, yes. Not because we are stupid. Because, like the woman in the film, we are colonized.

So Jane Campion tells us what she is going to have to do right before she does it. And for her selfish pleasure of exercising her cinematographer's art at the highest level of resources, she had degraded herself and her art by putting both at the service of the rapist-pornographers of the culture. What has she gotten for her pains? First place at Cannes. That should be good for at least two keys, if not three.

But heed your own metaphor, Jane, lest along the way to buying back your art, you should end up like your heroine—with your faculties amputated by the rapist. And there will be no sterling silver prosthesis for a woman's severed soul.

Choosing Among Alternative Recycling Systems: An Economic Analysis*

Gerald D. Stedge
Virginia Polytechnic Institute and State University

John M. Halstead
University of New Hampshire

Abstract. Due to the increasing concern over the disposal of municipal solid waste, municipalities have begun searching for ways to recycle a larger percentage of their waste stream at a reasonable cost. This report examines bag-based recycling. This system, due to its efficient collection and separation method and its convenience, should be able to capture a larger share of the waste stream at a lower cost per metric ton than conventional recycling programs. Using a case study approach, a bag-based program is compared with a curbside-sort program and a drop-off program. Using time/motion analysis, a garbage composition study, a household survey, and the recording of set-out rates of a sample of dwelling units, the efficiency of the three programs was defined and estimated. The efficiency of the bag-based system was also estimated for three areas with distinct household densities. Although the curbside-sort program was found to divert a larger percentage of the residential waste stream than the bag-based system, the cost per metric ton of the bag-based system is so much lower that it clearly is the most efficient of the three programs. The drop-off program had a very low cost per metric ton; however, it failed to divert the minimum acceptable level of the waste stream. The bag-based system proved to be more efficient in areas with higher household densities.

Introduction

Due to increasing concern over the disposal of municipal solid waste, municipalities have begun searching for ways to recycle a larger percentage of their waste stream. However, as municipalities began incorporating recycling as a component of their solid waste management plans, they realized that recycling programs were expensive to administer, especially those that included curbside collection of recyclables. The desire to recycle the greatest amount of waste for the least amount of money has led to innovation in recycling collection and separation systems. Although municipalities are investing heavily in a wide array of recycling programs, little is known about the performance and cost of these efforts. Although several studies have attempted to estimate the costs of existing recycling programs

*Gerald D. Stedge and John M. Halstead. "Choosing Among Alternative Recycling Systems: An Economic Analysis." *The Environmental Professional* 16 (March 1994), pp. 40–48. Reprinted by permission of Blackwell Science, Inc.

Choosing Among Alternative Recycling Systems *(cont'd.)*

(Stedge, 1991), the methodology differs substantially enough across studies to make comparisons impossible. This study establishes a common ground on which to compare recycling programs and then uses this new methodology to compare a relatively new collection system, bag-based recycling, with two more established systems, curbside-sort and drop-off.

The bag-based system, because of its relatively capital-intensive collection and separation system and its convenience, could prove more cost-effective than either the curbside-sort or drop-off systems. The bag-based system requires participants to presort their recyclables and place them into two specially marked plastic bags. One bag may contain both newspaper and mixed paper (junk mail, computer paper, and any other clean paper). The second bag contains "heavy" recyclables—glass, plastic, and metal cans. Bags are collected by a rear-loading packer truck each week on the same day as regular trash pick-up. The truck, manned by one "runner" and a driver, is equipped with a sweeper arm to push bags back but not damage them. The bags are then transferred to a material recovery facility (MRF) where the bags are opened and the recyclable material is separated by type in an assembly-line fashion using both equipment and labor.

Given the positive externalities and uncertain future benefits associated with recycling, a new method of determining the optimal level of recycling activity must be developed. In evaluating recycling programs, the recycling industry has long, used two standards—diversion rates and program costs per metric ton. However, these two standards are often contradictory. Since no definitive weight can be given to either of these goals, they are treated equally in the definition of efficiency used in this article. An efficiency factor is calculated as the net cost to operate the program divided by the percentage of the residential waste stream diverted. The program with the lowest efficiency factor is therefore the most efficient. The efficiency calculation assumes that municipalities not only were trying to minimize their residential solid waste (RSW) disposal costs (recycling to the point where recycling's marginal cost equals its marginal benefit) but also were willing to trade off between increased diversion due to recycling and increased current disposal costs. This study compares the efficiency of this trade-off between programs.

Methods

Three principal tasks were undertaken in the comparison of the three systems: (1) full-cost analyses of the three systems, including time/motion analysis of collection, diversion rates, and revenue/marketing issues; (2) a garbage composition study of a random sample of households participating in the bag-based program, to measure program recyclable diversion success; and (3) a survey of a subsample of bag-based program households. The data used in the analysis were collected from three case studies of municipalities, each employing one of the three recycling systems. A description of each of the three case studies is given below.

Choosing Among Alternative Recycling Systems *(cont'd.)*

Case Study Descriptions

BAG-BASED SYSTEM: CONCORD, NEW HAMPSHIRE

The city of Concord, New Hampshire (population, 30,400), put into effect a pilot bag-based recycling program on November 6, 1990, scheduled to run for 26 weeks. In 1990, the city collected and burned 13,219 metric tons of RSW. The bag-based recycling program was made available to the approximately 2,100 residential buildings on the Tuesday refuse collection route. This route's RSW averaged 39.8 metric tons per week for the 52 weeks prior to the start of the bag-based recycling project. The Tuesday route was chosen because it could be broken down into three distinct subroutes which possess different population densities. Subroute one was an urban area containing a high percentage of multifamily dwelling units, with approximate dwelling unit density of 55 units per road kilometer. The traffic flow in this route was heavy, and many of the streets were unidirectional. Subroute two was a suburban area with dwelling unit density of 29 units per road kilometer. All dwelling units were single-family. Subroute three was the most rural section of the route, with a dwelling unit density of 7 single-family units per road kilometer. This subroute is linear and must be driven twice in order to make the return trip.

Resource Conservation Services, Inc. (RCS), provided recycling services to the Tuesday collection route and processed the recyclables at their newly built MRF in Hooksett, New Hampshire, 27.4 kilometers south of Concord. Materials included in the program were newspaper, mixed paper, cardboard, magazines, aluminum, tin, glass, high density polyethylene (HDPE), and polyethylene terephthalate (PET). If other materials were found in the recycling bags by the collection personnel, the bags were not collected and a bright orange notice was affixed to the bag.

DROP-OFF PROGRAM: CONCORD, NEW HAMPSHIRE

Concord operates its drop-off recycling program on a citywide basis. The center is located at the town landfill and is open year-round on Tuesdays, Thursdays, and Saturdays. The center is staffed by one employee on Tuesdays and Thursdays and two employees on Saturdays. The program accepts newspaper, glass containers, cardboard, aluminum containers, and tin containers.

CURBSIDE-SORT PROGRAM: DURHAM, NEW HAMPSHIRE

Durham, New Hampshire, has a population of 10,620 and is also part-time home to the University of New Hampshire's 13,000 residents. The town provided curbside pick-up of refuse from all residential properties. Materials included in the curbside-sort program were: clear glass, green glass, brown glass, aluminum, newspaper, HDPE, PET, cardboard, and tin cans. This study only included Durham's RSW stream so that a more precise comparison with Concord's bag-based system could be made.

Recyclable material was collected on five days by a two-man municipal crew, using a specialized compartmentalized recycling truck owned by the town. Card-

---

Choosing Among Alternative Recycling Systems *(cont'd.)*

board was collected one day per month from all residences by a town-owned packer truck. Residents separated their recyclables and placed them into plastic bins which were distributed by the town free of charge. The runner separated materials by type; any contaminants were left in the container and re-placed at the curb. Materials were brought to the recycling center, located at the town landfill, whenever one of the compartments became full. The recycling center was staffed by two employees to process the recyclable material for market.

Data Collected

A data base provided by RCS of the Concord bag-based pilot program area contained 2,173 household addresses and their corresponding dwelling unit types. This data base was broken down into the three subroutes (urban, suburban, and rural). A subset of 182 dwelling units was randomly selected for study of participation behavior and as subjects of a postproject survey.

DWELLING UNIT SET-OUT BEHAVIOR

To determine the percentage of dwelling units involved in the bag-based system that set out recyclables, and the frequency at which these units set the recyclables out, it was necessary to record the set-out behavior of the 182 sample dwelling units. This information was gathered on ten Tuesdays by visually inspecting the curb of each sample dwelling unit.

TIME/MOTION ANALYSES

Because the efficiency of the bag-based collection system in areas with different population densities needed to be determined, the time/motion study was done separately for each of the subroutes. Data collected in the Concord analysis measured the average time spent collecting recyclables at each stop (time/stop), the average time spent moving between stops (time in motion/stop), the average distance in kilometers between stops (km/stop), the total number of stops made during the route (stops), the time spent traveling between the route and the MRF (time in transit to the MRF), the distance accumulated traveling between the route and the MRF (km in transit to the MRF), and the time spent unloading recyclables at the MRF (time at the MRF). This information was needed to compare the relative efficiency of the bag-based system with that of the curbside-sort and drop-off programs.

The same information was collected during the Durham time/motion study, except that time and distance spent traveling between the route and the landfill were measured instead of time and distance traveling to the MRF. Data were collected on four days.

HOUSEHOLD SURVEY

After the completion of the Concord pilot recycling program, a survey was mailed to all 277 households residing in the 182 sample dwelling units. Surveys

Choosing Among Alternative Recycling Systems *(cont'd.)*

were returned by 118 households, an effective return rate of 42.6 percent. The survey was used to determine various socio-demographic characteristics of the households in the bag-based pilot program area (Stedge et al., 1992).

GARBAGE COMPOSITION STUDY

From the above-described Concord sample, 30 dwelling units were randomly chosen to be part of the composition study based on set-out behavior, subroute, and dwelling unit type, in order to assure a representative sample with a small sample size. A one-day sample of trash was collected from the 30 sample dwelling units. Each dwelling unit sample was separated into two subsamples—material that was set out for recycling and material that was set out for regular refuse collection—and analyzed. Also, the number of recycling bags used by each dwelling unit was recorded.

Results

Bag-Based System

DWELLING UNIT SET-OUT BEHAVIOR

The average percentage of dwelling units that set out recyclables every Tuesday ranged from a high of 70.3 percent to a low of 60.4 percent. The mean set-out rate was 65.3 percent. The cumulative set-out rate (the percentage of dwelling units that set out at least once) for the entire route was 95.1 percent. Approximately 60 percent of the dwelling units set out 70 percent of the observed weeks; therefore, a strong case can be made that households will take advantage of a weekly pick-up schedule.

CONCORD TIME/MOTION ANALYSIS

Table 1 contains the results of the time/motion analysis performed on the three Concord subroutes. The data were collected during four days of observation. A truck was followed on one trip from Concord to the Hooksett MRF. The following additional time/motion data were recorded: km in transit to MRF (round-trip) = 54.7; time in transit to MRF (round-trip) = 1.1 hours; and time at MRF = 0.5 hours. The average number of trips to the MFR per day (determined from tipping records) was 2.25.

THE GARBAGE COMPOSITION STUDY

Table 2 gives the results of the Concord composition study. It should be noted that these groups set out 41.7 percent of their RSW for recycling. This is not representative of the whole sample, for two reasons. First, 73 percent of the dwellings in the composition study subsample set out recyclables, but set-out data indicate that 65 percent of the dwelling units in the larger sample set out recyclables each week. Thus there is an overrepresentation of recyclers in the composition study subsample. Second, the sample size is quite small. However, the aggregate composition figures obtained from this study are not affected by the overrepresentation of recyclers in the sample and can be used in further analysis.

Choosing Among Alternative Recycling Systems *(cont'd.)*

TABLE 1. Concord Bag-Based Recycling ProgramTime/Motion Mean Values

	Urban Route	Suburban Route	Rural Route
Stops	705.25	138.75	59.00
(std. deviation)	(3.86)	(6.18)	(4.96)
Time/Stop	11.61	8.81	10.08
(std. deviation)	(1.01)	(1.28)	(0.59)
Time in Motion/Stop	14.72	14.02	33.09
(std. deviation)	(0.44)	(0.94)	(3.50)
Km/Stop	0.05	0.06	0.32
(std. deviation)	(.002)	(.006)	(0.15)

Note: All time is in seconds.

Of the 19 recycling dwelling units, 6 had contaminants (nonrecyclable material) in their recycling bags, which must be dealt with at the MRF. The average number of recycling bags used for each household that set out recyclables was 2.6. Finally, the average weight of the set-out recyclables was 10.84 kilograms. The average for those dwelling units in subroute one was 12.11 kilograms; for those in subroutes two and three, the average was 6.71 kilograms (this is due to the fact that subroute one has a high concentration of multi-family dwellings).

Table 2. Concord Bag-Based Recycling Program Composition Study Aggregate Results

Material	Refuse Set-Out	Recycle Set-Out	Total Set-Out	Percent of Total	Percent Recycled
Glass	13.27	45.56	58.83	12.62	77.4
Plastic	3.77	2.88	6.65	1.43	43.3
Ferrous	3.79	6.67	10.46	2.24	63.7
Aluminum	0.91	3.02	3.93	0.84	76.8
Paper	36.67	136.42	173.09	37.12	78.8
Other	211.90	1.38	213.28	45.74	0.65
Total	270.32	195.93	466.25	100.00	41.7

NOTE: OTHER is all material that is nonrecyclable by Concord's program. Contamination (nonrecyclable material in the recycling set-outs) level is .65 percent. This is subtracted from recycle set-out in order to determine percent recycled. All weights in kilograms. Figures may not add up due to rounding.

Choosing Among Alternative Recycling Systems *(cont'd.)*

THE HOUSEHOLD SURVEY

The survey of households on the Tuesday route contained six objective questions and two open-ended subjective questions. Using those responses, the Concord composition figures, and the New Hampshire per capita daily MSW figure of 1.71 kilograms per person per day (NHDES, 1988), it is possible to determine the average amount of material that is actually recycled each week by the sample households while holding per capita generation constant. The calculated mean set-out (kilograms per capita) includes: glass (1.19), plastic (0.12), ferrous metals (0.19), aluminum (0.06), and paper (3.19). This yields a mean total recyclable set-out for the sample households of 4.75 kilograms per capita per week (standard deviation of 1.40 kilograms).

The household survey provided several important insights into household recycling behavior. The households with school-aged children did not report recycling significantly more (0.05 level) than those households without school-aged children. Thus the recycling education programs in the Concord schools have yet to influence family recycling behavior. The households that reported having used the Concord drop-off program prior to the start of the bag-based program reported a significantly higher per capita recycling behavior than those who had not used the drop-off program prior to the inception of the bag-based system (0.05 level). Households that are located in multi-family units recycle significantly less per capita than do households in single-family units (0.05 level).

The cumulative (households, that participated at least once) monthly household participation rate was 94.1 percent. The average percentage of households setting out recyclables in any week was 82.4 percent. Multiplying the average amount of set-outs per month by the average number of bags used per set-out indicates that households use 6.7 bags per month on average.

With respect to the two open-ended questions, several clear patterns emerged. In response to the question, "If you don't recycle all of each of the above materials, please tell us why," three main reasons were dominant. First, people were confused as to which of the plastics and paper items were accepted. Second, they did not want to spend the time cleaning "messy" bottles and jars. Lastly, they stated that they did not use enough of a material to make a difference. Respondents were also asked to write any comments or suggestions concerning the program; in general, participants were very pleased with the program and would like to see it continued.

MATERIAL COLLECTED

The total amount of RSW collected from the Tuesday route during the pilot project averaged 41.2 metric tons per week. Since 8.98 metric tons were recovered and recycled, the percentage of RSW diverted due to the bag-based recycling program equalled 21.8 percent.

An audit performed on 2,660 kilograms of material received at RCS's MRF from the pilot program provided information concerning the composition of the material diverted for recycling. By using this information, along with the waste

Choosing Among Alternative Recycling Systems *(cont'd.)*

composition figures, it is possible to determine the percentage of each recyclable material that is actually being recycled (Table 3). Due to the fact that residue must be subtracted from the percentage of material brought to the MRF in order to ascertain the true diversion rate, the apparent 21.8 percent diversion rate of the bag-based system is actually better estimated at 20.4 percent.

PROGRAM COSTS

In computing the costs of the Concord bag-based program, several assumptions were made so that results could be generalized to similar bag-based systems. These assumptions were as follows: (1) All equipment was used at a 100 percent utilization rate. This implied that the equipment was in service for some purpose 40 hours per week, 52 weeks per year. Therefore, the equipment charge to the recycling

Table 3. Concord Bag-Based Recycling Program Percentage of Each Material Diverted

Material	RCS Sample Percentage	RCS Sample Percentage	Actual Kilograms*	Possible Kilogram**	Percent Recovered***
Aluminum		1.57	140.72	346.19	40.65
Tin		3.56	319.08	923.19	34.56
Glass					
Clear Glass	10.88				
Green Glass	4.91				
Brown Glass	18.55				
Total Glass		34.34	3,077.89	5,201.21	59.18
Plastic					
HDPE	1.84				
PET	1.35				
Total Plastic		3.19	285.92	589.36	48.51
Paper					
Newspaper	28.08				
Magazines	5.64				
Cardboard	4.96				
Mixed Paper	12.34				
Total Paper		51.02	4,572.92	15,298.64	29.91
Total Recyclables		93.69	8,396.52	22,358.59	37.55
Residue****		6.31	565.56		

   * Equals percentage of sample material multiplied by the average recyclable collection weight of 8.963 metric tons.
  ** Equals material composition percentage multiplied by the average total RSW weight of 41,214 metric tons.
 *** Equals actual kilograms divided by possible kilograms.
**** Residue is nonrecyclable material that is sent to MRF in recyclable collection.
Figures may not add up due to rounding.

Choosing Among Alternative Recycling Systems *(cont'd.)*

program was equal to its hourly depreciation (hourly depreciation = weekly depreciation/40). (2) All labor costs were computed using a straight hourly wage (no overtime), since municipalities were flexible and arranged collection routes so that no overtime was needed. (3) No downtime (breaks, maintenance problems, etc.) was included in the analysis.

Total collection costs of the Concord bag-based system were $912.83 per week. Since the average weight of recyclable material collected during the pilot project was 8.98 metric tons per week, the bag-based program had a collection cost of $101.65 per metric ton. The weekly cost can be broken down into the following major categories: $210.48 (23 percent) toward labor, $189.77 (21 percent) toward truck expenses, $159.08 (17 percent) toward overhead and administration, and $353.50 (39 percent) toward the cost of the bags.

Due to the fact that the recyclable material is being brought to a MRF, the processing cost facing the municipality and revenue received by the municipality were combined and incorporated into the gate fee charged by the MRF. For every metric ton of material it takes in, RCS charges Concord $39.69. Part of this cost is offset by revenue sharing between RCS and Concord from the sale of recyclables. The first $27.56 of recyclable revenue per metric ton is retained by RCS. Any revenue received beyond $27.56 per metric ton is divided equally between RCS and Concord. Revenue from the sale of recyclable material averaged $32.02 per metric ton. Since $2.23 per metric ton went to Concord, the net gate fee averaged $37.46 per metric ton.

The total cost per metric ton to collect and dispose of these recyclable materials was therefore $139.11 (collection cost plus the net gate fee). It should be noted that if households are purchasing the recycling bags through retail channels, $99.74 per metric ton would be borne by the general fund of the municipality while $39.37 per metric ton would be borne by the households directly.

The recycling program must be credited with the cost avoided by not having to dispose of this trash by some other means. Hence, the tipping fee which the municipality would have had to pay must be subtracted to attain the net total cost per metric ton. For this study, we used the tipping fee of $62.84 per metric ton which Durham is charged at the Lamprey Regional Solid Waste Cooperative Incinerator. (Due to Concord's cooperative agreement with the Penacook Incinerator Cooperative, no avoided cost exists for Concord regardless of the amount of material recycled. The tipping charge facing Durham was applied to each system to maintain consistency.) Therefore, the net cost per metric ton of the bag-based recycling system is $76.27. Finally, the efficiency factor of the bag-based system, which is the ratio between the cost per metric ton and percentage of the RSW stream diverted was 76.27/20.4 = 3.739. This efficiency factor is used to compare the curbside-sort and drop-off systems.

EFFICIENCY OF THE BAG-BASED SYSTEM IN THE THREE SUBROUTES

To compare the efficiency of the bag-based system in the different subroutes, the net total cost of the system in each subroute was determined. The cost per met-

Choosing Among Alternative Recycling Systems *(cont'd.)*

ric ton in subroute one was $69.55, $101.29 in subroute two, and $164.50 in subroute three. The percentage of the RSW stream diverted was assumed to be equal at 20.4 for each subroute. Therefore, the efficiency factors of the three subroutes were: 3.40 for subroute one, 4.67 for subroute two, and 8.06 for subroute three. It is clear that the bag-based system is more efficient in urban areas (subroute one) than in suburban (subroute two) or rural areas (subroute three). The efficiency diminished with the collection area's household density.

Curbside-Sort Program

QUANTITY AND COMPOSITION OF RECYCLABLES

The quantity and composition of Durham's recyclable collection was analyzed over 13 weeks. The average weekly weight of material recycled was 9.57 metric tons (Table 4). During the same 13 weeks the weight of RSW collected by Durham's municipal trucks and brought to the Lamprey Cooperative incinerator was 255.73 metric tons, an average of 19.67 metric tons per week. Thus, the Durham curbside-sort program diverted 32.7 percent of the RSW stream. In order to determine the percentage of each recyclable material that was actually recovered, the amount of each material in the total waste stream was determined. This was done by multiplying the composition percentages that resulted from the Concord waste composition study by Durham's weekly RSW stream of 29.24 metric tons. The results are shown in Table 4. The assumption was made that Durham and Concord have similar RSW composition.

A comparison of Tables 3 and 4 shows that Durham recycled a larger portion of each recyclable material than Concord. In fact, according to Table 4, Durham recycled 111.85 percent of the glass in its waste stream. This obviously is not possible and calls into question the use of the Concord composition percentages to determine the amount of recyclable material in Durham's RSW stream. However, this does provide one valuable insight. Durham's impressive diversion rate of 32.7 percent is not only a function of the effectiveness of the recycling program but also a function of Durham's large recyclable material base. This large recyclable base is

Table 4. Durham Curbside-Sort Recycling Program Percentage of Each Material Recovered

Material	Metric Tons Recycled	Possible Metric Tons	Percent Recovered
Metal cans	0.717	0.895	80.11
Glass	4.124	3.687	111.85
Plastic	0.394	0.406	97.04
Paper	4.331	10.848	39.92
All Recyclables	9.566	15.832	60.41

Choosing Among Alternative Recycling Systems *(cont'd.)*

evident, at least with respect to glass, when it is considered that Durham is recycling 14.1 percent of its RSW as glass, while the EPA estimates that only 6.34 percent of the national RSW stream is recyclable glass (EPA, 1990).

TIME/MOTION ANALYSIS

Durham's recycling route covers the entire town in four days every week. Residential cardboard was collected on one day per month using a separate truck. Table 5 contains the time/motion data for both the weekly regular recycling route and the monthly cardboard collection route. A comparison with Table 1 shows that the mean time stopped/stop is significantly higher for the curbside-sort than for the bag-based system.

PROGRAM COST

Using the time/motion data, it is possible to determine the collection costs of the curbside-sort system. In order best to compare the three systems, the same cost assumptions were used for each (labor cost, overhead, administration cost, etc.), except for program-specific costs (truck expenses, container cost, etc.). Since the Durham program consists of one weekly route and one that is run once every four weeks (cardboard) it is necessary to calculate the costs of the system on a monthly basis. The total collection cost of Durham's curbside-sort collection system is $4,747.52 per month. Since the average weight recovered per week is 9.57 metric tons, or 38.28 metric tons per month (including cardboard), the cost per metric ton

Table 5. Durham Curbside-Sort Recycling Program Time/Motion Results

Weekly Regular Recycling Route

Stops	1,042.00
Total Time in Motion (Hours)	6.84
Total Time Stopped (Hours)	13.95
Total Distance in Route (Km)	139.16
Time in Transit to Landfill (Hours)	1.40
Time at Landfill (Hours)	2.02
Distance in Transit to Landfill (Km)	104.42
Mean Time in Motion/Stop (Seconds)	23.64
Mean Time Stopped/Stop (Seconds)	48.20

Monthly Cardboard Route

Stops	138.00
Total Time (Hours)	6.50
Total Distance (Km)	180.06

Choosing Among Alternative Recycling Systems *(cont'd.)*

to collect the material is $124.02. In order to compare the curbside-sort collection system with Concord's bag-based system, it would be preferable to test each system on the same route. Although this is not possible, by adjusting Durham's time and distance of collection by using the average time in motion/stop (15.81 seconds) and distance/stop (0.045 km) of the Concord route, it is possible to put the systems on equal footing with respect to the household density of the route. The total monthly collection cost of the curbside-sort system after the time/motion adjustments are made was $4,303.55. The adjusted collection cost per metric ton was $112.47.

Information concerning the labor time and equipment necessary to process Durham's recyclables was obtained (Hodgdon, 1991). The costs were calculated using the same input prices as used in collection. The two employees work 25 hours per week each, and equipment was nonidle. The total monthly processing cost of the curbside-sort system is $4,208.37, and for 38.28 metric tons processed, the cost is $109.94 per metric ton. (These processing costs may be higher than the national average [Glenn, 1992].) Since the quality of the recyclable material collected is partially a function of the type of recycling system, the revenues generated by each system differ. Therefore, specific market information was obtained for each system. The net total monthly revenue generated from the sale of Durham recyclables was $1,078.65, or $28.19 per metric ton.

The gross total cost per metric ton of the curbside-sort system was therefore $205.77 (collection and processing cost less revenue generated). The adjusted cost per metric ton assumes $11.55 less in collection costs, so that the adjusted gross total cost per metric ton is $194.22. The avoided tipping charge of $62.84 per metric ton must be subtracted from the gross figures above. Therefore, the normal net cost per metric ton was $142.93, and the adjusted net cost per metric ton was $131.38. With a diversion rate of 32.71 percent, the curbside-sort program has an efficiency factor of 4.370. When the cost per metric ton to collect the materials is adjusted, the efficiency factor falls to 4.017.

PARTICIPATION

Durham town officials have estimated that 90 to 95 percent of the residential units in the town participate in the recycling program to some degree. From September 10, 1990, to March 15, 1991 (27 weeks), the average number of containers set out per week was 1,223. The total number of dwelling units in Durham has been estimated at 1,500 by town officials (mostly single-family households). Therefore, the approximate percentage of households setting out recyclables averaged 81.5 percent per week (Hodgdon, 1991).

Concord's Drop-Off Program

MATERIAL COLLECTED

From January to October 1990 (43 weeks), the amount of material brought to the Concord drop-off center averaged 9.73 metric tons per week. The RSW that was incinerated averaged 254.22 metric tons per week. Therefore, of the total

Choosing Among Alternative Recycling Systems *(cont'd.)*

weekly RSW stream of 263.95 metric tons, 3.69 percent was recycled at the drop-off center. The program recovered 6.78 percent of the recyclable material in Concord's RSW stream. Table 6 provides a breakdown of each material, including the metric tonnage of each material collected, the metric tonnage of the material in the waste stream, and the percentage of each material diverted. The figures were obtained in the same manner as the corresponding numbers in the curbside-sort analysis.

COSTS OF THE DROP-OFF SYSTEM

The total cost of running the drop-off center per week was $924.75. Since 9.73 metric tons of material were recovered per week, the cost to run the center was $95.04 per metric ton. The revenue generated by the drop-off program per week was $122.30. or $12.57 per metric ton. Therefore, the gross total cost of the drop-off program per metric ton was $82.47 (operation cost less revenue generated). The avoided tipping fee of $62.84 was subtracted from the gross total cost per metric ton of $82.47 to yield the net total cost per metric ton of $19.63. The efficiency factor for the drop-off program was 5.31.

PARTICIPATION

The survey of Concord residents on the Tuesday collection route can be used to estimate the cumulative participation for the Concord drop-off system. Assuming this route is a representative sample of Concord households, their response indicates that 35.6 percent of the households in Concord used the drop-off center at some time.

Conclusions

Although the curbside-sort program diverted a greater percentage of the RSW than either the bag-based system or the drop-off system, the cost per ton to do so was higher. Of the two curbside collection systems, the bag-based system is more efficient due to its less expensive collection and separation system. The curbside-

Table 6. Concord's Drop-Off Recycling Program Percentage of Each Material Recovered

Material	Metric Tons Recycled	Possible Metric Tons	Percent Recovered
Aluminum	0.124	2.222	5.58
Glass	3.040	33.370	9.11
Tin	0.150	5.870	2.56
Paper	6.460	98.220	6.58
All Recyclables	9.734	143.570	6.78

Choosing Among Alternative Recycling Systems *(cont'd.)*

sort system has a more expensive collection and separation process than the bag-based system for two reasons. First, the curbside-sort program sorts while collecting, so that expensive labor is utilized for a longer period of time than if collection and separation were segregated. Second, the MRF is able to separate the recyclables using a combination of less expensive unskilled labor and capital. A summary of results is given in Table 7.

This difference in separation technology could have an effect on an important characteristic of any recycling program—the quality of the end product. Since both the Durham curbside-sort program and the Concord drop-off program have been successful in marketing their recyclables, the best indicator of quality is the price at which they sold their material. The Concord bag-based system is new and thus has a very short marketing track record. However, data concerning the quality of the bag-based system end product are available. The Concord bag-based program averaged a residue level of 6.31 percent of the collected material, and from the composition study it was determined that 31.6 percent of the dwelling units that recycled set out contaminated bags (Stedge et al., 1992). Recent evidence indicates that the quality of material coming out of the MRF may be lower than originally determined by this study (Walker, 1992). Since a low-quality end product undermines the MRF's ability to market the end product, this could increase the overall cost of the system. However, since this is only one case study, it is impossible to draw definitive conclusions regarding marketability of the system's end product.

The bag-based collection system was more efficient in more densely populated areas. The costs per ton and efficiency factors of the three subroutes both proved to have an inverse relationship to the relative density of a subroute. This indicates that economies of continuity do exist in bag-based recycling and that route density must be considered when forecasting system costs (Stevens, 1978).

Although the bag-based system is more efficient overall, it is important to notice one area in which the curbside-sort system is superior. The annual depreciation per curbside-sort container is $1.46. The annual cost of recycling bags per household is $11.83 (6.8 bags per month at $0.145 per bag). This makes it clear that the curbside commingled bag-based system could be made more efficient if a less expensive recycling container could be used.

Table 7. Summary of Results

	Bag-Based	Curbside-Sort Adjusted	Drop-Off
Net Cost per Ton	$76.27	$131.38	$19.63
Diversion Rate	20.40%	32.71%	3.69%
Efficiency Factor	3.74	4.017	5.31

Choosing Among Alternative Recycling Systems *(cont'd.)*

Study Limitations

Two possible cost savings of recycling have been excluded in the cost calculations of all three recycling systems. First, the possible savings to the municipality in terms of reduced refuse collection were not included. Providing recycling services should result in a reduction in the truck and labor hours needed to collect the regular refuse. Also, the curbside-sort and bag-based systems' cost calculations included the cost of the recycling containers and bags, but if RSW is placed in the plastic recycling containers, less RSW will be placed in regular refuse containers. Thus, there may be a cost savings because fewer regular refuse containers need to be used for refuse disposal.

It is also important to note that the total cost per ton of both the bag-based and curbside-sort systems increased as the 100 percent utilization assumption was relaxed. This increase is due to equipment being depreciated over a smaller total tonnage (assuming the tonnage of material collected per hour is constant). For example, if the equipment used in the bag-based system was utilized only 20 hours per week, the net cost per ton rises from $76.27 under the 100 percent utilization assumption to $88.42 per ton. Therefore, individual municipalities must include any inefficiencies in their cost calculations. Also, the cost calculations in this article are based on single case studies of each program, and thus no claim can be made as to the generality of these results.

This report began with the assumption that since municipalities are recycling due to a concern about the external costs of municipal solid waste disposal, they should strive to minimize their waste disposal costs subject to some minimum level of recyclable material recovery (thus the "efficiency factor calculation"). It must be noted that this article was not a benefit-cost study of recycling. The possible external benefits of recycling (e.g., increased landfill life; decreased air, land, and water pollution) as well as the possible external costs of recycling (e.g., homeowner time and resources spent recycling) were not included in this analysis. These costs must be included in order to estimate correctly the amount of recycling that should take place to minimize the total cost of municipal solid waste disposal.

References

(EPA) U.S. Environmental Protection Agency. 1990. Characterizations of Municipal Solid Waste in the United States: 1990 Update. EPA/530-SW-90-042. EPA, Office of Solid Waste and Emergency Response, Washington DC.

Glenn, J. 1992. Editor, *BioCycle* magazine, Emmaus, Pennsylvania. Personal communication with John Halstead.

Hodgdon, G. 1991. Superintendent of Solid Waste and Water, Department of Public Works, Durham, NH. Telephone interview with John Halstead, November 1991.

(NHDES) New Hampshire Department of Environmental Services. 1988. *Solid Waste Management Plan for New Hampshire.* Concord, NH.

Stedge, G. D. 1991. Bag-Based Curbside Recycling: An Economic Analysis of an Alternative Recycling System. M.S. Thesis. Department of Resource Economics and Development, University of New Hampshire, Durham, NH, pp. 29–34.

Stedge, G. D., J. M. Halstead, and D. E. Morris. 1992. An Economic Analysis of Alternative Recycling Systems. New Hampshire Agricultural Experiment Station Report No. 127. Durham, NH.

Stevens. B. J. 1978. Scale, Market Structure, and the Cost of Refuse Collection. *The Review of Economics and Statistics* 60(3): 438–448.

Walker, T. 1992. Former Technical Assistance Coordinator, New Hampshire Resource Recovery Association. Durham, NH. Personal interview with John Halstead, April 21.

CHAPTER 8

SYNTHESIZING

INTRODUCTION

As you progress through college—regardless of your discipline—you can expect assignments which require you to *synthesize* written materials—or to write a *synthesis*. Each time you integrate information from two or more sources to arrive at your own conclusion, you are synthesizing.

To help you gain a more complete understanding of the word *synthesis*, you might consider the meanings of a couple of familiar, everyday terms that are derived from the same root word (*suntithenai*—Greek for "to put together"). As you probably know, in manufacturing, a *synthetic* material is one that does not appear in nature but is an amalgam of various fibers and chemicals, which results in an entirely new kind of material. Another related word, *synthesizer*, refers to a musical instrument that combines electronic circuitry to create sounds that cannot be made by other instruments or sounds that duplicate the sounds of other instruments. These examples are analogous to the cognitive process of synthesis. Synthesis occurs when two or more things are combined to create something new—whether it be a new idea, a new fabric, or a new sound.

Although the term *synthesis* can be used in various situations, this chapter will focus on the kind of synthesis that results in a written product. Professionals in all disciplines write *syntheses* (note the plural form of the word)—to determine a new solution to a problem, to assess events or processes, to arrive at a new state of knowledge, or perhaps to help themselves become informed about new situations. Because synthesis is important to all professions, instructors devise synthesis assignments—although they rarely call them that—to help students learn more about their field. Often such assignments will ask you to locate sources in the library and integrate them in a "research paper"; in this way, you will gain a more complete understanding of your topic. In other cases, synthesis assignments may ask you to do field research (observing, interviewing, or surveying) and integrate it in some way with your disciplinary knowledge (theoretical concepts, library research, textbook chapters, etc.).

As we have said, research papers are perhaps the most frequent kind of synthesis assignment that you will be expected to do in college; procedures for doing library research will be explained in Chapter 9. The present chapter will focus instead on the skill of synthesis and will offer suggestions for making connections among sources and for organizing those connections into written products.

SAMPLE ASSIGNMENTS

Now that you understand a little about what synthesis is, how pervasive a type of writing it is, and why college instructors assign it, let's examine in more detail some sample assignments from a variety of disciplines. As you will see, synthesis assignments vary. Sometimes library research is involved, and sometimes students must perform field research, observations, or interviews of their own.

Economics Assignment. After familiarizing yourself with the fundamental aspects related to a controversial issue, present and *defend* a particular conclusion in ten to fifteen typed (or word-processed), double-spaced pages. [NOTE: Ten pages is the minimum for this assignment; papers usually average about fifteen pages.]

The issue that you select should be related to any of the topics that we have covered in class; however, you will need to supplement assigned readings and class notes with additional research. The readings you select may come from a range of sources such as newspapers, business periodicals, news magazines, and scholarly books and journals. However, do not rely too heavily on sources written for more "general" audiences; be sure to consult a sufficient number of economic journals (indexed in the *Journal of Economic Literature*).

For this assignment, it is not sufficient to merely report on the solutions that others have proposed; you must evaluate these and propose and justify your own conclusion. In writing your paper, be sure also to examine arguments that challenge your conclusion as well as those that support it; explain why you have accepted arguments in support of your conclusion and rejected the counterarguments.

Because this is a formal writing assignment, you need to be aware of good writing style and to edit your paper carefully. If you use informal footnotes in the body of your text, you should include a bibliography; if you use more complete, formal footnotes, then a bibliography is unnecessary.

Computer Science Assignment. This assignment has three parts: You will (1) write a ten- to fifteen-page paper (double-spaced) on a topic related to software engineering that includes at least seven references (to be included in a bibliography); (2) provide a twenty-minute presentation to the class on material from your paper, using visual aids, demonstrations, and so on, where appropriate; (3) carefully read the papers of *two* of your classmates.

Your paper and your presentation will be evaluated on the basis of their contents and on how effectively they communicate. You will also be responsible for knowing the material from your classmates' papers when you take the final exam.

To provide broad coverage, paper topics will be assigned; however, I will make these selections largely from suggestions I receive from class members. Therefore, the first requirement for this assignment is to hand in brief (1-paragraph) descriptions of *three* advanced topics related to software engineering. Each description should also be accompanied by a list of *three* complete references for sources of information. I will select a topic for you, if possible, from the three that you have submitted.

Environmental History Assignment. As we have discussed in class, the environment—whether natural or developed—can be studied historically. That is to say, the environment can reveal the culture/values of the people who have inhabited it, as well as fortell future possibilities. Select some aspect of the local, or a nearby, landscape and craft a four-to-six page essay that demonstrates how it reveals the culture and/or traditions of the society that surrounds it. What does it suggest about past or current values of the surrounding population? What does it suggest about their aspirations for the future? In addition to informing your essay with assigned readings or class notes, you may wish to interview one or more residents of the community that surrounds the landscape you've chosen. Local records can also be found at the county courthouse and public library.

Literature and Film Assignment. For the past several weeks, we have been reading novels and viewing films that depict images of American young people and of American youth culture. All of these imply what it is (or should be) to be "young," "American," "attractive," "cool" (or not "cool"), and the like. Integrate the information from the materials on reserve at the library or other nonfiction sources of your choice with class notes and discussion, and craft a focused, unified essay that defends a thesis.

Your essay should be approximately four to five pages in length, double-spaced. Although you do not (necessarily) have to quote from the sources you consulted, be sure to reference those that particularly influenced your thinking, using appropriate documentation.

Here are some ideas to get you started in forming a thesis:

1. Are notions such as "Generation X," "Baby Boomers," "Generation Gap" largely fictional? What are some of the illusions about these labels that have appeared in the films and literature we've studied?

2. Most of the people (novelists, screenplay writers, and directors) who depict American adolescents or adolescence are adults. What do films and literature reveal about their past experiences as they perceive or remember them?

3. Several of the essays on reserve present factual information (race, ethnicity, level of income, employment data, etc.) about American adolescents and young adults. To what extent are depictions of young Americans in film and literature "accurate"?

As you can see from reading these samples, synthesis assignments are a very common type of college writing. They require students to become knowledgeable about a body of information from their class readings, from library research, or from additional research of their own. In addition, students who are completing a synthesis assignment typically must not a simply regurgitate what these sources say. They must become knowledgeable enough about their subject to present their own ideas about it—to propose solutions to problems, to offer insight into complex phenomena, to correct misconceptions, or to critique current understandings or actions.

Most of the sample assignments you have just read specifically instruct students to develop their own conclusions about the subjects they research. The Economics Assignment, for example, (to defend a particular conclusion about a controversial issue) directs students to determine their own perspective on their subject. Some assignments include a set of procedures that must be followed, in order to facilitate the construction of a particular kind of synthesis.

As you were reading the sample assignments, however, you may also have noticed that a few of them do not direct students to synthesize the information sources they research. The Computer Science Assignment, for example, requires a paper that includes information from at least seven sources. This assignment, which is typical of many college research paper assignments, does *not* specifically direct students to answer a particular question on their topic, to determine their own opinion on their subject, or to synthesize information in order to develop conclusions. Nor does it caution students to avoid simply summarizing other people's ideas. In our experience, whether or not assignments offer specific directives, most often instructors actually *are* expecting their students to synthesize the information from the sources they have researched. Should you receive an assignment that simply instructs you to research a topic, it's always a good idea to check with your instructor about what his or her expectations are.

The preceding assignments share one additional feature: They all require students to write knowledgeably about information gathered from some resource or resources. Most often synthesis assignments require the integration of library research and class readings. Synthesis assignments may also require students to conduct surveys or interviews of experts or to conduct observations or other field research. In addition, some may require students to synthesize information from their own experiences or from class discussions. The sample assignments indicate the variety of information sources students may be required to synthesize. The Literature and Film Assignment, for example, asks students to synthesize information from assigned course readings, class notes and discussion, movies viewed in class, as well as other published sources found in library research.

One additional matter to keep in mind is a point we will repeat several times in this chapter: Synthesis is not a specialized type of writing. Rather, it is a skill that can be applied to a variety of types of writing. Consequently, synthesis assignments may involve observing, reporting, critiquing, or evaluating—the types of writing we have discussed in earlier chapters. Regardless of the specific *type* of writing you may be directed to produce, synthesis assignments will require you to synthesize information about a topic from a variety of sources in order not simply to reiterate what others have said, but to arrive at your own perspectives or conclusions.

SYNTHESIZING INFORMATION

No matter what sources of information assignments require you to synthesize, you will always face several major challenges. Your instructors (and other readers) will expect you to present disparate information in a unified, focused piece of writing. This expectation, in turn, will require you to think of ways to integrate the information you synthesize, even if the information is contradictory or if the information sources are varied in nature.

Thinking of Your Purpose

One of the major challenges of synthesis writing is that it requires you to blend information from different sources. You must blend data skillfully, or your text will appear disjointed and incoherent to your reader.

To achieve unity, then, effective synthesis writing requires a clear purpose or thesis. If James Helmer, the author of "Love on a Bun," had chosen to string together summaries of *each* of the eighteen sources he lists in his bibliography, his readers would have been both confused and frustrated. Instead, Helmer's thesis— that McDonald's used familial images in its advertising to sell burgers—helped him determine how much of each source to present and where to include this pertinent information.

Because assignments involving synthesis often require writers to integrate a number of disparate sources, determining a unifying thesis can be difficult. Still, a good way to begin this process is to examine assignments carefully because they can provide explicit directives. The Environmental History Assignment in the Sample Assignments section of this chapter, for example, suggests a means of integrating information from disparate sources (assigned readings, class notes, and interviews). It invites the writer to "select some aspect of the local, or nearby, landscape and craft a[n] . . . essay that demonstrates how it reveals the culture or traditions of the society that surrounds it." Such an assignment implies that a successful thesis might describe a specific relationship between the selected aspect of landscape and significant features of the surrounding community, as shown in the following example:

> *For more than a century, citizens of Quail Hollow have valued the process of communal decision making. We know this from extensive historical records that depict. . . . It is not surprising, therefore, that the most important feature of the local landscape is the town square, which surrounds the City Green.*

Although synthesis assignments often provide some guidance about possible unifying theses, this is not always the case. The Computer Science Assignment in the Sample Assignments section of this chapter specifies "a ten- to fifteen-page paper . . . on a topic related to software engineering that includes at least seven references." Assignments of this nature, especially for long end-of-term "research papers" are quite typical. However, for most of these, it would be unwise to string together a series of source summaries. Notice, for example, that in the Computer

Science Assignment, the instructor has said that papers will be evaluated on "the basis of their contents and on how effectively they communicate." It has been our experience that even when instructors don't state outright that they will be evaluating papers on the basis of how well synthesized the writing is, they often do.

When you are assigned writing that requires synthesis and you are uncertain about how to discover a unifying thesis—either because the assignment doesn't provide any guidance or because it provides too many confusing options—it may be helpful to consider possible overall aims for writing. Such a consideration may lead you to discover more focused, defined theses. Theorists and contemporary writing texts often speak of four categories of writing based on aim or purpose: *persuasive, informative, expressive,* and *literary* (or poetic). Although most writing contains elements from more than one of these writing "types," usually one aim or purpose is dominant.

In *persuasive* writing, the writer's goal is to persuade an audience to take action or to adopt a particular point of view. Such writing is characterized by logically presented arguments and counterarguments and supportive detail or example. *Informative* writing emphasizes a body of information. In general, informative writing highlights subject matter and de-emphasizes the author's feelings and attitudes toward it. *Expressive* writing focuses on the writer's experiences, attitudes, and feelings and is often characterized by first-person point of view, narrative passages, and storytelling. In expressive writing, the author may speak solely from his or her own perspective or may take on the role of a spokesperson for a larger group. Finally, in *literary,* or poetic, writing the emphasis is on the language itself. In literary writing, style and structure are important ends in themselves and the crafting of dialogue, imagery, and the like, is vital. Writing that employs synthesis can fall into all four categories, although published academic synthesis writing (technical reports, scholarly articles, reference works, etc.) is most often informative or persuasive.

Although most writing assignments that require you to synthesize information sources will encourage you to produce persuasive or informative writing, you may have some latitude. Expressive writing is increasingly gaining acceptance within colleges and universities, especially within disciplines in which personal experience is considered a valid source of information. Even literary synthesis writing may be appropriate for some assignments—although we suggest discussing a literary approach with your instructor.

In determining a focus or thesis for a piece of writing that requires synthesis, you will find it useful to think about possible overall purposes or aims. Deciding whether you wish to provide information on a topic, persuade readers to adopt a point of view, or express feelings and attitudes may help you see different relationships among your sources and provide you with different options for integrating similar information or reconciling differences. For example, in "The Proper Study of Womankind," Carol Sternhell could have decided to *persuade* her readers that the books were or were not well researched based on various criteria (such as the accuracy with which they described women's studies). She could have chosen to *inform* her readers about the important aspects of women's studies programs and discussed each book in terms of these aspects. Instead, she chose to *express* her feelings about and personal experiences with women's studies programs and to assess each book in light of these feelings and experiences. Whether or not Sternhell toyed with all of these options, the strategy she chose gave her a unique way of integrating her sources into a focused, coherent structure.

 **Activity 1**

Discuss each of the following with your group partners. Prepare a summary of *one* of your discussions for presentation to the class.

"On the Relationship Between Television Viewing and Academic Achievement" is a piece of informative writing. How might Keith Mielke have integrated the *same* sources if he had wanted to craft an expressive essay in which he shared what his own experiences told him about the relationship between television and academic achievement as well as his attitudes toward the work of academic research in this field?

How might James Helmer have integrated the sources within "Love on a Bun" if he had chosen to write a persuasive piece? Imagine several different audiences (advertising executives, consumer advocates, or Burger King executives, etc.). What might he have tried to persuade his audiences to do or believe in each case?

Instead of crafting "A Wife's Story," Bharati Mukherjee might have written an informative essay about how American popular culture shapes attitudes toward people of color or about how American popular culture shapes immigrants' attitudes toward themselves. Imagine these essays. How might the thesis of either essay be expressed? How might each essay be structured? To what extent would the author's voice be present in either text? What kinds of information or documentation would be necessary to support the claims within either essay?

Integrating Sources

Usually the processes of synthesizing information and arriving at a tentative thesis for a synthesis paper occur simultaneously; that is, as you gain knowledge about your materials and begin to see relationships among them, you also will begin to see possibilities for a thesis. It is logical, then, that as you work to determine a tentative thesis for your synthesis essay, you automatically will begin to consider various strategies that you might use to integrate your sources into a unified paper.

As you can see, integrating sources requires careful planning. In synthesis writing, you cannot stop at merely listing your sources and summarizing their contents; instead, your job as a writer is to make clear the *relationships* among sources. You must illustrate how the sources overlap, how they agree, and how they disagree—while providing ample connections and metadiscourse to lead readers to see the relationships you see. Synthesizing in this manner appears throughout the most sophisticated papers; in fact, it is the writer's synthesis itself that informs the thesis or focus of the paper, determines the overall structure, determines the kind and amount of summarizing that will be necessary, and establishes the conclusion.

Assessing Sources. As you might assume, the first major step in preparing to synthesize is to think about and evaluate your sources. If you are synthesizing written texts, this process will include reading the texts critically, underlining important points, and making marginal notations. (For a thorough explanation of how to read a text critically, refer to Chapter 6.)

As you read critically and evaluate sources, you will need to think about their overall validity—and about their relative importance to your topic. The validity of a source has to do with its overall merit, which is determined by its accuracy, the extent to which it is fair and unbiased, and its comprehensiveness. The relative importance of a particular source is determined by how centrally it relates to your thesis and whether it contains information that is essential or only peripheral. Also, some sources are vital because they make an argument that is central to your thesis, as opposed to offering supporting details as examples.

As writers plan a structure for a synthesis paper, they ordinarily do not treat sources equally. Let's say, for example, that you have decided to work with five sources. Perhaps three of the sources offer essentially the same information, but each of the remaining two offers a new perspective on your topic. Rather than devoting an equal amount of space to each of the five sources, you might think about discussing the three similar sources together in one section of the paper and then devote more space to the other two sources, showing, in the process, how they work together to inform your topic. In addition, when you discuss the two sources that offer a new perspective, you may decide to devote more space to discussing one rather than the other because that source appears to be more accurate and comprehensive or because it discusses issues more closely related to your thesis.

Perceiving Relationships among Sources. In crafting synthesis writing, not only do you need to assess the validity and relative importance of each of your sources, but you also need to *think about* how your sources relate to one another. Contrary to what some students might think, the process of synthesis takes place not within the pages of the sources, but within the mind of the writer. Similarities among sources are quite evident when they express like-minded opinions about the same topic. However, this is not always the case. For example, although it is not immediately apparent, you could argue that "A Wife's Story" and "Love on a Bun" both contain information related to the ways in which aspects of American consumer culture shape people's identities and values.

How might you go about discovering such a similarity? While there are no easy ways, in general we recommend detailed note taking. Each time you read a source, jot down as many ideas about it as you can. In fact, brainstorming and the physical act of note taking often jog your thinking processes. It is also helpful to brainstorm again during your second reading of the sources—this time noting all possible topics related to each source. After noting possible topics, you can compare all of your brainstormed lists to see where they overlap. In addition, talking aloud about your ideas—whether to group members, your teacher, or others—often triggers new ideas that help you synthesize your material.

Regardless of the means by which you perceive relationships among sources, you must directly state what those relationships are in synthesis writing. Readers are trained to have certain expectations—and having connections made for them by an author is an important expectation. When connections are omitted from a piece of writing, readers do not attempt to supply them; instead, they become frustrated with whatever they are reading and decide that it doesn't make sense.

If you examine the readings in this chapter, you will see numerous passages that make connections among sources, and thereby help readers to readily understand the authors' points. The following examples illustrate several of the many ways such connections can be made:

> My discomfort is sparked by *The Feminist Classroom,* which seems to endorse exactly the sort of teaching the other books mock . . . . ("The Proper Study of Womankind")

> All three of these books tend to present women's studies as much more uniform than I've known it to be . . . . ("The Proper Study of Womankind")

> Huston et al. (1992), building on work by a task force of the American Psychological Association, reviewed and interpreted a wide range of research on the effects of television . . . . Their general conclusion is consistent with that reached by other social scientists . . . . ("On the Relationship Between Television Viewing and Academic Achievement")

> Moreover, this analysis [of multiple sources] suggests that familial images, when they are adapted to contemporary meanings, continue to carry considerable persuasive force in modern society. ("Love on a Bun")

As you can see, making connections for readers can be handled in numerous ways; the important thing in synthesis writing is to be sure that connections are always explicitly stated.

 **Activity 2**

Together with your group members, gather at least four concrete objects of the same type, such as dolls, fruits, paintings, and so on. Place the objects before you to allow you to compare them. As a group, brainstorm a list of common features or characteristics of the objects you are comparing. Be creative as you think of numerous possibilities.

Activity 3

> Suppose that you and the members of your group have been assigned to write a synthesis essay on three of the readings from this chapter. With the members of your group, brainstorm a list of the features you consider significant about each reading. Then determine what commonalities you see among the three.

Working with Differences

Along with developing an aim or purpose to unify your paper and integrating sources, you will need to think about how to work with various differences among your sources. When you are synthesizing sources of information, you will encounter differences in context and perspective, ranging from factual contradictions to opposing conclusions based on the same information. You will also face the challenge of integrating long-range, heavily documented published research studies with more informal, unpublished observations, interviews, or information learned from class lectures or discussions. You may also confront differences when you use a variety of sources that were intended to serve very different purposes from one another, (e.g., a scholarly research study, an expressive opinion piece, a persuasive proposal, and a fictional representation in a novel or movie).

When differences arise, writers, especially student writers, may be tempted to take what appears to be an easy way out—to ignore any differences among sources and to focus only on similarities or points of consensus. However, merely glossing over differences can construct an unacceptable ethos for a writer. In writing an argument advocating the adoption of a particular recycling system in a community, for example, the writer who glosses over arguments against that system will appear to be biased or uninformed. In addition, ignoring differences among sources may lead a writer to reach a superficial conclusion based on a simplistic understanding of the subject. The result, again, would be to create the impression that the writer was unknowledgable, unintelligent, or unwilling to perform necessary research on the subject. In our experience, the most successful synthesis writing does not ignore or gloss over differences. Rather, in successful synthesis papers, writers find appropriate ways of working with the differences among their sources and of using differences to help them better synthesize their own thesis or focus.

Understanding the Causes. When you work to integrate your sources, it will generally be helpful to identify the kinds of differences that arise and to try to understand their cause. One kind of difference that may arise among sources is a factual discrepancy. In researching a subject, you may find that your sources differ about when an event occurred, who first advocated a proposal, or other matters to which there is seemingly a "correct" or factual answer. In such a situation, you should do additional research to determine "the facts," by using standard research tools like dictionaries and encyclopedias. In addition, newspapers provide reliable sources for determining information about recent events; indexes are available for national newspapers like the *New York Times,* and often indexes are available locally for regional or local newspapers. When additional research does not resolve factual differences, you should try to determine which of your sources are more credible, considering such factors as the background and experience of the authors and the reliability or prestige of the publisher.

An additional kind of challenge you may encounter is when sources reach *different* conclusions about the *same* subject. This is especially the case when some writers stand to benefit by supporting a particular conclusion or have a strong bias on the subject. For example, for years now many physicians and medical researchers have felt—based on research studies—that smoking cigarettes causes various health problems, especially lung cancer. Not surprisingly, researchers whose work is sponsored by large tobacco companies continue to reach a differing conclusion, that smoking does not actually cause health problems. While it is not always possible to recognize what benefits could possibly accrue to the authors or publishers of a particular source, in your own research you may find such information by paying attention to background information about the authors, the journal or publisher, and any agencies that have provided grants to support the research.

Sources may present different conclusions because their authors have training in different backgrounds that leads them to view the subject in particular ways. Suppose that you were writing a research paper to determine causes of the Vietnam war in the 1960s. A specialist in Southeast Asian cultures may support one conclusion about U.S. involvement in Vietnam, an international economist may support another, and a political scientist still another. A writer who takes the time to understand why these authors differ will have a much broader understanding of the topic than one who simply dismisses two conclusions and blindly embraces the third.

In addition, sources may present seemingly contradictory information because of how they define the key terms. One sociological study might conclude that poverty in the city of Lansing is increasing, while another concludes that poverty there is decreasing. These different conclusions may well be due to how the term *poverty* is defined, with one author defining *poverty* as "earning less than the minimum wage" and another defining *poverty* as "qualifying for government assistance such as subsidized housing, Aid to Dependent Children, and food stamps."

A related cause of differences among sources has to do with data collection. Authors may present conflicting information or conclusions because they are relying on different kinds of information. To return to the previous example, the two authors could have reached different conclusions about poverty in Lansing if one author relied primarily on statistics from a variety of government sources—census records, public assistance records, employment bureaus, and the like—while the other relied primarily on personal observations at a local shelter for homeless people, on interviews with people living in subsidized housing, and on information gathered from local social workers. Recognizing that authors' beliefs are based on different sources of information can help a writer develop a fuller understanding of the subject.

Besides differences that arise from matters such as an author's background, definitions, and methods of data collection, differences may arise because authors hold different opinions on a particular subject. As obvious as this statement sounds, it's important to note that when a subject is both complex and significant, people will disagree about it. Suppose, for example, that in the class Biology in Contemporary Society, you read several articles on biomedical engineering, which discussed such procedures as in vitro fertilization, using fetal tissue for treating brain disorders, and cloning rain forest plants for producing cancer medications. The authors whom you read—like other people in American society—would undoubtedly differ in their opinions about the ethics of some or all of these procedures. Such disagreement is not simply a result of lack of information, ignorance, or unethical behavior among those on one side. Rather, disagreement may result when equally informed and concerned people hold differing convictions about a controversial issue. In synthesis writing, it's far better, then, to acknowledge such differences of opinion than to pretend that they do not exist.

Finally, another kind of difference can arise when writers try to synthesize sources that have been created to accomplish very different purposes. An expressive piece of writing such as an editorial from a newspaper usually doesn't provide background information on a subject. An informative chapter in a textbook may present information in a way that seems balanced or objective, but usually won't express an opinion. A critique such as a book review may present a well-supported and seemingly undeniable conclusion about the source it critiques while omitting information that might be important to understanding the subject as a whole. In general, then, when you recognize differences among your sources, it is often helpful to try to identify the purpose of each source.

Achieving a Resolution. In addition to understanding the reasons *why* sources may differ from one another, writers must be able to unify them in order to develop a synthesis. Actually, resolving *the differences themselves* is not necessary, and is in many cases impossible. However, in order to construct a well-written synthesis paper, writers need to find a way of unifying diverse and even conflicting sources in order to identify a tentative thesis and craft a cohesive paper. It may be helpful initially to begin by unifying the sources with respect to you—to your beliefs, opinions, growing knowledge of the subject, or experiences. That is, you can consider the extent to which you agree with each of the sources, the extent to which you learn from each of the sources, and the extent to which your experiences correlate with those reported in your sources. Taking notes or making a chart to indicate such relationships as you perceive them will be helpful.

Whatever your personal perspectives on your sources and your subject, however, the primary principle to keep in mind is the overall purpose of the synthesis paper itself. In working toward a tentative thesis and overall approach, think about the general aim or purpose you want your paper to serve. Doing so will help you determine what information from your sources is most relevant and decide what aspects of your notes should be emphasized in your paper. In short, the overall purpose serves as a unifying element for the paper.

To return to our discussion of overall purposes for writing, each of the four major aims has distinctive unifying elements. In *informative* writing, the thesis itself and the information provided are highlighted, as in the essay "Love on a Bun." The opinions and voice of the writer are ordinarily much less important in this kind of writing than information about the subject. In fact, the voice of the writer may be muted or even absent, creating the appearance of objectivity. In *persuasive* writing, on the other hand, the opinion of the writer is central, along with the beliefs of the intended audience. Emphasized are the arguments and supporting evidence that are presented, as in Keith W. Mielke's "On the Relationship Between Television Viewing and Academic Achievement." Ordinarily the voice of the writer is present and distinctive in persuasive writing. In a similar way, *expressive* writing stresses the voice of the writer. However, unlike persuasive writing, there is little attention to argument and evidence; rather, expressive writing focuses on expressing the experiences, feelings, moods, values, and beliefs of the writer in a distinctive way. For an example, you might think of the presence and distinctiveness of the voice of Carol Sternhell in "The Proper Study of Womankind."

Finally, *literary* writing is unified by stylistic elements in the writing, such as the way a story ends and begins; mood and tone; and devices such as metaphor, repetition, and imagery. The voice of the writer may be present, as with Bharati Mukherjee's "A Wife's Story," or absent, as in some types of fiction. Literary syntheses can be quite effective pieces of writing; however, because college assignments most often require informative or persuasive writing, we recommend that you consult with your instructor before attempting to write a literary synthesis.

Activity 4

Review the essays "Love on a Bun" and "On the Relationship Between Television Viewing and Academic Achievement" in the Readings sections of this chapter. Then together with your group partners, read and discuss the following questions about these essays. Take notes on your discussion and make a brief report of your answers for the rest of your class.

1. James Helmer, in his essay "Love on a Bun," uses a variety of different written information sources on two major topics: historical information about families in the United States and advertising information about McDonald's. What is Helmer's thesis? Is it directly stated in the essay? If so, where? How are various parts of the essay unified by the thesis?

2. Keith W. Mielke synthesizes many sources that report differing opinions or conclusions on the same subject in "On the Relationship Between Television Viewing and Academic Achievement." Note that Mielke does not simply ignore differences in opinion among his sources; rather, he makes such differences a central part of his argument. What is Mielke's thesis? Where does he state it? How does the thesis unify his survey of conflicting opinions and conclusions about his subject?

Activity 5

Using the same set of concrete objects that you brought to class for Activity 2, brainstorm with your group a list of *differences* among the objects. As before, put the objects where you can see them as you brainstorm, and take notes to use in the rest of this activity.

Next, assume that you and your group have to write a paper about your set of objects. Together, brainstorm a list of several possible thesis statements for that paper, using your lists of differences and similarities (Activity 2). You should generate as many statements as possible that could offer a way to unify some of the similarities and differences from your lists.

Choose one thesis from your group that seems most promising as a way to unify the similarities and differences of your objects. As a group, brainstorm how you could use the *same* thesis (with some variations) to develop a variety of *different* papers. Be as creative as possible here, and take notes on your brainstorming.

Finally, when you have a list of at least ten different papers you could write that would develop your group's thesis, analyze your list. What different kinds of papers did you think of? What overall aim or purpose would each paper develop—that is, would the aim be informative, persuasive, expressive, or literary?

WRITING A SYNTHESIS PAPER

While you may think that writing a synthesis paper sounds like an overwhelming task, you will find that it is actually quite manageable—that is, if you break the task into parts and allow yourself ample time to complete each part satisfactorily. We cannot stress strongly enough that to write successful synthesis papers—even very short ones—you will need to employ careful planning and time management. In this section, we offer guidelines for working through the processes of writing a synthesis paper. These processes are critical reading and assessing sources; arriving at a synthesis; structuring the paper; and revising it.

Critical Reading and Assessing Sources

The first and most fundamental part of writing a synthesis paper that makes use of written sources is to critically read and assess the sources you have chosen. This part of the process simply cannot be completed hurriedly: Critical reading and assessment of sources require careful attention and thought.

Preparing Your Sources. Preparing sources in order to make them easily usable is a part of the process that you may not even have thought about; however, there are a number of important recommendations to follow.

On occasion, a teacher may provide the written sources that you are to use in constructing a synthesis paper; usually, though, you will be required to locate your own sources, in the library or elsewhere. Because locating sources can take a lot of time, teachers ordinarily assign synthesis papers well in advance of their due date. Even if the due date is far off, we recommend that you begin a synthesis paper assignment at the time you receive it, because locating sources is not always the smooth process you would like it to be. Sometimes, for example, you will find that sources you would like to use are not available in your library, so you will need to order them through the Inter-Library Loan program; in this case, your research process already has been delayed. At other times, you may have chosen or been assigned a topic on which little has been written; again your process might be delayed as you get advice from librarians, your teacher, or others. Sometimes your most useful sources may be found not in the library but in interviews or question-naires you do yourself. Obviously, working with such sources will take extra time. The bottom line is this: Get started early.

Assessing Your Sources. As you locate sources and note them for later use, you will, of course, be making some decisions about their usefulness to your topic. However, after you have gathered and prepared the sources that you think you might use, it is necessary to do a more careful and complete assessment.

In assessing your sources, you will probably first want to consider the number you have found. We recommend that you skim the sources, eliminating any insub-stantial materials that provide little information. You will want to keep the "meati-est" sources—those that say a lot about your topic and offer the most interesting insights on your particular slant.

On the other hand, if you haven't been able to locate a sufficient number of sources to work with, it is time for you to discuss with your teacher the best way to proceed. Perhaps the problem is that topic is very recent or so narrow that not much has been written on it. In such situations, your teacher probably will be able to help you find ways to broaden or modify your topic to make it workable for you.

Another important consideration when you assess sources has to do with their currentness. For some topics (e.g., AIDS), it is necessary that your sources be as up-to-date as possible because information on the topic is changing almost every day. On the other hand, for other topics (e.g., historical figures), currentness is less important, and in fact, some of your most useful sources may have been written long ago. For some topics (tracing a trend or development, perhaps), your most use-ful sources might come from a variety of time periods. It is important that you think carefully about the currentness of your sources because instructors often assign syn-thesis papers to determine their students' familiarity with current works in their discipline or profession.

Finally, you will need to assess which types of sources are preferable for your particular topic or assignment. Sometimes students think that encyclopedias pro-vide quick and reliable information, so they want to use them as sources. However, while encyclopedias provide good background coverage, they ordinarily are not useful sources in a synthesis paper; they merely provide a starting point, not com-prehensive coverage or evaluation. Teachers may provide direction about the type of sources they prefer you to use. If you look at the sample Economics Assignment in the Sample Assignments section of this chapter, you will see that the teacher has instructed students not to rely "too heavily on sources written for more 'general' audiences" and instead has directed them to consult economics journals. Ordinarily for college assignments, students are expected to use scholarly sources rather than more popular or general ideas.

Reading Critically. Having prepared and assessed your sources, you are ready for the important task of reading them critically. You will need to allot quite a bit of time for this task because reading texts *critically* entails time and effort. Preparation for a synthesis assignment, in fact, generally demands that you read each source three times.

You should read a source the first time merely for comprehension, in order to understand the author's overall message. During the second reading, you should assess the text more carefully, considering its validity and how it relates to your topic. This time as you read, you should note information that is important to your topic and write down comments and notes on separate sheets of paper or note cards, jotting down page numbers and sources you have used. You also should notice each time a potential major topic emerges and record information on this topic on a separate sheet of paper (one sheet for each topic). (For more complete directions on note taking during the process of critical reading, you can refer to Chapter 6.)

During the third reading, you will be ready to begin synthesizing information. As you read this time, you should think about your sources all at once, rather than separately. With all sources in front of you, you should read to notice where ideas agree—where they conflict—or where they overlap. Although you took notes on separate sources during the second reading, you should plan to take notes again during this reading, this time keeping track of how the sources relate to one another.

 **Activity 6**

Let's say that you have been given an assignment that requires you to use readings from the end of this chapter to write a synthesis paper on the American Dream. With your group, select two readings that incorporate the topic in some way. You might define the American Dream and decide whether or not it really exists—or whether it exists only for certain groups of people. Alternatively, you might discuss the essential components of the American Dream—or focus on changes that have occurred in people's conception of it. After your group has chosen the pieces you will work with, you should read them independently—the first time for comprehension and the second time for underlining and making marginal notations. When your group members have become familiar with the materials, you should meet to discuss how they relate to each other and what they have to do with the American Dream. Write out common themes, list points of similarity, and plan strategies that could be used in a synthesis paper.

Creating a Synthesis

As you work at critical reading and assessment of your sources, you will also be thinking about how to unify your various notes and ideas in order to craft a cohesive essay. In order to construct your own synthesis of your ideas and sources, work on two primary areas: seeing patterns in your readings and notes and writing a tentative thesis. At this point, you should reread your assignment. Look for any questions that your instructor has directed you to answer. As well, look for any topics or issues to be addressed in the paper; these can help you identify patterns and craft your working thesis.

Seeing Patterns. You will probably have some initial ideas for synthesizing while you are critically reading your sources, writing your notes, or making informal charts. However, it is especially important to remember that the process of synthesis takes place inside your head, not on the pages of your sources. Thus after reading and taking notes on your sources, you need to allow time to look through your notes and think about what your sources have to say about your topic. We suggest that you start by assembling all your materials: copies of your sources, all the notes you have taken, and any materials from your class that might be relevant, such as class notes, textbooks, and a copy of your assignment.

When you have assembled your materials, you should review them to familiarize yourself with their content. Reviewing your notes might seem like an unnecessary step, but you should remember that the various stages of synthesis writing require much time to complete. Consequently, you may have materials that you have not looked at for several weeks. As well as refreshing your memory, reviewing your materials now will help you to see all of your information at one sitting and, thus, assist you in noting patterns and relationships among them.

At this point, we suggest that you use your notes to make several charts. Making charts is an easy and efficient way to summarize the content of your sources and to represent visually the emerging patterns and relationships among them. Charts can also be useful for showing relationships among diverse types of sources—interviews, research studies, surveys, arguments, and the like. To determine what kinds of charts to make, you should think about what similarities and differences you see across your sources, connections and contradictions among them, as well as common themes or any other patterns. Your own knowledge of your subject and sources should give you additional ideas about what sort of information to summarize in your charts; you should also make charts to show what your sources say about topics, issues, or questions specified in your assignment. Tables 8–1 and 8–2 are examples of two charts a student might make if working on the Literature and Film Assignment from the Sample Assignments section of this chapter.

From these two charts, you can see a particular pattern emerging among the sources. More general and popular-culture-oriented sources, such as the movie, *Time* article, and film and popular culture journals, generally portray members of Generation X in one way. More specialized and research-study-oriented sources, such the sociology journal, census information, and government studies, generally portray them in a different way. Based on the charts and your notes, you might

Table 8–1: Popular Stereotypes About Generation X'ers

SOURCE	Sees X'ers as whiny	Sees X'ers as self-indulgent	Sees X'ers as upper-middle-class
Reality B/movie	X	X	X
Time magazine	X	X	X
Smith/sociology journal			
Evans/film journal	X		X
Chin/government study			
Gonzalez/pop culture journal		X	X
Schwartz/government study			
Census info			
Gen X/book	X	X	X

speculate that the more popular sources perpetuate stereotypes that don't reflect the reality described by the more scholarly and presumably more reliable sources.

To make such charts, use several big sheets of paper. List your sources vertically on the left-hand side of one sheet, using the authors' names or a short form of the title. It will also be helpful to note briefly what kind of source each one is (an interview, survey, book review, etc.). Next, list the themes, patterns, issues, and so forth,

Table 8–2: Research Information About Generation X'ers

SOURCE	X'ers diverse ethnically	X'ers diverse in class	X'ers self-supporting
Reality B/movie			
Time magazine			
Smith/sociology journal	X	X	
Evans/film journal			
Chin/government study	X		X
Gonzalez/pop culture journal			
Schwartz/government study	X	X	X
Census info	X	X	
Gen X/book			

horizontally across the top. Draw lines to create grids, as in playing tic-tac-toe. Then fill in each of the grids with relevant information summarized from your sources. It may be useful to make charts with very large grids so that you can summarize more information or add quotes or details from each source. You should make several charts—one summarizing what position each source holds on a controversial issue, one showing similarities among sources, another showing differences across them, another highlighting common themes, and so forth. When you are working on a controversial topic, or when a particular issue seems to be controversial across your sources, it may be helpful to make a simple two-grid chart listing each of the sources and showing the position of each source (pro or con). If you write on the computer, you can easily make several charts by printing multiple copies with your sources listed on them.

Making charts is especially helpful when you need to integrate information from several different kinds of sources—interviews, movies, surveys, research studies, observations, and so forth. With some of these sources, the information may seem to be less coherent, more specialized, or otherwise hard to connect to your other sources. In such cases, you will need to be flexible and to do more interpretation.

Finally, charting can help you identify whether you need to do any kind of additional research. Your charts may help you determine whether you need to reread a source to fill in gaps in your notes on it, to do further library research or reading to gather additional information, to ask a follow-up question to clarify the beliefs of a person whom you interviewed, or to conduct an additional observation to check for crucial details you did not note initially.

Deciding on a Working Thesis. The ultimate goal of seeing connections among your sources is to construct a central point or main idea around which to develop your synthesis paper—in short, to write a tentative thesis statement. You may be tempted to develop the first thesis that comes to mind, or the one that seems most obvious to you in your initial survey of your sources and notes. Yet many student writers encounter problems in drafting synthesis papers when they have a poorly conceived main idea, when they try to argue a point they have no evidence to support, or when they fail to develop the most interesting, controversial, or unexpected aspects of their subjects. Thus, we recommend that you spend some time coming up with several possible thesis statements and evaluating them for their workability.

Return to the Literature and Film Assignment about the portrayal of Generation X in various media. Your charts may initially suggest a possible working thesis: *Stereotypes about Generation X'ers are inaccurate.* While this thesis may be promising, you should try to think about others that you could develop given your sources, ideas, and assignment. Through using clustering, you might develop a variety of statements such as these:

- *Generation X is a unique generation characterized by four key qualities.*
- *Generation X is a media myth that in no way reflects the reality of the lives of young adults today.*
- *Unflattering and inaccurate portraits of today's young people as "Generation X" are the creation of aging Baby Boomers, unhappy about their own lost youth.*

Whatever possible working thesis statements you create, you will need to consciously evaluate them to determine which ones will work best. One of the most important guidelines to keep in mind is the assignment or the instructor's expectations or requirements. In the case of the Literature and Film Assignment, students are specifically directed to "defend a thesis," suggesting that an argumentative stance is most appropriate. Three of the preceding thesis statements have an argumentative stance, so they should fit the assignment. However, the other possible statement, *Generation X is a unique generation characterized by four key qualities,* is more expository than argumentative and, thus, may not fit the assignment. If you were particularly interested in developing that thesis, you should check with your instructor to determine his or her expectations. Alternatively, you could revise the statement to make it more clearly defend a thesis: *While media stereotypes are repetitive and unidimensional, Generation X is actually a unique generation characterized by four key qualities.*

In addition, you should seriously consider only those thesis statements that you can support or develop with available sources. In evaluating your working thesis statements, consider the amount of information needed to support each one. Do you have sufficient information on all necessary points, or do you need to do additional research? To return to the previous examples, consider the last statement: *Unflattering and inaccurate portraits of today's young people as "Generation X" are the creation of aging Baby Boomers, unhappy about their own lost youth.* This thesis sounds promising, yet to support it, a writer would need to establish who perpetuates X'er stereotypes as well as what their motives are. If reliable sources offer solid evidence about the motives of people promoting stereotypes about Generation X, this thesis may be workable. However, without such information, a writer would be able to offer only weak, unsubstantiated speculation.

Two other guidelines can help you choose among your working thesis statements. Consider each statement in terms of its relevance to course goals. That is, are some of your possible thesis statements more closely related to the content of a course or discipline? For the previous examples of thesis statements, those most relevant for the Literature and Film course might be those that draw attention to media portrayals of the subject. A second guideline to remember is your own interest. If, in light of your evaluation of several working thesis statements, you find that there are two equally strong possibilities, choose the one that you are more interested in. Your own interest in supporting your thesis will help motivate you to do well and enjoy your work.

 **Activity 7**

As a group, continue your work from Activity 6. Use your notes, copies of the two readings you selected, and your discussion to construct several charts to show connections among the readings. To determine appropriate categories for your charts, remember that the general focus of the assignment is the American Dream. Think of common themes, controversial issues, similarities, and differences. Fill in each grid with relevant information, details, or quotes from your two readings.

When your charts are finished, together with your group brainstorm several possible thesis statements for a synthesis paper on the American Dream. One person should record all your group's ideas. When you have come up with several possibilities—at least five—evaluate each of them according to the guidelines previously suggested. What classes or disciplines would each thesis be most appropriate for? What kinds of information would you need in order to develop each thesis? Which theses would be most interesting to write on? If you were really writing a synthesis paper on the American Dream, which thesis would you select? Why?

Structuring Synthesis Writing

Once you have decided on a working thesis, you should plan an overall structure for your piece of writing. However, because synthesis is a skill that is required for many different kinds of writing, it is difficult to offer specific advice about a particular organizational structure. That is, a variety of structures may be appropriate, depending on the nature of an assignment you receive or the type of writing you are required to produce. Nevertheless, as you think about structuring a piece of synthesis writing, you will inevitably face two challenges: how to build an effective overall structure for your text and how to create connections between and within the major portions so that your writing becomes unified and coherent.

Overall Structure. Ironically, some of the best advice we can offer about structuring synthesis writing is to describe what type of organization to *avoid*. We have observed that inexperienced writers often rely on *copied structure* when they produce synthesis writing. *Copied structure* is a strategy writers sometimes use in initial drafting because it allows them to simplify their task by using (or "copying") the structure of whatever they are writing about to organize a text. We do not wish to imply that having a text reflect the structure of the information it includes is *never* appropriate. However, copied structure often obscures important relationships. As an example, let's suppose you were writing a review of a book that had *five* major chapters. Your first (but not your final) draft of such a review might have *five* parts, each devoted to a discussion of a chapter. A review about a book that has several major strengths and weaknesses should be organized to highlight those strengths and weaknesses. It is unlikely that a chapter-by-chapter organization would accomplish that goal effectively.

When a writer uses copied structure within synthesis writing often the overall organization of a text is determined by the number of sources the writer used. That is to say, synthesis writing exhibits copied structure if each major part of a text is devoted to a discussion of a different source. An essay about a controversial issue that contained information from *four* sources would exemplify copied structure if it were divided into *four* parts, with a discussion of the arguments from each source presented within *each* part. A research paper about fad dieting would evidence copied structure if *five* sources were used and if the paper were divided into *five* major parts, each one discussing a separate source.

A good rule to remember is that regardless of how many sources a piece of writing employs, its structure should reflect whatever points the writer thinks are significant. If a writer's intention is to explore the growth of fad dieting in the United States and this growth occurred in *four* major phases, then the paper should be divided into *four* main parts (one devoted to each phase), plus an introduction and a conclusion. The point is that although an early draft of synthesis writing might be structured to reflect the sources it includes, a finished, reader-friendly draft should employ some other means of organization.

As we have said, it is difficult to offer specifics about a particular form or structure for writing that involves synthesis because such writing manifests itself in so many ways. Still, we do recommend that you consider your *purpose* or aim for writing as you think about possible structures because informative, persuasive, and expressive writing often make use of characteristic organizational patterns. These types of writing—especially informative and persuasive writing—are also routinely assigned within a large variety of courses within many colleges and universities.

Informative writing tends to emphasize subject matter, and the nature of the subject matter may suggest possibilities about the arrangement of material. If, for example, a process or event is being described within a text, it may be appropriate to structure the text according to the steps or stages within the process or event. If an object (or group of objects) constitute the subject matter, a text may be usefully organized to reflect the significant features or aspects of the object(s). James Helmer's "Love on a Bun" combines both of these approaches. The first part presents discussions of several important *aspects* of the historical and cultural contexts that set the stage for McDonald's successful campaign. Then the essay describes the *progression* of that campaign. This description begins with an explanation of why McDonald's was able to "enter the 1980's in solid control of the fast food industry," proceeds through an analysis of the successful campaigns of the 1980s, and ends with a critique of the corporation's current advertising practices.

In contrast to informative writing, which highlights information or subject matter, persuasive writing relies on reasoning and example to convince readers to act or to adopt a particular point of view. It is not unusual, therefore, to encounter persuasive writing that is organized by argument (and counterargument) or example. In our experience, college students most often structure persuasive writing to reflect their arguments, and this is usually appropriate, even if the writing synthesizes information from several different sources. The structure of academic writing whose primary purpose is to persuade may reflect a series of arguments (and counterarguments), but this isn't always the case. In "On the Relationship Between Television Viewing and Academic Achievement," Keith Mielke challenges the accusation that television lowers the academic achievement of children, arguing that the claim is oversimplified, perhaps even unfounded. Essentially, the substance of Mielke's argument is presented in two parts: One part discusses the source of the "false" charge that he challenges, and one part presents a series of examples (evidence) that suggest a much more complex relationship between television and academic performance.

Expressive writing, though a less common form of academic writing, is becoming a more acceptable option within various disciplines. Because expressive writing emphasizes an author's attitudes, feelings, or experiences, it can be structured chronologically, in order to highlight major events within the writer's life that led to a particular insight or conclusion or to reflect the sequence of actions within one important occurrence. Expressive writing can also be structured in other ways; it can, for example, be structured to reflect the writer's progression of thoughts on various related topics. "The Proper Study of Womankind," although it is a piece of expressive writing, assesses three books on the basis of their accuracy in depicting women's studies. Its structure, therefore, has chronological elements as well as elements that reflect the author's reactions to the works she reviews.

Integrating Sources Skillfully. Synthesis writing, because it can contain information and opinions from a variety of sources, requires extra care with respect to structuring. Although a well-designed overall structure is important, so too are connections within and between paragraphs. These connections are vital in helping readers understand the nature of what they are reading (e.g., background information, an argument in favor of a central point, or an example that supports an argument) and how it contributes to the overall purpose or aim of the paper.

In general, when writers wish to make relationships or connections between material explicit, they use metadiscourse, which, as you know, is a type of writing that helps readers follow a text more easily. Metadiscourse, particularly in combination with headings, reinforces the overall structure within a piece of writing because it helps readers recognize the major parts and understand how these parts fit together. Notice, for example, how James Helmer's "Love on a Bun" employs metadiscourse to inform readers of the overall purpose: "This essay examines McDonald's television commercials broadcast in the 1980's to show how they connected to the cultural construct 'family.' " Helmer also uses metadiscourse to identify important segments within the text and to explain how they function: "To understand McDonald's great success it is necessary first to understand why Americans consume so much fast food of all kinds." The preceding sentence begins the part of the essay that provides readers with important historical information and follows the heading, **The Historical and Cultural Context of American Fast Food.**

Within most informative writing, metadiscourse plays an important role in reinforcing overall structure. However, in synthesis writing, metadiscourse is also important in helping readers see how different types of information fit together. In the previous example, the metadiscourse reinforces the overall structure of the text, but it also lets readers know that they are being given background information about American history and culture that is necessary for them to understand the success of McDonald's advertising campaign. In addition to helping readers recognize and understand the relevance of background information, metadiscourse can be helpful by informing readers that they are about to encounter a review of one or more sources. Within "On the Relationship Between Television Viewing and Academic Achievement," for example, Mielke informs his readers that he will summarize the results of some representative overviews of research in the text that follows: "Five of the key overviews will be briefly cited here . . . to illustrate the nature of the evidence that we do have about television and academic achievement." Metadiscourse—particularly when it employs the words *for instance* or *for example*—can also let readers know that they are being provided with one or more examples or pieces of evidence to support a main point.

Although metadiscourse can manifest itself in many ways, sometimes its function helps determine the forms it takes. As stated previously, when used to introduce examples or evidence, metadiscourse usually employs words such as *for example, for instance,* or related phrases. Because synthesis writing often presents readers with information from many sources, metadiscourse such as "An even stronger argument is made by . . . " or "Jones's evidence is corroborated by still other . . . " lets readers know that they are being given additional supportive evidence and examples. Words and phrases such as *However, Although, In contrast,* and *On the other hand* generally precede metadiscourse that introduces sources that contradict views presented earlier, for example: "Although many environmentalists agree that . . . , dissenters argue. . . ." Finally, when writers want to clarify the relationship between events that are presented chronologically, they often use metadiscourse that calls attention to time. Carol Sternhell uses this type of metadiscourse during her discussion of her past experiences with women's studies and feminism: "As a grad student in literature at Stanford University in the mid-1970's, . . . "

As with form, the placement of metadiscourse also depends, in part, on its function. Metadiscourse often comes at the beginning of a paragraph so that audience members will understand how to read and interpret any information or examples with which they are provided. Metadiscourse at or near the beginning of a paragraph orients readers and helps them form appropriate expectations about what they are to read. Metadiscourse at the end of a paragraph can provide readers with a summation of preceding material, reiterate a generalization, or make an interpretation explicit. Finally, metadiscourse found within paragraphs usually functions to help readers understand the proper relationship between what precedes and follows it. Such connective metadiscourse can help smooth the transition between a generalization and one or more illustrative examples or related subtopics. Metadiscourse within paragraphs can also provide a link between similar (or contrastive) examples, as shown in the first two paragraphs of Keith Mielke's essay. In paragraph 1, Mielke says, "Two puzzling questions keep nagging. . . ." In the two sentences that follow, he uses the words *First* and *Second* so that the reader can easily identify their contents as descriptions of the *two* puzzling questions. The next paragraph begins with the assertion that the popular press criticizes television. Following this assertion, the second sentence begins with the phrase "To pick just one recent example, . . . " Although metadiscourse within paragraphs often manifests itself in single words or brief phrases, it is, nonetheless, very important in helping readers comprehend and integrate the information in a text.

 **Activity 8**

Examine "Love on a Bun: How McDonald's Won the Burger Wars." How is the essay structured? Locate the thesis statement (statement of purpose). What are the major parts of the essay? In what way is evidence used to provide structure? Then examine "The Proper Study of Womankind." Describe the overall structure of this essay. Is there a statement of purpose? If so, where does it occur? What are the major parts or divisions of the essay? How does Sternhell use time (past, present, and future) to structure the essay? [NOTE: As you examine the structure of both essays, you might imagine how they would have been organized if either author had merely stitched together summaries of each of their sources.]

Share your analyses with your group partners. Do you agree about how each essay is structured? If not, how do you account for your disagreements?

 **Activity 9**

Refer to Activities 6 and 7, in which you began to think about how you would write a synthesis essay using two of the readings from this chapter. You have already performed a critical reading of the two essays you selected and located common themes and points (Activity 6); you have also created a chart in which you represented these commonalities and used this chart to craft a tentative working thesis (Activity 7).

Try now to outline a detailed plan or structure for your synthesis essay. Given your working thesis, what would be the major parts of your essay? What arguments, examples, evidence, events, and so forth would you include in each part? If possible, try to craft an opening sentence for each of the major parts of your essay. Share your plan with your group partners.

 **Activity 10**

Together with your group partners, carefully examine at least three of the readings in this chapter for examples of metadiscourse. Locate metadiscourse at the beginning and end of paragraphs or major parts (or sections) of each essay. (If one or more of the essays you select use headings, comment on how these interact with the textual metadiscourse.) Describe the function of this metadiscourse; that is, what does it do? Also locate metadiscourse *within* paragraphs and describe how it functions. What type of relationship does it create between the text that comes before and after it?

Revising Synthesis Writing

For synthesis writing to be effective, the relationship between the sources that it integrates must be clear. Therefore, although crafting a careful, detailed plan may help you produce a substantial first draft, we suggest that you revise synthesis writing several times before turning it in, in order to ensure that your text will be coherent and well structured and that quotes, paraphrases, and summaries are integrated appropriately.

Clarifying Structure. One of the challenges that synthesis writing presents to writers is deciding how much of their sources to include within a text. Clearly, a five-page synthesis essay that contains information from 4 ten- to fifteen-page sources can't reiterate everything from each of those sources. Moreover, the point of synthesis writing is to integrate a variety of information into a text that expresses a purpose *chosen by the writer.* That is to say, effective synthesis writing should not be dominated by source material; source material should merely emphasize, clarify, or substantiate the information, argument, or experience presented by the author. Still, it has been our experience that apprentice writers—in their zeal to include lots of sources—often allow these sources to take over their papers.

In revising synthesis writing, then, it is wise to examine a draft to determine how much text is devoted to quotes, paraphrases, or summaries of source material. One easy way to accomplish this to apply the "vertical line" test that we described earlier in Chapter 6. As a general rule, no more than 25 percent of a text should be devoted to quoting, paraphrasing, or summarizing material from sources. The majority of synthesis writing, then, should discuss, interpret, or draw conclusions about source material, rather than merely present it again in one form or another.

Another good way to ensure that reiterated source material doesn't dominate synthesis writing is to check for copied structure. Quite often copied structure and excessive quoting, paraphrasing, and summarizing go hand in hand because a text that is structured according to sources tends to overemphasize their contents. In assessing a draft, then, should you detect an overabundance of source material or copied structure, restructure your text so that it reflects the points you wish to make and replace or augment summary with appropriate examples, description, or discussion.

Paraphrasing, Summarizing, and Quoting. No matter how much attention you devote to representing and integrating source material as you write, it is prudent to check over how you have included your sources after a first draft is completed. Often, the difference between a fluent, satisfying piece of synthesis writing and a text that appears labored and choppy can be attributed to the skill with which summaries, paraphrases, and quotations are constructed or integrated within a text.

When summarizing and paraphrasing, it is important to satisfy yourself that you have been fair and accurate and that you have not unwittingly distorted or misrepresented someone's views. Summary and paraphrase, then, should reflect sources honestly. Although they are smaller, reduced portions of original material, they should convey the general intent of the writer.

In addition to reflecting a source accurately, a paraphrase should also be substantially different from the original passage it represents. In other words, a paraphrase is *not* a direct quotation in which a couple of words have been changed. To produce a fluent, original paraphrase, we recommend the following: First, read the part of the text you wish to paraphrase several times, in order to ensure that you understand its contents fully. [NOTE: You may need to review the entire source—or a significant part of it—to be certain that you have properly interpreted the portion you wish to paraphrase.] If the passage you are attempting to paraphrase is lengthy, you may wish to jot down a few notes, in the form of key words and phrases. Next, remove the source and write a paraphrase of the relevant portion *from memory*. Revise the paraphrase so that it is clear and fluent. Finally, compare your paraphrase with the original passage to be certain that it is accurate and that it conveys the information you wish.

Direct quotes add vividness to a text. However, excessive quotation within synthesis writing can overwhelm the writer's voice and cause a text to appear unfocused and disjointed. Excessive quotation can also interfere with the overall tone a writer has labored to create. To avoid these pitfalls, be sure that each time you insert a quote you have a specific reason for doing so. When the phrasing from an original source is so powerful that it cannot be recreated, this is a good reason to inject a direct quotation into a piece of writing. Another reason to include quotations within synthesis writing is to bolster the authority of a claim or to strengthen the force of evidence. "Expert" testimony, particularly in the form of direct quotation, adds credence to information or argument. To strengthen his claim that charges against television are overstated and unfounded, Keith Mielke quotes the findings of S. B. Neuman, a well-published researcher, directly: "[Neuman's] general conclusion, after a review of dozens of variables, arguments, and studies, was that: '[T]here are no deleterious effects of television on learning achievement' (Neuman, 1986, p. 49)." Similar to direct quotations of experts are quotations from informants within a study or people who have personal, "insider" knowledge on a topic. A research study about teenage pregnancy, for example, can only be strengthened by well-placed quotes from young unwed mothers.

In addition to determining whether to use quotes, in revising synthesis writing, it is useful to examine how the quotes you employ are integrated into your text. Generally, quotes should be preceded or followed with sufficient discussion or metadiscourse to make their function clear to the reader. Metadiscourse, while not essential in every instance, is also helpful since it provides explicit direction about how to interpret or the significance of direct quotation. Phrases such as *for example, as Hilkin's words illustrate,* or sentences that provide an introduction to a quote ("Perhaps the most representative example of the unexamined assumptions frequently expressed by Jones are these quotes from his address to the local Chamber of Commerce. . . .") are usually welcomed by readers. In any case, a good rule to follow when providing quotations is to *be explicit* about what the quotes are meant to accomplish. That is, be sure to sufficiently explain what each quote is illustrating or how it is relevant to the point you are trying to make.

Activity 11

Perform the "vertical line test" on "The Proper Study of Womankind" and "Love on a Bun." That is, while reading each one draw a vertical line in the right- or left-hand margin with a pencil whenever you encounter direct quotation, paraphrasing, or summarizing. Estimate the percentage (e.g., 15, 20, 25, or 30 percent?) of each essay devoted to direct quotation/paraphrasing/summarizing.

Once you have performed the tests, compare your results with those of your group partners. Do you agree or disagree about the amount of quoting, paraphrasing, or summarizing you identified? If one essay employed more quoting, paragraphing, or summarizing, discuss why you think the author included the amount that she or he did.

 Activity 12

Select two of the readings from this chapter, and highlight or underline all of the direct quotations within each. Together with your group partners, examine the discussion and metadiscourse that precedes or follows the quotations. When is metadiscourse used? When doesn't it seem to be necessary? Do authors tend to *precede* or *follow* quotes with the discussion that makes their function clear? Can you detect any particular patterns? Prepare a brief oral report of your findings for the entire class.

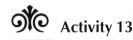 **Activity 13**

Examine several paraphrases from one or more of the readings in this chapter. How long do they tend to be? In each case, *what* was paraphrased?

In the first five paragraphs of "The Proper Study of Womankind," Carol Sternhell describes her relationship with women's studies. Reread these paragraphs and paraphrase Sternhell's attitude toward women's studies and feminism in a few sentences. Compare your paraphrase with those of your group partners. Which paraphrases do all of you prefer? Why?

WRITING ASSIGNMENTS

Writing Topics

Using the same process you used in Activities 6, 7, and 9, craft a synthesis essay in which you use a minimum of four sources. At least two of these sources should come from readings within this book. Your other two sources may come from readings within this book or from other sources (interviews, essays, book excerpts, etc.). Your instructor will provide more specific information about how he or she wants you to document your essay. [NOTE: If you use sources not published in this book, you should submit photocopies to your instructor along with your paper. If you interview someone as a source, you should turn in a copy of your notes or a transcript.]

Be sure that your essay has a focused topic (e.g., "the American Dream") and a thesis statement (*The American Dream does not really exist; The American Dream exists but only for certain people;* or *The American Dream exists for anyone who works to achieve it*). You may find it helpful to consider the overall purpose that you wish your essay to accomplish: Do you want to write an informative essay, a persuasive essay, or an expressive essay? The following are some topics to help you get started, or you may wish to choose your own topic (and thesis) in consultation with your instructor.

1. If you (with help from your group partners) have already begun to develop an interesting thesis relating to the topic "the American Dream," you may continue to work with this theme. Some possible ways of expanding sources within this chapter would be to interview several different people to gather a variety of perspectives. You may also wish to supplement your readings with those from a disciplinary perspective, particularly if you have already decided on an academic major or career interest. Although thinking of your audience is always important, if you choose a disciplinary perspective, be sure to use arguments, examples, and information that your readers will find appropriate.

2. Several readings refer directly or indirectly to the effects of gender on identity or self-concept. Think about your experience as a male or female, both what you have experienced personally and what you have observed. What relationships do you see between your experiences and the issues that you have encountered in the readings from this chapter? You might focus on areas such as gender and the effect of language use; gender and parent-child relationships; and gender and popular culture or media. Again, you may address your synthesis essay to a more general audience or you may choose a disciplinary or professional perspective. In either case, be sure your essay has a well-defined thesis and accommodates its audience appropriately.

3. The end-of-chapter readings throughout this textbook include numerous accounts of people who are pursuing a special interest or possibly even a career. Accounts of why some people enjoy writing appear in Chapter 1; accounts of people pursuing careers in geology and entomology appear in Chapter 3, as well as two accounts of why students enjoy reading. Referring to any of these— or to any other readings in this textbook—write a synthesis essay that explains influences that prompt people to pursue—or not pursue—a special interest or career.

4. In addition to the three preceding topics, here are some other themes that unite several of the essays in this book: "Family"; "The Role of Media in Shaping Attitudes"; "Immigrant Americans"; "Equity and Fairness"; Relationships between Men and Women." You may, of course, select a topic of your own; however, be sure to obtain your instructor's approval.

Writing Procedures

1. With a tentative topic in mind, select four or more sources (at least three sources must be readings from this chapter). Critically read and assess your sources (as described in the Writing a Synthesis Paper sections of this chapter), underline and make marginal notations. Jot down notes about how the sources relate to one another and to your tentative topic. Discuss your notes with your group partners and, using their feedback, determine if you want to work with the sources and topic you've selected; augment or replace one or more of your sources; or select a new topic and set of readings and repeat this process.

2. Reread the sources you have chosen, this time looking for similarities, differences, or other connections among them. Take detailed notes on these connections. At this point, you may wish to design a chart or diagram, using a large sheet of paper. Across the top of the chart, write out your major points; on the left side of the chart, list your sources vertically. Record your notes about each source within the appropriate grid.

3. Using your notes and your chart, write out a tentative thesis for your essay. Share your thesis and the notes or chart on which it is based. In response to the group's feedback, revise your thesis if necessary.

4. Using your tentative working thesis, outline a detailed plan for your synthesis essay. Be sure that the structure you devise reflects the significant points related to your thesis. Make sure that you do *not* organize your essay according to your sources. Describe the major parts of your essay, and try to include the arguments, examples, evidence, events, and so on that you would use to develop each part. You may want to craft an opening or topic sentence for each part. Share your plan with your group partners (and with your instructor) and revise it based on the suggestions you receive.

5. Using your plan and your notes from your sources, write a first draft of your synthesis essay. As you draft, make sure that you keep your purpose in mind. Be sure to include background information where necessary and to incorporate information from your sources with appropriate discussion and metadiscourse.

6. After you have completed your draft, bring it to class to workshop with your group. Use one of the draft workshop procedures described in Chapter 2. In this reading, group partners should attend particularly to overall structure. Is the essay structured to reflect points relevant to the thesis? Does the writer avoid copied structure? What is the proportion of quoted material to the overall essay? Is this proportion appropriate?

7. Based on the feedback you get from your group workshop or your instructor, revise your essay. In revising, you should pay particular attention to your structure. Each point should be clear and should be related to your thesis. Material from sources should emphasize, explain, or substantiate the points you make, rather than dominate your text.

8. After you have revised according to your partners' or instructor's suggestions, workshop your draft a second time with your group. Again, use one of the

ove on a Bun: How McDonald's Won the Burger Wars *(cont'd.)*

Chain Stores and Automobiles

The last quarter of the nineteenth century saw explosive growth in store chains—Woolworth's "Five and Ten Cent Stores," A&P grocery stores, and Walgreen's drug stores. The effects of this growth were the dissolution of neighborhood communities where local, independent retailers did business and the building up of what Boorstin calls "nationwide consumption communities," vast segments of the population connected by little other than the fact that similar clothes, furniture, food and implements were available to all of them from stores that looked identical. With the automobile, a city's radius no longer was limited to walking distance; no longer was there a need for businesses to concentrate at its center and no longer did one have to live near where one worked. The suburb was born. Largely a creation of land developers, the suburb promised to satisfy Americans' longing for a sense of place by offering a spot where one could erect a house of one's own and enjoy the grace and romance of country living at affordable rates. Of course, those who moved to the suburbs had no real bonds with the land or with their neighbors, except for the fact that they all shared in the consumption of housing, appliances, and automobiles.

Besides making movement faster and easier, the automobile changed what it meant to travel. *Going* somewhere, which implied an interest in seeing things along the way, lost its appeal. All efforts were bent toward *getting* somewhere. "Highways built to serve the automobile," Boorstin writes, "were insulated from the landscape, from pedestrians, and from people going about their business. The separated highway, on which more and more Americans would spend more and more of their waking hours, isolated citizens from one another and from their cities" (270).

Once Americans had become inured to the terrors of what Mumford calls "the Townless Highway," they had little further use for "the Highwayless Town" (Mumford, 1963). The coming of motion pictures and neighborhood movie theaters virtually eliminated the need to go downtown for spectacular entertainment, and the rise of television was even more successful in keeping citizens off city streets and in removing them from contact with one another. With the developments of suburban "shopping centers," begun in the 1920s, the transformation of the city and of community life was nearly complete. The time was right for the advent of fast food.

The Emergence of Fast Food

While the three decades of the 1920s, 30s and 40s had seen the appearance of a number of White Castle hamburger stores, Howard Johnson ice cream parlors and Jack-in-the-Box hamburger restaurants, it wasn't until after World War II that a full-fledged industry of fast food really emerged. As increasing numbers of young married couples moved to the suburbs, business too moved out of the cities into shopping centers amid networks of highways. For families wanting inexpensive and accessible places to eat out, the drive-in restaurant selling hamburgers and French fries was just the thing. While proximity and price were probably the key values for customers of early fast-food chains and the new ones—McDonald's, Burger King,

workshop procedures described in Chapter 2. In this reading, group partners should pay particular attention to how source material—especially quoting, paraphrasing, and summarizing—is integrated into the paper. Is there a sufficient amount of metadiscourse? Where is it located? Does the metadiscourse help make the relationship among sources evident?

9. Based on the feedback you get from your group workshop or your instructor, revise the final copy of your essay. Once you have completed your revision, edit carefully, being sure you have followed any format and documentation instructions your instructor has given you.

READINGS

Helmer, James. "Love on a Bun: How McDonald's Won the Burger Wars." *Journal of Popular Culture 26* (Fall 1992), pp. 85–97.

Mielke, Keith W. "On the Relationship Between Television Viewing and Academic Achievement." *Journal of Broadcasting and Electronic Media 38* (Summer 1994), pp. 361–366.

Sternhell, Carol. "The Proper Study of Womankind." *The Women's Review of Books* (December 1994), pp. 1–4.

Mukherjee, Bharati. "A Wife's Story," from *The Middleman and Other Stories.* New York: Grove/Atlantic, 1988.

Love on a Bun: How McDonald's Won the Burger Wars*

James Helmer

Whatever else it may be, television advertising is a persuasive form that not only reflects contemporary culture but shapes it. One arena in which the power of this persuasion is clearly evident is the marketing of fast food. In the United States, the fast food industry has managed not only to respond to the cultural values of mobility, economy and convenience but also to change irrevocably the nature of American family dining. Once a private act of perhaps the most intensely familial nature, eating together has become for many Americans a public act involving others in a variety of relationships, few of which are matters of blood.

No single purveyor of fast food has done more to advance this cultural change than McDonald's Corporation, whose influence is seen and felt in virtually every

*James Helmer, "Love on a Bun: How McDonald's Won the Burger Wars." *Journal of Popular Culture 26* (Fall 1992), pp. 85–97. Reprinted with the permission of the publisher.

Love on a Bun: How McDonald's Won the Burger Wars *(cont'd.)*

American community and in many places around the world. The 1980s offer a unique window on the ascendancy of McDonald's and its role in American culture because in this decade crucial dynamics were enacted through public messages. The first half of the 1980s was a period of intense competition among McDonald's, Burger King, and Wendy's, the latter two frequently using their television commercials to make direct and open attacks on the industry leader. But by just past mid-decade it was clear that McDonald's would not merely survive the burger wars, but win. McDonald's would win because it, better than any of its competitors, was able to catch up and exploit in its advertising a number of significant historical and contemporary developments in American community and family life. Built upon what Adams (1983) has called the "familial image," the persuasive strategy embodied in McDonald's advertising campaigns of the 1980s amounted to an attempt symbolically to reconstitute the family and relocated it under the golden arches.

This essay examines the McDonald's television commercials broadcast in the 1980s to show how they connected to the cultural construct "family." Specifically, it demonstrates how familial images were employed as a means of persuasion that ultimately portrayed McDonald's as a potential source of love and human happiness—as a place for *being* a family.

The Historical and Cultural Context of American Fast Food

To understand McDonald's great success it is necessary first to understand why Americans consume so much fast food of all kinds. To some observers, the attraction must seem inexplicable: much of the food is too salty, too full of carbohydrates and destitute of texture and taste. But fast food is best understood not as a gastronomic artifact but as a phenomenon that represents the convergence of several significant historical developments and cultural traditions: population mobility, advances in food technology, the rise of chain stores and the proliferation of the automobile. It is these phenomena, dating from early in the nineteenth century, that contextualize and inform the strategies of McDonald's persuasion late in the twentieth century.

A Tradition of Mobility

Americans have always been people in motion, moving often even before they had adequate means of movement. According to Stephan Thernstrom and Peter Knights (1970), the population of frontier communities was "extraordinarily restless and footloose"; in many townships and counties no more than 25% of the population stayed put through two consecutive decennial censuses (2, 3). Urban populations were highly volatile as well, with high rates of population mobility and turnover in both large and small cities (Thernstrom & Knights, 1970). "It might be said," write Thernstrom and Knights, "that American society in the [nineteenth century] was more like a procession than a stable social order" (35).

Love on a Bun: How McDonald's Won the Burger Wars *(cont'd.)*   L

One might wonder how, with so much movement going on, any cult tinuity at all was maintained. Thernstrom and Knights answer with two k vations: 1) that "certain aspects of this seemingly unsettling, chaoti process . . . were in fact stabilizing," and 2) that many features of nineteen tury America, such as the people's enthusiasm for joining voluntary asso and their devotion to political parties, "are best understood as efforts to ov or offset the 'excessive' mobility of the era . . . [and] testify . . . to the felt community" (36).

It is the persistence of this need for some kind of communal loyalty a struggle to maintain a sense of community that would help make Americans cious consumers of things. This voracious consumption, in turn, would cont to the success of chain stores and the franchise system, marketing concept McDonald's Corporation would come to epitomize.

Development in Food Technology

The proclivity to move had direct effects on eating habits and food technology example, Gail Borden's condensed milk, patented in 1856, was developed in par meet the traveler's need for portable, virtually imperishable foods. And progress industrial canning, pushed forward by the needs of Civil War soldiers in the fie brought not only Borden's milk but canned foods of all sorts into the American di

Mobility was obviously linked to the rise of transportation, and the rise transportation coupled with advancements in food technology and refrigeratio revolutionized the American way of eating. By the mid-1800s, the railroads ha made it possible for people throughout the United States to eat fresh fruits and vegetables, not just when they were in season but the whole year around. Refrigerated railroad cars, commercial ice manufacturing, the mechanical refrigerator, and Clarence Birdseye's discovery in 1912 of how to quick-freeze food further liberated the American diet from regional differences and the vagaries of seasons.

In the food of the United States there would be few surprises and little uniqueness. The country was on its way toward achieving what Daniel Boorstin (1973) calls "a novel environmental democracy":

> The American Democracy of Times and Places meant making one place and one thing more like another, by bringing them under the control of man. The flavor of fresh meat would be tasted anywhere anytime, summer would have its ice, and winter would have its warmth, inside and outside would flow together, and men would live and work not only on the unlevel ground but also in the homogeneous air. (307)

Two further developments would move the country to a fuller realization of the Democracy of Times and Places and complete the essential groundwork for an industry of fast food: the emergence of nationwide store chains and the introduction of the automobile.

Love on a Bun: How McDonald's Won the Burger Wars *(cont'd.)*

Pizza Hut—that were born in the middle of the 1950s, what would prove to be the most appealing for their patrons in the 60s was their capacity to save time.

The key trend that contributed to the popularity of fast foods, according to Thomas Anderson Jr., (1971), was the growth of industrial productivity through technological innovation and the resultant increase in affluence and leisure. The increase in discretionary time after World War II was what really boosted demand for convenience products—"t.v. dinners" and the like that could be quickly prepared and consumed at home as well as foods eaten at quick service restaurants.

In 1968 a report predicting that food consumed away from home would "increase at a rate in excess of that anticipated for food consumed at home" (Clausi 14) reflects not only increasing affluence and leisure time but also a growing American rootlessness that differed somewhat from the nineteenth century search for opportunity. Prompted—or, in some cases, forced—by political and economic developments or general disillusionment, Americans of all sorts, even entire organizations, hit the road. They went seeking alternate life styles, warmer weather, cheaper energy, lower taxes, more lasting love, greater adventure, better jobs.

All of this movement was what fast food chains were made for. Besides being highly visible to people traveling in cars, these restaurants offered a sense of familiarity and security. Indeed, however garish or unsightly the architecture, however little the food tastes like home cooking, the major fast food chain store is one place in an otherwise alien environment where one knows what to expect.

Much of the credit—or blame—for what fast food restaurants have become must go to the founder of McDonald's Corporation, Ray Kroc, a man whose vision and drive fired the entire fast service food industry while making his own chain the model for others. Kroc so systematized and standardized his version of the hamburger business that he has been called the Henry Ford of his industry. However unappealing it may be in other domains, predictability was just what Kroc sought in his restaurant—the buildings, the products, and the people—a consistency of service, quality, and taste that customers could count on regardless of where they ate or when. Ray Kroc was a key figure in the advancement of the American Democracy of Times and Places. As the automobile helped democratize the nation in the first half of the twentieth century, so would Kroc's hamburgers in the last half.

The Burger Wars and How McDonald's Won

McDonald's Corporation entered the 1980s in solid control of the fast food industry. Pumping hundreds of millions of dollars annually into advertising, it had cultivated a vast "consumption community," consistently reaping approximately 18% of the market, nearly three times the share of its closest competitor, Burger King. Moreover, McDonald's has tended to buy rather than lease land it would use for new store locations, a practice that in the beginning kept the corporation cash-poor. But while other chains took the initially less expensive route of leasing, McDonald's was acquiring property at a rate that by 1981 made it second only to Sears, Roebuck & Co. in real estate holdings, and that, according to *Business Week*

Love on a Bun: How McDonald's Won the Burger Wars *(cont'd.)*

(May 4, 1981), would produce "a huge competitive edge." The reason was simple: As other fast food chains grew in the 1960s, they commonly negotiated 20-year property leases. When those leases came up for renegotiation in the 1980s, standard $1,000-per-month leases had increased in some cases five-fold. McDonald's not only was less affected by these increases, but it was already paying off debts for its purchased properties, thus reducing fixed store costs.

Still, some observers felt that all that financial strength might not ensure McDonald's pre-eminence in the 1980s. The market and the competition were changing. *Business Week* (May 4, 1981) noted that in recent years "other chains have gotten more notice with seemingly fresher concepts" (161). McDonald's, under the advertising direction of Needham, Harper & Steers, returned in 1981 to its 1970 theme "You deserve a break today," thinking mainly of offering consumers relief from high prices. Meanwhile, Wendy's diversified its menu, and Burger King replaced its vague advertising message about lifestyle with the more direct "Aren't you hungry?" focusing on its Whopper, and it launched a bold attack against McDonald's (*Business Week* June 7, 1982).

McDonald's response to the heat from these other kitchens was to sack its advertising agency. McDonald's felt that it "was no longer able to distinguish itself from the increasingly sophisticated competition, and that the creative advertising of Needham, Harper & Steers, which generated much of the company's momentum in the 1960s and 1970s, would not suffice for the 1980s" (Millman 1). Executive interviewed by *Advertising Age* believed that the competition had caught up with McDonald's in many areas where the giant held a clear advantage in the 1970s:

> restaurant location, menu selection, operations and—perhaps most important—the image projected by the company in its advertising . . . McDonald's attitude scores, which measure consumer feelings about service, value, cleanliness, and convenience "have been eroding over the past year," one marketing executive said. McDonald's also could no longer convince consumers through its advertising that its products were significantly better or different than those of the competition. (Millman 1).

So it stopped trying. McDonald's in October 1981 hired the agency of Leo Burnett USA and "retooled" its advertising, taking attention off its products and venturing deeper into the realm of human feeling. Under the direction of Burnett, McDonald's creative strategy capitalized not only on Americans' traditional mobility and their need for convenience but also on the complex of more recent developments affecting American family and community life. More than any of its competitors, McDonald's worked to build a sense of community with consumers and went after the family market more vigorously than ever. McDonald's Corporation has always portrayed itself as philanthropic and community-minded through its contributions to health and service agencies, the establishment of Ronald

Love on a Bun: How McDonald's Won the Burger Wars *(cont'd.)*

McDonald Houses, and its support of various other community causes and non-profit organizations, and McDonald's has always called itself a family restaurant. But the ad campaigns of the 1980s took all this a good deal further. McDonald's moved its primary marketing emphasis off the food it sells and turned instead to marketing love, a sense of community and good feelings. Through Burnett's advertising, McDonald's aimed to reconstitute and relocate the American family—outside the home.

Targeting the Changing Family

What Leo Burnett's market analysis, if not its intuition, must have revealed was the American family in transition. Precipitated first by the Great Inflation that began in the 1960s and later by a rise in feminine consciousness (Harris 1981), the movement of women into the labor force wrought radical change on the home front. While in 1970 approximately 30% of mothers with children under age six were in the work force, within another decade "nearly one of every two had jobs outside the home. And nearly two-thirds of women with children between 6 and 17 were working in 1981—up from 49.2% in 1970. By [1982] 32 million children, or 55% of those under 18, had mothers in the labor force" (Shiels 29). While men and women in some cases learned to exchange or share roles, many mothers found themselves, either actually or for the intents and purposes of managing a household, on their own. Even for those families that clung to traditional roles and relationships the myriad and often conflicting demands and opportunities of modern life were making family life an increasingly frenzied and fragmented experience.

Traditional notions of family were further challenged by other developments as well. By 1980, cultural activity had repealed the marital and procreative imperatives (Harris 1981). And for years generations had been driven apart by wedges such as what Carey (1968) calls "age-graded" housing—retirement homes, young people's dormitories, age-segregated suburbs—which severely reduced inter-generational contact and increased the likelihood that more people would spend significant parts of their own lives, if not alone, then primarily with others like themselves. "Family" for some of these people no doubt meant these similar others, or perhaps the people with whom they worked or carried on some other activity. In any case, that most fundamental cultural unit was being reshaped into forms that had little to do with biology or institutional sanction.

So while McDonald's had for years called itself a family restaurant, if it were going to live up to that title in the 1980s it would have to appeal to this diverse group of people—all-of-us—for whom "family" was taking on widely varied meanings. What McDonald's would do was paint itself as many things that answered people's basic and powerful need for someone to mend the fragments with caring.

Constructing the Image of Family

The McDonald's advertising created by the Burnett agency has built on a kind of archetypal metaphor Adams (1983) identifies as the "familial image." Adams

Love on a Bun: How McDonald's Won the Burger Wars *(cont'd.)*

argues that relational images in rhetoric "act to unify audiences" by "entangling" listeners in an imaginative bond and a sense of common purpose. As "one of the oldest and most primary units of social cohesion," the family, used even in its figurative sense, carries "considerable 'ought weight' and therefore has deep reaching persuasive implications as a motive term" (Adams 56). The archetypal relationships suggested by familial imagery "tap into *essential* and *fixed* patterns of human caring. As such, they stand as bases of moral consciousness" (60).

McDonald's first full-fledged campaign from Burnett embedded familial images in a series of television commercials characterized as "heartsell" advertising, featuring slice-of-life vignettes. In the commercials, McDonald's appeared as hearth, healer, generational gap-bridger: the glue that holds friends and families together. All of the ads carried through the campaign's common theme of togetherness, captured in the line, usually sung or spoken as a tag, "Together, McDonald's and You."

Many of the commercials were mini-dramas in which a visit to McDonald's is reassuring of stability, security and love. In the commercial entitled "Back Home Again" a family returns to the father's hometown for the first time in many years. The neighborhood where he grew up is greatly changed, but a McDonald's remains. This and a chance encounter with an old friend bring back happy memories for the father. The voice-over sings, "In the night the welcome sight of an old friend feels so right—tonight at McDonald's again." Another vignette focuses on a small boy's anxiety when his pet is injured. While a veterinarian cares for the animal, the child nervously takes in a meal at McDonald's, after which he is happily reunited with his dog. In a spot called "Best Friends" two young girls with much in common, including hating their hair, share the activity that seems to be their greatest pleasure together and really shows they are friends: eating at McDonald's.

This first Burnett campaign, according to a McDonald's public information brochure, was designed to "appeal across a wide spectrum of age and race." It had to be "sensitive to emotional issues relevant to our black customers." So one commercial, entitled "Grandmother," showed a young black man taking his grandmother out for a meal at McDonald's as a demonstration of his love for her. To cut across generations, Burnett created a vignette called "Little Sister." In this spot a small girl sits on the living room floor in front of a television set, whose nearly round screen suggests the period is the late 1950s. With a mixture of envy and awe the girl watches her older brother leave with his friends for McDonald's. The years melt away until she is a young woman going to McDonald's with her own nearly grown-up friends. "We Grew Up Together, McDonald's and You," the ad says, suggesting that our visits to McDonald's, as those who accompany us change from parents and siblings to our own adult friends, serve as markers in our progress through life, much as a column of pencil marks on a doorframe tells the story of our growth.

In this commercial, the visit to McDonald's becomes a virtual rite of passage, part of the way this girl claims her independence and notifies the clan she is ready to shed the appellation "little sister" in favor of the new identity she will make for herself as a woman. The young woman's appearance at McDonald's with her own

Love on a Bun: How McDonald's Won the Burger Wars *(cont'd.)*

circle of friends also foreshadows her transition into other "families"—her play-mates and later her workmates. Buying a hamburger and fries at McDonald's becomes here not simply a pleasurable shared activity but a tribal act imbued with inevitability and necessity.

While McDonald's sold family, tradition and love, its major competitors pushed their food products, attempting with their slogans to remind consumers of what a restaurant should be about: "Aren't you hungry?" Burger King harangued, while Wendy's demanded to know "Where's the beef?" But McDonald's in 1983 still claimed 18% of the fast food industry's total sales of $38 billion and captured 42% of the $18 billion hamburger segment (*Business Week* January 30, 1984). Still, the direct and combative marketing approaches of the competition raised the concerns of McDonald's executive vice-president for marketing. *Business Week* (January 30, 1984) reported that in a fall 1983 study by Video Storyboard, Inc., a company that ad agencies hire to assess the pull of commercials, "only 6% of those surveyed mentioned McDonald's food after viewing several of its spots. Instead they commented on its characters, music and the family orientation. In a similar Burger King test, 22% said the food looked appetizing" (46). So the Executive V.P. for marketing wanted to spend more of McDonald's $360 million advertising budget on "harder-hitting, product-oriented spots" rather than the "good-feeling" promotions that Burnett continued to favor.

A new slogan—"It's a good time for the great taste of McDonald's"—suggests a compromise might have been struck: in this jingle there is at least an indication that McDonald's sells something to eat. As the Corporation itself reported, "McDonald's successful formula of 'food, folks and fun' took on a revised emphasis in 1984 of '*food, food,* folks and fun' " (Annual Report, 1984, 29). But it was hard to see the difference in the television commercials. In a few spots Big Macs and French fries were touted as "America's meat and potatoes," but again food was secondary to feelings—specifically, feelings of community in the elevated forms of patriotism and national pride. Occasionally, a "heartsell"-type mini-drama would crop up, too, such as the one entitled "Stranger in the House." In this vignette, a young boy struggles with pride and jealousy, love and hate as he watches his new baby sister come home for the first time. He feels forgotten, pushed aside until Dad comes to him, bends down, and asks, "You free for lunch?" Dad tells him, over a hamburger and fries, "Someone's going to have to show her the ropes." The boy smiles and saves a few French fries for his little sister as the viewer is reminded "It's a good time for the great taste of McDonald's." This same basic theme has continued to play out through a variety of more recent spots, all of which work toward the same end of establishing a sense of community—among family, friends, co-workers—and tying that up with good times at McDonald's.

Relocating the Family under the Golden Arches

McDonald's has attempted to reach out to the diverse elements of American culture and situate itself at the center of social life. Now spending upwards of $700 million annually on advertising heavy with relational images, it has attempted to

Love on a Bun: How McDonald's Won the Burger Wars *(cont'd.)*

reconstitute the community and the family and relocate them in the glow of the golden arches.

Recent evidence suggests the campaign has been for McDonald's a solid success. Its market share is estimated at 19%, more than twice that of Burger King, the nearest challenger, and consumer research indicates that McDonald's "caring" approach in advertising still makes a strongly positive impression (*Time,* April 13, 1987). The anti-McDonald's tone of its competitors' advertising has diminished and its rivals have generally slowed down their expansion. All of this suggests that McDonald's has indeed won the burger wars.

If its exploitation of love and general good feeling was not *the* reason for McDonald's victory, it was clearly a major contributor to the cause. McDonald's "won" in part by redefining the battleground, the terms of the conflict. McDonald's elevated the issue to a plane above simply satisfying hunger: Everyone will get enough to eat. The question is, who can give you a sense of place, where is home, who loves you? Legal scholar James Boyd White has suggested that the legal community might be thought of as a conversation about justice (White 1985). Might not the fast-food industry, then, be conceived of as a conversation about hunger and thirst, about hamburgers, chicken, pizza and soft drinks? If it is, McDonald's is speaking a different language.

White (1985b) has observed that the "process of law" is an art of persuasion which also creates the objects of its persuasion, and that the constitutive and creative functions of rhetoric are found not only in law but everywhere. That surely includes the hamburger business, for clearly discourse about how and what we are to eat—particularly as conducted through the medium of advertising—creates the objects of its persuasion, not only the goods but the audience as well.

Conclusion

What is suggested in the success of McDonald's recent advertising efforts is that, indeed, the American family recognizes the various human groups depicted in the commercials as reflections of itself. That is to say not only that the most fundamental cultural institution—the family—is much changed but that McDonald's public messages have helped make its variations acceptable and legitimate, thus playing an influential role in its reconstitution.

Moreover, this analysis suggests that familial images, when they are adapted to contemporary meanings, continue to carry considerable persuasive force in modern society. Time was when a restaurant built its success on selling "home cooking" or pies "like Mother used to make." But those images lack resonance today because fewer people are cooking at home and Mother has little time to make pies. McDonald's instead has provided a place for being a family, and in so doing has somewhat succeeded—at least in the minds of countless American youngsters raised on "Happy Meals"—in making eating there the same sweet obligation as coming home to supper.

Love on a Bun: How McDonald's Won the Burger Wars *(cont'd.)*

This, I think, is something to be concerned about. For McDonald's approach is nothing less than a strategy of control that works in insidious ways, as through the whines of a child who persuades his parent to stop at McDonald's when other restaurants are closer or offer tastier and more healthful fare. To raise objections on these grounds is fruitless, not only because these arguments often carry little weight with a child but because McDonald's has constructed the issue as inarguable: It's not about food; it's about caring. It's about home and family.

McDonald's use of this strategy and its success are troubling on two counts. The first is that anyone, adult or child, should feel so deprived of affection, belonging, and a sense of place that they should seek to satisfy their need at McDonald's. To be sure, people have always gravitated to social centers and these have been important focal points for cultures. But McDonald's has little interest in becoming one of those, for it actively discourages loitering. (That's why, for instance, you won't find a public telephone at McDonald's.) Its design elements, its seating, and its process all are coordinated to send a singular message: "Eat it and beat it."

What is perhaps more disturbing about McDonald's strategy is its contribution to the late twentieth-century American tendency to value form over substance. As both a reflection and a reinforcement of this mentality, this approach is not merely a marketing strategy. It is a political force. We have seen the way McDonald's has "democratized" the U.S. and there is the threat of the same sort of thing happening abroad, at least insofar as Americans experience foreign cultures. At this moment in the Underground stations of London there hang huge posters depicting a dozen of the city's most famous sights and giving the distance of each from the nearest McDonald's. These posters send an ethnocentric message, one that subtly devalues the experience of this great, historic city and attempts to homogenize it with the familiar. "So what's the big attraction?" the headline asks, while the tag assures us that "From Trafalgar Square to Chinatown, you're only minutes away from McDonald's." To an American standing on the platform, overwhelmed by "London's A to Z" and feeling far from home, the message is compelling.

Works Cited

Adams, J. "The Familial Image in Rhetoric," *Communications Quarterly* 31 (1983):56–61.

Anderson, W. T., Jr. *The Convenience-Oriented Consumer.* Austin: University of Texas, 1971.

Boorstin, D. J. *The Americans: The Democratic Experience.* New York: Random House, 1973.

Business Week, "McDonald's: The Original Recipe Helps it Defy a Downturn," 4 May 1981.

Business Week, "Pillsbury: Growth Could Suffer as Burger King Profits Shrink," 7 June 1982.

Carey, J. W. "Generations and American Society." *America Now* ed. J. G. Kirk New York: Atheneum, 1968.

Clausi, A. S. "Convenience Foods and Our Changing Social Patterns." *Marketing Insights* 11 Nov. 1968. Citied in Anderson.

Harris, M. *America Now.* New York: Simon & Schuster, 1981.

Millman, N. "Why McDonald's Switched." *Advertising Age,* 19 Oct. 1981.

Mumford, L. *Technics and Civilization.* New York: Harcourt, Brace & World, 1963.

Love on a Bun: How McDonald's Won the Burger Wars *(cont'd.)*

Shiels, M. "A Portrait of America—The Work Revolution." *Newsweek* 17 Jan. 1963. *Statistical Abstract of the United States,* 1965.

Thernstrom, S. and P. Knights *Men in Motion: Some Data and Speculation About Urban Mobility in Nineteenth-Century America.* Los Angeles: Institute of Government and Public Affairs, 1970.

Time, "Big Mac Strikes Back," 13 Apr. 1987.

White, J. B. Remarks delivered at the Conference on the Rhetoric of the Human Sciences, University of Iowa, March 1984. Cited in J. Lyne, "Rhetorics of Inquiry," *Quarterly Journal of Speech* 71 (1985): 65–73.

White, J. B. Remarks delivered at the Conference on the Rhetoric of the Human Sciences, University of Iowa, March 1984. Cited in H. W. Simons, "Chronicle and Critique of a Conference," *Quarterly Journal of Speech* 71 (1985): 52–64.

On the Relationship Between Television Viewing and Academic Achievement*

Keith W. Mielke

A perennial theme in the popular press is how poorly kids are doing in school because of how much television they watch. With some refinements, the criticism reaches all the way to the top of the policy food chain. Two puzzling questions keep nagging however. First, what is the real evidence that television is guilty as charged in lowering academic achievement? Second, if television is so attractive and powerful, and the needs of education so great, why should the devil have a monopoly on such an instrument? Why should we be advised to avoid the medium instead of using it aggressively in the service of raising academic achievement?

Popular press criticisms of television—the generic medium, the generic content on that medium—sound a steady drumbeat. To pick just one recent example, in *Newsweek's* "My Turn" column, Wyatt Townley (1994) calls for "video-free zones." Townley repeats many of the standard TV-bashing themes, including impact on achievement, so her piece is not atypical of the omnipresent genre. For example, she insinuates that there is a causal relationship between television viewing and (a) shortened attention spans, (b) decreased levels of concentration, (c) dissociation from literature, (d) decreased task perseverance, and (e) loss of capacity to think linearly. The attention-grabbing sentence in a *Los Angeles Times* article is even blunter: "Looking for a quick and cost-free fix for poor educational performance? Try pulling the plug on your TV set" ("A TV Guide," 1992, p. B6).

Is this standard media hype, perhaps relatively benign, or dangerous propaganda? Whatever the case, most treatment of this issue fails to reflect the rigor of a

*Keith W. Mielke, "On the Relationship Between Television Viewing and Academic Achievement." *Journal of Broadcasting and Electronic Media 38* (Summer 1994), pp. 361–366. Reprinted with the permission of the publisher.

On the Relationship Between Television Viewing and Academic Achievement *(cont'd.)*

serious search for truth. Instead, it skips the hard part and simply fingers television as the designated villain. The task gets complicated if "details" like different programming content, different viewer characteristics, and different viewing environments are taken into account. Those crisp conclusions are more difficult to reach in a single bound when the mental camera pulls back to reveal the writhing tentacles of dozens of indirect effects and moderating processes.

Oversimplifying Television's Effects

One of the many problems of oversimplification is its harvest of proclamation without progress. By avoiding the disciplined linkage of evidence and explanation, the oversimplifiers doom their issues to seemingly endless recycling. Simplistic pieces about television and academic achievement from 10 or 20 years ago could probably run in today's newspaper without seeming dated in the least. The arguments remain approximately the same. Oversimplification encourages single-factor explanations in a multi-factor reality, and is sustained by inattention to facts that do not fit in with the "polemics du jour." This viewpoint typically avoids arenas where scientific principles and tests of reasonableness would apply.

Blanket condemnation of the entire medium is demeaning to the many professionals in educational television who are working for, not against, the education of young people. Counting myself among that group, I insist that we are not the enemy. We do not join in concert to sing "my medium, right or wrong." We too are critical of some television programming and practices, and could easily be recognized as allies if there were enough precision of analysis to make the critical distinction between medium and message.

Of course not all of the prejudice against television comes in gross form from frontal salvos by the popular press. There are subtler varieties of anti-television bias, more complex in their contexts, more difficult to diagnose. These can take several forms: seeing some but not all of a picture; not applying common criteria across different media; or basing a serious policy argument on a fundamental assumption that has not itself been thoroughly probed and validated.

Elements of these subtler forms of bias against television can be found even among leaders in positions of highest responsibility. In 1991, for example, President Bush, lamenting a "dismal decline" in SAT verbal scores, pointedly asked: "And when our kids come home from school, do they pick up a book, or do they sit glued to the tube watching music videos?" ("Public Papers of the Presidents: George Bush," 1992, p. 1111). In his 1994 State of the Union Address, President Clinton praised parents " . . . who know their children's teachers and turn off the television . . . " ("Transcript," 1994, p. A17). Secretary of Education Richard Riley admonished parents: "Turn off the television and spend some time each evening working with your child or children" (Riley, 1993, p. 3). Pope John Paul II, seeing television as threatening to family life, urged parents to "simply turn the set off" ("Turn off Tube," 1994, p. 2).

On the Relationship Between Television Viewing and Academic Achievement *(cont'd.)*

For each of the four leaders cited above, a reading in fuller context would reveal their larger thesis to be that excessive television use can be one of several symptoms of inadequate parenting. This conclusion and the constructive motivations behind it are not questioned or challenged here. Nor can I imagine any serious educator not welcoming greater concern, responsibility, and involvement of parents in the well-being of their children. Even in such high-level commentary, however, the critical importance of content is not addressed specifically, although the content of a message is among the most basic elements of communication theory. Further, if television can be seen as a means and not an end, and a powerful force, why would it be unreasonable to expect similar high-level admonitions to watch television selectively? "Parents, watch these shows with your children and discuss them" should sound as comfortable and correct as "Parents, read these books with your children and discuss them." But I have yet to run across anything approaching this equality of media in serious policy talk.

It would be useful if popular press writers and policy spokespersons would both acknowledge the evidence that we already have about the relationship between exposure to television and academic achievement, and support efforts to find out more about it. The body of evidence in the scholarly literature is by no means complete, but enough of the complexity has been mapped out to be certain that simplistic cause-effect hypotheses are obscuring important, empirically demonstrated distinctions.

Examining the Real Evidence

There are hundreds of individual studies, and a smaller number of overviews and syntheses that try to get at the big picture. Five of the key overviews will be briefly cited here, not as an exhaustive review of this literature, but to illustrate the nature of the evidence that we do have about television and academic achievement.

A meta-analysis of 23 separate studies (Williams, Haertel, Haertel, & Walberg, 1982) exposes some of the complexity. Although their meta-analysis revealed a small overall negative association (−.05) between amount of TV viewing and academic achievement, even that weak linkage was not a constant across all children. The highest academic achievement was not found among the television abstainers, but among those who watched up to 10 hours per week. Those with the lowest achievement watched 35–40 or more hours per week, but this of course raises other questions. For example, what other problems might there be in a child's life, what other factors might account for both low academic achievement and such consuming levels of television viewing as 35–40 hours per week? Televiewing, the authors write, " . . . is neither the 'villain' nor the 'redeemer' some have claimed" (Williams et al., 1982, p. 35).

The U.S. Department of Education commissioned a major review of research literature on television's influence on cognitive development (Anderson & Collins,

On the Relationship Between Television Viewing and Academic Achievement *(cont'd.)*

1988). Despite the widely held belief that watching television hinders school achievement, no evidence was found to support that claim. Their review did, however, underscore the complexity of the relationship. The authors identify gaping holes in the pool of existing evidence and note inadequate attention to such seemingly obvious factors as the *content* of what is viewed on television.

Extending the meta-analytic work of Williams et al., Neuman (1986, 1988, 1991) examined the research evidence through the goggles of various hypotheses about the relationship between television viewing and academic achievement, particularly reading/literacy achievement. The themes of these hypotheses are diverse: Television replaces time that kids used to spend in more educational pursuits (the "Displacement Theory"); the television medium itself affects the processes through which we think and learn (the "Information Processing Theory"); television reduces perseverance, attention span, and concentration, while increasing impulsivity and demand for instant gratification (the "Short-Term Gratifications Theory"); television, as "window on the world," exposes children in an informal learning setting to a wide range of information and motivation (the "Interest Stimulation Theory"). Neuman (1991) notes that none of these theories argues that television affects academic achievement directly: "Rather, each details a mechanism to describe how television might indirectly relate to achievement by affecting what children might bring to and take away from school" (p. 9). In Neuman's view, none of the theories garnered enough support to explain differences in academic achievement.

One of Neuman's follow-up studies is large in scope, synthesizing data from eight statewide reading assessments, as well as the 1984 reading test conducted by the National Assessment of Educational Progress, and involving data from two million children (Neuman, 1986). Neuman found a curvilinear relationship between amount of viewing and level of achievement: Specifically, a modest positive association emerged for moderate viewers (two to three viewing hours per day), and a negative association for heavy viewers (four or more hours per day). Even though she found a small, overall negative association, television viewing accounted for so little variance in achievement that she considered these results to be "null findings." Her general conclusion, after a review of dozens of variables, arguments, and studies, was that: "[T]here are no deleterious effects of television on learning achievement" (Neuman, 1986, p. 49).

Huston et al. (1992), building on work by a task force of the American Psychological Association, reviewed and interpreted a wide range of research on the effects of television. Children were among the specific demographic groups emphasized, and academic achievement was among the issues examined in the review. Their general conclusion is consistent with that reached by other social scientists:

> Television viewing is associated with low school achievement and low reading ability, but these effects appear to be due to or confounded by low levels of intellectual ability among heavy viewers. On the positive side,

On the Relationship Between Television Viewing and Academic Achievement *(cont'd.)*

properly designed television can teach reading skills and motivate children to read (Huston et al., 1992, p. 140).

Finally, an extensive probing of the relationship between television viewing and academic achievement was conducted by Comstock and Paik (1991). They asked the central question about the repeatedly found overall negative association: "Is television the root or the fruit?" (p. 120). Their bottom line: " . . . the evidence indicates a modest causal contribution by television to lesser achievement, with viewing in excess of a modest-to-moderate amount the major factor" (p. 138).

Building upon the existing literature, Comstock and Paik (1991) propose a complex model through which television viewing can be associated with, and moderated by, dozens of factors in a child's environment. A multivariate approach such as this might evolve into a general conceptual framework capable of handling the natural complexity in this relationship between television and academic achievement. Explanatory theories could map out the interconnections among many different data streams, and develop a higher level understanding of how they work together. Certainly mapping this complexity is preferable to either ignoring it or drowning in the morass.

In our future theoretical models, we should not only find solid reasons for avoiding some kinds of television, but also solid reasons for engaging others. Then, instead of our leaders advising us to avoid our most powerful medium of communication, they might exhort us to use it both actively and intelligently in pursuit of our highest goals and our most deeply held values.

References

A TV guide. (1992, May 29). *Los Angeles Times*, p. 86.

Anderson, D. R., & Collins, P. A. (1988). *The impact on children's education: Television's influence on cognitive development* (Working Paper No. 2). Washington, DC: Office of Educational Research and Improvement. (ERIC Document Reproduction Service No. ED 295 271)

Comstock, G., & Paik, H. (1991). *Television and the American child*. San Diego, CA: Academic Press.

Huston, A. C., Donnerstein, E., Fairchild, H., Feshbach, N. D., Katz, P. A., Murray, J. P., Rubinstein, E. A., Wilcox, S. L., & Zuckerman, D. (1992). *Big world, small screen: The role of television in American society*. Lincoln: University of Nebraska Press.

Neuman, S. B. (1986, April). *Television and reading, A research synthesis*. Paper presented at the annual meeting of the American Educational Research Association, San Francisco, CA.

Neuman, S. B. (1988). The displacement effect: Assessing the relation between television viewing and reading performance. *Reading Research Quarterly, 23*, 414–440.

Neuman, S. B. (1991). *Literacy in the television age*. Norwood, NJ: Ablex.

Public Papers of the Presidents: George Bush. (1992). *Remarks to students and faculty of the Lewiston Comprehensive High School in Lewiston, Maine, September 3, 1991* (Vol. 2, pp. 1107–1111). Washington, DC: United States Government Printing Office.

Riley, R. W. (1993). *Prepared remarks: New Rochelle Magnet School, New Rochelle, New York*. Washington, DC: United States Department of Education, Office of the Secretary.

On the Relationship Between Television Viewing and Academic Achievement *(cont'd.)*

Townley, W. (1994, January 31). A plea for video-free zones. *Newsweek*, p. 8.

Transcript of President Clinton's message on the State of the Union. (1994, January 26). *New York Times*, pp. A16–A17.

Turn off tube, Pope warns. (1994, January 25). *New York Newsday*, p. 2.

Williams, P. A., Haertel, E. H., Haertel, G. D., & Walberg, H. J. (1982). The impact of leisure-time television on school learning: A research synthesis. *American Educational Research Journal, 19,* 19–50.

The Proper Study of Womankind*

Carol Sternhell

The way Harold Bloom talks about literature—besotted, defensive, grateful, aggrieved, proprietary—that's how I feel about feminism. Feminism saved my life, became my life, invented my life. For me, the awakening—that famous, rich experience of "revision" that 25 years ago felt truly like an unblinding—was as much intellectual as personal or political; in a way, I found my mind. I went to graduate school for only one reason: I wanted to learn everything, in every discipline, that could possibly explain how the world had gotten organized so oddly—that could possibly explain why humans everywhere seemed to think that women were the "second" sex.

My question, of course, was much too simple (and these days feminists disagree about what people "everywhere" think), but it's no wonder that it led me to a brand-new field called "women's studies." As a grad student in literature at Stanford University in the mid-1970s, I agitated for the creation of a women's studies program and met in constant informal study groups with feminist grad students in other fields (Stanford's excellent program in Feminist Studies began after I left). As a new assistant professor of journalism at New York University in the early 1980s, I worked for years with other faculty members to start a women's studies program; after I got tenure, I spent five years as our small, belated program's director. I've attended my share of National Women's Studies Association conferences, including a conference or two for directors of women's studies programs; I was a charter subscriber to *Signs* and *Feminist Studies* and have served as associate editor of *Women's Studies: An Interdisciplinary Journal;* I've written for *Ms.* and *The Women's Review of Books.* Women's studies and I go back a long, affectionate way. So why does the prospect of reviewing these particular books make me wish we'd never met?

*Carol Sternhell, "The proper study of womankind. *The Women's Review of Books* (December 1994), pp. 1–4. Reprinted with the permission of the author.

The proper study of womankind *(cont'd.)*

Well, let's be honest; we're all girls here. For the last few years, women's studies and I, we've had something of a love-hate relationship. For me, the nadir was the 1991 NWSA program directors' conference in Washington, DC that opened with pop-psych "self-esteem" exercises intended to eliminate racism and ended in a "healing circle." NWSA in general—the oppression olympics, the identity politics promenade—depresses all the feminists I know. The mind-numbing litany of race/class/gender/sex-preference/age/ethnicity/ability/weight/dry-cleaning-fluid allergy often seems to substitute both for serious thought and for serious political action.

But competing oppressions aren't all there is to NWSA, and NWSA isn't all there is to women's studies. The women's studies I've known and loved is a field of genuine scholarship that in many cases has challenged—successfully—the theoretical and methodological premises of traditional disciplines. Courses I've taken—and taught—have been intellectually rigorous, not CR groups and certainly not group therapy. The point was, and is, knowledge: although my field was literature, in grad school I studied anthropology with the late Michelle Rosaldo because I wanted to know how people "everywhere" organized and thought about gender; I studied psychology with Sandra Bern because I wanted to know if "sex differences" were real. I studied history with Carolyn Lougee and Estelle Freedman because I wanted to know what women's lives had looked like in other eras.

When I teach women's studies now, it's because I want to share similar information (backed by fifteen or twenty years of additional scholarship) and stimulate students to ask lots of questions about what they think they already know. Do I also hope they'll turn out to be feminists? Well, sure I do—just as Professor Bloom hopes his students will fall in love with great literature, just as academics everywhere believe better education makes better human beings. It would be odd if a committed teacher *didn't* want her students to value what she most values; but it's this often troubled alliance—among utopian, visionary feminism, the real-world fractious women's movement, and women's studies—that confuses feminists and inflames our critics.

What is the *purpose* of women's studies? In a way, that question runs through these three books now sitting on my desk, the three books I don't want to review. Their answers, assumptions and attitudes are quite different, but, read collectively, they paint a portrait of the field that I find very disturbing. My first reaction was to protest that the portrait was unrecognizable, that I'd never seen that frowsy face before, but of course that isn't true. I know her, yes; I even know her well—but she isn't always like that. The portrait is unrepresentative, partial, a series of snap-shots taken on a very bad day.

And it's probably unfair to read these books together. One, Christina Hoff Sommers' *Who Stole Feminism?*, is a well-known right-wing attack on feminism and secondarily on women's studies, financed by several conservative foundations (including the Olin Foundation, which also backed Dinesh D'Souza's *Illiberal Education* and David Brock's notorious screed, *The Real Anita Hill*). A second, *Professing*

The proper study of womankind *(cont'd.)*

Feminism: Cautionary Tales from Inside the Strange World of Women's Studies, by Daphne Patai and Noretta Koertge, is also intensely critical of women's studies—and agrees with Sommers on many points—but is written by two feminist academics who believe that the field they once embraced has become anti-intellectual, doctrinaire and self-destructive. The third, *The Feminist Classroom* by Frances A. Maher and Mary Kay Thompson Tetreault, is an enthusiastic feminist study of feminist pedagogy: where Patai and Koertge believe the teaching methods "that have become normative in many Women's Studies programs are ill-advised and destructive to women in the long run," Maher and Tetreault describe "a thoroughgoing revolution in curriculum content and pedagogy" that has "led to educational approaches that break the illusions and silences, and transform the visions of students."

Well, fine. We have two attacks on women's studies—one so mean-spirited and dishonest it's easy to dismiss—and one solid feminist rebuttal (endorsed by thinkers I respect, from Barrie Thorne to Johnetta Cole to Jonathan Kozol). My heart's in *The Feminist Classroom,* after all, and if aspects of Patai and Koertge's portrait seem accurate, the picture is lopsided, incomplete. My reluctance here isn't to face criticism; women's studies, like any academic field, can be mined for evidence of foolishness, close-mindedness and infighting, but also for evidence of brilliant scholarship and great teaching. My discomfort is sparked by *The Feminist Classroom,* which seems to endorse exactly the sort of teaching the other books mock, the sort of teaching I would have insisted—*will* insist—isn't representative of women's studies.

Critics first. According to Sommers, who describes herself as a feminist (although she earlier remarked in an *Esquire* interview that "There are a lot of homely women in women's studies. Preaching these anti-male, anti-sex sermons is a way for them to compensate for various heartaches—they're just mad at the beautiful girls"), feminism today is bad feminism, what she calls "gender feminism." Gender feminists—everyone from Gloria Steinem to Naomi Wolf to Catharine MacKinnon to pretty much all teachers of women's studies—believe that women are systemically oppressed, that our social/political arrangements assume and support male dominance "A surprising number of clever and powerful feminists share the conviction that American women still live in a patriarchy where men collectively keep women down," Sommers announces breathlessly:

> American feminism is currently dominated by a group of women who seek to persuade the public that American women are not the free creatures we think we are. The leaders and theorists of the women's movement believe that our society is best described as a patriarchy, a "male hegemony," a "sex/gender system" in which the dominant gender works to keep women cowering and submissive. The feminists who hold this divisive view of our social and political reality believe we are in a gender war, and they are eager to disseminate stories of atrocity that are designed to alert women to their plight. The "gender feminists" (as I shall call them) believe that all our institutions, from the state to the family to the grade schools, perpetuate

The proper study of womankind *(cont'd.)*

male dominance. Believing that women are virtually under siege, gender feminists naturally seek recruits to their side of the gender war. They seek support. They seek vindication. They seek ammunition. (p. 16)

Practitioners of good feminism, what Sommers calls "equity feminism," mostly seem to have died a hundred years ago. They simply want equal rights under the law; they don't feel like "victims" and they aren't mad at men. (Although those nine-teenth-century suffragists Sommers claims to admire seemed pretty darn mad in my reading of history.) It's something like the differences we used to see between radical and liberal feminism, except that Sommers (like PC-bashers everywhere) includes most contemporary liberal feminists in her bad-fem pile. *Who Stole Feminism?* spends most of its time appearing to debunk various feminist books, studies and ideas by pointing to factual errors; Sommers' "facts"—many of which are intended to prove that male violence against women isn't really all that much of a problem—have in turn been debunked in publications ranging from *Democratic Culture* to *The New York Times Book Review.* I don't have the space or energy to rehash all those arguments, and in a way they're beside the point. (Feminist authors, like anti-feminist authors, do sometimes make mistakes.) And her broader strokes are familiar by now: feminism is hostile to men; political correctness has swept through academia, browbeating freethinking faculty; women's studies is unscholarly and intolerant of dissent.

As someone who has spent most of the last 25 years on one college campus or another, I'm stunned by Sommers' portrayal of university life. Where I see small, underfunded women's study programs, she sees monoliths of thought control; where I see attempts to make traditional curricula less exclusionary, she sees the vicious destruction of Western culture; where I see faculties that are still predomi-nantly white and predominantly male, she sees a vast network of feminist deans and search committees who refuse to hire anyone who doesn't toe the party line. "As the number of doctrinally correct personnel grows," she warns, "they, too, will see to it that only candidates of like qualifications are hired in the future. Ironically, the ongoing self-selection of faculty of the right feminist persuasion is being carried out in the name of 'diversity' and 'inclusiveness'."

Sommers shares many criticisms of women's studies with Patai and Koertge— I'll get to them in a minute—but she shares a tone, that smug, self-righteous hos-tility, with self-proclaimed exterminators of "political correctness" everywhere. What I can't stand about this crowd, from D'Souza to Sommers to Richard Bern-stein, from The *National Review* to *The New Republic,* from Bloom to Bloom, is its dishonesty. I'd welcome a direct, honest attack on my *ideas.* But the bashers turn everything inside out—a call for tolerance becomes proof of intolerance; a racist remark becomes a blow for free speech—until they've committed every sin they accuse feminists of committing. Women's studies professors are accused of politi-cizing education, while rants like *In Defense of Elitism* by the late William A. Henry

---

The proper study of womankind *(cont'd.)*

3rd—"The unvarnished truth is this: You could eliminate every woman writer, painter and composer from the cave man era to the present moment and not significantly deform the course of Western culture"—are quoted approvingly in *The New York Times Book Review*. ("It is painful to admit it, I know, but Henry is right," allows the obnoxious Roger Kimball.)

Feminists practice victimology? Oh no, it's the unfeminists who are the true victims, hounded across campus by angry dominatrixes. Feminists invent conspiracies? Listen to the unfeminists describe our well-organized cabal. "The New Feminism has been rapidly colonizing and 'transforming' the American university," says Sommers. "Being morally convinced that they are not bound to adhere to rules of 'fair play' devised by the oppressor, these gender feminist ideologues have no scruples about bypassing normal channels in gaining their ends."

Well, I'm undoubtedly one of those gender feminist ideologues. But I've frequently criticized other gender feminist ideologues, and they've frequently criticized each other and me. (Sommers draws on those criticisms whenever they suit her purpose, which ought to defuse the cabal thing, but doesn't. My own complaints about one NWSA conference make it into her footnotes, but where did she find these complaints reported? In that notorious gender feminist publication, *The Women's Review of Books*.)

All three of these books tend to present women's studies as much more uniform than I've known it to be, as much less combative, fragmented and self-conscious. In *Professing Feminism*, for instance, Patai and Koertge accuse women's studies both of essentialism and of something they call "BIODENIAL," a cute name for social constructionism. (Their coy names for serious charges—IDPOL for identity politics and ideological policing, or TOTAL REJ "for the game that results from the feminist move of totally rejecting the masculinist, patriarchal, Eurocentric, capitalistic cultural heritage"—are consistently annoying.) While they later, quite thought-provokingly, claim that in fact women's studies programs tend to be essentialist when talking about men and social constructionist when talking about women, I think the wider truth is that some feminists favor essentialist arguments and some feminists favor constructionist arguments; that this split is well-known and indeed a source of much tension.

In many ways, Patai and Koertge, who built their book out of thirty interviews with disaffected faculty members, students and staff from women's studies programs around the country, offer a convincing critique of some currently popular foolishness, but they rarely seem to acknowledge that these charges have been made before—by other feminists and women's studies professors. For every feminist who complains about the presence of men in her class, there are ten who are thrilled to have male students. For every women's studies teacher who claims that what "women need most is not practice in the subtleties of scholarly analysis, but a nurturing atmosphere capable of leading them to empowerment," there are twenty feminist scholars gagging in the ladies' room.

The proper study of womankind *(cont'd.)*

The authors of *Professing Feminism* nod at this diversity, but believe feminist orthodoxy is widespread:

> Women's Studies programs have enjoyed the substantive protections afforded by the principle, and indeed the reality, of academic freedom. It is, in our view, the existence of the essentially liberal value of academic freedom that has allowed Women's Studies programs to develop in the diverse ways in which we observe them today. But our own experiences and those of many colleagues with whom we spoke have led us to conclude that some programs now deny the very values that allowed them to come into being. If Women's Studies does not promote, indeed does not stand for, open inquiry, critical exploration of multiple perspectives (even threatening ones), and scholarship not tethered to the political passions of the moment, what is there to be said for its presence in the academy? (p. xvii)

Not much, they eventually conclude:

> It would be far better to introduce courses on women and gender as part of the regular curriculum, insisting on sound scholarship and high professional standards on the part of those who teach and those who learn. Students and faculty should be encouraged to fight sexism and other injustices on their campuses and beyond, but they should not expect to receive academic credit or tenure for doing so. . . . Advocacy is often appropriate, sometimes necessary, in the street. But in the classroom, the more flexible values of liberal education should prevail. (p. 210)

Women's studies today, say Patai and Koertge—echoing Sommers—is a morass of anti-intellectualism, separatism and dogma, of pseudoscholarship in the service of political activism. Professors proselytize, encouraging "personal" rather than intellectual work; the classroom process silences dissent. TOTAL REJ, "throwing away the master's tools"—the feminist challenge to epistemology—has degenerated into a nihilist rejection of all prior human thought. Even feminist academics' alternative "support networks, conferences and journals" are seen as "all too reminiscent of the efforts of 'creation scientists' to represent themselves as the intellectual and professional equals of mainstream researchers" (although if there's an academic field alive today that doesn't produce its own "separatist" journals I'd like to meet it). Just as creationists want to deny "atheistic" radioisotope dating,

> Many feminists, for their part, find the values of objectivity, parsimony and consistency shot through with patriarchal bias, and they argue—with breathtaking simplicity of mind—that these intellectual virtues were designed, and are being used, to enforce the entrenched power of the white male European elite. (p. 184)

The proper study of womankind *(cont'd.)*

A decade ago, maybe even a few years ago, I would have been outraged by *Professing Feminism*. Today I find it sometimes infuriating, sometimes just silly, sometimes accurate—accurate at least about *some* attitudes popular among *some* feminists. Its descriptions of life within women's studies don't at all reflect my experiences here at New York University, but they do reflect my experience at NWSA meetings. (One explanation, of course, is that many of the best feminist scholars tend to bypass NWSA meetings, presenting their work only within their own disciplines. Despite Sommers' fantasies of feminist takeover, being directly identified with women's studies doesn't seem to help spark academic careers.)

And sometimes Patai and Koertge seem to be afraid of the genuinely destabilizing implications of feminist analysis; like Sommers, who complains that "gender feminists are convinced they are in the vanguard of a conceptual revolution of historic proportions," they suggest that learning about women is fine, but the "radical reappraisal of all the assumptions and values found in traditional scholarship" is dangerous.

Well, it's supposed to be dangerous. I often feel, when I think about these questions, like a head with two faces, a consciousness split down the middle, confusion walking a line. I've no desire at all to burn Western culture's Great Books, abandon linear thinking or smash my computer and write in "mother's milk"—but our intellectual history really *does* look profoundly different when viewed from a woman-centered perspective. Radical reappraisal—rigorous, scholarly, informed—is called for. Patai and Koertge point to evidence of feminist knownothingism, but our traditional "assumptions and values" are often rooted in misogynist knownothingism. Patai and Koertge claim feminist scholars, victims of "gendelirium," see gender everywhere—but it seems to me gendelirium is an apt description of the assumptions and values of much of Western culture.

And what about this man-hating thing anyway? Like most feminists, I'm fond of many, love some; I have a son. But if you know anything about the world you know that a real pattern of male atrocities against women really exists; women do plenty of rotten things, but the pattern simply isn't replicated if the genders are reversed. So I go through life believing both that human beings are human beings, that there's good and bad in all of us and gender shouldn't matter, *and* that the other gender has been systematically hurting mine all over the world.

My consciousness feels especially schizophrenic when I'm thinking about what Patai and Koertge call "IDPOL," the reduction of absolutely everything to categories of identity politics. It's my main complaint about the women's movement today—the caucuses keep getting narrower as the grievance checklist expands—but if I don't believe identity politics has some validity, how come I've spent the last quarter-century in a *women's* movement?

Which brings me, finally, to *The Feminist Classroom*. According to Patai and Koertge, feminist pedagogy is bad for women; according to Frances Maher and Mary Kay Thompson Tetreault, it's terrific. But the pedagogical practices they

The proper study of womankind *(cont'd.)*

describe—after extensively observing seventeen feminist teachers at six very different institutions—are remarkably like the pedagogical practices *Professing Feminism* deplores. Patai and Koertge complain that feminist pedagogy values feeling good over becoming competent; Maher and Tetreault describe one classroom as "communal and supportive" in nature, a haven where "learning was not understood to be an individual attribute or achievement." Patai and Koertge bemoan the "therapeutic aims of feminist pedagogy"; Maher and Tetreault describe one professor's effort to create a "supportive climate" for incest revelations and "validate all of the students who struggled with disclosing private experience in public." Patai and Koertge deplore reductionist identity politics; Maher and Tetreault explicitly endorse identity politics as the basis of what they call "positional pedagogy."

There's much to admire in the more interactive, less hierarchical pedagogy described in *The Feminist Classroom;* I try to practice it myself. These methods, and the understanding that all knowledge is partial, are familiar to anyone concerned with progressive education. Maher and Tetreault offer fascinating descriptions of real classrooms and are always scrupulously aware of their own roles as involved observers; the book works well as a sort of ethnography of education. And it was certainly a pleasure to hear from investigators who hadn't written their concluding chapter first. Unlike the authors of the other two books, these began with questions, not answers or denunciations. But ultimately it was *The Feminist Classroom*—not the two scathing attacks on women's studies—that left me feeling depressed.

Classroom after classroom, school after school, subject after subject, all anyone seems to talk about in *The Feminist Classroom* is race/class/gender/etc. The courses all ran together in my head like characters in a bad Russian novel; I had to keep checking back to see if I was reading about Literary Theory or the Sociology of Sexuality. Maher and Tetreault think this is good, even necessary: "Until professors and students explicitly define themselves as differently positioned by the hierarchies of knowledge, power and achievement in the academy, then the hopes of authentically challenging traditional hierarchies, or imagining the possibility of genuine social change, will be dim." San Francisco State University is described approvingly as an institution where students frequently "introduce their remarks in classes by saying, 'As a white, Jewish, lesbian feminist,' or 'Because I am an Asian-American working-class woman'." A professor at Lewis and Clark College, on the other hand, is criticized for wanting her students "to speak theoretically, to move beyond personal perspectives to a comparison of approaches in the abstract." Her emphasis on theory, say Maher and Tetreault, while understandable, "divested the discussion of the experiential, positional groundings it might have employed to move students beyond the dichotomies of gender and class."

Yes, the world looks different depending on where you stand, and it's probably true that marginalized social groups see some things more clearly than the folks at the top of the mountain. But if I really thought women's studies could be reduced to a sharing and sparring of "positions," I swear I'd give it all up tomorrow. Maybe today.

The proper study of womankind *(cont'd.)*

But I'm not giving it up, because I know what women's studies can be—I've seen the rest of the portrait, the angles forgotten here. I've learned too much, and taught too much, and thought too much; and hey, it isn't easy changing the world. Women's studies, you heartbreaker, you still have my heart.

 A Wife's Story*

Bharati Mukherjee

Imre says forget it, but I'm going to write David Mamet. So Patels are hard to sell real estate to. You buy them a beer, whisper Glenngarry Glen Ross, and they smell swamp instead of sun and surf. They work hard, eat cheap, live ten to a room, stash their savings under futons in Queens, and before you know it they own half of Hoboken. You say, where's the sweet gullibility that made this nation great?

Polish jokes, Patel jokes: that's not why I want to write Mamet.

Seen their women?

Everybody laughs. Imre laughs. The dozing fat man with the Barnes & Noble sack between his legs, the woman next to him, the usher, everybody. The theater isn't so dark that they can't see me. In my red silk sari I'm conspicuous. Plump, gold paisleys sparkle on my chest.

The actor is just warming up. *Seen their women?* He plays a salesman, he's had a bad day and now he's in a Chinese restaurant trying to loosen up. His face is pink. His wool-blend slacks are creased at the crotch. We bought our tickets at half-price, we're sitting in the front row, but at the edge, and we see things we shouldn't be seeing. At least I do, or think I do. Spittle, actors goosing each other, little winks, streaks of makeup.

Maybe they're improvising dialogue too. Maybe Mamet's provided them with insult kits, Thursdays for Chinese, Wednesdays for Hispanics, today for Indians. Maybe they get together before curtain time, see an Indian woman settling in the front row off to the side, and say to each other: "Hey, forget Friday. Let's get *her* today. See if she cries. See if she walks out." Maybe, like the salesman they play, they have a little bet on.

Maybe I shouldn't feel betrayed.

Their women, he goes again. *They look like they've just been _____ by a dead cat.*

The fat man hoots so hard he nudges my elbow off our shared armrest.

---

*From *The Middleman and Other Stories* by Bharati Mukherjee. Used by permission of Grove/Atlantic, Inc. Copyright © 1988 by Bharati Mukherjee.

A Wife's Story *(cont'd.)*

"Imre. I'm going home." But Imre's hunched so far forward he doesn't hear. English isn't his best language. A refugee from Budapest, he has to listen hard. "I didn't pay eighteen dollars to be insulted."

I don't hate Mamet. It's the tyranny of the American dream that scares me. First, you don't exist. Then you're invisible. Then you're funny. Then you're disgusting. Insult, my American friends will tell me, is a kind of acceptance. No instant dignity here. A play like this, back home, would cause riots. Communal, racist, and antisocial. The actors wouldn't make it off stage. This play, and all these awful feelings, would be safely locked up.

I long, at times, for clear-cut answers. Offer me instant dignity, today, and I'll take it.

"What?" Imre moves toward me without taking his eyes off the actor. "Come again?"

Tears come. I want to stand, scream, make an awful scene. I long for ugly, nasty rage.

The actor is ranting, flinging spittle. *Give me a chance. I'm not finished, I can get back on the board. I tell that asshole, give me a real lead. And what does that asshole give me? Patels. Nothing but Patels.*

This time Imre works an arm around my shoulders. "Panna, what is Patel? Why are you taking it all so personally?"

I shrink from his touch, but I don't walk out. Expensive girls' schools in Lausanne and Bombay have trained me to behave well. My manners are exquisite, my feelings are delicate, my gestures refined, my moods undetectable. They have seen me through riots, uprootings, separation, my son's death.

"I'm not taking it personally."

The fat man looks at us. The woman looks too, and shushes.

I stare back at the two of them. Then I stare, mean and cool, at the man's elbow. Under the bright blue polyester Hawaiian shirt sleeve, the elbow looks soft and runny. "Excuse me," I say. My voice has the effortless meanness of well-bred displaced Third World women, though my rhetoric has been learned elsewhere. "You're exploiting my space."

Startled, the man snatches his arm away from me. He cradles it against his breast. By the time he's ready with comebacks, I've turned my back on him. I've probably ruined the first act for him. I know I've ruined it for Imre.

It's not my fault; it's the *situation*. Old colonies wear down. Patels—the new pioneers—have to be suspicious. Idi Amin's lesson is permanent. AT&T wires move good advice from continent to continent. Keep all assets liquid. Get into 7-11s, get out of condos and motels. I know how both sides feel, that's the trouble. The Patel sniffing out scams, the sad salesman on the stage: postcolonialism has made me their reference. It's hate I long for; simple, brutish, partisan hate.

After the show Imre and I make our way toward Broadway. Sometimes he holds my hand; it doesn't mean anything more than that crazies and drunks are crouched in doorways. Imre's been here over two years, but he's stayed very old-

A Wife's Story *(cont'd.)*

world, very courtly, openly protective of women. I met him in a seminar on special ed. last semester. His wife is a nurse somewhere in the Hungarian countryside. There are two sons, and miles of petitions for their emigration. My husband manages a mill two hundred miles north of Bombay. There are no children.

"You make things tough on yourself," Imre says. He assumed Patel was a Jewish name or maybe Hispanic; everything makes equal sense to him. He found the play tasteless, he worried about the effect of vulgar language on my sensitive ears. "You have to let go a bit." And as though to show me how to let go, he breaks away from me, bounds ahead with his head ducked tight, then dances on amazingly jerky legs. He's a Magyar, he often tells me, and deep down, he's an Asian too. I catch glimpses of it, knife-blade Attila cheekbones, despite the blondish hair. In his faded jeans and leather jacket, he's a rock video star. I watch MTV for hours in the apartment when Charity's working the evening shift at Macy's. I listen to WPLJ on Charity's earphones. Why should I be ashamed? Television in India is so uplifting.

Imre stops as suddenly as he'd started. People walk around us. The summer sidewalk is full of theatergoers in seersucker suits; Imre's year-round jacket is out of place. European. Cops in twos and threes huddle, lightly tap on their thighs with night sticks and smile at me with benevolence. I want to wink at them, get us all in trouble, tell them the crazy dancing man is from the Warsaw Pact. I'm too shy to break into dance on Broadway. So I hug Imre instead.

The hug takes him by surprise. He wants to let me go, but he doesn't really expect me to let go. He staggers, though I weigh no more than 104 pounds, and with him, I pitch forward slightly. Then he catches me, and we walk arm in arm to the bus stop. My husband would never dance or hug a woman on Broadway. Nor would my brothers. They aren't stuffy people, but they went to Anglican boarding schools and they have a well-developed sense of what's silly.

"Imre." I squeeze his big, rough hand. "I'm sorry I ruined the evening for you."

"You did nothing of the kind." He sounds tired. "Let's not wait for the bus. Let's splurge and take a cab instead."

Imre always has unexpected funds. The Network, he calls it, Class of '56.

In the back of the cab, without even trying, I feel light, almost free. Memories of Indian destitutes mix with the hordes of New York street people, and they float free, like astronauts, inside my head. I've made it. I'm making something of my life. I've left home, my husband, to get a Ph.D. in special ed. I have a multiple-entry visa and a small scholarship for two years. After that, we'll see. My mother was beaten by her mother-in-law, my grandmother, when she'd registered for French lessons at the Alliance Française. My grandmother, the eldest daughter of a rich zamindar, was illiterate.

Imre and the cabdriver talk away in Russian. I keep my eyes closed. That way I can feel the floaters better. I'll write Mamet tonight. I feel strong, reckless. Maybe I'll write Steven Spielberg too; tell him that Indians don't eat monkey brains.

We've made it. Patels must have made it. Mamet, Spielberg: they're not condescending to us. Maybe they're a little bit afraid.

A Wife's Story *(cont'd.)*

Charity Chin, my roommate, is sitting on the floor drinking Chablis out of a plastic wineglass. She is five foot six, three inches taller than me, but weighs a kilo and a half less than I do. She is a "hands" model. Orientals are supposed to have a monopoly on the hands-modelling business, she says. She had her eyes fixed eight or nine months ago and out of gratitude sleeps with her plastic surgeon every third Wednesday.

"Oh, good," Charity says. "I'm glad you're back early. I need to talk."

She's been writing checks. MCI, Con Ed, Bonwit Teller. Envelopes, already stamped and sealed, form a pyramid between her shapely, knee-socked legs. The checkbook's cover is brown plastic, grained to look like cowhide. Each time Charity flips back the cover, white geese fly over sky-colored checks. She makes good money, but she's extravagant. The difference adds up to this shared, rent-controlled Chelsea one-bedroom.

"All right. Talk."

When I first moved in, she was seeing an analyst. Now she sees a nutritionist.

"Eric called. From Oregon."

"What did he want?"

"He wants me to pay half the rent on his loft for last spring. He asked me to move back, remember? He *begged* me."

Eric is Charity's estranged husband.

"What does your nutritionist say?" Eric now wears a red jumpsuit and tills the soil in Rajneeshpuram.

"You think Phil's a creep too, don't you? What else can he be when creeps are all I attract?"

Phil is a flutist with thinning hair. He's very touchy on the subject of *flautists* versus *flutists*. He's touchy on every subject, from music to books to foods to clothes. He teaches at a small college upstate, and Charity bought a used blue Datsun ("Nissan," Phil insists) last month so she could spend weekends with him. She returns every Sunday night, exhausted and exasperated. Phil and I don't have much to say to each other—he's the only musician I know; the men in my family are lawyers, engineers, or in business—but I like him. Around me, he loosens up. When he visits, he bakes us loaves of pumpernickel bread. He waxes our kitchen floor. Like many men in this country, he seems to me a displaced child, or even a woman, looking for something that passes him by, or for something that he can never have. If he thinks I'm not looking, he sneaks his hands under Charity's sweater, but there isn't too much there. Here, she's a model with high ambitions. In India, she'd be a flat-chested old maid.

I'm shy in front of the lovers. A darkness comes over me when I see them horsing around.

"It isn't the money," Charity says. Oh? I think. "He says he still loves me. Then he turns around and asks me for five hundred."

What's so strange about that, I want to ask. She still loves Eric, and Eric, red jump suit and all, is smart enough to know it. Love is a commodity, hoarded like

---

A Wife's Story *(cont'd.)*

any other. Mamet knows. But I say, "I'm not the person to ask about love." Charity knows that mine was a traditional Hindu marriage. My parents, with the help of a marriage broker, who was my mother's cousin, picked out a groom. All I had to do was get to know his taste in food.

It'll be a long evening, I'm afraid. Charity likes to confess. I unpleat my silk sari—it no longer looks too showy—wrap it in muslin cloth and put it away in a dresser drawer. Saris are hard to have laundered in Manhatten, though there's a good man in Jackson Heights. My next step will be to brew us a pot of chrysanthemum tea. It's a very special tea from the mainland. Charity's uncle gave it to us. I like him. He's a humpbacked, awkward, terrified man. He runs a gift store on Mott Street, and though he doesn't speak much English, he seems to have done well. Once upon a time he worked for the railways in Chengdu, Szechwan Province, and during the Wuchang Uprising, he was shot at. When I'm down, when I'm lonely for my husband, when I think of our son, or when I need to be held, I think of Charity's uncle. If I hadn't left home, I'd never have heard of the Wuchang Uprising. I've broadened my horizons.

Very late that night my husband calls me from Ahmadabad, a town of textile mills north of Bombay. My husband is a vice president at Lakshmi Cotton Mills. Lakshmi is the goddess of wealth, but LCM (Priv.), Ltd., is doing poorly. Lockouts, strikes, rock-throwings. My husband lives on digitalis, which he calls the food for our *yuga* of discontent.

"We had a bad mishap at the mill today." Then he says nothing for seconds.

The operator comes on. "Do you have the right party, sir? We're trying to reach Mrs. Butt."

"Bhatt," I insist. "*B* for Bombay, *H* for Haryana, *A* for Ahmadabad, double *T* for Tamil Nadu." It's a litany. "This is she."

"One of our lorries was firebombed today. Resulting in three deaths. The driver, old Karamchand, and his two children."

I know how my husband's eyes look this minute, how the eye rims sag and the yellow corneas shine and bulge with pain. He is not an emotional man—the Ahmadabad Institute of Management has trained him to cut losses, to look on the bright side of economic catastrophes—but tonight he's feeling low. I try to remember a driver named Karamchand, but can't. That part of my life is over, the way *trucks* have replaced *lorries* in my vocabulary, the way Charity Chin and her lurid love life have replaced inherited notions of marital duty. Tomorrow he'll come out of it. Soon he'll be eating again. He'll sleep like a baby. He's been trained to believe in turnovers. Every morning he rubs his scalp with cantharidine oil so his hair will grow back again.

"It could be your car next." Affection, love. Who can tell the difference in a traditional marriage in which a wife still doesn't call her husband by his first name?

"No. They know I'm a flunky, just like them. Well paid, maybe. No need for undue anxiety, please."

A Wife's Story *(cont'd.)*

Then his voice breaks. He says he needs me, he misses me, he wants me to come to him damp from my evening shower, smelling of sandalwood soap, my braid decorated with jasmines.

"I need you too."

"Not to worry, please," he says. "I am coming in a fortnight's time. I have already made arrangements."

Outside my window, fire trucks whine, up Eighth Avenue. I wonder if he can hear them, what he thinks of a life like mine, led amid disorder.

"I am thinking it'll be like a honeymoon. More or less."

When I was in college, waiting to be married, I imagined honeymoons were only for the more fashionable girls, the girls who came from slightly racy families, smoked Sobranies in the dorm lavatories and put up posters of Kabir Bedi, who was supposed to have made it as a big star in the West. My husband wants us to go to Niagra. I'm not to worry about foreign exchange. He's arranged for extra dollars through the Gujarati Network, with a cousin in San Jose. And he's bought four hundred more on the black market. "Tell me you need me. Panna, please tell me again."

I change out of the cotton pants and shirt I've been wearing all day to put on a sari to meet my husband at JFK. I don't forget the jewelry; the marriage necklace of *mangalsutra*, gold drop earrings, heavy gold bangles. I don't wear them every day. In this borough of vice and greed, who knows when, or whom, desire will overwhelm.

My husband spots me in the crowd and waves. He has lost weight, and changed his glasses. The arm, uplifted in a cheery wave, is bony, frail, almost opalescent.

In the Carey Coach, we hold hands. He strokes my fingers one by one. "How come you aren't wearing my mother's ring?"

"Because muggers know about Indian women," I say. They know with us it's 24-karat. His mother's ring is showy, in ghastly taste anywhere but India: a blood-red Burma ruby set in a gold frame of floral sprays. My mother-in-law got her guru to bless the ring before I left for the States.

He looks disconcerted. He's used to a different role. He's the knowing, suspicious one in the family. He seems to be sulking, and finally he comes out with it. "You've said nothing about my new glasses." I compliment him on the glasses, how chic and Western-executive they make him look. But I can't help the other things, necessities until he learns the ropes. I handle the money, buy the tickets. I don't know if this makes me unhappy.

Charity drives her Nissan upstate, so for two weeks we are to have the apartment to ourselves. This is more privacy than we ever had in India. No parents, no servants, to keep us modest. We play at housekeeping. Imre has lent us a hibachi, and I grill saffron chicken breasts. My husband marvels at the size of the Perdue hens. "They're big like peacocks, no? These Americans, they're really something!" He tries out pizzas, burgers, McNuggets. He chews. He explores. He judges. He loves it all, fears nothing, feels at home in the summer odors, the clutter of Manhattan streets. Since he thinks that the American palate is bland, he carries a bottle

A Wife's Story *(cont'd.)*

of red peppers in his pocket. I wheel a shopping cart down the aisles of the neighborhood Grand Union, and he follows, swiftly, greedily. He picks up hair rinses and high-protein diet powders. There's so much I already take for granted.

One night, Imre stops by. He wants us to go with him to a movie. In his work shirt and read leather tie, he looks arty or strung out. It's only been a week, but I feel as though I am really seeing him for the first time. The yellow hair worn very short at the sides, the wide, narrow lips. He's a good-looking man, but self-conscious, almost arrogant. He's picked the movie we should see. He always tells me what to see, what to read. He buys the *Voice*. He's a natural avant-gardist. For tonight he's chosen *Numéro Deux*.

"Is is a musical?" my husband asks. The Radio City Music Hall is on his list of sights to see. He's read up on the history of the Rockettes. He doesn't catch Imre's sympathetic wink.

Guilt, shame, loyalty. I long to be ungracious, not ingratiate myself with both men.

That night my husband calculates in rupees the money we've wasted on Godard. "That refugee fellow, Nagy, must have a screw loose in his head. I paid very steep price for dollars on the black market."

Some afternoons we go shopping. Back home we hated shopping, but now it is a lovers' project. My husband's shopping list startles me. I feel I am just getting to know him. Maybe, like Imre, freed from the dignities of old-world culture, he too could get drunk and squirt Cheez Whiz on a guest. I watch him dart into stores in his gleaming leather shoes. Jockey shorts on sale in outdoor bins on Broadway entrance him. White tube socks with different bands of color delight him. He looks for microcassettes, for anything small and electronic and smuggleable. He needs a garment bag. He calls it a "wardrobe," and I have to translate.

"All of New York is having sales, no?"

My heart speeds watching him this happy. It's the third week in August, almost the end of summer, and the city smells ripe, it cannot bear more heat, more money, more energy.

"This is so smashing! The prices are so excellent!" Recklessly, my prudent husband signs away traveller's checks. How he intends to smuggle it all back I don't dare ask. With a microwave, he calculates, we could get rid of our cook.

This has to be love, I think. Charity, Eric, Phil: they may be experts on sex. My husband doesn't chase me around the sofa, but he pushes me down on Charity's battered cushions, and the man who has never entered the kitchen of our Ahmadabad house now comes toward me with a dish tub of steamy water to massage away the pavement heat.

Ten days into his vacation by husband checks out brochures for sightseeing tours. Shortline, Grayline, Crossroads: his new vinyl briefcase is full of schedules and pamphlets. While I make pancakes out of a mix, he comparison-shops. Tour number one costs $10.95 and will give us the World Trade Center, Chinatown, and the United Nations. Tour number three would take us both uptown *and* downtown

A Wife's Story *(cont'd.)*

for $14.95, but my husband is absolutely sure he doesn't want to see Harlem. We settle for tour number four: Downtown and the Dame. It's offered by a new tour company with a small, dirty office at Eighth and Forty-eighth.

The sidewalk outside the office is colorful with tourists. My husband sends me in to buy the tickets because he has come to feel Americans don't understand his accent.

The dark man, Lebanese probably, behind the counter comes on too friendly. "Come on, doll, make my day!" He won't say which tour is his. "Number four? Honey, no! Look, you've wrecked me! Say you'll change your mind." He takes two twenties and gives back change. He holds the tickets, forcing me to pull. He leans closer. "I'm off after lunch."

My husband must have been watching me from the sidewalk. "What was the chap saying?" he demands. "I told you not to wear pants. He thinks you are Puerto Rican. He thinks he can treat you with disrespect."

The bus is crowded and we have to sit across the aisle from each other. The tour guide begins his patter on Forty-sixth. He looks like an actor, his hair bleached and blow-dried. Up close he must look middle-aged, but from where I sit his skin is smooth and his cheeks faintly red.

"Welcome to the Big Apple, folks." The guide uses a microphone. "Big Apple. That's what we native Manhattan degenerates call our city. Today we have guests from fifteen foreign countries and six states from this U.S. of A. That makes the Tourist Bureau real happy. And let me assure you that while we may be the richest city in the richest country in the world, it's okay to tip your charming and talented attendant." He laughs. Then he swings his hip out into the aisle and sings a song.

"And it's might fancy on old Delancey Street, you know . . . "

My husband looks irritable. The guide is, as expected, a good singer. "The bloody man should be giving us histories of buildings we are passing, no?" I pat his hand, the mood passes. He cranes his neck. Our window seats have both gone to Japanese. It's the tour of his life. Next to this, the quick business trips to Manchester and Glasgow pale.

"And tell me what street compares to Mott Street, in July. . . . "

The guide wants applause. He manages a derisive laugh from the Americans up front. He's working the aisles now. "I coulda been somebody, right? I coulda been a star!" Two or three of us smile, those of us who recognize parody. He catches my smile. The sun is on his harsh, bleached hair. "Right, your highness?" Look, we gotta maharani with us! Couldn't I have been a star?"

"Right!" I say, my voice coming out a squeal. I've been trained to adapt; what else can I say?

We drive through traffic past landmark office buildings and churches. The guide flips his hands. "Art deco," he keeps saying. I hear him confide to one of the Americans: "Beats me. I went to a cheap guide's school." My husband wants to know more about this Art Deco, but the guide sings another song.

"We made a foolish choice," my husband grumbles. "We are sitting on the bus only. We're not going into famous buildings." He scrutinizes the pamphlets in his

A Wife's Story *(cont'd.)*

jacket pocket. I think at least it's air-conditioned in here. I could sit here in the cool shadows of the city forever.

Only five of us appear to have opted for the "Downtown and the Dame" tour. The others will ride back uptown past the United Nations after we've been dropped off at the pier for the ferry to the Statue of Liberty.

An elderly European pulls a camera out of his wife's designer tote bag. He takes pictures of the boats in the harbor, the Japanese in kimonos eating popcorn, scavenging pigeons, me. Then, pushing his wife ahead of him, he climbs back on the bus and waves to us. For a second I feel terribly lost. I wish we were on the bus going back to the apartment. I know I'll not be able to describe any of this to Charity, or to Imre. I'm too proud to admit I went on a guided tour.

The view of the city from the Circle Line ferry is seductive, unreal. The skyline wavers out of reach, but never quite vanishes. The summer sun pushes through fluffy clouds and dapples the glass of office towers. My husband looks thrilled, even more than he had on the shopping trips down Broadway. Tourists and dreamers, we have spent our life's savings to see this skyline, this statue.

"Quick, take a picture of me!" my husband yells as he moves toward a gap of railings. A Japanese matron has give up her position in order to change film. "Before the Twin Towers disappear!"

I focus, I wait for a large Oriental family to walk out of my range. My husband holds his pose tight against the railing. He wants to look relaxed, an international businessman at home in all the financial markets.

A bearded man slides across the bench toward me. "Like this," he says and helps me get my husband in focus. "You want me to take the photo for you?" His name, he says, is Goran. He is Goran from Yugoslavia, as though that were enough for tracking him down. Imre from Hungary. Pana from India. He pulls the Leica out of my hand, signaling the Orientals to beat it, and clicks away. "I'm a photographer," he says. He could have been a camera thief. That's what my husband would have assumed. Somehow, I trusted. "Get you a beer?" he asks.

"I don't. Drink, I mean. Thank you very much." I say those last words very loud, for everyone's benefit. The odd bottles of Soave with Imre don't count.

"Too bad." Goran gives back the camera.

"Take one more!" my husband shouts from the railing. "Just to be sure!"

The island itself disappoints. The Lady has brutal scaffolding holding her in. The museum is closed. The snack bar is dirty and expensive. My husband reads out the prices to me. He orders two french fries and two Cokes. We sit at picnic tables and wait for the ferry to take us back.

"What was that hippie chap saying?"

As if I could say. A day-care center has brought its kids, at least forty of them, to the island for the day. The kids, all wearing name tags, run around us. I can't help noticing how many are Indian. Even a Patel, probably a Bhatt if I looked a hard enough. They toss hamburger bits at pigeons. They kick styrofoam cups. The

A Wife's Story *(cont'd.)*

pigeons are slow, greedy, persistent. I have to shoo one off the table top. I don't think my husband thinks about our son.

"What hippie?"

"The one on the boat. With the beard and the hair."

My husband doesn't look at me. He shakes out his paper napkin and tries to protect his french fries from pigeon feathers.

"Oh, him. He said he was from Dubrovnik." It isn't true, but I don't want trouble.

"What did he say about Dubrovnik?"

I know enough about Dubrovnik to get by. Imre's told me about it. And about Mostar and Zagreb. In Mostar white Muslims sing the call to prayer. I would like to see that before I die: white Muslims. Whole peoples have moved before me; they've adapted. The night Imre told me about Mostar was also the night I saw my first show in Manhattan. We'd walked down to Chelsea from Columbia. We'd talked and talked and I hadn't felt tired at all.

"You're too innocent," my husband says. He reaches for my hand. "Panna," he cries with pain in his voice, and I am brought back from perfect, floating memories of snow, "I've come to take you back. I have seen how men watch you."

"What?"

"Come back, now. I have tickets. We have all the things we will ever need. I can't live without you."

A little girl with wiry braids kicks a bottle cap at his shoes. The pigeons wheel and scuttle around us. My husband covers his fries with spread-out fingers. "No kicking," he tells the girl. Her name, Beulah, is printed in green ink on a heart-shaped name tag. He forces a smile, and Beulah smiles back. Then she starts to flap her arms. She flaps, she hops. The pigeons go crazy for fries and scraps.

"Special ed. course is two years," I remind him. "I can't go back."

My husband picks up our trays and thrown them into the garbage before I can stop him. He's carried disposability a little too far. "We've been taken," he says, moving toward the dock, though the ferry will not arrive for another twenty minutes. "The ferry costs only two dollars round-trip per person. We should have chosen tour number 1 for $10.95 instead of tour number four for $14.95."

With my Lebanese friend, I think. "But this way we don't have to worry about cabs. The bus will pick us up at the pier and take us back to midtown. Then we can walk home."

"New York is full of cheats and whatnot. Just like Bombay." He is not accusing me of infidelity. I feel dread all the same.

That night, after we've gone to bed, the phone rings. My husband listens, then hands the phone to me. "What is this woman saying?" He turns on the pink Macy's lamp by the bed. "I am not understanding these Negro people's accents."

The operator repeats the message. It's a cable from one of the directors of Lakshmi Cotton Mills. "Massive violent labor confrontation anticipated. Stop. Return posthaste. Stop. Cable flight details. Signed Kantilal Shah."

A Wife's Story *(cont'd.)*

"It's not your factory," I say. "You're supposed to be on vacation."

"So you are worrying about me? Yes? You reject my heartfelt wishes but you worry about me?" He pulls me close, slips the straps of my nightdress off my shoulder. "Wait a minute."

I wait, unclothed, for my husband to come back to me. The water is running in the bathroom. In the ten days he has been here he has learned American rites: deodorants, fragrances. Tomorrow morning he'll call Air India; tomorrow evening he'll be on his way back to Bombay. Tonight I should make up to him for my years away, the gutted trucks, the degree I'll never use in India. I want to pretend with him than nothing has changed.

In the mirror that hangs on the bathroom door, I watch my naked body turn, the breasts, the thighs glow. The body's beauty amazes. I stand here shameless, in ways he has never seen me. I am free, afloat, watching somebody else.

CHAPTER 9

WRITING RESEARCH PAPERS: WORKING WITH LIBRARY SOURCES

INTRODUCTION

The previous chapter discussed writing *synthesis* papers. This chapter will discuss writing *research* papers, which involves the process of synthesis in a specialized way. You probably are aware of the vast amount of information available to you: books and periodicals in your college library, computer and database services, national and international computer networks, and so forth. In addition, books or periodicals not available in the library can be obtained through inter-library loan, and information from experts of all kinds can be obtained through telephone conversations, e-mail, or fax transmissions. As a college graduate, you also will be expected to know how to retrieve the information you need, evaluate it, apply it, integrate it with other information, and share it with others. Hence, a major function of college research paper assignments is to help you to learn these skills.

Because the ability to access and synthesize available information is so important, this textbook will devote two chapters to writing research papers. Chapter 9 will focus on strategies for writing research papers using traditional sources housed in libraries: books, journals, popular magazines, newspapers, and other publications. Chapter 10 will expand your notion of "research" by focusing on how research papers can be written using "nonlibrary" sources such as questionnaires and surveys, interviews, observations, media, public records, and public lectures.

Whether you use library or nonlibrary sources or both in writing a research paper, the ultimate goal is to *synthesize* your sources—that is, to integrate them in order to reach and support your own conclusions. As with any synthesis paper, your research paper should have a thesis that helps you organize your writing according to the main points you wish to make about your subject. Although the previous chapter introduced you to four categories of synthesis writing that are based on purpose (persuasive, informative, expressive, and literary), in college you ordinarily will be asked to write informative or persuasive research papers.

In addition to sharing many of the features of synthesis writing, research papers require other elements. Research papers must document sources according to a specialized format. These specialized formats include requirements about bibliographies, quotations, title pages, headings, margins, fonts, and the use of charts or graphs. Of course, teachers who assign research papers frequently add their own format requirements.

Learning format requirements is just one challenge student writers face with research papers. Another challenge is how to determine the paper's scope. Narrowing a topic and creating a thesis that can be treated in a balanced, appropriate manner takes careful planning. Knowing the expected length of a final draft helps you determine the scope of a topic, which is why teachers often provide length requirements for research papers.

Another challenge that student writers (especially inexperienced ones) encounter in writing research papers is how to allot sufficient time for locating sources, drafting, and revising. Student writers often fail to understand how much time is necessary for identifying and securing source material, especially if they are unfamiliar with on-line catalogues and electronic data bases. Materials may be unavailable if they have been checked out or the library does not own them. Thus, beginning research as early as possible will enable you to put a "hold" on a book that is checked out or to request materials through the inter-loan service.

Because such challenges are instrumental to learning, teachers often assign research papers. Writing them helps develop problem-solving skills you can use in college and in your professional life. You will also develop skills important to your personal life: how to find medical information, investigate companies to invest in, choose products to purchase, and so on. Writing research papers helps prepare you to be a lifelong learner.

SAMPLE ASSIGNMENTS

Library research paper assignments vary considerably from one teacher to another and from one discipline to another. The samples we have gathered illustrate this range as well as many of their common features.

Psychology Assignment. This paper is worth 30 percent of your grade. Due date: *No later than noon, May 3*. The requirements and guidelines for the final research paper are as follows. Research papers must contain a minimum of *ten references* and be well edited. All topics must be *approved* by the *end of the second week of class*. Documentation must follow APA guidelines. The research paper must contain the following sections and headings:

a. **Introduction**

b. **Statement of Problem or Thesis**

c. **Review of Related Literature**

d. **Summary of Major Findings**

e. **Conclusions**

f. **Recommendations**

Political Science Assignment. One of the requirements for this course is a four- to five-page paper, worth 20 percent of your final grade. (The paper may exceed 4–5 pages, but should be under 10 pages.) You may hand the paper in early, but the final due date is December 1, at the beginning of class. Late penalties—one letter grade per day reduction—will be assessed. Your topic must be approved by me at least one month in advance of submitting your paper.

Purpose: This paper is assigned so that you will improve your writing and research skills, clarify your understanding of important course concepts, and apply those concepts to contemporary events.

Topics: Your paper must involve the application of *two or more* core course concepts to analyze an *event* or *issue* in contemporary politics. Core course concepts from which you should make your selection are listed on the attached sheet. The following are examples of appropriate events or issues; you may, of course, use others:

Events: The Gulf War; Peacekeeping Forces in Liberia; GATT Negotiations

Issues: Global Warming; Acid Rain; Nuclear Proliferation; Hunger; Farm Subsidies; The Emergence of a European Common Market

Sources: A minimum of *three* sources about the event or issue you have selected are required. These should be articles from reputable news sources, academic journals, and regional reviews; you may also use books. You may use more than three sources; however, be sure that you correctly cite the sources that you employ. Failure to do so is plagiarism. I do not specify the conventions that you should use for citing your sources, but you need to select a documentation system and use it consistently.

Evaluation: Your paper will be evaluated according to (1) grammar, format, and spelling; (2) content; and (3) sources.

Introduction to Ethnic Studies Assignment. An important requirement for this course is the group research project or report, for which you must select *one ethnic group* or *an issue related to ethnic studies* covered in this class. When completed, your research project should be in the form of a booklet with a preface, table of contents, charts, graphs, illustrations (where appropriate), and so on. Although I prefer not to specify length, in the past, each group member has produced about five to seven pages of text (double-spaced). Groups with three members tend to produce fifteen- to twenty-page booklets. Your audience should be junior high school readers, because we will be donating the best booklets produced by class groups to the Evans Junior High School library. To supplement course information, each research project (booklet) should include additional information from a minimum of *ten* scholarly sources. These should be listed in a bibliography; use APA format.

Because the collaborative nature of this project is important, 10 percent of your evaluation will be based on the quality of your group's interaction. Subsequently, I will be distributing a questionnaire that will require group members to record meeting times and dates, describe the tasks performed by each group member, and assess the quality of each person's contribution.

English Grammar Assignment. As you studied English grammar this term, you discovered a great many controversies. For your final project, select one controversy, describe it (What is the controversy? Who expresses which views and why?), and explain your own position about it in ten to twelve pages. An example of a suitable controversy is the use of the generic *he.* Should we continue to use sentences like, "An artist must study for many years to perfect his craft"? Or do these sentences exclude females?

Be sure to explore sufficient scholarly sources with respect to your issue so that you present a comprehensive view of relevant historical information. You must cite at least *ten* sources in your paper, although you may list more in your bibliography if you consult but do not cite them. Please follow the documentation conventions listed within the *MLA Handbook.*

Although the paper is due no later than Wednesday of Final Exam week, this schedule of requirements precedes the final due date: *February 2—A two-page* description of your issue and a list of *three* of the sources that you will use are due. *February 27—*An annotated bibliography (1-paragraph annotations) of your ten sources is due. *March 20—*A first rough draft of your paper is due. Please bring four copies and the original to class for workshopping. *April 4—*A second rough draft of your paper is due. Again, bring four copies and the original to class for workshopping.

As the preceding examples illustrate, library research paper assignments vary considerably. Nonetheless, such assignments share many features. They require writers to do library research and consult relevant sources in writing the paper. They also require the use of a documentation system whose conventions students are expected to follow precisely. Whatever documentation system is required, all library research assignments also require students to bolster their own ideas or arguments by drawing on source materials. Whether writers use endnotes or footnotes, paraphrases or direct quotations, they must follow conventions about identifying sources and distinguishing their own ideas from those of their sources.

Library research paper assignments are usually major assignments. Often a library research paper is the only written assignment in many classes. Even when there are other writing requirements, a research paper is generally worth a significant portion of the course grade—often as high as 40 to 50 percent. Because library research papers are a major assignment, teachers also usually have higher expectations for them than they do for other kinds of writing. Library research papers should show a writer's best effort in all aspects of writing—selecting a pertinent topic, narrowing it, researching it, developing original ideas, structuring a cohesive and readable paper, using documentation appropriately, and editing and proofreading.

While the specifics of assignments may vary, writing a library research paper requires time and planning. Whether teachers provide direct assistance, the following activities can help you complete a library research paper successfully:

- Set up an overall schedule.
- List intermediate deadlines.
- Allow time for library research.
- Develop an efficient system for finding, assessing, and recording information from sources.
- Learn and use an appropriate documentation system.
- Draft, revise, and edit your paper so that it shows your best writing.

In addition, whatever the specific requirements of your instructors, all good research writing includes these following features:

- A clear thesis or overall purpose
- A clear structure
- Well-integrated or synthesized sources
- Appropriately integrated quotes, paraphrases, and summaries
- Appropriate documentation
- Polished writing.

WORKING WITH LIBRARY SOURCES

Throughout your college years, you can expect to spend many hours in the library on your campus. By "library," we mean the place where published materials (books, newspapers, journals, etc.) are kept for reading, reference, or lending. On some campuses this facility may have a different label, such as "learning resources center." Because a campus library typically is a very large facility, sometimes housed in more than one building, we recommend that students familiarize themselves with the one on their campus as soon as they begin college, rather than wait for a research assignment. Familiarizing yourself with the library as soon as possible is a good idea, especially if you find the place a bit overwhelming. To begin this process, simply go there and look around. Most libraries provide a map or other handouts to indicate what is located where, and they place them near the entrance, in an area labeled "information," or at the circulation desk—the area where books are checked out and returned.

At the circulation desk or in the information area, you can find out about library tours, which provide a good introduction to various collections, resources, and services. Although many libraries offer such tours during orientation programs or at the beginning of terms, some also offer them throughout the year. If your library does not offer them, be resourceful and take yourself on a "self-guided tour," following the maps or other handouts.

Acquainting Yourself with Library Resources

Housed within your library are numerous kinds of resources with which you must become familiar in order to do research. Among the more familiar are newspapers, magazines, microform materials, videotapes, recordings, and books. Resources that may be less familiar to you include special collections of books (such as rare books, oversized books, and books written by a local author who has become famous); computerized indexes; government documents (which take the form of books, pamphlets, and sometimes even computer disks); archives (primary records and other original source materials), and various special collections (perhaps of maps, artwork, manuscripts, or books for browsing, for example).

Reference materials constitute another large group of library resources; although you are probably familiar with some of these materials, there are undoubtedly others that you will benefit greatly from using. In general, reference materials fall into two categories: resources that provide specialized information and resources that serve as guides in locating information. Included among the hundreds of resources that provide specialized information are encyclopedias (not only general encyclopedias that cover all fields of knowledge, but also specialized encyclopedias such as the *Encyclopedia of Psychology, Encyclopedia of the Occult,* or *Encyclopedia of the Vietnam War*) and dictionaries (not only general, such as *Webster's New World Dictionary,* but specialized, such as the *Biographical Dictionary of Actors, Actresses, Musicians, Managers, and Other Stage Personnel in London, 1660–1800*). Other resources that provide specialized information include fact books; directories of notable people, businesses, and organizations; and even telephone directories from different cities.

The other kind of reference materials, those designed to help you locate information, comprise an even larger group of resources. These reference materials come in a variety of forms: books, pamphlets, computerized indexes, and even people—the reference librarians. Some examples are bibliographies that list books and journals on particular topics or disciplines; collections of abstracts that describe the content of source materials; and indexes to journals, magazines, newspapers, and book reviews. As you become familiar with this group of reference materials, you will encounter noncomputerized sources such as the *Book Review Index* and *Guide to the National Archives of the United States;* and computerized indexes such as *Periodicals Abstracts* and *ABI/Inform,* a specialized index for business information. As you locate and use such sources for the first time, we recommend that you consult with a reference librarian who can direct you to specific reference materials related to your topic and assist you in using them. Reference librarians are trained to help you—and they are happy to do so.

Learning about Library Facilities and Services

In addition to resources such as reference materials, most libraries house a variety of facilities and services. To use the library to your best advantage, you should be aware of these; they can range from simple equipment such as staplers to entire rooms or areas that house specialized collections. In general, library facilities and services can be classified into several different types. Some help users locate material that is in a special form or that is not generally accessible. For example, library personnel in a closed stacks area are available to retrieve restricted materials. Microfilm and microfiche readers, for example, assist library patrons in using microform materials, and of course, videotapes and musical recordings require special equipment and perhaps, special assistance. Other facilities enable researchers to duplicate library resources and prepare research papers. Examples of these are photocopiers, typewriters, computers or computer labs, and miscellaneous workroom equipment. Finally, most libraries provide their users with a variety of areas to accommodate their different needs. Study carrels, for example, provide quiet, private work areas; reading rooms offer comfortable, informal surroundings. Major service areas such as the circulation desk, the reserve room, and the newspaper and periodicals desk are staffed by trained library personnel who are able to assist you.

When you need to locate resources within a library, if you have no idea where to begin your research, or if you do not have a topic yet and are starting from scratch, the best place to go is the Information, Reference, or Circulation desk. If you have a topic but don't know where to begin researching, personnel at the Information or Circulation desk may direct you to the Reference desk, where a librarian will be able to direct you to an appropriate index or bibliography. If you do not have a topic, a reference librarian may direct you to any of several places where you could browse—the current periodicals, specialized indexes, the catalogue (which might be a card file or might be on-line), or a computerized data base.

 **Activity 1**

When you have one to two hours to spare, go on your own to the library and locate the following:

- The title page of a specialized encyclopedia
- A page from an out-of-state telephone directory where your surname is or would be listed
- Census information from the decade when you were born
- A map or floor plan of the library, if provided
- A one-page computer printout of sources on the topic of "dogs"
- A photocopy of the front page of a newspaper on microform from the day you were born
- A page that has listings related to gender in a specialized index or bibliography.

Bring photocopies of your findings to your next class so that you can compare them with those of your group partners.

Evaluating Sources

In writing library research papers, writers not only need to become familiar with library resources and facilities, they also need to assess the sources they find. Actually, evaluating sources is a crucial step in writing library research papers. Simply put, all the published sources available on a given topic are not equally credible. Instructors frequently require particular kinds of sources—ones that are current, scholarly rather than general, and those written by well-respected professionals. In specifying which kinds of sources are acceptable, instructors are evaluating the general worth of different kinds of sources—and are expecting their students to learn to make such distinctions themselves. Whether instructors directly state such specifications in research paper assignments, they always expect students to write using the *best* sources available, not simply the *first* ones students find.

Whether in college or outside of college, evaluating sources is crucial in library research for an additional reason: Published sources often contradict one another. A person who wants to assess the safety of the public water supply in a city, for example, might find contradictions in several sources—for example, an Environmental Protection Agency study of water quality, an environmental action group's study, a public relations announcement by a local pesticide producer, and a medical research article on the incidence of cancer in young children who drink city water. To determine which conclusions you should believe about this topic—or any other—would involve evaluating each of the sources using criteria such as accuracy, comprehensiveness, reliability, relevance, and fairness.

Determining the Reliability of a Source. Just as you do not believe everything you hear, so also you should not believe everything you read; instinctively you know this already. You aren't likely to believe the tabloid headlines you read in line at the grocery store ("College Student Gives Birth to Own Grandfather"). It may seem at first that the sources uncovered in research at a college library must be reliable simply because they appear to be more serious publications than tabloids. However, even with scholarly writing, readers should be skeptical of what they read, and this is particularly true of information found on computer sources such as discussion groups and electronic journals. Formal documentation or specialized jargon may mask a variety of factors that make a source unreliable. Luckily, however, there are several general principles that can help you determine the reliability of sources.

First, writers should consider bias on the author's part. While no person can really be totally objective about a subject he or she cares deeply about, authors can try to be fair and openly acknowledge their biases to their readers. Authors may, for example, directly state their personal beliefs, their political leanings, or their experience with their subject in order to alert readers to biases that may shape the conclusions of a piece of writing. Even when conventions promote the appearance of objectivity and personal information might be perceived as intrusive, authors can still try to write with fairness; for example, when presenting a controversial subject, they can take care to discuss both strengths and shortcomings of differing views.

In addition to bias, you should take the author's expertise into consideration when you evaluate a source. Formal education, training, and professional experience are relevant factors. Many publications highlight background information about authors in special sections. Authors may also discuss their experience or training in their writing. In addition, you can consider an author's other books or articles on the same subject or on a closely related one. Related publications may be listed in the bibliography of the source you are evaluating or in bibliographies of other sources you find.

In addition to bias and authorial expertise, you should consider what background information is available about the publisher or journal when evaluating sources. Often periodicals print editorial policies that state political leanings or other values they promote: "This journal promotes research into the social causes of adolescent deviance," or "As a labor-oriented activist journal, we solicit articles on equitable labor policy legislation at the state and national levels." Such policies are usually printed inside the front cover of journals or on the editorial page of newspapers. Electronic journals may store copies of their policies in an archives file. Journal titles may also reveal information about the general interests of the editors and readership; for example, you would expect to find a pro-ecology stance expressed in articles published in the *Journal of Environmental Policy* or to find views favorable to feminism in *Women's Studies Quarterly*.

An additional consideration when assessing sources is the documentation used in published sources. The exact style and level of formality of documentation is usually determined by the publisher, not by the author; to some extent, then, documentation—or its absence—reflects the reliability of both the author and the journal, newspaper, or publishing company. Don't, however, equate the absence of *formal* documentation with unreliability. *Smithsonian* and *National Geographic*, both well respected magazines, do not use formal footnotes or endnotes, presumably because they are directed toward a general reading audience, not a scholarly one. These magazines, instead, use informal documentation; information about a source is provided within the text, in the same way that reputable newspapers document their sources. Whether a publication uses a formal or informal documentation, the important thing to evaluate is whether documentation is used at all, and how consistently it is used. When an author makes claims such as "experts have proved that . . . ", are they backed up with references to sources, or are they left unsupported? When statistics are used, how much information is provided about their origin? With a quotation, is information provided about who the speaker is, or is the speaker unnamed (e.g., "a source close to the Royal Family")?

You must also consider the distinction (in terms of reliability) between journals directed toward a scholarly audience and popular magazines directed toward a general audience. Many college instructors direct students to use scholarly journals because these are believed to be more reliable than popular magazines. Scholarly journals have rigorous standards for what they publish; often they reject 50 to 90 percent of submissions. Usually, articles published in scholarly journals have been reviewed first—or refereed—by three or more readers who are experts in the appropriate subject. By contrast, when articles are published in more general magazines, they may have been reviewed by a general editor or by a staff lawyer, but only rarely by people with expertise in that particular subject. To determine the reviewing procedures of a periodical, readers can look in sections entitled **"Information for**

Prospective Authors" or **"Editorial Policy";** such sections are often printed on the inside front cover. In addition, journals usually print the names of an **Editorial Board,** along with their academic positions; such information indicates the background and professional training of people who review papers submitted for publication. With electronic journals, however, it may be difficult and sometimes impossible to assess the level of reviewing used. Therefore, these sources should be used with caution, and, wherever possible, claims made within them should be checked against other sources.

In addition to these general considerations about all sources, there are several considerations to keep in mind when evaluating particular types of sources, such as books, scholarly articles, newspapers, or magazines. An important consideration that varies across types of sources is the breadth and depth in which a subject is discussed, or comprehensiveness. Obviously, when a three-hundred-page book and a three-hundred-word newspaper article are written on the same topic, the book will offer a more comprehensive discussion. Generally speaking, then, some types of sources are more comprehensive and others are less so.

A particular kind of scholarly book you should be aware of is the comprehensive, multivolume work. Usually painstakingly researched and documented, multivolume books may present the most comprehensive treatment of their subject available and, hence, can be an extremely good resource. However, such books take so many years to research and write that they may be out of date by the time they are published. In considering the comprehensiveness of a source, then, you shouldn't simply look for the most comprehensive sources available and dismiss all newspaper and journal articles as "too short" and, therefore, not comprehensive. It's more important to weigh this one criterion against others in assessing the overall value of a particular source.

When assessing different types of sources, you must consider how up to date they are. Usually instructors expect students to use the most current sources available on a topic, along with well-respected "classics" that present especially comprehensive, revolutionary, or important discussions. Consequently, again, rather than simply looking for only the most recent sources and dismissing older ones, you should weigh the currentness of a particular source along with other criteria to assess its worth overall. In assessing the currentness of a particular source, it's extremely important to note what *type* of source it is. Scholarly books may be comprehensive, but they take a long time to publish—perhaps three to four years for an author to research and write, and another two years before publication. Articles in scholarly journals tend to be more current than books, because most journals publish several issues each year and it usually takes less time for an author to write an article than a book. However, it is not uncommon for a scholarly journal to take a over a year to be published. Not surprisingly, the most current sources often are newspapers, which are committed to publishing information quickly. While newspapers may not offer comprehensive or detailed discussions—assuming instead that readers follow news coverage daily—they frequently present the most up-to-the-minute information about recent events, findings, or trends. In addition to newspapers, the Internet, which is constantly expanding in size and scope, contains a multitude of up-to-the-minute information. This is a difficult source to use, however, because the information is often too new to be easily verified.

You should also consider the specific values and limitations of specialized sources such as government documents, archival materials, and local history collections. Such materials are produced and collected for particular uses and, thus, can give researchers an advantage or disadvantage depending on their exact needs. For example, to find out about the daily lives of rural women in your community during the last century, you might read diaries and letters written by rural women. Yet you would probably find inconsistencies between the women's experiences, handwriting that is difficult to read, and slang terms that you cannot understand. In evaluating such sources, then, writers need to be aware that the needs of their own research projects may be at odds with the purposes for which such specialized sources were written.

Evaluating the Relevance of a Source. In addition to using the general criterion of reliability, it is also important to evaluate sources on the basis of their relevance to a general topic. If you do not consider how relevant your sources are to your central idea, you may end up writing a research paper based on sources that treat your topic as a tangent, an endnote or sidenote, or as a minor part of the central discussion. Relying substantially on sources that treat your topic in a minor way will cause a significant problem in developing and supporting your own ideas. That is, instead of having an author's full discussion of your topic to draw on, learn from, and critique, you'll be forced to use only a cursory treatment of it. As a result, you probably will not have sufficient detail or evidence to use in developing your own paper.

Although it is important to use sources that are relevant to your topic, locating these can be challenging because sources may be catalogued under several subject headings. A particular book may be listed under different headings in a bibliography, an index, and a card or on-line catalogue. Multiple listings occur not because librarians are trying to complicate your research, but because complex writings, especially lengthy journal articles or books, are related to a variety of related topics of interest to many researchers. In researching your topic, then, you can expect to identify initially many more sources than you actually end up deciding to use, because many of the sources you identify will be only marginally relevant to your research paper.

In evaluating the relevance of a source, consider how your topic relates to the information you actually discover in your research. How you conceive and write about your topic should generally reflect the information actually found in your research. Preconceptions about your subject as well as your own point of view should not unduly restrict how you represent the information that you find. To illustrate what we mean, assume that you are writing a research paper on "world hunger" for a sociology class. After some research, you might narrow your focus to "UN programs to combat world hunger." While initially you might expect your paper to describe agricultural programs, you might find in several sources that the UN has also developed family planning programs as a way of combating world hunger. If your personal convictions do not support the use of contraceptives, however, you might feel conflicted about discussing these programs and consider omitting any mention of them from your paper. Yet if you simply omitted any mention of them, you would misrepresent your topic. In such a situation, it would be far better to shift the focus of your paper, for example, from "UN programs to combat world hunger" to "UN agricultural programs to combat world hunger."

Assessing Conflicts between Sources. In evaluating sources, writers must not only assess the reliability and relevance of sources; they must also determine how to resolve conflicts between different sources. When you do research, you can expect to find that sources conflict over areas ranging from the inconsequential to the significant. Conflicts over factual details can be resolved through additional research. More difficult to handle, however, are conflicts over interpretations or conclusions. These can be resolved only by assessing the sources and determining which sources are more credible, based on their reliability and relevance. For example, a newly established electronic journal whose editorial policies are unknown is most likely a less credible source than a highly refereed journal published by a national professional organization. In making such an evaluation, the general considerations we have discussed will help you.

To return to the previous example, in writing a research paper on the UN's role in combating world hunger, you might find that some sources conclude that the UN has no business involving itself in such decisions as family planning, while others conclude that family planning programs are essential to solve world hunger. To better understand and deal with these conflicts among your sources (and to better develop and articulate your own position in your paper, when doing so would be appropriate), you should assess the reliability of the sources in question. You might note the presence of bias if an author is opposed to all forms of contraception, or if a source that praises UN programs was published by the UN. You should also assess whether your topic is a central or only a minor part of the discussion in the sources. These considerations can help you determine which of your sources are most credible and should have the most influence on your position and your research paper.

Activity 2

Use the previous discussion of reliability to evaluate "Adolescents and Their Music" at the end of this chapter. Together with your group, discuss the essay in terms of the following criteria: expertise, education, and training of the authors; absence or presence of bias; background information about the publisher or journal; presence, absence, or consistency of documentation; reviewing policies of the publisher; comprehensiveness; currentness; and generic characteristics of this type of source. Based on these criteria, do you find the essay to be generally reliable or unreliable, or is your group's judgment mixed? Explain your assessment.

Relating Topic to Task

On receiving a writing task, many students ask, "How long does the paper need to be?" Such queries are reasonable because the nature of a writing task determines many things about the text that is constructed in response to it—including length. Just as it would be inappropriate to submit a forty-page detailed analysis of a product to a client who had requested a "brief, preliminary report," it would be unreasonable to turn in a two-page essay in response to a major term paper assignment. What this suggests is that the scope of a research project, as well as the resulting paper, is very much determined by the expectations of the instructor and how these expectations are manifested within an assignment. For this reason, research writing assignments usually specify the number and type of sources to be used as well as the minimum number of pages that will fulfill the assignment adequately.

Specifications about length and scope are also important in research assignments because there is no such thing as an inherently minuscule subject or a topic about which nothing can be written. For example, an assignment to research "the manufacture of paper clips" might cover the materials paper clips are made of and an explanation of how those materials are fabricated. Because every entity, object, or process has characteristic features as well as a unique history, all topics are potentially complex.

In a sense, then, imagining or formulating a topic is a major challenge in writing a research paper. Even potential topics suggested in an assignment are often merely starting points. An initial topic must be shaped and redefined by the writer during the course of researching and writing. The English Grammar Assignment in the Sample Assignments section of this chapter, for example, suggests that one suitable topic is the controversy over the use of the generic *he*. However, numerous articles have been written on the subject, ranging from historical origins of the generic *he* to the effects of its use on cognition. An entire class might research the generic *he* and produce substantially different papers. A history major might focus on the role of the prescriptive grammar movement in promoting the use of the generic *he*. A journalism major, on the other hand, might choose to research publication policies regarding the use of inclusive pronouns in contemporary magazines, journals, and newspapers.

The fact that topics don't "make themselves" and must be created by the researcher and writer often presents students with another challenge, that of narrowing or focusing an overly broad topic. Many students with whom we've worked pick vast topics (e.g., "The Civil War" or "nonverbal communication") to be sure that they have "enough to write about." These students are often reluctant to narrow such broad topics, even when they discover numerous subtopics (eye contact, body distance, gestures, smiling, etc.) and hundreds of related sources.

Distinguishing Your Voice from That of Others

Although research paper assignments often focus a good deal of attention on how sources should be referenced, documentation is principally a mechanical matter. Yet despite its rather mechanical aspects, careful documentation is important because it allows writers to acknowledge ideas and information that they have gotten from other sources. In addition, proper documentation also indicates whether the information and ideas the writer presents are being reported directly or indirectly. This is an important distinction because a paraphrase, no matter how carefully crafted, can never fully reproduce the meaning and intent of actual words from an original source. Suppose, for example, you read an article by John Jones, who ended his piece with the following statements:

> *In reviewing the research that attempts to correlate television viewing and violence among adolescents, I could find no clear patterns. Despite my own experience that suggests that there is a connection, at this time I cannot conclude anything other than that the overall picture is complex and contradictory.*

In referencing John Jones, you could quote him directly. You could also quote him indirectly by paraphrasing his opinion:

> *John Jones found that no clear correlation exists between television viewing and adolescent violence.*

> *John Jones concluded his study by asserting that no correlation existed between television viewing and adolescent violence.*

> *Although his personal experience suggested that there was a correlation, John Jones described the results of research studies that attempt to establish a connection between television viewing and adolescent violence as being inconclusive at this time.*

As the previous variations illustrate, all three paraphrases are similar recreations of John Jones's original statement, yet they manifest subtle differences in emphasis and, thus, meaning. The first two paraphrases, for instance, resemble one another a great deal, but the second one contains information about where the statement was located ("John Jones *concluded* his study. . . .") and interprets Jones as having asserted his conclusion ("concluded his study by *asserting* that. . . ."). Because paraphrases necessarily alter the original wording of a source, it is important for readers to know when they are being presented with a person's exact words and when they are experiencing the original words through the interpretive lens of the writer.

Direct quotations suggest that they are "true" representations of other voices within a text, so it is essential to be accurate when quoting. Even a minor, accidental alteration can seriously misrepresent or distort ideas and information. Imagine what a misplaced decimal place could do to the statistic in this quote: "Beswith found that 3.4 percent of students had committed armed robbery while attending college."

Contractions and negatives (e.g., *no* and *not*), though they are small, can also significantly change the meaning of a sentence. However, even those mistakes that don't affect meaning dramatically can be serious, particularly if the individual being quoted is a well known for his or her speeches or writings.

In addition to accuracy, you must also be sure to reproduce quotes and paraphrases in such a way that they accurately represent a person's views. The phrase "quoting out of context" has become quite commonplace, suggesting (unfortunately) that the practice of deliberately distorting the intent or opinion of a writer or speaker by lifting (or paraphrasing) an unrepresentative passage occurs frequently. Certainly, it would be inaccurate to refer to John Jones (from the previous example) as an authority who recognizes the existence of a positive relationship between television viewing and violence and to quote him as saying that his "own experience suggests that there is a connection." Such a reference would distort his conclusion that "the overall picture is complex and contradictory."

Taking matters related to documentation seriously is very important because inaccuracies, when detected, make a writer seem sloppy and careless at best and unethical or dishonest at worst. However, failure to acknowledge when ideas or information have come from other sources is called *plagiarism* and is a major offense, *whether the writer has erred because of ignorance or design.* Unfortunately where plagiarism is concerned, pleas about inexperience or "honest" mistakes often fall on deaf ears.

There are several reasons why plagiarism is a serious offense. One has to do with a particular cultural practice, the right of individuals to own property. Ideas, which people often labor to create and develop, are seen as *intellectual* property. If you worked to earn money to buy a new stereo, you would feel distressed if someone stole it. Similarly, if you labored hard to develop and write out an idea or to synthesize different kinds of information in a unique way, you would be upset if someone took parts of your paper and put his or her name on them. Moreover, although having your ideas "stolen" can be painful in and of itself, plagiarism can cause more than bad feelings. Grades in college classes are often determined substantially by what students write, and in many professions, people's income, professional advancement and job retention are affected by what they publish.

Plagiarism also implies insensitivity toward or a lack of respect for others. In general, when people do something worthwhile, it is courteous to acknowledge them. If a group of your friends were discussing a serious problem and one of you proposed an ingenious solution, it would be unfair for one person to take credit for it later. The principle here—and it's a good one—is to give credit where credit is due. Treat others' ideas with respect by acknowledging them for those ideas. Although it is not always easy to keep track of "who thought of what"—particularly in a collaborative writing group—it is good to develop the skill of noticing what contributions others have made to your work. The acquisition of such a skill may motivate you to be sensitive to and thus credit such contributions.

Of course, while the principle of giving credit where it's due is a good one, writers don't *always* have to be acknowledged for *everything* they say. Some information is considered common knowledge. It is not necessary to acknowledge the sources for commonly held opinions ("College educations are becoming more expensive") or widely known facts ("George Washington was the first president of the United States"). Indeed, members of your audience would find it odd to read a sentence like the following: "According to John Evans, George Washington was the first president of the United States." On the other hand, *opinions* about George Washington's presidency would need to be documented, particularly if they were controversial: "According to John Evans, George Washington's only significant contribution as a president was that he came first." Also, unusual facts about Washington's life would need to be credited. If, for example, a researcher discovered that young George liked to play mischievous jokes on people, that scholar should be credited for her discovery, for example: "According to May Belle Jarvis, George Washington as a young boy developed a reputation for being an incorrigible prankster."

 **Activity 3**

The following are several sets of topics. The first is the most broad; the final is the most focused or narrowed:

- Nonverbal communication—eye contact—the effect of culture on eye contact
- Rock music—rock music of the sixties—the contribution of the Grateful Dead to rock music of the sixties
- Computer networks—commercial network services—commercial network services for secondary school teachers.

Together with your group, select a minimum of three broad topics with which two or more of you are familiar and describe how you might narrow and focus these for one or more of following assignments:

1. A six- to eight-page research paper with at least three sources on an issue related to contemporary American culture for an introductory course in contemporary American literature.

2. A ten- to fifteen-page research paper requiring at least eight sources on a controversial issue for a course titled Contemporary Issues in Political Science.

3. An eight- to ten-page research paper requiring a minimum of six sources about a current environmental crisis for an introductory course in ecology.

 **Activity 4**

Select two of the readings from this chapter, and find in each reading *four* direct quotes and *four* paraphrases or summaries that are credited to others. Compare these, especially noting how quotes and paraphrases are integrated into the text and how the author is cited. Also locate four statements or claims that represent widely held beliefs or acknowledged facts that are *not* credited to others. Discuss with your group partners the sorts of opinions and information you could offer *without citation* within a research paper on the topic "selecting an undergraduate major for the nineties."

WRITING YOUR RESEARCH PAPER

This section provides advice to guide you through writing a research paper. The phases in this process include working with bibliography cards and note cards, narrowing your topic, developing a thesis and structure, documenting sources, and of course, revising and editing. Although we will discuss each phase as a separate step and in sequential order, we are not suggesting that the phases necessarily are separate, sequenced steps. In fact, when writing research papers, most people ordinarily do not follow a linear process; instead, they move back and forth between researching and writing.

Working with Bibliography Cards

An extremely useful tool to anyone writing a research paper is a set of bibliography cards—index cards on which writers put relevant publication information about their sources. Bibliography cards can be referred to throughout the research process as well as when it's time to construct your **Works Cited** page or bibliography. For bibliography cards, three-by-five-inch index cards (lined or unlined) are preferable because the remaining cards in a packet can be used for note taking. One bibliography card should be created for each of your sources. As a rule of thumb, we recommend that you write out a bibliography card *before* you start the taking notes on a source. If you establish such a routine, you will always remember to write out a bibliography card and never lose track of an important source.

Before beginning to write bibliography cards, though, you need to know what documentation format to use. Most often, college writers must use one of the three documentation systems used most widely in scholarly writing—the MLA (Modern Language Association), APA (American Psychological Association), or CBE (Council of Biology Editors) styles. If you do not know which system to use for the discipline in which you are writing, you should ask your instructor for guidance. Various formats require different bibliographic information and in differing orders, so you will need to be sure that you are following the correct format and that your bibliography cards are written correctly, down to the smallest detail. You should also ensure that your documentation format (usually found in a handbook or style sheet) is current; disciplines occasionally revise their formats.

Figures 9–1 and 9–2 are two sample bibliography cards for a book by a single author. Notice how the first card, which follows the MLA format, differs from the second card, which follows the APA format.

A.

Sadker, Myra, and David Sadker. <u>Failing at Fairness: How America's Schools Cheat Girls.</u> New York: Scribner's, 1994.

Figure 9–1 MLA Format.

A.

Sadker, M., & Sadker, D. (1994). <u>Failing at</u>
<u>fairness: How America's schools cheat girls</u>. New York:
Scribner's.

Figure 9–2 APA Format.

Notice also that each card has been written with the letter *A* in the upper-right-hand corner. We recommend that you label each new card with a consecutive letter. (The next source card would have a *B* in the corner; the next one would have a *C*; and so forth.) Doing so will be useful when you begin the process of writing out note cards, as you will soon see.

Working with Note Cards

Note cards, or index cards on which you take notes from the sources you are reading, are also helpful research tools for a couple of important reasons. First, they are not fastened to each other as are sheets of paper in a spiral-bound notebook, so they can be arranged in various patterns to help you determine the most effective organization for your research. Note cards can also be arranged according to subtopics so that you can see if you have subtopics on which you will need to go back and gather additional information—or subtopics that you should eliminate. Still another advantage of using note cards is that doing so will help you avoid copied structure. As we have said, you ordinarily will write a more effective paper when you organize it according to *ideas* rather than *sources*.

We don't want to give the impression, however, that note cards are so advantageous that they can replace the other kinds of note taking we previously have discussed. Before you are ready to bring note cards into your research process, you need to read critically and take notes on each of your sources. (For a more complete discussion of the critical reading and note-taking processes, refer to Chapter 7.) Only when you have prepared in this manner will you be ready to write notes on your cards.

As you write notes on the cards, we recommend a few basic guidelines. Although index cards can be purchased in a variety of sizes, we recommend three-by-five-inch cards, which provide ample space, but not so much that notes might be too long and cumbersome to work with. We also recommend that you write on only one side of each card, and that you use a second one to finish writing down related information when necessary. Writing on both sides of a card may prevent you from experimenting with different ways of arranging your notes and organizing your paper. In addition, it's not necessary to fill up all the space on each card; cards are more useful when they are not crammed with too much information. Finally, in general you should write note cards using your own words rather than the author's—although you should take care to accurately represent the author's meaning. However, especially powerful phrases or particularly salient quotations (punctuated with quotation marks) should be copied word for word for later use.

If you look at the sample note cards that follow, you will see that the first two are typical note cards that record information in the student writer's own words. The third, however, records a direct quotation that the writer may want to use in her research paper.

Because all of these note cards were taken from the same source (Myra and David Sadker's *Failing at Fairness*), they have been labeled with an *A* in the upper-right-hand corner. Next to the *A* is the page number from which the information was taken. Keeping track of page numbers in this manner is essential to allow you to quickly return to information you wish to reread and to help you document your paper correctly.

A. p. 48

There are 3 kinds of students in a classroom. The first is made up of "star students," who volunteer to answer questions and catch the teacher's attention. They constitute about 10 percent of a class. The second group is composed of "nominal students," who are 70 percent of a class and answer 1–2 questions from the teacher but don't try to catch his or her attention. The third group, about 20 percent of a class, comprises shy or silent students who don't say anything at all.

Figure 9–3 In the Student Writer's Own Words.

A. p. 43

These researchers have found that teachers often forget about the rule of raising your hand to talk, with boys anyway. Usually boys begin calling out their ideas without raising their hands, and the teacher pays positive attention to them. But when girls call out their ideas, most often the teacher reprimands them for not raising their hands.

Figure 9–4 In the Student Writer's Own Words.

A. p. 50

"Unlike the smart boy who flourishes in the classroom, the smart girl is the student who is least likely to be recognized."

Figure 9–5 A Direct Quotation from the Source.

 **Activity 5**

Write out a bibliography card (using a documentation format of your choice) and at least five note cards for "Adolescents and Their Music." Then meet with your group members to discuss the correctness of your bibliography cards, paying close attention to differences in documentation formats that may have been used. Also discuss the kinds of information that were included on the note cards and any passages that were chosen as direct quotations.

Narrowing Your Topic

When assigned a research paper, writers often begin exploring a topic by reading a few related sources. As they read, these sources help them envision ways of narrowing or modifying their initial ideas. Narrowed or modified topics, in turn, help writers select still more sources. The resulting chain reaction—of sources leading to potential topics leading to more sources leading to more topics—continues until a writer is satisfied that the topic is well defined and researched.

To see how this process works, let's say that you were given the Introduction to Ethnic Studies Assignment in the Sample Assignments section of this chapter and that you and your group partners selected "Irish Americans" as the ethnic group you wished to explore. It would be difficult to write a term paper of the length specified without narrowing the topic. Still, without reading any information on the subject, it would be difficult to begin the narrowing process, unless one or more members of your group were already well informed. From some initial reading, however, you would begin to discover different avenues to explore (e.g., when Irish settlers left

Ireland and came to the United States"; "conditions in Ireland that caused the Irish to emigrate"; or "the predominant occupations of the persons who emigrated"). These ideas could suggest additional, more focused topics: "religious practices of Irish Americans"; "occupations and incomes of Irish Americans"; "Irish American literature"; "famous Irish Americans (e.g., John F. Kennedy)."

The list of questions and subtopics related to Irish Americans in the preceding paragraph (which is by no means exhaustive) suggests that the topic is rich with possibilities. However, the process of shaping a specialized focus for a research paper would undoubtedly be affected by the nature of the sources encountered during that process. If, for example, you and you group discovered many sources on ties between Ireland and Americans of Irish decent, you might settle on a final topic like this one: "How conditions in Ireland have influenced the lives of Irish Americans." On the other hand, if during the course of the narrowing process you and your partners became particularly interested in sources that discussed Irish American literature, art, dance, and music as well as the contexts (e.g., holidays or festivals) in which these were produced and performed, you might decide to narrow your topic to "Irish American cultural practices."

Once you have begun the researching and topic-narrowing process, you may find yourself in a pleasing treasure hunt, in which one source or idea leads to another in a path that promises a clear, satisfying resolution. This may not always happen, for a variety of reasons. Sometimes an initial topic may be so broad that the number of subtopics may be overwhelming. In this case, you might attempt to locate a broad source that presents an overview of the topic and divides it into subtopics. Books devoted to a particular subject often contain introductory essays that provide such overviews.

Another frustrating problem that researchers often encounter is difficulty locating sources related to a topic about which little has been published. In this situation, *one* scholarly book or article—with a *bibliography*—can be very valuable. Students who can't get started because they "can't find any sources" become productively engaged in the researching and topic-narrowing process once they locate a piece that cites other sources.

Perhaps the greatest challenge for a writer who wishes to research and narrow a particular topic is knowing how to proceed when there just *aren't* any sources (or perhaps merely one or two). Novice researchers should select another topic, if possible. However, seasoned researchers may create new research topics in such a situation. Melissa, an English education major, decided to research the topic "students negotiating their own writing grades." However, she could find only one source on the subject, an essay that was a class handout. When she inspected its bibliography, she discovered that the author had cited books and articles on broad related topics, rather than sources that dealt in particular with the subject of the essay, "students negotiating their own writing grades." In response to this challenge, Melissa read sources from the bibliography of her one essay, which lead her to other essays and books on related subjects such as "portfolio evaluation," "self-evaluation," and "peer writing groups." From her various readings and her initial idea, she created a new, focused topic of her own: "Adapting various techniques to allow students to

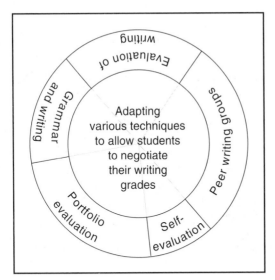

Figure 9–6 The Process of Forming a New Topic.

negotiate their writing grades." As Figure 9–6 illustrates, Melissa formed her topic by combining ideas and information that she selected from a number of related "old" topics. Creating new topics from the intersection of more established, recognized ones is an exciting—if challenging—way to integrate your research and topic-narrowing processes.

 **Activity 6**

With your group partners, select a tentative topic from those listed in the Writing Assignments section of this chapter. You and other members of your group will research this *one* topic, whether you write papers separately or submit one group project. After selecting your tentative topic, follow these steps:

1. Individually consult the reference works discussed earlier in the chapter (computerized indexes, newspaper indexes, specialized bibliographies, etc.) and locate on your own *six* sources related to your group's topic; read and take notes on these. Bring your sources and notes to class. You may carry actual sources to class; however, we recommend that you *also* photocopy journal articles, book chapters, and important excerpts from larger works, if allowed.

2. Discuss your sources and notes with your group. If your group will be writing *separate* papers, discuss the sources that each of you have read and assist each person in devising a detailed,

narrowed topic. Which sources from all those in the group should each person select to further develop his or her topic? What additional research should each person do?

If the group will be producing *one* research paper, together decide on a detailed, narrowed topic for that paper. Based on the narrowed topic you have devised, decide which of the sources located by individual group members should be read by everyone. Also decide if the group needs to do additional research and reading on your narrowed topic.

Developing a Thesis and Structure

Once you have a concrete idea of your topic and feel satisfied with the number of sources you've read and taken notes on and the information in them, you are ready to develop both a tentative thesis and a structure for your research paper. At this point, using the invention techniques you have learned will help you to come up with initial ideas for thesis statements. Clustering and brainstorming or even discussing your topic with interested parties on the Internet are especially effective techniques when you have finished reading and note taking but are not quite sure what main ideas to develop in your paper. Moreover, you should pay particular attention to instructions from your teacher about matters such as particular topics to be addressed, suitable focuses, and requirements about using particular sources. Any such requirements should guide your decisions in developing a thesis and structure for your research paper. In structuring your paper, it is also important to keep in mind disciplinary and professional conventions, as we discussed in Chapter 5.

As you begin to develop a thesis, remember that a research paper is a specialized kind of synthesis writing. Thus, like any other synthesis paper, your research paper should be unified by a thesis statement that presents your own synthesis—shaped by your research—of ideas on the topic. As we discussed in Chapter 8, considering what your primary aim is in writing will help you in developing a thesis statement. While it is conceivable that a few research paper assignments might permit literary or expressive papers, usually teachers will expect papers that are persuasive or informative, because that is conventional for most disciplines. In developing your own thesis, then, you should reread your assignment to determine whether an informative or a persuasive paper is expected or ask the teacher for clarification. It is also a good idea to write out a tentative thesis statement and solicit your teacher's feedback on it, including whether your primary purpose—that is, to persuade or to inform—is acceptable for the assignment.

Planning for Thesis and Structure. Whether the primary aim of your research paper is informative or persuasive, the key principle to keep in mind is that all the major parts of your paper should relate to your thesis statement. Thus, as you write a tentative thesis, you should also sketch out a brief plan or outline of the major parts of your paper. As you consider different thesis statements, you should note how each implies certain points to be supported.

Assuming, say, that you are writing a research paper on undergraduate student life earlier in this century and have narrowed your interest to "student activism." In your research, you discover that while people ordinarily associate college student activism with the 1960s, it has been a part of college student life since the beginning of the twentieth century. Here are some possible thesis statements that you might consider:

1. *Student activism has been a part of college student life since about 1900.*

2. *The relatively peaceful and largely ineffective student activism of the early part of the twentieth century foreshadows the more violent, and effective, student activism of the 1960s.*

3. *Those of us who grew up hearing about sit-ins, peace marches, and college students commandeering the offices of college presidents might assume that student activism began in the 1960s. However, the violence and intensity of activism in the 1960s is preceded by a more peaceful yet still important sixty-year history of activism among college students.*

4. *Just as college student activism in the 1960s helped to change national politics, activism among college students in the early decades of this century was an important influence on interest in socialism in the United States.*

In reading through these thesis statements, note that while they are all on the general subject of the history of student activism, they make different claims about that subject. Necessarily, then, they would each require different discussions to support or develop them. For example, thesis statement 2 would require the discussion of several major areas—what forms of activism there were in the early part of the twentieth century, what effects those early forms had, what forms of activism were popular in the 1960s, and what effects resulted from 1960s activism. Similarly, thesis statement 3 would require discussion of major events that promoted activism among students (e.g., World War I, the Spanish Civil War, and the Great Depression) or of the various forms activism took (e.g., involvement in campus-based organizations, involvement in national political parties, and involvement in underground organizations).

As you can see, in reviewing several thesis statements, writers should consider the main topics each implies, for such topics must be developed or supported in the resulting research paper. Moreover, as illustrated by the previous examples, small changes in the wording of thesis statements can translate into major changes in the structure of a paper. Consequently, when considering several possible thesis statements, rather than focusing on the thesis statements alone to make your decision, you should write out tentative outlines or plans for each, indicating what major topics would be discussed. Make your final decision based on your consideration of both elements, the thesis and the overall structure it implies.

To generate possible thesis statements, it is helpful to reread your note cards and review all the other notes you have taken. Again, at this stage clustering, freewriting, and brainstorming can help you move from note taking to a synthesis of your ideas. As ideas for a thesis occur to you, jot them down on a sheet of paper; record all your ideas on a single sheet of paper if possible so that you can look at them all together. These ideas may consist of complete sentences or groups of sentences that are possible thesis statements. If you have words and phrases that identify particular topics you want or need to address, try drafting complete sentences or revising existing ones to incorporate them. Identify topics about which you have little information and will, thus, need to do additional research on, and mark these clearly with a highlighter, asterisks—or perhaps a yellow "caution" flag. Using asterisks or a highlighter, mark the thesis statements that seem most workable to you.

Once you have generated several thesis statements and chosen a promising one by comparing the statements and the brief plans or lists of topics that you have devised for each, you are ready to design the overall structure of your paper in more detail. A detailed plan should be divided into the major sections that are implied in the thesis statement. In addition, each section of the plan should indicate the major content to be discussed and list the important information that will be used to develop that content: specific examples and details, definitions of key terms, particular arguments, refutations of particular arguments, and so forth. Finally, each part of the plan should list the sources that will be used.

Writing a plan this detailed may seem like an extra step that you could skip. However, we have found that time spent writing a detailed plan soon translates into easier and more efficient drafting. Because of the complexities of research papers— the length of time involved in researching a topic, the length of the final paper, the intricacies of working with several information sources—we recommend writing a detailed outline before drafting.

Planning for Connections. In addition to planning the overall structure of your research paper, you need to think about planning of a different kind: how to connect the major parts of the paper to one another. Such planning is important in writing research papers for two reasons. First, research papers are usually divided into several sections or topics and the relationship between these must be clear to readers. Second, research papers are long and writers must pay more attention to making the connections within them explicit for readers. You may have noticed this principle in reading a variety of longer writings: Books and long newspaper or magazine articles routinely use headings and metadiscourse to make connections clear.

Perhaps the most important area to plan for is how to inform readers of the overall structure of your research paper. Writers usually do so in what we call an *overview sentence,* which identifies the major sections or topics of discussion in a paper in order to give readers an idea of what the major parts are and how they are connected to the thesis and to one another. While the overview can be written as a part of a thesis, the two are not the same thing and often are written as two separate sentences. In practice, the thesis usually asks a particular question or makes a general claim, while the overview sentence explains how the paper will answer the question or support the claim posed in the thesis.

Examine, for instance, the article "Risks and Chemical Substances" by Avrom Blumberg. Both thesis and overview sentences are stated at the end of Blumberg's introduction, in the third paragraph of the article:

> We are exposed to about **50 thousand** of these [chemical substances] in various amounts and it is natural to ask how safe we are from this contact. This paper will look at how we become exposed within our homes, then examine three important ways in which we identify and evaluate hazardous substances, and finally try to suggest a rational picture of the risks we all face.

The first sentence, the thesis, describes a condition and asks a question about it—which the paper itself will try to answer. However, the following sentence is the one that provides the overview of the structure of the paper.

In addition to writing an overview sentence, you should also plan to use metadiscourse consciously at key parts of your paper. In research papers, writers should pay particular attention to transitions from one major section of the paper to the next. Suppose that you were writing a research paper supporting this thesis (taken from the examples on page 372):

> *The relatively peaceful and largely ineffective student activism of the early part of the twentieth century foreshadows the more violent, and effective, student activism of the 1960s.*

Assume also that you had decided to organize the paper into two major sections (early activism and sixties activism) and to subdivide each section into two parts (forms of activism and effects of activism). Under these circumstances, you would need to consciously plan transitions to connect the various parts of the paper. Statements and phrases such as the following might be appropriate for this purpose:

> *To understand the general ineffectiveness of early student activism, it is important to acknowledge the great variety of forms it took in the earlier parts of this century. . . .*

> *Given the great variety of forms that early student activism took, student voices and energies were spread over a wide number of local or regional causes. Hence, it should come as no surprise that early student activists were most effective at the local level and only rarely effective nationally. . . .*

> *Early student activist movements, then, generally encompassed a variety of issues and were most influential at changing local policies and practices. In contrast, student activism in the 1960s centered on a few issues perceived to be of national importance and became very influential on both local and national levels. . . .*

Transitional sentences are useful not only to let readers know what connections are being drawn between parts of a papers. They also remind writers engaged in a large project about the connections they must develop in the course of drafting their research papers. In fact, it is a good idea to jot down such transitional sentences or phrases on your detailed outline as you draft it.

 **Activity 7**

Reread the sample thesis statements on activism among college students from earlier in this section. For thesis statements 1, 3, and 4, write out a tentative plan of the major topics you would have to discuss in a research paper. Use the discussion of thesis statement 2 to guide your work.

Activity 8

Drawing on the work you have begun on your own research paper (Activity 6), read and take notes on your sources. Be especially sure to take notes carefully on any electronic sources because retracing the exact steps by which you located a source may be difficult. If your group is collaborating on one paper, by now you will have decided what sources to read. With your group, share and discuss your notes and information you have learned from your reading. Based on this discussion, together devise and write out at least three possible thesis statements. Next, write out a tentative plan of the major topics or sections required for supporting *each one* of the thesis statements. Discuss the merits of each thesis and plan, and select one to work with. Make any revisions you feel necessary, based on your group discussion. Write out your thesis statement and a short plan of the major sections or topics you will discuss, and submit them to your instructor for commentary.

If you are working on an individual paper, share and discuss your notes with your group partners. On the basis of their feedback, devise and write out at least three possible thesis statements and plans. With your group, discuss the merits of each one and decide on a final selection. Write out your thesis statement and a short plan of the major sections or topics that you will discuss, and submit them to your instructor for commentary.

Activity 9

Whether you and other members of your group have each developed your own tentative thesis and plan, or whether your group has devised these together, follow these steps:

1. Revise your thesis and plan based on the feedback from your instructor.

2. Using your revised thesis and plan as a guide, write a *detailed* plan or outline of your research paper; your plan should be a minimum of two pages long. Begin your plan by stating your thesis and writing an overview sentence. Also, you should describe the major parts or sections of

your paper. For each major part or section, indicate the following types of information that you will use to develop or support your major claims: definitions, specific examples, background information, arguments, counterarguments, and so forth. Be very detailed as you fill in this information, noting, for example, specific sources and page numbers where appropriate.

3. Once you have completed your detailed plan, estimate how many pages you think each section will take. Also, write out transitional sentences or phrases that you can use to connect the parts to one another.

4. Discuss your plans and thesis statements with your group. Make any necessary revisions, and submit the plan to your instructor for feedback.

Documenting Sources

Once you have determined a thesis and structure for your research paper and are engaged in the process of drafting, you will need to be concerned with documentation. By "documentation," we mean a discipline's guidelines on the **format, annotations, citations,** and **bibliography** of a scholarly paper. As we have said earlier in this chapter, procedures for documentation vary greatly from discipline to discipline, so you will need to obtain a good handbook or style manual for the discipline in which you are writing and follow it closely. Ordinarily, all of your particular concerns about documentation will be addressed in your handbook or style manual; however, we offer the following general information to give you an overall understanding of the kinds of procedures for which you will be accountable.

Considering Format. The numerous format considerations that you will face as you construct your research paper constitute an important aspect of documentation. In general, these many considerations fall into two basic categories: those on the construction and placement of parts within the paper and those on mechanical matters. The construction and placement of a paper's parts include how the title page should be written (if one is required); whether an abstract should be included (and, if so, how it should be written and where it should be placed); whether headings should be used (and, if so, how they should be written and where they should be placed); whether graphs and charts should be included (and, if so, where they should be placed—in the body of the paper? in an appendix?); and so on. Format considerations on mechanical matters also include a range of issues: what size margins and fonts should be used; how pagination should be handled; whether the writer's name should appear only on the title page or on each page of the paper (and, if so, where? in the upper-right-hand corner? centered at the bottom of the page?); and so on.

While most of these format considerations will be specified by disciplinary conventions (which actually makes the writer's task easier), sometimes you will have to make choices. That is, sometimes a handbook may offer options on a format consideration. If this is the case, it is important that you choose *one* option and use it consistently throughout your paper. Of course, you should keep in mind that your teacher may have specific format requirements for your research paper. Pay close attention to your assignment; if your teacher has provided you with specific guidelines, these should take precedence over any guidelines in your handbook.

Including Annotations. Another important aspect of documentation is the use of annotations, sometimes referred to as "explanatory notes" or "informational notes." An annotation is information provided in a note rather than in the body of the text. Annotations often appear at the bottom of a page, although sometimes they are listed at the end of a chapter or at the end of a book in a section labeled "**Notes.**"

The purpose of annotations is to provide readers with information that would seem digressive or obtrusive in the body of the paper itself. Let's say, for example, that you are writing a research paper for an education class on ways that portfolios are being used in the teaching of writing. In the introduction you write:

> *In the past six years or so, the use of portfolios in the teaching of composition has proliferated. Professional conferences have included numerous sessions on various aspects of portfolio pedagogy, school districtwide support groups have been established, and portfolio newsletters[1] have been started across the country.*

You are satisfied that this is a good opening sentence for your paper and wish to continue with your explanation of the current popularity of portfolios. However, as you researched your topic you located the titles and addresses of two newsletters about portfolios and you believe that some of your intended readers might be interested in knowing about them. You realize, though, that including such information in your introduction probably would seem obtrusive and out of place. The rhetorical problem just described can be easily solved through the use of an annotation. If you are using MLA documentation you simply can place a raised (superscript) number 1 after the word *newsletter.* (Look at the raised number 1 in the previous block quotation.) This indicates to your readers that additional information having to do with newsletters appears in an annotation below. You would then insert a footnote such as the following at the bottom of the page:

[1] *See, for example,* Portfolio Assessment Newsletter *(Five Centerpointe Drive, Suite 100, Lake Oswego OR 97035), which supports an information network for educators interested in portfolios and portfolio assessment and* Portfolio News *(c/o San Dieguito Union High School District, 710 Encinitas Boulevard, Encinitas, CA 92024), which contains reports of individual projects and discussions of concern in portfolio assessment.*

Any subsequent annotations would be identified by the numbers 2, 3, and so on. If you are using a documentation method other than MLA, your handbook may direct you to handle annotations in a slightly different fashion.

Handling Citations: Internal Documentation, Footnotes, and Endnotes. Although you may not previously have used annotations in your writing, you probably have had some experience with using citations, which constitute another important part of documentation. The three kinds of citations—internal documentation, footnotes, and endnotes—all serve the same function: to let readers know that an idea in the text was borrowed from a source and did not originate with the writer.

There are two basic principles behind citations. One is that writers should give credit to all sources from which they borrow information; the other is that writers should provide readers with the publication information necessary to locate an original source. Based on these principles, then, writers are expected to indicate immediately within their text whenever an idea has been taken from a source and to provide the necessary publication information.

Citations are handled in one of three ways, depending on the documentation requirements of the discipline. In current scholarly writing, the most commonly used citation method is internal documentation, sometimes referred to in handbooks as "parenthetical citation." Internal documentation requires the writer to include brief information about the source within parentheses immediately following the sentence or sentences in which information or ideas have been borrowed. The following passage taken from the research paper on portfolios is an example of internal documentation using MLA format:

> *Tracy and Cantlebary, who teach at a high school in the Columbus, Ohio, area, ask their students to prepare a "showcase portfolio" by removing selections from their various computer disks and combining the selections on a "portfolio disk." The teachers claim that the students are able to retain the work for "reflection, self-evaluation, and comparisons to later works" (Tierney, Carter, and Desai 51).*

As you can see, the writer has included parentheses at the end of her passage to indicate the source of her information. Because she is following MLA format, she includes the names of the authors and the page from which the information was taken. For additional publication information, the reader can turn to the bibliography of this paper, where the full publication information will be written. If writers were using another documentation format, the information that they would include in the parentheses might vary. Some internal documentation formats require publication dates, some require commas or semicolons between pieces of information, and so on.

Another citation method that you will encounter in your readings—but which is seldom required for current writers—is footnotes. When using footnotes, a writer ordinarily indicates that a source has been used by placing a raised number immediately following the borrowed passage. The publication information on the source is then given at the bottom of the page, in whatever order is required by the discipline. The following passage from the research paper on portfolios is shown again, this time with a footnote rather than with internal documentation:

> *Tracy and Cantlebary, who teach at a high school in the Columbus, Ohio area, ask their students to prepare a "showcase portfolio" by removing selections from their various computer disks and combining the selections on a "portfolio disk."*

The teachers claim that the students are able to retain the work for "reflection, self-evaluation, and comparisons to later works."[1]

[1]Robert J. Tierney, Mark A. Carter, and Laura E. Desai, Portfolio Assessment in the Reading—Writing Classroom *(Norwood, MA: Christopher-Gordon, 1991) 51.*

As with internal citations, footnotes vary depending on the discipline and the nature of the source. The information provided in the previous footnote follows former MLA requirements for a book by three authors. Within footnotes, information can vary depending on the number of authors a source has, if author information is available at all; whether the source is a book, a popular magazine, a scholarly journal, a government document, a chapter from a book, or whatever; whether the source is an original edition or a reprinted or revised edition; whether the source is part of a series; and so on.

Endnotes, the final kind of format documentation, are handled in the same way as footnotes—with one major difference. Instead of appearing at the bottom of the page on which a source is mentioned, endnotes are listed in sequential order on a page at the end of the text. This page ordinarily is labeled "**Endnotes**," or often simply "**Notes**."

Regardless of the citation method you are required to use, it is important for you to keep track of your sources as you draft your paper. On the other hand, as you draft you don't want to lose a good idea simply because you are stopping to write out citations. Therefore, we recommend that you devise an abbreviated system for keeping track of source information as you complete a first draft. Later as you revise, you can refer to your note cards and bibliography cards to complete your citations completely and correctly.

Constructing Bibliographies. Bibliographies—lists of sources that appear at the end of a paper or other scholarly work—are the final part of documentation. As we have discussed before, bibliographies work in concert with citations to provide readers with full publication information about sources. In general, bibliographies list all works that are cited within a paper. Sometimes, though, they also include sources that the writer has consulted but has not actually referred to in the paper. In some cases disciplines may require writers to include both a "**Works Cited**" page and a "**Works Consulted**" page at the end of their text to distinguish how the sources were used; in other cases, disciplines require that all sources—whether cited or consulted—appear in one listing labeled "**Bibliography**." As with internal citations, follow a handbook or style manual closely to be sure that you are adhering to the requirements of the discipline for which you are writing.

Constructing a bibliography ordinarily is not a difficult task—if you have written out bibliography cards as you read and taken notes on your sources. Under these circumstances, it is a fairly easy matter to wait to construct your bibliography until after your paper has been written and revised. Most bibliographies are organized alphabetically; therefore, you can alphabetize your bibliography cards and transform the information into a list, using the appropriate disciplinary or professional requirements.

✿ Activity 10

Using the readings at the end of this chapter as well as others from your research, locate and bring to class examples of the following kinds of citations:

- Book written by a single author
- Coauthored book
- Selection from an anthology or edited collection
- Newspaper article
- Coauthored journal article.

Notice differences among the documentation systems and formats in your examples. Working by yourself, use your handbook or style manual to create a bibliography following *one particular documentation system,* preferably the one you will use in your research paper. Compare your bibliography with those constructed by the other members of your group, and discuss any differences.

Revising, Editing, and Polishing Your Documentation

Earlier in this chapter we explained that it was important to work out a detailed plan or outline before drafting a research paper because such a plan enables you to devise a structure that develops points or supports claims that are related to your thesis. In addition, well-conceived plans or outlines can offer guidance about where in your paper to insert details (quotes, statistics, etc.) from your notes. Besides being a valuable drafting aid, however, detailed plans are also helpful in the revision process because they can help you compare what you *actually wrote* with what you *intended to write.*

Once you have completed a draft of your research paper, then, you should carefully compare it with the plan you devised in order to see how closely you have adhered to it. One of the best ways to do this is to outline your completed draft and then to compare that outline with your plan. This method is more time-consuming than simply reading over a draft with your original plan or outline nearby, but it's worth the extra effort because an outline of a draft can show precisely where it has deviated from your plan. Such an outline may, for example, show you that you have digressed and written an entirely unplanned (and unnecessary) section. After you have ensured that the draft of your research paper follows the overall structure you intended, you should read it again to assess how well you have integrated sources and to determine if connections between each part are clear. As you recall, skillful integration requires you to provide sufficient background information that clearly demonstrates the relevance of each source. It may also be necessary to give information about the authors whom you quote or paraphrase so that readers understand why you have included them.

Besides paying attention to the amount and nature of background information, you should use metadiscourse to skillfully integrate sources and make relationships between parts of your paper clear. Because research writing—which may contain a great deal of information from a variety of sources—can be difficult to follow, readers often appreciate metadiscourse that previews what is to come. Here is an example of such metadiscourse:

> *Before I discuss the importance of Overhulse's contribution to computer technology, however, I will provide a brief overview of the development of that technology over the last decade.*

Statements, such as the following, that explain the relevance of quoted material are also helpful to readers:

> *As the above quote illustrates, Dill did not change his mind about private education until after he had completed two terms in the state legislature.*

> *The following excerpts show that Barwell's conversion was a gradual process.*

Although paying attention to the care with which you have integrated quotes and paraphrases is an important step in revising research papers, so too is attending to the overall *proportion* and *accuracy* of this information. Source information, no matter its form, should support, illustrate, and elaborate on the information or arguments that *you* have chosen to present; it should not dominate or take over a text. That is to say, a research paper should not be a collage of source information pasted together.

In attending to quotes and paraphrases, you must ensure that you have indicated clearly when information and ideas originate from other sources and that you have quoted or paraphrased accurately. When revising, then, take care to designate quotes and paraphrases as such and provide information about where they originated. Carefully compare each quote with the original text or with the relevant note card to be sure that your wording is accurate. Finally, check paraphrases to be certain that you haven't distorted the sense of the original text, and review each quote and paraphrase to be sure that they are not taken out of context.

Although your voice should be evident within a research paper (as well as distinguished from those that originate from other sources), the *extent* to which you should call attention to your own perspective is something to consider during revision. Disciplinary conventions (as well as the requirements of individual instructors) often limit the degree to which a writer may emphasize himself or herself within a text. Whether personal narratives or the use of the first-person point of view (*I/we*) is acceptable varies. So too do other matters related to style, such as tone (humor, for example) and level of formality. Generally, research papers tend to be formal documents in which slang and informal usage are ordinarily inappropriate. Other options such as whether passive voice is permitted or whether contractions may be used are not so clear-cut. In revising, then, once you have assured yourself that your text is well organized, that your discussion is detailed and coherent, and that your sources are well synthesized, you should review your style for appropriateness and consistency.

Editing—the stage in which a text is polished and rendered as error-free as possible—is particularly important for research papers. Unlike other texts, research papers require attention to format and documentation. Many instructors take off points if a cover page is improperly prepared or if a footnote or bibliographical entry is inaccurate. The final preparation of a research paper, then, requires time. Despite the smallness of many details associated with documentation and format, however, time spent during this stage of research paper preparation is well justified. The substitution of a semicolon (;) for a period (.) within a bibliographical entry can cause a citation to be improper, and an accumulation of such "small" matters can create an impression of sloppiness, which can undermine a writer's credibility. In addition, matters related to documentation and format aren't necessarily low-level details. Inconsistent headings can easily confuse readers about how a text is structured. Incorrect spacing can also interfere with readers' ability to comprehend a text. For all these reasons, then, an important, final step of writing a research paper is to check format and citations.

Although many of the revision strategies we have offered in this section are similar to the suggestions we made in the preceding chapter, we included a few additional steps because some aspects of research writing distinguish it from other synthesis writing. One unique aspect of research papers is that they are often assigned to groups rather than to individuals. When research papers are assigned as group projects, students are usually able to decide how to divide the various writing and research tasks. In our experience, a common practice is for each person to be responsible for writing, revising, and editing one section of the research paper; then these sections are put together and handed in to the instructor when the paper is due.

While this method of dividing the workload of a research paper is popular, however, it can be problematic. When group members are responsible for producing *particular portions* of a text, rarely does anyone take responsibility for revising and editing the text *as a whole*. A common result is a paper that is unevenly edited and composed of parts that don't fit well together. If assigned a research paper as a group project, then, you should make sure that the group assigns at least one person the responsibility of revising and editing the entire paper, including the cover page, bibliography, appendixes, and so forth.

WRITING ASSIGNMENTS

Writing Topics

Your primary assignment in this chapter is to write a research paper based on a minimum of six library sources. You should use a formal documentation system such as MLA or APA, or another system that your instructor requires. Your topic should be chosen from the following list or from any additional topics your instructor provides. Working together, each group should choose one topic to research. Depending on your teacher's instructions and your preferences, your group may choose to write one longer paper coauthored by all members or to write individual papers separately.

1. Identify a particular career or occupation that you would like to know more about. Use library resources to find out such information as typical salary levels, the education and training required for entry-level jobs, job availability locally and nationally, daily work of professionals, and the level of job satisfaction reported by professionals in this area.

2. Who killed Malcolm X? What happened to the body of labor leader Jimmy Hoffa? Was there a second person shooting from the grassy knoll when President John F. Kennedy was killed? What happened to Charles Lindbergh's baby? For your research paper, investigate a well-known but unsolved crime. What are the facts of the case? What areas are unknown? What theories have been offered in attempts to solve the case?

3. Despite the advances of modern science, there are a number of phenomena about which people can offer only theories. For example, why did the dinosaurs become extinct? Does a Loch Ness monster really live in the lake in Scotland? Does a creature named Bigfoot really roam the Pacific Northwest? How was the Sphinx built? Choose a seemingly inexplicable event, occurrence in nature, or artifact such as these, and investigate it. What is known about your topic? What areas are the subject of speculation?

4. You probably have learned quite a bit about undergraduate student life at your college in recent months, including what majors and intramural sports are most popular, who hangs out at what local nightspots, as well as local campus legends. But what was college life like in generations past? For this topic, investigate student life among undergraduate college students in the United States before 1950. Depending on your interests and the library resources available, you may narrow this topic to "college life at your university."

5. Whether you grew up using computers or are just learning to use them, and whether you surf the Internet or use computers only for writing papers, you are undoubtedly aware that computers have become an important part of contemporary culture. Select an aspect of computer technology to research: information sources available on-line, social relationships formed and maintained through the Internet, legal issues such as copyright protection for software or penalties for hacking, and so forth.

6. From the very beginning to contemporary times, the United States has had a rich and varied ethnic background. Select a particular ethnic group within the United States to research. In your research, consider such questions as the following: Where did the ethnic group originate? How large and dominant is this group within the United States? What are the group's significant cultural or religious practices? What important contributions has this group made to American life and culture? What are some important historical events that have significantly affected members of your group?

Writing Procedures

Rather than giving you a list of instructions to follow, we are providing a check sheet to follow as you continue work on your research paper assignment. In our experience as writers and teachers, check sheets are a good way of visually listing the steps and activities involved in a large project like writing a research paper. Moreover, they help teachers and students keep track of the work completed and the work still to be done.

Use the following check sheet—or one your instructor provides—to help break the task of writing a research paper into a series of manageable tasks and to help you create deadlines. You will probably find it easier to photocopy the check sheet and keep the copy with your research materials, where you will need it most. In places, we have indicated that your ideas or writing should be workshopped with your group. To do so, use one of the procedures from Chapter 2. In addition, your instructor may require you to submit your work for approval at several parts of the process.

RESEARCH PAPER CHECK SHEET

Your Name:

Your Research Topic or Question:

Documentation Format You Will Use:

Tasks	Target Date	Date Completed
Written research proposal approved (minimum 1/2 page typed or word-processed)		
Final sources selected		
Bibliography cards completed		
Critical reading and underlining completed		
Note cards completed		
Tentative thesis and brief plan submitted to instructor		
Detailed plan or outline submitted to instructor		
First draft completed		
First draft workshopped with group		
Revised draft completed, based on feedback from group, instructor, or writing center		
Editing for mechanics, usage, and spelling completed		
Format and documentation checked and corrected		

READINGS

Professional Models

Blumberg, Avrom A. "Risks and Chemical Substances." *Journal of Chemical Education 11* (November 1994), pp. 912–918.

Brown, Elizabeth F., and William R. Hendee. "Adolescents and Their Music." *Journal of the American Medical Association* (September 22–29, 1989), pp. 1659–1663.

Lopez, Judith. "Buttonholes: Some Differences in Gender-related Front Closures." *Dress 20* (1993), pp. 74–78.

Student Models

Karrenbauer, Kelly. "Rita's Portuguese Education."

Huthmacher, David B. *"Dead Poets Society:* Heart Over Mind."

Questions

1. Examine the structure of these research papers. How is each organized? How are sources integrated to avoid copied structure? With respect to the student papers, how do the writers organize their essays to avoid copying the structure of the movie they are reviewing?

2. Determine the overall aim or purpose of each essay. Is each one more persuasive or more informative? In particular, examine "Risks and Chemical Substances," by Avrom A. Blumberg, which appears to be an informative paper. Do you think it advances interpretations about the effect of toxic substances with which some readers might take issue? To what extent, then, is this piece persuasive rather than informative?

3. Carefully examine the documentation used in each piece. What forms, for example, do the citations take? Which authors, if any, use annotations? Which pieces use headings or abstracts?

4. Find examples of quotes and paraphrases within each reading. How are these synthesized into the text? How is metadiscourse used?

5. Focus on the bibliographies for each reading. What range of sources (scholarly, popular, books, newspapers, etc.) does each employ? To what extent do these sources lend credibility to each text? As you recall, some sources vary in terms of comprehensiveness and currentness. Do the writers employ both comprehensive and current sources? If not, why do you suppose they have neglected to include these? Are up-to-date sources more important for some of the topics than for others? Explain.

Risks and Chemical Substances*

Avrom A. Blumberg
DePaul University, Chicago, IL 60614

Early in this century a discussion of environmental risk usually referred to the particulate matter, hydrocarbons, ozone, and oxides of sulfur, carbon, and nitrogen all present in the air and to the heavy metals and untreated sewage present in water. Infectious diseases such as pneumonia, influenza, and tuberculosis were collectively responsible for more deaths than heart and circulatory diseases; and each of these three was individually the cause of more deaths than all cancers combined (*1*). During this century there has been a steady, significant decline in mortality from infectious diseases, with the notable exception those related to AIDS. As our environment has become cleaner and more free of the obvious older pollutants, and mortality patterns have changed, more attention is paid to such things as polychlorinated biphenyls, alar, and dioxins, the safety of newer medicines and food additives, and the disposal of chemical waste, all of which may affect us within our homes.

There have been good reasons in the past for such worry because at one time there seemed to be no control over what substances could be used in foods, medicines, and cosmetics: arsenic-and-lead-containing hair dyes and fruit sprays; mercury salt freckle removers; thallium depilatories; turpentine lotions for diphtheria, tuberculosis, asthma, and cancer; radium rejuvenators; and nicotine for worms were just some of the products available (*2*).

Chemists have identified over 12 million different substances. They know the chemical formulas, melting points, boiling points, solubilities in several solvents, densities, colors, and perhaps a few reactions characteristic of each. We are exposed to about **50 thousand** of these in various amounts and it is natural to ask how safe we are from this contact. This paper will look at how we become exposed within our homes, then examine three important ways in which we identify and evaluate hazardous substances, and finally try to suggest a rational picture of the risks we all face.

Reasons for Exposure
Pharmaceuticals

As we gain insight about disease we devise chemical strategies about control and cure. The annual death rate in the United States has dropped from an estimated 3.5% in the year 1800 (which was 1 death per year per 28 persons) to 2% in 1900 and to less than 1% today (about 1 death per year per 110 persons). Pharmaceuticals play a major role in this. In addition to antibiotics, we have medicines for parasites, allergies, arthritis, depression, respiratory problems, anxiety, hormone imbalance,

*Avrom A. Blumberg, "Risks and Chemical Substances." *Journal of Chemical Education*, Vol. 1, No. 11 (November 1994), pp. 912–918. Reprinted with the permission of the publisher.

Risks and Chemical Substances *(cont'd.)*

obesity, gestation, gastrointestinal disorders, hypertension, cardiovascular problems, and certain neoplasms. These are widely available and almost all have undesirable side effects. Illicit drugs and the misuse of accepted medicines and household chemicals are also serious problems.

In Food

Chemical substances play a major role in our food. The success of American farmers in feeding us and in exporting agricultural produce depends on hard work, modern farm machinery, and the use of chemical fertilizers, pesticides, fungicides, growth and ripening agents, and antibiotics. A century ago grocers sold mostly staples such as flour, sugar, salt, rice, dried meal, a few spices, and not much else except fruits and vegetables in season for customers who did not grow their own. In 1945 a supermarket carried about 1500 separate items. Today, supermarkets stock about 10,000 and some larger warehouse-type supermarkets carry about 20,000 separate items. We use a larger variety of more convenient foods, prepared or packaged months before and at some distance from where we purchase them. The preparation of these foods makes use of about 3000 food additives. There are preservatives to retard spoilage, flavoring agents, acidulants to impart tartness to, for example, citrus-flavored foods, antioxidants to prevent rancidity in the more healthy unsaturated fats and oils, artificial sweeteners, emulsifiers to keep aqueous and oily fluids mixed, thickeners, bleaches and colors, anticaking agents for powders and grains, moisture retainers to give baked products a good feel, nutritional supplements, and sequestrants as scavengers for metals which give food an off taste (*3–5*). Food additives may be natural materials, such as cinnamon and pepper; synthetic but identical to natural substances, such as artificial vanilla and fruit esters; or entirely synthetic, such as saccharin, ferrous sulfate, and the antioxidants BHA and BHT (butylated hydroxyanisole and butylated hydroxytoluene). And sometimes there are accidental migrations of substances from the packaging material or processing equipment into food. What follows will deal mostly with evaluating the risks from new drugs, food additives, and incidental chemical substances (*6–9*).

Epidemiology

The first broad way of identifying dangerous substances is by looking at human mortality records and hoping to discover patterns: epidemiology (*10, 11*). In the United States the annual death rate is slightly less than 0.9%, or about 2¼ million deaths per year. About 38% of these deaths are from diseases of the heart; another 10% from cerebrovascular diseases; and about 1.5% from atherosclerosis. In all, about half the deaths each year in the United States are related to cardiovascular conditions. About 19% of the mortalities, 450 thousand deaths each year, are from malignancies. Other major causes of death in the United States are accidents, 5.3%; respiratory diseases, 3%; diabetes mellitus, 1.8%; cirrhosis of the liver, 1.6%; and suicide, about 1.4%.

Risks and Chemical Substances *(cont'd.)*

Mortality rates are gender-related, about 1% per annum for men in the United States, and 0.78% for women. Women have a lower mortality from all cardiovascular disorders, a slightly higher rate from cancers of all types (20 versus 19.4%), but less than half the male death rates from accidents, from suicide and from cirrhosis. Mortality shows an age pattern, also. Accidents are the leading cause of death of males up to the age of 44, and in females up to 24. Malignant neoplasms are the leading cause of death among females from the age of 25 to 64. Above that age, diseases of the heart are the primary cause of death for women in the United States. But the male death rate from cancers of all types exceeds the female rate at all ages except 25–44 years.

Cancer

Factors and Patterns in Cancer

We know how to associate cancer with certain factors. Radiation was responsible for the higher than average occurrence of cancers among uranium miners, and early workers in nuclear science and X-rays. There are family patterns, where cancers of the stomach, ovaries, breast, and intestines in successive generations are more likely in some families than others. Yet we are not entirely sure what part genetics and life style play in this clustering.

There are hormonal influences. Some tumors flourish during pregnancy and wane after. Early removal of ovaries lessens the incidence of breast tumors. Women who have children at an earlier age, and have more pregnancies, and breast-feed their infants longer, are at lower risk from breast cancer. In addition, family history seems important. And Oriental women and Blacks have lower incidences than Caucasian women.

Infectious agents may play a role. The Epstein–Barr herpes-type virus is suspected to be a factor in Burkitt's lymphoma. Kaposi's sarcoma, once relatively rare and found almost exclusively among older Italian and Jewish men, and in Zaire, after 1982 began appearing among younger non-Mediterranean-type men and pointed to a new health problem, AIDS. Now we think some tumors can be rejected unless the immune system is damaged (*12,13*).

There are important national differences in total occurrence and in specific-site cancer incidence rates. Data in Table 1 are selected from a more extensive list of 20 developed countries (*14*). Males from Scotland and women from Denmark in 1976–1977 had the highest overall cancer fatalities. Japan and Israel, among industrialized nations during the same year, have relatively low death rates from all cancers. Nevertheless, Japanese men and women led all other nations in the group of 20 in deaths from stomach cancer, although Chilean men and women are not far behind in this kind of mortality. Israeli women head the list of leukemia-caused deaths among females. We cannot easily sort out environment, including food, from heredity and life style, but migrants from other countries to the United States often show shifts in mortality patterns (*14*). For example, in Japan, stomach cancer

Risks and Chemical Substances *(cont'd.)*

TABLE 1. Cancer Deaths per 100,000 per Year from Selected Causes in Six Selected Countries and by Gender M/F (*14*)

	all causes		colorectal		lung		stomach	
	M	*F*	*M*	*F*	*M*	*F*	*M*	*F*
Scotland	269.8*	165.8	32.7	26.5	108.5*	23.7	25.4	13.4
Denmark	232.1	170.9*	32.4	25.9	62.0	15.2	19.0	9.7
US	213.6	136.3	26.2	20.2	68.1	17.2	9.2	4.4†
Chile	197.7	153.8	9.9†	10.0†	25.3†	6.9	64.9	30.4
Japan	186.7	108.7†	15.0	11.1	28.3	8.2	70.2*	34.9*
Israel	170.5†	141.3	21.4	16.6	32.9	10.5	18.4	9.2

*denotes country with greatest incidence of indicted cancer deaths and
†denotes lowest incidence, among the 20 countries with adequate data.

causes more deaths than any other cancer and is more than seven times more common in Japan than in the United States. However, among Japanese families living in the United States, stomach cancer death rates diminish over successive generations. In contrast to the sharp differences between countries in stomach cancer mortality, the *ratio* of male-to-female stomach cancer deaths is relatively steady (between 1.86 and 2.13), suggesting a gender-related factor inasmuch as the normal diets or other exposures in these countries are not expected to be different for men and women.

Chemical Carcinogens

But when we think of cancer we usually think of chemical carcinogens—substances which cause cancer. And we look for unusual occurrences of unusual types of cancer in special populations to give us some idea about chemical carcinogens (*15*).

The eighteenth century British physician, Percival Pott, recognized that soot wort, a rare form of scrotal cancer, seemed to be found only among chimney sweeps and concluded that something in soot was responsible. This may have been the first time an environmental factor was recognized as a cause of cancer.

Vinyl chloride is the starting substance for polyvinyl-chloride, e.g., neoprene, used as shower curtains and synthetic leather and in many other products. It had also been used as an aerosol propellant and as an ingredient of surgical anesthetics. When a relatively uncommon angiosarcoma of the liver was found among workers who had been exposed to prolonged high levels of this gas, it was easy to conclude that vinyl chloride is a carcinogen. It is no longer used as a propellant or in anesthetics, and working conditions in that industry are safer (*16*). Recently an increased miscarriage rate was noticed among pregnant women handling ethylene glycol ether in semiconductor manufacture, leading to a phasing out of that substance (*17*).

Risks and Chemical Substances *(cont'd.)*

The Role of Tobacco

Probably the most ambitious epidemiological studies ever conducted have to do with the increasing incidence of lung cancer. In the year 1900 lung cancer was a rather uncommon disease; the annual death rate is estimated to have been about 0.3 per 100,000 men, or probably no more than 120 lung cancer deaths that year in a total population of 76 million. In 1940, with a population of 132 million, the lung cancer death [rate] was 8 per 100,000 population among U.S. men, for about 5000 lung cancer deaths. In 1960 our population was 179 million and the male lung cancer death rate was at 30 per 100,000. An estimated 29,000 men died in 1960 from lung cancer. By 1980 and with a population of 227 million, the death rate was over 80 per 100,000, for 90,000 male deaths from lung cancer. During the same time stomach-cancer mortality dropped from 38 per 100,000 men in 1930 to 9 per 100,000 in 1980. In 1950 the increasing mortality from lung cancer and the decreasing mortality from stomach cancer crossed at 24 per 100,000. The improved stomach cancer health statistics are attributed to the greater use of refrigeration, the wider availability of fresh vegetables and fruits throughout the year, less consumption of moldy and otherwise spoiled foods, and much reduced use of pickled, smoked, or otherwise preserved foods in the United States (*14*).

Thoracic surgeons observed in the 1930's that in nearly all cases of lung cancer patients were also heavy cigarette smokers (*1*). During the 1960's several studies of mortality and cigarette smoking were undertaken and all showed a positive correlation. In 1966 E. Cuyler Hammond published the results of his extensive study on smoking and death rates (*18*). Using a small army of 68,116 volunteers, data were collected over a period of 3 years and 9 months on over one million men and women residing in 1121 counties in 25 states. For all deaths the rate was 1.88 greater for the younger smokers, as compared to the younger nonsmokers, and 1.43 greater for the older smokers. Death rates were correlated to the number of cigarettes smoked each day. For women in the early 1960's, heavier cigarette smoking produced 3.63 times the death rate from lung cancer, and 1.80 the death rate from heart and circulatory causes, compared to women who never smoked; however, as women had not then (1962) begun smoking in great numbers Hammond's data were most useful for the 440,558 men monitored, both smokers and nonsmokers. He found that the death rates from all cancers of men smokers was about double that of men who never smoked. In the age group 65–79 the mortality rate from lung cancer was 11.4 times higher for the smokers, and for the 45–64 group, 7.9 times greater. The rate from heart and circulatory diseases was 1.9 greater for the smokers aged 45–64, and 1.3 greater for the 65–74 age group. With so many subjects, Hammond was able to make comparisons between smokers and nonsmokers in the same types of work environment, at the same age, and in the same urban or rural settings. Clearly, cigarette smoking seems to be the important factor in lung cancer.

Risks and Chemical Substances *(cont'd.)*

Limitations to Epidemiology

There are three obvious limitations to such epidemiological studies, however. First, cancers have long incubation periods, perhaps 20 years, and during that time there can be other factors involved: exposure to X-rays, or inhaled metal dust, or now-recognized carcinogenic solvents, or asbestos fiber. It is difficult to isolate one factor from another. Second, we learn of the danger of a substance only long after many people are exposed. Cigarette smoking increased somewhat among men in World War I, and more markedly during the World War II. Men in uniform and veterans in hospitals were given free cigarettes by tobacco companies, until the cause and effect relationship was established. And third, if an increase in a type of cancer is not concentrated in a particular industry, life style, or geographical area, it may not be noticed at all. Pott was able to associate soot wort with chimney sweeping because this kind of cancer was seen only among those engaged in that line of work. Similarly, primary liver angiosarcoma were found among the 27,000 workers exposed to prolonged high levels of vinyl chloride and hardly at all elsewhere. The much wider use of aerosols containing vinyl chloride exposed large numbers of widely scattered persons to much lower doses; only the higher industrial vinyl chloride concentrations made the identification possible and brought about the removal of vinyl chloride from household use. The same number of angiosarcoma deaths distributed over the general population probably would not have been recognized and even less likely would a connection have been made between vinyl chloride in household aerosol cans and this cancer. Deaths so widely and seemingly randomly distributed would have failed to attract attention.

Animal Tests

Animal tests are useful for the routine testing of new medicines or other chemical substances *before* these are introduced into the human community. We select animals whose physiologies and body chemistries are closest to ours: mammals such as dogs, monkeys, rats, and mice. Infrequently, volunteers such as prisoners have been used also.

Riojan Kinoshita, in 1936, concerned over the high incidence of liver cancer in Japan, directed his attention to the yellow dye used in butter. Cows eat less fresh green grass during winter months and the natural yellow xanthophyll pigments are in reduced amounts in their diets. Winter butter thus is paler than the richly yellow butter of summer months. Because yellow butter looks and is thought to taste better than pale white butter, yellow dyes are commonly added to butter. Kinoshita prepared a relatively concentrated solution of yellow butter dye in vegetable oil, and mixed this with normal solid rat food. An unexpectedly high number of rats died within a month from a variety of causes other than liver cancer, and most of those surviving a half year had liver tumors. Repeating the experiment with lower doses of butter yellow dye, Kinoshita observed fewer early deaths and a lower but still high incidence of liver tumors (*19*).

Risks and Chemical Substances *(cont'd.)*

Kinoshita learned several important things about using animals for tests. An increase in human mortality by 10 extra deaths per 100,000 (which would amount to an additional 13,000 deaths in Japan today) is 1 extra death per 10,000 humans each year. Statistically the addition of 1 more death to the 80 or so deaths annually in a random sample of 10,000 Japanese would not be significant and not noticed. Assuming that rat mortality is equal to human mortality (expressed as mg of substance per kg of body mass), one would need many more than 10,000 rats to observe a statistically significant effect. Such a large number, about 100,000 or more of test animals treated with the low doses humans are likely to be exposed to is impractical. Alternatively, one can use higher doses and a more manageable number of test rats (40–200 rats is common). But Kinoshita observed that high doses can produce other toxic effects in addition to the liver tumors he was looking for, obscuring the significance of his tests. A compromise must be struck between low doses in large numbers of test animals, and high doses in smaller numbers of animals.

This is a very serious problem inasmuch as food additives are normally present in low concentrations and it is necessary to extrapolate effects from higher animal test doses to lower doses in humans. In typical tests several cages of animals are used such that all the animals in a given cage are fed the same amount of test substance, and the amounts fed vary from zero, in the control cage, to some level high enough to kill all or almost all the test animals within some accepted test time interval. Plots of dose (along the horizontal axis, as mg/kg) versus response (i.e., test-animal mortality, along the vertical axis, from 0 to 100%) are s-shaped curves: as the dose is increased from 0 there is at first a slow increase in deaths, then the curve increases more rapidly, and then it slows down again and asymptotically approaches 100% mortality. The characteristic toxicity of the substance tested is the lethal dose to kill exactly 50% of the animals (written as LD_{50} (or LD50 in some publications)). This can be read from the s-shaped curve. A substance with an LD_{50} of 2.6 mg/kg is more toxic than one with an LD_{50} = 143 mg/kg.

Confidence in Animal Test Data

A high response such as 50 or 80% mortality is established by comparing the mortality in test cages with mortality in the control (no dose) cage. Such tests can be done in duplicate or triplicate to confirm reproducibility of results. For example, if the control cage has a 2.5% ± 1.5% mortality (that is, with 68% confidence the normal death rate among these animals is between 1.0 and 4.0%) and one set of cages has 77.5% ± 3.0% mortality, we can with high confidence say that the second cage dose produced an increase in mortality about 75.0% ± 4.5%, that is, with 68% confidence, between 70.5 and 79.5 % above the normal rat mortality. At low doses there is less confidence in and less agreement on how to interpret the data. If the animals in one cage are treated with a low dose and exhibit a 3.4% ± 1.0% mortality there is less confidence about a real increased mortality at the low doses. To examine very low dose effects we look at, for example a dose range from 0.0 to 5.0 µg/kg of body weight, and mortality (*thought* to be above the normal background

Risks and Chemical Substances *(cont'd.)*

rate) from 0.000 to 0.005%. Recall that short segments of curves, even s-shaped ones, can be approximated by linear line segments. The large relative errors obtained in subtracting two small numbers, at the option of the data handler, may be thought to have the response curve go through the origin: no dose, no increased mortality, but even a very low dose will result in an increase in mortality. (Draw a line between the points (0.0 $\mu g/kg$,0.000%) and (5.0 $\mu g/kg$,0.005%).) In this view there is no threshold of safety. A small dose, 0.5 $\mu g/kg$ in this example, would be attended by an increase in mortality of 0.0005%. In the United States today that represents an additional 1280 deaths. One half that small dose can be expected to cause the death of half that number or 640 more people. Persons who favor the nonthreshold line argue that it is prudent whenever possible not to take chances with these additional deaths. A contrary option is to draw the dose-response curve so it intersects the dose axis at some small positive value, e.g., at 2.0 $\mu g/kg$. Low confidence in data allows for this kind of judgment. This is equivalent to stating that there will be no adverse effects for doses lower than this threshold of 2.0 $\mu g/kg$. Arguments for a threshold are that the human body can tolerate small amounts of toxic substances without harm, for example, by conversion to safer substances by the liver. Our livers can handle low levels of toxic substances but can be overwhelmed by larger doses. It is also known that some substances seem to be necessary in very low amounts for our well-being but they are toxic at higher levels. The elements fluorine, copper, and selenium are good examples, as is vitamin A. In this interpretation a threshold dose exists below which there is no harmful effect; one does not have to worry about very low level exposures.

Kinoshita also discovered that the original yellow butter dye molecule was quickly converted to something else in the rats' bodies. It very likely was not the dye itself but a metabolite that was carcinogenic. A further problem is that metabolism in rats is not necessarily the same as in humans for all substances. Benzidine, once used in forensic police work to detect traces of blood, is known to produce bladder cancer in humans, liver cancer in rats, and gall bladder cancer in hamsters. Another human cancer-producing substance, beta naphthylamine, once used in dye manufacture and as a rubber antioxidant, is carcinogenic in dogs but not in rats. Nicotine has a mouse LD_{50} of 0.3 mg/kg when applied intravenously, 9.5 mg/kg intraperitoneally, and 230 mg/kg when taken orally. Rodents and dogs evidently can eat all kinds of things that would make us ill. Therefore, it is important to use more than one kind of test animal and a variety of administration methods to lessen the chance that a harmful to humans substance will slip by.

The Delaney Amendment

The 1958 Delaney amendment to the Food, Drug and Cosmetic Act states that no food additive which, in any amount, produces cancer in any experimental animal or in man, is permitted in any amount in food for human consumption. That the Delaney amendment is concerned solely about carcinogens reflects the common greater concern over cancer compared to other kinds of morbidity. Arguments supporting

Risks and Chemical Substances *(cont'd.)*

the Delaney amendment state that the rule is unambiguous, removes the Food and Drug Administration from unwanted outside pressures, and is consistent with the no-threshold view of hazardous substances. Contrary arguments state that there is no possibility for judgment. For example, a human might have to consume unreasonably large amounts of a soft drink each day to be exposed to the amounts of artificial sweetener that produce tumors in test animals (*20, 59*).

The ideal of having "no amount" of any substance that produces undesirable effects at higher doses has some interesting aspects. The pesticides heptachlor and dieldrin have been banned from food. Before 1964, milk from surrounding states was shipped to the District of Columbia without worry because neither substance could be found. But in 1964 more sensitive chemical analytical methods were developed that did detect very low levels of heptachlor and dieldrin, which made the milk then unacceptable. Knowledge about the presence or absence of a dangerous substance depends on whether or not we have sensitive enough means of detecting it. Better analytical methods permit a more careful control of these substances.

Carcinogenicity is not the only effect that must be tested for in animals. In 1955 a European pharmaceutical company introduced a new, mild sleeping pill with obvious advantages: there was no "hangover" characteristic of other sleeping pills; it was not toxic (an entire bottle could be swallowed without causing illness); it was inexpensive; and, having passed appropriate tests, was approved for over-the-counter sales. In 1961, physicians in Germany and Britain, who in the past might have seen perhaps 1 case in 25 years of the congenital disorder phocomelia (characterized by severe shortening or absence of forearms and, often, missing eyes and ears, and seizures) were seeing 1–15 cases in 1 year. The new sleeping pill, thalidomide, was implicated. It affects development during the first few weeks of pregnancy and was somehow missed in routine animal testing (*21–25, 60*). As a consequence the U.S. Congress mandated more stringent testing for toxicity, teratogenicity (producing misformed offspring, as in phocomelia), mutagenicity (affecting chromosomes and thus heredity), carcinogenicity, and thrombosis-formation; and administration of doses by inhalation, in feed, intravenously, by injection, painting on skin, and implantation (*61*). Testing with animals requires large but manageable numbers of test animals, at least two species, both sexes because some toxic or carcinogenic substances are gender-specific, testing over the normal two-year life span because susceptibility changes with age, and with pregnant animals too. The last is necessary because the drug thalidomide is toxic to human embryos a few weeks old, but had not been evaluated using enough pregnant rodents. The dose given to each test animal must be below the toxic level if the tests are for carcinogen or mutagen activity, to not complicate the investigation with multiple effects. Detailed organ analyses are needed to discover a variety of different effects. And one must consider the natural mortality and natural occurrence of tumors in test animals (*31*). Understandably, the cost of new drug applications rose by several orders of magnitude, with a concomitant drop in the number of such applications for approval by the FDA (*27–30*).

Risks and Chemical Substances *(cont'd.)*

Animal Rights

Using animals in testing for the safety of substances is criticized by animal rights proponents (*31–33*). The procedure most widely objected to is the Draize test, dating from the 1940's and used more for cosmetics than medicines, consisting of treating one cornea of albino rabbits with the substance to be tested and after 72 hours examining that cornea for severity of lesions (*34*). Proponents of animal testing state that there is no wholly satisfactory alternative and that perhaps three-fourths of modern medicine and surgery is made possible through animal testing.

Short-Term Screening

The expense and long times involved in animal tests and the limitations of epidemiology point to a need for a testing procedure that can be done more quickly and cheaply. The Ames test, developed by the biochemist Bruce Ames, is one such method (*35, 36*). The microorganism *Salmonella typhimurium* ordinarily can synthesize the amino acid histidine and can thrive without histidine in its diet. A particular mutant of *S. typhimurium* cannot synthesize histidine and will not survive unless histidine is present in the cell's immediate environment. Certain chemicals called mutagens can cause the mutant microorganism to revert to its natural state of flourishing independently of histidine. Mutagens alter DNA in an inheritable way and often can also cause cells to become malignant.

The mutant bacteria are placed in a culture dish with nutrients but not with histidine, and with a substance to be tested as a mutagen. If the *S. typhimurium* does not survive, the test substance is not a successful mutagen for reversion; if it survives and grows, the substance is a mutagen. Then the assumption is made that such a mutagen for *S. typhimurium* is likely to be a human carcinogen (*37*).

How well this works can be judged from one early demonstration in testing 300 substances for mutagenicity, using 256 known human carcinogens and 44 substances known not to be carcinogens. Of the 256 known carcinogens, 226 were also mutagens (an 88.3% success rate); the other 30 known carcinogens were not mutagens. These were false negatives: 12% of these known human carcinogens were incorrectly passed as safe. Thirty-nine of the 44 known noncarcinogens were also not mutagens, but 5 were mutagens: there was a false positive rate of 11%. In more recent versions, liver enzymes are present in the medium, to simulate the activity of livers that convert chemical substances to their metabolites and could change a harmless substance into a carcinogen. With this there are fewer false negative results. Work on tissues and with other cells indicate that such rapid screening tests are useful, primarily to set priorities for animal tests (*34, 38*).

A List

Now we can examine some of the toxicity data, collected in Table 2, which contains a selection of substances, their toxicities (as mg of substance/kg of rat), and an estimate of how many 70-kg humans on the average would die from 1 g of the substance (*39*).

Risks and Chemical Substances *(cont'd.)*

TABLE 2. List of Toxicities (*39*)

substance	LD_{50} mg/kg	human deaths/g
aspirin	1750	0.008
ethyl alcohol	1000	0.014
phenobarbital	660	0.022
morphine	500	0.028
Tylenol	338	0.042
caffeine	200	0.07
heroin	150	0.095
codeine	120	0.119
lead	20	0.714
cocaine	17.5	0.816
arsenic trioxide	12	1.19
sodium cyanide	10	1.43
nicotine	2	7
strychnine	0.8	18
soman	0.4	36
rattlesnake toxin	0.08	179
tetrodotoxin	0.005	2900
ricin	0.00002	600,000
tetanus toxin	0.00000010	120 million
botulism toxin	0.00000005	250 million

Aspirin has a lethal dose of 1.750 g/kg of test animal and, we think, per kilogram of human. An average 154-lb man, with a mass of 70 kg, would require 122.5 g of aspirin, the amount contained in 380 aspirin tablets for a lethal dose. For a 22-lb or 10-kg infant, 17.5 g or about 50 tablets would be lethal. Not surprisingly, aspirin although low on this list is one of the riskier chemical substances found around the house and is the main reason why medicines have so-called "child-proof" caps.

The value for ethyl alcohol is extrapolated from rat data to humans. Enough epidemiological data exists to know that this value is too low for our species. A better value for LD_{50} is 300–500 g for a 70-kg man, which is more than but not seriously far from the 70 g computed from the listed value. Acetaminophen, the ingredient in Tylenol and other similar over-the-counter medicines, has an LD_{50} of 338 mg/kg of animal or man. This is about five times as toxic as aspirin. A 70-kg man would have to ingest nearly 70 of these to be at serious risk, and for a 10 kg infant, only 10 tablets. Lead, present in old plumbing, old white paint, and in some car exhaust, has an LD_{50} of 20 mg/kg. Our average 70-kg man needs only 1.4 g for a lethal dose. Arsenic oxide, that old favorite of gardeners, and sodium cyanide,

Risks and Chemical Substances *(cont'd.)*

have LD_{50}s of 12 and 10 mg/kg. The 70-kg man would die, half the time, with 0.84 and 0.70 g of these poisons.

Nicotine, a naturally occurring substance found in tobacco and once used widely in agriculture and gardening, has an LD_{50} of 2 mg/kg in rats. A 70-kg man needs only 0.14 g for a lethal dose, which is three drops! The nerve gas soman has LD_{50} of 0.4 mg/kg. For the 70-kg man only 28 mg, or only a half drop, is fatal. Another way of looking at this is that 1 g or 20 drops of soman is enough to kill 36 human adults.

Toxins

A *toxin* is any poisonous substance produced by a living organism and which is toxic without that organism being present. Tetrodotoxin, from the puffer fish, has an LD_{50} of 0.005 mg/kg of mammal. A 70-kg adult male would find only 0.35 mg, slightly more than 1/3000 of a gram or 1/150 of a drop lethal. One gram of this toxin is enough to kill 2500 people. Ricin, found in castor beans, has an LD_{50} of 0.00002 mg/kg. One gram is enough to kill over 600,000 adults. The tetanus toxin has the remarkably low LD_{50} of 0.00000010 mg/kg of adult. One gram is enough to kill over 140 million adult humans. And the most toxic substance we think we have been able to identify is the botulism toxin, with an LD_{50} half that of the tetanus toxin (*40*). A gram of this is enough to kill 280 million adults, or the entire U.S. population. By far, the most deadly of the toxic substances we are exposed to are natural rather than manmade. Among carcinogens we think that aflatoxin B, produced by molds on peanuts or corn, is the most potent at least in some animal tests.

Conclusions: Toxicity versus Risk

Toxicity is not the same as risk. The botulism toxin was more of a threat when we did more home canning of garden produce. Today botulism poisoning is relatively uncommon (*41, 42*). There are more deaths each year from salmonella poisoning than from botulism because more persons are exposed to the former. Lead, much less toxic than the botulism toxin, is a continual source of concern as it is found in paint in old houses, plumbing fixtures, and soil near roadways (*43, 44*). "Lead poisoning is one of the most common and preventable pediatric health problems today" (*45*). There is an extensive literature about risk as distinguished from toxicity (*46, 47*). The aflatoxins are perhaps the most potent carcinogen we know of (and are also toxic with an LD_{50} of about 400 mg/kg (*39*)), but exposure to less potent cancer-producing substances is more common for more persons (beryllium in broken, old fluorescent bulbs; formaldehyde evolving from plywood adhesives; safrole in soaps and perfumes; et al. (*16*)).

There are trade-offs between risk and benefit. Mortality is significantly lower from all causes, in part from the use of chemical substances. Other health indices: in 1900, life expectancy in the United States was 50 years; today it is over 70 years. Infant mortality dropped from 1 death per 18 live births in 1900, to 1 per 68 today;

Risks and Chemical Substances *(cont'd.)*

and maternal deaths from childbirth from 1 per 167 live births to now 1 in 8000 live births. We accept traces of pesticides because obvious insect parts in food are unacceptable in our society. Nitrates and nitrites are used to preserve bacon from botulism, which is more of an immediate worry than the formation of nitro-samines, a carcinogen, when bacon is heated at high temperatures (*48*).

Natural substances, particularly the toxins, are far more deadly than anything humans can synthesize in a laboratory. Foods themselves may naturally contain harmful substances. Sassafras bark, used in making root beer, contains the carcino-gen safrole. Favism is the severe allergic reaction produced in some persons by eat-ing the fava or flat bean. Certain peas of the genus *Lathyrus* may affect the central nervous system, as in lathyrism. Oxalic acid is found in rhubarb leaves.

Level of exposure must be considered in dealing with risk. With each breath we take in and exhale very small amounts of carbon monoxide. Vitamin A deficiency, defined as a normal adult ingestion of less than 0.8–1.0 mg daily, causes poor night vision, and growth retardation and impaired vision in children. Therapeutic doses of 10–20 mg/day help in recovery from this deficiency disease. But daily diets with 100 mg or more produce, in hypervitaminosis A, intracranial pressure and vomit-ing, and there are reports of birth defects. We consume between 2 and 5 mg of cop-per each day in a normal diet. Much less than this produces an anemia and, in children, psychomotor retardation; but more than 15 mg of copper each day pro-duces nausea, vomiting, abdominal pain, and in severe cases coma and death. Less than the recommended daily intake of 4 mg of pyridoxine (vitamin B6) produces another kind of anemia but too much (2 or more g a day) causes lower limb impair-ment (*39, 49*).

Absolute purity is unattainable and purity beyond some practical limit is unaf-fordable for most substances. Examining recent chemical catalogs, one can see that 99% pure zinc is available for $1.80 per 100 g; and 99.9999% pure zinc sells at $98 per 100 g. Reducing the amount of impurity in 100 g of lead from 1 g down to 0.0001 g increases the cost by a factor of five and a half. Reducing impurities fur-ther will boost the cost even more sharply. At the same time, the sensitivity of chemical analysis has been increasing from parts per million to parts per billion and eventually for many substances to parts per trillion. This ability to detect substances present at extremely dilute concentrations can be both a comfort and disquieting. On one hand it permits a careful monitoring of what we eat to an extent unavail-able until recently, and a much clearer idea of what is harmful (*50–53*). The list of harmful and banned substances increases continually and our contact with them decreases. On the other hand, we can find almost anything we want to in a food if we use fine enough techniques. Even broccoli and its family of related healthful vegetables contain toxic substances but in amounts too minute to be of any concern. Peaches have trace amounts of cyanide in the fleshy fruit pulp, from the nut within peach pits. A similar kind of worry obtains over radioactivity. A typical human body is 18% carbon; a 70-kg man contains 12,600 g of carbon. We know each gram of carbon in any living organism contains enough carbon-14 (with a half life of

Risks and Chemical Substances *(cont'd.)*

**TABLE 3. Best Estimates of Causes of All Cancers,
The Surgeon General's Report 1982 (*58*)**

diet	35%
tobacco	30
reproductive and sexual behavior	7
occupation	4
alcohol	3
geophysical	3
pollution	2
industrial	1
medicines	1
Total	86%

5770 years) to have 15 ß-particle emissions per minute. The standard 70-kg person is continuous subjected internally to over 3000 ß-particle emissions per second. This is an unavoidable part of our existence (*54*).

Synergism in the enhanced effect observed when two substances act together. For example, both cigarette smoking and exposure to asbestos fibers are hazardous, but the combination is greater than simply adding the individual effects (*55–57*). It is likely that many individually harmless substances can be dangerous when present together. With 12 million substances known, there is no hope of screening each individually, much less in pairs. Limiting attention to just those 50,000 substances in common use, there are still over a billion pairs, and over 20 trillion triplets. There is no still hope of testing even a very small part of these combinations.

To balance this pessimistic point about synergism, the Surgeon General in 1982 assembled the best information available about known causes of cancer, and this is shown in Table 3 (*58*).

The first three factors account for 72% of cancers and are to a significant extent under our individual controls. We know that fresh fruit and vegetables, and low fat and high fiber diets, contribute to our well-being. The relationship between cigarettes and lung cancer and other illnesses is well-established. We have much less control over the factors we tend to worry about more such as the industrial and environmental pollution, which, even combined, are less important than either of the first two factors.

The author thanks the Quality of Instruction Council of his university for its support.

Literature Cited

1. Hammond, E. C. "The Effects of Smoking," *Sci. Am.* **1962** (July), 207, 39.
2. Lamb, R. deF. *American Chamber of Horrors: The Truth about Food and Drugs;* Farrar and Rinehart: New York 1936; Arno Press: New York, 1976.

Risks and Chemical Substances *(cont'd.)*

3. Sanders, H. J. "Food Additives," *Chem. Eng. News* **1966** (10 October), 100–120; (17 October), 108–128.
4. Grenby, T. *Chem. Brit.* **1992**, *28*, 791.
5. "Food Chemistry"; *Chem. Brit.* **1991**, *27*, 1001–1032,
6. "Identification, Characterization, and Control of Potential Human Carcinogens: A Framework for Federal Decision-Making"; Office of Science and Technology Policy, Executive Office: Washington, DC, February 1, 1979.
7. "A Review of Risk Assessment Methodologies"; report for Subcommittee on Science, Research and Technology, Committee on Science and Technology, HR 98th Congress; Congressional Research Service, Library of Congress: Washington, DC, March 1983.
8. Wilson, R.; Crouch, E. A. C. "Risk Assessment and Comparisons: An Introduction"; *Science,* **1987**, *236*, 267.
9. Butterworth, K. R. *Chem. Soc. Rev.* **1978**, 7, 185.
10. *Health United States 1988* U.S. Department of Health and Human Services; PHS Publ. No. (PHS)89–1232, U.S. Government Printing Office: Washington, DC, 1988.
11. *Charting the Nation's Health, Trends since 1960* U.S. Department of Health and Human Services; PHS Publ No. (PHS) 85-1251; U.S. Government Printing Office: Washington, DC, 1985.
12. Woodburn, J. H. *Cancer, the Search for Its Origins;* Holt Rinehart and Winston: New York, 1964.
13. Doll, R.; Peto, R. *The Causes of Cancer, Quantitative Estimates of Avoidable Risks of Cancer in the United States Today;* Oxford Medical Publications: Oxford and New York, 1981.
14. *Cancer Rates and Risks,* 3rd ed.; U.S. Department of Health and Human Services, PHS; NIH Publication 85–691; U.S. Government Printing Office; Washington, DC, 1985.
15. Reif, A. E. "The Causes of Cancer"; *Am. Sci.* **1981**, *69*, 437.
16. *Sixth Annual Report on Carcinogens; 1991 Summary;* U.S. Department of Health and Human Services, PHS, National Toxicology Program; U.S. Government Printing Office: Washington, DC.
17. Ember, L. "Glycol Ethers Linked to Increased Miscarriage Rate"; *Chem. Eng. News* **1993** (14 June).
18. Hammond, E. C. *Smoking in Relation to the Death Rates of One Million Men and Women;* National Cancer Institute Monograph 19; National Cancer Institute: Washington DC, 1966.
19. Kinoshita, R. *Chem. Abst.* **1938**, *32*, 4652[6]; *Trans. Soc. Path. Japan* **1937**, *27*, 665.
20. "Forum on the Delaney Clause"; *Chem. Eng. News* **1977**, (27 June), 24–46.
21. Maxwell, K. E. *Chemicals and Life:* Dickenson: Belmont, CA, 1970.
22. Turner, J. A. *The Chemical Feast;* Grossman: New York, 1970.
23. Mintz, M. *The Therapeutic Nightmare;* Houghton-Mifflin: Boston, 1965.
24. Modell, W. *Science* **1967**, *156*, 346.
25. Brody, Jane. "Thalidomide on Trial"; *New York Times, Week in Review* **1968**, (2 June).
26. Goldberg, A. M. "Alternatives to Animals in Toxicity Testing"; *Sci. Am.* **1989**, *261*, 24.
27. "Stiffer Drug Laws in Wake of Thalidomide"; *Chem. Eng. News* **1973**, (22 January), 11.
28. Burger, A. "Behind the Decline in New Drugs"; *Chem. Eng. News* **1975**, (22 September), 37–41.
29. Spark, R. "Breaking the Drug Barrier"; *New York Times Magazine* **1977**, (20 March), 64–71.
30. Kelly, J. "Bridging America's Drug Gap"; *New York Times Magazine,* **1981**, (13 September), 100–108.
31. Hanson, D. "Better Risk Assessment Emerges from More Sophisticated Science Data"; *Chem. Eng. News* **1992**, (14 December).
32. Hubbard, R. C.; Young, C.; et al. *J. Am. Med. Assoc.* **1984**, *252*, 3249; **1985**, *254*, 56.
33. Feder, B. J. "Beyond White Rats and Rabbits"; *New York Times, Business* **1988**, (28 February), 1, 8, 9.
34. Noever, D. A.; Matsos, H. C. *Bioconvective Assay Device as an in vitro Alternative To Ocular Irritation Testing in Rabbits;* NASA Tech Briefs; MFS-26162; U.S. Government Printing Office: Washington, DC, 1991.
35. McCana, J.; Choi, E.; Yamasaki, E.; Ames, B. N. *Proc. Nat. Acad. Sci.* **1975**, *72*, 5135; **1976**, *73*, 950.
36. Fox, J. L., "Ames Test Success Pathway for Short-term Cancer Testing"; *Chem. Eng. News* **1977**, (12 December), 34–36.
37. Cairns, J. *Nature* **1981**, *289*, 353.

Risks and Chemical Substances *(cont'd.)*

38. Devoret, R. *Sci. Am.* **1979,** *241*(August), 40.
39. Windholz, M. Ed. *The Merck Index;* Merck: Rahway, NJ, 1983.
40. Lamanna, C. *Science* **1959,** *130,* 763.
41. Bernarde, M. A. *The Chemicals We Eat;* American Heritage Press: New York, 1971.
42. Sokolov, R. "Deadly Dinner"; *New York Times, Week in Review,* **1971** (1 August).
43. de Mora, S. J.; Harrison, R. M. *Chem. Brit.* **1984,** *20,* 900.
44. Wessel, M. A.; Dominski, A.; *Am. Sci.* 1977, *65,* 294.
45. *Preventing Lead Poisoning In Young Children;* Centers for Disease Control; U.S. Department of Health and Human Services; U.S. Government Printing Office: Washington, DC, October 1991.
46. Ames, B.; Gold, L. S.; et al. "Risk Assessment of Pesticides"; *Chem. Eng. News* **1991,** (7 January), 5, 27–55.
47. Wilson, R.; Crouch, E. A. C.; Ames, B. N.; et al. "Risk Assessment and Comparisons"; *Science* **1987,** *236,* 26, 271; letters, **1987,** *237,* 235, 128–84; **1988,** *240,* 1043–47.
48. Smith, P. J. *Science* **1980,** *209,* 1100.
49. Berkow, R., Ed. *The Merck Manual,* 15th ed.; Merck: Rahway, NJ, 1987.
50. Searle, C. E. "Chemical Carcinogens and Cancer Prevention"; *Chem. Brit.* **1988,** *22,* 211.
51. Harvey, R. G. *Am. Sci.* **1982,** *70,* 386.
52. Stevenson, R.; Thompson, K. *Chem. Brit.* **1985,** *21,* 893.
53. Nero, A. V., Jr. *Sci. Am.* **1988,** *258,* 42.
54. Lindsay, D. G. *Chem. Soc. Rev.* **1981,** *10,* 233.
55. Zurer, P. S. "Asbestos"; *Chem. Eng. News* **1985,** (4 March) 28–41.
56. Sherrill, R. "Asbestos, the Saver of Lives, Has a Deadly Side"; *New York Times Magazine* **1973,** (21 January) 12, 13, 58–64.
57. Hammond, E. C., Selikoff, I. J., Seidman, H. *Ann. N.Y. Acad. Sci.* **1979,** *330,* 473.
58. *Cancer Control Objectives for the Nation: 1985–2000;* NCI Monograph; U.S. Department of Health and Human Services, PHS; NIH 1986 #2; U.S. Government Printing Office: Washington, DC, 1986; pp. 1–105.
59. Hanson, D. "Flaws in Delaney Clause Make Change Imperative, But Congress May Balk"; *Chem. Eng. News* **1994,** (10 October), 16, 17.
60. Stinson, S. C. "Chiral Drugs" *Chem. Eng. News* **1944,** (19 September), 71.
61. Grasso, P., "Carcinogenicity Testing and Permitted Lists"; *Chem. Brit.* **1970,** *6*(1), 17–22.

 ## Adolescents and Their Music*

Elizabeth F. Brown, M.D. and William R. Hendee, Ph.D.

During adolescence, teenagers are expected to develop standards of behavior and reconcile them with their perceptions of adult standards. In this context, music, a powerful medium in the lives of adolescents, offers

*Elizabeth Brown and William Hendee, "Adolescents and Their Music." *Journal of the American Medical Association,* Vol. 262, No. 12 (September 22/29, 1989), pp. 1659–1663. Copyright © 1989 The American Medical Association.

Adolescents and Their Music *(cont'd.)*

conflicting values. The explicit sexual and violent lyrics of some forms of music often clash with the themes of abstinence and rational behavior promoted by adult society. Identification with rock music, particularly those styles that are rejected by adults, functions to separate adolescents from adult society. Some forms of rock musics extended well beyond respectability in fulfilling this definitional role. Total immersion into a rock subculture, such as heavy metal, may be both a portrait of adolescent alienation and an unflattering reflection of an adolescent's perception of the moral and ethical duplicity of adult society. Physicians should be aware of the role of music in the lives of adolescents and use music preferences as clues to the emotional and mental health of adolescents.

(*JAMA.* 1989;262:1659–1663)

Traditionally the role of physicians has been to conquer disease and promote health. For physicians who treat adolescents, this role has become increasingly challenging. Often an adolescent presents with a seemingly trivial physical complaint that, after questioning by the physician, expands into a set of complex problems related to the teenager's psychosocial environment. Frequently the tragic health problems of teenagers, such as unplanned teen pregnancies, accidents, and violence, have strong roots in the psychosocial environment. Prevention and intervention in these health problems require the physician to be more sensitive and knowledgeable about the environment of adolescents.[1]

Health promotion and disease prevention in the adolescent encompass multiple dimensions of health care. They go beyond the traditional advocacy of a healthy diet, exercise, and avoidance of health risks such as tobacco, drugs, and excess alcohol to an understanding of the sociocultural forces that influence adolescents as they experience the transition into adulthood. Appreciation of this environment not only yields insights into the challenges facing adolescents but also enables the physician to identify adverse psychosocial problems and intervene before their consequences are expressed as health problems. One aspect of the adolescent environment that has been a source of concern since its appearance in the 1950s has been the role of rock music, specifically its lyrics. This concern has been enhanced by the visual imagery of rock music videos.

The term *rock music* is frequently used generically to encompass any type of music listened to by teenagers. However, the music associated with adolescents has, over the years, splintered into a wide variety of styles, including punk, heavy metal, rap, hip-hop, and house music, to name a few. The latter three styles are particularly identified with black adolescents. In this article, we have chosen to define rock music more narrowly, as music that might also be referred to as popular music and is typically played on the top-40 radio stations. This type of rock music is most

Adolescents and Their Music *(cont'd.)*

often listened to by white adolescents. Much of the communications research has focused on this type of rock music and consequently on its effects on white adolescents. This article reviews and analyzes the recent communications literature on the impact of rock music on the lives of adolescents.

The Role of Rock Music

Music long has been recognized as a powerful communicative force that affects attitude, mood, emotions, and behavior. Anthropologist A. P. Merriam in his book *The Anthropology of Music* says, "The importance of music, as judged by the sheer ubiquity of its presence is enormous . . . there is probably no other human cultural activity which is so all pervasive and which reaches into, shapes and often controls so much of human behavior."[2]

For today's adolescents, music is particularly ubiquitous. During the early years of rock music, radios were heavy, bulky, and essentially stationary. Music became portable with the advent of transistor radios. Recent innovations in miniaturization and the development of light high-quality headphones have made it possible for teenagers to envelop themselves constantly in rock music. Between the seventh and 12th grades, the average teenager listens to 10,500 hours of rock music, just slightly less than the entire number of hours spent in the classroom from kindergarten through high school.[3] During this period, television viewing decreases and music becomes an increasingly powerful medium in an adolescent's life.[4]

Unlike television, for which the patterns of viewing are often subject to family discussion and parental control, music is largely uncensored. Parents frequently do not appreciate the sound of rock music and therefore ignore it. In the home, teenagers often listen to music in the privacy of their bedrooms,[5] and the ideas presented in the music are interpreted privately, without modulation or guidance by parents. Unlike television, music is controlled by the user; a song can be replayed anytime, anywhere, any number of times.

Music is important to adolescents in many ways. For example, music plays a large role in adolescent socialization. As adolescents gain independence, they turn to music as an information source about sexuality and alternative lifestyles, subjects that are largely taboo in both home and school.[6,7] Music can also introduce adolescents to political topics via the various concerts organized around political causes—for example, Amnesty International, Live Aid, or Farm Aid.

For young people, music is an important symbol in their search for independence and autonomy. Identification with a particular musical style may indicate resistance to authority, provide an outlet for personal troubles or conflicts with parents, or yield a sense of relaxation, release, and security in new environments. Music can be used to heighten emotions and encourage movement, such as dancing or clapping, or can be used to soothe emotions and provide relaxation. Music

Adolescents and Their Music *(cont'd.)*

can be used alone, as background for other activities, or as the focus of events such as concerts.[8–10]

While rock music may generally symbolize adolescent rebellion and search for autonomy, the forms it takes differ among different cultures—the preference of black adolescents for rap or house music has already been mentioned—and also between sexes. For example, heavy metal music with its loud beat and performers with aggressive and startling stage antics attracts primarily white male adolescents. On the other hand, adolescent girls tend to be more attracted to soft, romantic, nonthreatening music. Weinstein[11] proposes that these musical preferences reflect the different types of struggles that boys and girls face as they make the transition to adulthood. As children, boys are typically allowed more freedom, to behave more aggressively, and to be slightly naughty. In contrast, as an adult, strict conformity and supervision is the rule. Heavy metal music then, though an extreme example and certainly not appealing to all boys, represents this conflict. A salient struggle for adolescent girls is the emergence of sexuality and the initiation, or at least contemplation, of sexual activity. Soft, romantic music serves to ease tensions about sexual activity in a nonthreatening way.[11]

Knowledge of rock music is used as a criterion of expertise by many adolescents, and music and musical personalities are often the subject of adolescent conversations. Shared enjoyment of music can be the basis of new friendships and form the basis of peer groups. Rock music has spawned many "cultural accessories" such as T-shirts, posters, and dress styles that are a prominent part of the adolescent's life.[6] Some youth subcultures such as punk rockers and heavy metal stylists can be immediately identified by music and sartorial preferences that imply a common bond with other devotees of the same musical genre.

In some cases, identifying features of adolescent preferences transmit a strong message of adolescent alienation. For example, Roe[10] proposes that there is a causal link between school performance and music preference. Specifically, academic performance defines status; negative status can lead to antischool activities, which then in turn result in alignment with an adolescent subculture. Therefore, students who perform well in school will be more likely to embrace the values taught in school, while those who perform poorly are more likely to react negatively toward the institution that labeled them failures. A heavy involvement in rock music by low achievers may be an adaptive reaction to their failures as students and an expression of their alienation from school and the learning experience. Affiliation with a particular teen subculture provides these youngsters with an identity and reputation that has been unattainable through academic performance.[10]

A longitudinal study of the academic performance and music preference of Swedish youths from age 11 to 15 years support this hypothesis. Successful students, including those from low socioeconomic backgrounds, exhibited a preference for mainstream music, less interest in punk and rock music, and less involvement in peer

---

Adolescents and Their Music *(cont'd.)*

groups. Lower school achievement was indirectly related to a preference for rock music through an intervening factor of greater involvement with peer groups. In addition, a negative commitment to school, identified on a questionnaire, was directly related to a preference for punk and rock music.[10]

Roe[10] states that "the findings unequivocally support the argument that music preferences are dependent on earlier levels of school achievement." This analysis challenges the widely held assumption that music, as a competitor for the time and commitment of young people, has a deleterious effect on school. It also suggests that teenage immersion into a rock subculture may be primarily symptomatic of alienation and hostility toward adult society.

Television is the entertainment medium for mainstream America, whereas rock music represents the adolescent peer culture. A study by Larson and Kubey[5] revealed that adolescents who preferred to watch television spent more time with their families and were reasonably well integrated into mainstream American culture. Similarly, heavy involvement with rock music is associated with a greater commitment to peer groups and less association with family.

Rock Music Lyrics and Videos

Against a backdrop of the pervasive presence of music, its multiple roles, and its power in communicating messages, the lyrics and images of rock music have been a persistent controversy. As a reflection of its origin in rhythm and blues, rock music espouses the themes of rebellion and sex. Even the words "rock 'n' roll" have strong sexual connotations. Attempts at censorship have occurred since the inception of rock music. For example, the BBC banned the line "I'd love to turn you on" in the Beatles song, "A Day in the Life." To appear on the *Ed Sullivan Show* the Rolling Stones were required to change the lyrics and title of their song from "Let's spend the night together" to "Let's spend some time together" (*New Republic.* August 12, 1985;19:14–16).[12]

Such concerns seem quaint in light of the explicitness of the lyrics of current rock music. Parents groups and other concerned citizens have characterized many rock lyrics as sexually explicit and violent. For example, the song "Darling Nikki" by rock star Prince (which sold 10 million copies) speaks crudely of masturbation, and other songs by this artist refer to fellatio and incest. Ozzy Osborne's "Suicide Solution" distinctly advocates suicide.

Heavy metal music, a musical style more rebellious than mainstream rock music, features a loud pulsating rhythm and abounds with lyrics that glorify hatred, abuse, sexual deviancy, and occasionally satanism. While rock and roll has always symbolized rebellion, it has only recently embraced outright hatred and rejection through the style of heavy metal.[13] In earlier music that preceded rock and roll, connotations were implicit, often using the word "it" as an euphemism for sexual

Adolescents and Their Music *(cont'd.)*

experiences, such as in Cole Porter's "Birds do it, bees do it." Even the Beatles proposed, "Why don't we do it in the road?" In the 1980s the word "it" is no longer needed; the most deviant sexual activities can be described.[3]

Preteens and teenagers are highly impressionable and many have speculated that they may be particularly sensitive to the messages of rock music. In *The Closing of the American Mind*, Bloom[14] calls music the "medium of the human soul." He finds rock music barren and a "junk food for the human soul." Young teenagers with emerging concepts of sensuality and sexuality are not nurtured slowly and carefully by rock music; they are bombarded with messages about adult sexuality and perversities at an age when they have immature concepts of love, caring, and commitment. According to Bloom, the pervasiveness of rock music undermines parental control over a child's moral education.

In 1985, there were well-publicized discussions about the sexual and violent content of lyrics, prompted in part by a citizens group, The Parents' Music Research Center, which culminated in hearings before the Senate Commerce Committee in September 1985. Much of the discussion and controversy centered on adults' perceptions of the meanings of rock music. However, several studies indicate that an adult's interpretation of rock lyrics might be entirely different from that of a teenager.[15] A complete understanding of rock lyrics that is consonant with an adult's interpretation of the lyrics often requires sophistication beyond the reach of young persons. The symbolic meaning of a song, represented more by the rhythm of the music and personalities of the artists, may transcend any explicit appreciation or interpretation of its lyrics and may be the primary attraction for adolescents. For example, few teenagers in a survey of Southern California high schools correctly identified sex, drugs, or violence as subjects of their favorite songs. In 37% of songs listed as their favorites, the students were unable to identify any theme. Sex, drugs, or violence were identified in only 7% of the songs and even then the students' interpretations of the lyrics were frequently quite literal and unsophisticated; the teenagers very infrequently understood the symbolic meanings of the lyrics. The most prevalent items identified by the students were love and friendship and other themes that generally reflected experiences of teenage life.[15]

In a study of upper-middle-class 4th 8th, and 12th grade and college students, Greenfield et al[16] found that a surprisingly few number of students correctly interpreted the general theme of Bruce Springsteen's song "Born in the U.S.A.," even though the song was familiar to most students and the students were questioned directly after listening to it. The "correct" interpretation of alienation vs the common "incorrect" interpretation of "Born in the U.S.A." as a patriotic song increased with the age of the students, but still barely 50% of the college students identified the "correct" theme.[16]

Even though adolescents' understanding of the lyrics might be unsophisticated, their individual appeal and symbolic importance cannot be discounted.

Adolescents and Their Music *(cont'd.)*

These young persons may be responding more to the themes of independence and rebellion against parental authority symbolized by rock music than to its actual verbal messages, for music is more than lyrics, rhythm, and melody. It is an interaction of these attributes with the listener's personality and receptivity and includes a perception of attitudes and style manifested by the performer.[17]

The visual dimensions of rock music have also been an enduring concern from the era of Elvis Presley's swiveling hips to the frankly sexual or violent stage antics of today's performers such as Prince and Ozzy Osborne. Music videos have added yet another visual dimension to rock music. Typically, rock videos have a surreal, dreamlike quality with dramatic visual effects.[18] There is concern that the marriage between television and music is powerful and synergistic. Multisensory input reinforces any message, specifically by enhancing learning and recall.[13] As an example, one study of music video found that individual meanings for a music video version of a song were more favorable and potent than the audio version alone.[19]

The violent and sexual content of the video images are disturbing to many. In one content analysis of 200 concept videos (distinguished from performance videos in which the predominant theme is a studio or concert performance), violence occurred in 57% of the samples and sexual intimacy in 75%. Of the videos containing violence, 81% also contained sexual references. Half of all women who appeared in the video were dressed provocatively.[20] Another study showed that 59.7% of a random sample of rock videos had sexual themes, and 53.2% had violent themes.[21] In an analysis of sexism in a sample of rock videos, 57% of those depicting women portrayed them in a condescending manner while only 14% depicted women as fully equal to men.[22]

Studies of the effects of television violence may also apply to music videos. These studies strongly suggest, but do not verify, that there is a causal connection between television violence and subsequent aggressive behavior.[23] Gerbner and coworkers[24,25] argue that television violence also may have a more subtle influence on social relationships. They hypothesize that the violent world of television portrays a pattern of domination, sexism, and inequality that colors viewers' perceptions of the real world. Those who view an excessive amount of television tend to regard the world as mean and hostile.

However, television and music videos may not be strictly comparable. For example, the negative imagery in the visuals of music videos may be mediated by their surrealistic and abstract qualities. Burns and Thompson[26] suggest that music videos may help young people to confront the real problems of adolescents growing up in our society. The frequent themes of holocaust and apocalypse presented in music videos, while irrational and dreamlike, may offer a subjective way of addressing these threatening problems in contrast to the depressing and sometimes complacent presentation by the news media of the threat of nuclear war.

Walker[27,28] argues that the total media profile of a viewer must be assessed before the influence of any one medium can be analyzed. High levels of violence on

Adolescents and Their Music *(cont'd.)*

videos would be a significant concern, for example, only if they are associated with high levels of violence on the television programs watched by the viewer. However, Walker found that music video exposure is negatively related to watching televised crime and action programs.[27,28]

Some researchers have suggested that music videos, by supplying a visual image, inhibit the imagination. When a listener hears a song previously seen on a music video, the video image comes to mind instead of an individual and personally meaningful one. In this way music videos destroy the potential of music to evoke special feelings and memories for the viewers.[29] In an informal empirical study of the effect of music videos on the imagination of fifth and sixth graders, Greenfield and coworkers[16] found that those students who had watched a music video had less imaginative responses to a series of questions than those students who had only heard an audio version of the same song. The students themselves commented that seeing a music video before hearing the song on the radio inhibited their imaginative thinking about the song. In their studies of 587 high school students, however, Sun and Lull[30] found that although students enjoyed the visual images of music videos and used them in interpreting the music, they also were actively involved in selecting the music and had some perspective on music videos' content.

The Effects of Rock Music

The lyrics and images in rock music and rock music videos are certainly disturbing. However, there have been few studies of the effects of these new trends in music. Such a study is methodologically very difficult. Rock music audiences are not totally passive, uncritically absorbing the lyrics and images of rock music. That is, adolescents are active participants in the rock music experience and are not "victims" of rock music.[9] Rock music, or any music for that matter, is processed through several complex steps in each individual. The listener first chooses certain music to satisfy a specific need. Then the message of the music is interpreted by the individual and assimilated and applied to the listener's daily life. In this way interpretation and use of a particular message provided by music are intervening variables between the verbatim lyrics and any possible effects.

In addition both the choice of the music and the way in which it is used by its fans are heavily influenced by such variables as social class, age, education, race, religion, or gender. While both a 13-year-old girl and a blue-collar worker both might enjoy the music of Prince, for example, their interpretation of the music and the way it fits into their lives is probably very different. Music can also be but one component of an immersion into an adolescent subculture. For example, the subculture represented by punk and heavy metal music is intimately linked with distinct dress codes, language, and attitudes.[8] Quite simply, music can mean different things to different people at different times. Music is a very individual and complex experience and thus resistant to traditional research.

Adolescents and Their Music *(cont'd.)*

The effects of music and its lyrics on teenagers are subtle and cumulative and could only be definitely studied in a carefully controlled longitudinal study. This type of study is unrealistic. Therefore, it is also unrealistic to expect that any direct causal role of music on the behavior of teenagers can be easily identified.

The evidence of possible effects of explicit rock music, specifically heavy metal, has so far been anecdotal and circumstantial. Heavy metal music is of particular concern since it is such a strong expression of rebellion and sometimes alienation. For example, several murders have been correlated with a fascination for heavy metal music. The "Night Stalker," a serial murderer on the West Coast, was said to be obsessed with the heavy metal band AC/DC. A 14-year-old girl, also fascinated with heavy metal music, stabbed her mother to death (*US News World Rep.* October 28, 1985:46–49). In a study of chemically dependent adolescents, 60% named heavy metal as their first choice of music, leading the author to suggest that such music is associated with and may promote destructive behavior in susceptible individuals.[31] Healthy well-adjusted teenagers, on the other hand, may be minimally affected by explicit rock music.[32]

In a laboratory study of the effect of music television (MTV), Greeson and Williams[33] found that 7th and 10th graders, after watching 1 hour of selected musics videos, were more likely to approve of premarital sex compared with a control group of adolescents. Whether there were any long-term effects or whether the music videos actually changed the behavior of the adolescents was unknown. Another behavioral study found that violent music videos desensitized viewers to violence immediately after viewing.[34] Lack of human effects studies on heavy users of music videos and rock music, particularly heavy metal, leaves a major gap in our current knowledge.

An obvious question to ask is why there has been such an upsurge in the violent and sexual imagery of rock music. The explicitness of rock music today may be due in part to the aging of rock and roll. Rock music has always functioned to define the adolescent culture as distinct from adult society. As it has aged, however, much of the rock-and-roll culture has been absorbed into the mainstream and no longer separates "them" from "us." Former hippies and baby boomers are now parents of adolescents and many rock stars have become accepted if not embraced by the establishment. Rock music has become the voice of corporate America.[35] Eric Clapton, Phil Collins, and Steve Winwood endorse beer, the song "Revolution" by the Beatles is used to promote tennis shoes, and Michael Jackson is seen shaking hands with President Reagan. The album "Purple Rain" by rock star Prince, which contained the offensive song "Darling Nikki," has won both an Oscar and a Grammy.

The sexual freedom and recreational drug use that once were the exclusive property of young people have become an accepted part of adult behavior. The lyrics of rock and roll in the 1960s, which once so shocked parents, today seem quite tame. Adult society is already sexually and behaviorally explicit, and in order for rock music to express rebellion and autonomy, the explicitness must be taken to a higher level (*New Republic,* August 12, 1985;19:14–16).

Adolescents and Their Music *(cont'd.)*

For teenagers who identify with an alienated youth subculture, rock music must go beyond respectability to fulfill its definitional role. For these teenagers, nihilistic, violent, and at times sadistic music may express their reaction to the adult world in which they see no consistent and logical set of moral values. The music may be both a portrait of their alienation and an unflattering reflection of their perception of moral and ethical duplicity of adult society.

Conclusion

Adolescence is a challenging period under any circumstances. Young people are expected to develop a set of moral values and reconcile them with their perceptions of adult standards and behaviors. In this context, music, a prominent medium in the lives of adolescents, sends conflicting messages. Rock music, reflective of the adolescent peer culture, symbolizes the adolescent themes of rebellion and autonomy. Increasingly it does so with disturbing lyrics that connote violence and pornographic sexual imagery. In contrast to these media messages are the themes of abstinence and reasoned, responsible behavior promoted by authority figures such as parents, teachers, and government officials. At the very least, commitment to a rock subculture is symptomatic of adolescent alienation from these authority figures.

Whether, in addition to revealing adolescent alienation, explicit lyrics are also a lasting influence on adolescent values remains to be seen. Research into the effects of media messages has been problematic because of the very pervasiveness of music and its individual appeal and meaning. The effects of rock music, particularly heavy metal music, have not yet been studied extensively. As an important agent of adolescent socialization, however, the negative messages of rock music should not be dismissed.

In interactions with adolescents and their parents, physicians should be aware, and promote awareness, of the messages of music, and should nurture and encourage alternative responsible sources of information about sexuality and responsible behavior. Physicians should also educate parents about the potential influence of both music and music videos and encourage parental awareness of an adolescent's exposure to media.[32] Inasmuch as music can be representative of an adolescent subculture, questions about music preference can be corroborating evidence when other affective behavior of the adolescent suggests potentially destructive alienation. An extreme example is total immersion into a heavy metal subculture with total identification with such bands as Slayer and Metallica. Evidence, although anecdotal, suggests that these adolescents may be at risk for drug abuse[31] or even participation in satanic activities.

At the other end of the spectrum may be parents who are concerned about the explicit rock music that their well-adjusted adolescent child is listening to. Although perhaps not entirely comforting, the physician can point out that so far there is no evidence that this music has any deleterious effect on the behavior of adolescents. As a measure of its potential effect, physicians can encourage parents to question their

Adolescents and Their Music *(cont'd.)*

children, in a very nonjudgmental way, about their interpretation of the music and what role it plays in their lives.

References

1. Blum RW. Contemporary threats to adolescent health in the United States. *JAMA.* 1987;257: 3390–3395.
2. Merriam AP. *The Anthropology of Music.* Chicago, Ill: Northwestern University Press; 1964:218.
3. Davis S. Pop lyrics: a mirror and molder of society. *Et cetera.* Summer 1985:167–169.
4. Avery R. Adolescents' use of the mass media. *Am Behav Scientist.* 1979;23:53–70.
5. Larson R, Kubey R. Television and music: contrasting media in adolescent life. *Youth Soc.* 1983; 15:13–31.
6. Lull J. Listeners communicative uses of popular music. In: Lull J, ed. *Popular Music and Communication.* Beverly Hills, Calif: Sage Publications; 1987:212–230.
7. Lull J. On the communicative properties of music. *Comm Res.* 1985;12:363–372.
8. Grossberg L. Is there rock after punk? *Crit. Stud Mass Comm.* 1986;3:50–70.
9. Grossberg L. Rock and roll in search of an audience. In: Lull J. ed. *Popular Music and Communication.* Beverly Hills, Calif: Sage Publications; 1987:175–197.
10. Roe K. The school and music and adolescent socialization. In: Lull J. ed. *Popular Music and Communication.* Beverly Hills, Calif: Sage Publications; 1987:212–230.
11. Weinstein D. Rock: youth and its music. *Pop Music Soc.* 1983:9:2–16.
12. MacDonald JR. Censoring rock lyrics: a historical analysis of the debate. *Youth Soc.* 1988;19: 294–313.
13. Steussy J. *Testimony for the United States Senate Commerce Committee.* September 19, 1985.
14. Bloom A. *The Closing of the American Mind.* New York, NY: Simon & Schuster; 1987:68–81.
15. Prinsky L, Rosenbaum J. 'Leer-ics' or lyrics: teenage impressions of rock 'n' roll. *Youth Soc.* 1987;18:384–396.
16. Greenfield PM, Bruzzone L, Koyamatsu K, et al. What is rock music doing to the minds of our youth? a first experimental look at the effects of rock music. *J Early Adolesc.* 1987;7:315–329.
17. Hyden C, McCandless N J. Men and women as portrayed in the lyrics of contemporary music. *Pop Music Soc.* 1983;9:19–25.
18. Aufderheide P. Music videos, the look of the sound. *J Comm.* 1986;36:57–77.
19. Rubin RB, Rubin AM, Perse EM, et al. Media use and meaning of music video. *Journalism Q.* 1986;63:353–359.
20. Sherman RL, Dominick JR. Violence and sex in music videos: TV and rock 'n' roll. *J Comm.* 1986;36:79–93.
21. Baxter RL, DeRiemer C, Laudini A, et al. A content analysis of music videos. *J Broadcast Electron Media.* 1985;29:333–340.
22. Vincent RC, Davis DK, Bronszkowski LA. Sexism in MTV: the portrayal of women in rock videos. *Journalism Q.* 1987;64:750–755,941.
23. National Institute of Mental Health. *Television and Behavior: Ten Years of Scientific Progress and Implication for the Eighties. Summary Report.* Washington, DC: Dept of Health and Human Services; 1982. Publication 82–1195;1.
24. Gerbner G, Gross L, Signiorelli N, Morgan M, Jackson-Beech M. The demonstration of power: violence profile No. 10. *J Comm.* 1978;28:176–207.
25. Gerbner G, Gross L, Morgan M, Signiorelli N. The 'mainstreaming' of America: violence profile No. 11. *J Comm.* 1980;30:10–29.
26. Burns G, Thompson R. Music, television and video: historical and aesthetic considerations. *Pop Music Soc.* 1987;11:79–89.
27. Walker JR. How viewing of MTV relates to exposure of other media violence. *Journalism Q.* 1987;64:756–762.

Adolescents and Their Music *(cont'd.)*

28. Walker JR. The context of MTV: adolescent media use and music television. *Pop Music Soc.* 1987;18:177–189.
29. Abt D. Music video: impact of the visual dimension. In: Lull J. ed. *Popular Music and Communication.* Beverly Hills, Calif: Sage Publications; 1987:96–109.
30. Sun SW, Lull J. The adolescent audience for music videos and why they watch. *J Comm.* 1986;36:115–125.
31. King P. Heavy metal music and drug use in adolescents. *Postgrad Med.* 1988;83:295–304
32. Frith S. *The Sociology of Rock.* London, England: Constable; 1978.
33. Greeson LE, Williams RA. Social implications of music videos for youth: an analysis of the contents and effects of MTV. *Youth Soc.* 1986;18:177–189.
34. Rehman S, Reilly S. Music videos: a new dimension of televised violence. *Penn Speech Comm Ann.* 1985;41:61–64.
35. Frith S. Trends in the music industry. In: Lull J, ed. *Popular Music and Communications.* Beverly Hills, Calif: Sage Publications; 1987:75, 76.
36. Committee on Communications, American Academy of Pediatrics. The impact of rock lyrics and music videos on children and youth. *Pediatrics.* 1989;83:314–315.

BUTTONHOLES: Some Differences in Gender-related Front Closures*

Judith Lopez

Even though "there is nothing intrinsically feminine or masculine about any particular fashion . . . ,"[1] the "gender convention"[2] of fastening right-over-left (ROL) for women and left-over-right (LOR) for men is observed in Western civilization today. Theatrical costumers, however, hypothesize that early men and women held animal skins around their bodies for protection with the left hand[3] because they were predominately right-handed.[4] This ROL closure would have left the right hand free for more demanding tasks such as wielding a weapon. Whether this was the case or not, experts on armor from the fourteenth century state:

> To insure that an enemy's lance point would not slip between the plates, they overlapped from left to right, since it was standard fighting practice that the left side, protected by the shield, was turned toward the enemy. Thus, men's jackets button left to right even to the present day.[5]

European men's upper garments have LOR front closures that appear to have been codified by the eighteenth century, if not earlier.[6] Moreover, according to

*Judith Lopez, *Buttonholes: Some Differences in Gender-related Front Closures. Dress 20* (1993), pp. 74–78. Reprinted with the permission of the publisher.

BUTTONHOLES: Some Differences in Gender-related Front Closures *(cont'd.)*

French law, only male tailors could construct fitted fashionable clothing,[7] and the clothing they made fastened LOR for women as well as for men.[8]

When did the ROL standard develop in American women's dress? Nineteenth century accounts do not agree. Fashion plates and extant garments found in the United States document differences in closures until the early twentieth century.

This research sought to monitor the direction of front closures between 1860 and 1920 to discern how the standard to ROL emerged for women. Whether this change was slow, but pervasive, or if it occurred quickly over a short period of time also was a concern.[9] The following questions were asked.

1. Were the ready-to-wear (RTW) industries instrumental in mandating that front closures fasten LOR for men and ROL for women? While women could purchase RTW outerwear by the 1840s and RTW underwear in the 1880s,[10] the highly ornamented fitted styles of daywear that were popular in the nineteenth century were impossible to mass produce at a reasonable cost.[11]

2. Will the influence of RTW allow some categories of garments for women to exhibit ROL closures sooner than others?

3. Will a difference in front button closures be found between fashion illustrations and extant garments? Creekmore and Pederson and Richards found that fashion illustrators exaggerate style elements for emphasis.

Method

Illustrations of clothing in periodicals published between 1860 and 1920[12] were compared with extant garments from the same period in historic collections.[13] Every woman's and man's garment that clearly showed front button closure or overlap was coded as to type of garment, direction of overlap, date, and gender of wearer. No back openings were considered since their sidedness might or might not relate to front opening sidedness.

The issue of reversed images in print sources constantly plagues the historic researcher. This study documents the influence of fashion illustrations *as they were printed*. The question is whether/when women were influenced by those illustrations, regardless of the original sketch. Furthermore, since the comparison is with *extant clothing*, no attempt was made to distinguish between RTW and custom-made garments.

Findings

Illustrated Garments

The sample of 1,251 fashion illustrations (women=1,013, men=238) included everything from work clothes to high fashion and underwear to outerwear. Overall, ROL openings in this sample of illustrated women's clothing increased steadily from 66% in the 1860s to almost 100% by 1919 (Table 1). About three-fourths of

BUTTONHOLES: Some Differences in Gender-related Front Closures *(cont'd.)*

TABLE 1. Illustrated garments for women between 1860 and 1919

	Under/Sleepwear		Daywear		Outerwear		Decade Totals	
	ROL	*LOR*	*ROL*	*LOR*	*ROL*	*LOR*	*N*	*%ROL*
1860–1869	**3**	0	**24**	15	**13**	7	62	65
1870–1879	**24**	10	**164**	79	**65**	21	363	70
1880–1889	**14**	1	**108**	8	**15**	2	148	93
1890–1899	**12**	5	**99**	35	**57**	6	214	79
1900–1909	**1**	2	**24**	3	**6**	0	36	86
1910–1919	**1**	0	**97**	1	**87**	4	190	97
Total N	**55**	18	**516**	141	**243**	40	1013	
Category %	75	25	78	22	86	14		**80.5**

the illustrated under/sleepwear and day garments fastened ROL. An additional ten percent of the outerwear fastened ROL.

Soon after publication began in 1867, *Harper's Bazar* stated unequivocally that buttons for women's clothing were "sewed on the left side".[14] While the publishers may have believed that ROL was the norm, the 1860s were still a period of transition for women. Fashion illustrations of an 1868 wedding party show one dress buttoning LOR and another fastening ROL.[15]

ROL closures exhibited an unusual peak in the 1880s. English dressmakers,[16] followed by American fashion illustrators, encouraged women to button ROL. It is not clear why this change occurred in Europe. J. P. P. Higgins suggested that the recurring decimation due to bubonic plague resulted in "a new concept of gender distinction" that was reflected in clothing by the late seventeenth and early eighteenth centuries. Additionally, the 1880s seem to have been a decade of standardization in the United States.[17]

The ROL standard for women resumed its natural climb in the 1890s while garments continued to exhibit a variety of front button closures. Whether decorative or functional, ROL and LOR closures could be found in one garment.[18] Unlike the firm statement that women sewed their buttons on the left side in 1868, by the 1890s, publications suggested that ladies "usually" fastened their clothing ROL.[19] In *School Needlework* Olive Hapgood stated, "the side of the garment in which the buttonhole is made is a matter of choice, but it is wise to decide upon one side and adhere to it."[20]

As in women's fashion illustrations, the surge towards standardization during the 1880s is evident in men's fashion illustrations (Table 2). Again, outerwear fastened LOR more consistently than did the other categories of clothing.

BUTTONHOLES: Some Differences in Gender-related Front Closures *(cont'd.)*

TABLE 2. Illustrated garments for men between 1860 and 1919

	Under/Sleepwear		Daywear		Outerwear		Decade Totals	
	ROL	*LOR*	*ROL*	*LOR*	*ROL*	*LOR*	*N*	*%LOR*
1860–1869	0	**0**	6	**17**	1	**4**	28	75
1870–1879	3	**12**	7	**26**	4	**17**	69	80
1880–1889	0	**0**	0	**4**	0	**3**	7	100
1890–1899	1	**2**	5	**36**	0	**31**	75	92
1900–1909	0	**15**	1	**26**	0	**13**	55	98
1910–1919	0	**0**	0	**2**	0	**2**	4	100
Total N	4	**29**	19	**111**	5	**70**	238	
Category %	12	88	15	85	7	93		**88.6**

Surprisingly, men's LOR closures found in illustrations in all categories, and over four decades, lag up to 15% behind the 100% LOR rate found in extant garments. This trend is the reverse of that seen in women's garments.

Extant Garments

Extant garments dated 1860–1919 from four historic collections and photographs were analyzed. Front openings meant to be invisible in women's garments were examined. Where LOR and ROL occurred in the same garment (i.e. inner and outer bodice closures), neither was included in the data. The sample of 457 garments (women=398, men=59) was primarily daywear.

Less than half of the women's garments in this sample dated prior to the Civil War exhibited ROL front closures. American seamstresses continued making as much female clothing fasten LOR as had earlier French tailors. Ambivalence toward ROL openings for women prevailed. Photographs of a man and his wife show that both of their clothing buttoned LOR in 1868.[21] Even in the period 1910–1919, only 78% of the women's clothing in this sample fastened ROL.

Compared to the 80% ROL closures found in illustrated women's clothing, the 66% ROL closures exhibited by extant clothing suggests that women were unexpectedly persistent in fastening their clothes "men's way" (Table 3).

Perhaps due to the RTW industry, 87% of the extant women's outerwear found fastened ROL. As expected, less (70%) daywear did so. Surprisingly, since RTW under/sleepwear was available in the 1840s, only 65% of that found fastened ROL.

Women seem to have followed the dictates of fashion illustrators in the clothing that others could see more often than in garments not meant to be seen. *More importantly,* if LOR fastenings occurred in more than one-third of women's most

BUTTONHOLES: Some Differences in Gender-related Front Closures *(cont'd.)*

TABLE 3. Extant garments for women between 1860 and 1919

	Under/sleepwear		Daywear		Outerwear		Decade Totals	
	ROL	*LOR*	*ROL*	*LOR*	*ROL*	*LOR*	*N*	*%ROL*
1800–1859	**0**	1	**14**	16	**0**	0	31	45
1860–1869	**1**	0	**34**	21	**0**	0	56	63
1870–1879	**6**	0	**19**	15	**0**	1	41	61
1880–1889	**2**	2	**52**	17	**4**	3	80	73
1890–1899	**1**	3	**36**	13	**3**	0	56	71
1900–1909	**2**	1	**55**	12	**6**	0	76	83
1910–1919	**1**	0	**37**	13	**7**	0	58	78
Total N	**13**	7	**247**	107	**20**	4	398	
Category %	65	35	70	30	83	17		**72.7**

intimate and utilitarian apparel, it seems evident that there was no physical reason for women to change to ROL fastenings in other clothing, either.

All menswear found closed LOR (Table 4). The many ROL fashion illustrations in men's clothing seem to have had no effect on actual garments.

Summary

The development of ROL closures for women grew steadily between 1860 and 1920, but LOR had become the norm for men at least a century earlier. All of the extant menswear found buttoned LOR, but only two-thirds of the womenswear

TABLE 4. Extant garments for men between 1860 and 1919

	Under/sleepwear		Daywear		Outerwear		Decade Totals	
	ROL	*LOR*	*ROL*	*LOR*	*ROL*	*LOR*	*N*	*%LOR*
1800–1859	0	**0**	0	**3**	0	**1**	4	100
1860–1869	0	**0**	0	**2**	0	**0**	2	100
1870–1879	0	**1**	0	**2**	0	**0**	3	100
1880–1889	0	**0**	0	**2**	0	**0**	2	100
1890–1899	0	**2**	0	**1**	0	**0**	3	100
1900–1909	0	**0**	0	**30**	0	**1**	31	100
1910–1919	0	**0**	0	**14**	0	**0**	14	100
Total	0	**3**	0	**54**	0	**2**	59	**100**

BUTTONHOLES: Some Differences in Gender-related Front Closures *(cont'd.)*

found fastened ROL. Women's under/sleepwear was more resistant to change from LOR to ROL than was daywear or outerwear. Outerwear may have been influenced by the womens' RTW industry as more extant garments than illustrations fastening ROL were found. Fashion illustrations showed fewer LOR closures for men, and more ROL closures for women than did extant garments.

This work examined when the change between men's and women's front closures occurred. Further research is needed to document why.

References

[1]Claudia Kidwell and Valerie Steele, *Men and Women, Dressing the Part* (Washington D.C.: Smithsonian, 1989): Plate 2.

[2]Kidwell and Steele, *Men and Women*, 2.

[3]This theory was submitted by George Riddle, actor in the Broadway play, *Fantastics*, after an article concerning this research appeared in the *New York Post*.

[4]Marcel Kinsbourne, in "Handedness" in *Speech and Language, ed.* Doreen Kimura (Boston: Birkhäuser, 1987) 19. Kinsbourne, states that "the non-right-handed population is said to amount to about 10% . . . across many different cultures . . . for many thousands of years." Ibid.

[5]Helmut Nickel, Stuart Phyrr, and Leonid Tarassuk in *The Art of Chivalry.* (New York: Metropolitan Museum of Art, 1982),18.

[6]All of the illustrations in DeMarly's *Fashion for Men* (London: B. T. Batsford, 1985) dated between 1470 and 1730, fastened LOR.

[7]Nora Waugh, in *The Cut of Women's Clothes,* states that French tailoring guilds excluded women until 1675 when seamstresses were permitted to make only loose untailored garments. Restrictions were gradually lifted until 1789 when women were constructing any garment they chose (London: Farber and Farber, 1968, 102). Diana DeMarly in *Working Class Dress,* maintains that poor and common people made do with garments that pulled on over the head or ones that fastened with ties; button holes took too much time to make (London: B. T. Batsford, 1986, 80, 131). Furthermore, buttons were restricted by English sumptuary laws from 1363 until the 17th century (DeMarly, *Fashion for Men*, 19.)

[8]While only 13 pre-1700 women's garments with front closures were found in European sources, all fastened LOR.

[9]Special thanks to the reviewers of *Dress* in helping to clarify this point.

[10]Claudia Kidwell and Margaret Christman in *Suiting Everyone, The Democratization of Clothing in America* (Washington D.C.: Smithsonian Institution Press, 1974), 94.

[11]Claudia Kidwell. *Cutting a Fashionable Fit* (Washington D.C.: Smithsonian Institution Press, 1979), 98.

[12]Fashion illustrations were taken from the *Delineator,* 1888; the *Des Moines Register* (also published as the *Iowa State Register* and the *Register and Leader*) 1862, 1866, 1877, 1880, 1885, 1888–1915; *Demorest's Monthly Magazine,* 1866, 1870, 1878, 1880–1885; *Harper's Bazar* 1867, 1868, 1871, 1875, 1876, 1878, 1879, 1891–1894; the *Ladies Home Journal,* 1906, 1907; the *Montgomery Ward and Company Catalogue,* Spring and Summer, 1895; the *New York Herald* 1913–1915; the *San Antonio Express,* 1910; the *Sears Roebuck Catalogue,* 1902, and the *Woman's Home Companion*, 1911.

[13]I would like to thank Elaine Sullivan, Assistant Collections Manager at the Texas Memorial Museum in Austin; Cecila Steinfeld, Curator at the Witte Museum in San Antonio; Dr. Jane Farrell-Beck, Curator at the Department of Consumer Science historic collection at Iowa State University; and Kathryn Stocking, Registrar at the Iroqois facility in Cooperstown, New York for the use of their collections, their help and encouragement.

[14]*Harper's Bazar,* (November 14, 1868): 869.

[15]"Wedding Party," *Harper's Bazar* (December 12, 1868):929.

BUTTONHOLES: Some Differences in Gender-related Front Closures *(cont'd.)*

[16] Madame Vevay, in "Notes on Dressmaking" which appeared in *The Ladies Treasury* ([April, 1881]: 229), replies to a reader's question: "Yes, the button holes of a dress should be on the left-hand side, not on the right, as dressmakers usually put them. . . ."

[17] According to Dr. Hamilton Cravens, Professor of History, Iowa State University, the width of train rails, time zones, and weights and measures in foods, among other things, were standardized in the 1880s, (personal correspondence, 1987).

[18] "Wool Walking Dress," *Harper's Bazar* (November 26, 1892):965.

[19] *Harper's Bazar* (February 2, 1898): 1.

[20] (Boston: Ginn and Co, 1893), 59.

[21] "Engagement Photo of Vice President Schuyler Colfax and Ella M. Wade." *Harper's Bazar* (December 5, 1868):921.

Bibliography

Creekmore, Anna M. and Elaine Pedersen. "Body Proportions of Fashion Illustrations, 1840–1940, Compared with the Greek Ideal of Female Beauty." *Home Economics Research Journal 7* (July, 1979): 379–388.

DeMarly, Diana. *Fashion for Men*. London: B. T. Batsford. 1985.

——. *Working Class Dress*. London: B. T. Batsford. 1986.

Hapgood, Olive. *School Needlework*. Boston: Ginn and Co, 1893.

Higgins, J. P. P. *Cloth of Gold, A History of Metallised Textiles*. London: The Lurex Company, LTD. 1993.

Kidwell, Claudia. *Cutting a Fashionable Fit*. Washington, D.C.: Smithsonian Institution Press, 1979.

Kidwell, Claudia and Margaret Christman. *Suiting Everyone, The Democratization of Clothing in America*. Washington D.C.: Smithsonian Institution Press, 1974.

Kidwell, Claudia and Valerie Steele. *Men and Women, Dressing the Part*. Washington D.C.: Smithsonian Institution Press, 1989

Kinsbourne, Marcel. "Handedness." *Speech and Language*, edited by Doreen Kimura, 19–20, Boston: Birkhäuser, 1987.

Nickel, Helmut, Stuart Pyhrr, and Leonid Tarassuk. *The Art of Chivalry*. New York: Metropolitan Museum of Art, 1982.

Richards, Lynn. "The Rise and Fall of All: The Hemlines and Hiplines of the 1920s." *Clothing and Textiles Research Journal 2* (1983–1984): 42–48.

Vevay, Madame. "Notes on Dressmaking." *The Ladies Treasury*. (April, 1881): 229.

Waugh, Nora. *The Cut of Women's Clothes, 1600-1930*. London: Farber and Farber, 1968.

"Rita's Portuguese Education"

Kelly Karrenbauer

Conscientizacao. It's a word from the Portuguese penned not by Elizabeth Barrett Browning but by Brazilian educator Paulo Friere. For those of us who don't speak Portuguese and are not well versed in educational theory, *conscientização* in plain English means to be conscious of the social, political and economic forces which shape our lives, and to fight against those oppressive forces to gain our individual freedom.[1] "What," you may ask, "has this gibberish got to do with a quiet little film

"Rita's Portuguese Education" *(cont'd.)*

called *Educating Rita?* The answer: If you watch the film while eating a bowl of popcorn and talking on the phone, not much. But if you watch this film with the close attention it deserves, you will be inspired to follow Rita into a battle which you didn't even know existed. And when the smoke clears, you will find the end of the film both disturbing and inspiring.

Rita is, by most accounts, a nontraditional student. Not only is she married and older than most students, but her working class vocabulary and ideas don't fit within the ranks of the "proper," more educated members of the University. Yet her strong desire to "discover meself" before settling for the expectations of her family, that is, having babies, leads her through the walls of academia into the sanctuary of Frank's office.

Frank is a former poet, a professor who has somehow lost himself in the disheartening realization that his academic world exists mostly as a forum for the academics to hear themselves speak. His students rattle on about the metaphysical aspects of Blake's poetry, and Frank is forced to earn a living listening to them.

Enter Rita. Whether admiring the view from Frank's window or expressing her opinion of the staging difficulties in a production of Ibsen's *Peer Gynt*, Rita's editorial opinions clear the fog from Frank's dreary, mundane life. Rita is determined to transform herself into an educated person, and she demands Frank's help. After warning her that she will have to learn to discipline her mind in order to learn literary criticism, Frank begins educating Rita.

Rita knows that "if you want to change, you've got to do it from the inside," but she doesn't follow her own advice. Frank watches in frustration as Rita willingly dons the uniform of the academic, her personality becoming obscured behind the "right" voice and the "right" clothes, the "right" books and the properly "educated" answers. Richard Rodriguez remembers doing the same as a student, idolizing his teachers, using their diction—reading and thinking what he was told in an effort to somehow absorb the confidence and knowledge of others.[2] Rita perfects this mimicry, and with Frank's help, learns to conform her individual style to the confines of academic rhetoric.

Rita immerses herself in the system of academia, the oppressor of gut feelings and free thought. She seems completely integrated and assimilated.[3] She parrots Blake along with the rest of the good little soldiers, without attention to her own offbeat but equally valid ideas. Frank knows the importance of one's personal views. He knows that true knowledge emerges not from listing someone else's thoughts but by searching for one's own, asking for oneself, and valuing one's own unique discoveries.[4] While he himself has lost the ability to use this method of learning, he tries to explain it to Rita. He praises her passionate critique of *Macbeth*, but must admit that as far as exams are concerned, it's worthless. "It shouldn't be, but it is," he adds. He wants to encourage Rita's gut feelings, her uniqueness, but she wants the academically acceptable truth.

True to movie form, Rita doesn't disappoint us. Frank angrily accuses her of settling not for a *better* life, but just a *different* life, but not until one of her idols proves false does Rita "get it." Literally overnight she recognizes that while her student guise is useful for fooling the academic bureaucrats, it won't stand up to inspection in the real world.

"Rita's Portuguese Education" *(cont'd.)*

A true idealist would have told all the academics to "sod off" by writing her unique analysis of the ways to overcome the staging difficulties in a production of Ibsen's *Peer Gynt*. But Rita is a realist. "Do it on the radio" wouldn't have gained Rita any ground in her battle for education. In the end, Rita received more than just the "load of quotes and empty phrases" that Frank felt he had given her. Without these tools of traditional education, Rita would not have learned which traditions were uniquely valuable to her.[5] She wouldn't have had the choice. Because of the education Frank had given her, however, she had the weapons to fight for an education uniquely valuable to her.

Educating Rita is an inspiring story of one student's education. Not so inspiring is the identification of the bureaucratic system of education that remains firmly entrenched in our society. But there is hope for change. As the Sophist Protagoras taught, if "there can be opposing, and equally valid arguments to any given case,"[6] then anyone can be taught to argue any side of an argument, if given the right tools. Rhetoric, the conscious and deliberate use of language, supplies the right tools.[7] Every idea, every invention, every discovery Rita will make in her life will add to her power to persuade others to join her rebellion against the oppressive system that inhibits individual thought. Maybe Rita will be the one to change the system. Maybe it will be one of us. After watching "Educating Rita," you will know a little Portuguese yourself. How you use this knowledge is up to each one of you.

Notes

[1] Paulo Friere, "The 'Banking' Concept of Education," *Ways of Reading*, 3rd ed.(Boston: Bedford, 1992), 210.

[2] Richard Rodriguez, "An Achievement of Desire," *Ways of Reading*, 3rd ed.(Boston: Bedford, 1992), 485, 489.

[3] Friere, 210.

[4] Ibid., 208.

[5] Victor Villanueva, *Bootstraps*, (Urbana, Ill: National Council of Teachers of English, 1993), 75.

[6] Villanueva, 79.

[7] Ibid.

Dead Poets Society: **Heart over Mind**

David B. Huthmacher

Thousands of viewers cheered as Todd Anderson led his class in a "desk standing" tribute to his teacher Mr. Keating. It was a move of calculated rebellion against an oppressive system of education. Just before, the viewers had wept as Neil Perry

---

Dead Poets Society: **Heart over Mind** *(cont'd.)*

placed cold steel against his skull to end his life when he found he did not have the courage to face the same opponent. And numerous times earlier, the audience had smiled and laughed through scenes of adolescent life, influenced by a giant symbol of artistic independence and individual thinking, the one and only Captain of Welton Academy. He is the sacrificial Socrates of our time, the doomed hero who inspired them all. Americans and people in many other parts of the world felt the same inspiration after seeing this 1989 film, Peter Weir's *Dead Poets Society.*

The film is often used to illustrate the conflict between a traditional form of literacy that focuses on order and discipline, and a new, humanistic one that emphasizes critical thinking and creative expression. But does the film achieve this goal adequately? Does the film ever intend the discussion of this theme to be its thesis? The answer is simple. In the tradition of Hollywood box-office greats, *Dead Poets Society* is more concerned with creating dramatic effects to influence the audience emotionally than with exposing competing notions of literacy to challenge it intellectually.

The most obvious evidence stems from the unrealistic notion that debates about literacy can be reduced to two sides, namely, one that is "good" and one that is "evil." This blatant dichotomy in no way represents the dynamics and complexity of literacy struggles in America. A casual glance would reveal many different approaches to literacy, some humanistic and some traditional, as well as some that are more pluralistic in nature. And an objective stance would have to admit that each of the various approaches to literacy has a number or advantages and disadvantages that make acceptance of only one to be very problematic. But the film instead chooses to present only two simplistic sides, both very general and abstract, to represent a very complex issue. Quite literally, as critic David Payne puts it in his review of the movie, "order, tradition, authority, institutions, and social status are a unified and monolithic evil, against which one is pitted in the struggle for autonomy and meaning" (14).

As a discussion on literacy, this one-sided presentation is unacceptable. However, as an effective film technique, it is brilliant. Any sharp division between "good" and "evil" renders them more manageable and thus heightens the audience's emotional response. If a film makes it clear who is bad and who is good and leaves little gray area in between the extremes, the audience does not have to think about whom to support or oppose but can instead invest all energies and emotions in supporting or opposing. Payne writes:

> By making the physical and social environment one of stifling oppression, and by offering images and enactments of free expression, the text attempts to exaggerate the audience's experiences of comic and tragic themes (15).

One can see that the makers of *Dead Poets Society* were far more concerned with making us feel than with making us think.

Not only is the horizontal view of literacy greatly simplified, but so is the vertical picture. In reality, one's literacy is a combination of environmental factors, including issues of class, gender, and race. But *Dead Poets Society* avoids this vital

Dead Poets Society: Heart over Mind *(cont'd.)*

aspect of literacy when it concentrates solely on Welton's white upper-class male society. The film hints at the effects of gender, in that it emphasizes the boys' future role as "breadwinner." Social class is remotely discussed through Mr. Perry's demand that his son Neil move to a higher class than his own. But otherwise, pluralistic facets of literacy are a mute issue. Even the contrast between the elite private school and the rural public school offers no social commentary. The film had an opportunity to expand its discussion of identity and literacy in these matters, but obviously chose not to.

Again, to do so would have contradicted the film's purpose of creating emotionally dramatic effects. Such a discussion would have required the audience to consider these complexities in the mind when the film is aimed instead at the heart. Other films have attempted serious discussion and/or social commentary, and have done so successfully. But they have sacrificed substantially the title of "feel good movie of the year," as *Dead Poets Society* was billed (Payne 13).

For example, the 1984 film *Educating Rita* provides a more thorough discussion of literacy in relation to such pluralistic themes. Rita, a working-class woman, seeks education as a means to raising her social position in society. As the contrast between her working-class environment and academia develops, we come to appreciate the rather complex and problematic situation surrounding her. It is not an oversimplified dichotomy between two obvious sides of right and wrong but an honest struggle between two distinct classes in society that have both good and bad qualities. The resolution of the film does not present one notion of literacy overpowering the other, and no specific favor is given to either. Rather, Rita discovers that education is merely an understanding of the choices each of us have. True, this resolution may not carry with it a grand emotional finale of tears and overabundant joy, but the audience is left to further ponder the situation they had witnessed.

Finally, *Dead Poets Society* sacrifices the character development of its golden boy, John Keating, to strengthen the dramatic effect even more. In order to canonize a hero, make him or her a god, that person must be portrayed as flawless, as Keating is. While in *Educating Rita*, Rita's professor Frank struggles with his own notions of literacy and his effectiveness as an educator, in *Dead Poets Society*, Keating never makes a mistake. He never questions his methods or the possible consequences of producing a class of "free-thinkers." As critic Mark Collins notes, "His performance never falls flat or disappoints because it must satisfy the wish-fulfillment of film-goers" (74).

In addition, the movie presents Keating's class as a problem-free environment. He never loses student control, even after he grants them a seemingly endless supply of freedoms. Not only does this group of adolescent boys control this freedom responsibly in Keating's class, we never see them rebel in any of their other, more structured classrooms. With the exception of "Newanda's" telephone-call-from-God stunt, the boys never overstep the bounds of acceptable behavior. The movie thus avoids discussion of the practical consequences of freedom and instead presents Keating as an infallible hero. The result is a make-believe classroom that

Dead Poets Society: **Heart over Mind** *(cont'd.)*

"involves the cult of personality and a romanticized view of change" (Collins 74). Although this technique makes the viewer an instant and eternal disciple of Keating, it creates a frankly unrealistic view of schooling.

I don't want to take away from the film's magic and inspirational qualities. In its own objective, the film is quite successful. But it achieves little more than idealistic inspiration. Rather, as Collins writes, the "simplistic dichotomy of institutionalized authority and student freedom sheds little light on a complex reality" (75). But please, go see *Dead Poets Society* again. It has a special message: Use every second at hand. But just remember, as in all fairy tales, it's simply make-believe.

Works Cited

Collins, Mark. "Make-Believe in *Dead Poets Society*." *English Journal.* Dec. 1989: 74–75.

Payne, David. "Political Vertigo in *Dead Poets Society*." *The Southern Communication Journal.* Fall 1992: 13–21.

CHAPTER 10

WRITING RESEARCH PAPERS: WORKING WITH NONLIBRARY SOURCES

INTRODUCTION

In the preceding chapter, we offered guidelines for writing research papers using library resources. However, as you probably realize, professionals and students also often rely on other sources to support their findings. In some disciplines, such as those in the sciences, lab research provides the primary foundation for study. In other disciplines, too, professionals often must do "empirical" research, which means that they conduct investigations themselves. As you would imagine, library and nonlibrary sources work well in concert with one another; some of the most useful research studies rely on both kinds of research.

Many kinds of commonly used nonlibrary sources are at a researcher's disposal. Among them are interviews, surveys, information from observations, data obtained from the media, public records (such as court records, records housed within historical societies, and records kept by agencies like the Department of Human Services), and information obtained from public presentations (such as lectures or panels). Still another important nonlibrary source is the Internet, commonly nicknamed "the Information Superhighway." Many colleges and universities are now making computer terminals and software readily available to help students access this source in libraries, residence halls, student unions, and other locations.

It is important to keep nonlibrary sources in mind when you are conducting research because the best sources sometimes simply are not found in the library. If you are researching a current issue in your local community, for example, your most immediate, up-to-date information will come from nonlibrary sources. The people you interview, your own observations, the public forums you attend, and so forth, would be credible primary sources of knowledge and experience that have not been recorded anywhere.

Because nonlibrary research very often complements library research, researchers frequently combine these two kinds of sources. Using nonlibrary sources can, for example, provide a means of confirming (or questioning) published information. For example, let's say that you are investigating whether social workers are overworked. You have found some publications in the library that discuss the topic, but they are not recent. Under these circumstances, you might arrange to observe a social worker on the job, noting her various activities and how much time she has to do them. You also might arrange to interview her about her own opinions on her working conditions. In this way, you not only could gain new perspectives that are not recorded anywhere, but you would be able to comment in an informed way on the sources you found in the library.

As a college student, you can expect to be assigned nonlibrary research; such assignments are given for a variety of reasons. Some disciplines rely heavily on nonlibrary research; students cannot fully understand important information or learn how to critique concepts within the discipline until they learn how the research is conducted. For students majoring in sociology, for example, learning how to design and conduct surveys and present findings may be an essential part of their career preparation.

A related reason for assigning nonlibrary research papers is that they prepare students for the kind of writing they will be expected to do as professionals. As you might imagine, reporting the results of an experiment, observation, interview, or survey entails special techniques that cannot be learned from other kinds of writing assignments. Thus, nonlibrary research papers provide students with practical "hands-on" writing experiences that serve as preparation for their future careers.

There are also a couple of other—perhaps less apparent—reasons why nonlibrary research papers are assigned. One is that students who have written such papers become better consumers of published studies. That is, because they have a first-hand understanding of the research process, they are able to make critical judgments about the research findings of others. Still another reason for assigning nonlibrary research papers is that they broaden students' perspectives on whatever topic they are researching. Students may get one perspective when they read journal articles about "welfare mothers," for example, and quite a different perspective if they spend time with or interview several women who receive public assistance.

In this chapter, we will introduce you to a variety of ways to conduct nonlibrary research and to report your findings. Writing a research paper based on library sources or one based on nonlibrary sources requires similar skills, so you should view this chapter as an extension of the preceding one. That is, you should use this chapter after you have worked through Chapter 9—or in conjunction with it, if you are writing a paper using both library and non-library sources.

SAMPLE ASSIGNMENTS

Now that you understand a little about what non-library research is and why college instructors assign it, let's examine in more detail sample assignments from several disciplines. As you will see, assignments involving nonlibrary research vary in a number of respects. (For example, library research may or may not be required, and students may receive a great deal or a minimal amount of instruction.)

Chemistry Assignment. The following handout describes the Special Project which is due by December 1 at 5 PM. It is worth fifty points.

To complete this project, your group will select a compound and report on how you would prepare one kilogram of it, including the cost of manufacturing it as well as the amount of profit you expect to realize. Part of your discussion should also include a justification for making the compound and a description of whom you intend to sell it to. Finally, you will need to provide a detailed procedure for the compound's preparation, including descriptions of the following:

- Quantities of starting materials
- The order in which you will mix the starting materials
- The temperature employed
- Any catalyst that would be required
- How you would isolate and purify your compound
- The equipment you would need. [NOTE: you can use *only* the equipment that would be available in a typical General Chemistry Lab or Organic Chemistry Lab.]

Although you and your group members should work as a team, every member should be given a specific assignment; you will need to include a list of the roles for each member of your team at the end of your report. Here are some suggestions for various tasks that might be assigned to group members:

1. Providing an analysis of profit and cost of doing business
2. Determining safety considerations in preparation
3. Researching patent considerations
4. Researching environmental considerations.

These and other tasks will require library research, but they also may require you to gather other sorts of information. You may need to make trips to local sites (such as manufacturing plants), conduct interviews with various individuals, and so forth.

Before you will be "allowed" to make your compound, you must secure the approval of "the government." That is, by November 11, you must get approval from Dr. Jones (Room 100 in Chemistry Hall), who will be playing the role of a rigorous public servant. Dr. Jones will want to know (among other things) whether your compound can be made legally; whether there are patent restrictions on it; and how the environment, local citizens, and the workers (who manufacture your compound) will protected. Dr. Jones is no pushover. Be prepared for his questions because *you cannot produce your compound without his written approval.* Your entire group should prepare for your presentation to Dr. Jones; **if you do not get his approval, your group will forfeit all fifty points.** (Attached is the checklist that Dr. Jones will use to assess your chemical compound.)

Language Arts Education Assignment. An important assignment for this class is the term research project (using a minimum of 10 sources), which will require you to investigate and write about a topic that deals with an aspect of language arts education. The paper should be approximately twelve pages in length, not counting bibliography and appendixes; it should employ APA style.

You will need to get your topic approved in advance; to do this, please submit a description of approximately one hundred words by October 12. By November 9, you will need to turn in research notes, a partial draft, or other evidence of work-in-progress. The final paper is due on December 10.

Attached is a list of broad topics; these are meant to be starting points. If, for example, you pick topic 3, "grammar and writing," you will need to decide how you wish to narrow it. One possibility might be to trace the attitudes of educators toward grammar instruction over the last fifteen years.

As you investigate your topic, you may need to include data from a variety of sources. If you are researching the topic "portfolio assessment and proficiency testing," for example, local public school teachers who are currently instituting state requirements via this mechanism may be the *only* source of up-to-date information. Under these circumstances, the results of interviews or surveys would be an important part of your final paper. In addition, the Internet may also provide you with useful documents or put you in contact with individuals in other school districts nationwide who may offer you valuable information or perspectives on your topic. [NOTE: Methods for preparing and conducting interviews and surveys are discussed in Part IV of Gruber and Gruber, which is on reserve at the main library.]

Linguistics Assignment. On pages 343–348 of our text, the authors describe the procedure for studying a sociolinguistic variable. For this semester project assignment, you will be using that procedure to conduct your own research. Select at least two groups (men and women, for example) and report your findings with respect to one of the variables on the attached list.

As the description in your text suggests, you will need to organize your study into two parts: First you should observe your subjects' use of language; then you should interview them. Before you begin, you will need to design your own data recording sheets for your language-use observations and for your follow-up interviews. [NOTE: These will need to be included in the appendix of your paper.] In addition to including interviews and information from your observations in your research paper, you will need to discuss a minimum of *four* scholarly sources related to your topic.

Although I won't prescribe a particular format for this paper, a good way to organize it would be to describe what others have found out about the variable that you are studying and then to report the results of your own research. If your results are different from those that have been reported, offer an explanation for those differences. Be sure to present your findings clearly; you should describe your results in writing *and* show them in a table, if at all possible. Your paper should be twelve to fifteen pages in length (*not* including the appendixes and bibliography) and should employ consistent documentation.

Due Date: Noon, May 1.

From reading the preceding examples, you will have noticed that assignments for nonlibrary research require *synthesis* writing. For all of these assignments, it would be inappropriate to simply present information in the order in which it was discovered and leave to readers the task of assimilating and integrating that information. Even in situations in which an assignment does not specifically instruct students to synthesize information discovered in research, you should assume that doing so is expected.

The sample assignments also show that most often nonlibrary research papers are major assignments. In part, this is because performing adequate research—especially nonlibrary research—is time-consuming. Hence, instructors may assign only one research assignment a semester and weigh it heavily in the total course grade; 40 percent to 60 percent of the course grade is common. The Linguistics Assignment specifically describes a "semester project," implying that the instructor expects students to work on it throughout the term. In addition, you can see that the Chemistry Assignment requires students not only to research their topic in the library but also to conduct experiments in the lab and gather information from experts or from manufacturers of products needed to produce a compound. Performing the nonlibrary research for this assignment would necessitate scheduling research work around times that the lab is open and available for student use, in addition to locating appropriate experts and scheduling convenient interview times during working hours. Assignments such as these, then, require a major commitment of time and effort and, thus, are major projects. Consequently, instructors have high expectations for them. In addition to expecting thorough research, both in and outside the library, instructors will want final papers to be well written, typed (or word-processed), and proofread.

Although all nonlibrary research assignments are major projects that require synthesis, they vary from one another in one important way: the amount of instruction students are given to perform the required nonlibrary research. In some instances, detailed instructions may be provided, as in the case of the Language Arts Education Assignment ("Methods for preparing and conducting interviews and surveys are discussed in Part IV of Gruber and Gruber, which in on reserve at the main library"). In contrast, students may be instructed to "interview experts" or to "survey students," with few direct instructions from instructors on how to perform such research. Instructors of advanced courses may not provide detailed instructions because they expect students to already understand how particular types of research are performed within the discipline. Note that in the Chemistry Assignment, students are expected to perform laboratory experiments to produce a compound, but no specific directions are given on how to isolate and purify a compound. Whether direct instructions are provided in an assignment, however, you should be aware that disciplines have very stringent guidelines for how nonlibrary research is performed, and college instructors will most often use such guidelines in assessing their students' research. Consequently, you should treat the nonlibrary research component of these papers as an important part of such assignments.

A related feature of these assignments is that students are expected to present the results of their research within their paper. The results of surveys, interviews, experiments, or observations must be discussed within the paper; writers are also expected to describe the particular methods by which their information was collected. Often assignments require students to present such material or explanations in a table, a chart, or an item in the appendix. The Linguistics Assignment, for example, instructs students to design "data recording sheets" for their observations and interviews, and to include these sheets in the appendix of the paper. Whatever the specific requirements of your instructors, good nonlibrary research papers include these features:

- A clear thesis or overall purpose
- A clear structure
- Appropriate synthesis and integration of information from library and nonlibrary research
- Appropriate presentation of information from nonlibrary research, including explanations of research methods, tables, or appendix items
- Appropriate documentation
- Polished writing.

WORKING WITH NONLIBRARY SOURCES

When you are assigned a research project, you should remember that library sources may not necessarily provide the only—or the best—resources for your particular investigation. With each research assignment you receive—even if you have not been specifically directed to include nonlibrary research—we recommend that you weigh the possible merits of its inclusion. A variety of nonlibrary sources are widely available for use in many research assignments. However, the availability of such sources necessitates careful assessment on your part to determine which would be the most appropriate for your research. To help you make such judgments, we offer the following overview of frequently used nonlibrary sources, including reasons why researchers use them.

Using the Internet One nonlibrary resource that is rapidly gaining in popularity is the Internet—the system of sources, information, and interactions available on computer networks. If you do not currently use this important resource, we recommend that you begin to do so at once. Most colleges and universities have computer labs where staff members can assist you with securing an e-mail (electronic mail) account and learning to use the Internet. When you have access to "the Net," you will find that you suddenly have at your disposal a number of journals, newsletters, and other texts that exist electronically. Information on virtually any topic can be located: lesson plans that were collected by state departments, government data about pesticides, nutritional information about various foods—the possibilities are endless. Other particularly useful sources found on the Internet are directories (or lists) of resource persons, clearinghouses (organizations that will help you locate information on specific topics), and societies you may wish to join (the Hemlock Society or the Rocky Horror Picture Show Fan Club, for example). When you consult the various directories, you may find the names of people whom you would like to contact—and contacting them can be easily accomplished through the use of e-mail. E-mail, a common form of interaction on the Net, allows you to engage in electronic conversations with individuals or interest groups.

As you can see, when you use the Internet, the information readily available to you increases enormously. You should be aware, however, that because this information is constantly changing and growing by accretion, it cannot be neatly organized. Therefore, powerful "search engines" such as Yahoo (a comprehensive subject index) and Lycos (a tool that searches by looking for key words) have been—and are being—developed to help you navigate your way through the Net. In addition, the number of books and directories that have been printed to assist Net users has grown astronomically, as a visit to the "Computers" section of any bookstore will show. You probably also can acquire information on using the Net from your college library and through the computer services on your campus.

By now you probably can see many advantages for using the Internet as a resource. One is that the Net makes the most current information immediately available to you, before there is even time for it to be printed in books. Of course, the Net also provides information that *never* will be printed in books; the only place it is available is on the Net. Through the technology of the Internet, you can also contact numerous people around the globe to find out their opinions and perspectives on given topics—and you can do so at your leisure. Still another advantage is that the Net allows you to search the archives of electronic conversations held by interest groups, which allows you to read over conversations that took place in the past. Because the Internet has so many advantages, it is a nonlibrary resource you cannot afford to overlook.

Conducting Interviews. Another important nonlibrary source is the interview, which is a face-to-face (sometimes telephone-to-telephone—or electronic) conversation held to solicit information, attitudes, or opinions from one or more knowledgeable individuals. Interviewing provides a couple of important advantages for the researcher. First, people who are being interviewed do not have much time to think about their answers before they give them; therefore, interview responses generally are spontaneous and uncensored. Such responses can bring appeal and a high level of detail to research papers; particularly salient responses make powerful direct quotations, often bringing "life" to potentially mundane topics. Second, through interviewing, researchers may be gathering information from the most knowledgeable sources of all—that is, the people whose time is devoted to working in a particular area rather than writing about it. This distinction is important because the people with the most direct experience may have perspectives that differ from those presented in library sources.

Taking Surveys. Professionals across the disciplines frequently perform surveys as a means of gathering information. In general, surveys are lists of questions that are distributed to groups of people whose responses are then tabulated and interpreted. The questions may take a variety of forms (true/false, multiple choice, short answer, etc.) and are administered in paper form or through telephone contacts.

In several unique ways, surveys are a useful means of gathering information. First, people in surveys remain anonymous; therefore, their responses may be more honest and forthright. Second, surveys often cull information from large groups of people, hence, the researchers are able to do far more than merely tally responses to the questions; they can also look for relationships or patterns within responses. There is one shortcoming of surveys, however, that you should be aware of: Because surveys ask for short responses, they simply cannot elicit they kind of detail that might be provided by other research methods. Therefore, we recommend that when you perform a survey, you ordinarily should supplement your findings with library research or other nonlibrary resources. An example of such a nonlibrary resource is the "General Social Survey," which contains attitudes and opinions of a randomly selected group of Americans. Data bases of this sort may be available at your university.

Making Observations. Another important nonlibrary resource is the observation—a careful examination of people, objects, events, or processes. Observations are so important to research that some disciplines are largely built around them. The sciences and social sciences, for example, focus on teaching students different methods of making and reporting their findings in specified formats. Of course, in varying degrees throughout the other disciplines, too, students are regularly asked to make observations. (For a detailed discussion of observing, you can refer to Chapter 4 in this book.) Observations are advantageous to researchers because they provide first-hand information, rather than information that has been filtered through other people's perspectives. In addition, observations can provide a wealth of detail and information for researchers; often the results of an observation include far more than the researcher originally set out to learn.

Using Agencies and Resource Centers. Two useful sources of information that are all too often overlooked by student researchers are agencies and resource centers. Agencies and resource centers (such as Planned Parenthood, Big Brothers—Big Sisters, the County Board of Education, the Department of Human Resources, the Historical Society in your community, and the Women's Resource Center on your campus) provide not only services—but specialized information to those who request it. Sometimes information from these resources can be provided during a short chat or an interview with a staff member; often, though, information is available to you for the asking in the form of brochures, pamphlets, data sheets, data bases, or World Wide Web pages. Public records, housed at your county courthouse and open for your perusal, provide another good source of information on many topics you might be investigating.

Because agencies and resource centers provide specialized information—including statistics, records of community events, and information about how services are provided—they offer perspectives that may not be found in library sources. In fact, if you are researching a local issue, the information you need might not be found in print anywhere other than in agencies or resource centers. Another major benefit of using these sources is that the information they present usually is up-to-date and detailed.

Using Public Presentations. Because you live in—or at least spend much of your time in—a community that has at least one college or university, you undoubtedly have easy access to another important nonlibrary source: public presentations. As the name suggests, public presentations include lectures, debates, speeches, panels, demonstrations, news conferences, and any other presentations that are offered in a public forum. If you peruse the pages of your college or community newspaper or read the posters on local bulletin boards, you certainly will see announcements for upcoming campus presentations on a wide variety of topics. Surfing the Internet may also alert you to on-line conferences about topics in which you are interested.

As sources for research papers, public presentations have their own special kinds of advantages, one of which is that they allow members of an audience to experience news right while it's being made. Another advantage of public presentations is that the presenters at such forums typically are prominent (because of their training, expertise, position, experiences, etc.); therefore, taking notes on (or taping) their words and incorporating these into a research paper adds a sense of authority to your findings. Audiences are often given an opportunity to ask questions at public presentations, which is yet another advantage; if you have a specific concern that was not addressed during the formal part of the presentation, you can ask the presenter(s) to elaborate on it for you. Finally, making use of the Internet as a public forum has additional kinds of advantages. Because "conferences" on a wide range of topics are increasingly becoming available through the Internet, interested individuals all over the country or even the globe are able to "attend" and "converse" with other conference participants through the use of special discussion lists. In other instances, the Internet makes available to anyone copies of papers read at conferences where the participants physically attended.

Using the Media. An important nonlibrary resource by which you are bombarded every day is the media; in our definition of *the media,* we are including film, television, radio, and advertising. Because the media is so prevalent in our daily lives, people doing research sometimes overlook it as a useful source of information. While you probably recognize that the function of the media often is to disseminate information (as is the case in news reports or documentaries), you might not immediately recognize that it can be a useful source in another way. Different media can be *interpreted*—even when their primary function is to entertain (sitcoms or films) or to sell a product (advertisements). In interpreting various media, you can look for underlying messages—about our culture, political issues, social issues, and so on. Interpretation of the media is an especially interesting endeavor, since people working with the same materials may reach very different conclusions because of their own backgrounds, biases, and perspectives.

Using the media as a resource has a great deal of merit—especially if you are investigating aspects of our culture. Through a close look at the media, you quickly can assess what is popular at any given time; sometimes the entire country may be interested in a court case that is taking place; at other times people may be consumed with interest in a political scandal—or in a controversy involving professional sports, for example. The media can also be perused for other kinds of information about our culture—including general attitudes on race and ethnicity, gender, health, and education; the possibilities are limitless. Because the media is designed for the population at large—rather than for special groups of people—the information it contains is easily accessible. For any topic you are researching, the chances are high that you will be able to supplement your findings with information gleaned through the media.

As we have discussed, if you want to become a skillful researcher, you will need to expand your concept of "research" to include a wide variety of nonlibrary sources. Please realize, though, that the list of nonlibrary sources we have discussed here is far from exhaustive; we have commented on these seven sources to help you start thinking of the many possible sources of information that are available to you.

 **Activity 1**

Meet with your group to select an issue that currently is receiving widespread coverage in the news. Then each group member should work independently to gather information on the issue, being sure to locate at least three nonlibrary sources. Nonlibrary sources for this activity might include notes from a television news program, notes from an interview, or a brochure or pamphlet. After members of your group have found their sources, meet again to discuss and compare your findings and to prepare a brief report for the class about your group's investigation.

Constructing Interpretative Frames

When you are working with nonlibrary sources, there is an especially important process you need to be aware of. This is constructing the interpretative frame through which you will present your sources. In part, interpretive frames are necessary when working with nonlibrary resources because of the nature of the information or data acquired. Research methods such as surveys, interviews, or observations produce an accumulation of data that writers must sift through, select from, and organize for readers. Other nonlibrary sources, such as resource centers or electronic data bases, contain a wide array of information, only part of which is relevant to a particular writer's research; similarly, information from these sources must be sorted, selected, and organized. In either case, the meaning of such materials is not immediately apparent to people who read them. Consequently, writers must bring their own knowledge, values, and expertise to bear as they work with these materials, select relevant aspects, and construct interpretations of the meaning of these materials. To put this principle another way, readers do *not* expect to read *all* the information a writer has gathered. Instead they expect a writer to construct an interpretive frame to give meaning to the data. In developing a particular thesis, writers may omit some aspects of an interview and highlight others. They may delete portions of their observation notes that seem unrelated to their research questions. They may organize their information in a particular order or pattern that seems logical or coherent to them.

As a reader, then, you should be aware that you are reading not a simple recital of "the facts" but a writer's interpretation, selection, and arrangement of information. And as a writer, you should remember that you will be selecting and shaping the information you collect, using it to support a particular thesis or conclusion.

 **Activity 2**

To complete the following activity, you will need to read the following excerpted interview transcript and the excerpted discussion of it. Both are taken from a research study conducted by Mike Rose, *Writer's Block: The Cognitive Dimension.* In his study, Rose relied on interviews and observations of several college students, including Liz, whose interview is excerpted here.

1. Read the excerpts that follow, and compare Mike Rose's discussion to the actual interview transcript. What interpretation does the writer present of the interview subject? How does the writer's interpretation slant or shape your impressions of Liz and her writing abilities?

2. Assume that you are using the transcript of Liz's interview in a research project of your own. For the thesis statement that follows, which parts of the interview excerpt would you omit? What parts would you use in your own paper? Would you summarize the parts you use or quote them?

Thesis Statement: *If Liz's experience is typical, writing teachers should pay more attention to teaching strategies for organizing papers.*

Researcher: You say it's difficult to organize and get all these associations straight, and yet it's interesting that you never work out any kind of outline.

Liz: I've tried that a couple of times. . . . It works on a specific kind of paper.

Researcher: What kind of paper?

Liz: It works on the kind of paper where you're supposed to . . . report on six or seven things, what somebody said, and that's easy.

Researcher: What kind of an outline did you use?

Liz: I just put [the points] in order.

Researcher: You mean number 1, number 2?

Liz: Yeah, 1, 2, 3, and then I tried to, well, I tried to do it like you're supposed to, with the 1 and the A.

Researcher: But for other sorts of papers, . . . you tend not to outline?

Liz: Sometimes if I've got a . . . real tough paragraph, I'll try and do it for that one paragraph.

Researcher: Does that help?

Liz: I don't know. . . . I think it's probably a pretty good tool. It's just that I don't know how to use it. . . . I wouldn't know how to outline something [in a way] that would benefit me.

Researcher: Didn't . . . grammar school teachers teach you an outline form?

Liz: Well . . . they didn't tell you why you put in I, A, B, C, . . . It's like a research paper where they . . . tell us "O.K. write a research paper of about 12 pages." And the way they told us to do it was just to get quotes and string them together. So this paragraph is from this book. This paragraph is from that book. This paragraph is from that book.

Mike Rose. *Writer's Block: The Cognitive Dimension.* Carbondale and Edwardsville: Southern Illinois University Press, 1984, pp. 51–52. Copyright © 1984 by the National Council of Teachers of English. Reprinted with permission.

The previous excerpt suggests that Liz does not rely on pen-and-paper structuring and focusing aids because she does not have them in her repertoire. The outline she knows (but claims not to fully understand) is the old standard. She does not possess other techniques . . . that are flexible and suited for generating and guiding complex discourse. . . . In a sense, then, she lacks the quintessential strategy for complexity: an aid to balancing intertwining or conflicting issues. Perhaps this lack explains why she plans in increments, in "blocks of information" not unlike the disconnected quotations in her research paper analogy.

Mike Rose. *Writer's Block: The Cognitive Dimension.* Carbondale and Edwardsville: Southern Illinois University Press, 1984, p. 52. Copyright © 1984 by the National Council of Teachers of English. Reprinted with permission.

WRITING YOUR RESEARCH PAPER

The process of writing a research paper with nonlibrary sources is quite similar to the process of writing a paper with library sources. Despite this similarity, however, two matters related to using these sources deserve some explanation. Sometimes nonlibrary sources can create special challenges for the researcher, especially if she or he doesn't know what to expect or how to prepare in advance for using them. In addition, integrating both library and nonlibrary sources into the same piece of writing may cause inexperienced writers some difficulties. After discussing these two topics, we will provide a brief summary of the process of writing a research paper with varied sources and a checklist to help you manage this complex task. You may also find it helpful to review the Writing Your Research Paper section of Chapter 9 when you begin to research and write the assignment for this chapter.

Special Challenges in Using Nonlibrary Sources

In our experience, many students enjoy assignments that require them to use nonlibrary sources because acquiring information in a variety of ways is quite interesting.

Attending public events or performances, conducting on-site observations, interviewing people, searching for information or conversing with knowledgeable individuals on the Internet are absorbing—even exciting—ways of spending time. However, the very features of nonlibrary sources that make them exciting to use—their diversity and unpredictability—can frustrate even the most seasoned researcher. For this reason, people who are experienced in using nonlibrary sources rely on their knowledge to help them adjust their expectations and guide their advance preparations. Clearly, the descriptions that follow cannot take the place of actual experience with any of these sources, but they may help you anticipate some of the problems you might encounter.

The Internet. Because it is vast and constantly expanding, the Internet is a powerful source of information. However, whether you employ network technology to locate information or to conduct conversations, it can present you with a variety of special challenges. Once such challenge is the time—often unanticipated—that it can take to locate information. For this reason, we cannot overemphasize the importance of allowing yourself a sufficient opportunity to exploit this resource. Unlike libraries, which select and catalogue sources in a particular manner, the Internet is sprawling and reflects no particular system of organization; it contains *anything and everything* people have put into it—in no order whatsoever. Moreover, because the Internet is constantly growing and changing, even user-friendly software that enables you to search through it can often take you to dead ends. You may, for example, spend ten minutes trying to locate a promising source, only to find that although listed, the source contains nothing because its "authors" haven't finished designing it yet.

If you are going to use the Internet as a source of information, then, you need to allow for plenty of time to accomplish whatever is appropriate for your project. Budgeting time to spend within the Internet is important because searching through it is not easy, as we have explained. Moreover, during certain hours, it may be difficult to make connections with the locations of particular sources because of heavy traffic on the Internet. It is wise, therefore, to investigate the best times of the day (or night) for you to work productively with this resource.

Another challenge that can face the Internet researcher is the time and skill it may take to learn to use different kinds of software. We cannot hope to explain even the most common "search engines" (means of finding information) here because computing—and thus the Internet—undergoes constant change. Moreover, even currently available, easy-to-use engines such as Yahoo and Lycos will take novice users some time to master. Taking full advantage of network technology, then, may require you to learn how to use specialized software to find information, communicate with others, print information from your computer screen, and so forth. Even experienced "Net surfers" must regularly upgrade their knowledge and skills.

Once useful information is located on the network, it is important to take thorough notes, not only on the source itself but also on the means by which it was located. Because of the chaotic nature of the network, it is not always easy to find a source a second time, especially for inexperienced users. In fact, if it is possible (and reasonable) to do, sources—including related information about authors, copyright, and so on—should be downloaded (i.e., printed) in entirety for future reference.

Printing sources—which may require money and which always requires time—is also a helpful way of winnowing information. The Internet contains so much data that sifting through it can be quite overwhelming. Each Internet researcher, therefore, needs to develop strategies for evaluating the currentness, relevance, and reliability of potential source material. Although commonly used strategies for assessing information are helpful (see Chapter 9), these may need to be supplemented from time to time when the Internet is the source of information. Because of the nature of the medium, even the words of respected authorities may appear in vastly different forms—from offhand remarks to carefully documented treatises.

In addition to the challenge of locating, recovering, and evaluating information, the researcher who uses Internet sources may experience difficulty in integrating facts, opinions, and interpretations from these sources with information from other more "traditional" reference works and periodicals. Because much of the information of the Internet is new, the views implied or expressed within such information may not fit well within frameworks determined largely by older, more established ideas.

Observations, Public Presentations, and the Media. Observation plays an important role in many academic fields, and within some disciplines it is central. Therefore, notes from observations—whether of field or laboratory research, public events, or media presentations—can be an important, even a necessary, part of a research paper. Although objects of and circumstances surrounding observation vary dramatically, regardless of the nature of the observation, careful preparation is always necessary. As you recall, Chapter 4 offered a detailed discussion about how to prepare for an observation, take notes, conduct follow-up observations, and so forth. If you make use of any of the sorts of nonlibrary sources that require observation and note taking, you should review this chapter carefully.

Agencies and Resource Centers. As with objects, events, or processes that you may observe, making use of information that can be obtained from public or private agencies and resource centers requires preparation. For an initial contact, unless an agency or center is located within easy walking distance, it is best to phone in advance to determine regular hours, set up appointments with appropriate personnel, or find out where the information you seek is housed. A phone conversation can also help you determine whether the records or documents you seek are available to the public or whether you need to make special arrangements or secure permission to use them.

Generally, agencies and centers house a variety of resources, the most common of which are records and documents, informational material, and the staff workers themselves. When you visit these sites, you should plan to take advantage of as many resources as you can. Although you may not intend to interview staff members when you visit an agency or center, it is wise to prepare for such an opportunity—should it present itself—by bringing writing implements and (if you wish) a small, lightweight tape recorder. In addition, during one of your visits, you should plan to gather copies of any relevant informational material that is available to the public.

Interviews. One of the most common nonlibrary sources of information is the interview. Interviews can range from informal conversations between two individuals, to highly structured, controlled events that can involve two or more informants. In fact, within several of the social sciences, specialized interviews are a significant means of gathering information; it is not unusual, therefore, to find upper-level and even graduate courses devoted entirely to this topic.

Because the importance of interviews as information-gathering tools varies across disciplines, so too do the guidelines that specify how they are to be conducted. If you wish to use interviews as a source of information for a research paper, it is a good practice to ask your instructor whether you should follow a particular format, both in conducting the interviews and in reporting the results. However, if you are not required to use particular disciplinary or professional conventions, there are some general guidelines that you can follow. Because the process of preparing for and conducting an interview is similar in many ways to preparing for and conducting an observation, you should review Chapter 4. The information in that chapter will complement the following pointers:

- *Think about your informants.* Although it may seem obvious to suggest this, the first thing you should do in preparing for an interview is to consider carefully how many persons you need to talk with and who they should be. Sometimes one informant is sufficient and the choice is obvious. In other instances, however, informant selection requires careful consideration. Suppose, for example, you were interviewing student peers to determine their attitudes about a local event or issue. You would need to carefully consider how many persons you wanted to query and how members of your "sample" complemented one another. If you wanted to contrast the attitudes of men versus women or first-year students versus juniors and seniors, you would need to interview an equal number of each group. In considering informants, you might also wish to explore other options besides face-to-face interactions. Network technology can allow you to interact in "real-time" with persons located just about anywhere; depending on your topic and your access to and familiarity with computers, you may decide to utilize this resource.

- *Make arrangements in advance.* Particularly if you are going to interview more than one person or if your informants have busy schedules, you need to set up times for your interviews well in advance. Waiting until a week (or less) before an assignment is due to schedule and conduct one or more interviews is risky. Your informants may cancel your appointment, and, as with observations, you may need to conduct one or more follow-up interviews. Remember, also, that if you wish to tape-record an interview, you should ask for permission in advance to do so.

  Besides arranging for your interviews, it is also wise to consider what materials and physical space requirements you will need for your sessions and begin securing, designing, or gathering these. We recommend that you think about the materials you will require at the same time that you make arrangements for interviews so that you can, for example, secure a room with good acoustics and electrical outlets if you decide to tape your sessions.

Considering the materials you need well in advance may also prompt you to design and prepare tally sheets, a list of typed (or word-processed) questions, and so forth.

- *Prepare questions in advance.* The best interviews are ones in which the interviewer gets the kind of information and opinions that he or she intended. To prevent meandering, unfocused conversations that yield little of value, it is important to devise questions related to specific goals or topics that you have articulated *in advance* to guide your informants' responses. If, for example, you are interviewing several people about their behavior as writers, you would be more likely to get concrete, detailed responses if you thought of focused topics in advance. Questions about how your informants drafted their essays, what they did to prepare for writing, or how they felt when they got stuck might prompt more detailed answers than general queries like "Describe your behavior as a writer" or "Tell me what you do when you write."

  In addition to crafting questions that reflect particular goals or focuses, it is wise to create questions that allow your informants to reflect their own opinions in their own words. The question, "Do you dislike writing?" is not well phrased because it predisposes the informant to answer in a particular way; it also encourages a rather minimal response ("yes," "no," or "maybe") When you devise questions for your interview, you should be prepared to issue follow-up questions that encourage detail. If, for example, you ask an informant to describe how she felt when she began drafting her most recent paper, and she responds with "overwhelmed" or "frustrated," be ready to ask a follow-up questions such as, "Can you remember any details?" "Did any thoughts cross through your mind?" or "Did you experience any physical sensations?" Finally, if you have a willing friend or roommate, it is always a good idea to test your questions in a pre-interview to see how they work; you may decide to revise and refine some before you conduct interviews with your actual informants.

- *Take careful, detailed notes.* Careful, detailed notes are essential if you are to make the best use of the results of your interviews. Chapter 4 provides both explanation and examples of how to take notes during an observation. Because the process of taking notes is similar for interviews and observations, we suggest that you review the discussion within that chapter carefully. Of course, should you choose to conduct an on-line interview, you will easily be able to print a written transcript.

- *Examine and rewrite your notes immediately after each interview.* As is explained within Chapter 4, what you do immediately *after* an observation is very important. This is also true with respect to interviews. Because portions of your notes will necessarily be in "shorthand" and because your notes may not reflect patterns or ideas for follow-up questions, it is good practice to go over them immediately after each interview.

Surveys. As with interviews, surveys can range from a series of questions put together by persons with little formal training to highly sophisticated instruments.

Some advanced, graduate-level social science courses cover the design, implementation, and interpretation of surveys. Unless you receive a great deal of specialized training, therefore, the surveys you conduct will be informal and offer interesting detail, rather than reliable information. It is wise to explain this within the text of your paper when you report your results.

Surveys are meant to yield information about groups of people rather than individuals. As you design and execute your survey, you should think about the number of informants you wish to include and identify the groups you think they characterize. For example, if you design a survey to gauge first-year students' attitudes toward their introductory composition course, you might wish to compare women's responses with those of men. Or, instead of comparing men and women, you might wish to see whether students' courses of study affect their attitudes. In this case, you might distribute surveys to equal numbers of business, music, chemistry, and English majors. Of course, you also will need to consider the means by which you will disseminate any survey you design. Although it is common to distribute copies by mailing them out or handing them to people, you also might consider distributing them to members of a discussion group on the Internet.

Besides considering your informants, when you conduct a survey you need to think about the survey instrument itself, particularly the questions you will use. There are several types of survey questions; some common ones are *yes/no (true/false) questions, multiple-choice questions, ranking scales, checklists, and open-ended questions.* If you leaf through Chapter 1, you will see many examples of most of these. Here is a brief discussion of each type of question.

- *Yes/no questions* generally provide informants with two choices only, yes/no or true/false. Sometimes informants may be given a third option, to indicate uncertainty. Here are two examples:

I am a confident writer.

    _____ yes

    _____ no

My writing has improved as a result of the instruction I've received.

    _____ true

    _____ false

    _____ uncertain

- *Multiple-choice questions* give informants a range of responses from which to choose. These questions often invite persons to answer by checking or circling their answers or by circling a numeric rating:

Circle the appropriate response.

When I draft, I worry over every sentence.

Always   Usually   Sometimes   Never

Check the appropriate response.

When I draft, I worry about every sentence.

_____ always

_____ usually

_____ sometimes

_____ never

Circle the number on the numerical scale.

When I draft, I worry about every sentence.

1   2   3   4   5   6   7

- *Ranking scales* are interesting because they invite respondents to compare a number of options and rank them with respect to one another. In combination with other types of questions, ranking scales can provide a different perspective on a topic or issue. Here is an example:

What you do when you get stuck while drafting?
    Use a *1* to indicate your most common behavior, a *2* to indicate your next most common behavior, and so on—until you have ranked each option.

When I get struck while drafting, I

_____ panic

_____ quit for the day

_____ take a short break

_____ try freewriting

_____ review my plan for writing

- *Checklists* allow persons to select as many options as they wish, in contrast to multiple-choice and yes/no questions, which prompt informants to choose one response.

For each of the following questions, check all of the responses that describe how you feel.

Before I begin writing, I feel

_____ anxious to begin

_____ excited about what I'm going to say

_____ worried that my mind will go blank

_____ confident that I'll finish

_____ worried that I won't be able to finish

_____ worried about my grade

- *Open-ended questions*—unlike the type of questions previously described— do not rigidly constrain the answers informants might provide. However, because open-ended questions require more work, people often ignore them and/or do not provide helpful information. In general, then, if you design a survey, you should include only one or two open-ended questions and place them at the end of your instrument. Here are two examples:

Briefly describe your attitude toward writing:

_____

_____

_____

What change in your writing behavior would be the most beneficial? Why?

_____

_____

_____

Because surveys can vary with respect to the amount and types of questions they include, it is difficult to prescribe a particular length for them. However, short surveys (2 pages, maximum) can be very effective. The majority of people are quite busy and may discard a survey if it looks as if it will take a long time to fill out. Remember that in most instances completing a survey is voluntary; you should design your instrument so that it is attractive, simple to use, and easy to return.

Another matter to consider when designing a survey is confidentiality. It is always wise to design surveys that protect the identity of those who fill them out, even if you query your friends and acquaintances about a topic that you consider to be trivial or nonthreatening. As you may know, what one person is comfortable about revealing, another may find highly sensitive. When you distribute surveys, if you need to keep track of the identity of your subjects or record information about them (age, gender, etc.), you should provide a tear sheet that can be separated from each survey, after you have recorded your data.

Finally, although it may seem obvious to say so, if you conduct a survey as a means of gathering information for a research paper, your instructor will expect you to include a copy of the instrument you used (usually in an appendix) and explain the important aspects of your method. How many persons you surveyed (20? 40?), the conditions under which you surveyed them (the same time each day? after they'd completed a particular task or activity?), and important characteristics about your informants (age? gender? academic major? class ranking?) may all be relevant. You should preface your discussion or your interpretation of results with an easy-to-read summary of your findings. A chart or table is often the best way to present such a summary. (You may wish to review the discussion of charts and tables in the Using Supplemental Materials section of Chapter 5.)

Activity 3

Read and examine the selections in the Reading section of this chapter, and find places where information from nonlibrary research is employed. How is methodology described? How are results reported and discussed or interpreted? How much detail from particular sources is provided? For example, if the results of interviews are included, do the authors include excerpts from them?

Integrating Nonlibrary Resources

In Chapter 9, we offered suggestions for integrating library resources into a research paper. As you probably assume, many of those suggestions apply equally well to integrating nonlibrary resources. However, working with nonlibrary resources presents several additional challenges of which you should be aware. Here we will explain these challenges and suggest ways of dealing with them.

As you certainly know, regardless of the kind of paper you are writing, you need to be careful that you only make claims that are warranted; in working with nonlibrary resources, however, you need to be *especially* careful. This is because when you use nonlibrary resources, you must rely on your own interpretation of findings. If, for example, you have interviewed a social worker on his perception of a specific social problem, you must be careful not to imply that his opinion speaks for *all* social workers; instead, you will have to make it explicit that this is the opinion of just one social worker. A possible strategy for concluding your paper might be to suggest that future studies be done to see whether other social workers share this person's view. You should keep in mind that professional survey-designers spend years learning how to design their materials, distribute them to an appropriate sample of people, and interpret the findings. As a college student, you obviously are not expected to possess the expertise of a professional survey-designer and, therefore, are not expected to conduct surveys that prove anything with certainty. Instead, professors will expect your paper to contain qualifying phrases such as "This small sampling suggests that . . . ; however, more formal, rigorous research is warranted in order to. . . ." Regardless of the type of nonlibrary resources you are using, then, you will have to interpret your findings and suggest what they *may indicate* as opposed to what they *prove.*

Another challenge in working with nonlibrary resources involves effectively fitting your discussions of them into your paper. Doing so requires careful metadiscourse: You cannot suddenly shift from discussing a library resource to discussing a nonlibrary resource without confusing your readers. To help your readers through your text, you need to explain how the nonlibrary resource accommodates your thesis and how it substantiates—or refutes—any library sources in your paper. You also need to provide explanations of your rationale for using the nonlibrary resource and your particular methodology. By "methodology," we mean, for example, a description of your survey instrument, including explanations of how forms were disseminated and how many people responded. In effect, you will need to (1) consider the kinds of questions your readers might have about your use of a nonlibrary resource and (2) address these clearly within your paper.

When inexperienced writers try to integrate nonlibrary resources with one another, they often find it hard to maintain consistency in matters such as tone, level of formality, point of view, and verb tense. Inappropriate shifts sometimes occur as writers attempt to integrate library research that is written in a formal style with nonlibrary research that they conducted themselves. In this situation, writers sometimes use a formal style as they write about the library sources and abruptly shift to an informal style as they write about their nonlibrary research. Such shifts cause papers to lack fluency, thereby making the overall readability problematic.

To avoid this pitfall, you should pay attention to the style and level of formality you are using. If you are using a serious tone and a formal style ("Based on the careful analysis of my reading, I ascertain that. . . ."), you should try to maintain that style rather than making an abrupt shift to a lighter, less formal one ("So it's no wonder that my interview was such a big flop. Case closed."). As you might imagine, such inappropriate shifts would confuse readers about your intentions or create the impression that you are not serious about the research you conducted.

There might be occasions, however, as you move from writing about a library source to writing about a nonlibrary source, when you deliberately want to make shifts within your paper—from active to passive voice, from third-person to first-person point of view, or from past to present tense. Such shifts sometimes are needed to allow writers to express themselves in the clearest, most effective ways possible. In these situations, you will need to incorporate some metadiscourse into your text to ensure that readers are prepared for the shifts and that the shifts occur smoothly. The best strategy for deciding whether the shifts you make are smooth and appropriate is to read your paper aloud; your ear often can tell you whether there are problems.

Writing, Revising, and Editing

Because the process of writing a research paper with library sources is similar to that of writing a research paper with nonlibrary sources, the descriptions of the various aspects of that process in the preceding chapter will help you craft a competent text regardless of the sources that you employ. Of course, you should consult a handbook or style manual for methods of proper documentation. In the event that the handbook or manual that you are using does not describe how to cite a particular source that you have employed, you should find a similar item and adapt the format specified for that item so that it is appropriate for your source. For example, if your handbook explains how to cite a personal or telephone interview but not how to cite an Internet interview, use the format for the telephone interview, but change the wording from *Telephone Interview* to *Internet Interview*.

To assist you with the process of researching and writing a research paper with both library and nonlibrary sources, we have provided the following checklist.

Although the tasks specified are listed in a particular order—as required by the format of a checklist—you may perform many of them simultaneously or work back and forth between them as you research and write your paper.

Process Checklist

_____ Read your assignment. Think about possible approaches and select the most promising one.

_____ Determine which library and nonlibrary sources to use.

_____ Make arrangements to secure nonlibrary information. (Arrange interviews; investigate films to view; design survey instruments; etc.)

_____ Begin working with library sources. Make bibliography and note cards.

_____ Begin working with nonlibrary sources. Make bibliography cards and note cards.

_____ Narrow your topic. Use information from both library and nonlibrary sources to do so.

_____ Devise a thesis and map out brief overall plans or structures for your paper. You may wish to develop several theses and plans and select the best one.

_____ Write a detailed outline for your paper. Indicate which sources (both library and nonlibrary) you will use in each part.

_____ Write a first draft of your paper, including an informal bibliography of your sources.

_____ Share your draft with your group members and your instructor for feedback.

_____ Revise your draft, attending to the feedback you receive and paying particular attention to the draft's overall structure, the connections between and within its parts, the integration of background information, material from sources, and so on.

_____ Edit your draft for punctuation, usage, sentence structure, and spelling.

_____ Edit your draft for format (documentation, bibliography, tables, etc.).

WRITING ASSIGNMENTS

Writing Topics

Your assignment in this chapter is to write a research paper in which you use a minimum of three library sources and two nonlibrary sources. You should use a formal documentation system such as MLA, APA, or another that your instructor requires.

Your topic should be chosen from among the writing topics listed in the preceding chapter. As in Chapter 9, your writing group should research one topic together. Your group may wish to continue working with the same topic that you choose for your library research paper, augmenting your library research with nonlibrary materials. However, you may wish to choose a new topic to research. As before, depending on your teacher's instructions or your preferences, your group may choose to write one longer paper coauthored by all members or to write individual research papers separately.

We have provided some suggestions here for incorporating nonlibrary research into each of the writing topics from Chapter 9. In deciding which topic to work with for your nonlibrary research paper, you should read the following discussion as well as the Writing Topics part of the Writing Assignments section of Chapter 9. In addition, in deciding which topic to research, you should consider whether members of your group have access to particular nonlibrary sources for some of the topics and discuss what types of nonlibrary research your group could perform for each topic. Each of the numbered topics that follow parallel those in Chapter 9.

1. *Research a particular career or occupation.* In addition to researching library sources, for this topic you could interview one or more professionals in the field or distribute surveys among several of them. You might also interview professionals through the Internet or find similar relevant electronic information sources. You could visit local information resource centers, for example, the local Department of Human Services, to research the career of social work or a local nursing home to investigate the field of gerontology or medical administration. For some careers or professions you also might conduct observations at professional worksites—such as a law court or a research laboratory. A valuable resource center for this topic would be the Placement or Career Office on your campus, where you may find specialized computer data bases and other relevant sources.

2. *Investigate a well known but unsolved crime.* To incorporate nonlibrary research into this topic, you could conduct a survey to determine public opinion and attitudes about the crime you are researching, the victims involved, or the alleged criminals. You may also be able to view television documentaries or films that focus on the crime you are researching or to view original news broadcasts of the crime and related trials. If possible, you may be able to visit a relevant site, such as the crime site or other sites important to the background of the principal persons involved. You may be able to interview persons involved in the crime, such as the police officers who originally investigated it, or you may interview legal experts to learn their opinions on the case. Don't necessarily limit yourselves to a crime committed nearby, however. If you're researching Jack the Ripper, the Internet might be able to put you in touch with experts in London, England.

3. *Research an inexplicable event, occurrence in nature, or mysterious artifact.* With this topic, you could survey public opinion to find out how much people know about your topic or what they believe about it. A good source would also be interviews with experts such as biologists, geologists, or naturalists, who may be available on your campus. You may be able to identify special interest groups on the Internet; there might, for example, be a Loch Ness Monster Club—or a discussion group for people who believe they have been abducted by aliens. You may also be able to visit an important site related to your topic.

4. *Research undergraduate student life at colleges in the United States before 1950.* For this topic, one of the most useful resource centers will be the Alumni Office at your college, where you may be able to find out about local meetings of alumni or the names of persons you could interview. You may also be able to attend class reunions held in conjunction with Homecoming Weekend or visit the college

archives to read early yearbooks, newspapers, or personal papers donated by former students. Another good source could be interviews with current or retired faculty who were college students before 1950, or with current or retired staff members.

5. *Research an aspect of computer technology.* To expand this topic, you could observe people who are learning to use computers in a lab or computer class. You could also visit a mainframe lab to observe people working there. Interviews with computer science majors or with people who have used particular hardware or software can also be good research sources. You could observe people surfing the Internet or interview those who are regular users. An additional research source could be popular movies that center on computers or that use computer technology—real or imagined—to advance key aspects of the plot; some examples are *Sneakers, 2001: A Space Odyssey, War Games,* and *Jurassic Park.*

6. *Research a particular ethnic group within the United States.* Good research sources for this topic could include interviews with members of the ethnic group you are researching and visits to local or regional museums or resource centers. You may be able to visit and observe seasonal or religious festivals and other celebrations. There may be special interest groups available on the Internet. You may also be interested in watching and critiquing depictions of this ethnic group in popular media such as advertising, popular television shows, and movies.

Writing Procedures

As in the preceding chapter, we have provided you with a check sheet to follow as you work on your research paper assignment. You should use it to help you break the task of writing into a series of manageable steps and to help you create a series of deadlines. Where we have indicated that you should solicit the feedback of your group on your work, use one of the workshop procedures described in Chapter 2. You will probably find it useful to photocopy this check sheet so that you can mark your deadlines and progress on it or submit it to your instructor.

READINGS

Professional Models

O'Neill, Barry. "The History of a Hoax." *New York Times Magazine,* 6 March 1994, sect. 6, pp. 46–49.

Kouri, Kristyan M., and Lasswell, Marcia. "Black-White Marriages: Social Change and Intergenerational Mobility." *Marriage & Family Review 19* (1993), pp. 241–254.

Student Model

Riffle, Jennifer. "Selling the Frontier Dream to the American Public: The Frontier West and Advertising."

RESEARCH PAPER CHECK SHEET

Your Name:

Your Research Topic or Question:

Documentation Format You Will Use:

Tasks	Target Date	Date Completed
Written research proposal approved (minimum 1/2 page typed or word-processed)		
Final sources selected		
Arrangements for nonlibrary research completed		
Bibliography cards completed		
Critical reading and underlining completed		
Note cards on library and nonlibrary sources completed		
Tentative thesis and brief plan submitted to instructor		
Detailed plan or outline submitted to instructor		
First draft completed		
First draft workshopped with group		
Revised draft completed, based on feedback from group, instructor, or writing center		
Editing for mechanics, usage, and spelling completed		
Format and documentation checked and corrected		

Questions

The following questions will help you examine the readings in this chapter. These questions call your attention to how nonlibrary sources are integrated, reported, and utilized. Notice that in all of the readings, both library and nonlibrary sources are employed within each paper.

1. Both of the professional models employ data from interviews, but they report that data differently. Find examples in each of the articles to illustrate how the authors report what their informants said. Compare the functions each method serves within each piece, given its overall purpose and audience. (Note that "The History of a Hoax" is directed to a popular readership while "Black-White Marriages" has been taken from an academic journal.)

2. As with library sources, nonlibrary sources can be documented informally or formally. "The History of a Hoax," published in a popular magazine, is informally documented; how does O'Neill employ nonlibrary sources in it? How does his

nonlibrary research supplement the library research he tried to do? How does he establish authority for his interview subjects in the text of his article?

3. When nonlibrary research sources are used, writers generally must provide some rationale for using them and explain exactly what nonlibrary research was used and how it was conducted. Go through each of the readings to identify exactly where the writers provide such explanations. What different rationales are provided for conducting the nonlibrary research? What descriptions of methodology are provided? How detailed are they?

4. Consider the point of view used by the different writers. Which writers use first-person pronouns, and where? Is the point of view consistent throughout a piece, or does it change? Similarly, consider verb tense; is it consistent throughout, or does it change? Do any of the shifts you find occur when writers discuss their nonlibrary research? In pieces where such shifts in point of view and/or tense occur, do the overall tone and level of formality also shift, or instead remain consistent?

5. When the authors use direct quotations, how are they formatted? When are direct quotations integrated within a paragraph, and when are they set off in block quotes? What kind of introductory phrases are used to integrate quotations into the rest of the text?

 ## The History of a Hoax*

Barry O'Neill

We often define ourselves more by our misdeeds than by our accomplishments. Twenty years after my father died, I leafed through his school diaries and found a side of him that I hadn't known. The events he considered worth recording weren't his successes but the trouble he got into: "fought with Jimmy Egan," "running in the hall, broke statue of Virgin Mary," "teacher took my slingshot."

For many worried adults, the offenses of young people have become a measure of America's well-being. Last April someone tacked a survey on a Yale bulletin board comparing the top problems of public schools in the 1940's and 1980's. In the 40's the problems were: 1. talking; 2. chewing gum; 3. making noise; 4. running in the halls; 5. getting out of turn in line; 6. wearing improper clothing; 7. not putting paper in wastebaskets.

The top problems in the 80's had become: 1. drug abuse; 2. alcohol abuse; 3. pregnancy; 4. suicide; 5. rape; 6. robbery; 7. assault.

Something stopped me. The old-time problems seemed too trivial, the contrast between then and now too tidy. My father could have bested the 1940 list any day,

*Barry O'Neill, "The History of a Hoax." *New York Times Magazine,* 6 March 1994, sect. 6, pp. 46–49. Copyright © 1994 by The New York Times Company. Reprinted by permission.

The History of a Hoax *(cont'd.)*

and in my own school years I worried about bullies starting fistfights or stealing my lunch, not kids cutting in line at the drinking fountain. A 1984 Gallup poll asking teachers to name the biggest school problems recorded the top two as parent apathy and lack of financial support, but drugs were near the bottom. In 1991 the National Center for Education Statistics asked specifically about discipline and safety issues, and educators' prime complaints were tardiness, absenteeism and fighting. Again drugs fell near the bottom, well below tobacco.

Puzzled by these inconsistencies, I tried to locate the source of the list of school problems. The list on the bulletin board had been taken from a book published by the Young & Rubicam Foundation, an arm of the ad agency that created the slogan "A mind is a terrible thing to waste." But it attributed the research to the California Department of Education. I scoured computer bibliographies and data bases, but could find no specific title or date or author. I began to suspect that the lists were folklore, like the famous alligators crawling through New York's sewers.

If so, they were a rare variety, folklore of the eminent and powerful. William Bennett, a former Secretary of Education, used them in television talks, editorials and speeches to promote "The Index of Leading Cultural Indicators," his 1993 book on America's moral decay. The lists were not just the oratory of conservatives: Anna Quindlen, Herb Caen and Carl Rowan included them in their columns. A former Harvard president, Derek Bok, recounted the lists to the Harvard Club of Chicago. Joseph Fernandez, former chancellor of New York City's schools, used them to argue for his curriculum reform, and the publisher Mortimer Zuckerman saw them as an outgrowth of television violence. Dr. Joycelyn Elders, then the Surgeon General nominee, said they showed the need for social-service and health programs.

Senators, mayors, state education officials, university professors, deans—these were notables who would never stand up to announce the discovery of alligators underneath New York, but they accepted the lists as factual. They were reported in all the major news magazines. In addition to the Quindlen column, The New York Times printed them five times (not as fact but in quotes of various people), and they became commonplace in grass-roots America, popping up in Dear Abby, Ann Landers and countless letters to the editor. They have become the most quoted "results" of educational research, and possibly the most influential.

We will never know who first said "Let's do lunch," but this was a different case—an item from popular culture that had circulated widely through the news media, leaving a traceable record. I was determined to find its origin.

I wrote letters to users asking them where they had found their versions, and paged through education journals looking for the originator. After several months I found him. As I had suspected, his lists were not scientifically valid, but neither were they hoaxes. He had offered them simply as his opinion, never meaning to hoodwink the experts. It was later users who added background details, like William Bennett's elaboration about an "ongoing" survey asking teachers "the same question" over the years.

The History of a Hoax *(cont'd.)*

Some felt free to modify the lists. Rush Limbaugh, for example, cited the authority of Bennett but added a few school offenses of his own. Others advanced the date, making the results sound more current; in November 1992, when The Wall Street Journal reprinted the lists from the CQ Researcher, the modern survey's date jumped from 1980 to 1990. If there was any hoaxing, it was users hoaxing themselves.

Their originator was T. Cullen Davis of Fort Worth, a born-again Christian who devised the lists as a fundamentalist attack on public schools. Davis was born again through a remarkable course of events. He and his brother Ken had built the family business in oil equipment into a billion-dollar conglomerate, but in 1976 Cullen was arrested for a double murder, accused of shooting his stepdaughter and the lover of his estranged wife. The sensational trials, which featured lurid tales of his wife's drug and sex parties at his mansion, became the talk of bridge tables and barrooms across Texas.

After his aquittals, Davis turned from the fast life to Christianity. One night at his home, he and James Robison, a television evangelist, took hammers to Davis's million-dollar collection of jade and ivory statues, smashing them as false religion. He plunged into a reading program on public schools, fought plans for sex education and lobbied for the teaching of creationism.

Sometime around 1982, Davis constructed the lists and passed them around to other fundamentalists. His 1940 offenses were closes to the seven on the Yale bulletin board: 1. talking; 2. chewing gum; 3. running in the halls; 4. wearing improper clothing; 5. making noise; 6. not putting paper in wastebaskets; 7. getting out of turn in line. But he listed 20 modern problems: 1. rape; 2. robbery; 3. assault; 4. personal theft; 5. burglary; 6. drug abuse; 7. arson; 8. bombings; 9. alcohol abuse; 10. carrying of weapons; 11. absenteeism; 12. vandalism; 13. murder; 14. extortion; 15. gang warfare; 16. pregnancies; 17. abortions; 18. suicide; 19. venereal disease; 20. lying and cheating.

I asked him how he had arrived at his items. "They weren't done from a scientific survey," he told me. "How did I know what the offenses in the schools were in 1940? I was there. How do I know what they are now? I read the newspapers."

His recollection that he formed the lists entirely from scratch must be faulty. His first 10 modern offenses are almost identical in wording to items on a questionnaire from a survey by the National Center for Education Statistics, which asked principals whether they had reported certain *crimes* in their schools during a five-month period in 1974–75. This survey was published in the Safe School study of 1977–78, which was widely distributed. Rape, robbery and assault held the top places not because they were the top problems, but because the researchers used a standard ordering in crime reports: first crimes against people, then crimes against property, then others. Curiously, murder does not appear among the serious items at the head of Davis's modern list. It shows up only after playing hooky and vandalizing. The reason is that the survey relied upon a list of crimes for which researchers could interview the victims, so murder obviously was left off.

The History of a Hoax *(cont'd.)*

Thus, Davis's modern list is made up not of survey answers but of the questions. His list of 1940 problems, however, seems genuinely to date from that time. It is close to the wording of a 1943 list in a Texas teachers' magazine and fits with dozens of old research reports collecting teachers' most common classroom problems. Talking usually ranked high and gum-chewing close behind.

Davis's 1940 list may be based on real data, but it cannot in any event be compared with his 1980's list. It gave the answers to a discipline, while the new list was an inventory of crimes. You can't learn how times have changed if you change your question.

In the early 1980's some of Davis's conservative colleagues took up his creation. The Rev. Tim LaHaye put the lists in a book promoting family values, and the anti-feminist activist Phyllis Schlafly used the idea in an essay about her school days. The lists gained wide circulation in the fundamentalist community when they appeared in a newsletter published by Mel and Norma Gabler. These were the education activists who gained national fame for pressuring the Texas state textbook committee to purchase books that promote creationism, patriotism and a Christian life style. In their newsletter they reordered the old problems and shrank the new list to 17, knocking out lying and cheating, personal theft and weapons.

In 1984 David Balsiger, then of Costa Mesa, Calif., picked up the Gablers' version for the Presidential Biblical Scoreboard, a glossy magazine that rated presidential candidates on how closely their platforms followed biblical teachings. Although the print run for the Scoreboard was around two million, the lists had little visibility outside conservative religious circles. To gain wider circulation, they needed the imprimatur of a credible publication. That came, in a backhanded way, in March 1985, when Harper's printed the Scoreboard's version as a curious piece of Americana. Harper's slipped in clues that the lists were unscientific, noting that the Scoreboard wanted readers to "vote conscientiously for godly rule." Nevertheless, in April the Governor of California, George Deukmajian, included the lists in an address warmly received by the California Sheriff's Association.

Mary Weaver, a program administrator at the California Department of Education, circulated the table from Harper's in a March memo to her guidance and counseling staff, and used it for workshops on discipline and safety. The department had set up a liaison group with the police across the state, and a police officer from Fullerton began presenting the lists in his talks in his home community.

Simply by quoting the lists the Fullerton police and the California Department of Education put their stamp on them, and many would later claim that they were the originators. This is the best-source-yet rule: The most credible party to date to recite or publish the lists becomes the source. Following the best-source-yet rule, various later users would say that the survey was compiled by CBS News, the CQ Researcher or the Heritage Foundation, whose staff, according to John McCaslin of The Washington Times, found the 1940 offenses in an old survey.

During their time in Fullerton the lists underwent a crucial change—the drug shift. The public was alarmed about teen-age drug use, which a Gallup poll rated

The History of a Hoax *(cont'd.)*

the public's No. 1 worry about schools. The modern list could ride this concern if drugs were moved to the top. Most users had not explicitly claimed that the items were in order of worst first, so shifting them around seemed permissible. The four self-destructive offenses—drugs, alcohol, pregnancy and suicide—got promoted as a block, and rape, robbery and assault fell to fifth, sixth and seventh. My earliest record of the new ranking comes from a January 1986 meeting in a Fullerton junior high school. Most recent lists feature the drug shift, a clue that they descended from the Fullerton version.

According to a University of Michigan study, drug use by high-school seniors dropped by about one-half between 1980 and 1990. But the public thought just the opposite was true. In Gallup polls over the decade, the proportion of respondents naming drugs as an important school problem rose from 14 percent to 38 percent. In other words, when drug use was most severe, the school lists were sounding the klaxon about rape, robbery and assault, and they focused on drugs just as students were using them less. The experts and reporters repeating the lists were not providing the public with real information, just reflecting public opinion back to the public.

In 1986, with pseudo-credentials from California educators and the Fullerton police, and a new look from the drug shift, the lists of school problems spread across the country. They popped up frequently in the literature of the anti-drug movement, which became another crucial conduit from the religious right to the mainstream.

The first national writer to publish the lists as factual was George Will, in his Newsweek column of Jan. 5, 1987. He gave no source. A month later a CBS News reporter, Bernard Goldberg, featured them in a story about child criminals. Will's and Goldberg's modern lists were cut to seven: drug abuse, alcohol abuse, pregnancy, suicide, rape, robbery, assault. Fundamentalists wanted to leave no sin unmentioned, but trimming the list gave it wider appeal. Seven elements seem to be the approximate limit to people's apprehension, according to George Miller, a psychologist. There are seven colors in the rainbow, seven deadly sins and seven wonders of the world, among many other examples. Seven versus seven gave a balanced comparison of old and new, and let some public speakers go sideways across the columns, contrasting yesterday's abuse of chewing gum against today's drugs and alcohol abuse.

CBS News changed the wording slightly, and this became the preferred form among the elite, like Senator John Glenn, whose speech was picked up by the CQ Researcher for an article later copied by The Wall Street Journal and The International Herald Tribune. In a 1989 syndicated documentary on youth morals, Tom Selleck delivered the CBS News version of the list "like a punch in the solar plexus," according to one reviewer, and he also changed the wording slightly, generating another family of the lists.

Time magazine's 10-item version in 1988 included "bombings" as a top problem. F.B.I. data for 1987 show that the total reported damage done by bombs to all the schools and universities across America was only $30,000, just a drop in the

The History of a Hoax *(cont'd.)*

budget. So many in the new media had seen the lists so often that they assumed they were valid.

After collecting close to 250 versions of the lists, I tackled a harder question: Why have Americans found them so attractive? One clue is the way they change, like a folk song or folk tale, as they are passed on. When people hear an item of folklore they remember its core emotional meaning, not its exact words, so when they want to reproduce it they reconstruct it around that meaning. The elements of a folklore item that are not essential to this meaning change or fall away. Those that endure through successive versions often reveal its emotional significance for the group.

The items on the original 1940 list have hardly changed at all. Constant also is the location in the public schools. The date of the old list is semi-stable, usually 1940, although it has been put at anywhere from "the Depression" (Ross Perot) to "five years ago." The modern problems usually stay in the recent past, so their date moves forward as time passes.

The feature that varies widely, sometimes even slips away, is just what the inventory represents. If it is the answer, what is the question? Sometimes the lists are "top" problems, sometimes discipline problems, offenses or worries. None of these fit all the items, but no one seems to mind calling suicide a discipline problem. Logically an answer should be judged against its question, but at its core the list is an emotional expression, not a logical assertion.

In fact, the school lists are remarkably close to the Puritan jeremiads of 300 years ago, and what made them the rage may be working for the school lists now. Jeremiads were formulaic political sermons. First the preacher reminded the congregation of its covenant with God and God's blessings on their ancestors; next, he catalogued the afflictions of the day, like Indian wars, fires or caterpillar plagues, or, in later versions, the congregation's evil habits. These were God's punishment for breaking the covenant and his warning to them to reform. Finally, he called for a renewal, after which God would grant them fulfillment.

In their nostalgic contrast of then and now, the school lists constitute a jeremiad. On their face they are criticizing schools but their real target, like the jeremiad's, is society in general. They place drugs, pregnancy, rape or suicide as problems in the public schools. But is a typical school more hazardous or immoral than its surrounding area? Blaming the schools is illogical, but it is rhetorically right, since responsibility for schools falls on all Americans.

The second and third generations of Puritans felt a tension, for which the jeremiad provided a release. Their religion had sanctioned ambition for the good of the community, but now that virtue was promoting greed, worldliness and sin. Springing from "grief and a sickness of soul," says Perry Miller, the great scholar of Puritan intellectual history, the Puritans' sermons were "professions of a society that knew it was dong wrong, but could not help itself, because the wrong thing was also the right thing." Through public lamentations, they paid tribute to their sense of guilt over betraying their ancestor's ideals.

The History of a Hoax *(cont'd.)*

Americans today regard their country as the richest, freest and fairest, with the best social system, but cannot square this with the social problems of America's youth. And what does this disorder promise for the future? The tension felt by modern Americans, like that of the Puritans, demands release. The school lists are a collective moan of anxiety over the gap between ideals and reality. When Puritans or modern Americans enumerate their faults, they are declaring their dedication to their ideals, reassuring each other that at least their goals remain high.

The spread of the school lists proves that jeremiads, at least, are not in decline. The lists are not facts but a fundamental expression of attitudes and emotions. They overlook the successes of American public education, its great expansion since 1940 and its high quality despite taxpayer resistance. The lists' broad sweep ignores that some public schools are devastated by violence and substance abuse and others hardly touched at all. They should not guide our choices on education policy.

Black-White Marriages: Social Change and Intergenerational Mobility*

Kristyan M. Kouri
Marcia Lasswell

SUMMARY. The majority of marriage partners in the United States are of the same race, although a growing minority are choosing to intermarry (Lieberson & Waters, 1988). In this article, we examine why black and white individuals living in the greater Los Angeles metropolitan area chose to marry each other. Explored are characteristics such as social class background and family upbringing which might influence a decision to go against the societal norm of racial endogamy.

Black/white interracial marriages were known to exist soon after the first blacks came to this country as indentured servants in the seventeenth century. Soon afterwards, however, black/white marriages were outlawed in most states. Such marriages were almost nonexistent, as a consequence, until the Emancipation when a slow but steady growth commenced until 1900. There was a decline between the turn of the century and 1940 followed by slightly increasing numbers until

*Kristyan M. Kouri and Marcia Lasswell, "Black-White Marriages: Social Change and Intergenerational Mobility." *Marriage & Family Review 19*, No. 3/4 (1993), pp. 241–255. Copyright © 1993 by The Haworth Press, Inc., Binghamton, New York.

Black-White Marriages: Social Change
and Intergenerational Mobility *(cont'd.)*

1967, when miscegenation laws were declared unconstitutional by the United States Supreme Court (Porterfield, 1982). Between 1970 and 1988, black/white interracial marriages rose from 65,000 to 218,000 (Monroe, 1990). Even with this increase, black/white marriages continued to be the exception rather than the rule (Lieberson & Waters, 1988).

Studies of interracial marriage which have attempted to understand why a few choose to marry outside their racial boundaries have resulted in two broad categories of theoretical explanations: the structural theory and the racial motivation theory.

According to the structural approach, interracial marriages are more frequent when the community structure sanctions such unions. For example, lack of kinship controls in urban environments makes personal characteristics more likely to be valued than categorical traits such as race, ethnic background, religion, or social class (Kvaraceus, 1969). The structural theories propose that interracial couples marry for the same reasons that racially homogeneous couples do; they meet, they discover similar interests, they fall in love, and they decide to marry. Over the past several decades desegregation of neighborhoods, schools, and the workplace has facilitated propinquity and the opportunity for those from different races to come to know each other (Farber, 1973). In addition, there has been a gain in status for many blacks as a result of the civil rights movement allowing their education levels and incomes to rise (Heer, 1974). Structuralists suggest that those blacks who have achieved higher socioeconomic status find more white partners in their pool of eligibles and that as a result of their higher status, blacks come to be viewed more favorably and hence as more suitable partners by a growing number of white persons.

Still another explanation of interracial marriage from a structural point of view is that as interracial marriages increase in number, society becomes desensitized to what previously may have been socially unacceptable to most of the population. Early studies of black/white marriages, for example, indicated that such unions were relatively isolated from their families of origin (Golden, 1953; Pavela, 1964; Smith, 1966). By 1978, Porterfield reported that families were more supportive and couples felt less negative social pressure (Porterfield, 1978).

In considerable opposition to the structural approach, the racial motivation theory proposes that many interracial marriages occur precisely because of the racial differences instead of in spite of them or with indifference toward them. It is suggested that, for example, those who marry persons of another race may find them more physically appealing. It is reported that curiosity about those who are different creates heightened sexual interest for some (Grier & Cobbs, 1968). In addition, this theory suggests that individuals may go against the social norm of racial endogamy as a form of rebellion or as a sign of independence. Social psychologists have suggested that some persons who profess to be independent and liberal may, in fact, be counterconformists who have a desire to act in opposition to socially accepted norms.

To explore these two very different frameworks, in-depth interviews with twenty-nine black/white interracial couples living in the Los Angeles area were conducted.

Black-White Marriages: Social Change
and Intergenerational Mobility *(cont'd.)*

The interviews sought information concerning why the partners chose each other, how they bridged cultural differences, how their families of origin reacted to their choice, how they coped with prejudice, and how they were rearing their children.

Recent Literature

The most extensive study of interracial couples in the United States to date was conducted by Ernest Porterfield (1978) who interviewed forty black/white couples, seven of whom consisted of black women married to white men and thirty-three in which white women were married to black men. Twenty of these couples resided in Illinois, eleven in Ohio, seven in Alabama, and two in Mississippi. Porterfield concluded that the majority of the couples in his sample had married because they had the opportunities to meet in integrated settings and to fall in love. Porterfield argued that the structural theory, which speaks of increased opportunities for the races to intermingle, explained why the majority of his respondents married outside their own race.

Porterfield reported that a small number of his respondents indicated that, although they chose to marry on the basis of overall compatibility, they also had a strong attraction to persons of another race for reasons such as societal rebellion and/or physical attraction. It was, therefore, concluded that racial motivation theories for intermarriage could not be entirely ruled out.

In the early 1970's, British anthropologist Susan Benson (1981) interviewed twenty black/white interracial couples, fifteen of whom were black men married to white women and five who were white men married to black women. They lived in a mixed black/white working-class neighborhood near London. Like Porterfield (1978), Benson discovered that her respondents met in integrated settings such as school, work, through friends, or casually on the street. Five of the white female respondents were judged too economically vulnerable and socially disadvantaged to stand a good chance to find a suitable white partner. According to Benson, these five women elected to marry established black men to obtain economic security. The implication was that, had their circumstances been different, they may have married endogamously.

Benson further reported that seven white women and two white men in her sample had weak links to their extended family members which limited any family pressure to discourage marriage. A question exists as to whether weak family linkages are a consequence of intermarriage; however, Benson did not address this issue and concluded that the individuals in her sample chose to marry for a variety of motives that could not be accounted for by any single theory.

The Sample

The studies reviewed were conducted in the Midwestern and Southern United States and in Great Britain. This led to the question of whether couples residing in

Black-White Marriages: Social Change and Intergenerational Mobility *(cont'd.)*

the West, and in particular in one of the largest and most ethnically and racially diverse cities in the world, Los Angeles, may or may not marry for the same reasons as black/white couples in those regions studied by Porterfield, Benson, and others. In addition, were couples motivated to marry by factors associated with the structural view or the racial motivation view of intermarriage, a combination of the two, or that neither explained their choices of mates?

Because interracial couples are relatively few in number, large populations of couples from which to draw a scientific-random sample do not exist. For this reason, a snowball procedure was used in obtaining the couples rather than random sampling. This procedure was facilitated by the knowledge that many interracial couples are likely to be known by other interracial couples. The snowball began by identifying black/white couples shopping in a supermarket located in a middle class neighborhood. This, in turn led to other couples suggested by the original supermarket interviewers.

The use of this sampling procedure and the large multi-racial, multi-ethnic mix in the Los Angeles population, not necessarily characteristic of other locales in the United States, limit the generalizability of the findings of this study to other populations. The findings presented, therefore, are exploratory rather than definitive.

Twenty-six of the twenty-nine couples interviewed were legally married while the other three were cohabiting. It is appropriate to note here that California laws do not provide for nonceremonial marriage, so the length of time of cohabitation does not affect marital status. The range in length of legal marriage was from four months to twenty-two years; the range for the cohabiters was from six to eight years.

Twenty-three of the couples interviewed consisted of a black male and a white female; six were white male and black female. In the United States, 3.6% of American black males are married to nonblacks; 1.25% of American black females marry nonblacks (U.S. Bureau of Census, 1985). For Los Angeles County, these figures are slightly higher with 6.6% of black males married to nonblacks as compared to 2.6% of black females married to nonblacks (Tucker & Mitchell-Kernan, 1990). This overall pattern is reflected in the Los Angeles sample, Porterfield's Midwestern and Southern sample, and Benson's British sample.

The socioeconomic statuses of the couples were defined by occupation, education, and income. Some of the husbands' occupations included: truck driver, meat cutter, computer programmer, entrepreneur, and university professor. The wives' occupations included: real estate agent, registered nurse, entrepreneur, bank loan officer, cartoonist, and university professor.

Each pair of respondents was asked to give a self-rating of their socioeconomic statuses as well as their perceptions of the social classes of their families of origin. A scale of lower, lower-middle, middle, upper-middle and upper was provided for estimating social class. In impressionistic terms, the couples ranged from lower-middle to upper-middle class when self-reports of the social statuses of their families of origin were considered along with their own socioeconomic variables. Many

Black-White Marriages: Social Change and Intergenerational Mobility *(cont'd.)*

of the respondents volunteered that they had experienced upward mobility in education, income, and occupation beyond their parents' respective socioeconomic statuses. This was particularly likely to be the case among blacks in the sample.

The Interview

The interviews were loosely based on the issues Porterfield (1978) developed. Questions centered on the couples' meeting place, decision to marry, family reaction to the marriage, and housing issues. Questions were structured in such a manner that they left room for any additional information the respondents wished to add. Interview time ranged from forty-five minutes to two and one-half hours. Additional visits and telephone calls were made to respondents when further information was needed. All of the interviews took place in the homes of the couples and, in all cases, both of the spouses were present. Interviewing husband and wife together had both methodological limitations and advantages. On the one hand, in each other's presence partners sometimes avoid talking about issues that would upset their spouse (Rubin, 1976). On the other hand, interviewing couples together allows observation of how the spouses interact with each other (Reinharz, 1991) and elicits each couple's shared notion of reality (Berger & Luckman, 1967).

Finally, it should be noted that the interviewer was a white female. There is the possibility that this may have biased the responses of both black and white respondents.

Integrated Social Contact

The structural theory of interracial marriage stresses the social acceptance of such marriages due to socially accepted interracial contact in schools, at work, and in leisure-time activities. Six of the couples in this study were introduced by family or friends, lending support to the acceptance of interracial social contact. The remainder met in public, racially-integrated settings: seven at work, four in night clubs, five at school, one at a health club, and one on a public bus. The way the couples in Los Angeles met is very similar to that of couples interviewed in Porterfield's (1978) southern and midwestern sample as well as Benson's (1981) British sample. It appears clear that while housing and recreational segregation between blacks and whites still exists, structural changes that have desegregated society have nevertheless led to increased contact in these areas as well as in school and at work. Interracial encounters which previously were discouraged or prevented by institutionalized policies or practices prior to the civil rights movement have improved. To this extent, interracial marriages appear to have been facilitated by structural changes. In the Los Angeles sample, many of the respondents had lived in racially-mixed neighborhoods and had attended integrated schools. Many had dated those from other races and ethnic groups and in some instances, so had other family members and their friends.

Black-White Marriages: Social Change and Intergenerational Mobility *(cont'd.)*

The structural perspective holds that the decrease in prohibitions related to mate selection outside one's own group in American society has, by default, fostered an increase in positive factors in interracial mate selection (Lasswell & Lasswell, 1991). As the strength of propinquity, social class, racial, ethnic, and religious filters diminishes in mate selection, the physical attraction and psychodynamic influences increase in importance (Klimek, 1979, p. 13). Consequently, when interracial couples can transcend the institutionalized opposition to marriage, they are more likely to marry for the same reasons that racially homogeneous partners do.

Similarities

Forty-four of the individuals in the Los Angeles sample stated that they were attracted to their partners because of similar values and interests which led to overall compatibility. A response heard repeatedly was "We could talk to one another." Many of the respondents reported being friends before they became romantically involved. The following comment characterizes the sentiment of many of these couples:

> We were friends for a long time before we became involved and then it got serious very quickly. We came from totally different backgrounds with nothing in common but we have the same values, the way we think, goals and what's really important in life.

These individuals further stated that their marriages were strong and stable. Another statement frequently heard was:

> I know interracial couples are supposed to have many problems, but our marriage is different.

The respondents indicated that the fact that one of them was black and one of them was white was not the most salient feature in their marriage. Consistent with Porterfield's (1978) findings, the partners reported that the only time they thought of each other as being black or white is when they were reminded of it by others.

Thus, the majority of the Los Angeles sample reported that they met and married because they became friends and had similar values. The reasons the couples reported for why they were attracted to one another and why they chose to marry were almost identical to what Porterfield found in Illinois, Ohio, Alabama, and Mississippi.

Interracial Attraction

The racial motivation approach to explaining changes in the nature and number of interracial marriages holds that interracial couples marry because, as individuals,

Black-White Marriages: Social Change
and Intergenerational Mobility *(cont'd.)*

they have a special attraction to novel or different behaviors that are unconventional in the social environment in which they live. In extreme cases this may take the form of social rebellion. While six of the couples were initially drawn to each other primarily by sexual attraction, these feelings were soon intertwined with a general liking for one another. They reported no thoughts of social rebellion. As one black husband put it:

> The attraction was immediate but I suppressed it. We taught together, worked well together, and finally realized that we loved each other.

One of the black women and six of the black men in the sample reported they had always been attracted to white partners. Seven of the white females indicated that they found black men especially appealing. Two of these women spoke of an ardent concern for the plight of blacks and a love of black culture. Two of the white men in the study found black women particularly alluring and one of these men reported a strong empathy for the racism which blacks encounter. While the findings from the majority of the couples showed support for the structural theory, there were a number of couples who married because they were especially attracted to a person of the other race. These findings suggest that the racial motivation theory for interracial marriage is not without foundation.

Racial motivations for interracial marriage were also reported by Porterfield (1978) and Benson (1981). Porterfield indicated that nine of his black male respondents, two of his white female respondents and one of his white male respondents listed race-related reasons for their marriages. Benson (1981) also reported that four of the white respondents in her sample married blacks in rebellion against their families. None of the Los Angeles respondents, however, indicated that they married a person of another race to rebel nor did any possess characteristics or past histories that precluded them from finding a partner of their own race as Benson reported in her population.

Social Class Characteristics

Merton's (1941) theory of reciprocal compensation proposes that black men of high economic standing will sometimes marry white women of lower social class status in an exchange of economic security for what they perceive as a greater social status attached to being white. Because men traditionally play a larger part in determining the socioeconomic status of their families, it has been suggested that women are reluctant to marry men of lower status, black or white.

Porterfield (1978), on the other hand, found most of the couples who married interracially were of equal socioeconomic status at the time of their meeting. This pattern also held true for the Los Angeles sample although there was a distinct tendency for the black men to be upwardly mobile as compared to their parents while white males and most of the women, black or white, did not show this mobility.

Black-White Marriages: Social Change
and Intergenerational Mobility *(cont'd.)*

Each spouse was asked his or her social class of origin. The data were analyzed to determine whether women married up, married down, or married someone with the same social class, to determine whether Merton's theory of reciprocal compensation held for the women in the Los Angeles sample. Of the white women, five married up, nine of the women married down, and nine married equals. Of the black women, four married up and two married social class equals. Women (black or white) who had bettered their social class of origin were generally fewer than those who married down or married equals. This raises the distinct possibility that unlike the tendency for the Los Angeles sample not to use racial motivation for marrying one of another race, social class considerations may have played a part in women's mate selection.

Kinship

The structural position suggests that the lessening of kinship controls over mate selection and the consequent rise in the number of interracial marriages has been a result of a broader spectrum of social change. The racial motivation theory, on the other hand, implies that persons who marry interracially often are countercultural and may be rebelling against social or family norms. Benson (1981) discovered that four of her respondents married a person of another race to rebel against their families; two of the four had parents who were reported to be extremely prejudiced and a third said she had an extremely racist ex-husband. None of the respondents in the Los Angeles sample reported any feelings of rebellion against their families or against society's norms concerning race.

Porterfield's (1978) results indicated that there was still rejection by twenty-six of the white families even after the couple had been married for a period of between one and four years. Black families were more receptive to their children's interracial marriages and most of those few families who initially opposed the marriage had gradually come to accept it.

The majority of the families in the Los Angeles sample stated that their families had accepted their marriages. While many black and white families initially disapproved of their children's interracial marriage, black families were somewhat more likely to have accepted the relationship from the beginning. Over time, though, any disapproval was often removed as families became acquainted with their sons-in-law and daughters-in-law and after the birth of grandchildren. Benson (1981) found this same pattern among the British respondents and argued that parents abandoned their antipathy toward their daughters-in-law and sons-in-law when they realized they might lose contact with their children and grandchildren.

In the Los Angeles population, seventeen of the black men reported that their families had accepted their marriages immediately, two had eventually accepted the marriage, and one had not accepted it by the time of the interview. Of the white respondents, six women reported that their families had accepted their marriages immediately, eleven that they had accepted it in time, and six that their families had

Black-White Marriages: Social Change
and Intergenerational Mobility *(cont'd.)*

not accepted their marriages to date. Three of the black women's families were reported to have accepted their marriages immediately, and two were said to have accepted them later. Four of the white men replied that their families accepted their black wives right away, one that they accepted her later. All in the white husband-black wife category reported that their families had accepted them as a married couple. Two white women described typical family responses:

> There were major problems with my father at first, but now he and my husband are good friends.

> Although I was introduced to him by my brother, my family was a bit uncomfortable with the interracial part. But when they met him and got to know him as a person they just thought the world of him.

Two black husbands commented:

> My mom loves her; my father loves her; my brothers are happy they have a sister.

> Although my mother accepted her, they were not behind us one hundred percent.

The respondents whose families accepted their interracial unions from the inception were typically families reported to have little racial prejudice. Some respondents, whose families disapproved of their interracial unions, were taken by surprise since they had assumed approval because their parents had previously expressed positive attitudes about interracial marriages. Other respondents said they had assumed their parents would approve of their marriages even though their parents had never voiced approval of such unions because their parents had never voiced disapproval of black and white couples. For example, one white woman's family advocated racial integration and had encouraged her to form friendships with people of other races since childhood but reacted negatively when she married a black man. Similarly, Benson (1981) reported that one young man's mother encouraged him to spend time with a black young woman from their church, but was quite distressed when her son chose to marry the woman.

Overall, these findings suggest that family disapproval did not discourage interracial mate selection for these couples. Twenty-three of the twenty-nine couples chose to marry despite initial opposition from one or both of their sets of parents. The fact that sixteen of the twenty-three who did not approve of the marriage initially came to accept the marriage in time supports the structural notion that desensitization to interracial marriages can occur. Of course, it is known that many racially homogamous marriages are not initially supported enthusiastically by the families of both the bride and groom; some come to be accepted in time, and some never do.

Black-White Marriages: Social Change and Intergenerational Mobility *(cont'd.)*

The results from the Los Angeles survey lend substantial support to the structural theory of increasing acceptance of interracial marriage. The picture painted by respondents illustrates that increased socioeconomic mobility of blacks in Los Angeles has provided greater opportunity for interracial contact leading to marriage through housing, schools, work and leisure activities. The increase in the number of interracial marriages has, in itself, helped to desensitize the population to such marriages. The fact that the spouses are of similar social class origins has undoubtedly influenced the degree of family acceptance and approval of racially different marital partners.

A minority of our respondents did reveal racial motivations for their marriages ranging from white's feelings of compassion for blacks to a heightened sexual attraction on the part of both races. Although support for the structural view is indicated more often, the racial motivations for interracial marriages must also be included in any analysis of interracial mate selection.

Those individuals who reported racial motivations for their marriages also reported that they met in integrated settings and indicated that they were highly similar to their mates. Perhaps structural and motivational theories work hand in hand. While the relative desegregation of workplaces, neighborhoods and schools give people of different racial backgrounds the chance to meet, fall in love, and marry, propinquity may also provide individuals who are especially attracted to people of a different race the opportunity to act upon their desires.

The two theories about the increasing number and increasing acceptance of interracial marriages that have been mentioned in this paper each have support, but neither alone seems sufficient to explain everything about such unions. Mate selection is a complex process (Lieberson & Waters, 1988) and it is clear that different people marry for different reasons. To speak of interracial marriages as though they were all alike assumes that all members of a race are alike, a patent fallacy.

Discussion

This small exploratory study is not intended to be generalized to all black/white interracial relationships in all regions in the country or in different parts of the world. Los Angeles, which is now purported to be the most cosmopolitan major city in the world, is not typical of most cities in the United States. Yet, when it comes to the partners' reasons for marrying an individual of another race, Los Angeles couples are markedly similar to Porterfield's (1978) respondents who resided in Ohio, Illinois, Mississippi, and Alabama. Benson's (1981) British findings are somewhat similar even though there is greater support for the theory of racial motivation than in the studies in the United States.

Results from Porterfield's study (1978) and those of the Los Angeles study were derived from qualitative intensive interviews and qualitative procedures and cannot be declared definitive. They do suggest that interracial couples residing in different parts of the United States are marrying for similar reasons. Moreover,

Black-White Marriages: Social Change and Intergenerational Mobility *(cont'd.)*

because the Los Angeles study was conducted approximately ten years after Porterfield's, it can be assumed that this trend has persisted for at least a decade.

Because of the multi-ethnic nature of Los Angeles, one might assume that interracial couples living in Los Angeles have had different experiences from their counterparts living in Illinois, Ohio, Alabama, and Mississippi. However, Tucker and Mitchell-Kernan (1990) found that black Los Angeles residents who married persons of another race were not usually native to the area. Instead, the majority of blacks who married a person of another race were either foreign-born or had migrated to California from the Northeastern and Northcentral parts of the United States. Tucker and Mitchell-Kernan indicated that blacks born in Los Angeles were no more likely to marry a person of another race than blacks born in the South. Tucker and Mitchell-Kernan argue that just because the environment in which interracial couples live is more tolerant toward such unions is not sufficient to explain interracial marriage. Couples must also have grown up in a racially permissive environment to overcome their own prejudices. Such persons often are motivated to move away from their community of birth for a variety of reasons; among the important reasons may be to find a more tolerant atmosphere. As a consequence, blacks who marry interracially are often removed from their kinship networks and consequently avoid much of the disapproval from their families.

Some of our Los Angeles respondents were born in different parts of the country and were unable to see their families on a regular basis. Many, however, were born in Southern California or had migrated with their families when they were children and continued to have close contact with their families. This is in no way meant to contradict the Tucker and Mitchell-Kerner findings since exact data on where couples in our sample were born or reared was not analyzed.

References

Benson, S. (1981). *Ambiguous Ethnicity: Interracial Families in London.* London: Cambridge University Press.

Berger, P. L., & Luckman, T. (1967). *The Social Construction of Reality.* Garden City, New York: Doubleday.

Farber, B. (1973). *Family and Kinship in Modern Society.* Glenview, Illinois: Scott Foresman.

Golden, J. (1953). Characteristics of Negro-White Intermarried In Philadelphia. *American Sociological Review* 18, 178-.

Grier, W., & Cobbs, P. (1968). *Black Rage.* New York: Basic Books.

Heer, D. (1974). The prevalence of black-white marriages in the United States. *Journal of Marriage and the Family.* 27, 262–273.

Klimek, D. (1979). *Beneath mate selection and marriage: The unconscious motives in human pairing.* New York: Van Nostrand Reinhold.

Kvaraceus, W. et al. (1969). *Negro Self-Concept: Implications for School and Citizenship.* New York: McGraw-Hill.

Lasswell, M., & Lasswell, T. (1991). *Marriage and The Family.* (3rd ed.) Belmont, California. Wadsworth, Inc.

Black-White Marriages: Social Change and Intergenerational Mobility *(cont'd.)*

Lieberson, S., & Waters, M. (1988). *From Many Strands: Ethnic and Racial Groups in Contemporary America.* New York: Russell Sage Foundation.

Merton, R. K. (1941). Intermarriage and the social structure: fact and theory. *Psychiatry* 4 (8) pp. 361–74.

Monroe, S. (1990). Love in black and white: the last racial taboo. *Los Angeles Times Magazine,* December 9, 1990.

Pavela, T. (1964). An Exploratory Study of Negro-White Intermarriage in Indiana. *Journal of Marriage and The Family.* 26, 209–211.

Porterfield. E. (1978). *Black and White Mixed Marriages: An Ethnographic Study.* New Jersey: Prentice-Hall, Inc.

Porterfield, E. (1982). Black-American intermarriage in the United States. *Marriage and Family Review.* 5, pp. 17–34.

Reinharz, S. (1991). *Social Research Methods: Feminist Perspectives.*

Rubin, L. B. (1976). *Worlds of Pain: Life in the working class family.* New York: Basic Books Inc.

Smith, C. (1966). Negro-White Intermarriage: Forbidden Sexual Union. *The Journal of Sex Research,* 2, 169–178.

Tucker, B., & Mitchell-Kernan, C. (1990). New trends in black American interracial marriage: The Social Structural Context. *Journal of Marriage and The Family.* 52, pp. 209–218.

U.S. Bureau of the Census (1985). *Census of the Population, 1989* (Vol. 2). Subject Reports: Marital Characteristics. Washington DC: Government Printing Office.

 ## Selling the Frontier Dream to the American Public: The Frontier West and Advertising

Jennifer Riffle

To survive as a business, it is an absolute necessity to advertise in our American capitalistic society of today. The purpose of business is getting the customer to buy a product or service, and although advertising cannot make a person buy a product, "it can make a person more ready to buy" (Baldwin 8). Advertising invades us every day of our lives in many different ways, such as the commercials on radio and television; in newspapers, magazines, and other publications; on billboards and buses; on computer bulletin boards; in classrooms and educational settings (Channel 1, the video jukebox); and even on the highly visible brand name splashed across some articles of clothing, shoes, and other products of the fashion world. To stand out in the highly competitive field of advertising, the business or corporation must create a commercial that catches the attention of the audience and places the brand name in their minds. Not only does the advertiser face the challenge of attracting new customers, he or she has the added dilemma of keeping the current ones. There are three very basic components to a good commercial. These are "1. Create a memorable

Selling the Frontier Dream to the American Public:
The Frontier West and Advertising *(cont'd.)*

impression for the consumer, making it both intriguing and familiar. 2. Communicate the intended message to the consumer, presenting it as simply and explicitly as necessary. 3. Stir the consumer's attitude, creating or reinforcing a positive image to associate with the product" (Baldwin 14–15). Businesses have struggled for years to develop the perfect advertising strategy. Following the guidelines for a good commercial, the advertisers have found that using Western themes catches the attention of the audience and induces a favorable reaction to products that may be related to the frontier West.

The American fascination with frontier history has existed from the times of the Westward expansion until the present day. The influence of the frontier west can be seen in many different segments of our society, including movies such as *Unforgiven* and *Wyatt Earp*, books by authors such as Larry McMurtry, and the work of many fashion designers. The form of media that most consistently uses the influence of the West is quite possibly the advertising world. From "a turn of the century Levi's catalog that shows men on horses roping cattle, with copy that says 'All over the west they wear Levi Strauss & Co. copper riveted overalls'" (Downey 274), to the modern-day Marlboro campaign and its internationally known spokesman, the Marlboro Man, the advertising industry has influenced us to buy products by connecting them to the cherished notion of Westward exploration and the glorified but often less than truthful image of "cowboys and Indians." The industry powers are well aware of the power that this imagery holds, and they use this power to their best possible advantage. In *The New Icons?* the author emphasizes the importance of advertising in our society, stating "we never forget that commercials have become icons for part of the American culture. The TV commercial has become our folklore" (Rutherford 3). This function of folklore is very evident in the portrayal of the cowboy in commercials.

Because "the cowboy could not be portrayed accurately and interestingly at the same time" (Savage 113), there is little relation between the modern-day concept of a cowboy and historical fact. The true cowboy, as opposed to the image portrayed in the movies and commercials, was looked down on by most of society in his time because of "his tacky appearance, his violent behavior, and his disregard for the peace and quiet of Sunday mornings, church socials, and family picnics" (Savage 110). For the most part, he led a solitary life caring for the cattle in his trust, usually without the beautiful women, wild gunfights, and the exciting life that so many fictional cowboys share. Also, every cowboy was not the very picture of rugged handsomeness and the personification of a real man. In fact, the rigors of cowboy life produced scruffy, often malnourished men who were not a picture of decent health and hygiene, much less of romance and physical perfection. A fact often not considered in the modern representation of cowboys is the reality that cowboys were men of many different races, including Blacks and Hispanics. To be hired as a cowboy, a man didn't need much in the way of formal education or skills. He just had to be willing to work for a few dollars a month. This greatly contrasts with the

Selling the Frontier Dream to the American Public:
The Frontier West and Advertising *(cont'd.)*

modern cowboy hero who is skilled, inventive, and articulate. Possibly the most exaggerated fact about the modern cowboy is that he was satisfied with the cowboy life and chose it willingly. Because the economic conditions in our country at that time were hard, the sons of many small farmers took up the occupation out of desperation. Others looked to the life on the range as an adventure, but most only found a hard job with few dramatic occurrences.

One of the first acts of commercialization dealing with the cowboy was a prominent romanticizing effort by William F. Cody. In 1884, searching for a new attraction to add to his Wild West Show, he introduced William (Buck) Levi Taylor to his audience, selling his attributes which included family history, size, physical strength, remarkable dexterity, and genial qualities (Savage 111). After Taylor became a hit attraction, he became a feature of the dime novel. The relatively small scale of this first effort to capitalize on the cowboy image had a large influence on the enormous presence of the cowboy in advertising today. As the cowboy became popular in radio, movies, and television, he was used to endorse many products that did not exist in the frontier West, such as wristwatches, pocket watches, alarm clocks, cough drops, headache remedies, pickup trucks, oil filters, shock absorbers, and even United States Savings Bonds (Savage 114–17). His image as well as the testimony of popular characters was used as an authority on nutrition and good health when personalities such as Tom Mix, Roy Rogers, Sky King, Red Ryder, Hopalong Cassidy, and Buck Jones promoted items for Ralston Purina, Quaker Oats, Peter Pan, General Mills, and Grape-Nuts. In more recent years, cowboy imagery has been used to sell a diversity of non-frontier-related items, including Frito-Lay Barbecue-flavor Chips, Philips 66 Motor Oil, Toyota Trucks, and Miller Beer, as well as bath soap, cigars, juice, razors, snuff, barbecue sauce, flashlight batteries, and laundry detergent (Savage 119).

As a research tool for this report, I have collected several different ads from recent magazines that display a dominant western theme. A majority of these are for Marlboro cigarettes. In the 1950s, Philip Morris ranked fifth out of the six large tobacco companies, and the Marlboro brand was a cigarette marketed primarily to women. Attempting to rescue the company from this poor ranking, Philip Morris went to the Leo Burnett advertising agency for a campaign that would target men as the new consumers of Marlboros. The first version of the new campaign featured a cowboy along with other stereotypically male characters, "usually sporting a tattoo, which suggested an air of mystery and intrigue, and an interesting past" (Baldwin 39). Influencing Philip Morris sales to jump 13 billion in two years, the campaign was a success, and market research revealed that people especially liked the cowboy in the Marlboro ads. Deciding to make cowboys the exclusive focus of the new ads, Burnett filled the commercials with strong imagery, theme music from *Magnificent 7*, and slogans emphasizing the Marlboro's flavor such as "A man's world of flavor," "You get a lot to like," "The flavor that won the west," and "Flavor you can get hold of" (Baldwin 40). Some of the very early commercials depict an

Selling the Frontier Dream to the American Public:
The Frontier West and Advertising *(cont'd.)*

"urban cowboy" lighting up a cigarette and being instantly transported to Marlboro Country. This mystical Marlboro Country is the focus of the ads, a place where the cowboy's West exists forever, and every man is a cowboy.

Other commercials explained the origins of the mysterious Marlboro Man, and how he'd ridden out of Richmond in some past time to leave "his brand throughout the country" (Baldwin 40). Over the years, the ads stressed some degree of authenticity, even going so far as to use an operating ranch as the background and true cowboys instead of actors. There was also a great push to show actual details as far as riding, roping, and driving the cattle was concerned. The actors were told to "act natural, in particular to smoke only when that seemed appropriate" (Baldwin 40). Although the dominant slogan in most of the ads is "Come to Marlboro Country," a few of the other slogans used in the Marlboro campaign were "This is my country. It's big, open, makes a man feel ten feet tall"; "The simple things mean a lot out here: a dry blanket, hot cup of coffee, a good smoke—Marlboro"; and "Wherever you go, that's Marlboro Country" (Baldwin 41). This image of Marlboro Country was meant to be compared to the pressures and problems of everyday life, and with that comparison Marlboro Country seemed much better than reality, especially to urban consumers. The best summary of the motivation behind the Marlboro campaign can be found in this excerpt from *The Cowboy Hero:*

> The Marlboro Man had plenty to do, looking after horses and cattle, riding through deep snow, and so forth. Regardless of the activity, he would need a smoke, of course, and while he puffed and looked rugged, the audience would be encouraged to "come to Marlboro Country," where the flavor was. The Marlboro Man himself never said a word, but the complex message was clear. You came to Marlboro Country by smoking Marlboros, and since the trip took place in your head anyway, while you were at it you might as well pretend you were a cowboy. When the last television commercial ran in September, 1970, the narrator could state with some certainty, "Today the West is everywhere." (Savage 113)

Of the fourteen ads and promotions that I examined for this report, six of them are for Marlboro cigarettes. In the first ad is a man wearing a leather vest, cowboy hat, gloves, and chaps. Against the backdrop of a barely visible fence, he is carrying a saddle and rope, and is, of course, smoking a cigarette. The copy reads "Come to Marlboro Country." The second ad shows an extreme close-up of a man wearing cowboy boots and spurs, blue jeans, and chaps, the only visible part being his legs. The copy is promoting the new Medium 100"s and reads "A special place in Marlboro Country. The low tar cigarette that's long on flavor." In the third ad is a picture of five men dressed in jeans, chaps, boots, spurs, work shirts, vests, and cowboy hats climbing over a wooden fenced in an area that holds a bull. The copy reads "Most times, cowboys don't like fences." The fourth ad shows a cowboy riding his

Selling the Frontier Dream to the American Public:
The Frontier West and Advertising *(cont'd.)*

horse down a sand dune in an obviously western area. The message of the Marlboro Man has become so familiar that the man isn't even shown smoking in this ad. Just as in the first ad I examined, the copy reads "Come to Marlboro Country."

My fifth subject of examination is a promotional offer by Marlboro. For a limited amount of time, there are five "country store miles" printed on each package of cigarettes. By accumulating a specified number of miles, the consumer can receive various items. The copy throughout the eighteen-item catalogue is abundant with western-terms, but the first page is a good example of the frontier and cowboy imagery used throughout the whole catalogue. It says:

> Marlboro Country. Mile after mile, it stretches out. Great. Wide. And open. Taking on a land this big takes a special kind of gear. From jackets to shirts, hats to bags. All of it, built tough enough for a working day. And good enough for a night on the town. So have a look around the Marlboro Country Store. And get the gear made for the great wide open.

The sixth piece I examined is a sweepstakes promotion, also linked to the Country Store promotion. When the consumer enters, he is certifying that he is a smoker at least twenty-one years old, and he has the chance of winning twenty-one different prizes, including a mechanical bull, a registered quarter horse, and a cowboy bunkhouse. The first page of copy reads "Win the best Marlboro Country has to offer." Even though the true relationship between cowboys, smoking, and the frontier is severely stretched, cigarettes and smoking did exist on the frontier. This makes the Marlboro campaign credible, if not entirely accurate.

The seventh piece, an advertisement, is for the Wrangler brand. It has George Strait acting as a spokesman, wearing a cowboy hat and western-style belt buckle and holding a guitar. The copy mentions "cowboys" and "the West" several times, and the articles of clothing advertised are the Cowboy Cut jeans and a Gold Buckle shirt. In fact, the logo for the Wrangler Company is its name written out in twisted rope, stamped on a leather tag. Underneath the logo, the ad says "The Western Original." The ad is making the highly questionable connection between country music and cowboys. Although George Strait may take inspiration from cowboys, he earns his living singing, not herding cattle. The eighth piece is an ad for Skoal, which pictures two men standing on an otherwise empty stage wearing cowboy boots, jeans, belts with western-style buckles, and cowboy hats. This is set off against a mountain backdrop at sunset. Although the copy doesn't say anything about "cowboys" or "the West," the imagery is clear without words. Again, this ad is making a connection between country music and cowboys. The ninth piece is an ad for Chuck Wagon dog food. The particular flavor is called "Stampede." The ad shows two dogs chasing after a man driving a frontier-style chuck wagon that is pulled by a horse. With the proof of purchase from a bag of this dog food, the consumer has the chance receive a free country music cassette in the mail.

Selling the Frontier Dream to the American Public:
The Frontier West and Advertising *(cont'd.)*

The tenth piece, an ad for Roper Shoes, contains the image of a young woman dressed in a cowboy hat, plaid work shirt, jeans and the advertised shoes, squatting by an outdoor fire at dusk, with another figure standing nearby carrying a rope and wearing jeans and the same shoes. The name of the style of shoe is HorseShoes. The copy reads "There's a new footprint on the American West. HorseShoes by Roper are designed for the active Western lifestyle with the comfort and versatility to work, play or ride the range." This ad is particularly absurd, because despite the obvious use of cowboy imagery, the shoes themselves are not a western style at all. The eleventh piece I examined is a sweepstakes offer from A & W Rootbeer. In the picture is a man drinking a root beer standing by a country store that is made of wood and has a tin roof. The man is wearing cowboy boots, jeans, a work shirt, and a cowboy hat. The prizes for the sweepstakes are a pickup truck and tickets to the Academy of Country Music Awards. The influence behind this ad may have been the fact that it appeared in Country America magazine, because the ideas of soda pop and the frontier West are not often combined.

The twelfth piece is a special promotional collector's item beer stein by the Coors Company. It salutes the American rodeo with a painting of a cowboy riding a bucking horse, images of rope trimming and bull horn decoration, and a statuette of another cowboy riding a bucking horse topping the stein. Of course, the brand name *Coors* is also written several times on the stein, qualifying it as a promotion. The thirteenth piece is an ad for Lady Stetson. It pictures a woman in jeans, a white shirt, and a leather jacket, holding a cowboy hat. The copy reads "The spirit of the west. The power of a woman. The fragrance that captures it all. Lady Stetson—It's how the west was won." Despite the fact that women did not work as cowboys on the frontier, the very idea of linking a perfume and cowboy life is a contradiction. The cowboy life did not concern itself greatly with simple personal hygiene, let alone the luxury of perfumes and colognes.

The fourteenth and final piece I examined is a brochure from the U.S. Postal Service; its purpose is to advertise a new commemorative line of stamps featuring legends of the West such as Buffalo Bill, Jim Bridge, Annie Oakley, Chief Joseph, Bill Pickett, John Fremont, Wyatt Earp, Geronimo, Kit Carson, Wild Bill Hickok, and Sacagawea. In addition to the stamps, the Postal Service is also offering a commemorative album, an exclusive uncut sheet, first day program, and postal card set. The order form states "Round 'em up now—before they're history," and the title of the brochure is "The Legends Ride Again." Although I do not question the sincerity of the tribute, there is strong emotional wording connected to the promotional merchandise that is purely for profit. These fourteen examples are a mere sample of the many print ads that use the ideas and myths of the Western frontier to sell products, relying on the emotional response of the consumer to persuade them to buy that product. Hundreds of similar ads exist, in all of the different forms of media used by advertisers today.

Selling the Frontier Dream to the American Public: The Frontier West and Advertising *(cont'd.)*

Because of the obvious success of the Marlboro campaign and others similar to it, advertisers will probably continue to exploit America's fascination with its frontier heritage. Specifically trained to find ways to draw an emotional response from their audience, the advertisers construct relationships between products and the West that would become ludicrous if they were given some thought by the consumers who receive the ads. If glamorizing a period in history and using it to make money for modern-day businesses seems like an insult to the lives of the people who lived in the frontier West, it is the responsibility of viewers to be educated enough to realize that the image they are receiving is not accurate; they should not be swayed to purchase something by the imagery they see, because as soon as an advertising strategy becomes ineffective, it will be abandoned. However, it is possible that through keeping the tradition of the frontier West in the minds of the people, no matter how distorted, that fascinating time will not become just another event in the history books.

Works Cited

A & W advertisement. A & W Rootbeer Co. 1994.

Baldwin, Huntley. *Creating Effective TV Commericals.* Chicago: Crain, 1982.

Chuck Wagon advertisement. Ralston Purina Company. 1994.

Coors advertisement. Coors Brewing Company. 1994.

Downey, Lynn. "Levi Strauss Invented Western Work Clothes for Miners, Cowboys, and Engineers." *The American Frontier.* Ed. Bruno Leone et al. San Diego: Greenhaven Press, 1994.

Lady Stetson advertisement. Coty Inc. 1994.

Marlboro advertisment. Philip Morris Inc. 1989.

Marlboro advertisment. Philip Morris Inc. 1992.

Marlboro advertisment. Philip Morris Inc. 1994.

Marlboro advertisment. Philip Morris Inc. 1994.

Marlboro Country Store. Philip Morris Inc. 1994.

Marlboro Sweepstakes. Philip Morris Inc. 1994.

Roper advertisement. HorseShoes by Roper. 1994.

Savage, William W. *The Cowboy Hero: His Image in American History & Culture.* Oklahoma City: U of Oklahoma P, 1979.

Skoal advertisement. U.S. Tobacco Co. 1994.

U.S. Postal Service pamphlet. 1994.

Wrangler advertisement. Wrangler Co. 1993.

Bibliography

Baldwin, Huntley. *Creating Effective TV Commericals.* Chicago: Crain, 1982.

Chapman, Simon. *Great Expectorations: Advertising and the Tobacco Industry.* London: Comedia, 1986.

Churchill, Ward. *Fantasies of the Master Race: Literature, Cinema and the Colonization of American Indians.* Monroe, ME: Common Courage, 1992.

Selling the Frontier Dream to the American Public:
The Frontier West and Advertising *(cont'd.)*

Downey, Lynn. "Levi Strauss Invented Western Work Clothes for Miners, Cowboys, and Engineers." *The American Frontier.* Ed. Bruno Leone et al. San Diego: Greenhaven Press, 1994.

Johnson, Douglas J. *Advertising Today.* Chicago: SRA, 1978.

Rutherford, Paul. *The New Icons? The Art of Television Advertising.* Toronto: U of Toronto P, 1994.

Savage, William W. *The Cowboy Hero: His Image in American History & Culture.* Oklahoma City: U of Oklahoma P, 1979.

Taylor, William B. and Franklin Pease, Ed. *Violence, Resistance, and Survival in the Americas.* Washington: Smithsonian Institute, 1994.

White, Barton C. *The New Ad Media Reality: Electronic over Print.* Westport, CT: Quorum, 1993.

HELPING READERS GET THE MOST OUT OF TEXTS: THE EDITED COLLECTION

Although a college education can prepare an individual for a particular career, such as accounting, most educators assume that an undergraduate degree also provides graduates with skills that they will use in many different contexts, not just on the job. Of course, reading is one such skill. The ability to understand, assimilate, and use ideas and information from a piece of writing is absolutely vital, and not just for success in class. We live in a society in which written works contain just about everything from information about insurance coverage or advice about how to repair a roof to ideas about what constitutes morality and ethics.

Still, as important as most people acknowledge reading to be, we know that adult readers possess different levels of skill. We also know that many texts challenge even the most skilled readers because of complex ideas or information or because of a style or format that is difficult to penetrate. For this reason, many readers frequently rely on writing that explains or provides pathways through other pieces of writing. As a student, you have already encountered a great deal of discourse of this nature. Think, for example, of the literature textbook that you used in your high school or college English class. We imagine that such a textbook would have contained selections of fiction, poetry, and drama accompanied by readings to help you understand and enjoy these selections. Or recall a textbook from a consumer education class; such a text might have contained a section on how to read warranty agreements with reproductions of several different agreements, each accompanied by an explanation or analysis of its contents and form.

Up to now, you have probably been a reader of texts that reproduce and explain other texts, but not a writer of them. Perhaps, therefore, you might like to switch roles. Can you envision publishing a collection of poems, stories, or essays, accompanied by your own insightful commentary on them? Are there poets, short-story writers, film reviewers, or essayists within your writing class or in your residence hall or in your community whose work deserves to be published with explanations, discussions, and critiques? Is there an issue or current event about which a great deal of commentary has been published? It might be interesting to gather a selection of essays that offer a variety of perspectives on a particular topic (say, global warming or a recent presidential election) and to explain and evaluate these.

If you are interested in publishing a collection of works (essays, profiles, recipes, stories, poems, personal reflections, descriptions, etc.), your project will require you and members of your group to engage in several activities. First, of course, you will need to agree on the types of texts you want to include in your collection.

SELECTING THE TYPE OF WORKS
FOR YOUR COLLECTION

We cannot recommend the type of collection your group should produce, but we think that shared interests and expertise as well as group members' familiarity with other collections should be important determinants. For example, if more than half of the members of your group write poetry and short stories or if many members are avid readers of such works, you might seriously consider producing a critical edition of poetry and fiction—containing either works by your favorite "established" writers or works by students or friends. Another advantage of this option is that most group members are likely to be familiar with this kind of collection. Certainly, there are many such works that could be used as models for your finished product.

On the other hand, if every person in your group is addicted to daytime soap operas or science fiction films, you might consider gathering, organizing and commenting on essays that have been written about either of these topics. Then again, members of your group may be interested in what it was like to have attended college earlier in this century. Under these circumstances, all of you might decide that it might be fun to compile a collection of materials (essays, photographs, excerpts from student journals, portions of residence hall behavior codes, student newspaper articles, photographs, etc.) that depict student life from a particular decade or era (the Roaring Twenties or the depression years) and write commentary to accompany and explain the selections you've chosen.

 **Activity 1**

Brainstorm a list of possible collections you might like to produce. Then select your favorite and freewrite about it for a few minutes. Afterwards, write out the answers to these questions: Why does this collection appeal to you? Would you prefer to collect works with which you are already familiar or ones that are new to you? Explain your preference. Do you think that other people in this class would be interested in your collection? Explain why or why not. Describe the audiences that would find your collection interesting, instructive, entertaining, or useful. Share your freewriting with your group partners.

Activity 2

Together with other members of your group, rank preferences for collections. What type of collection is the group's top choice? Is there a close second? If group members cannot agree on the type of collection to produce, we recommend that you explore together the possibility of consolidating two types of collections into one through the use of a unifying theme. (For example, reviews of films that depict the values and habits of young adults and articles that provide actual information about this same age group could be published together, with accompanying commentary, in a volume entitled "Images of Generation X: Fact and Fiction.")

Once your group agrees about the type of collection members wish to produce, everyone should read the rest of this section carefully before proceeding with the project. Of course, if a consensus does not emerge or if the group cannot combine or consolidate the types of works to be collected, we recommend that other projects be considered.

After selecting the type of text that you will collect and comment on, your group will need to engage in several activities. At the very least, you and your partners will need to do the following:

1. Devise a procedure for gathering, selecting, and arranging works you want to include.

2. Decide what kinds of commentary (and other materials, such as diagrams, glossaries, and illustrations) to provide and where to provide them.

3. Determine a procedure for writing, revising, editing, and producing your project.

GATHERING, CHOOSING, AND ARRANGING YOUR SELECTIONS: THE ORGANIZING THEME

Once your group has determined the types of texts to be collected and commented on, the first challenge you will face is how to gather possible candidates for inclusion. Whether you have decided to produce a collection of poems and short stories, essays about attending college, reviews of films or television shows, analyses of current events or contemporary issues, you will want to gather a wide variety of texts from a number of sources so that you will have many options.

Local libraries and your college or university library are good sources from which to gather pieces of writing for your collection. Trade magazines, professional journals, and other edited collections may contain the types of writing you are seeking. As always, your library's reference librarians can give you ideas about the sources you will find most useful. In addition, you may find it useful to review the discussions within Chapter 9 of different types of library sources and how to locate these.

If you are collecting works that are likely to be possessed or produced by individuals (poetry, fiction, letters, excerpts from journals or diaries), your group will need to decide where people should be approached (residence halls? church gatherings? social gatherings? family gatherings?) as well as the best means for approaching them. Time permitting, it might be interesting to put a few ads in your school or hometown paper soliciting the types of works you will be collecting—if this isn't too costly. Alternatively, your group might decide to duplicate some announcements and place these in strategic places such as residence hall, church, social, or classroom bulletin boards.

 **Activity 3**

> With other members of your group, brainstorm locations (libraries, residence halls, etc.) and sources (books, journals, other students, etc.) that are likely to include or possess the types of texts you will include in your collection. Then together decide how you will manage the task of assessing these sources. Here are some questions you might consider: Should individual members consult selected sources and report the results of their findings so that the group can reassess its list of sources and locations? Should group members work individually, in pairs, or in different configurations to assess sources?

At some point, either before or after you start gathering works, you will need to determine a theme or focus for your collection. *When* you begin to determine a focus will depend, in part, on the number of works that are potentially available to be included in your collection. If your group has decided to produce an edited collection of film reviews or short stories by established writers, the possibilities for inclusion will run into the hundreds—or thousands; you may, therefore, need to create a theme or focus *before* you begin gathering possibilities so that you and others in your group will not be overwhelmed during the selection process.

On the other hand, the works you have decided to collect may be scarce or difficult to obtain, in which case limiting selections to conform to a pre-chosen focus or organizing principle may cause difficulty. For example, suppose your group has decided to produce a collection of family recipes that represent a particular ethnic group, accompanied by discussions of how and why these recipes are culturally significant or commentary about their historical development. It may be premature to decide on a thematic focus for your collection until *after* you assess the range of recipes you have acquired as well as the nature and scope of appropriate commentary that you can locate in your school library or in other local sources.

In any case, whether your group decides on a focus or organizing principle for your collection before, during, or after you begin gathering works, such a focus will be essential in helping you to select and organize the texts you want to include. Let us suppose, for example, that you and your partners decide to produce a collection of student-written poetry and prose and that the group has gathered fifty pieces, thirty-five of which are of good quality. How will you select what to include? If more than twenty works will produce a collection that is too long, how can fifteen selections be eliminated? If all thirty-five works can be included, how should they be arranged? An organizing theme or focus such as "Leaving Home for the First Time" might facilitate selection and suggest possible chapter headings (**Missing Family and Friends, The Exhilaration of Freedom, Loneliness,** etc.)

Activity 4

Before you begin collecting texts for possible inclusion in your collection, discuss as a group whether you should decide on a focus or organizing principle *before* or *after* you begin the gathering process. Here are some factors your group should consider before making a decision:

- Do you anticipate that there will be many sources for possible works to include?

- How accessible will these sources be?

- Will there be a good number of works from which to choose or a wide range of possibilities?

- Should the group send out one or two "scouts" to do a preliminary check on the plentifulness and availability of sources or works?

- If there are many possible texts that might be included in your collection, what are the advantages of coming up with a focus before group members start gathering samples? What are the disadvantages?

- Would it be useful to come up with a one or two preliminary focuses that could be revised as the project progresses?

 Activity 5

Examine the following list of collections and brainstorm *an organizing principle* and *four* possible chapter headings or subtopics (related to each organizing principle).

Example: a collection of essays written by college women

> *Organizing principle:* Why women attend college: dreams and aspirations

> *Possible chapter headings:* (1) **Career Plans,** (2) **Acquiring Skills for Life-Long Learning,** (3) **Building Confidence,** (4) **Expanding Horizons**

1. A collection of essays/commentaries about a recent election

2. A collection of film reviews

3. A collection of articles and essays about the censorship of contemporary music or music videos

4. A collection of student-authored poems, short fiction, and essays

⚛ Activity 6

> With your group, brainstorm possible organizing principles for your collection. Discuss which ones seem to be the most viable. Can any closely related focuses be combined into one organizing principle? Select and articulate an organizing principle. Try to put this principle in writing.

Group Writing Assignment: Prepare a brief two-page report of your progress; this report should be handed in to your instructor. In your report, be sure to respond to each of the following prompts. (1) Describe in detail the nature of the works that you will include in your collection. (2) Describe the audience to whom your collection is addressed, and explain why readers will find the collection to be informative, entertaining, interesting, provocative, useful, and so forth. (3) Describe the principle or focus around which the works in your collection will be organized. (4) List possible sections (parts? chapters?) for your collection, and provide a brief explanation for each.

CHOOSING THE NATURE AND SCOPE OF YOUR COMMENTARY

Once you have selected a tentative focus for your collection and chosen a group of items for possible inclusion, you need to start to plan the nature and scope of the commentary you will include. However, before you begin this process, you need to assess carefully the texts you have gathered so that you can make your final selections. As you might imagine, whether you have gathered fiction, poetry, critical essays, or other types of texts (recipes, journal entries, commentary, etc.), you need to be sure that you have included a set of writings that are uniform in quality. Moreover, depending on your intention, you may also wish create a set of readings that presents a balanced, comprehensive point of view on a particular issue or event. To help you assess and select your readings for final inclusion, you will need to read them carefully, taking notes where necessary. A review of Chapter 6 should help you with the process of critical reading and evaluating.

Having a clear sense of the range of pieces for your edited collection should guide you in determining what sort of commentary to include. In addition, examining some published models for ideas about form and content is also a good idea. You and other members of your group undoubtedly own or have access to several different edited collections. For example, if some of you are taking introductory history, psychology, or sociology courses, one or more of the textbooks you are using for these classes may be a collection of essays with accompanying commentary. Others in your group may own edited collections of literature or cookbooks that contain recipes accompanied with or preceded by explanations, notes, or personal anecdotes. Before you decide what commentary to include in your own work, then, we recommend that you and your partners examine a few edited collections so that you can familiarize yourselves with some of the options available.

As we have suggested, besides the works that you have gathered, your project should contain materials that you and your group partners have designed and written. These might include (1) a general introduction, (2) brief essays preceding each chapter, (3) notes, anecdotes, or discussions about each work, and (4) other materials such as glossaries, illustrations, diagrams, questions, cartoons, bibliographies, and the like.

Including a General Introduction. If you examine several edited collections you will find that they almost always contain introductions. Introductions are important because they explain the general nature of the collection, provide basic information about the works in the collection and any concept that is related to them, and set forth the purpose of the collection as well as who might find it useful or interesting. As you might imagine, introductory essays usually involve the process of *synthesis;* therefore, in preparing to write an introductory piece, it would be wise to review Chapter 8.

Sometimes collections are introduced by very friendly, informal essays that tell readers quite a bit about the likes and dislikes of the editors as well as about the items within the collections; often, however, introductions focus their attention entirely on the works being collected and provide very little information about the editors. Depending on a number of factors, introductory essays can be brief, perhaps five hundred words (two typewritten or word-processed pages), or they can be lengthy, running up to twenty or thirty pages, if the authors wish to provide extensive information about the history of the collection, how it was gathered, or how items in the collections are received by the public.

Here is an example of an introduction from a collection entitled *Science Fiction: A Historical Anthology* edited by Eric Rabkin. The introductory essay, which is addressed to a general audience, attempts to define *science fiction* as well as trace its historical development.

 ## Introduction from *Science Fiction: A Historical Anthology**

Welcome to the world of science fiction!

> *The last man on Earth sat alone in a room.*
> *There was a knock on the door. . . .*

What had happened? Had there been a nuclear holocaust? An interplanetary war? A terrible man-made plague? What would happen? Would there enter the first of a race of horrible mutants? A conquering Martian? The last woman? Perhaps a forlorn wind is merely swinging a torn tree limb against the door. This tiny story,

*From *Science Fiction: A Historical Anthology* by Eric S. Rabkin. Copyright ©1983 by Oxford University Press, Inc. Reprinted by permission.

Introduction from *Science Fiction: A Historical Anthology* (cont'd.)

usually attributed to Frederic Brown, exemplifies much of what characterizes science fiction. The story concerns alienation, whether through the presence of an alien or the simple isolation of the the human: humanity made strange in the world or the world made strange for humanity. The story is fantastic, reversing rules to gain attention: the last man on Earth should, at first thought, be in a situation that prohibits a knock on the door—but the knock comes nonetheless. The story calls up a background of science, quite different from the tone one would hear in a story that concerned simply "the last man . . . in a room" and quite full of inventive possibilities. And the story functions in extremes to indulge what Sam Moskowitz calls "a sense of wonder": this is not the next-to-last man in a life raft but the last representative of our race. Science fiction is a world of exaggerated drama.

On our Earth, overloaded by change and inundated by violence, drama often needs to be exaggerated to be felt at all. On a spinning globe smoldering with ambiguous conflicts between countries we once ignored, the clear good-and-evil battle for possession of a galaxy has made *Star Wars* the most financially successful film of all times. In cities terrorized by crime we see foreshadowing of *A Clockwork Orange*. At night, troubled by visions of biotechnology and industrialization gone beyond our comprehension, we grow fears that are given shape as *The Andromeda Strain* and long for the good green safety of *Silent Running*. With so many machines let loose around us, even if no real monsters rise from Tokyo Bay, our "brave new world" seems ever more fearful, and the ancient wish for a Garden of Eden innocence becomes a poignant nostalgia for a time before we knew so much. Science fiction is sometimes exuberant about the young strength of new knowledge—the flash of light sabers delights us—but it is also fearful of the way the human mind has apparently set the world out of control. We want a simpler world. Light sabers, after all, are still sabers, the understandable weapons of lusty Vikings and handsome princes; the fairy tale needs to go on.

Science fiction is everywhere in our dangerous world. All forms of art have their science fiction branches; motorized statuary, light show rock-and-roll, the impossible drawings of M. C. Escher. The alienation we all too often feel takes shape as the misunderstood monster (*Frankenstein*) or the outcast genius (*Altered States*) while the hopes we yet cherish continue to promise a transformation of humanity into something better than itself (*Close Encounters*). While once we prayed for miracles to save us from disaster, now we pray for "miracle cures" to save us from industrial cancers. We live at the very edge of a gleaming new future, but the year is 1984.

The literature of all this ferment is vast and diverse, associating in one section of the bookstore gloriously self-indulgent mass gratifications with thoughtful and difficult social commentaries, vigorous tales of adventure with quiet ruminations on the difficulties of defining oneself in the world. The names of the subspecies include Sword-and-Sorcery, alternate time streams, utopian and dystopian literature, speculative fiction, lyric romance, and doomsday fiction. The novels and short stories offer power fantasies, mystic experience, intellectual challenge, and always excitement. This wealth seems almost beyond definition.

Introduction from *Science Fiction: A Historical Anthology* (cont'd.)

The easy—and perhaps appropriate—way to define science fiction is to approach it through sociology. Science fiction is what sells under the name of science fiction, and the needs it serves are those of its audience, a group for a time composed of almost all broadly literate readers. When Poe and Hawthorne wrote works we would now call science fiction, they spoke to widely sensed fears as do Pynchon and Calvino today. A more narrowly defined market study would force us to attend especially to the enormously successful Verne and Wells and then to mass culture giants such as Edgar Rice Burroughs and "Doc" Smith. The reintegration of the mass culture with the elite culture is a phenomenon of our times, dominated as they are by art produced through expensive technology but made affordable by inexpensive duplication (films, records, comic books). Science fiction is now gathered in one place in the bookstore, but may also be scattered through the sections for general fiction, children's literature, poetry, reference, and even religion and self-help. It turns up on calendars and T-shirts and instructions for programming your home computer to run "Space Invaders."

Perhaps no single definition could do justice to this extraordinary wealth of production. Speaking primarily of its literary branches, different critics have attempted nonetheless to trace some order in this universe. Brian Aldiss has written of science as a variety of Gothic romance; this definition is useful if we wish to emphasize the literary heritage and typical moods of much of science fiction. Darko Suvin calls science fiction the literature of "cognitive estrangement"; this definition is useful if we wish to emphasize the intellectual devices of much science fiction. My definition of science fiction as the branch of fantastic literature that takes scientific knowledge as its background is useful if we wish to emphasize the literary techniques and reader responses associated with much science fiction. While no single definition seems to have been fully satisfactory for all discussions, all definitions rely on the recognition that the worlds of science fiction are, often aggressively, not our world and yet, often quite subtly, the worlds of our inner doubts and wishes.

A purist definition that once seemed appealing held that the ideal work of science fiction made one and only one assumption, preferably based on an unlikely but not absolutely impossible scientific notion, and "extrapolated" a narrative world from that, keeping all other rules of our world otherwise unchanged. Although no extended work ever fulfilled that definition, Wells's novels came close. *The Time Machine* (1895) postulates the vehicle of its title, but the projected futures it reveals are based on ideas about human nature and society widely held at the time of writing. Yet even in a classic short story like "The Star," Wells himself not only postulated a radical new astronomical event but, in the last paragraph, adds the postulation of a non-human race. As the progress of science has itself demonstrated, once one decides to start inventing, it is very difficult—if not impossible—to stop. Sometimes the unlikely assumption that characterizes science fiction, then, may be of the "Star Trek" kind; assuming a spaceship that can go absolutely anywhere, you can always decree a new planet that has anything you can think of. So much for careful extrapolation.

Introduction from *Science Fiction: A Historical Anthology* *(cont'd.)*

The assumptions made by science fiction are usually those that do induce "wonder," or at least supply us with drama so exaggerated that the symbolic power of the tales is assured: Frankenstein's demon walks through our culture and Superman flies above it. Because the symbols of science fiction are so palpable they sometimes seem unsubtle; delicacy of characterization does sometimes fade in this strong light. Science fiction has often been criticized as a literature more concerned about "ideas" than about "characters"—as if that were an obvious fault! Science fiction *is* often about ideas, just as science is about knowing and the quest for knowing. The quest for knowing is the theme of much of our literature, a fundamental aspect of the tale of the Fall, of the myth of Prometheus, of the versions of Faust, and of all narratives of initiation and coming of age. Who would complain that the character of Prometheus is not drawn in the manner of the psychological realist or that we have no hints of Faust's toilet training? In fact, many science fictions do deal with subtly defined characters, but the special hallmark of the field is that the characters live in dramas that speak to our whole culture or to whole aspects of the human condition, rather than to the particularities of a brief cultural moment intersecting a person at a fleeting stage of life. While so-called mainstream fiction is set in its own here-and-now, science fiction is removed into the there-and-then, the distant land or planet or galaxy, the future or past or sidewhen. Because such removal inevitably affords contrast, exaggerated contrast, with our own world, science fiction becomes a literature not only of wonder, but of commentary, not perhaps of character analysis, but of serious inquiry. What does it mean to suppose a government overwhelmingly more powerful that the citizenry? How can the act of invention change a person? Does the world look the same through the eyes of another? Science fictions may help readers explore their world, their society, their life, their vocation—these are among the highest uses of art.

Just as no single definition can satisfactorily confine and describe science fiction in the abstract, no modest anthology could exemplify science fiction in its fullness. Nonetheless, it is possible to present some of the best of science fiction, some of its enormous variety, and suggest some of the ways in which the field has developed. Especially with that last aim in mind, this collection is organized historically.

In Part 1, we see science fiction emerging as a vehicle for satire, a literature constructed to highlight by contrast the foibles of the world of its readers and writers. Science fiction is particularly well suited to such contrasts because it simply postulates the most dramatic alternative worlds one might wish, and beginning in the seventeenth century science itself made such postulation seem worth considering. By the nineteenth century, as we see in Part 2, the workings of science were already becoming problematic, calling human nature into question and suggesting how it might be improved or, more frequently, revealed as beyond redemption. In the beginning of the twentieth century, well into the Industrial Revolution, science was remaking the world in surprising, sometimes hopeful, but often frightening, ways. The stories in Part 3 show fiction concerned with these developments, aiming to help us outgrow our past selves and warning against our insignificance and pride.

Introduction from *Science Fiction: A Historical Anthology* *(cont'd.)*

Despite the technological successes coincident with and growing from the effort of World War II, the wide reading public became more scared by the bomb than delighted by penicillin. Besides, fiction need not help us learn to live with penicillin; something was clearly needed to help us live with the bomb. In Part 4, we see some visions of science trying, and usually failing, to create a better world. In the expansive post–World War II period, such pessimism was a minority view in mass literature and science fiction was a ghetto literature read by a small group of fans who often shared qualities of hope and timidity and alienation. This readership had grown out of the pulp readership of the earlier part of the century but was more literate and not nearly so massive as had been the audience for Burroughs or as was the audience for detective stories or Westerns, and certainly not so representative of the society at large as had been the audience of Wells or as would be the audience of Vonnegut. But by the modern period, when the world itself had in some sense become the world of science fiction, the literature of science fiction began again to speak to everyone. In Part 5, we see stories that clearly grow out of the traditions of science fiction but that are readable by all.

Science fiction can be connected to fanciful satire and utopian literature going all the way back to the ancients, but as a separately definable sort of literature it truly emerges in the seventeenth century, when science begins to take hold. The first utterly science fictional novel is perhaps *Frankenstein* (1818), a work that haunts our culture to this day. But our culture has come around to science, become defined by science, and what in the nineteenth century had developed as a separate thread in the fabric of literary history has been woven back into the whole cloth. Science fiction—its techniques and concerns and attitudes—is not the common stock of all writers. How science fiction began, grew, and finally joined the society of letters is a historical question. This collection presents some of the materials from which to construct an answer.

Providing Essays That Precede Chapters. Whatever works your group has decided to gather together, you can assume that your collections should be preceded by an introduction. However, its length and scope will depend, in part, on the extent to which you include additional commentary and information elsewhere within your collection. Your collection, for example, may require several parts or chapters, each of which might be preceded by a short essay of one or two pages that resembles "mini" introductions. However, rather than inform readers about the history or nature of the entire collection, such essays explain important issues related to or provide information about the topic of the chapter. The following excerpt from an essay illustrates the types of information an introduction to a chapter or unit within a collection might provide. The portion we have selected is from the introduction of Chapter Six, "The Democratic Revolution," from *Great Ideas* by Thomas Klein, Bruce Edwards, and Thomas Wymer.

The Democratic Revolution*

Imagine being stranded on a desert island with a group of your peers. There is ample food and shelter, and the climate is hospitable. You feel assured of rescue but believe that it will come only after a prolonged stay. The central problem and challenge of your group, then, is to organize yourselves so that certain necessities of living can be obtained and evenly distributed. You are aware that without this organization, harm may come to those who are weaker and less able to fend for themselves. In fact, any individual or group, whether weak or strong, becomes vulnerable if unfair organization results in a faction that gains a disproportionate share of power. Clearly, the island scenario above reflects the story in William Golding's novel *Lord of the Flies,* and is one view of the continuing story of individual human beings thrown into groups and left to prosper or die.

The central problem of any group, then, that assembles to live together, whether on a mainland or a deserted island, whether as a family or a society, is balancing the conflicting claims of freedom and authority, of individual liberty and communal need. All government starts by recognizing the validity of these claims and then by attempting to resolve the conflicts rising among them. One example of this conflicting claim is the wartime military draft, which requires individuals to relinquish their rights to personal liberty by submitting to the defense needs of their country (as was so controversial during the Vietnam war). Other familiar claims raise similar controversial issues: prayer in public schools (how can the interests of those who do not want to pray and those who do want to pray be simultaneously respected?), and capital punishment (is the community protected and is it justified in denying the "right to life" of the few who may have committed a capital offense?). A society earns its right to call itself successful and civilized when it works out an optimal balance between these conflicting claims. At the same time that it protects or maximizes individual needs and liberties, it also provides for a reasonable degree of security and protection of the public good. The history of democracy in the last 2500 years reveals increasingly effective ways of working out this balance.

Societies have not only sought a balance of individual freedoms and collective goods, but they have also appealed to different kinds of authority to work out that balance. While the early Jews and Christians appealed to revelation and the word of God as their authority, the ancient Greeks appealed to reason, dialogue, and debate. Rather than kings and rulers dictating what was acceptable, the freemen of Athens, through a representative council of free male citizens, governed the city. They gained the right to do this through heredity (by virtue of being free Athenian

Excerpt from *Great Ideas: Conversations Between Past and Present* by Thomas Klein, Bruce Edwards, Thomas Wymer, copyright © 1991 by Holt, Rinehart and Winston, Inc., reprinted by permission of the publisher.

The Democratic Revolution *(cont'd.)*

males), and chaotic as the system was, taxes, laws, wars, and the rights and obligations of citizenship were debated regularly by hundreds of men in the assembly or town square. Thus, the institution of the city-state that was governed by principle and reason was born. The Greek "democracy," sadly though, only lasted several hundred years.

Employing Notes, Anecdotes, and Discussions. Not only might your collection require essays preceding chapters, it might also be enhanced by bits of information or personal anecdotes on individual works. Such pieces of discourse are usually brief, often ranging from a short paragraph to a page in length, but they can be crucial in creating links between each work in a collection and the reader. Sometimes such brief entries can also give important information about a particular work in a collection that cannot easily be provided in any other format.

As examples, examine the following pieces. One, a brief description of the life and writings of the novelist and essayist Virginia Woolf, precedes her story "Lappin and Lapinova," within the collection *Women of the Century: Thirty Modern Short Stories.* The other short writing, a brief passage that provides information about a recipe, appears in *Sundays at Moosewood Restaurant,* a cookbook that contains ethnic and regional recipes as well as cultural and historical information about the groups from which the recipes are taken.

 ## Virginia Woolf
from *Women of the Century: Thirty Modern Short Stories**

edited by Regina Barreca

The daughter of a Victorian scholar, editor, and critic, Virginia Stephen read incessantly and was educated by her parents, but envied her brothers' school and university careers. As an early modernist and a member of the Bloomsbury group, she violated the conventions of traditional fiction and sought to awaken the reader to the intensity she recognized in both life and art. She married Leonard Woolf in 1912. Amid several suicide attempts and severe breakdowns, she wrote such celebrated novels as *The Voyage Out* (1915), *To the Lighthouse* (1927), *Orlando* (1928),

from *Women of the Century: Thirty Modern Short Stories* (cont'd.)

and *Mrs. Dalloway* (1928). Her definitive essay on women and writing, *A Room of One's Own* (1929), which was based on lectures she gave at a women's college at Cambridge, asserts that a woman must have £500 a year and her own private room in order to write to her full capacity. In 1941 Woolf drowned herself.

Recipe
from *Sundays at Moosewood Restaurant**
Hamantaschen

These yummy pastries, traditionally filled with poppy seeds and honey, are served during Purim, a holiday that celebrates the story of Queen Esther of Persia. She helped bring down wicked Haman, who had planned to kill all Persian Jews. Jewish people worldwide remember this story with special foods. German Jews make little triangular pastries, shaped like Haman's tricornered hat. Italian Jews have a variation called "Haman's Ears," after his ears, which were supposedly shaped like a donkey's. In Holland, Jews make a Haman gingerbread man, and the Sephardim have a pasta dish called "Haman's Hair."

Jewish history is often transmitted through a particular food. Special local celebrations have sometimes been created to commemorate some averted disaster within a particular Jewish community. Prune-filled Hamantaschen are said to have been created in 1731 in Bohemia where a man named David Brandeis was falsely accused of selling poisonous plum jam but was later proven innocent. Hence a town holiday called "Brandeis Purim" resulted, and now prune-filled Hamantaschen are a holiday pastry served all over the world.

Yields 40 Hamantaschen

Dough	*Filling*
1 cup butter, softened to room temperature	*1 cup pitted prunes*
2 cups sugar	*$\frac{2}{3}$ cup raisins*
2 eggs	*$1-\frac{1}{3}$ cups prune butter (see note)*
4 teaspoons baking powder	*$\frac{1}{2}$ cup unsweetened grated coconut*
5 cups flour	*$\frac{2}{3}$ cup chopped walnuts*
4 teaspoons orange juice	
2 teaspoons pure vanilla extract	

For the dough, cream the butter and sugar until smooth. Add the eggs and mix well. In a separate bowl, stir the baking powder into the flour until well distributed. Add the flour mixture and juice alternately to the creamed mixture. Stir in the vanilla. Refrigerate for at least ½ hour.

Recipe from *Sundays at Moosewood Restaurant* *(cont'd.)*

Meanwhile, for the filling, put the prunes and raisins into a saucepan with water to cover. Bring to a boil, turn down the heat, and simmer for 5 minutes. Drain. Immediately purée the hot prunes and raisins with the prune butter in a food processor or blender. Be careful not to overprocess. If you use a blender, you'll need to stop it often to push down the prunes and raisins. Mix the purée with the coconut and nuts.

To make the filling by hand, finely mince the prunes and raisins and then, in a mixing bowl, combine with the prune butter, coconut, and nuts.

Allow the filling to cool to room temperature.

Preheat the oven to 375°.

Work with half of the chilled dough at a time. On a well-floured surface, roll the dough out to ¼-inch thickness. Cut into circles with a 3-inch cookie cutter or glass. Put one teaspoon of filling in the center of each circle. Pull 3 points of the circle of dough up over the filling to the center to form a triangle. Pinch the dough together along the top seams. Place the filled Hamantaschen about 2 inches apart on a buttered baking sheet. Rework the scraps of dough to get about 20 pastries from each half of the chilled dough.

Bake for 20 to 20 minutes, until lightly browned.

Notes: Hamantaschen freeze very well. Put them in a plastic bag when they're cool and then into the freezer. When ready to serve, thaw them at room temperature for an hour or two. Truly, it's as if they were never frozen.

Prune butter is found in supermarkets shelved near apple butter.

Providing Supplemental Materials. Finally, although you may provide readers with a great deal of knowledge about your collection in your introduction, chapter essays, and notes related to each work, you may find it desirable—or necessary—to offer additional information through the incorporation of supplemental materials such as glossaries, bibliographies, charts, diagrams, prefaces, acknowledgments, or postscripts. If your group is compiling a collection of works for a "general" readership, a glossary that defines key terms might be well appreciated. If the works in your collection are related to a complicated topic, graphics, charts, graphs, diagrams, or illustrations might help your readers better understand the contents of these collected works or your related commentary. As you may recall, several of the chapters in this book can offer you suggestions about how to produce these and other materials. Chapter 5 includes a discussion of supplemental materials such as charts, graphs, and illustrations; Chapter 9 offers information about different types of bibliographies.

The following are two examples of the sorts of supplemental material that are often included within edited collections. From *Language: Introductory Readings*, a collection of essays about aspects of language, we have excerpted a portion of the glossary found at the back of the volume. From *Sundays at Moosewood Restaurant*, we have reproduced a part of a bibliography of additional readings.

Glossary
from *Language: Introductory Readings**

acoustic phonetics.   The study of the properties of human speech sounds as they are transmitted through the air as sound waves.

affix.   In English, a prefix or suffix (both are bound morphemes) attached to a base (either bound or free) and modifying its meaning.

affricate.   A complex sound made by rapidly articulating first a stop and then a fricative. Affricates appear initially in the English words *chin* and *gin*.

allophone.   A nonsignificant variant of a phoneme.

alveolar.   A sound made by placing the tip or blade of the tongue on the bony ridge behind the upper teeth (e.g., the initial sounds of the English words, *tin, sin, din, zap, nap,* and *lap*); also, a point of articulation.

alveolar ridge.   The bony ridge just behind the upper front teeth.

ambiguity.   Having more than one meaning; ambiguity may be semantic or syntactic.

American Sign Language (ASL, Ameslan).   A system of communication used by deaf people in the United States, consisting of hand symbols that vary in the shape of the hands, the direction of their movement, and their position in relation to the body. It is different from finger spelling, in which words are spelled out letter by letter, and Signed English, in which English words are signed in the order in which they are uttered, thus preserving English morphology and syntax.

aphasia.   The impairment of language abilities as a result of brain damage (usually from a stroke or trauma).

articulatory phonetics.   The study of the production of human speech sounds by the speech organs.

aspiration.   An aspirated sound is followed by a puff of air; the English voiceless-stop consonants /p, t, k/ are aspirated in word-initial position (e.g., *pot, top, kit*).

assimilation.   A change that a sound undergoes to become more like another, often adjacent, sound.

back formation.   A process of word formation that uses analogy as a basis for removing part of a word; *edit* was formed by back formation from *editor*.

base.   In English, a free or bound morpheme to which affixes are added to form new words; *cat* is a free base, *-ceive* is a bound base.

bilabial.   A sound made by constriction between the lips (e.g., the first sound in *pet, bet,* and *met*).

Black English.   A vernacular variety of English used by some black people; more precisely divided into Standard Black English and Black English Vernacular.

Glossary from *Language: Introductory Readings* (cont'd.)

blending.   A process of word formation, combining clipping and compounding, that makes new words by combining parts of existing words that are not morphemes (e.g., *chortle* and *galumphing*).

borrowing.   A process in which words, and sometimes other characteristics, are incorporated into one language from another.

bound morpheme.   A morpheme that cannot appear alone. In English, prefixes and suffixes are bound morphemes, as are some bases.

Broca's area.   One of the language centers in the left hemisphere of the brain.

Suggested Reading List
from *Sundays at Moosewood Restaurant**

Vegetarian Cookbooks

The Moosewood Cookbook, Mollie Katzen. Ten Speed Press, Berkeley, 1977.
New Recipes from Moosewood Restaurant, The Moosewood Collective. Ten Speed Press, Berkeley, 1987.
The Vegetarian Epicure, Anna Thomas. Alfred A. Knopf, New York, 1972.

Africa South of the Sahara

The Africa News Cookbook, African News Service Inc., ed. Tammi Hultman. Penguin Books, New York, 1986.

Armenia and the Middle East

The Best Foods of Russia, Sonia Uvezian. Harcourt Brace Jovanovich, New York, 1976.
The Best of Baghdad Cooking, Daisy Iny. Saturday Review Press/E. P. Dutton, Inc., New York, 1976.
A Book of Middle Eastern Food, Claudia Roden. Alfred A. Knopf, New York, 1974.
Armenia, Cradle of Civilization, David Marshall Lang. George Allen & Unwin, London, Third Edition (corrected), 1980.

The Caribbean

Caribbean Cookbook, Rita G. Springer. Evans Brothers Ltd., London, 1968.
Caribbean Cookbook, Using the Foods We Grow, Lisa Miller. Kingston Publishers Ltd., 1979.

*Reprinted with the permission of Simon & Schuster, from *Sundays at Moosewood Restaurant*, by Vegetable Kingdom, Inc., pp. 693–694 Copyright © 1990 by Vegetable Kingdom.

Suggested Reading List
from *Sundays at Moosewood Restaurant* (cont'd.)

Caribbean Fruits and Vegetables, Beryl Wood. Longman Caribbean Ltd., Trinidad, 1973.

The Complete Book of Cribbean Cooking, Elisabeth Lambert Ortiz. Ballantine Books, New York, 1973.

A Merry Go Round of Recipes from Jamaica, Leila Brandon. Golding Printing Service Ltd., Kingston, Jamaica W.I., 1963.

China

Asian Vegetarian Feast, Ken Hom. William Morrow and Co., New York, 1988.

Chinese Meatless Cooking, Stella Lau Fessler. New American Library, New York, 1980.

Classic Chinese Cooking for the Vegetarian Gourmet, Joanne Hush. Smallwood and Stewart, New York, 1984.

Finland

Classic Scandinavian Cooking, Nika Standen Hazelton. Scribner, New York, 1987.

The Cooking of Scandinavia, Dale Brown. Time-Life Books, New York, 1968.

The Finnish Cookbook, Beatrice Ojakangas. Crown Publishers, Inc., New York, 1964.

 **Activity 7**

Together with your group, brainstorm a list of possible items to include in your collection. Besides an introduction and the works themselves, will you need chapter discussions? commentary pertaining to each work? a glossary? a bibliography of other similar works or collections of works? charts, diagrams, cartoons, illustrations? a rating system? After you have finished brainstorming, see whether group members can agree on a tentative list of items.

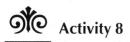 **Activity 8**

Once the group has agreed on the contents of the collection, you and your partners should begin to plan your introduction. Keeping in mind the list of items that will be included in your collection, individually freewrite a description of the introduction: What sort of information should be included in it? How detailed should it be? How many pages do you think it should be? If you envision a rather lengthy introduction, should it be divided into sections? If so, what topic (or topics) should be covered in each section? After each member of the group has completed his or her freewriting, share the contents of these with each other. Can you reach a consensus or will you have to defer some decisions about the introduction until after you have discussed the other sections of your collection?

Group Writing Assignment: Prepare a brief (2-page) description of your project for your instructor, in which you do the following: (1) describe the scope and contents of your introduction; (2) list the titles (or brief descriptions) of the works that you will include in your collection; and (3) list and briefly describe the types of additional commentary you will provide (chapter discussions, personal anecdotes, glossaries, etc.) and what information you plan to include in each. If your group has not made some of the decisions needed to complete tasks 1, 2, and 3, explain why. Your description can be presented in the form of a report, an outline, or a combination of these.

WRITING AND PRODUCING YOUR PROJECT

By now you and members of your group have already begun to plan various parts of your project; in fact, some of you may have already started to draft pieces as you planned what to do. Still, if your group hasn't together decided which members are going to write what portions, and how this is to be accomplished, it's time to make these determinations.

Although you and your group partners have invented and planned pieces of writing together, each of you has probably done the actual writing alone. This is a common form of collaborative writing, in which a group, together, decides what is to be written but then individuals are assigned to write specific parts. If you all feel most comfortable with this way of proceeding, then it may be best to divide up the writing tasks so that each member is responsible for writing a particular part of the project.

As an example, suppose that your group intends to produce a work entitled *Images of a Generation,* which consists of two parts: a collection of articles describing the characteristics of the twenty-something generation ("Generation X") and a collection of reviews about films that depict persons of this age. Let's also assume that you have decided to write and include (1) a brief (1- or 2-page) general introduction; (2) two short (2- or 3-page) essays that describe or discuss each of the two major parts of the collection; and (3) one or two paragraphs of commentary to accompany each article and film review. Under these circumstances, if your group has four members, you might decide that three members could each write the general introduction and the two chapter essays, respectively; the fourth member would be responsible for writing all of the paragraph commentaries.

On the other hand, depending on the number of people in your group and on individual preferences, you may wish to divide the writing tasks into larger chunks that two (or more) members can write together. If you and your group partners haven't experienced writing with someone—where you sit together at the word processor or take turns writing and dictating with pen and paper—you might like to experiment with this option. However, whatever configuration your group chooses, before individuals or pairs go off to draft their portions of the project, the group should have completed one or more invention techniques and planned each portion so that the members will have some ideas about what to write and how to proceed. In addition, as we explained in Chapter 9, it is imperative that at least one person (or two) be assigned the task of compiling and integrating all of the parts and assuring that they fit together well. You will not be sure that your project is coherent and unified unless one or two persons are specifically assigned this important responsibility.

 **Activity 9**

As a group, determine how you wish to divide up the parts of your project so that these portions can be drafted. Do you want to divide up and assign *all* of the commentary to group members, or do you think it would be wise to assign just a *portion* of it (e.g., the general introduction) and meet to assess the quality of the drafts, the difficulty group members had in writing these, and so forth, before assigning the remainder? If you divide up all of the commentary, should the group meet once during the drafting process to provide support for those who are having problems or who need some additional guidance? Once drafts are completed, should the group assign one or two members to type these on a word processor and save them on a disk so that revisions can be easily made?

At some point, either during or after the process of completing drafts of the commentary for your project, you and your group partners will need to devise a procedure for revising, editing, and producing your collection. Depending on the size of your group and how you have divided up the tasks, you may prefer to engage in group revising sessions or your group may assign revising, editing, and production to individuals or subcommittees. If you decide to revise in one or more group sessions, consider devising a set of questions or criteria to use as a guide for revision suggestions. For example, you may wish all members to answer the following prompts as they read over a draft of an introductory essay: (1) Describe the order in which the information is presented. How might the organization be modified to make the overall structure and the relationship between each part clearer? (2) What is the weakest part of the draft? What suggestions can you offer for revision? (3) What is the strongest part of the draft? Explain why it is effective.

Once your group has critiqued the drafts of each part of the commentary and offered suggestions for revision, the same people who wrote each section can do the actual rewriting or a different group or individual can be assigned to do it. A particularly large group (6 or more individuals) may decide to appoint a two- or three-member subcommittee to do all of the revising. But it is probably wise, no matter the circumstances, for every member of the group to read and comment on all drafts before these are revised. This reading and commenting can occur during a group meeting, or individual members can read and comment on copies of the drafts alone and then give these copies, with their comments, to the individuals responsible for rewriting.

Because writing and revising the commentary for your collection will be a challenging process no matter how your group divides up the work, it may be easy to overlook matters such as editing and producing your project. However, the quality of your collection will be very much enhanced if it is well edited and professional-looking. For this reason, we recommend that either a committee of several persons or the entire group do a final, careful editing *after* the revising and rewriting has been completed and all of the parts have been fitted together. In addition, you and your group partners might consider word processing your project and producing it with a letter-quality printer, such as an ink jet or laser printer, if you can gain access to such equipment. Especially if your project is to contain materials such as charts, diagrams, special headings, or drawings, you might want to explore the possibility of using a word processor that has graphic capabilities. Your instructor may be able to suggest some sources for these, or perhaps, the director of the Writing Center at your college may be of help.

Group Writing Assignment. Together with members of your group, devise a procedure for revising, editing, and producing your project. Then write up a report of this procedure along with a timetable that suggests when the various activities you describe will be completed. Hand this report in to your instructor.

PROJECT 2

IMPROVING YOUR SURROUNDINGS: THE ACTION PROJECT

Throughout your life, you have undoubtedly observed or experienced many situations that you want to change. However, actually making the commitment to change a situation can be difficult, perhaps because you don't have the time, the expertise, or the tools to alter existing circumstances. What can *I* do, many people have wondered. While people often feel overwhelmed by conditions that they feel unable to change, this initial feeling doesn't stop many from taking action to improve their surroundings.

If you have already participated in an effort to provide a needed facility or service for people or to modify an unjust practice or policy, you know that such efforts can be rewarding, even if the outcome is not what you wished for. In fact, some might argue that the experience of working on behalf of other people is its own reward.

Now that you are attending college, is there something that you would like to accomplish, either on your campus or within a nearby community? Although you may not have an immediate response to this question, you might discover a project that you'd like to work on rather easily. Consider some of these issues, for example:

- If a large portion of the students at your school are parents, does your school provide any assistance with child care?
- Does your college or university offer low-cost legal aid or health insurance to students who need these services?
- Does your residence hall (if you live on a residential campus) encourage students to recycle waste?
- Are prospective students within the local community informed about student grants and loans and work study programs offered by your college?
- Does your school provide an adequate escort service to enable female students to use its facilities after dark?

- ■ Would students, either at your college or at a local high school, benefit from a workshop or program that would teach them a useful skill or provide them with important information?

If you and your group partners have responded with interest to these issues or if these issues have prompted other ideas, you might consider working on an action project together and reporting the nature and results of this project to your instructor. Depending on their nature or scope, most action projects require a variety of tasks, including designing and writing different sorts of texts—proposals, petitions, letters, ads, flyers, announcements, and so forth.

SELECTING AN ACTION PROJECT

In general, action projects can culminate in one of two ways: They can culminate in a specific one-time event, or they can set a process in motion. Suppose, for example, that you and your group partners want to sponsor or copresent—with one or more guest speakers—a Saturday morning workshop on how to improve study skills for students in your residence hall. Under these circumstances, your action project will produce a workshop, and the tasks in which you and your group partners engage will involve planning one or more of the sessions, publicizing the event, securing accommodations, and so forth.

Although planning and preparing for a particular event is rewarding, you and your group partners may, instead, prefer to choose an action project that sets a process in motion. Such a process may involve the establishment of an ongoing group whose aim is to educate members on a particular topic or issue and disseminate the information to others. Alternatively, you may want to organize a letter-writing campaign to convince an institution, group, or organization to examine and change its practices, or begin the process of establishing a needed facility or service for students at your school.

As you consider the kinds of action projects you and members of your group might select, try to build on interests and convictions you already share. For instance, are any of your group partners already members of an organization (or organizations) that could benefit from a one-time event? Do one or more members of your group share a "pet peeve" about something at your school or in your community? Have one or more of your group members thought of establishing an organization or ongoing network of some sort? What speakers would group members like to bring to your campus? What types of workshops would group members like to attend? What new service or facility do your group partners agree is most needed at your school?

If some interesting ideas about possible action projects don't readily come to mind, you and your group partners might try freewriting individually, sharing the results, and brainstorming a wish list of changes you would enact at your school (or in your residence hall or in your neighborhood), if it were in your power to do so. Here, also, are some exercises and activities to help you make a selection.

Activity 1

On your own, brainstorm a list of topics about which you think your campus community should be informed. After each topic, jot down some different ways in which a group could get information about the topic (through a speaker, panel, workshop, etc.). In addition, write down the names of dynamic speakers, either well known or known to you, who are informed about these topics. Indicate whether these speakers would be most effective as individual performers or as members of a panel. Share your list with other members of your group.

Activity 2

On your own, brainstorm a list of events, activities, facilities, changes in rules and procedures, and so forth, from which your campus community could benefit. Do not censor any ideas that come to your mind at this time, no matter how extravagant they seem to you. If ideas like a women's film festival, a daylong workshop on combating racism, a weekend career fair, a legal aid service, or an International Students' Center come to mind, jot them down. Once you have generated your list, select the event, activity, or facility that seems most exciting, and freewrite for five minutes about it. In your freewriting, try to explore ways in which your idea for an action project could become sufficiently manageable so that your group might actually consider selecting it. Share your list and your freewriting with your group partners.

Activity 3

Once your group has produced a list of ideas for an action project, organize it into two columns, one that contains projects that culminate in a one-time event and one that contains projects that will create an ongoing organization or process. At this point, your group may wish to rank the items in each column or decide whether it wishes to pursue one type of project or the other. For example, if everyone wants to do a project that culminates in a one-time event, the list of process projects can de discarded.

   To arrive at a final consensus, you and your partners might consider several factors regarding the execution and nature of your project: (1) How realistic is your goal? Is the problem (or piece of the problem you've chosen to attack) manageable? Is the event you want to sponsor or the process you wish to inaugurate feasible? (2) What type of activities will your project require?

publicity? fund-raising? letter-writing? (3) What will be the impact of your project's outcome; how many people will be affected and for how long? As always, once your group arrives at a consensus, you all should read the rest of this section before embarking on an action project.

PLANNING YOUR PROJECT

Handling the One-Time Event

Although you may have been enlightened by a well-run, informative workshop, excited by a stimulating event (such as a panel or international festival), or inspired by a dynamic speaker, you probably don't know how much work and planning such affairs demand. At a minimum, these activities require organizers to spend time selecting and contacting speakers and arranging accommodations for the event itself and for the speakers, as well as publicizing the event so that it is well attended.

If you and your group partners decide to bring in a speaker or to sponsor an event that others will present, you will need to become proficient at communicating precisely what you expect of your presenters and at designing and disseminating a variety of documents (circulars, posters, ads and articles for the local newspaper) that describe your event and generate interest and curiosity. (Of course, a well-known speaker will automatically attract a sizable audience without much publicity, but such an individual may require a hefty honorarium, or payment, in addition to travel expenses.) On the other hand, if you and your group partners wish to present an event or workshop yourselves, an important part of your task will be designing the activity and producing written documents for distribution (handouts that highlight or provide additional information, evaluation forms, lists of useful resources, etc.), where appropriate.

Because there are so many possible events for your group to chose, we cannot advise you precisely about what procedures to follow; however, here are a few guidelines to help you plan and execute your project. If you have decided to sponsor an event, such as a panel or a speaker, to be presented entirely or in part by people who are *not* in your group, you will be responsible for selecting and securing presenters, arranging for the room in which the event will be held, publicizing it, and, perhaps, raising funds. Obviously, the more in-demand or busy a prospective speaker or panelist is, the more difficult it will be for you to get him or her; even administrators, advisors, and faculty at your school have full schedules and may need to be committed well in advance. It is best, therefore, to have several "backups" or alternatives in mind for speakers or panelists so that individuals can be substituted if your first choices are not available.

After your group has selected a group of speakers, panelists, workshop presenters, and alternates, but before you contact these individuals, you should come up with several possible times and dates for your event. Following this, a group member should contact the office that handles room assignments at your school to determine whether appropriate rooms are available for those times and how those rooms can be secured. [NOTE: Reserving a room may involve help from you instructor.] If rooms are available for the times you've selected, these should be tentatively reserved while speakers or presenters are approached. You will need to contact these individuals rather quickly and secure a commitment from them as soon as possible so that you can hold a room permanently and begin to plan a publicity campaign. Your publicity campaign should involve announcements in your school newspaper several days to one week before the event, as well as flyers that you can post on public bulletin boards or distribute to prospective attendees (one week before the event). If your campus has one, an electronic bulletin board can also be a good means of publicizing your event.

If your group has decided to do a project entirely on its own, corresponding with speakers and participants will, of course, be unnecessary; most of the work will involve planning and publicizing the affair. You and your group partners should begin designing your affair (workshops, panel, fund-raiser, etc.) right away so that you will have plenty of time to rehearse, work out "bugs," prepare materials for distribution, and so on. It is also advisable to reserve a room as soon as possible. Once your affair takes shape, a publicity campaign should be prepared so that announcements, fliers, and the like, can be sent out at least one week in advance.

 **Activity 4**

Write a description (1 to 2 pages) of the event your group will sponsor; then make a list of all of the tasks that must be done in advance, such as getting speakers and participants, reserving a room, and designing the event. Create a timetable that indicates when the event and each task leading up to it will be completed; submit these materials to your instructor for a response.

Handling the Ongoing Process

An action project that involves the establishment of a group (a study group, social issues discussion group, local chapter of Amnesty International, etc.) or begins a long-term process to create a facility (a day-care center, legal aid service, etc.) or attempts to change a policy may not be completed during the time that you are enrolled in your writing class, especially if it is successful! You and your partners should attempt, therefore, to create enough momentum so that the activity you started continues—even after one (or all) of you have ceased to be involved in it. If you all have opted to create a group or local chapter of some sort, you will need to publicize and secure space for your meeting; however, these efforts will probably be minimal because you won't have a large audience. Instead, the bulk of your efforts will involve working closely with your attendees (perhaps keeping logs of meetings) and planning subsequent gatherings and activities that meet the needs of participants. Such activities might include a series of guest speakers, field trips, letter-writing campaigns, group reading or film viewing, and materials exchange.

Unlike offering a one-time event or establishing an ongoing group, changing an institution—whether by convincing authorities to offer new services and facilities or to modify unjust policies and practices—can take years. This is not meant to discourage you and your group partners from embarking on such a project, however. Long-term efforts have to begin somewhere, and you and your partners may have the drive and commitment to get the ball rolling. Although an action project of this nature may require a public meeting (for which a room must be reserved) we expect that the best approach for starting a process that will culminate in the desired end is to conduct a needs assessment and submit a report of this to your student government association and to the appropriate administrators. If your group has opted to start work on establishing a day-care center, for example, other people, such as student peers, school administrators, or community leaders, will need to be convinced that there is a genuine need for such a facility before they devote time, much less money, to the project. If your group wants, say, to begin a process that will culminate in the modification of the "course repeat" policy at your school, those individuals who are responsible for creating and changing such regulations will need to be convinced that many students and faculty find the current policy to be unjust and inefficient.

At least two sources of information can be very persuasive in the early stages of a long-term effort: (1) research that shows that other schools have experienced—and dealt with—similar needs and problems; (2) research that illustrates student need or dissatisfaction at your school. We suggest, therefore, that you and your group partners research the facility, service, or policy that you are addressing. You might find it appropriate to conduct several observations of a site, or to survey students (and faculty, administrators, etc.) In addition, you should review our discussion of surveys and other nonlibrary research sources in Chapter 10.

 **Activity 5**

> Together, write a description of the ongoing process your group will attempt to inaugurate. Be sure to address the following issues: What are the final goals of the process? What steps will you take to create initial interest in your project? What steps will you take to provide continuing momentum? If your project will require a report of the results of research or a survey, to whom will your report be addressed? Do you have an idea of how the report might be organized? Hand in this description, which should be at least two pages long, to your instructor for a response.

WRITING AND PRODUCING YOUR PROJECT

As you read the previous section about how to plan and carry out various action projects, you may have noticed that the projects require different kinds of writing. Many require correspondence and publicity pieces; others require surveys and reports. What follows are a few pointers about how to produce some of the specialized documents you may need in the course of executing your action project.

Composing Letters

As with all other kinds of writing, a letter should show a clear purpose and be appropriate for the audience to whom it is addressed. In the course of arranging your event, you may need to compose several different kinds of letters in order to achieve different ends. Some of the letters your group will write may be letters of inquiry to determine one or more of the following:

- Whether a person is willing to be a speaker, panelist, or participant for your event
- What topics a particular speaker or panelist can discuss
- What a speaker or panelist charges for an appearance
- Whether a speaker is willing to make his or her own travel arrangements, if necessary
- Whether a speaker is available at particular times or on a particular date
- Whether an individual (or group) will cosponsor or contribute money to support your event
- What rooms are available at a particular time and date
- Information about available rooms (seating capacity; way in which chairs can be arranged; whether food and beverages are allowed in the room, etc.).

In addition to writing letters of inquiry, you may need to correspond in order to confirm particular arrangements, provide requested information, or report unanticipated problems or changes in schedule.

We suggest that before you begin drafting, you and your group partners jot down the general purpose of a letter (e.g., to inquire, to report, or to respond to questions) and list the specific points you need to cover. For example, if you are writing a letter to inquire whether a particular individual would be willing to deliver a talk, your notes might look like the following:

purpose:

   inquire

points to cover:

   inform person who we are and why we're writing

   ask if person is willing to come to Bowling Green

   ask person what he or she charges (including expenses)

   ask person to list topics on which he or she would be willing to speak

   ask person if she or he would be available on any of the following dates

   ask person to respond by letter or phone by February 10th

Once you've generated a list of points, you can decide on the order in which you'd like to present them and jot down additional notes about what information to include in the letter. The letter described in the previous notes will certainly require you to provide the name, address, and telephone number of a contact person in your group to whom your speaker can send a response. In addition, if the contact person can be reached at certain times, that information should also be provided: "Please call before 9:00 A.M. or after 8:00 P.M., Monday through Thursday."

After you have completed a satisfactory draft of a letter that exhibits a clear purpose and contains the necessary information, revise it for tone. We recommend a courteous, friendly approach. Overly formal prose that tries to sound "intelligent" or "cultured" may, instead, seem awkward or pretentious.

Here is a simple format that you can use for most of your correspondence:

---

221 B Fairview
Bowling Green, OH 43402
February 27, 1996

Professor Jackie Fields
Education Department
221 Williams Hall
Bowling Green State University
Bowling Green, OH 43403

Dear Professor Fields:

I am writing on behalf of a group of BGSU students who are sponsoring a panel discussion on the proposed legislation the Ohio Legislature is considering on changes in how local districts are funded. We plan on having from three to five speakers on the panel, from the local university and the county Board of Education. We hope that the panel discussion will inform local students and other voters about the intent of the proposed legislation and its possible effects so that they will in turn express their views to their representatives in the State Legislature.

Would you be able to speak at our discussion? Tracy Collins, one of your students, has indicated that you are following this legislation closely and have discussed it at length in you EDCI 312 class.

We have tentatively scheduled the panel discussion for Tuesday, March 28 from 7:00 to 8:30 P.M. If you are willing to speak, please contact our Workshop Coordinator, Marsha Hill, by next Monday, March 6. You can reach Marsha by phone at 372–5555 before 9:30 A.M. or after 6:00 P.M. You can also reach her by e-mail at this address: marhill@bgsu.opie.edu. Marsha can provide you with additional details about the other speakers on the panel and the kinds of questions you may want to address in your talk.

Thank you for considering our request. With the cooperation of knowledgeable persons in the local area like you, we are hoping to inform the university community better about this very important issue.

Sincerely,

Edward Floyd

Edward Floyd

Publicizing an Event

Publicity for a speaker, panel, workshop, food drive, and the like, can take a variety of forms. You and your group may need to produce several pieces. These may range from simple announcements (ads or flyers) of a few sentences that inform readers about the time, date, and place of an event to articles of one or two pages that provide considerable information about the person, panelists, and participants, the content of the event, and ways in which participants can benefit from attending. The following two pieces of writing were both created to publicize an event and to present the reader with different kinds of information.

Example 1
Run for Life:*

Kappa Sigma and Alpha Chi Omega are running in a 24-hour marathon to raise money for Muscular Dystrophy Association. University President Paul Olscamp helped kick off the philanthropy Wednesday evening. The event runs until tonight at 6 in the Union Oval.

Example 2
Lambda Chis to host leadership conference†

by Jennifer Taday
staff writer

More than 600 Lambda Chi Alphas will be attending the chapters' 23rd annual leadership conference at the University this summer.

Jon Bush, Lambda Chi Alpha President, said delegates from the 223 chapters representing 48 states and three Canadian provinces will attend the conference Aug. 7–11, which is entitled, "Designing the Lambda Chi Alpha Experience."

The leadership conference is being hosted at the University because "our chapter has always been a strong one in the eyes of National—especially in regard to our strong scholarship—and the location is ideal for all of the chapters," Bush said.

*"Run for Life," *BG News.* Reprinted with the permission of the publisher.
†"Lambda Chis to host leadership conference," by Jennifer Taday. *BG News,* 3 May 1991, p. 5. Reprinted with the permission of the publisher.

Lambda Chis to host leadership conference *(cont'd.)*

Various seminars including risk management, public relations and member involvement will be presented during the conference, he said.

"Risk management is a new topic added to the schedule and the chapters have been working on our fraternity education system, which is unique to other fraternities," Bush added.

> "Our chapter has always been seen as strong in the eyes of National—especially in regard to our strong scholarship— and the location is ideal for all of the chapters."
>
> —Jon Bush, Lambda Chi Alpha president

"This system is still being implemented, but it treats all the members the same—no distinction is made between members and associate members."

Featured speakers will be National Football League Hall of Fame Green Bay Packers' quarterback Bart Starr, the keynote speaker, and NASA space shuttle pilot Captain Richard Richards.

Richards, a Lambda Chi, will be receiving an achievement award from Lambda Chi Alpha.

An initiation will also be conducted in which the 200,000 Lambda Chi Alpha will be inducted, he said.

"The 200,000th active brother will be presented with a jeweled pin that Richards took up in space with him in the last space shuttle mission," Bush said.

This initiation will be special because the one thing that ties all Lambda Chi Alphas together across the country is the ritual, he added.

Bush said more than two-thirds of his chapter will be participating in the week's events and these members will also assist in registration and transportation.

One University Lambda Chi will be on the international ritual team, "which is compared to a sports all-star team," and another member applied for a position on the student advisory committee, he said.

"I've never seen the morale in this house so high," Bush said. "Our chapter is really excited for the conference."

Creating Helpful Materials

Especially if you and your partners are sponsoring an event that is meant to inform people about a set of skills, or provide information about a process, procedure, or organization, attendees will appreciate one or two helpful handouts that they can refer to subsequently. For example, if your group is sponsoring a panel on how to prepare for a job interview, people in the audience will surely appreciate receiving a printed list of pointers about how to dress, topics to avoid, ways to answer "difficult" questions, and so forth. Here are a few more examples of possible events accompanied by ideas for ancillary materials you and your partners might create and distribute:

- *A workshop on how to study for finals:* a handout that details a procedure for memorizing information; a description of a step-by-step process for note-taking or highlighting information; a list of quiet places to study on campus or coffee shops that are open all night.
- *The first meeting of an effort to establish a university day-care center:* an agenda that outlines the topics to be covered at the meeting; a list of tentative steps—for discussion—that the group might adopt to begin the process; names and addresses of directors of local, private day-care centers that group members might interview to gather information about issues such as cost.
- *A panel discussion for local high school students about applying for admission and financial aid at your college:* a list of useful names and phone numbers; a timetable of the steps to follow for admission and financial aid; sample admission and financial aid forms correctly filled out. [NOTE: Any such materials should be checked over by an appropriate person in your Admissions/Financial Aid offices to ensure accuracy.]

Reporting Results of Information Gathering

Those groups who have chosen an action project that will, if successful, culminate in the establishment of a needed service, facility, or change in policy may need to conduct an opinion survey and gather other relevant, persuasive information. Such data, whether gathered from a survey or from a variety of other sources (e.g., books, pamphlets, and interviews), cannot be presented in raw form because your readers (the dean of students? the president of the university? members of the university's Union Advisory Council?) will want to spend as little time as possible determining the gist of your information. Besides, you can always provide more complete information—even a survey and *all* of the results—in an appendix (or at a later date), if it is requested.

Depending on your audience and the nature of your goal, it is advisable to summarize the results of your data gathering and research in a two- to three-page letter in which you and your group offer to provide more complete data (a copy of the survey you used; complete tallies of responses to questions; and copies of relevant materials such as articles and pamphlets) on request. Your group may prepare, instead, an actual report of your findings accompanied by a brief (1-paragraph) letter that explains the contents of the report. Regardless of the format you choose to present your information, we suggest that you refer to Chapter 5, Chapter 8, and Chapter 10 for suggestions about how to construct informative texts that are well organized, clear, and persuasive.

❖ Activity 6

> With your group, brainstorm all of the written documents you will need to produce in the course of executing and completing your action project. List written texts your project will require and write brief descriptions of each; turn in the list and descriptions to your instructor for feedback. If you have already produced some drafts, we suggest that you include copies of these with your list and descriptions.

MATERIALS TO HAND IN TO YOUR INSTRUCTOR

Your instructor will want to evaluate your project, so you will need to create a packet of materials to hand in. Some action projects will require groups to research, gather data for, and write a report addressed to an appropriate individual or committee. If your group produces such a report, a copy may be submitted to your instructor, along with any additional material you and your partners wish to place in an appendix (such as a survey you designed and distributed). However, if your action project does not culminate in a report, your group will need to turn in other written documents. We recommend that you hand in at least the following items:

1. **A written description of your project.** Whether your project was to sponsor a speaker, to present or sponsor a panel, workshop, or food drive, or to inaugurate an ongoing group or process, your description should provide basic information such as what happened at the event or meetings, who did the speaking and under what circumstances, the type of materials distributed, the number of attendees, and so forth. You may wish to include notes, informal agendas, and portions of scripts. We recommend that you consult your instructor about how much detail she or he would like your group to provide.

2. **A written description of the process you went through.** Depending on the nature of your project, your and your partners can include summaries of discussions, explanations about how you planned and wrote correspondence, publicity, and other documents, and how you solved problems. You may wish to include timetables, logs of activities, portions of notes or minutes taken from the meetings, and other similar materials.

3. **A written assessment of the success of your project.** Unless you hand out evaluation forms to participants, you won't be able to provide a formal assessment of the success of your project. Still, matters such as attendance and audience participation and response can be useful ways of determining whether your project was worthwhile. You and your group partners may also want to discuss your own level of satisfaction with the project and suggest ways in which it could have been improved.

4. **Copies of every piece of "formal" writing your group produced during the course of your project.** By "formal" writing we mean writing *other* than notes, preliminary drafts, and the like. Such writing might include correspondence, ads, flyers, newspaper articles, explanatory materials, lists of resources, surveys, and evaluation forms.

Group Writing Assignment. One or two weeks before your project is due, hand in to your instructor a brief (1- to 2-page) progress report. This should include a description of what your group has accomplished to date as well as a final list of materials you expect to turn in after your project is completed.

DIVING INTO CONTROVERSY: WRITING ABOUT A LOCAL ISSUE

After national elections, whether for president of the United States or for members of Congress, public commentators often discuss the small percentage of eligible citizens who voted, citing apathy, disgust, helplessness, or hopelessness as possible causes for their lack of participation. As you have probably noticed, however, this lack of involvement is not unusual; people rarely become involved in civic projects and activities unless a particular issue has captured their imaginations or fired their emotions. Think, if you will, of what it would take to motivate you or one of your friends to express his or her opinion publicly in a letter to a magazine or newspaper editor, for example, much less to invest time in attending rallies, raising funds, doing volunteer work, and so forth.

Of course, nothing motivates people like personal experience. Individuals who live near a toxic-waste dump that infuses their home with chemical odors may become committed to preserving the environment for the rest of their lives. Adult victims of child abuse may devote a great deal of time and effort to combating this tragic problem so that future children might be spared. Unfortunately, however, those who haven't had direct experience with something usually don't feel strongly enough about it to do more than offer an opinion now and then to a friend or to get in an occasional heated discussion over dinner—unless they can be made to feel strongly about the matter. That is, if people can be made to feel a powerful emotion such as anger, distress, or outrage about an event, issue, or condition—even though they may have never personally experienced anything remotely similar—they may adopt someone else's commitment as their own.

If you accept our reasoning that people who become emotionally charged with a matter can become personally invested in it (even if they have no prior experience with it), you will probably agree that skillful and impassioned writing often inspires a good deal of emotional intensity among readers. Of course, other forms of communication such as live speeches, television, and film can operate similarly, but these forms are considerably less accessible to the average person.

At this time, your writing group may already be fired up about a campus or local issue; if so, this is a wonderful opportunity to increase the number of people who are impassioned about it. Of course, the members of your group may be fired up about a topic on which you do not agree; if this is the case, it might be a stimulating and valuable experience to attempt to reach a consensus. If your group cannot resolve your differences of opinion, you may wish to construct two essays that present strong opposing arguments. However, even if you and your group partners are unaware of any debates that are raging on your campus, you may still be intrigued by the idea of bringing a matter to the attention of your reading community through a skillful piece of writing that takes a forceful, if controversial, stand.

 ## Activity 1

Read the following essay, which was written by a college student and published in his college newspaper. Discuss the essay with your group members and answer the following questions: What issue is the writer addressing in his essay? What is his stance on the issue? How would you characterize the writer's approach? Was this approach effective? Why or why not?

 ## Schools must sink to our level*

Roark Littlefield

Last week a riter named Penny Brown rote we students is dumb cause we watch too much TV. Lots of people go round saying stuff like that, and me for one is sick an tired.

Many articles now say that schools in the United States is no good. People says we oughta make our schools like the ones they gots in Europe and Japan. They say that our schools should be more hard. MORE HARD? Don't make me laff.

We young people today have lots to do. It's not like when our parents were kids. In those days kids didn't have television and cars and stuff. Plus history classes didn't have to go as far.

Different story today. Now we gots problems like getting jobs. If a college don't help you get a job, then what's it for? Some kind of liberal agenda? You bet!

I think the liberals have gone too far. I looked, and you can even get a degree in Liberal Arts. Try that one on for size.

*"Schools must sink to our level," by Roark Littlefield. *BG News,* 8 February 1995, p. 2. Reprinted with the permission of the author.

Schools must sink to our level *(cont'd.)*

Plus classes start too early! In high school we could skip all we wanted. I never went to class until one o'clock. I got to watch Jerry Springer, Rolanda, Sally, and all kinds of stuff. But try that in college! They pile on the work, and say, "Read this, read that!" Hey, I got a life!

High school. Now those were the days! We could get our learnin' done without it interfering with our lives. But even then there was nerds who said American schools were too easy. There was one guy named Marvin. He thought he was so smart. They voted him most likely to suck seed. Hey, I was the same age as him, and I been suckin' seed since I was eight. Then I came here to BGSU. They told me I had to take classes about lots of things, like philosophy and languages. I have to take four classes in German! What for? Isn't this America? I feel just fine talking good ole American, thank you very mutch.

My freshman year I had to take a class called English 110. What for? My advisor said I only had to take one foriegn language.

I'll never forget that class. The teacher had us do stuff that was real hard. I closed my eyes and thunk. Deep inside my brain I heard a voice say, "I don't got time for this!"

Everyone in class musta thought the same thing, 'cause So a guy in front row said, "Hard! Hard, teacher! More easy! No hard!"

Then a girl goes, "He right! We ain't like English teachers or somethin'. Don't you know we got other classes and not just yours?"

I got all filled with angir. I stood up and said, "She's right! No hard! No hard! Easy! Easy!"

Didn't do no good. Plus I got F.

Now I has to take English 110 all over again. Not only that, I then has to take English 111, and then other numbers. How long will that take? I can't take class after class. English, German, Philosophy, Shakespeare. When's a man supposed to get his beer drinkin' dun? Plus my teachers gave me homework over the weekend, when I'm supposed to spend Saturday shootin' squirrels off the front lawn with my grandpappy.

Enuff is enuff. I say we join together and demand a lower standard. But I need your help. I can't do it alone. I tried talkin' to my philosophy teacher about this. She said that higher education wasn't just for getting a job. She said it teaches you how to think for yourself. I got two words for that. "Haw! Haw!"

Can't I already think for myself? You bet I can. This column proves it. Know how I learned? I learned by listening to Rush Limbaugh. He never finished collidge, and he one smart cookie.

Rush says multiculturalism is a bunch of gobbledygook. I agree. America is king, and we don't need to know what they're doing in places like Brazil where they ain't even got enough decency to talk American. Sometimes I think they make us study certain things because they want to undermine. I used to know what undermine means but I forgot.

Like I said before, this is America. Why do we need women's studies, for example? Women don't need studies, they just need a good stiff one.

Schools must sink to our level *(cont'd.)*

Here is what I think in a nutshell. America is already strong. These people who say we oughta improve our school worry too much about the future. Right now we are richer and more better than anybody else. Why should it change anytime soon?

My other teacher told us that in China they know more about America that we know about China. Duh! It's 'cause there ain't nothin' goin' on in China. Jeez!

Sure, maybe they got harder schools in Japan and Germany. But don't forget everybody is starving in those countries too! Who wants to be like that? We in U.S. is just fine the way we are with our schools the way they currently is.

The end.

SELECTING AN ISSUE

Before you and your group members can construct a powerful piece of writing about an event or issue, you will need to do a bit of research to find out what is being talked about on your campus. Perhaps people are discussing matters that are unique to your school, such as a new universitywide course requirement, a campuswide ban on smoking, or a disturbing local incident; or they may be talking about community, state, or national matters such the election of a controversial politician, a particular law or social policy, or a well-publicized incident or event. Although your campus or the community surrounding your campus may already be engaged in a wide-scale, well-publicized controversy, your writing group should still spend some time investigating the range of conversations occurring on and around campus. In this way, you may discover a lesser-known matter that deserves attention *and* that arouses your interest and emotions more readily.

One way to begin getting a sense of the issues that have been affecting your campus is to survey the front page, the editorial essays, and letters to the editor of your school newspaper for the last month or two. In order to do this, you probably will be able to read back issues at your college library or at the newspaper office. As you and your group members construct a list of topics that seem to have generated debate in recent months, we suggest that you keep a log of the types of writing you noted (e.g., front-page articles or editorial essays and letters) as well as the dates of the newspapers and page numbers of the writings so that you can refer to them later. If several members of your writing group are assigned the task of surveying newspapers, your group might consider constructing a simple form that each member can use to record information. Such a form can easily be duplicated and might contain categories such as the following: topic; type of article (letter, essay, etc.); page numbers; date and edition.

After you and your partners have gained a sense of the topics that are being discussed in your school (or local) paper, you should consider acquiring additional information about the issues that concern your student peers by surveying them. Many students may be concerned about issues that have not generated much attention in your local newspapers, and a simple survey may reveal this. Such a survey should probably ask students to circle (or check) items from a list that you provide, but it should also invite informants to write in topics that you may have omitted. You also should ask people to assign ratings to their selections (from 1 "Very Important" to 4 "Slightly Important," for example). Lastly, your survey should solicit the informants' names (if they wish to provide them), class (e.g., first-year), gender, and any other information you may find useful (such as race, ethnicity, or age) as well as their willingness to be interviewed. Prospective interviewees should be asked to provide phone numbers and hours when they can be reached. When you select the issue about which you will write, interviews can provide quotes that will lend immediacy and vividness to your final text. To find out how to conduct interviews efficiently you should review the Conducting Interviews section in Chapter 10.

Once you have gathered information about the issues that have aroused emotions or stimulated controversy among your student peers, you and your group will need to agree on which one to pursue so that you can research and—ultimately—write about it. This process may be simple, if your group began to approach a consensus while members were collecting information. On the other hand, your group may have turned up a number of controversial matters that have grabbed the imaginations and emotions of several members. In this case, it may be difficult for you and your partners to settle on one. If your group is experiencing difficulty in selecting an issue, you might consider the guidelines that follow.

First, all group members should be willing to express their personal attitudes toward and feelings about each issue under consideration. If members hold strongly opposing points of view on a matter (smoking in residence halls, a controversial candidate, the legal drinking age, a schoolwide course requirement, or a local incident), everyone should know that. Some groups may consider such opposition a liability and eliminate that particular topic; others may consider it an asset because of the debate it will generate. The point is, your writing group should be able to decide whether *or not* you wish to (or are able to) work with a divisive topic. This is an important selection criterion.

Another matter you and your group members should consider is your collective level of familiarity with an issue. If none of you knows enough about it to explain to one another why the matter is important or controversial, you may find that your interest level doesn't increase—even after you've all gathered information and generated discussion. Then you may be in the uncomfortable position of having to decide whether to continue with an issue that bores most of you (but in which you've invested time and trouble) or switch to a more interesting topic, and begin again rather late in the process.

 **Activity 2**

Together with your group members compile a list of issues that you all gathered from your survey of newspapers (and from surveys that you circulated). Then, on your own, rank these in order of their appeal or interest.

After deciding which issue seems the most interesting to you, freewrite (on your own) about your top selection, considering the following questions: Why does this topic or issue interest you? Do you have personal experience with it? What is your opinion or point of view about it? Can you describe the different points of view members of the campus community hold in regard to it? To what extent are these points of view incompatible? How controversial is the topic or issue?

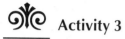 **Activity 3**

As a group, discuss each individual member's freewriting. If two or more persons wrote about the same issue or topic, discuss whether they expressed similar or different attitudes, opinions, or points of view. Assess the level of information the group has on each potential issue. Determine how contentious or divisive each issue might be for the group and how easy or difficult it will be to discuss each issue within the group. Try to reach a consensus about the best topic for your group to work with. If you cannot choose one, then narrow the choices down to two.

 **Activity 4**

Together with your group members, describe the issue your group has selected in a two-page report for your instructor. Include the following:

1. A one-paragraph description of the issue.

2. A one- or two-paragraph explanation of the major points of view members of the campus community hold on the issue and why they hold these views. *Be sure to include copies of surveys or transcripts of interviews that have been conducted.*

3. A one- or two-paragraph description of the group members' attitudes toward the issue, which includes an assessment of the intensity of different points of view within the group.

4. A one-paragraph conclusion that explains why the group chose this topic.

If your group cannot decide between two issues, include in your report responses to items 1, 2, and 3 from the previous list with regard to both issues. In place of item 4, write a one- or two-paragraph explanation of why you cannot decide between your two finalists. To proceed to the next step, you and your group may have to vote to determine the issue about which you will write, after a discussion with your instructor.

GATHERING INFORMATION ABOUT YOUR TOPIC

As you and your group members were surveying campus or local newspapers to discover issues or events that created interest and controversy among your peers, you recorded the nature and location of various articles, editorials, and essays. Now that you have selected your issue, you need to go back and take notes on those writings that are related to your topic. The information and opinions offered in these texts will stimulate discussion within your group and will suggest ideas and strategies for when you and your partners write your piece. In the course of discussing and assessing the texts you gather, you may wish to review relevant information in Chapter 6 and Chapter 7. Depending on the nature of the topic, issue, or event you have selected, you may need to gather other information.

Using Interviews

Nothing adds immediacy and creates a personal dimension with regard to an issue better than a personal story: "This happened to me. . . ." "My friend experienced this and I experienced it with her. . . ." It is often difficult for people to imagine the impact of a policy, practice, event, or set of circumstances (real or potential) on an individual's life unless they have experienced something related or similar. For this reason, you and your group members should again interview several friends or acquaintances or survey willing informants to determine their attitudes about the issue you've chosen and to find out why they have these attitudes.

If possible, you should try encourage interviewees to relate personal experiences that shaped their attitude toward your group's issue, if the experiences are not too private. Such narratives may play an important part in helping you and your group members sort out your own attitudes and responses with respect to the matter, or they may provide you with a convincing level of detail to include in your final piece of writing. Reviewing the rhetorical models in Chapter 3 may also give you ideas about the types of questions to ask and how to incorporate the information you acquire into your final text.

To ensure that each member of your group who conducts one or more interviews draws a breadth of information as well as detail from every informant, we suggest that your group draw up a list of questions to use during each interview *and* that you test these questions in a mock or practice interview. That is, after your group has generated a list of questions, one member of the group should interview another member using the list, while the others observe and jot down notes that suggest ways to improve the questions or that describe practices that group members should use or avoid when they conduct their interviews. Here are some matters that the rest of your group might consider as you observe one another conduct a mock interview:

- What questions on the list might be modified or eliminated?
- What new questions might be added?
- What techniques might interviewers use to get informants to clarify, explain, or elaborate on what they're saying?

- What types of questions and techniques might interviewers use to get informants to add more detail?
- How does the interviewer change the topic or get the informant to answer the "next" question?
- What practices should be avoided during an interview because they silence the informant or influence him or her too much?

Because you will be conducting a number of interviews, you may wish to tape them, if possible. Of course, you will need to ask your informants for permission to tape their responses and inform them when you have turned the recorder on (and off). For additional information about how to prepare for and conduct interviews, we suggest that you and your partners read Chapter 10.

One final reminder: Regardless of whether you and your group members consider any information divulged during the course of an interview to be sensitive, you should treat all information as confidential and not reveal your sources either verbally or in your final writing to anyone other than your group members and your teacher. You will, however, need to inform interviewees that these individuals will have access to notes and tapes of the interviews. As you complete your project, you should discuss with your instructor whether he or she wishes you to turn in tapes and notes of interviews along with your final piece of writing.

Using Other Sources of Information

As you and your group members gather information from newspaper articles, editorials, essays, and interviews that you conduct, you may discover that you need to find answers to questions that are raised (but not answered) with respect to the issue you have chosen. Suppose, for example, that students and faculty on your campus are arguing heatedly about whether smoking should or should not be permitted in residence halls. If your group has selected this issue to research and write about, you may find that neither the newspaper articles you've gathered nor the informants you've interviewed know the answers to questions that your group considers crucial for forming and defending an opinion.

Reliable information about the extent to which cigarette smoke in the air (passive smoke) is or is not harmful to nonsmokers, whether (or not) the administration at your school has explored the feasibility of establishing a residence hall (or setting aside special areas) for smokers, and the quality of the ventilation systems in areas within residence halls that must service smokers and nonsmokers may be central to this debate. But that doesn't mean that those who hold a strong opinion on one side or the other necessarily possess that information.

If your group wants to convince readers of your point of view, factual information can intensify the powerful effects of personal narratives about experience. The library, newspapers, and interviews with "experts" are all sources for the types of supplemental information you might wish to provide. To allude to our smoking-in-the-residence-hall issue once more, information that addresses the questions we raised could be secured from science journals, government reports, popular magazines and from interviews with the head of your student Health Center and with the Director of Residence Life (or Housing) at your school.

 Activity 5

On your own, brainstorm a list of questions that you and your group might use during interviews. Share your questions with your group, and together devise a list that two of you will use during a mock interview.

 Activity 6

With your group, conduct a mock interview (as described previously) within your group. Your group might consider doing this several times so that every member has a chance to interview, to be interviewed, and to observe. Based on your experience as an interviewer, interviewee, and observer, suggest modifications for the list of questions to be used during the actual interviews and write out a list of practices that you think your group should use or avoid when interviews are conducted. Share your suggestions for modifications to the list of questions and your list of interviewing dos and don'ts with your partners.

 Activity 7

Together with your group members decide on and write out a final list of questions you all will use during your interviews. Also decide on and write out a list of procedures all members of your group will use during interviews. Hand in a copy of your list of questions and procedures to your instructor.

WRITING AND PRODUCING YOUR PROJECT

Before you and your group partners actually begin to draft a piece of writing (or several pieces of writing) for this project, you need to consider several factors. First, it is important for all of you to articulate your views with respect to the issue you've selected—even if you don't necessarily agree with one another. In addition, it is vital to consider your audience and the context in which you will be publishing your position papers. Once these matters have been addressed, when you write your text you will need to frame your arguments and counterarguments carefully and construct an effective ethos.

Reaching a Consensus

During the course of gathering information about the matter you are investigating, you and your group members may have reacted similarly to the articles and essays you read and the interviews you conducted, in which case you may have developed or strengthened similar opinions about your topic. Under these circumstances, we suggest that your group work on broadening and strengthening your consensus by imagining points of view that oppose or are different from your own, and by considering who might hold these attitudes and whether the attitudes seem reasonable and justified. How would you answer individuals who held opposing stands? How would you respond to their arguments? On the other hand, if your group is already divided on the issue or event you've chosen to write about and if your readings and interviews support (or do not seriously undermine) the controversy within your group, you and your group members should explore this disagreement to understand and develop opposing points of view.

If possible, we recommend that you and your group partners try to reach a consensus regarding your issue or event—if you all can, in good conscience. Two factors that you might consider during this process are the quality and range of the information or personal anecdotes you've all gathered that support one view as opposed to the other and the level of detail and persuasiveness with which various group members support and express their views.

To assess the quality and extensiveness of the information you've gathered, you and your partners might list factual data, possible quotations, arguments, narratives, and the like, contained within your readings and interviews that could be used to support each "side" of your issue. If one set (array) of information seems much broader, more detailed, and more convincing than the other, people within your group may find it sufficiently compelling to modify their views so that a consensus can be reached. Again, a review of the chapters on critiquing and evaluating (Chapters 6 and 7) might assist you with this process.

It is, of course, more difficult to assess or evaluate the persuasiveness and expertise of individual group members with respect to one another (because you can't make lists and compare them.). However, you and your group members might try having each person (one at a time) argue his or her position and counter opposing points of views. Alternatively, you might pair up individuals who hold opposing points of view and have them debate with each other while the rest of the group watches and decides who is more persuasive.

Although the strategies we've suggested—as well as others that you and your group might try—may eventually help you reach a consensus on the issue you've selected, we cannot guarantee such results. The members of your group may not be able to agree on one stand that they are willing to articulate publicly and persuasively. In this case, you will need to consider how you all will respond to this dilemma. You and your group may wish to create two pieces of writing, one that argues one side of the issue and a second that presents an opposing argument. Or you may decide to construct one piece of discourse (a dialogue? a series of "letters to the editor" that "argue" with one another?) that presents both points of view in a detailed, passionate manner.

 **Activity 8**

Using the procedures we have just described or other methods, reach a group consensus, or one point of view. If this is not possible, articulate and settle on two opposing stances. In one or two pages, describe the stance or stances you and your group have decided to adopt on your issue; then list and describe in a sentence or two the data, arguments, examples, and personal anecdotes you will use to support your position(s). Turn your report in to your instructor.

Selecting a Forum in Which to Publish Your Writing

As you were reading this project you may have noticed that we have refrained from calling the culminating piece of writing an "essay." This is because although you and your group partners may wish to produce this type of writing, you don't have to do so. What is most important is that your group construct a convincing piece, addressed to "real" readers, that will jog individuals who have no opinion on the subject out of their complacency. If your writing is published, and effective, it should spark a few nerves or perhaps help inaugurate a controversy.

Because you want to construct a text that will reach a particular audience effectively, you and your partners need to decide on the forum in which you wish to publish your piece before you begin writing so that you can select content and strategies appropriate to the size and nature of your readership. As you begin to consider publishing opportunities in your campus or local community, you and your group members may draw a blank. "Who would publish something we wrote," you might ask. There are several answers to this question, the most obvious of which is your school newspaper—especially if it has a policy of regularly printing unsolicited editorial essays or articles. If your group wishes to pursue this possibility, one or more of you will need to investigate the paper's editorial policy (what—besides the work of newspaper staff writers—gets published, and how often?) as well as length and format constraints, to maximize your chances of getting published.

Although the readership of a school newspaper is an obvious forum for your writing, you and your group partners may also wish to investigate others, because these may afford you a greater opportunity to get published, a more diverse (or larger) readership, a more specialized readership, and so on. If your school paper does not publish writing from persons who are not on the newspaper staff, you and your partners should see if your school has organizations (The African American Student Union? Women United for Women? Nontraditional Student Organization? Business Student Association?) that publish their own newsletters, magazines, or newspapers. These materials may reach a smaller audience, but it may be easier for you to get published in one of them. Moreover, your readers (a self-selected group) might become more committed to your issue than "average" student readers—if your writing is skillful.

Similarly, a student group or organization may already support the point of view your group wishes to articulate, in which case the organization members may wish to distribute copies of your piece at a forthcoming meeting or rally they will be sponsoring. Then, too, some schools permit organizations to periodically staff booths or tables in central locations (such as a hallway in a major classroom building) from which students who pass by may request information and pick up printed materials. Such an organization may welcome the opportunity to pass on a well-written pamphlet or circular provided by your group.

Lastly, to reach a diversity of students without the help or approval of an organization or newspaper, you and your partners should consider publishing your piece yourselves and distributing it at common gathering places on campus (such as the Student Union) or posting it on public billboards. Pamphleteering, in which a writer or group of writers compose, produce, and—if necessary—distribute an essay or treatise on a current issue or topic, is a time-honored practice by which persons who have something important to say reach large numbers of readers without relying on a socially established means of dissemination, such as a newspaper or publishing company.

Finally, be sure to investigate publishing opportunities thoroughly and select a forum for your piece before you begin writing it so that you can adapt the strategies for envisioning your audience and for developing and expressing convincing arguments.

Considering Arguments and Ethos

Once you have articulated your point of view and the arguments that support it, you need to consider the best way of presenting these within your writing, if you are to be persuasive. In addition, the ethos projected by your writing will assuredly affect your readers' reception of your ideas.

Earlier, as we discussed how you might reach a consensus, we suggested that you write out in as much detail as possible different points of view on your issue as well as personal anecdotes, factual data, quotations, and so on, that supported these viewpoints. In planning and writing your piece, it is essential that you incorporate both sides of the argument while at the same time convincing the reader that your stance is the most reasonable. Neglecting to anticipate and answer persuasive arguments that contradict your own will weaken your case—particularly if many of your readers do not share your point of view. For example, suppose (again) that you are writing a piece that argues for a campuswide ban on smoking. An obvious counterargument is that such a ban would deprive smokers of a right to engage in an activity that is entirely legal. Moreover, smokers rights' advocates might reasonably ask why special vented areas for smokers (which would protect nonsmokers from passive or secondhand inhalation) could not be created? A strong argument should anticipate these responses and explain why they are unwarranted, impractical, too costly, and so forth.

In general, structuring arguments and counterarguments can be done in one of two ways. One strategy is to present (following a general introduction) the entire opposing viewpoint first, followed by a persuasive rebuttal. Next, all of the arguments in favor of the writer's viewpoints would be explained at length accompanied by supportive information and example. The other strategy, which works best if arguments pro and con are parallel, is to present alternating points of view. That is, a series of arguments against the writer's point of view would be addressed one at a time, each followed immediately by a persuasive rebuttal, which would also make the writer's case. For additional advice on structuring a persuasive essay, you might also wish to consult Chapter 8.

Besides crafting a structure carefully and including sufficient argument and example to support your view, good persuasive writing needs to project an effective ethos. As you recall, *ethos* refers to the way a writer presents himself or herself within a text. In general, an effective ethos projects good sense, good character, and good will—all of which are important if writing is to be persuasive to its attended audience. For a review of ethos, we suggest that you look over the portion of Chapter 5 that explains good sense and good character as well as the portion of Chapter 7 that explains good will.

The following selection is an editorial from the *BG News*, the campus newspaper of Bowling Green State University. Read and examine it carefully. How does the piece appeal to students *and* perhaps to administrators who are responsible for designing and enforcing local policy?

 ## Cardholders Take the Blame*

Food Op should admit more theft responsibility

An open letter to the Food Op Director

I am disappointed by the response of your department to two recent incidents of theft of monies via the "debit cards" which Food Operations administers.

Your public information officer was quoted in *The BG News* saying that "usually 'we' guard our credit cards from any type of misuse." You said that "Food Operations cannot be responsible for the charges made on the card."

*"Cardholders Take the Blame," by James E. Youll. *BG News*, 15 October 1991, p. 2. Reprinted with the permission of the author.

Cardholders Take the Blame *(cont'd.)*

I am a graduate of the University with a degree in computer science, a member of Computer Professionals for Social Responsibility, and a businessman who deals daily with issues of computer security, data integrity, business management and customer service. As such, I respectfully submit my observation that the stance that all blame for these thefts rests with cardholders is not an appropriate response in the "information age," and tender my suggestion that you correct what seem to be insufficiencies in the security offered by the debit card system.

Bowling Green's Public Information Officer draws parallels to credit cards. But credit cards have a ceiling loss of just $50. No matter when a credit card is stolen, or how much money is charged to it, the cardholder cannot be liable for more than $50 of those fraudulent charges. The BGSU system and policies, in contrast, apparently hold cardholders liable for all charges up to the entire balance on the card.

All cash-card operations I have seen, including credit cards, automatic teller machines (ATMs) and commercial debit cards, have safeguards to protect the consumer. If you or your programmers are not familiar with these methodologies, I encourage you to find out more. I would be glad to share my knowledge of system security with you at any time.

Some examples of commercial systems designed to safeguard the money they hold include bank ATMs. These limit the funds they will release to a "reasonable" amount. And ATM cards are inherently more secure that BGSU debit cards because they require a secret passcode. BGSU debit cards require no passcode when used in unattended vending machines.

Credit card companies offer another example. They watch for "unusual" levels of credit card activity, and may take additional action to verify the identity of the cardholder before authorizing a large charge. American Express has used such spot checks for years.

ATM networks and credit card verification centers are worldwide operations, spanning hundreds of computer networks, dozens of languages and currencies, and thousands of points of sales. The BGSU debit card system, in contrast, runs on a single computer system with a few dozen points of sale on one square mile of land. I think that most of your consumers would agree that it would be reasonable for the system to shut down the stolen card after more than $20 or $30 is charged to vending machines in a short period of time.

I hope you would agree that no person of moderate income should carry hundreds of dollars of cash in his wallet. The risk of loss is simply too great, and "moderate income" suggests that there's probably not much left after each paycheck to replenish that money. Now imagine that those hundreds of dollars were the person's entire food budget for four months, and the money's been stolen.

To avoid the risk of losing their entire food budget, most prudent individuals keep their "hundreds" in the bank and carry enough cash for a few meals and a tank of gas. They don't walk about flashing hundreds of dollars when they know they are only out to spend ones and fives. But the BGSU debit card system forces cardholders, in effect, to put hundreds of dollars on the line every time they want a 50-cent can of soda or a $3 salad. This does not seem reasonable.

Cardholders Take the Blame *(cont'd.)*

The cards require no secret "Personal Identification Numbers" (PINS) to force cardholders to prove their identities. There are no "sanity checks" in the size or frequency of transactions. There is apparently no policy to protect cardholders from fraud, yet debit card and residence hall policies mandate that 6,400 students at BGSU carry these cards or go hungry. This is not reasonable, as it offers nothing to assure the integrity or security of the account attached to a debit card.

You have said that cardholders should "immediately" report a card is "lost" as soon as it's lost. I do not dismiss the cardholder's duty to act responsibly when a card is lost. But the consumer's penalty for a lost or stolen card is just too high under the present rules. No person should starve or be forced to leave school because he or she lost a piece of plastic, and I think it's certainly possible that such a financial tragedy could occur.

In a perfect world, everyone's wallet and credit cards are safely tucked into the sock drawer every night, and nobody tries to steal them. This is not a perfect world. People lose things. Those who don't may have them stolen anyway. If we as systems designers and policymakers ignore such realities, then we invite their consequences. If we further enforce these consequences in a web of unfeeling policy and programming, then we have done a disservice to our clients and our profession.

I call on you to bring Food Services' level of responsibility up to par with commonly accepted and expected practices of customer assurance and responsibility by implementing electronic checks of reasonableness in all card transactions, by assuming financial responsibility for fraudulent charges made on debit cards, and by changing policies to reflect concern for the well-being of your card-carrying consumers and the funds they have entrusted to you. Protecting these funds will demonstrate that Food Operations is as concerned about the financial safety of its customers as it has historically been about their physical health. The fact that you hold student money on account, I believe, implies in spirit if not in law a responsibility for the safekeeping of that money.

 **Activity 9**

With your group, brainstorm possible forums in which to publish your piece. Create a chart in which you describe each possibility with respect to (at least) these criteria: ease or difficulty of publication; size of readership; nature of readership; means of dissemination (how and where would your piece be distributed?); and publication constraints (length, format, and so forth). After you all have completed the chart, together evaluate each possibility and try to come up with a selection.

❦ Activity 10

Together with your group partners, state your point of view in several sentences; write out and describe the arguments and supporting information you will use in a tentative plan. Submit this to your instructor for feedback. [NOTE: If you will be crafting two or more pieces expressing different points of view, do the above activities for each.]

Group Writing Assignment. At least two weeks before your project is due, write and turn in to your instructor a three-page report in which you describe (1) the forum in which you have chosen to publish; (2) the size and nature of your intended readership; (3) the point(s) of view your group will be advocating and the supports you will include; and (4) the additional materials you expect to hand in with your project (survey forms, excerpts from interviews, etc.). [NOTE: This project requires both the preparation and distribution of surveys as well as the conducting of interviews to gauge local opinion.]

❦ INDEX